THE ROMAN EMPIRE
350 CE

Caspian Sea

ARMENIA

Serûg

Callinicum

MESOPOTAMIA

Damascus
azareth
sarea
usalem
em

INDIA

Red
Sea

Arabian Sea

© 2008 Jeffrey L. Ward

P9-EGC-516

AUGUSTINE

— AND THE —

JEWS

RIDLEY BRANCH LIBRARY

AUGUSTINE
— AND THE —
JEWS

♦♦♦

A CHRISTIAN DEFENSE OF
JEWS AND JUDAISM

PAULA FREDRIKSEN

DOUBLEDAY

New York   London   Toronto   Sydney   Auckland

GUDLEY BRANCH LIBRARY

DD
DOUBLEDAY

PUBLISHED BY DOUBLEDAY

Copyright © 2008 by Paula Fredriksen

All Rights Reserved

Published in the United States by Doubleday, an imprint
of The Doubleday Publishing Group, a division
of Random House, Inc., New York.
www.doubleday.com

DOUBLEDAY is a registered trademark and the DD colophon
is a trademark of Random House, Inc.

Endpaper maps by Jeffrey L. Ward

LIBRARY OF CONGRESS CATALOGING-IN-PUBLICATION DATA
Fredriksen, Paula (1951–   )
Augustine and the Jews : a Christian defense of Judaism /
Paula Fredriksen.—1st ed.
p.   cm.
Includes bibliographical references and index.
1. Augustine, Saint, Bishop of Hippo. 2. Augustine, Saint,
Bishop of Hippo—Relations with Jews. 3. Christianity and
other religions—Judaism. 4. Judaism—Relations—Christianity.
5. Judaism—History. 6. Church history. 7. Christianity and
antisemitism—History. I. Title.
BR65.A9F74 2008
261.2'6092—dc22
2008003023

ISBN 978-0-385-50270-2

PRINTED IN THE UNITED STATES OF AMERICA

1 3 5 7 9 10 8 6 4 2

FIRST EDITION

12/08

for Zev

CONTENTS

AUGUSTINE

—— AND THE ——

JEWS

PROLOGUE

Whoever saves the life of a single person,
it is as if he saved the entire world.
MISHNAH SANHEDRIN 4.6

In 1146, for the second time in fifty years, Christians in the Rhine Valley responded to the call to liberate the Holy Land from Muslims by first laying waste to communities of European Jews. The earlier slaughters of 1096, the bloody prelude to the First Crusade, had startled contemporaries. This time, however, a learned churchman was prepared, and he preached against those inciting anti-Jewish violence. His good deed was gratefully noted by a Jewish contemporary, Rabbi Ephraim of Bonn:

> The Lord heard our outcry, and he turned to us and had pity on us. In his great mercy and grace, he sent a decent priest . . . named Abbot Bernard, of Clairvaux in France. . . . Bernard said to them: "It is good to go against the Ishmaelites [Muslims]. But whosoever touches a Jew to take his life is like one who harms Jesus himself . . ., for in the book of Psalms it is written of them, 'Slay them not, lest my people forget.'" All the Gentiles regarded this priest as one of their saints. . . . When our enemies heard his words, many of them ceased plotting to kill us.[1]

Reading Psalm 59.12 in this way—as an injunction addressed to Christians on how to treat Jews ("Slay them not")—was not Bernard's own idea. The Abbot of Clairvaux had drawn his instruction from one of the greatest authorities of the Latin church, Augustine of Hippo.

Some seven centuries before Bernard's day, in what turned out to be the twilight of the Western Roman Empire, Augustine presented his interpretation of Psalm 59 in his great masterwork, *City of God.* He argued there that the Jews, alone of all the religious minorities within the (newly) Christian state, should be unimpeded in their religious practice. Why did the Jews merit this unique exemption? Because, said Augustine, their religious practices devolved from a unique author: God the Father. The same god whom Christians worshiped was himself the source of Jewish scripture, Jewish tradition, and Jewish practice. Thus God himself, Augustine insisted, wanted the Jews to remain Jews. Let them preserve their ancient books, he urged; let them live openly according to their ancestral practices while scattered among the Christian majority. In so doing, Augustine taught, the Jews performed a valuable service of testimony for the church.

> By the evidence of their own scriptures they bear witness for us
> that we have not fabricated the prophecies about Christ. . . . It
> follows that when the Jews do not believe in our scriptures, their
> scriptures are fulfilled in them, while they read them with blind
> eyes. . . . It is in order to give this testimony which, in spite of
> themselves, they supply for our benefit by their possession and
> preservation of those books [of the Old Testament] that they are
> themselves dispersed among all nations, wherever the Christian
> church spreads. . . . Hence the prophecy in the Book of Psalms:
> "Slay them not, lest they forget your law; scatter them by your
> might."
>
> CITY OF GOD 18.46

This paragraph sums up Augustine's justly famous "witness doctrine." His teaching on the Jews' special status, and on the special service that their presence and their religious visibility rendered to the church, remained a singular aspect of his great theological legacy. With the collapse of the Western Roman Empire, this legacy passed into the traditions of medieval Christian Europe. In that more violent society, Augustine's witness doctrine provided authority for later learned churchmen, who used it—as Bernard, in the bleak days of the Second Crusade—to deflect and defuse Christian violence against Jews.[2]

Augustine and the Jews tells the story of how Augustine came to conceive this unique teaching, which was original to him. Thanks to the happy survival of so many of his writings, whose sequence we know, we can see the development of his thought on this topic in an astonishing degree of detail: philosophically oriented treatises and commentaries just after his conversion in Italy in 386, his failed commentary on Genesis once back in North Africa, short essays and attempted bigger projects on the Pauline epistles, transcripts of debates with heretical opponents, sermons, letters. And then, suddenly, dazzlingly, four brilliant and original works, produced in overlapping, rapid succession, beginning in 396—*To Simplicianus* (on Paul), *Christian Teaching* (on reading the Bible), *Confessions* (on knowing God), and *Against Faustus* (on the Bible, against the Manichees). We have them all. These works chart the way to his teaching on Jews and Judaism. Augustine's writing is so vivid, his intellectual energy so fierce, the force of his personality so present, that we can practically *hear* him thinking. Tracing his thought through these closely dated works is like viewing time-lapse photography. We can watch—phrase by phrase, problem by problem, insight by insight—how he gets to where he goes.

Prior to this question of Augustine's teaching on Jews and Judaism, however, and in a sense framing it, stands the more fundamental one already put to us by our glance at the Crusades: Why and how did relations between Christians and Jews ever become so terrible in the first place?

◆◆◆

THE HISTORY OF CHRISTIAN ORIGINS makes this distressing question that much more difficult to answer. Christianity had been born and nurtured within Judaism. Its message of bodily resurrection, divine judgment, and messianic redemption is quintessentially Jewish. The earliest Christians, themselves Jews, had proclaimed the good news of this impending redemption in terms drawn entirely from Jewish scripture. Fanning out from Jerusalem, the Christian movement in its first generation, and indefinitely thereafter, incubated within diaspora synagogue communities. In brief, ancient Christianity was itself a type of Judaism. Nonetheless, by Augustine's day—in fact, well before—an important shift had occurred. Even though Christianity's past was incontrovertibly Jewish, its future was resoundingly gentile.

This shift in Christianity's ethnic base came with shifts in traditions of textual interpretation. Which change came first, or whether both came together, is now impossible to say. The texts in question were themselves also originally Jewish. The larger and vastly older collection was the ancient Jewish scriptures in their "modern" Greek translation, the Septuagint (largely complete by the early second century B.C.E.). The fewer and more recent texts were, preeminently, Paul's letters to his gentile communities and some or all of the gospels—also Jewish, also in Greek—that were eventually collected into the churches' New Testament canon.

Both bodies of literature preserved condemnations of the social and religious practices of outsiders, and they particularly condemned the images of the outsiders' gods. But this literature also preserved hostile caricatures of *insiders,* heated polemics by their Jewish authors against other Jews. The scriptural prophets, for example, roundly condemned those Jews whose practice and interpretation of Jewish law differed from their way; and their way, they proclaimed, was God's way. Asserting similar authorization (for he saw himself as "an apostle neither from human beings nor through them, but through Jesus Christ and God the Father"; Galatians 1:1), Paul energetically repudiated other Christian Jews who construed the gospel message in ways different from his own. And the evangelists present Jesus himself as condemning various Jewish contemporaries: scribes, Pharisees, priests, and occasionally others of his own followers who in some way dissent from the position championed by the particular gospel writer. (Matthew 7:15-23 provides a particularly clear example of this internal debate, which in its original historical context would have been "internal" with respect to Judaism no less than with respect to Christianity.) Diversity, it seems, was worse than dangerous: it was damnable. Yet, clearly, diversity was also typical. At least, we have very many ancient Jewish texts—including paleo-Christian Jewish texts—that complain about or condemn such diversity.

In the Christian literature that begins to appear early in the second century, however, these arguments against other Jews transform into condemnations of Judaism itself. From this point on, many gentile authors, whether disputing with Jewish contemporaries or contesting with each other over questions of authority and identity, increasingly expressed the principles of their various Christian beliefs and practices by appealing to a vast web of interconnected anti-Jewish themes. They authorized their arguments by referring to biblical texts and, above all, to statements in the letters of Paul. By Augustine's period, after three hundred years of vigorous development, this interpretive anti-Judaism had become a defining feature of orthodox identity and of orthodox theology. Scholars speak of this invective as the *adversus Iudaeos* or *contra Iudaeos* tradition: Christian teachings "against the Jews."

These teachings appear throughout every form of early Christian literature known to us: in epistles, sermons, and commentaries; in apologies and in learned theological treatises. Eventually, from the early fourth century on, they echo in the legislation of church councils, in the mosaics ornamenting basilicas and baptisteries, and in the legal language of the imperial government. Yet, intriguingly, no correspondingly robust tradition *contra Christianos* appears in extant Jewish literature of the same period, from the second to the early fifth century. The bulk of these texts originates with the rabbis: the Mishnah, the Jerusalem Talmud, and the great homiletical commentaries (*midrashim*). They collect and preserve traditions whose focus is Jewish custom and community, whose language is Hebrew or Aramaic, and whose provenance is the Land of Israel. The voices of that vast portion of the Jewish population living west of the Land of Israel, however, the voices of the Greek- and Latin-speaking Jewish Diaspora, fall curiously silent. The abundant Jewish literary culture in Greek, which had flourished in the Hellenistic and the early Roman periods, and whose momentum had led, centuries before our period, to the translation of the Jewish scriptures into Greek, simply dries up.[3]

This imbalance in the evidence complicates efforts at explanation. What social context can accommodate the production of such hostile rhetoric, and why would this rhetoric be so heavily developed and so copiously represented on one side alone?

Current efforts to explain the scope and the energy of the *contra Iudaeos* tradition and to reconstruct a plausible social context within which our lopsided evidence might make some sense look back particularly to the late nineteenth century, to the work of the great church

historian Adolf von Harnack (1851–1930). Harnack made three interpretive proposals. The first was that, after the Roman destruction of
Jerusalem's temple in 70 C.E., Jewish communities began to turn inward, withdrawing from active relations with and involvement in
the outside, gentile world. (This conjecture accounts for the general
lack of early Jewish responses to Christian anti-Jewish invective). His
second proposal was that the stereotypical quality of Christian statements about Jews suggested that their usual source was not encounters with Jewish contemporaries but interpretations of Old Testament
texts, especially of those of the prophets. (This second conjecture accounts for the repetitive and abstract quality of so much anti-Jewish
criticism: hearts that are always stony, hard, or uncircumcised; necks
that are always stiff; and so on.) And, third, Harnack suggested that
contra Iudaeos invective was most often stimulated by Christians'
polemical contacts not with Jews but with the much larger population
of potential converts, which is to say, with pagans. Skeptical and hostile, these pagans would have pointed out to Christians that Jews did
not follow the gentile Christian lead when interpreting what were
clearly Jewish books. Christian anti-Jewish argument responded to pagans by making the case that the Jews had their interpretations all
wrong.[4]

Other scholars challenged Harnack's contentions. Two of these
scholars, who published their work in the years just after World War
II, stand in the immediate background of the present study. The first
scholar, Bernhard Blumenkranz, minutely analyzed a late sermon of
Augustine's, traditionally identified as the "Sermon against the Jews,"
in *Die Judenpredigt Augustins* (1946). The second scholar, his friend and
contemporary Marcel Simon, wrote a wider study: *Verus Israël. Études
sur les relations entre Chrétiens et Juifs dans l'empire romain* (A.D. *135–425*)
(1948). In this book, Simon surveyed the pan-Mediterranean context
of Christian–Jewish relations from the period after Rome's defeat of
the Judean rebel Bar Kokhba through the reign of the Christian emperor Theodosius II. Both scholars argued that the force, the scope,
and the sheer ubiquity of Christian *adversus Iudaeos* polemic could not
be accounted for by conjecturing, as Harnack had, that diaspora Judaism had all but disappeared. ("Do men rage so persistently against

a corpse?" Simon famously asked.) On the contrary, urged these scholars: The church inveighed against the synagogue because the synagogue posed an active threat to the church.[5]

The many complaints within ancient Christian literature about gentile Christians who "Judaized"—that is, who voluntarily assumed some Jewish practices—and the occasional criticisms of and imperial laws against gentile conversions to Judaism provided the evidence in support of this new description of the late Roman religious and social context. But Blumenkranz and Simon went further, arguing that this evidence attested not only to the attractiveness *of* the synagogue but also to strenuous efforts to be attractive made *by* the synagogue. The Jews of late antiquity, argued Blumenkranz and Simon, exactly like their contemporary Christian counterparts, actively engaged in *missions,* seeking to persuade Gentiles, whether pagan or Christian, to become Jews. The noise and the quantity of Christian anti-Jewish invective, they urged, indexed the younger community's insecurity in the face of its much more established Jewish rival. Christian polemic *contra Iudaeos,* they concluded, actually reveals the intensity of the church's rivalry with the synagogue as both communities competed for a limited resource: new converts.[6]

From that time to this, an enormous volume of fresh research, new data, and different arguments have refined, softened, or reinforced the two interpretive options represented by Harnack to the one side and by Blumenkranz and Simon to the other. New archaeological finds have offset the silence of post-first-century Hellenistic Jewish literary texts. The monumental remains of the great synagogue at Sardis, integrated into the heart of that city; a wealth of inscriptional evidence and of mosaic donor plaques, attesting to close interactions between Roman-era Jews and Gentiles whether pagan or Christian; new ways of reading rabbinic literature in order to perceive contacts and influences across the confessional divide: Scholars now have much richer and more varied evidence to consider.[7]

Earlier interpretations have also been modulated and new ones proposed, as scholars have paid increasing attention to the ways that polemics ostensibly directed against outsiders work rhetorically to establish definitions of community for insiders. And also, while much of the formal Christian literary evidence (such as sermons and commentaries) bespeaks hostility between Christians of various kinds, Jews, and pagans, much of the nonliterary and nonecclesiastical evidence (inscriptions, papyri, decorative artifacts) and indeed, some of the complaints made within the literary evidence, attest to various, often friendly contacts between members of these different communities, up to and including co-celebration and marriage. A second gap thus begins to open up, this one between the extremely hostile *contra Iudaeos* rhetoric and a surprisingly open and accommodating Mediterranean urban social reality. Whence the strength, the ubiquity, and the stability of this anti-Jewish invective, then, absent an explanatory social context of equally universal and intense competition or hostility?[8]

These difficulties of interpretation notwithstanding, we need to have a sense of the history and the role of Christian anti-Jewish rhetoric in Augustine's culture in order to see how his bold revisions challenged this tradition. I propose to tell his story, then, by beginning with a different one: a broad and brief history of Greco-Roman Mediterranean civilization from its dawn in the conquests of Alexander the Great (d. 323 B.C.E.) to its incipient twilight in the fifth-century western Christian empire. From this aerial view of Augustine's social and religious culture, we will move into our closeup of Augustine's life and thought and thence, finally, to the evolution/revolution of his theology of Jews and Judaism.

Thus Part I, "The Legacy of Alexander," examines the interactions of the two most important populations in antiquity: gods and humans. We will see how these gods and their humans—including the Judean god and his humans—formed units that were imagined and understood as family groups. We will also see how empire and the new "global" culture of Hellenism affected the ways that different ethnic and, thus, religious groups perceived and described themselves and others; and we will explore the various practical ways in which ancient people sought to maintain good relationships both with their own god(s) and with the gods of others. Next, we will consider elite traditions of Hellenistic education—chiefly rhetoric but also philosophy—to determine how these shaped social, political, and intellectual encounters and activities. As we trace the spread of the Christian movement within this erudite culture, we will examine how its leaders saw their enterprise, at least in part, as a conflict over the interpretation of texts. And finally, we will explore some of the variegated evidence noted earlier—inscriptions, archaeological remains, different kinds of literature—to gain a sense of the social world of Roman antiquity, of the ways in which pagans, Jews, and Christians interacted among themselves and with each other in the shared space of the Greco-Roman city.

Part II, "The Prodigal Son," explores the immediate context of Augustine's teaching on Jews and Judaism: his own intellectual and spiritual development. This story of Augustine's life ranges from his student days in Carthage (370s C.E.), during which he joined the outlawed Christian sect of the Manichees, through to his early years as a catholic bishop, when he composed his amazing prayer to God, the *Confessions* (circa 397). Here I highlight the particular questions that impelled him first to the heresy of Manichaean Christianity and, later, to a cosmopolitan version of his childhood church. What is the relation of spirit to flesh? Of a good god to the problem of evil? Of text to meaning? Of time to eternity? Grappling with these questions drove Augustine ever more deeply into the problem of interpreting the Bible. The challenge that these questions posed, and which his commitments to Manichaeism had greatly intensified, provoked in the later 390s an outpouring of original theology. The axial point around which these old questions and his new answers revolved is the issue of divine justice and human moral freedom. Scripturally—and thus both theologically and historically—that issue was embodied for Augustine in the ways that he imagined the relationship between God and the Jews.

Part III, "God and Israel," begins with the literary confrontation between Augustine and an old teacher of his, Faustus the Manichee. Faustus' book the *Capitula* had attacked the principles and traditions of Augustine's church. Its strategy was in one sense commonplace: Faustus the Christian defined and defended his Christianity as true Christianity by using anti-Jewish rhetoric to revile a rival group of gentile Christians, accusing them of the same moral and spiritual errors by which that rhetoric had long characterized "the Jews." But the *Ca-*

pitula had surprising polemical power, which arose from Faustus' ingenious combination of two originally quite distinct traditions: the rhetoric *contra Iudaeos* of heretical Christianity and the rhetoric *contra Iudaeos* of orthodox Christianity. In Augustine's response to Faustus we can see in microcosm the applications and the effects of traditions of Greco-Roman rhetoric, philosophy, textual interpretation, and cross-ethnic relations explored in the macrocosm of Part I. But we can also see, in wonderful detail, the effect that the particular contingencies of Augustine's own life had on his thought. His education and its limits; his relations with other Latin Christian intellectuals; the circumstances specific to late-fourth-century North Africa, with its communities of Jews, pagans, and dissenting Christians; the instability of Latin versions of the Bible; the particular conclusions that he had come to in understanding the biography as well as the theology of the apostle Paul: all of these factors combined to lead Augustine to the stunning achievement of his teaching on Jews and Judaism.

◆◆◆

I OWE READERS some preliminary remarks to explain several peculiarities of this book. First, I have capitalized the word *god* only when it acts as the name of the biblical deity: thus, "God spoke to Moses" but "the god of Moses spoke." This decision reflects my effort to put all of our ancient actors on the same level playing field. Traditional capitalization seems like a form of special pleading. I did not want to write about "the god of Plato" if I wrote about "the God of Abraham."

Second, modern English uses two words, *Gentiles* and *pagans*, where the Greek on which these both rest has only a single word, *ta ethnê*, "the nations." The two English words have different connotations. *Gentile* makes a statement about a person's ethnicity: The person is not a Jew. *Pagan* refers to a person's religious beliefs: The person is neither a Jew nor a Christian. When Christianity began to appear in first-century diaspora synagogues, however, mutatis mutandis, pagans were Gentiles, and Gentiles were pagans. (The exceptions to this virtually universal rule are explored in the text.) The distinction between religion and ethnicity created by the two English words is an anachronism for the first several centuries of the Christian Era, one that makes the quarrels within the first generation of the movement and the reasons for later pagan anti-Christian persecutions harder to see. I note where this vocabulary presents problems, and I offset these problems by using the one word when modern usage expects the other. The reader should prepare for encountering "pagan Christians" when we look at the first generation of the Christian movement in the Diaspora.

Third, throughout the present study I have tried to compensate for one of the abiding problems in the field of ancient Christian studies: the language of the winners. Surveys of pre-Constantinian Christianity often identify various Christian communities, marginalized only during the power struggles of the fourth century and later, as already "heretical" in the late first century, or in the second, or in the third. Such an approach seems to grant to the "orthodox" their own claim, namely, that their version of Christianity was the defining one, always the same from the beginning and therefore authentic and in some special sense "true." It thereby invites and promotes anachronism. Before Constantine, each of the various Christian communities thought that its own views were correct and that the views of others, if different, were false. Before 312, what we have is variety. After 312, we still have variety. By that point, however, events had led to a clear, functional definition of *orthodoxy:* the views that enjoyed the support of the emperor. After 312, in brief, what primarily distinguished orthodox Christians from their rivals was power. To think otherwise is simply to recapitulate in modern academic language the ancient rhetoric of the orthodox bishops. (To see some version of rabbinic Judaism as "orthodox" Judaism projects the same error onto ancient Jewish communities.)

Nonetheless, we remain stuck with the vocabulary of the winners. Scholars habitually identify various second- and third-century Christian groups by the names of their prominent leaders: Valentinians (the followers of Valentinus), Marcionites (the followers of Marcion), Manichaeans or Manichees (the followers of Mani). And we identify the community that names them this way as proto-orthodox or as orthodox. For clarity, I have had to acquiesce. The reader should remember, however, that in their own eyes, all of these people were simply followers of Christ and, therefore, "Christians."

Fourth—a different version of the same problem—how should we identify Paul and his Jewish contemporaries in the first generation of the movement that formed around the memory and the message of Jesus of Nazareth? To call them "Jews" leads to confusion, because they are a particular kind of Jew, and it is their particularity that gives them their historical importance. (So too, for example, with those Jews who were members of other first-century Jewish schools or sects, such as the Pharisees or the Essenes.) To call this first generation "Christian" risks anachronism, however. The term, and arguably the concept, did not exist during their lifetimes. By their own lights, these particular Jews saw themselves—when they were not arguing with each other—as Jews who had the correct understanding of the Jewish god, the Jewish messiah, and the Jewish scriptures. The problem is no less acute when trying to speak about the non-Jews who joined with them. Are these people "converts"? (If so, in this period before a separate Christianity exists, then to what?) Or are they "Judaizers," that is, pagans who adopt some but not all Jewish practices? (Which ones? In what ways? And why?) I have finally opted to use "Christian," while acknowledging the many points made by good arguments against such usage. Where this label leads to problems of historical analysis, I mention it in the text.

Fifth, I have designated the fourth-century Christian victors as both "catholic" and "orthodox." This too reflects their own claim, especially in the age after Constantine, to represent universal (*catholica*) and right-thinking (*orthodox*) Christianity. Those later and more localized churches, (Latin) Roman Catholicism and (Greek) Orthodoxy, descend from this community, but in our period they do not yet exist. Thus Latin theologians in the fourth and fifth centuries can be "orthodox" (like Ambrose, or Augustine); and Greek prelates in the eastern Mediterranean (like Athanasius of Alexandria), in claiming to represent an international and uniform Christian tradition, can be "catholic." I hope that the use of lower-case letters will help avoid confusion. Of course, important fourth-century communities that self-identified as Romans and as orthodox Christians lived outside of the immediate Mediterranean linguistic world of Greek and Latin. Vital traditions also flourished in Coptic and in Syriac, and some of these contributed also to the development of Christian anti-Jewish invective. Augustine, however, felt the impact of those traditions that came through Greek and especially through Latin texts. For that reason, the present study concentrates on them.[9]

Sixth, while I have availed myself wherever possible of standard translations of Greek and Latin texts, I have usually altered and adjusted them. (This is true even when I used translations that I have previously published myself.) Biblical quotations in English, often but not always, draw on the text of the Revised Standard Version (RSV), though frequently I have adjusted these as well. Last, quotations of biblical texts made by ancient authors often do not conform to the received texts and authorized translations of today. Sometimes this is because the author is quoting from memory; sometimes it is because his text (especially if in Latin) differs from the Greek or the Hebrew that stands behind modern scientific editions of the Bible. In these instances, of course, I have kept their readings and translated accordingly.

Seventh, and finally, my notes here are discursive and only minimally bibliographical: I did not intend them to be exhaustive. Two considerations prompted this decision. The first was practical. The earlier academic publications on which the present study rests are readily accessible thanks to the Internet. Readers who want a fuller complement of scholarly bibliography and argumentation than I give here can consult my webpage at Boston University, where my earlier essays are available in PDF format (www.bu.edu/religion/faculty/fredriksen). My second consideration, however, was literary, thus aesthetic. The conclusions that I have reached in the course of several decades' work on a wide variety of questions, in related but different areas, emerged only severally. In *Augustine and the Jews,* I wanted to retell the results of that research in one sweeping story.

PART ONE

THE LEGACY OF ALEXANDER

The roots of Christianity run deep in Judaism. And the roots of anti-Judaism run deep in Christianity.

To grasp the force and complexity of these two facts—and of Augustine's singular response to them—requires a sense of their historical matrix, the culture that enabled their birth, sponsored their growth, and fed their long-lived, manifold interactions. That culture was born nearly seven hundred years before the brilliant bishop reconceived his ideas about God, creation, and history; some three centuries before the message of the risen Christ began its reshaping of Mediterranean society. Understanding the traditions of Christian anti-Judaism, in order to see how Augustine's ideas on Jews and Judaism ultimately challenged them, begins with an understanding of the world in the wake of Alexander the Great.

✦ ✦ ✦

1 ✦ GODS AND THEIR HUMANS

A task was set for me, which caused me deep anxiety. . . .
I was to recite the speech of Juno in her anger and grief
that she "could not keep the Trojan king out of Italy."
AUGUSTINE, *CONFESSIONS* 1.17,27

Born in North Africa in 354, Augustine began life some four decades after Constantine's momentous decision to link the fortunes of the Roman Empire with those of the church. Augustine's father, Patricius, though not baptized until near the end of his life, was Christian; his mother, the formidable Monnica, was a fervent believer. Augustine's native province, with its illustrious history of saints and martyrs, was the cradle of Latin Christianity. Nonetheless, it was the tales of ancient heroes and the classical gods that filled and formed the imagination of this bright little boy: furious Juno and Virgil's doomed lovers, Dido and Aeneas; wicked Medea flying through the air; Zeus and Athena, Achilles and Odysseus, and the whole noisy throng of Homer's outsize deities and warriors. Augustine's formal education—a benefit that his Christian parents made considerable sacrifices to secure for him—was thoroughly and unapologetically pagan.[1]

How did these gods become so established in traditions of learning? Why would Augustine's parents want this sort of education for their son? How did Augustine learn to read and to think with pagan literature, and how did this education ultimately affect his reading of the Bible and thus his interpretation of Judaism? To answer these questions, we have to look back across nearly seven centuries, to the birth of the world that Augustine lived in. Odd as it may seem, the story of Augustine and the Jews begins with the conquests of Alexander the Great.

✦✦✦

BY THE TIME HE WAS THIRTY, Alexander the Great (d. 323 B.C.E.) presided over a vast and variegated empire that stretched from the eastern Mediterranean and Egypt to the edges of India. Though his empire was short lived—at his death, it fractured into much smaller kingdoms and city-states—his underlying cultural achievement endured. In the wake of his conquests, Alexander had planted Greek colonists and veterans from his army in new settlements. He organized these settlements along lines reminiscent of the Greek city, or *polis.* Urban life in Alexander's new establishments pulsed around the agora, the central public space that served as the commercial and social nerve center of the city. At public feasts, civic altars smoked with the flesh of animals offered to the gods. Schools and gymnasia educated the next generation in public speaking and athletics, training the sons of the elite for future leadership. The *boulê* (town council), the library, the theater, the hippodrome: all served simultaneously as sites for social interaction and for the enactment of public piety.

These organs of the classical Greek city, widely transplanted abroad, enabled the growth of a new international culture, which scholars call *Hellenism.* Greek itself became antiquity's English, the international language par excellence. As such, it facilitated trade and travel, the exchange of goods and ideas, and the workings of government and of diplomacy across vast expanses of territory. Hellenism, in brief, was the West's first great experience of globalization.

Thanks to the gymnasia—institutes of learning for the adolescent sons of civic elites—education was also globalized. Adapted classical curricula brought the patrimony of high Greek culture, *paideia,* to local elites abroad. To the degree that citizens participated in the political, intellectual, and cultural life of their cities, to that degree they lived and thought in Greek. So penetrating was this linguistic accomplishment that by the second century B.C.E., Jews in the Mediterranean Diaspora had dropped their native vernaculars and translated their ancient sacred writings from Hebrew (or Aramaic) into Greek. So perduring was this linguistic accomplishment that most of the texts from the first several centuries of the Christian movement, even those composed in the "Latin" West—in Rome, for example, or in Lyon—were in fact written in Greek. The lineaments of Augustine's curriculum in fourth-century North Africa, and Homer's place within it, give the measure of Alexander's long-lived cultural achievement.[2]

Vernaculars of course persisted, and Hellenism itself was a mongrel phenomenon, expressed in local accents whether in Egypt, Syria, or Asia Minor (modern Turkey). (Artifacts from the kingdom of the Ptolemies, for example, one of the dynasties that emerged in the power struggle after Alexander's death, are at once recognizably Greek and unmistakably Egyptian.) Its myriad variations notwithstanding, however, Hellenism facilitated communication and spread cultural coherence across vast distances. Adapting and adopting it, Rome exported this civilization even further, adding to the Hellenistic repertoire its own variations on urban structures: the forum, the basilica, the circus, the public bath. By the end of the first century c.e., thanks to Rome's conquests, the expanse of territory from Britain in the west to the edge of Persia in the east, from the Danube in the north to the African breadbasket in the south, formed an identifiable, if not uniform, cultural whole.

Trade and government, art and literature: these abstractions sit atop a rougher reality. Throughout the 750 years that stretch between Alexander and Augustine, war and its aftermath, peace, brought different, distant peoples closer together. Contact with other cultures achieved initially through military conquest often meant disempowerment, deportation, and dislocation for the losing side. Defeated peoples might remain where they were, cooperating with and accommodating themselves to the new order. Or they might move, whether as refugees, exiles, or slaves. But these empires, Hellenistic or Roman, also established domestic peace. Peace enabled and encouraged interior travel and less traumatic forms of migration. Merchants, enticed by the wider horizons and the increased opportunities for trade brought by empire, could travel in safety. So could pilgrims, who celebrated festivals and journeyed to famous temples and holy sites. Populations mixed as soldiers married, and they and their families garrisoned military colonies in frontier areas. Ancient empire thus not only spread the unifying global culture of Hellenism but also facilitated the mixing and mingling of populations, bringing foreigners—slave and immigrant alike—"home." (Different people, as we shall see, greeted this new proximity to strangers with different attitudes.) And, since all ancient peoples had their own pantheons, these ancient empires also brought into closer contact many different gods.

◆ ◆ ◆

GODS AND HUMANS were the two key populations of ancient empire, which could prosper only if they cooperated. To understand how ancients solicited this cooperation, we need to imagine the world as they did, a world that was filled with gods.

Though, often, these gods lived in the heavens, they also lived on earth. Ancient gods tended to be local in two senses. They attached, first, to particular places. Sometimes their holy sites were natural: a grove or a grotto, a spring or a sacred mountain. No less often, however, these sites were man made. Gods, like men, were also urban creatures, and cities held shrines. Temples might be visited or statues temporarily tenanted by the god to whom they were sacred. The Gospel of Matthew, written in Greek probably toward the close of the first century C.E., provides a nice statement of this extremely common ancient idea. In that work, Jesus observes that "he who swears by the Temple [in Jerusalem], swears by it and by *him who dwells in it*" (Matthew 23:21)—that is, by the god of Israel, who abides in his temple.

At festivals and solemn occasions, whether in town or in country, ancient gods joined worshipers around their altars. There gods and men could enact a fundamental and binding social ritual: they "ate" together. The fat, bones, and flesh of blood offerings, the cereals and wine brought by worshipers, provided the medium of this encounter, which was cautiously scripted according to purity rules that (often) the god himself had revealed. Mistakes made gods angry; proper ritual and piety—all indices of affection, loyalty, and respect—pleased them and disposed them to be gracious. Humans, in consequence, took care to safeguard the purity, sanctity, and financial security of these altars and holy sites because, in a simple way, the god was there. (Much later into the Christian period, when anti-pagan polemic demoted both the moral and the celestial status of these divine beings to that of "evil demons," their presence around their altars was still assumed.)[3]

But ancient gods were local in another sense. They attached not just to places, but also to peoples. Put more concisely, ancient "religion" was inherited. It characterized ethnic groups. In antiquity, gods ran in the blood.

I put "religion" in scare quotes because of the important differences between the ways that modern people tend to think of religion and the ways that ancient peoples maintained good relations with their gods. For the modern Westerner, religion is a detachable aspect of individual identity. Largely personal or private, modern religion seems first of all a question of beliefs. And beliefs themselves often relate to individual psychological states, the sincerity or commitment or conviction or inner disposition of the believer.

In the ancient Mediterranean, by contrast, the closest social analogue to our concept of religion would be *cult*, those protocols and practices whereby humans enacted their respect for and devotion to the deity, thereby securing heaven's goodwill. Cult focused on deeds. It was communal, both across generations (cult acts, or rituals, were performed according to ancestral tradition) and among members of the group. This is not to say that individual households and, indeed, persons might not have their own particular protocols of piety: They could and they did. And this is not to say that religious activities always involved an entire urban population. On the contrary, smaller groups gathered around particular deities whom they chose to worship, such as Isis or Dionysus. Various immigrant communities had their own liturgical calendars and traditions that served, precisely, to indicate who was in the group and who was not. Still, ancient worship in general emphasized actions that were public, communal, and (especially at the civic and imperial levels) what we would identify as political.[4]

To the degree that cult was inherited, to that degree it was also ethnic—that is, cult was most often specific to a people (*ethnos* in Greek). Cult thus functioned as a type of ethnic designation, binding a group together across time as well as space, defining one's kinship group, the *genos* (Greek) or *natio* (Latin). Herodotus, the Greek historian of the fifth century B.C.E., gives a clear example of this way of thinking, when he defines "Greekness" (*Hellenismos*) in terms of shared blood, language, altars, and customs (*Histories* 8.144.2–3). Or, more simply, deities, peoples, and places could all be identified in terms of each other: the god of Israel, the gods of Rome, the god at Delphi, and so on. "Great is Artemis of the Ephesians!" (Acts 19:28).

Hellenistic Jews, in distinguishing their way of life from that of outsiders, invented a word similar to Herodotus' term for Greekness: *Ioudaismos,* "Jewishness" or (perhaps better) "Judeanness." Thus the heroes of the passage in the Second Book of Maccabees, where this word first appears, fight for "the temple, the city (Jerusalem), and the laws" (2 Maccabees 2:21). Centuries later, sometime in the 50s C.E., another Greek Jew, the apostle Paul, defined Jewishness in ways that again recall Herodotus' categories of Greekness. "My brothers, my kinsmen according to the flesh," wrote Paul, "are the Israelites. To them belong . . . the glory [Greek: *doxa*], the covenants [*diathêkai*], the giving of the Law [*nomothesia*], and the worship [*latreia*]" (Romans 9:3–4 RSV). In other words, Paul explains to the (gentile) Christian community in Rome that his kinsmen (*syggenoi*) are distinguished by their customs, their cult, and their god.

The Greek word that Paul uses, which implies several of these ideas, is *doxa.* The Revised Standard Version (RSV) translates this word as "glory." But Paul's phrasing draws on the Jewish scriptures, so that beneath his Greek *doxa* lies the Hebrew word *kavod. Kavod* also translates as "glory," but the word refers most specifically to the glorious divine presence and thus to the particular place of this presence—that is, the altar of Israel's god in his temple in Jerusalem (Romans 9:4). Paul also lists customs as defining his people, their covenants (*diathêkai*) and laws (*nomothesia*), by which he means Torah. And as another ethnic identifier in this list, Paul names service or cult: *latreia* in his text, translated rather bloodlessly by "worship" in the RSV. But *latreia* specifically means "offerings," most often blood offerings; the biblical Hebrew behind Paul's Greek would be *avodah.* In the context of Paul's letter, then, this word *latreia* refers both to Torah, which communicated God's protocols for sacrifice, and also to the Temple in Jerusalem, where the cult was performed before his altar. (Romans 9:4–5. Note that neither the author of 2 Maccabees nor the apostle could follow Herodotus in using "shared language" to indicate shared ethnicity.)[5]

Thus, like their humans, ancient gods (including, emphatically, the Judean god) were ethnic also. Their ethnic relation to their humans was sometimes presented in terms of the family bond of descent. Myths of primordial breedings between a god and a mortal often recounted such a relation between heaven and a ruler. Alexander the Great claimed descent from Heracles; according to another legend, Alexander's mother, Olympias, had conceived him through the god Zeus. Aeneas, hero of Virgil's great poem, was the child of the goddess Venus, a connection that later served his descendant Julius Caesar very well.

Cities as well as rulers found such divine connections politically useful. A city whose citizens were descended from a god could negotiate treaties and reach understandings with other peoples by invoking newly discovered bonds through ancient divine–human relationship. Hellenistic and later Roman diplomats, availing themselves of these traditions, wove intricate webs of kinship diplomacy among cities. These diplomats could appeal to an ancient past when prolific deities and semidivine heroes, in the wake of their considerable wanderings, left behind human offspring, who were the ancestors of the parties to the treaty under negotiation. So too did Hellenistic Jews, who paired the offspring of their patriarchs with lesser Greek divinities. This ancient bond of shared "blood" served to stabilize current agreements.[6]

The Jewish god himself was austerely removed from such divine–human couplings. He had children nonetheless. Biblical claims of divine sonship are a strong way of asserting intimacy with God. "You are my son; today I have begotten you," God says on the coronation day of an Israelite king (Psalm 2:7). "I will raise up your offspring after you," God promises David. "I will be a father to him, and he shall be a son to me" (2 Samuel 7:12,14; later Christians referred such passages to Jesus). So too with the entire people of Israel, whose historical (thus ethnic) descent ran from Abraham through Isaac to Jacob. "Israel is my first-born son," God announces in Exodus 4:22, and the image recurs often throughout Jewish scripture. The apostle Paul, repeating this biblical commonplace, distinguished his *genos* from others by referring to their sacred "sonship" (for example, at Romans 9:4). Those members of the nations whom Paul evangelized achieve this filial status through "adoption." Baptism brings them into the family as "sons"; like Christ, they can address Israel's god as "Abba, Father" (e.g., Galatians 4:5–7; Romans 8:15). Later, in the second and third centuries, when non-Jewish Christian communities sought to formulate their identity, they too fell back on this native Mediterranean language of divinity and blood kinship or ethnicity, claiming that their community constituted a new "race" (*genos*).[7]

◆ ◆ ◆

WHAT DID THESE IDEAS about gods and humans mean practically for the way that ancient peoples lived? They meant that, first, in an age of empire, gods bumped up against each other with some frequency, even as their humans did. The larger the political unit, the greater the number of different peoples and thus the greater the number of gods. And the greater the number of gods and of peoples, the greater the plurality of cultic practices, because different peoples naturally had their own ancestral customs. Ancient empires, in other words, accommodated as a matter of course a wide range of religious practices. To see this accommodation as "religious tolerance" is to misunderstand it. Ancient society was not liberal in the sense that modern civil societies tend (or try) to be. But it was, of practical necessity, pluralistic. Religious differences were a normal fact of life. Put differently: A mark of successful empire (the subordination of many different peoples to a larger government) was the variety of gods and the range of traditional practices that it encompassed (since many peoples meant, naturally, many gods).

Second, the existence or nonexistence of the gods of outsiders (those of a different *genos* or *natio*) was not at issue. Ancient peoples generally assumed that various gods existed, just as their humans did. When these gods, with their humans, were encountered, various kinds of recognitions and acknowledgments might occur. When Alexander conquered Egypt, for example, a priest of the god Ammon greeted him as Ammon's son. Deified himself, Alexander was depicted on coins in gorgeous Hellenistic profile, the ram's horns of the Egyptian deity growing out of his head. As cultures encountered each other, their gods might be identified with, associated with, or assimilated to each other. Thus the Roman Jupiter took on characteristics of the Greek Zeus; statues of the Roman Minerva replicated aspects of Athena; indigenous Semitic gods (such as *Ba'al shamin,* "lord of heaven") gained currency by being presented under Olympian names ("Zeus"). When different peoples clashed, their gods were imagined as fighting, too. But this was not always the case. The Romans, ever practical, began sieges by addressing the presiding deities of the enemy. Through rituals of *evocatio* ("calling out"), the Romans summoned the city's gods to come over to them, promising in exchange for victory to respect and to continue their cult.[8]

The Bible reveals a similar sensibility. Accustomed as we are to seeing our own modern monotheism mirrored in its verses, scripture's messier monotheism can be harder to discern. Other gods, nonetheless, still peek through the biblical text. "Who is like you, O Lord, among the gods?" sings Moses (Exodus 15:11). "You shall have no other gods before (or besides) me," the god of Israel insists (20:3). "All the peoples walk, each in the name of its god," says the prophet Micah, "but we will walk in the name of the Lord *our* god forever and ever" (Micah 4:5). Both in law and in prophetic texts, ancient Jews condemned "images" or "idols," those human productions that represented the divine personalities worshiped by other nations. The god of Israel, in his self-revelation at Sinai, forbade his people this style of worship (and Exodus 32, the story of the Golden Calf and God's response to it, preserved a standing cautionary tale). Later Jews in the western Diaspora certainly thought that idol worship lowered the moral tone of pagan society: Paul in Romans 1:18–32 rendered a particularly full-throated indictment. Some Jewish writers, like the author of the Book of Tobit (second century B.C.E.?), looked forward to the day when the nations would wake up and destroy their man-made images (14:6). The idols, however, were not the divinities themselves.[9]

The Bible's casual acknowledgment of the existence of other gods stands in stark contrast to its repeated injunction that Israel must worship only Israel's god and must never use images to do so. In the Hellenistic and Roman periods, these two characteristics of Jewish religious practice—a principled cultic exclusivism and aniconic worship—were often remarked on by outsiders. But ancient Jews lived in the same world as their pagan contemporaries, which means that they lived with other gods as well. Jews thought that their own god was the best, the truest, the mightiest. Jews of an apocalyptic bent, as we shall see, looked forward to the day when the gods of the nations, together with their humans, would acknowledge the god of Israel alone as supreme. In the meantime, however, these other gods continued to inhabit the human landscape too.

The existence of these lesser divinities was a matter of experience, not a question of "belief." Paul, for example, complained that these beings attempted to impede his mission. "The god of this cosmos," he protested to one of his communities, "has blinded the minds of unbelievers" (2 Corinthians 4:4). Such beings, he tells gentile Christians in Galatia, are not gods by nature but mere *stoicheia* ("elements"), celestial lightweights unworthy of fear or of worship (Galatians 4:8-9. Note that Paul only demeans the cosmic status of these beings; he does not deny their effects and thus their existence). Idols—those figural representations of gods that are made by men—Paul insists are "nothing" (1 Corinthians 8:4, 10:19). The gods represented by these idols are actually only demons (and thus of lower status than the "living and true" God; 1 Corinthians 10:19-20; 1 Thessalonians 1:9. The Septuagint, centuries earlier, had identified them as such: "The gods of the nations are *daimones*"; Psalm 95:5). Both earth and heaven hold "so-called gods"—"indeed there are many gods and many lords," Paul notes to his Gentiles in Corinth. Nonetheless, he insists, his congregations must turn from these other, lower gods and lords to worship the god of Israel alone, together with the one lord, Jesus Christ (1 Corinthians 8:5-6). When the risen Christ returns, Paul explains, he will defeat these cosmic entities, who at that point will themselves acknowledge the god of Israel (1 Corinthians 15:24-27). They too will bend knee to the victorious Jesus (Philippians 2:10).

But Jewish apocalyptic convictions, such as Paul expresses to his communities, represent an extreme attitude toward foreign gods and thus are by definition exceptional. On a day-to-day basis, for Jews as well as for others, what mattered was deciding how to deal with the gods of outsiders while dealing with their humans as well. This was a practical question: Any god by definition was more powerful than any human, and gods as a group tended to be incensed when slighted. In general, most people opted for a sensible display of courtesy, showing and (perhaps just as important) being seen to show respect. Such courtesy went a long way toward establishing concord both with other gods (who, if angered, could be dangerous) and with their equally sensitive humans.

Third, this ancient identification of gods and peoples in the Greco-Roman world meant that piety required first of all the honoring of one's *own* gods according to ancestral custom. Ethnicity and antiquity were the measure of religious respectability and sources of pride. The terms designating proper religious behavior reflect this definition. *Ta patria êthê, patria nomima, mos maiorum, paradosis patrikôn:* All these phrases translate as "ancestral custom." No matter how odd a practice might seem—and other people's practices could strike outside observers as odd indeed—if it were ancient and traditional, it could to that degree be understood and accepted as appropriate to that particular *ethnos*.[10]

Fourth and finally, the dense religious and thus ethnic multiplicity of ancient empire was offset by the binding power of two transethnic cultic institutions: civic organization and the cult of the ruler. Both were key aspects of the legacy of Alexander, and both had a lasting effect on Roman religion and politics, even after the Roman Empire became Christian.

To civic organization first. Moderns tend to think of cities as densely populated secular space: Individual communities within a city might be "religious," but the city itself is neutral. In antiquity it was otherwise. Ancient Mediterranean cities were themselves religious institutions, which their citizens and residents were collectively responsible for maintaining. The urban elites who manned antiquity's town councils were, as magistrates, also priests. So were Roman emperors themselves, beginning with Augustus. Through innumerable public and communal rituals—processions, blood sacrifices, dancing, hymns, plays, competitions both athletic and musical—citizens and residents displayed their respect for the heavenly patrons of their city, thereby ensuring divine favor. Further, the opening of a city council, the convening of a court of law, the enjoyment of and participation in cultural events such as rhetorical, theatrical, or athletic competitions—all activities that moderns experience as religiously neutral—in antiquity honored the gods.[11]

Public displays of piety measured civic responsibility. Indeed, to be a citizen meant to take responsibility for the cult of the city's gods. These forms of social activity, by publicly demonstrating respect for the gods who superintended the well-being of the city, likewise bound the city's inhabitants together while articulating the social rankings organizing them. Civic cult frequently involved shared eating, and shared eating forged bonds between citizens and other residents, just as the sacrifices through which the gods "ate" forged and maintained the bonds between heaven and earth. Thus ancient civic ritual established and consolidated necessary relations with powerful patrons both celestial and (since rulers, too, received divine honors) terrestrial. Neglect of these responsibilities was impious, and impiety risked divine anger, which could be manifest in any number of dangerous ways—drought, flood, plague, earthquake, invading armies. Proper cult pleased gods. When gods were happy, cities prospered.

Finally, the cult of the ruler, introduced into the Mediterranean world through Alexander, was adapted and adopted by Rome. The emperors from Augustus on ruled and protected the commonwealth as heaven's special agent on earth. After death, translated to a higher realm, they continued to serve as the empire's special agents. Imperial cult served both soldier and civilian, focusing the allegiance and piety of the army while notionally binding the empire's wide-flung municipalities both politically and religiously (terms that are virtually synonymous in this context). Establishing a cult to the emperor and his family brought honor to one's city and the possibility of imperial patronage. And to offer to the emperor, as to the goddess Roma (the divine personification of the city), was to offer as well for the empire.

Inscriptions identified the ruler as "divine" (*divus*). In provincial temples and private shrines, the emperor whether living or dead could also be referred to as "god" (*deus* in Latin; *theos* in Greek). Temples, priests, feast days, blood offerings, images, incense, processions, ritual prostrations, festive gladiatorial combats: Through all these means, citizens of the empire enacted divine honors to the emperor. (Jewish citizens, in light of their ancestral customs, were excused from such liturgies.) After 312 C.E., with his decision to become a patron of the church, Constantine eventually banned blood offerings, but all the rest of the imperial cult perdured long into the Christian period. (Jews once again were excused.) And deceased Christian emperors, like their earlier pagan counterparts, continued to be venerated as heaven's special residents, well-placed celestial patrons of the empire below. In short, like the civic cults, the ruler cult served to bind citizens together even as it bound together heaven and earth. It too helped establish and maintain the *pax deorum* ("the peace of the gods") or, after Constantine, the *pax dei* ("the peace of God"), that benevolent concordant between humanity and divinity upon which depended the commonweal.[12]

*It is a marvel to be greatly respected that, while all the
nations subjugated by Rome went over to the rituals of
Roman worship, taking up those sacrilegious customs and
celebrations, the Jewish nation under foreign monarchs
whether pagan or Christian has never lost the sign of their
law, by which they are distinguished from all other
nations and peoples.*

AUGUSTINE, *AGAINST FAUSTUS* 12.13

The Greek Diaspora caused by Alexander's victories pulled other
peoples in tow. His conquests led to the wholesale resettlement of
Greek veterans and merchants in his new territories. Immigrants followed in their wake. Among them were ancient Jews.

Israel's experience centuries earlier under the Babylonian Nebuchadnezzar had been traumatic. In 586 B.C.E., that king destroyed
Solomon's temple and Jerusalem, sending captive Judeans into exile in
Babylon. Under and after Alexander, by contrast, Jews relocated voluntarily. As supporters of Hellenistic regimes, whether as merchants,
mercenaries, or regular soldiers, they willingly chose to move out into
the broader Hellenistic world: *Diaspora* ("dispersion") was not exile.
These Mediterranean Jews (or Judeans; either word translates the
Greek *ioudaioi*) came in time to view their diaspora communities as
"colonies" of the *metropolis,* the "mother city" Jerusalem. Their city of
residence became for them a *patria,* their "fatherland" and home.[1]

By the dawn of the Christian era, Jews had been settled for centuries everywhere throughout the Hellenistic world and in Italy as
well. 1 Maccabees, a Jewish text composed in the mid-second century
B.C.E., mentions substantial western Jewish populations in Egypt,
Syria, the cities and principalities of Asia Minor, the Aegean islands,

Greece proper, Crete, Cyprus, and Cyrene on the northern coast of Africa (1 Maccabees 15:22–23). The Jewish historian Josephus, a contemporary of the evangelists, preserves a remark by the pagan geographer and historian Strabo, himself an elder contemporary of Jesus of Nazareth. "This people," Strabo noted, "has made its way into every city, and it is not easy to find any place in the habitable world which has not received [them]" (Josephus, *Antiquities* 14.115).

Establishing themselves in their new cities of residence, these Jews, over the course of the centuries after Alexander, absorbed and adapted Greek language and culture. As their vernacular shifted from Aramaic to Greek, their scriptures shifted too. By about 200 B.C.E., Jews in Alexandria had completed the Septuagint (LXX), the translation of their sacred texts into Greek. Through this medium, traditional Jewish ideas about divinity, worship, creation, ethics, piety, and practice came to be broadcast in the international linguistic frequency. And due to this same fact of translation, the vocabulary of *paideia*—Greek high cultural ideas about divinity, humanity, cosmology, and government—was established within the biblical text. This creative interpenetration of Jewish and Greek ideas had enormous consequences for Western culture. Indeed, without the Septuagint, it is impossible to imagine the eventual spread and growth of Christianity.

Living among Greeks in the cities of the western Diaspora, Jews also lived among Greek gods. Their new environment encouraged an attitude toward this pantheon that differed markedly from their scriptures' contempt for the pantheons of the Canaanites and Philistines. The Bible often reviled the other Semitic gods for inspiring human idolatry, sexual licentiousness, and infanticide. The behavior of Greek gods, as described in ancient poetry, was no less unsavory. Yet the classical deities, deeply integrated into the life of the polis, eventually acquired "culture" via the ingenious interpretations of their well-educated human followers. Through the literary canon that shaped Hellenistic education—Homer and Hesiod; Sophocles, Euripides, and Aeschylus; comedians, grammarians, literary critics, rhetoricians—these gods dominated education itself. To the degree that western Jews availed themselves of the opportunities offered by their new Hellenistic environment, to that degree they made their peace with Greek gods, around whose cults pulsed the political and cultural life of their cities. The Alexandrian translators of the Septuagint, moving their sacred text from Hebrew into Greek, seem to have acknowledged, delicately, their new circumstances. Coming upon the Hebrew of Exodus 22:27, they altered the prohibition against reviling "God" (*elohim*, a Hebrew plural form used for the singular Jewish deity) to "Do not revile *the gods*" (Greek: *tous theous;* Exodus 22:28 LXX).[2]

Hellenistic city life put Jews in a potentially awkward situation. Like everyone else, Jews (or "Judeans") had their own ancestral, thus ethnic, traditions. But unlike anyone else, Jews were in principle restricted by their traditions to worshiping only their own god. Some pagan observers commented irritably on this fact, complaining of Jewish civic irresponsibility or disloyalty or impiety or at least discourtesy. But majority culture was extremely capacious, and respect for ancestral tradition was the bedrock of Mediterranean religious, political, and legal civilization. Thus, despite evidence of pagan irritation or offense, we also have evidence of pagan patience and even sympathy. By and large, these people were prepared to make allowances for Jewish religious difference even on this point of Judaism's (odd) cultic exclusivism, precisely because of Judaism's ethnicity and antiquity.[3]

But how exclusive were ancient Jews? They served as town council members, as athletes, as actors, as patrons of pagan festivals, as officers in gentile armies: All of these activities touched on cult to other gods. All such Jews obviously managed to find ways to benefit from and to contribute to local Greek culture, serving both their own traditions and those of their cities. They learned how to live with non-Jewish neighbors and/or fellow citizens, and thus with their gods as well.

To repeat: That these other gods existed was a matter of experience, not a question of belief. Sometimes we find evidence of Jews' acknowledging these gods and demonstrating respect for them. In the third century B.C.E., two local deities appeared in a dream to Moschos son of Moschion, ordering him to free one of his slaves. He did so, installing the record of his obedience in their temple. Nonetheless, in this inscription, Moschos identified himself as *Ioudaios*, "Judean" or "Jew." (Either translation works, because ancient ethnicity and religion stand on the same continuum.) A century later, one Niketas from Jerusalem gave a hundred drachmas in support of a festival dedicated to Dionysus. Higher up the social scale, we find the example of Herod the Great, king of the Jews (d. 4 B.C.E.). Famous for keeping the purity and food laws of his people, Herod insisted that a Gentile who sought marriage with his sister first be circumcised; and he also gloriously refurbished the Temple in Jerusalem. Yet Herod also built temples to foreign gods and to the emperors, and he sponsored Olympic games, dedicated to Zeus. Diaspora Jews seem no less flexible. Pious inscriptions from the Bosporus, consigning new freedmen to the care of the synagogue, open with praise to the "almighty god" and close with a nod to heaven, earth, and sky: Zeus, Gaia, and Helios. (Cf. Isaiah 1:2: "Hear, O heavens, and give ear, O earth!") And Jews might install inscriptions to their own god in pagan temples.4

How do we understand this behavior? Were ancient Jews not "monotheists"? By modern measure, yes and no. Their god, the god of Israel, was for them the highest and mightiest god. By living according to ancestral custom ("the traditions of my fathers," as Paul says; Galatians 1:14), Jews enacted their respect for and their fidelity to their own god. (Both Jews and outsiders identified these customs most commonly with Sabbath, food laws, and, for males, circumcision.) But these Jews were *ancient* monotheists. This meant that they (like the apostle Paul) knew that heaven and earth held other, lower divine personalities and forces as well. In certain circumstances, these divinities could be, and were, acknowledged.

The circumstances mattered. The manumission inscriptions mentioned earlier record pious individual acts, not civic communal ones. And Herod, by contrast, was a very public figure and the empire's loyal client: His political status obligated him to make lavish displays of largesse and of loyalty to Rome. Neither set of activities need be seen as contravening "Jewish tradition," which (then as now) was interpreted differently by different Jews in different places. But when in the second century B.C.E. a foreign king, Antiochus IV, introduced Greek cult into Jerusalem's temple, the Maccabaean revolt erupted, eventuating in the establishment of a Jewish kingdom under the victorious family of the Hasmoneans. And Caligula's effort to put his own statue in the Temple in 40 C.E. led to a massive strike in Judea and Galilee and grim predictions of an empirewide revolt. (Caligula's assassination averted the crisis.) The worship of images—especially in the Temple in Jerusalem—was for Jews expressly forbidden by their tradition. For this reason (the unhappy exceptions of Antiochus and Caligula to one side), authorities routinely excused Jews, whether as loyal provincials or as Roman citizens, from obligations to the gods of majority culture.

The schools and the courts, the councils, the theaters: All of these organs of the city provided one context for shared social (and to that degree, religious) activity between pagans and Jews in the Diaspora. Jewish adolescents received good Greek educations in their cities' gymnasia and so joined the ranks of the *ephebes,* young adolescent males whose municipal duties entailed participating in competitions dedicated to the gods. Jews participated both as contestants and as spectators at these events. (Again, given the intrinsically religious nature of such activities, the modern analogy is less to the Super Bowl or to Carnegie Hall than to high mass.) Every time we find a Jewish ephebe, a Jewish town counselor, a Jewish soldier or actor or athlete, we find a Jew identified as a Jew who nonetheless spent part of his working day demonstrating courtesy toward gods not his. And while Jews in principle did not join actively in the sacrifices attendant upon the ruler cults native to Hellenistic and, later, Roman culture, they dedicated their synagogues to these rulers (who were divine figures for the local majority) and in Jerusalem made offerings on the emperor's behalf. Prayers were offered not to rulers but for them.[5]

✦ ✦ ✦

TWO JEWISH INSTITUTIONS—one local, one distant—served to express and to instill a special sense of Jewish identity while at the same time providing, as these foreign cities did, a context for shared social and religious activities between Jews and pagans.

The local institution was the "synagogue." Ancient literature and inscriptions sometimes use the term *synagôgê* to designate the assembly of the local Jewish community itself. *Proseuchê* ("prayer house"), another common term, certainly implies an actual building; and other Greek or Latin terms for these associations of Jews also appear (*col-*

legium, synodos, politeuma, communitas). From Italy to Syria, from the Black Sea to North Africa, remnants of these foundations have been recovered. Wherever there were Jews, it seems, there were synagogues.

Ancient synagogues appear to have functioned as community centers. They were also a type of ethnic reading house, where Jews could gather at least once every seven days to hear instruction in their ancestral laws. ("From early generations Moses has had in every city those who preach him," remarks James, Jesus' brother, in the Acts of the Apostles, "for he is read every Sabbath in the synagogues"; 15:21.) On the analogy of pagan temples, synagogues could serve as places where manumissions were enacted and recorded; and some pagan rulers gave synagogues, like temples, the status of places of asylum. Synagogue organizations hosted community fasts, feasts, and celebrations; they held archives of community records and copies of sacred books. They settled issues of community interest: announcing the calendar of festivals, negotiating access to appropriate foodstuffs with the civic authorities, adjudicating internal disputes. They sponsored fund drives, and they honored conspicuous philanthropy with public inscriptions.

An intriguing number of big donors to diaspora Jewish communities were not themselves Jews. They were pagans, and the record of their benefactions affords us a glimpse of the mixed population that supported synagogue activities. One especially striking inscription, from Acmonia in Phrygia, recalls the generosity of a first-century Roman noblewoman, Julia Severa. This distinguished lady, a high priestess in the imperial cult (thus publicly responsible for the worship given the Julian emperors), had paid for the synagogue building itself. Another very wealthy pagan lady in the third-century C.E., one Capitolina, recorded that she had (lavishly) furnished a synagogue interior. Jews in Aphrodisias in Asia Minor, sponsoring a fund drive of some sort (fourth or fifth century C.E.), inscribed their donor monument with names of sponsors specified by affiliation: "native" Jews, converts to Judaism ("proselytes"), and gentile sympathizers ("god-fearers"), whether pagan or (in view of the inscription's late date) perhaps Christian. Nine in this last group were members of the town council. And synagogues elsewhere benefited from the patronage of city magistrates, whose generosity they duly proclaimed in stone.[6]

This same picture of mixed populations in diaspora Jewish communities, teased from epigraphy, is supported by varied literary evidence. Professional magicians, for example, evidently dropped by the synagogue to hear stories of a powerful god whom they could later evoke in their own spells. In the recipe books that they left behind, we find "magical" Hebrew (or Hebrew-like) words, as well as biblical episodes—badly garbled—that could easily have been picked up by listening to the Septuagint read and expounded, as Jewish communities were known to do every week. And ancient Jews, like their pagan counterparts, frequently celebrated their holy days out of doors, singing, dancing, processing, eating. The visibility of such celebrations invited the interest and the participation of outsiders, as Philo of Alexandria (d. 50 C.E.?) attests. Philo describes an outdoor meal on a beach just outside the city proper, "where not only Jews but also multitudes of others cross the water to do honor to the place [the site according to tradition where the Septuagint was translated] . . . and also to give thanks to God" (Life of Moses 2.41–42).

Both modern scholars and ancient observers refer to these interested pagans as "god-fearers," and indeed that is how they referred to themselves. Another word used, both then and now, is "Judaizers." The terms are elastic, which fits the imprecision of our ancient data and of the phenomena that they witness to. Occasional pagan involvement stands at one end of this behavioral spectrum, but levels of engagement were known to increase. As pagan, Jewish, and later Christian sources tell us, interested pagans sometimes chose to assume some specifically Jewish observances and to involve themselves in more sustained ways with the activities of their Jewish neighbors. Ancient sources speak (and the non-Jewish ones complain) most often about pagans who assume dietary restrictions or Sabbath observance or who participate in major Jewish fasts (such as Yom Kippur) or feasts (such as Passover). The Gospel of Luke tells the story of a centurion in Capernaum in the Galilee, evidently a Gentile, who solicits a cure from Jesus. In support of his request, the Pharisees praise him as one who "loves our nation, and he built us our synagogue"—an example of the god-fearer-as-patron (Luke 7:5). Another centurion, Cornelius, is identified explicitly as a god-fearer. Though a worshiper of Roman gods (since he is a commander in Rome's army), Cornelius distinguishes himself through pious acts that Jews habitually associated with Judaism: conspicuous charity to the poor and constant prayer to God (Acts 10:2). Acts also depicts a significant gentile presence within the Jewish communities of the Diaspora: *Sebomenoi*—that is, pagan "god-fearers"—hear the gospel through the synagogue.[7]

The point, for our present purpose, is that these pagans, when they so chose, participated *as pagans* in Jewish communal activities. For pagans, multiple religious allegiances were entirely normal; indeed, majority culture usually accommodated this sort of openness to various cults. These Gentiles freely assumed as much or as little of Jewish ancestral practices as they cared to, while continuing unimpeded (as the case of Julia Severa demonstrates) in their own cults as well. No formal constraints from the pagan side seem to have abridged this ad hoc, improvised, voluntary, and evidently comfortable arrangement.

Nor, it must be stressed, did Jews impose constraints on this pagan support: After all, the demand for exclusive worship had been given by Israel's god to Israel alone. Welcoming the material support and encouraging the interest and even the admiration of those from the host pagan majority, furthermore, simply made good sense, both socially and politically. Exclusive for insiders (Jews in principle were not to worship foreign gods), Judaism was thus inclusive for outsiders (interested Gentiles, whether pagan or, eventually, Christian, were welcomed). In the cities of antiquity, it seems, no fences made good neighbors, and the give-and-take among communities within these cities contributed to the maintenance of the interethnic, thus interreligious urban ecosystem.

As with synagogue buildings in the Diaspora, so with the Temple in Jerusalem: It too provided a common space for Jews and pagans. The Temple was the prime Jewish institution that served to focus Jewish identity at home and abroad, while also accommodating interested outsiders. Jews from everywhere within the empire and beyond came to Jerusalem on pilgrimage. For the late spring festival of Shavuot (Greek "Pentecost"), the Acts of the Apostles in the New Testament lists Jewish pilgrims from Parthia, Mesopotamia, the Black Sea, Asia Minor, Egypt, Libya, Crete, Roman Arabia, and Rome itself (Acts 2:9–11). Interested pagans came as well, especially for the grand festivals: Both the Gospel of John and Josephus mention such people, especially in connection with Passover (John 12:20; *Antiquities* 14.110). Those Jews who did not make the journey—the vastly greater majority—could contribute annually to defray the Temple's overhead expenses. This voluntary donation of the "Temple tax," a half shekel or two drachmas, in effect enabled Jews far off to participate in the enactment of their people's ancient cult. The funds they collected could be so considerable that their cities of residence occasionally sought to appropriate these monies for more local use. But pagan authorities honored the Jews' ancestral custom and guaranteed their right to collect and to send this donation on to Jerusalem. As a result of these voluntary donations, Jerusalem ran in the black for as long as the Temple stood.[8]

Under Herod the Great, king from 37 to 4 B.C.E., the Temple reached the acme of its splendor. Herod expanded the area around the old sanctuary to some thirty-five acres, enclosing it with a magnificent wall that ran nine-tenths of a mile along its perimeter. Concentric courtyards of graduated size ringed the Temple's interior sacred space. Its innermost sanctum was entirely empty, given over to the presence of the people's god. Next, dedicated to his service and regulated by ancient purity codes, stood the court of his priests, who supervised offerings at the altar. Two other courts circumscribed this area, the inner one for Jewish men, the outer for Jewish women. But the whole was surrounded by the vast and beautiful stone tundra of the Gentiles' Court, or the Court of the Nations. Gentiles and Jews would mingle in this space, which Jews necessarily traversed to reach their own courts for cult activity. As in the diaspora synagogue, so in Jerusalem's temple: Pagans as pagans had a place to show respect for Israel's god ("a house of prayer for all the nations" in the prophet's famous phrase; Isaiah 56:7). In fact, at the Temple, they had the largest court of all. Israel's priests, meanwhile, burned offerings at God's altar on behalf of the imperial family and the empire. Traditional piety, ethnic pride, international politics, tourism, public pomp: It all came together in Herod's extraordinarily beautiful building.

✦✦✦

THIS PICTURE of comfortable Jewish–pagan interactions should not suggest that patience with foreign gods was embraced universally as a virtue, or that social life was friction free. When they so desired, Hellenistic Jews could formulate their own teaching of contempt, taking aim at pagan contemporaries, expatiating on the immoral and demeaning consequences of idolatry. "How miserable are those, their hopes set on dead things, who give the name 'gods' to the works of human hands," chides the (Alexandrian?) author of Wisdom of Solomon, sometime in the first century B.C.E. (Wisdom 13:10). Such people kill children in their initiation ceremonies and give themselves over to frenzied reveling; they defile their own marriages with adultery, their societies with treacherous murders; they prophesy falsehoods and commit perjury; they lie, cheat, and steal (Wisdom 14:23–28). Paul the apostle, a hundred years later, repeats and amplifies Wisdom's themes. Pagans degrade themselves with passions and with unnatural sexual acts; their minds are debased, their ways malicious, their societies violent (Romans 1:18–32). This rhetoric could heat up real life. The disastrous war against Rome began in Caesarea, where pagan sacrifices, provocatively staged close to a synagogue, goaded local Jews to riot and eventually led the country into open rebellion (*Jewish War* 2.285–288). And during the mysterious uprising of the Jews of Cyprus and Cyrene in the years between the first Judean revolt (66–73 C.E.) and the last (132–135 C.E., under Bar Kokhba), the bloodshed was accompanied by the deliberate desecration and destruction of pagan temples.[9]

Ancient pagan evidence also bespeaks various grievances, these directed against diaspora Jewish communities and against other resident foreign groups. Then as now, globalization and multiethnic, multicultural empire provided opportunities for the cultivation of ethnic stereotyping, racial prejudice, and occasionally (as—notoriously—in Alexandria, that most cosmopolitan of ancient cities) fits of interethnic violence. Greek and Roman intellectuals sounded xenophobic themes in their writings: Foreigners, they feared, would pollute the blood, the traditions, and the moral fiber of their culture. In the capital itself, the governing elite was particularly zealous to guard the purity of Roman religion. From time to time the Senate ordered the expulsions of foreigners and their cults—along with astrologers and magicians—from the city.[10]

These classical authors penned bilious remarks. They complained that Jews were antisocial, hateful to outsiders, sexually profligate, lazy (because resting one day out of every seven), and cannibalistic. Modern readers, looking back through the anti-Semitic horrors of mid-twentieth-century Europe and the violence of medieval Christian anti-Judaism, are particularly sensitive to the anti-Jewish prejudices expressed by these ancient writers. This sensitivity easily obscures the fact that classical authors, in maligning Jews and Judaism, conferred no special distinction upon them. Egyptians, Parthians, and Persians; Gauls, Britons, and Germans: All came in for their share of swingeing insults and derogatory descriptions, many of them the same as those aimed at Jews. (Egyptians, said these writers, were also lazy; like Jews, Britons, and Germans, they also ate human flesh; and so on.) In the world of learned Greco-Roman ethnic prejudice, as one historian has noted, even the stereotypes were stereotyped.[11]

One ancestral tradition particular to Judaism, however, did single Jews out for vituperation of a special sort. Jewish piety in principle focused on the Jewish god alone. The sorts of practical accommodations that some Jews occasionally made to lesser deities did not soften, for ancient contemporaries, the insult of this aspect of Jewish behavior. Again, the fact that Jewish practices were ancient and ancestral for the most part legitimated them both socially and even legally, and helped Jews to obtain various exemptions, protections, and considerations. Majority culture valued ethnic loyalty as the index of piety.

But this ancient premium on ethnic loyalty is also and precisely what accounts for a special category of pagan anti-Jewish hostility. The target of this hostility was not Jews as such, but rather those pagans who decided to make an extreme commitment to Jewish ancestral practices. That is, some pagans slid from associating in synagogues with Jews, to voluntarily keeping some Jewish customs, to deciding, finally, to "become" Jews themselves. In modern idiom, pagans sometimes converted to Judaism.

Antiquity had no word for "conversion," and conceptually the act itself was odd. Ancient gods traveled in the blood; ethnicity anchored piety. How then could an individual change his ancestors, his past, and his traditions? The closest analogue in Roman society was legal adoption, another ritual creation of fictive kinship. Adoption was regulated and authorized by magistrates, who were themselves priests. An adopted person, crossing kinship lines, moved also from his own family's private religious obligations (which focused on ancestors) to assume those of his adoptive family.

For Jewish society, this crossing of the ethnic frontier, the extreme degree of association that we term "religious conversion," was most readily understood on the analogy of forging political alliances. Thus, said Philo, pagans who became ex-pagans joined the Jewish body politic (the *politeia*; *On the Special Laws* 4.34.178). Hostile pagan writers thought similarly, and saw in such behavior a species of treason. Roman elites in particular objected to conversion to Judaism as by definition conduct unbefitting a Roman. The convert spurned Roman law to take up Jewish law; he abandoned his own ancestral rites, gods, fatherland, and family to assume foreign ones. Lower-class people who made this extreme act of affiliation were evidently at small or no risk. Aristocratic Romans, however, born into special obligations to the gods and to the state, were in a different situation. The emperor Domitian executed some members of the Roman upper class precisely for lapsing into "atheism," that is, for spurning their own gods on account of treasonable loyalty to "the customs of the Jews" (Dio, *Roman History* 67.14.1–2).[12]

The problem with Judaism, in the eyes of these pagan critics, was not its peculiar customs per se. The idiosyncrasy of any ethnic culture—special days, special foods, special gods, special rules—was what marked it as specific to a particular people. *But to make a commitment to a foreign god to the point of forsaking the gods of one's own people*—a condition unique to Judaism in the pre-Christian period—*was to behave with alarming and insulting disloyalty.* And the prime marker of the male convert to Judaism—namely circumcision—was derided by majority culture with particular revulsion. Thus the main pagan objection to "god-fearing" (that is, to other pagans' Judaizing voluntarily) was the fear that such Judaizing could lead to a kind of ethnic treason, which we call "conversion." And the problem with conversion to Judaism as such was its principled exclusion of all other cult. The cultic exclusivism of born Jews was excused—sometimes grudgingly—because of the antiquity of Jewish custom. But in the convert's case, such exclusivism was adopted, not inherited; foreign, not native. The choice did not sit right, especially with patriotic Romans.[13]

Yet pagans did convert to Judaism in this period as in others, and majority culture did acknowledge these peoples' (oddly altered) status. Their turning to the laws of another nation and their consequent dropping of what was their own nonetheless seemed to some to insult the "family," the birth/blood connection that one had to one's native *genos* or *natio*. This was especially so (as we saw earlier, in the case of the emperor Domitian) if those converting were aristocrats, whose social rank came with special responsibilities for the safety and prosperity of their city. And accordingly, since people inherited their gods, such behavior could place the whole family, or city, at risk. Respect for one's own ancestral customs defined piety. To abandon these customs was impious. Impiety angered gods. And angry gods usually made for unhappy humans.

The complex religious ecosystem of the Greco-Roman city provided the social context for the growth and spread of a very peculiar type of mid-first-century Hellenistic Judaism, namely, early Christianity. Like other Hellenistic Jewish communities, Christian ones welcomed sympathetic pagans; unlike those others, however, Christian Jews actively solicited these pagans to join and to commit to their assembly (Greek, *ekklêsia*). This vigorous mission to pagans marks Christianity as a Jewish movement specific to the Diaspora: The Diaspora, after all, was where (most) pagans were. But the very earliest Christianity was not a diaspora phenomenon at all. If we take seriously the tradition's own claims as embodied in the gospels, Christianity originated specifically in the Jewish homeland, in the mission and message of Jesus of Nazareth.

Renowned as an exorcist and as a holy man, Jesus had taught within the overwhelmingly Jewish context of rural Galilee and early-first-century Judea. Like John the Baptizer before him and like many of the prophetic figures in that region who preached in the decades after him, Jesus announced the impending arrival of God's kingdom. (Jesus' first statement in Mark's gospel, for example, is "The time is fulfilled, and the Kingdom of God is at hand!"; Mark 1:15). The Roman prefect Pontius Pilate evidently heard sedition in his message, or feared that others did. He arrested Jesus in Jerusalem during the Passover holiday and crucified him as a rebel (around 30 C.E.). But shortly after Jesus' execution, a sizable group of his followers reassembled. They were convinced that they had seen Jesus again, risen from the dead.[14]

Jewish ideas about the resurrection of the dead had germinated centuries earlier, within the context of speculations about the End of the Age. Developing out of the prophecies of consolation that had flourished especially in the wake of Nebuchadnezzar's destruction of Jerusalem (around 586 B.C.E.), Jewish apocalyptic literature particularly flourished in the two centuries to either side of Jesus of Nazareth's lifetime, roughly from the period of the Hellenistic kingdoms after Alexander to the years of the high Roman Empire. The sufferings of the righteous; a final battle between Good and Evil— sometimes led by God himself, sometimes by an archangel, sometimes by a messiah (or two, according to one of the Dead Sea Scroll texts)—the ingathering of the scattered people of Israel; the restoration or enlargement of Jerusalem and of the Temple; the punishment of the wicked; the destruction of idols; the foundation of enduring, universal peace: These various anticipated events, presented variously and in various combinations in various apocalyptic texts, would signal the coming of God's kingdom and would mark its establishment.

Apocalyptic thought, in other words, represents neither a "doctrine" nor even a universal set of expectations. Rather, it expresses a particular mentality of urgency, coupled with intense religious conviction. If times were terrible, if the wicked flourished and the righteous languished, that must mean that God would soon intervene to put things right, which was the way that they should be. The god of Israel was just, good, and powerful. He would not tolerate for long this inversion of moral order. He would not permit history to drift indefinitely. (The identities of the "wicked" and of the "righteous," of course, depended on the perspective and the circumstances of the visionary writer.) Once one knew how to read these signs of the times, the codes for which were often revealed in apocalyptic texts, one could know when the End would come, when God would fulfill his long-postponed promise of redemption.

Within these varied and variable traditions about the End time, the resurrection of the dead was conceived as a communal event. The idea represented an extension of the prophetic idea of the ingathering of Israel. The prophecy in Ezekiel 37, for example, can be read in this light. God and Ezekiel together ponder a valley of dry bones. The Lord commands; Ezekiel prophesies. The bones rise up, assemble, bloom with flesh, stand on their feet, and live.

> "Son of man," he said to me, "these bones are the whole house of Israel.... [S]ay to them, Thus says the Lord: Behold I will open your graves, and I will raise you up, O my people; and I will bring you home into the land of Israel.... Behold, I will take the people of Israel from the nations among which they have gone, and I will gather them from all sides.... My servant David shall be king over them.... My dwelling place shall be with them; I will be their god, and they shall be my people."
>
> EZEKIEL 37:11–27

In other visions, this idea of communal resurrection and home-coming extended even more broadly. Not only all of Israel, living and dead, would reassemble in Jerusalem; *all* of the dead, the nations as well, would be raised, and everyone judged. The wicked would receive their well-deserved reward; at last, so would the just. Establishing finally his unchallenged reign, God would plant Israel back in the Land, while giving the nations a place also alongside the Jews in his kingdom.[15]

The earliest disciples' experiences of the risen Jesus thus represented an anomaly in the perspective of this tradition. The resurrection of the dead had been imagined as a communal event, not an individual episode; and in any case, resurrection was not to precede these other prophesied End-time events. And what possible meaning could an individual resurrection have, especially as the world continued on just as it had before?

Jesus' followers made a bold inference. The miracle of his resurrection, they proclaimed, confirmed Jesus' original prophecy: The kingdom really *was* at hand, the redemption of Israel and the transformation of the world really was about to begin. And Jesus himself, they declared, was the kingdom's messiah. His first coming had ended not with his crucifixion but with his glorious resurrection. His second coming would restore life to the dead, defeat once for all the power of evil, gather in the elect, and establish God's kingdom.[16]

This good news of the imminent redemption of Israel spread rapidly. Fired by their convictions, some of Jesus' early followers took this message from Jerusalem throughout Judea, along the seacoast and up into Asia Minor, following pathways laid out by the network of synagogue communities. There they encountered what was for them a new social reality: These diaspora synagogues, unlike their counterparts in Galilee and Judea, held interested pagans in significant numbers. Together with some of the synagogues' Jews (such as, eventually though not initially, Paul), some of these pagans also responded positively to earliest Christianity's apocalyptic message.[17]

How did these early Jewish missionaries, so shortly after Jesus' execution, react to this unanticipated pagan response? As we can see from Paul's letters, mid-first century, the first generation did not know quite how to proceed. Some missionaries (like Paul and those in his circle) argued for these Christian Gentiles to be received, though provisionally, *as* Gentiles. As long as they behaved in certain ways—and above all, as we shall shortly see, in a specifically public, Jewish way—they could join in and with the new community. Other Christian missionaries strongly dissented from this view and pressed for more formal affiliation to Judaism—not only the same Jewish public behavior that Paul insisted on but also Jewish private behavior: circumcision for male pagans, attention to Israel's calendar, and the committed maintenance of Jewish ancestral custom. In other words, conversion to Judaism.

The confusions and vigorous disagreements of this first generation of Christian Jews imply that Jesus himself had never directly addressed the gentile question. When we move from Paul's letters to the New Testament's next strata of historical evidence, the Gospel of Mark (probably written sometime shortly after the Temple's destruction in 70 C.E.) and the traditions preserved in Q (material common to Matthew and Luke that is not found in Mark), we can see that instruction concerning sympathetic pagans is scarce in the gospel material itself. And even though all four canonical gospels presuppose the existence of a gentile mission—indeed, by the time that they were written, in the final third of the first century, that mission seems to be already well established in the Diaspora—these gospels do not feature Gentiles with any prominence in their respective narratives about Jesus' mission. All of this literary evidence accords with what we can surmise was the case historically: Pagans did not figure prominently among Jesus' original hearers in Galilee and Judea. Nor, evidently, did they occupy a major place in his teachings.

Nonetheless, the question still remains: Even absent clear teachings from Jesus, *why should this enthusiastic pagan response to the good news of the coming kingdom have been a problem for the young movement in any case?* After all, Jewish communities in the Diaspora had accommodated and benefited from the interest and even the participation of outsiders for hundreds of years by this point; and they would continue to do so for long after. With all these centuries of such successful precedent to look to—and a precedent specific to diaspora synagogue life—why did the missionaries of this new messianic movement not simply use the traditional model, and welcome pagans *as* pagans into the fold?

One part of the answer lies with the fact that the Jesus movement *was* messianic. That is, the convictions and commitments of its disciples, the very way that they defined the mission and message of Jesus and articulated beliefs about his second coming, drew upon larger traditions of apocalyptic thought. These traditions focused squarely on the redemption of Israel: the people's return to the Land; their rededication to Torah; their feasting and rejoicing on God's mountain, the home of his house, the Temple in Jerusalem. What role in such imagined scenarios did foreign nations play?

Speculations on the eschatological fate of Gentiles lie scattered throughout apocalyptic literature. We can cluster them at two poles. At the negative extreme, God in his wrath crushes these nations, destroying them and their cities. Thus, for example, the vision of "Enoch": "The [Gentiles'] towers shall be engulfed in flame, and removed from the whole earth. They shall be thrown into the judgment of fire, and perish in wrath and in the force of the eternal judgment" (1 Enoch 91:9). At the End, teaches 4 Ezra, a late-first-century C.E. apocalyptic text, the nations will assemble near Mount Zion. There they will be "reproved for their ungodliness ... reproached for their evil thoughts," and they will be destroyed (4 Ezra 13:32–38). "Rouse your anger and pour out your wrath," exhorts Sirach, or Ben Sira, a text from the early second century B.C.E. "Destroy the adversary and wipe out the enemy. . . . Let him who survives be consumed in the fiery wrath, and may those who harm your people meet destruction. Crush the heads of the rulers of the enemy" (Sirach 36:7–10). Consoling Israel, "Baruch" promises, "Your enemy has overtaken you, but you will soon see their destruction, and will tread upon their necks" (Baruch 4:25, probably edited in the second or first century B.C.E.).

At the positive pole, by contrast, we find traditions that look forward to the nations' inclusion in the Kingdom of God. "In those days ten men from the nations of every tongue will take hold of the robe of a Jew, saying, 'Let us go with you, for we have heard that God is with you'" (Zechariah 8:23). After witnessing the eschatological ingathering of Israel, says "Tobit" (some time in the second century B.C.E.), "all the Gentiles will praise the Lord ... and all who love the Lord God in truth and righteousness will rejoice, showing mercy to our brethren," (Tobit 14:7). "All the nations shall flow to it," prophesies Isaiah about Jerusalem in the new age. "Many peoples shall come and say, 'Let us go up to the mountain of the Lord, to the house of the god of Jacob'" (Isaiah 2:2–3). This inclusive apocalyptic tradition, in other words, envisaged the social makeup of life in the kingdom as mirroring that of everyday reality. (Confusingly, many of these writings, such as Isaiah and Sirach, express *both* extremes, those traditions about final punishment and those about final inclusion.) Jews and Gentiles, in the positive view, would reside together at the end of days in God's kingdom.[18]

So far, this eschatological tradition of gentile inclusion seems

little different from the noneschatological practice of receiving interested pagans *as* pagans in the diaspora synagogue. But there was a
huge difference, one that we will see more clearly if we attend to a
problem with our English usage. In the preceding paragraphs, I have
used the two words *gentile* and *pagan* interchangeably. In so doing, I
have tried to have my usage reflect that of the New Testament's first-
century Greek. In English, *gentile* and *pagan* obviously are two different
words, and they have different connotations. *Gentile* registers ethnicity.
It is a neutral way to indicate Jewish status—that is, the person in question is not a Jew. *Pagan* on the other hand indicates religion: not only
"not Jewish religion" but also "not Christian religion." And, until very
recently, *pagan* would also register a note of disdain or disapproval.
This last is no surprise because the word applied this way is a derogatory coinage of the fourth-century church, which wished to distinguish biblical religions from the worship of the gods.

Only a single Greek word, however, stands behind both English
ones: *ta ethnê*, "the nations." This word translates the Hebrew *ha goyim*,
"peoples." In the Septuagint the word denotes everyone who is not
part of Israel. As with the paired terms *Greek* and *barbarian*, so too
with *Israel* and *the nations:* The two words taken together stand for "all
humanity," divided up roughly as "us" and "them." And, since "race"
and "religion" stood in the same continuum in antiquity, the biblical
paired words *Israel/ta ethnê* distinguished humans according to ethnic
group and, at the very same time, according to "religion" (better, "ancestral custom"). The ethnic distinction was the religious distinction
was the ancestral distinction. (Hence Paul's comparable division of
humanity into *tâs peritomâs* and *tâs akrobustias*, "the circumcised" and
"the uncircumcised," or, more literally, "the foreskins"; Galatians 2:7.)

Barring what we think of as conversion to Judaism, *all* Gentiles—
even those benefactors variously associated with Jewish communities as
god-fearers—were pagans. They worshiped the gods native to them,
however many other gods (including Israel's god) they might add on.
This point marks out the *crucial difference between the diaspora synagogues'
actual practice of including pagans and the apocalyptic traditions' ideas about
including pagans.* The synagogue's Gentiles were pagans. The kingdom's
Gentiles, however, were a theoretical category: ex-pagan pagans or (to

use the wiggle room created by our two English terms) ex-pagan Gentiles. When the lord of the universe reveals himself in glory, say these Jewish apocalyptic texts, the nations will repudiate their gods (who will themselves at this time worship Israel's god), destroy their idols, and worship Israel's god together with redeemed Israel. In other words, these Gentiles would also be included in the kingdom, and they would be included *as* Gentiles. But they would not worship other gods anymore.

This last point needs stressing. The nations' destruction of their idols in this literature did *not* imply that, at the end of time, they converted to Judaism. The marker of conversion in Judaism—universally named as such by Jews, by pagans, and later by Christians—was circumcision. No known apocalyptic text mentions or alludes to circumcision in the event. Rather, when God redeems Israel, these texts proclaim, the nations will *turn from* the lower gods whose images they had worshiped and *turn to* the god of Israel. *"Turn* to me!" cries God, not only to Israel but also to the nations (Isaiah 45:20–22). Similarly Tobit: Once God brings Israel back to the Land, "all the nations will *turn* in fear to the Lord God . . . and they will bury their idols" (Tobit 14:6).

Turning is a good biblical and post-biblical prophetic locution. But because of the accidents of translation—Greek into Latin into English—this idea of the apocalyptic *inclusion* of Gentiles, which is what this term represents, becomes garbled. The words for "turn" in Greek—*-strephô* with various prefixes—come into Latin as *conversus* words; and *conversus* words come into English as "conversion." But in these ancient texts, these theoretical, eschatological Gentiles do *not* "convert"—that is, they do not receive circumcision and/or in some way "become" Jews. Nor do they turn to "Judaism" and thus to Jewish ancestral custom. What they turn to is Israel's god, who is the god of the whole universe. It is as Gentiles that they worship him. So too, mutatis mutandis, opined Paul, in a letter pulsing with apocalyptic conviction. "You turned to God from idols," writes Paul to his pagan Christians in Thessalonika, "to worship the true and living god" (1 Thessalonians 1:9).[19]

This passage from Paul's letter to the Thessalonians leads us back into the mind-set of the earliest Christian Jews who traveled throughout the western Diaspora. When those pagans who were affiliated with synagogues began turning to the gospel, the new mission absorbed them, because such a prospect cohered with those apocalyptic traditions already shaping their worldview. The ancient traditions of gentile inclusion evidently helped the early missionaries to improvise in their unanticipated situation, as time stretched on between Jesus' postresurrection appearances and his anticipated triumphant return. These new communities saw themselves as the vanguard of the fast-approaching kingdom: dead to the evil powers of the present age, filled with the spirit of God so that they could exorcise and prophesy, living in anticipation of the return of God's son to consummate his mission of redemption. And, consistent both with general Jewish social practices in the Diaspora and with the inclusive traditions of Jewish apocalyptic expectation, the earliest missionaries neither asked nor encouraged these pagans to commit exclusively to Judaism and thus, for men, to receive circumcision. It was *as* Gentiles that these people joined the assembly (*ekklêsia*) of Christ.

But their acceptance into this new movement was provisional. The proviso was this: *Christian Gentiles—who were Christian pagans—could no longer worship their native deities.* This condition, which again cohered with apocalyptic speculations about pagans at the End of the Age, was socially unprecedented on a large scale: Jews had never before run *missions* to solicit pagan interest in Judaism. And this surprising new policy—encouraging pagans to act like Jews but not to "become Jews"—placed these people in a completely new (and ultimately dangerous) situation. Earlier, as synagogue-going god-fearers, they had never faced such a demand. The custom of the diaspora synagogue—long-standing, eminently practical, and, within the larger context of ancient Mediterranean piety, entirely normal—was simply to receive sympathetic outsiders. Well before the birth of Christianity, these synagogues had welcomed such pagan Gentiles. And well after the birth of gentile Christianity, these synagogues continued to welcome pagan Gentiles. (Much to the annoyance of later bishops, diaspora synagogues even continued to welcome Christian Gentiles.)

But the mid-first century diaspora *ekklêsiai*, these tiny, Jewish, messianic convocations, seem universally to have insisted that sympathetic pagans renounce their native gods as a condition of belonging fully to the new community. The question that (only eventually) split the early mission was not *whether* to accept these ex-pagan Gentiles as members, but whether these people should become Jews more formally, thus for men to receive circumcision and for all to assume other specifically Jewish practices: dietary customs, the Jewish calendar of holy days, and so on. ("Whoever receives circumcision"—that is, who converts fully to Judaism—"is responsible for the whole of the Law," Paul warned the ex-pagan pagans of Galatia; Galatians 5:3). About the necessity of these pagans' relinquishing their own gods to join the church, however, both Paul and his Jewish opponents, those other Christian missionaries whom he calls "the circumcisers," seem to have had no dispute.

By constructing their demand in this way, the first generation of missionaries, faced with their unanticipated reception among the synagogue's pagans, creatively applied an element of the hoped-for apocalyptic future to their present situation. Gentiles joining the movement were to *act as if* they were "eschatological" Gentiles—which, given the new community's convictions, they were. Unencumbered by the greater part of Jewish ancestral practice, they nevertheless were required, by Paul as by others, to assume precisely that very visible public behavior that was most resented by pagan culture and that pagan critics universally associated with Judaism: Christian Gentiles could not participate in cult to their native gods.

In the long run, however—precisely what these early missionaries were convinced would never be—this requirement turned out to be extraordinarily disruptive. It threatened to unsettle the centuries-long stability of Jewish–pagan relations not only within the synagogue community itself but also—indeed, especially—within the larger social and religious context of the Greco-Roman city. By declining to participate in their own familiar cults, these non-pagan pagans alienated and offended members of their own households. (For centuries hereafter, Christianity would be accused of ripping families apart and disrupting normal patterns of household authority.) And by *not* converting to Judaism (a position most associated with the apostle Paul, though others also held it), these Christian Gentiles maintained their social status and, in a sense, their civic or legal status as members of majority culture.

By removing themselves from the worship of those gods who were theirs by birth and blood, these people walked into a social and religious no-man's-land. Exemption from such worship was an accommodation extended to Jews alone, and that primarily on account of Jewish ancestral custom. These new Christian pagans, the Gentiles-in-Christ, were violating their own ancestral customs. Perhaps worse, they behaved in a way that their families, friends, and neighbors could identify only as Jewish and could associate only with the synagogue. In consequence, these people were open to charges of "atheism" and "impiety," failing to show respect to their own gods. They thus became the focus of local anxieties over public endangerment. Gods, deprived of cult, grew angry. When gods were angry, people paid.

The Acts of the Apostles, written around 100 C.E., offers vivid and historically plausible depictions of the urban response to the socially disruptive message of this tiny messianic Jewish subculture. Itinerant Christian missionaries were repudiated by their host synagogues, run out of town by irate pagan citizens, and occasionally punished by cautious Roman authorities attempting to keep the peace. The unprecedented Christian "policy" of separating pagans-in-Christ from their native cults was enormously disruptive. It provides us, however, with a gauge of the apocalyptic convictions that motivated members of these fledgling communities in their first few decades, both those of pagans who made such a commitment to the gospel and those of the messianist Jews who received them into community. Everyone expected that this anomalous and inherently unstable situation would be speedily and finally resolved. The kingdom was at hand. Christ would return soon.[20]

But as Christ delayed and the kingdom tarried, improvisations, confusions, and conflicts mounted within the Jesus movement itself. Some baptized pagans evidently resumed their participation in public cult, perhaps confused because their ancestral worship had caused no problem back when they had been non-Christian god-fearers in the synagogue. ("Do not associate with any one who bears the name of 'brother,' " thunders Paul, around 50 C.E., "if he is guilty of immorality or greed, or if he worships idols!"; 1 Corinthians 5:11, cf. 8:7–12; 10:14). In urban centers like Antioch, mixed groups meeting in households, Christian Jews and Christian pagans, became entangled in confusions over the kosher status of community food. (Galatians 2 gives Paul's account of these events; Acts 15, another.) Competing missions offered differing messages. (This too is evident from Paul, who reserves his greatest vituperation for his Christian competition.) By the late 40s, evidently, some missionaries made a principled case that Christian Gentiles should regularize their devotion to Israel's god by assuming for themselves the practices commanded by this god, thus converting to Judaism (Galatians passim; cf. Philippians 3:2 ff. Paul did not like his colleagues' idea). Such a policy would be no less socially destabilizing to diaspora synagogue communities, which might still bear the brunt of their pagan neighbors' resentment. But perhaps Christian Gentiles themselves might gain some relief. Precedent existed. As converts to Judaism, they would have some place, socially and religiously, to stand. Majority culture had long acknowledged such pagan transitions to Jewish ancestral practice.

✦ ✦ ✦

WHAT HAPPENED NEXT is difficult to say. As early as we have evidence from the Christian movement—that is, with Paul's letters, mid-first century—we hear the noise of roiling debate. The noise continued unabated ever after. Christian Jews argued with Christian Jews: This is the noisiest fight that we overhear in Paul's letters. ("Are they Hebrews? So am I. Are they Israelites? So am I. Are they descendants of Abraham? So am I. Are they ministers of Christ? . . . I am a better one"; 2 Corinthians 11:22–23 RSV.) They also argued with non-Christian Jews, who argued back: Some of these quarrels are retrojected back into the lifetime of Jesus and shape the gospel stories, especially those in Matthew and in John. ("Woe to you, O scribes and Pharisees! Hypocrites!" Matthew 23:13.) Christian Jews argued with Christian Gentiles: Should not these people, who had been swept up in the redemption promised to Israel, also keep the Sabbath, the food laws, or any of the other practices that God had revealed to Israel? And finally—the arguments for which the most abundant evidence remains—Christian Gentiles argued bitterly with each other. Vigorous variety characterized early Christianity no less than it characterized the Judaism that was its matrix.

Christian variety, and its attendant arguments, only increased with time. But beginning in the early second century, these arguments come to be expressed with increasing sharpness and clarity. This is so because rhetorically and philosophically trained intellectuals, formerly pagan, began to make their own contributions to evolving Christian movements. In articulating their commitment to Christian revelation, these men had to make sense of the literary medium of that revelation: the Septuagint first of all, but also the burgeoning body of specifically Christian writings (various gospels; collections of apostolic letters, especially Paul's; sermons; apocalypses, and so on). To do so, they interpreted these Greek texts, and defended their interpretations, in light of their shared rhetorical and philosophical culture, high Greco-Roman paideia.

In short, Christian theology itself was another late child of Alexander's success.

> *These [pagan] philosophers have been raised above the*
> *rest by a glorious reputation, which they thoroughly*
> *deserve. They recognized that no material object can*
> *be god . . . and that nothing changeable can be the*
> *supreme god.*
>
> AUGUSTINE, *CITY OF GOD* 8.6

In modern parlance, *theology* often means something like "religious thoughts." In antiquity the term had greater precision. *Theos* in Greek means "divinity" or "god." *Logos* has a very broad range of meanings: In the standard Greek lexicon, its definitions stretch for over five columns of very fine print. "Word," "reason," "discourse," "order": all these can translate *logos*. *Theologia* as the Greek word for our word "theology" means "systematic, rational discourse on the nature of the divine."

In the Greek world, this intellectual enterprise had been conceived not in temples or around altars but within ancient academies. Theology was in this sense a special branch of philosophy, which was itself distinct from traditional cult. The ways in which philosophers conceived divinity coordinated with the ways in which they imagined other aspects of reality—matter, time, soul, reason, cosmos, and so on. *God* was a key term within a larger, coherent and rational system of thought.

As a specialized exercise in reasoning, and as a study that implied an entire way of life as well as a training in particular modes of thought, philosophy stood to one side of the civic curriculum. The schools of the classical Greek polis had emphasized athletics, poetry, music, mathematics, and rhetoric. Their purpose, eminently practical, was to train the next generation of aristocrats to lead the city, whether as soldiers or as statesmen. Philosophy entered into advanced and specialized curricula only eventually, and only once the writings of philosophers (like Plato's dialogues) had themselves acquired the status of literary classics.

In the late fourth century B.C.E., following Alexander's conquests, this mode of education and these forms of intellectual culture began to be exported on a large scale. Hellenism, the new international form of Greek culture, was disseminated precisely through the social and physical structures of Alexander's new cities. These cities looked to the older classical polis as their model, and they adopted classical Greek writings as their literary canon. Rome's encounter with Hellenistic culture resulted in its adoption and adaptation of the Hellenistic curriculum as well. As a result, educated urban elites from one end of the Roman world to the other shared a common literary culture, originally mediated through the Hellenistic gymnasium.

The curriculum for these young men was exceedingly stable. From one generation to the next they read, memorized, and studied the great Greek epic poems and tragedies. (Romans eventually added Latin classics such as Virgil and Cicero to this curriculum; and well into the late empire—Augustine's lifetime and beyond—Roman education remained in principle bilingual.) These young men were trained in forensic rhetoric—that is, in how to craft persuasive oral arguments and to discredit the arguments of others—as part of their formation as future leaders in municipal and (later) imperial government. And at the highest levels, such students might advance to specialized schools offering a particular type of philosophy. Here they studied the writings of earlier masters, or at least became acquainted with them through summaries of or excerpts from their works. This mix of rhetorical and philosophical culture represented the acme of ancient education.

Those forms of philosophical paideia that owed most to Plato can properly be called monotheist. Beneath the multiplicity of physical existence, Platonists detected the effects of a single, transcendent deity, the ultimate source of everything else. This highest god—variously called "the One" or "the Father" or "the Being" or, more simply, "the god"—was imagined in self-defining terms as perfect, changeless, good, single, simple, utterly without body of any sort. He (or it) was utterly unique and uniquely self-generated. Everything else in some sense derived from or depended upon him; he alone derived from and depended upon only himself. Further, since he was absolutely without body, he could not be represented (unlike the lower cosmic deities) through any image: The high god, said these philosophers, could be "seen" only by the mind.[1]

Centuries later, philosophically educated Hellenistic Jews would interpret these pagan philosophical claims in light of their own traditions of imageless worship. They further imagined that Plato could have learned such a manifestly "Jewish" theological principle only through contact with Torah. Later still, Christian Gentiles made a similar claim: Since Plato had gotten his theology (at least on this point) "right," he could have learned it only from Christ himself as the pre-Incarnate Logos. The presupposed chronology of these two arguments, which impute the origins of Platonic theology either to Judaism or to Christianity, neatly reverses the true intellectual line of descent. Theological interpretations of the Bible, whether Jewish or Christian, depended fundamentally upon pagan philosophical paideia.

How did this high god of pagan philosophy relate to everything else? The cause but not the maker of the universe, this purely spiritual deity stood at the opposite end of an imagined continuum whose other terminus was the physical cosmos, the earth that stood at its center, and finally matter itself. The universe that could be perceived by the senses was, especially for Platonists, a sort of shadow cast by the divine world "above." The One/the many, mind/body, spirit/matter, above/below, truth/error: All of these contrasting pairs simultaneously implied a cosmology, a moral hierarchy, and an epistemological divide. The structure of the physical cosmos itself revealed to the wise the true order of things, wherein what was truest, best, and most "real" was visible not to the fleshly eye but only to the "eye of the soul," that is, to the mind. To train the mind to "see" these eternal verities, to know them and to look beyond them to the ultimate god to which they pointed, was the goal of this philosophy.

The serenely transcendent high god was in no sense a "creator."

Such a function would have compromised his perfection, implicating him in change by imputing to him an act of will. Nor could so perfect an entity be directly involved with the myriad imperfections—and, indeed, the evils—that characterized experience in the realm below the moon. Matter itself, that unstable substratum of physical reality, indeed could seem to be the god's cosmic opposite: tangible, defective, nonrational, perennially inclined to change and nonbeing. The intrinsic unruliness of matter was held to account for much of the difficulty with physical existence itself. (To see matters as "bad" since god and spirit were obviously "good" was a temptation inherent in the Platonic system itself, one that most Platonists strenuously attempted to avoid.)[2]

Divine intermediaries filled in the gap between the all-good, unchanging high god and the physical universe that only approximately reflected him. Lower gods, designated variously as the "craftsman" (demiurge in Greek) or "world ruler" (kosmokrator) or "divine reason" (logos), took on the function of organizing and sustaining the material universe according to the principles of divine order. Stars and planets, thought to be ensouled and intelligent beings themselves, likewise stood between the high god and humanity, luminous witnesses to the perfection of the upper realms. The gods of traditional pantheons, assorted cosmic envoys (angeloi in Greek), still lower local divinities called daimones (whence the English demon): All these subordinate powers helped to bind the universe together and to communicate truths about transcendent divinity to the human mind trained to understand their message.[3]

The great epic poems and plays of Greek culture, however, related quite different ideas about divinity. Literature's gods had strong individual personalities. As characters in stories, they constantly did things. They had bodies, which they used, occasionally with abandon. They forgot and remembered, grew calm or angry; they raged and plotted, lied and raped, and frequently behaved in ways that one would not tolerate in humans. The deities of classical literature, in brief, did not oblige the moral categories of rhetoric or the metaphysical categories of philosophy. How then could this cultural patrimony serve as a literary medium of divine truth?

To spin the straw of traditional narratives into the gold of intellectually and morally elevating theology, educated pagan Hellenists often availed themselves of sophisticated theories of reading. One
such—grounded in the conviction that texts held multiple levels of
meaning—was *allegory*. *Allos* in Greek means "other"; *agorein* means "to
speak." Allegory—"other-speak"—was a disciplined technique whereby
the enlightened reader could see through what a text merely said to
what it actually meant. The uneducated might simply savor the action
in ancient tales—Chronos eating his children, Zeus raping Ganymede,
Odysseus sleeping by the cave of the nymphs. The learned few, however, could see beyond the simple or "literal" meaning that was available to just anyone and instead detect the text's *huponoia*, its
"undersense," and thereby grasp its moral message, its eternal, luminous truth. Divine cannibalism? No: Time (*chronos* in Greek) is subdi-
vided into units. Divine rape? No: The soul experiences divine rapture
when it is seized by its contemplation of the One. A sleeping homesick
hero? No: The human soul yearns to leave the physical body and to return to its true home in the upper cosmos. As with humans, said the
intellectuals, so with texts: The body of flesh was the lower, irrational,
mortal part; the spirit the upper, rational, eternal part. The fleshly
body of the text—that is, the obvious narrative meaning available even
to the uneducated—had to be "looked through" in order to grasp the
text's "soul," its higher spiritual and intellectual import.[4]

Paideia did not produce atheists. Well-educated young men did
not deny the existence of the traditional gods, nor did they think that
traditional worship was unimportant. Quite the contrary. Groomed
by gymnasia to take their place in municipal councils as their cities'
leaders and wealthy patrons, these men built and endowed temples
and underwrote the celebrations—the games; the free provision of
wine, oil, and meat; the prizes awarded for excellence in dedicated
competitions—through which their city's celestial patrons were honored. As magistrates, they served as priests in their cults. Traditional
piety toward the lower gods, like appreciation of their myths, stood on
the same cultural continuum as philosophy itself. For the vast majority of ancient peoples, showing the gods honor was the best way to
avoid their anger and to protect against ill fortune. For those pious pa-

gans of philosophical bent, however, the traditional gods, their stories, and their cult all pointed the way to the One.

+ + +

JEWS IN THE GREEK-SPEAKING DIASPORA plunged into learned Hellenistic culture. They paid it the ultimate compliment and claimed that it was fundamentally, originally Jewish. What the Greeks got right, these Jews maintained—chiefly philosophy, but also mathematics, music, and astronomy—they actually got from the Jews. Plato, some argued, had studied Torah and developed his doctrines in Egypt, using a (since lost) Greek translation of the Bible made centuries before the Septuagint. One writer depicted Abraham as bringing civilization to the Egyptians, an argument for the greater antiquity of the Jews in a culture in which older was better. Hellenistic Jews forged pagan prophecies, wherein ancient sibyls hymned Jewish excellence in Homeric hexameters. Others presented "histories": King Ptolemy sought out Jewish wisdom, commissioning translations of the Torah into Greek for the royal library in Alexandria. Young Moses, in one story, received instruction from the wisest teachers of both Egypt and Greece, but of course outstripped them all; in another, he taught music to Orpheus. Jews turned out Greek poetry in praise of their own culture while ascribing authorship to the literary heroes of the Hellenistic curriculum: Aeschylus, Sophocles, Euripides. (These forgeries turn up centuries later, preserved in the texts of church fathers concerned to demonstrate the superiority of the Bible to pagan culture.) One pagan sage, Numenius of Apamea, finally conceded the point by asking, "What is Plato but Moses speaking Greek?" Ingeniously, tirelessly, Hellenistic Jews worked to liberate paideia from its pagan matrix. They thus gave it a new "native" culture: their own.⁵

When turning to their own sacred texts, however, educated Hellenistic Jews encountered the same problems that their learned pagan counterparts did when reading Homer. The first sentence of the entire collection got things off on the wrong foot by proclaiming, "In the beginning God made. . . ." (Genesis 1:1). According to the principles of philosophical paideia, either the god doing the making was not the high god (since the high god, perfect and changeless, by definition "did" nothing), or else he could not actually be "doing" anything. As with Homer, so with Moses: To transmute venerable stories into philosophically elevating truths, the simple meaning of the words had to yield to spiritual understanding. Through the efforts and imagination of erudite Hellenistic Jews, biblical theology was born.

Theology in this sense—its ancient sense—was intrinsically philosophical. The modern phrase "philosophical theology" (to put this idea another way) would be to ancient ears a redundancy. The philosophical reinterpretation of sacred ancient texts defined theology. For educated Jews attracted to this project, the fact that their scriptures were now in Greek made the task of reinterpretation much easier. Jews coming to the Septuagint's rendition of Moses at the burning bush discovered that the name of God, in Hebrew "I am" (*ehyeh,* Exodus 3:14), stood in their text as *ho Ôn,* "the Being"—exactly what anyone with a decent education, Jew or pagan, would expect as the designation of the high god. When this god established the heavens, he did so "by a word" (Psalm 33:6 RSV). The Hebrew *davar* ("word") became the Greek *logos.* For Jewish readers with allegiances to Platonism and/or to Stoicism, framing the heavens through logos, divine rationality, made good philosophical sense.

Biblical theology comes into full flower in the works of Philo of Alexandria (20 B.C.E.?–50 C.E.?). An elder contemporary of Jesus and Paul, Philo put his extensive Greek learning at the service of scriptural interpretation. He saw in the Septuagint the very best philosophical thought of his age. Indeed, he referred to Moses quite simply as "the philosopher."

In his commentary on Genesis, Philo gracefully conformed the offending elements of this ancient Semitic creation myth in its new Greek mode to the canons of philosophical rationality. The days of creation in Genesis 1, Philo observes, cannot refer to time, since (the high) God does not act in time. Rather, "days" refer to sequence and order: they are Moses' way of describing the rational process whereby God intellectually conceived the universe. The actual material realization of the plan, described in Genesis 2, was left to "the divine Logos," the image of God according to which (or whom) humanity itself was made (Genesis 1:26). Of course God has no form, Philo remarks; nor is the human body godlike. The human *mind* is what is made "after God's image and likeness." And who or what is this image and likeness? The divine Logos himself, God's own Word and Reason (*On the Creation* 23.69).

But what about the rest of the biblical creation story—the fruit tree, the wily serpent, the deceived woman, the disobedient man? "Now these are no mythical fictions such as the poets and sophists delight in," scolds Philo. Rather, Jewish stories (unlike, he insists, pagan stories) "are modes of making ideas visible, bidding us to resort to allegorical interpretation" (*On the Creation* 56.157). Where the story, if read on a simple or "literal" level, gives most offense, the educated reader finds his clue—the invitation in and from the text itself—to think on a symbolical or spiritual level, to interpret allegorically. (To be fair—and Philo isn't, here—pagan sages used exactly this same argument to justify retrieving philosophical truths from unsavory episodes in Greek myth.)[6]

Genesis 2–3, then, does not relate a story about a snake deceiving the primal woman who eats forbidden fruit and gets her husband to do the same. Such a simple understanding of the sacred text, thought Philo, indicted only the ignorance of the unphilosophical reader, not the meaningfulness and timeless validity of scripture. Understood spiritually, as the text itself demanded, these chapters relate the way that the senses ("Eve"), perennially turned toward lower, earthly things ("the serpent"), can distract even the mind ("Adam") from its pursuit of divine truth. What else should we expect from Moses, who "had attained the very summit of philosophy" (*On the Creation* 2.8)?

Not only biblical stories but also traditional practices received this same sort of spiritual interpretation. The food laws, the holy days, Shabbat, the details of animal sacrifices, the command to circumcise: Far from being the arbitrary directives of a detail-obsessed deity, these laws symbolized profound moral instructions and commitments. Circumcision, Philo observed, spiritually understood, connotes the excision of pleasure and passion (a good aim for the wise). God does not care about festivals and seasons in themselves; these symbolize the gladness and gratitude that the soul feels toward God. To live according to the Law meant to practice virtue, the goal of true philosophy.

Some educated Jews went a step further than Philo. Understanding the spiritual significance of the Law, they declined to enact its "lower" or "literal" protocols. What would be the point? After all, these commands at their most profound level were allegories of moral excellence. Once one grasped, for example, that the spiritual meaning of circumcision was self-discipline, then one lived one's commitment to the traditions of Israel by being so disciplined. Why perform a mere physical action, conforming to a literal interpretation of the command, when the purpose of the command itself was to point to this higher and more important moral truth?

The allegorizing Jews had a good point. And Philo affirmed that these Jews did indeed grasp the more profound meanings of Jewish observances. But, he said, such people acted as if they were disembodied souls instead of men living in society. Accordingly, he concluded, they were poor philosophers because philosophy entailed not only a way of thinking but also and consequently a way of living. "We should look on all these outward observances as resembling the body," he urged, "and their inner meanings as resembling the soul. It follows that, exactly as we have to care for the body because it is the abode of the soul, so also we must attend to the letter of the laws." The discipline of scrupulousness in matters of Jewish practice, Philo concluded, can only enable and enhance wisdom. "If we keep and observe these, we shall gain a clearer conception of those things of which these are symbols" (*The Migration of Abraham* 16.89–93).

In other words, for Philo as for the type of Hellenistic Judaism that he represents, true wisdom and true philosophy were not generic wisdom and generic philosophy. They were, quite specifically, Jewish wisdom and Jewish philosophy. And these were attainable only through close reading, spiritual understanding, and disciplined adherence to Jewish practice as encoded in divinely revealed Jewish scripture. The true identity of the philosopher's god, Philo insisted, was the god of Israel; but most pagans, mired in their idol worship, could not realize this. Those who did, he said, and who in consequence became proselytes, did nothing less than recapitulate the journey of Abraham, going out from the idols of their fathers' houses to the true homeland of the One God (*On the Special Laws* 4.178; *On the Virtues* 20.102–104).

Philosophical understandings of scripture, as we have just seen, could vary quite significantly among Jews who otherwise shared strong commitments. Both Philo and the allegorists whom he addressed in *The Migration of Abraham,* for example, concurred on the importance, the sanctity, the philosophical depths, and the spiritual heights of scripture. Yet they nevertheless strongly disagreed on the best way to enact their common convictions.

Paul, their younger contemporary, offers another interesting comparison with Philo. Though neither as highly educated philosophically nor nearly as prolific literarily, Paul too could offer spiritual understandings of the Septuagint much as Philo did, convinced, as was Philo, that such readings revealed the deeper significance of the text. Like Philo, Paul also saw in idolatry a standing indictment of pagan culture that gave the lie to pagan claims to wisdom. "Claiming to be wise, they became fools, and exchanged the glory of the immortal God for images" (Romans 1:22–23; for the whole passage, 1:18–32). Like Philo, Paul believed in the superior value of his own understanding of the Law's spiritual meaning. Jews who understood the Law differently from his way, Paul opined, do not understand Moses at all. "That same veil [that Moses put over his face when bringing the Torah down from Sinai] remains unlifted, because only through Christ"—the point of orientation for Paul's reading—"is it taken away" (2 Corinthians 3:14). And again like Philo, Paul valued Jewish law deeply. ("The Law is holy, and the commandment is holy and just and good"; Romans 7:12.) As a Jew who was committed to a new messianic movement, Paul had views on the ultimate meaning of scripture that distinguished him in important ways from Philo. Yet as a Jew whose first language was Greek and whose education was in good measure Greek, Paul also had much in common with Philo, not least of all the same Greek text of the Bible.

After Philo's and Paul's lifetimes, however, the Septuagint (and *testimonia,* collections of excerpts from the Septuagint) began to circulate ever more widely within communities that were increasingly independent of diaspora synagogues. We can attribute this broader circulation quite specifically to the spread of Christianity. By the late first to early second century, versions of the Christian message had found adherents among the educated class of the Roman world, as becomes evident in the types of intra-Christian disputes that we can begin to overhear in our sources. Those formerly pagan intellectuals who entered the Christian movement took upon themselves the relatively recent revelations attributed to Jesus. In so doing, these men also took upon themselves an intensified form of the same problem that troubled educated Jews about the depiction of the god of Israel in the Septuagint, and that troubled educated pagans about the depiction of the traditional gods in their own literary canon (Homer, Hesiod, Euripides, and so on).

In its starkest form, that problem was relating the perfect and changeless high god of philosophical paideia to the imperfect world of time, change, and matter. Theology in all three modes—pagan, Jewish, and Christian—was the specific expression of this more general intellectual problem. All theology proceeded by making philosophical sense of sacred texts. In the case of Christianity, however, this challenge was additionally complicated by the fact that gentile Christians for a long time had few sacred texts of their own. Paul's letters, letters written in Paul's name, gospels (many more than would ultimately appear in the New Testament's collection), various apocalypses and revelations, and a rich assortment of pseudonymous epistles all circulated widely; and different communities respected different textual collections. But for many, perhaps most, Christian communities throughout most of the second century and even into the third, their fundamental scriptures were those that they shared with the synagogue, namely, the Septuagint. This simple fact ultimately had enormous consequences, social as well as theological, for Jews and for Christians—and, as we shall see, for pagans as well.

◆ ◆ ◆

THEOLOGY, AS WE NOTED EARLIER, differs from other types of religious thought in its effort to be systematic, to coordinate the various elements of its views on divinity, humanity, and the cosmos in order to achieve an intellectually coherent whole. To be "religious" requires belonging to some sort of community, but to be "theological" requires an effort at systematic thought. For this reason, the core texts of the

New Testament collection—Paul's letters and the four gospels (Mark, Matthew, Luke, John)—are theological only incipiently. They communicate their new message through story (the gospels) and through proclamation (Paul, too). Where they appeal to philosophical terms or issues—such as the Gospel of John's brief presentation of Jesus as "logos" (John 1:1–5), or Paul's naming Christ as an agent in creation ("through whom all things are and through whom we exist," 1 Corinthians 8:6 RSV)—they offer no systematic reflection on the idea. Eventually these texts will become the subject of and occasion for theological reflection. But even once they attained that status of "scripture" themselves—an uneven and contested process not definitively concluded until the era of the imperial church—they were always understood in relation to the much larger, much older, and much more prestigious biblical canon that had preceded them: those Jewish scriptures that eventually became the Christian "Old Testament."[7]

We catch an indirect indication of more ambitious theological reflection on the Christian message in some of the later New Testament texts. In the writing known as 1 John (probably from the late first century), the author warns against "false prophets." These prophets are other Christians. What makes these Christians "false," John argues, is that they deny that "Jesus Christ has come in the flesh" (1 John 4:2). "This is he who came by water and blood, Jesus Christ, not with the water only but with the water and the blood" (1 John 5:6). In another short letter also attributed to this John, the author warns again against listening to these other Christians. "Many deceivers have gone out into the world, men who will not acknowledge the coming of Jesus Christ in the flesh. Such a one is the deceiver and the anti-Christ" (2 John 7).

Why would some Christians claim that Christ had had no fleshly body? What sort of sense would that make? We can understand what is at stake in this early dispute, and what compelled these repudiated Christians to teach that Christ did not have flesh, if we think with the principles of philosophical paideia.

"High" claims about Jesus occur in the very earliest stratum of our evidence, from mid-first century: the letters of Paul. Paul speaks of Jesus as the divine and preexistent son of God, his agent in creation, the one "through whom all things are" (1 Corinthians 8:6). Before

Jesus' mission on earth, said Paul, he was "in the form of God"—a claim for his divinity, surely—but that he then "emptied himself" and took on "the form of a slave," was born "in the likeness of men" and "in human form" (Philippians 2:5-10). When on earth, Jesus had assumed "the likeness of sinful flesh" (Romans 8:3). Paul elsewhere describes Jesus as a human being (*anthrôpos*), albeit "from heaven" (1 Corinthians 15:49); a man born of woman, under the Law—that is, a Jew (Galatians 4:4; Romans 9:5); a fleshly descendant in fact of King David (Romans 1:4). Frequently at still other points, Paul speaks of Christ's blood and of his death on a cross. And he proclaims Jesus' bodily—though not fleshly—resurrection (1 Corinthians 15:42-55).

These assertions of Paul's seem to pull in different directions. His claims for Christ's elevated, eternal, superhuman qualities—Christ's divinity, in brief—sound shocking coming from a Jew and thus from someone whom we habitually identify as a monotheist. Here, again, the modern version of the concept—belief that there is only one god—obscures both Paul's meaning and his historical context. Ancient monotheism left scope for many gods. Only one supreme god was "on top," but various other gods in this divinity-congested universe ranged beneath, lower than and in some sense subordinate to the high god. Were these lower gods "demons"? Educated pagans were comfortable with the claim. Plutarch, an intellectual of the early empire (46 C.E.?– 120 C.E.?), commented that such lower divinities were flattered when addressed by the name of the higher god whom they served. And the third-century Neoplatonist Porphyry observed that demons presided over oracles, local altars, and shrines: "They were regional deputies, not very exalted cosmic powers." In short, for pagans, *demon* (Greek: *daimon*) was a synonym for "lower god."[8]

The Septuagint reflects this neutral usage. Centuries afterward, however, when some Jews and, later, Christians impugned the moral status of these lower gods, the term assumed the negative aspect that it still has in modern English. "The gods of the nations are *daimones*," sang the Psalmist in Greek (Psalm 95:5 LXX). "What [other] pagans sacrifice they offer to *daimones*, and not to God," Paul tells *his* pagans, to whom he forbids such practices (1 Corinthians 10:20). The question of these powers' moral orientation to one side, however, the point is that their existence was assumed universally, by highly educated churchmen no less than by others. By the early fifth century C.E., Augustine could insist that *god* and *demon* were merely interchangeable terms. "If the [pagan] Platonists prefer to call these 'gods' rather than 'demons,' and to count them among those whom Plato their master writes about as gods created by the highest god, let them say what they want . . . for then they say exactly what we say, whichever word they may use for them" (*City of God* 9.23).

People of sufficient education who thought philosophically about relations between levels of divinity might see these lower gods as contingent upon the high god, meaning that their existence depended somehow on his. Less philosophically inclined monotheists were content to assert that their own particular god was the oldest or the highest or the best god. In other words, ancient "monotheism" easily accommodated the idea of multiple divinities, as long as a single deity stood at the absolute pinnacle of holiness and power. Claims for the divinity of various other beings did not compromise commitment to a single highest being, as Paul himself illustrates. And by speaking of the preexistent son as God's agent in creation—much, indeed, as pagan Hellenists spoke of the *demiurge* or *kosmokrator* and as both pagan and Jewish Hellenists spoke of the divine *logos*—Paul explicitly subordinated the divine Son to God the Father.

What about Paul's description of Jesus as *anthrôpos,* "human"? Again, thinking with the ancient context helps. Paul lived in a society comfortable with ascribing divinity to special human beings. (Heroic figures such as Heracles had started out human and ended up divine; so too, mutatis mutandis, did the emperor.) Jews famously took a different view on this matter from that of their neighbors, the pagan majority, though Philo can speak of Moses, or of the patriarchs, as representations of the divine. For moderns, Paul's assorted declarations about Jesus—that he was a man and that he appeared in the form of a man (Philippians 2:5–8), that he was truly divine and yet he truly died—can seem to stand in tension with each other. For ancients, while these claims about Jesus in particular might have seemed unusual, they were certainly not in themselves unthinkable: The universe was filled with divine personalities who manifested themselves in a vast va-

riety of ways. And on the evidence, Paul himself noticed no fatal con-
tradiction. He simply described Jesus as human and as divine, as heavenly and as historical, as having flesh and blood and as simply
assuming their "likeness."[9]

The Christians denounced in 1 and 2 John probably lived at least
one generation, perhaps two, after Paul. We know nothing about what
or which Christian writings they would have known. We do know that
collections of Paul's letters were beginning to circulate and that they
confused people. ("There are some things in them," warned a late-first-
century Greek-speaking Christian, "that are hard to understand, which
the ignorant and unstable twist to their own destruction"; 2 Peter 3:15–
16). The position that these repudiated Christians are accused of taking, however, makes sense in terms of the sorts of "high" claims for
Jesus' divinity that we find in Paul and in certain passages of the
Gospel of John. Undergirding these later Christian ideas about Jesus'
flesh, or lack of it, are the principles of philosophical paideia and the
imagined architecture of the Hellenistic cosmos.

This mental picture of the universe, inherited from Greek philosophers and reinforced by ancient science, organized reality along a vertical axis. What was physically "up" was also morally "good." Thus the
bodies of the stars—luminous, beautiful, stable, eternal—declared their
moral and metaphysical superiority to the planets, which wandered;
just as the planets in turn were superior to the moon itself, which altered in its monthly courses. Below the moon, matter grew thick and
recalcitrant. Flesh and blood—the constitutive elements of animal and
thus of human bodies—were relegated to the earth, which stood at the
universe's center, where the heaviest matter had sunk. Labile both
physically and morally, flesh was subject to insult and to death; susceptible to appetite, it distracted the mind, the highest part of the
soul. How could the fleshly body possibly be the native home of the
soul? Surely the soul came from above. (This last idea was extremely
congenial to thinkers with allegiances to Plato.) Once freed of its entrapment in the flesh, whether through sleep, spiritual ecstasy, or finally death, the soul could begin its ascent through the universe, back
up past the moon and on to its point of origin in the celestial realm.[10]

It is this worldview that probably prompted those Christians attacked in 1 and 2 John to ask a reasonable question: Had Christ at any point really had a fleshly body at all? If Christ were "from heaven," if he were divine, and if he ascended back to heaven, then why suppose that he had really inhabited animal flesh for the brief moment when he appeared on earth? And if Christ had been "raised" at his resurrection to be seated "at the right hand of the Father"—that is to say, in the highest heavens—why insist illogically (and unscientifically) that he had been in a fleshly body when he had been raised? (After all, Paul himself had explicitly taught otherwise: "Flesh and blood cannot inherit the Kingdom of God, nor can the perishable inherit the imperishable"; 1 Corinthians 15:50.) Such bodies, whether for humans or for Christ himself, belonged only in the realm below the moon. The higher the claims for Christ's divinity, in other words, the less coherent was the thought that he had ever actually had a body of flesh. If those Christians who thought this way had had access to Paul's letters and to the Gospel of John, they could easily have found support there for their own views.

Paul himself, mid-first century, does not seem to have reflected systematically on this aspect of the evolving Christian message. But evidently these later Christians did. Their theological understanding of Christ—that he had only seemed to have a fleshly body—scholars have labeled "docetic Christology" or, more simply, "docetism." The term rests on the Greek *dokeo*, "to appear." Docetism is "appearance-Christology."

For many moderns, docetism seems an odd and even a counterintuitive idea. After fifteen centuries of Christian art (and nearly one century of innumerable biblical movies), we are long accustomed to seeing Jesus represented as an embodied human male. In this formative period of Christian theology, however, gods and their messengers, the *angeloi*, were not imagined as having bodies of earthly flesh. "Not all flesh is the same," Paul had observed. "There are heavenly bodies and there are earthly bodies" (1 Corinthians 15:39–40). For those later Christians who attempted to think systematically, and thus who attempted to organize their religious assertions rationally, their belief in Jesus' divinity readily invited the coordinating claim that Jesus had neither appeared nor been raised in a fleshly body.

Docetic Christology potentially provided one way to coordinate a whole host of related and difficult issues: how to read the Bible, especially Genesis; how to conceptualize both God and those beings made "after his image and likeness" (Genesis 1:27); how to wring some overarching consistency out of Paul's letters; how to imagine salvation. If the god described in Genesis had made the physical universe, for example, how could he be the highest god? If the stories about that god stood in Jewish scriptures commonly known as the Law, and if Paul so frequently contrasted Law and gospel, how should the Christian regard those scriptures and that god? God is spirit; humans are made after his image; flesh (as Paul frequently asserted) battles against the spirit. How then could *salvation* mean anything other than the redemption of the human spirit from this lower cosmos of flesh, sin, and death, and its transfer to the divine realm of spirit, love, and life eternal?

But docetic Christology did more than provide a plumb line for theology and exegesis. It also implied an answer to a question of social import. In the view of docetist Christians, "flesh" coordinated theologically with the god who, according to Jewish scriptures, had made flesh. It was a short move from this position to a more general interpretive principle, namely, that Jews and Judaism were also particularly concerned with things of the "flesh." These Christians, by contrast, saw themselves as concerned with things of the "spirit." Their docetic Christ pointed the way to coherently relate the Jewish god to the revelation of Christ, the Jewish Law to the Christian gospel, the Jewish synagogue to the Christian church. A Christ without human flesh heralded a Christianity without Judaism.

These positions, as we shall shortly see, characterized the theologies of docetist Christians later on, in the early to mid-second century. We cannot know how many of these ideas were affirmed by those first-century Docetists whose existence we can only glimpse behind the polemics of the epistles of John in the New Testament. But they stand as the anonymous origins of a strong theological current that courses through major Christian thinkers in the second century and on to Augustine himself in the fourth. The young Augustine, encountering philosophy for the first time as a gifted "undergraduate" in the early

370s, shed his childhood faith to adhere for over a decade to the outlawed church of the Manichees. This community introduced him to the docetic Christ and to the anti-Jewish Paul. The intellectual coherence of the Manichaean position, and its unnerving resonance with more mainstream Christian paideia with its traditions of anti-Judaism, haunted him long after he returned to the Roman church. Augustine's teachings on Jews and Judaism have the clarity and the power that they do in no small part because Augustine had to pitch them against the clarity and the power of Manichaeism.

✦ ✦ ✦

ETERNITY AND HISTORY, god and cosmos, time and redemption, spirit and matter. Philosophical paideia dictated the terms and the problems that intellectual Christians thought with when they tried to frame a theology. But it also, through allegory, offered a means by which to reach answers. This was because Christian paideia, like its Jewish and pagan elder siblings, relied profoundly upon textual interpretation. The premier text was the Septuagint. Through their applications of allegorical interpretation, Christian thinkers could achieve an understanding of the Septuagint which disclosed its "true," spiritual meaning as a revelation of Christ.

Paul's own letters once again provide our earliest instance of this sort of reading. Christ was the focal point for Paul's new perspective on scripture. Once he joined the Christian movement, Paul was certain that his native traditions and Israel's scriptures themselves, properly understood ("according to the spirit, not according to the letter"), actually enunciated his own current convictions. Thus, when speaking to his Corinthian community about the material support due Christian apostles, he suddenly recalled a teaching of Moses. Deuteronomy 25:4, he realized, clinched his argument. "Do I say this on human authority? Does not the Law say the same? For it is written in the Law of Moses, 'You shall not muzzle an ox when it is treading grain' " (1 Corinthians 9:4–9). Clearly, Paul urges, the Law seeks to communicate more than just suggestions on good animal husbandry. "Is it for oxen that God is concerned? *Does he not speak entirely for our own sake?*" (v. 10). The more profound meaning of Deuteronomy, in other words, does not coincide with what it plainly says: That much would be obvious to anyone hearing the text. Rather, understood spiritually, the Law reveals a crucial truth precisely pertinent to Paul's current situation: Christian apostles working in and for the spiritual well-being of the community ("treading grain") should not be restrained ("muzzled") from partaking of the community's material well-being.

Shortly thereafter in this same letter, referring to Israel's wandering in the desert after leaving Egypt, Paul retrojects Christ back into Exodus as a character in the biblical story and as an agent in Israel's past. The children of Israel drank water from a rock in the desert, Paul recounts, "and that Rock was Christ," (1 Corinthians 10:4). Nonetheless, Paul continues, some of these same Israelites later fell into idol worship (the Golden Calf, Exodus 32) and thence plunged into indiscriminate eating, drinking, dancing, and idolatry's invariable companion sin, fornication. God destroyed them. Paul's argument assumes that these historical events did occur. But the reason for their being recorded in scripture was in order that the lesson be preserved for his Corinthian community. "Now these things happened to them as a warning, *but they were written down for our instruction, upon whom the end of the ages has come*" (1 Corinthians 10:11; we will consider Paul's last phrase shortly). Paul's lesson here presumes a notion of Christ's preexistence, and the role of Christ as an actor in the foundational history of Israel. But the reason for which this story was preserved in scripture, he teaches, was to serve as a clear moral warning to Paul's gentile Christians: These Corinthians better not even *think* about worshiping idols again.

Scholars designate this last sort of reading *typology*. A genre of allegory, typology takes an episode or person or image from scripture and treats it as a model or "type" (Greek *tupos*) that serves to interpret a different situation, understanding, or event occurring outside the frame of the original story. In the example just given, the story of the Golden Calf is a cautionary tale. The Israelites of the generation of the Exodus serve Paul as a type of and a negative role model for the first-century gentile community whom he addresses. We can see Paul creating another such web of referents in Galatians 4, where he constructs a long lesson around Abraham, Sarah and Hagar, Isaac and

Ishmael, Jerusalem above and Jerusalem below, all oriented around the poles of spirit versus flesh (Galatians 4:21–31. "Now these things are being allegorized," he cues his listeners; v. 24). In Galatians his typology restates the message of the entire epistle: His Christian Gentiles in Galatia must not listen to other Christian missionaries who advise them to be circumcised.

In both of these instances—with the Corinthians about idol worship, with the Galatians about circumcision—Paul read the Bible typologically as a way to situate himself and his listeners in their current context. Pauline typology thus represents a radical updating of the Bible and, at the same moment, a radical reinterpretation of Jewish history. The prime purpose and function of these ancient stories, both religiously and historically, becomes understanding the (gentile, Christian) present, which in turn means revising older understandings of the Jewish past. Indeed, urges Paul, it was precisely for the benefit of his gentile Christian communities in their current historical moment that scripture contained these texts. As he says in his final letter, Romans, "Whatever was written down in former days was written for *our* instruction" (Romans 15:4).

All these styles of "spiritual" interpretation would go on to have long lives as techniques by which to render the Septuagint a Christian book. In this sense (as in others), later Christian interpreters owed much to Paul (as, indeed, they would also owe much to Philo). But Paul's situation was fundamentally different from that of his later theological heirs for two important and historically specific reasons. First, Paul thought of himself as a Jew and he thought of his message as Judaism. And, second, Paul was convinced that he stood on the edge of the End of time.

As a Jew, Paul understood the "true" meaning of scripture. He identified this with his own interpretation of the gospel, which he saw as confirming and conforming to the promises that God had made to Israel long ago through Abraham, Isaac, and Jacob. We hear him stating these ideas most clearly (and calmly) in his final letter, written to Christian Gentiles in Rome. "For I tell you that Christ became a servant to the circumcised to show God's truthfulness, in order to confirm the promises made to the patriarchs" (Romans 15:8). To be true to scripture, Christ's redemption had to encompass Paul's "kinsmen by race," his *suggenoi*, the Jews (Romans 9:3 RSV). Yet, as Paul knew, the good news of Christ had left many of his kinsmen unmoved. Did this mean, then, that the word of God had failed? Impossible (9:6). What, then, was the explanation for Israel's indifference or hostility to Paul's message?

In Chapters 9 through 11 of this letter addressed to the community at Rome, we hear Paul resolving this dilemma. Here he relies not on reading scripture allegorically, but rather on constructing a grand narrative that is at once historical—that is, set in the past—and, therefore, also prophetic. In this grand narrative, Paul develops a description of the ways that God has worked and will work in history, choosing individuals and nations to act (whether positively or negatively) as his agents, in order to achieve his purpose of redemption.

Paul begins by seeming to narrow the field of those encompassed by God's promise. He distinguishes two populations within Israel, those descended from Abraham according to the flesh and those descended through the child of the promise, Isaac (Romans 9:6–9). Abraham had children by other women, but by Sarah alone he had Isaac, his divinely designated heir. And even between children of the same mother—twins, no less; and still in utero—God chose one brother, Jacob, over the other, Esau, "though they were not yet born and had done nothing either good or bad" (9.10–13). What, then, of the question of fairness? "Is there injustice with God? God forbid!" (9.14). God, not man, controls history. God, not man, knows the divine plan (9.11). In pursuit of his purpose of election, "so that my name may be proclaimed in all the earth," God even hardened Pharaoh's heart so that Pharaoh could not respond to the divine call (9:16–18). Like a potter, God shapes the clay of humanity as he will, some vessels for mercy and others for wrath (9.19–23). All of this controlling and choosing and shaping rests absolutely with God's prerogative, and he owes humanity no explanation. "Who are you, O man, to answer back to God?" (9.20).

This, urges Paul, is the way to understand the justice of God. For now, God has evidently elected only *some* Jews (a mere remnant, Romans 9:27) and *some* Gentiles. God can and does pick whomever he wants to receive his mercy. He is under obligation to no one.

But Paul is committed to a much broader vision of redemption, and so is his god, so he does not leave matters here. It is true, he says, that in spurning the gospel, Israel has proven to be disobedient and contrary (Romans 10:4,18,21). Does Israel's rejection of God's plan mean that God in turn has rejected Israel (11:1)? "By no means!" Paul answers. The current situation, he urges, is both providential and temporary, for Israel's response to God's initiative is itself determined by God. For the present, God has chosen "by grace" only a remnant of Israel, just as back in the days of Elijah he kept 7,000 men from worshiping the god Ba'al. So too he has currently "hardened" the greater part of Israel, much as he once hardened Pharaoh (11:2–7, cf. 9:17 on Pharaoh). But God, explains Paul, has always intended Israel's "full inclusion" in redemption (11:12). True, the Gentiles have taken precedence with respect to the gospel, but this, Paul warns them, was not due to any merit whatsoever on their part, but solely to God's surprising plan. "Lest you be wise in your own conceits," Paul cautions his gentile hearers in Rome,

> I want you to understand this mystery, brethren. A hardening has come upon part of Israel, until the full number of the Gentiles come in, and so *all Israel will be saved.* . . . As regards the gospel, they are the enemies of God *for your sake;* but as regards election they are beloved for the sake of their forefathers. *For the gifts and the call of God are irrevocable.* Just as you were once disobedient to God but now have received mercy because of their disobedience, so they have now been disobedient in order that, by the mercy shown to you, they may receive mercy. For God has consigned all men to disobedience, *that he may have mercy upon all.*
>
> ROMANS 11:25–32 RSV

Examining Paul in the retrospect of history, we can sort through his convictions, identifying those that he would have had even if he had never encountered the Christian movement and those that he had specifically on account of his involvement in the Christian movement. And for clarity we label such beliefs "Jewish" or "Christian." In terms of Paul's own experience, however, such identifications are a gross anachronism, and they risk representing a false dichotomy. In his own view, Paul was always a Jew, in both phases of his life. In fact—and again in his own view—Paul was always an excellent Jew in both phases of his life. Before receiving his call, "I advanced in Judaism beyond many of my own age among my people" (Galatians 1:14); "As to righteousness under the Law, I was blameless" (Philippians 3:6). And given his own understanding of the message of Christ, he was also convinced that he was a superior Jew: chosen before birth by God himself to be an apostle to the Gentiles (Galatians 1:15–16), empowered by God's own spirit to prophesy and to teach (1 Corinthians 14 passim), superior to other missionaries to an extraordinary degree on account of his fortitude in suffering (2 Corinthians 11 passim) and on account of his elevated visions and revelations (2 Corinthians 12:1–5). "By the grace of God I am what I am," Paul proclaimed, adding (with no false modesty) "and God's grace toward me was not in vain" (1 Corinthians 15:10). Our analytic distinction between Paul the Jew and Paul the Christian simply does not carry over into his own life. He was both, and he saw the message of Christ as absolutely synonymous with his native religion and with God's promises to Israel, his "kinsmen by race" (Romans 9:3 RSV).

Paul's convictions as a Jew—that the god of Israel was both just and merciful, that his promises to Israel were irrevocable, that Israel's redemption was unalterably promised in the scriptures—might have conflicted with his convictions as an apostle of Christ. After all, by midcentury, when he wrote Romans, the gospel mission to Israel was not meeting with conspicuous success. And Paul's convictions specifically as a Christian Jew—that Jesus truly was the messiah, that he truly had been raised, that his resurrection truly heralded the establishment of God's kingdom—might have conflicted with his experience. After all, Christ had died and been raised nearly two decades prior to Paul's writing his letter to Rome, and still the End had not come. But instead, through his rereading of scripture, his bedrock confidence in God's promises to Israel, and his certainty that the End was indeed at hand ("nearer to us," he tells the community in Rome, "than when we first believed"; Romans 13:11), Paul ingeniously resolved the tensions between his convictions and his experience. He understood God's plan.

Because he had seen the risen Christ, Paul believed that he knew what time it was on God's clock. He was convinced that he lived and worked in the very last days, in history's final generation. For this reason he could tell his community that the End of the Age had *already* come upon them (1 Corinthians 10:11, quoted above). He would witness Christ's return, when "we who are alive, who are left until the coming of the Lord" would be caught up with the resurrected dead to meet Christ in the air (1 Thessalonians 4:15-17). "We shall not all sleep," he tells his Gentiles in Corinth, "but we shall all be changed" (1 Corinthians 15:51). Thus for Paul as for the other early apostles, Christ's resurrection was no solitary event. Indeed, the resurrection of Christ was incomprehensible without its communal dimension. "If the dead are not raised, then Christ has not been raised" (1 Corinthians 15:16). For Paul as for this first generation of apostles and missionaries, the risen Christ presaged the returning Christ, the imminent resurrection of all the dead and the transformation of the living, and the establishment of God's kingdom.

True, by the time that Paul wrote Romans, a gap of some twenty years had opened between Christ's resurrection and his second coming. But Paul knew why: God was giving Paul a little more time to complete his mission to the Gentiles. Soon, very soon, Christ would return. God would stop his miraculous hardening of Israel's heart, and everyone—the full number of the Gentiles and all Israel—would enter into the redemption promised in scripture (Romans 11:25). The entire biblical past was, for Paul, transparent upon current events (15:4). He wove his own experience in this new messianic movement together with his understanding of Israel's past as preserved in scripture to produce a single grand narrative of redemption. His experience of Christian pagans' turning from idols and false gods to the exclusive worship of the god of Israel, together with his own witness to the risen Christ, charged the present with eschatological significance. These events confirmed Paul in his conviction that the kingdom truly was at hand.

♦ ♦ ♦

THE KINGDOM, HOWEVER, did not arrive within the first generation of this vital new messianic movement. In consequence, its foundational prophecy—"The Kingdom of God is at hand!"—shifted meanings as the mission spread. Scattered communities of very diverse orientation were left to make sense of the gospel proclamation, of the Jewish scriptures on which it was based, and of the literary legacy of its early years, most especially the letters of Paul.

As forms of the Christian message reach erudite urban elites, we begin to see evidence (as with our anonymous late-first-century Docetists) of learned reflection on its various elements. Pagan intellectuals, committing themselves to Christianity, applied their training in systematic rational thought, forensic argument, and techniques of textual interpretation to these Greek Jewish texts. Rising to the challenge of finding meaning in the early message, these men defended their views using all the tools and skills of rhetoric and all the philosophical sophistication that their educations had made available to them. The result was an eruption of intra-Christian theological dispute.

By comparing the work of three prominent early gentile Christian theologians—Valentinus (fl. 130), Marcion (fl. 140), and Justin (fl. 150)—we can gain a sense of the issues that shaped this dispute. These men came from various corners of the empire: Valentinus from Alexandria in Egypt, Marcion from Pontus by the Black Sea, Justin from Neapolis (now Nablus) in Roman Palestine. For a moment, all three lived in Rome. Their common educational culture and their shared conviction that salvation was uniquely available through Christ did not preclude bitter enmity. All three theologians left behind teachings that contributed to the formation of long-lived, wide-flung, and mutually antagonistic churches. And their arguments established points of contention that shaped theological controversy for centuries, in their own period up to Augustine's day and beyond.

This antagonism might surprise us, because these men and their respective communities held so much in common. Two originally separate strands of ancient monotheism—from the pagan side through philosophy, from the Jewish side through the Bible and the literature of the early Christian movement—twined together in their works. All three theologians defined the high god philosophically: He was unique, perfect, good, changeless, incorporeal, utterly transcendent, and so on. And this transcendent deity, they agreed, was indeed the father of Jesus Christ. They all asserted, further, in light of their commitment to this definition of the high god, that the divine intelligence who had organized the material cosmos could only be a lower god. And this lower god, they concurred, was the creative deity described in Genesis and active throughout the Septuagint. And, finally, they all three asserted that the Septuagint, interpreted correctly—that is, with spiritual understanding—provided crucial insight into Christian revelation.[11]

Despite their broad agreement, however, these theologians were much divided on two questions. One, whose ultimate source in learned Mediterranean culture was the Platonic philosophical tradition, concerned the moral status of matter. Was matter good or bad? The second, whose source was the Christian message itself, concerned the status of the Septuagint. How were Jewish scriptures to be read and used to gain insight into Christian truth? The answer to one question immediately affected the answer to the other.

Of these three Christian thinkers, the first, Valentinus, was the most intellectually sophisticated, the most philosophically radical, and the most theologically original. At our current distance from his work, which was suppressed by the fourth-century Roman church, we cannot sort out the sequence of his convictions. Did his reading of the Septuagint prompt his belief that the material cosmos was evil? Or did his belief that matter was evil subsequently inform his interpretation of Genesis? However he arrived at his convictions, they led Valentinus to break with one of the prime positions of Roman-period Platonism, namely, that the cosmos was good, because its organization reflected the operation of divine mind. Valentinus and his followers, on the contrary, saw the material cosmos as a barrier rather than a bridge to the realm of light and love beyond. And as the Valentinian estimate of the moral status of the physical universe sank, so too did their opinion of the god of Genesis who had organized matter. Correspondingly, their opinion of the people who revered this god and kept his laws—that is, the Jews—sank as well.

Genesis and other books of the Jewish Bible did indeed reveal Christian truth, said the Valentinians; but one had to know how to read these texts with spiritual insight to arrive at this truth. Such understanding exposed the biblical god as an ignorant deity, obsessively concerned with blood sacrifices and sexual couplings. His distasteful and small-minded laws related exclusively to the Jews. Yet deep within this unelevating text lay the long-concealed message of the high god, revealed now to his elect by the coming of his son. This message imparted other, divine, spiritual laws that were in fact directed toward the enlightened Christian. Rules for how to interpret the Septuagint, transmitted through apostolic tradition, could aid the discerning reader in distinguishing these spiritual commands from all the others in the Bible that were directed solely to Israel according to the flesh.[12]

Marcion and his followers shared with the Valentinians the view that matter was the defective product of the lower god described in Genesis. They arrived at this position, however, by different textual means. Valentinian teachings had drawn on a huge, rich, and eclectic assemblage of books: the Septuagint (particularly Genesis), various gospels, apostolic letters, and a considerable volume of their own inspired writings ("a countless number!" complained their opponent Irenaeus, *Against Heresies* 1.20,1). Marcion concentrated his interpretive efforts much more narrowly. For him, what mattered most were the letters of Paul. The contrasting pairs that structured Pauline rhetoric— Law and gospel, works and grace, flesh and spirit, Jew and Gentile— Marcion read as absolute, antagonistic opposites. (In his suppressed theological work, the *Antitheses,* Marcion compared statements in Jewish scriptures to those in Christian writings to demonstrate what he saw as the intrinsic incompatibility of the two.) This reading of Paul led Marcion to formulate a radically new idea.

Using Paul to authorize his position, Marcion repudiated not only traditional Jewish religious practices (the "works of the Law") but also—this is Marcion's *novum*—the scriptures that enjoined them. Both, he said, were "fleshly" and thus intrinsically unacceptable to the true follower of Christ. The source of the Septuagint traditions was entirely the lower, justice-obsessed god of the Jews. But (gentile) Christians, urged Marcion, worshiped the high god, the father of Christ, revealed by his son uniquely through Paul to be an all-loving and all-good deity. Jewish scripture, then, should be utterly relinquished to the Jews, who in any case insisted that it was theirs. In its place, Marcion proposed a new, specifically Christian canon: a single gospel and the letters of Paul.

But what about those places in the Pauline corpus where Paul had praised the Law, invoking its authority and commending its holiness? When arguing that women should keep silent in community, Paul had urged that they "should be subordinate, even as the Law says" (1 Corinthians 14:34). "The Law is holy," Paul had declared, "and the commandment is holy and just and good" (Romans 7:12). Paul's Jewish enemies, Marcion concluded, had corrupted Paul's letters by introducing these and other similar assertions into later copies of them. Marcion purged these statements, which he regarded as interpolations. Elegantly, decisively, he thereby produced both a de-Judaized Apostle and a de-Judaized Christian canon, a "new" testament.[13]

Despite their very different views on what properly constituted Christian texts, both Valentinians and Marcionites shared a similar Christology and thus a similar idea of redemption. Since matter, thus flesh (they agreed), was the flawed medium of the morally derelict god of the Jews, there was no reason that Christ should have put it on when he entered history to perform his mission of salvation. Rather, he had only seemed to have a body: In reality, he had appeared in the "likeness" of flesh. (Paul's statement in Philippians 2:5–11 lent itself readily to this view.) Accordingly, nothing so crude as flesh was included in human redemption, either. (Had not Paul himself taught that "flesh and blood will not inherit the kingdom of God," 1 Corinthians 15:50?) Christ had been raised in a spiritual body, and that was the same sort of "body" that the redeemed Christian would have. (This position, too, was based on Paul: A dead human body at burial, he taught, "is sown a physical body, and it is raised a spiritual body [*soma pneumatikon*]. If there is a physical body, there is also a spiritual body"; 1 Corinthians 15:44.) Flesh was not truly part of the person; rather, flesh was the trap set by the lower god to ensnare the person, whose true self was his soul. Accordingly, the salvation of Christians would not be achieved *en masse* as a historical event. Rather, the individual soul, shedding the encumbrance of flesh at death, would rise through the material universe and out of it, to the transcendent realm of the Father above.

Against the positions of these two theologians stood their younger contemporary, Justin. For all his objections to them, however, Justin shared many of their views. Like Valentinus and Marcion, Justin defined the high god according to the canons of philosophical paideia.

Like Valentinus and Marcion, he also asserted that this high god was the father of Jesus Christ. And, again like Valentinus and Marcion, he too held that the busy deity who appeared in the Septuagint in so many places and in so many stories—here conversing with Abraham, there speaking with Moses—could not possibly have been the high god. Instead, Justin wrote, this deity had to be a *heteros theos,* another, lower god (*Dialogue with Trypho* 56). And he too maintained that Christian truth was made evident in Jewish scripture, providing one knew how to read with spiritual understanding.

But Justin held a philosophical position on the moral status of matter that distinguished him from his two Christian colleagues and aligned him more with his pagan intellectual contemporaries. Like philosophers in the mainstream Platonic tradition, Justin also viewed matter as defective but not in itself evil. This conviction in turn enabled and informed Justin's bold Christology, and his equally bold rereading of the Jewish Bible. Since matter was not evil, argued Justin, then neither was the lower god of Genesis who had formed matter. No reason, then, to think that that god was the cosmic opponent of the divine son and of his father. But, no less obviously, this active god could not possibly be the high god himself. Therefore, urged Justin, the identity of the creator god of Genesis, the chief divine personality presented as an actor in Israel's history all throughout the Jewish scriptures, could only be the divine son, Christ himself, before his incarnation.

In one sweeping motion, Justin was thus able to argue that the Septuagint, in a direct and positive way, was a book of Christian revelation. Indeed, according to his interpretation, Christ *was* the god presented in the Jewish Bible. More boldly still, Justin was thus able to insist that Christ, on this account, was (and always had been) the proper object of *Jewish* worship. Christ was the god who had spoken with Abraham, Christ was the god who had redeemed Israel from Egypt, Christ was the god who had given the Law on Sinai, and so on (*Dialogue with Trypho* 56–62, cf. 38). Moses, the prophets, the psalmist—all the great spiritual heroes of Israel had realized this, Justin claimed. When read with spiritual understanding, their writings obviously spoke, whether symbolically or prophetically, of Christ.

Accordingly Justin argued that when Christ, the god present at Sinai, had given his laws to Israel, he was actually giving Israel a coded message whose deeper, spiritual meaning was himself. Alas, the Jews misunderstood him. As always, the Jews interpreted the Law in a fleshly way (*Dialogue with Trypho* 11-14, and frequently elsewhere). They performed as physical acts—blood sacrifices, purification rituals, and so on—what were meant either as allegories or as prophecies of Christ. Thus, in Justin's perspective, the Jewish Bible, in the most profound and direct way, *was* the Christian Bible: Its divine author, after all, was Christ. Nor was "Israel" actually the Jews: Once read correctly, the Bible clearly prophesied the rejection of the old Israel and the salvation of the True Israel, that is, of the gentile church (or, more precisely, of Justin's gentile church; *Trypho* 29; 135). Justin could, therefore, insist against his Christian opponents that nothing was wrong either with the Septuagint or with its message. The problem was not the Bible, but the Jews.

Further, argued Justin, since Christ himself was the god who had framed the material cosmos, nothing impeded his truly assuming flesh when he finally did appear in history. Not only had Christ lived in a real, fleshly body, Justin asserted; he had died in it, and he had also been raised with it. Neither flesh nor matter, then, was something that Christians needed to escape in order to be saved. The saints, like Christ, would be raised in their fleshly bodies, too. Thus, whereas Valentinus and Marcion defined redemption as the soul's escape from the material cosmos and its ascent to a transcendent heaven, Justin insisted on the resurrection not merely of a "body" but specifically and emphatically of the *fleshly* body, in a communal and historical event to be accomplished in the last days. The saints, raised to new life, would gather not in some spiritual, transcendent heaven, but right here on earth. (Where else could flesh and blood go?) Together with Christ, they would reign in Jerusalem for a thousand years (*Dialogue with Trypho* 80–82).

Justin's views, of course, did not go unchallenged. Valentinians and Marcionites continued to protest that the god of the Septuagint was fundamentally incompatible, morally and temperamentally, with Christian revelation. The Jewish god had demanded blood sacrifices. He commanded sexual procreation ("Be fruitful and multiply"), and occasionally he ordered the wholesale slaughter of peoples. The enlightened followers of Christ knew that their god would never have required blood offerings: Not only were such things fleshly in themselves but they came much too close to the rites of the idol-worshiping pagan majority. Further, they observed, Christ had valued virginity and sexual celibacy, not marriage and procreation, and he had praised those who would make themselves eunuchs for the sake of the kingdom of heaven (Matthew 19:12). Paul his apostle had taught that it was well for a man not to touch a woman (1 Corinthians 7:1, see also verses 28–38). Furthermore, Christians practiced love, patience, forgiveness; they eschewed violence. How then could the martial deity of the blood-soaked Jewish book have any direct relation to Christ or to his gospel? Finally, they argued, the incoherent and unspiritual belief in a fleshly resurrection and an earthly thousand-year reign of the saints—in Jerusalem, no less!—bespoke a carnal literal-mindedness that revealed the Jewish orientation of Justin's own style of reading. And why hold on to the Jews' book anyway, if the Christian were free of all those fleshly practices and rites that the text enjoined?

♦♦♦

THE CONTESTATIONS of these second-century theologians profoundly affected the patterns of later Christian thought. Their writings circulated broadly; their positions and the arguments against them developed further in the writings of later generations of theologians. Eventually, though, many of the main points of Justin's own position prevailed, thanks to the power of a belated patron, the fourth-century Roman emperor Constantine. In 312 C.E., Constantine chose to sponsor and to promote those Christian communities that had preserved the writings and expanded the arguments of Justin and of other like-minded thinkers. And, despite the considerable theological developments distinguishing the Constantinian church from the community of Justin's day, a common interpretive principle spanned their generations and bound them together, namely, that the Septuagint was a code for Christ. For these later Christian communities in the fourth century as for Justin's in the mid-second, Jewish scriptures, properly understood, were really the scriptures of the church.

But this later community also appropriated and preserved an im-

portant idea that had originated historically with Marcion. That idea
had to do with writings that were specifically Christian. *Scripture* for
Justin had denoted Jewish sacred literature, most especially the Law
and the prophets, particularly Isaiah. Relatively recent Christian writings, such as the gospels and various letters, even though these were
doubtless valued by his community, Justin referred to as the apostles'
"memoires" (*First Apology* 1.66.3). Their status did not equal the Septuagint's. Within forty years, however, this attitude appears to shift.
Those who succeeded Justin and preserved his writings nonetheless
held a body of specifically Christian texts as canon, as had the Marcionites before them. Unlike the Marcionites, however, these Christians used their newer canon to bind the Septuagint to the church:
The newer collection, they held, provided the necessary points of reference whereby to correctly interpret the older canon. By the time that
Constantine became its imperial patron, a century and a half after
Justin's lifetime, this church had long revered both the Jewish scriptures and this distinct collection of Christian ones as well.

Marcion's original canon had been small and heavily Pauline. The
later anti-Marcionite church gathered a much broader selection of
writings: four gospels rather than one; letters written by later Christians in Paul's name as well as seven genuine letters of Paul's; the Acts
of the Apostles, a continuation of Luke's gospel; various letters or sermons presented as letters, attributed variously to other apostles of the
first generation; the apocalyptic visions of John of Patmos. Canonized
as a "new" testament—de facto in the late second century, officially in
the fourth—this collection was regarded as correcting and completing
the revelations recorded in the Septuagint, now held as the "old" testament of the church.[14]

A prime feature of the fourth-century church's traditions of scriptural interpretation, however, gave a posthumous victory to all three
of our second-century contestants. This church read both parts of its
Bible, Old Testament and New, in ways that broadly repudiated Jewish
understandings of the Septuagint and that effaced the Jewish context
and content of the core texts of the New Testament canon. In so doing, fourth-century imperial Christianity recapitulated and further developed a prime interpretive position exemplified variously in the

work of all three of our earlier theologians, namely, that both the high god and his divine Son had utterly renounced Jews and Judaism.

In this ecclesiastical understanding, Jesus had come specifically to teach against the Jewish interpretation of Jewish law. For that matter, so had Moses and so had all of the prophets in the period before the incarnation. All of these holy men, the church taught, as well as the Son of God himself, had denounced the Temple and its blood sacrifices, had condemned fleshly circumcision, had criticized the Jewish observance of the Sabbath, and had censured Jewish practices generally. So too had Paul, and so too the other apostles of the first generation.

Articulating this conviction were three broad modes of mutually reinforcing arguments. One, which drew ultimately on values and concepts in Plato, was the derogatory comparison of flesh (lower and this-worldly) to spirit (higher, thus intrinsically better, and upper-worldly). *Flesh* in this rhetoric coded both intellectual inadequacy and moral turpitude. Christians who assigned "Jews" and "Judaism" to this negative pole thereby created not only a hostile construct of Judaism, but at the same time created a positive construct of themselves. And this construct could do double-duty, for it served to express the problem with those other Christian communities who were outside of this rhetorical and social fold. "True" Christianity was spiritual, and true Christians understood the scriptures spiritually; "heretical" Christianity and heretical Christians, condemned within this same value system, were obviously carnal and literal minded. In this way, through this invective, these other, repudiated Christians (who, like their opponents, were themselves Gentiles) were rhetorically rendered as "Jews."

A second genre of argument drew on a strongly biblical motif: the idea of prophecy and fulfillment. Christ, said these Christians, had obviously and perfectly fulfilled the Old Testament's prophecies about the messiah. If the Jews failed to grasp this fact, the fault was their own. They read the prophets with blind eyes and with carnal understanding. But all this had also been foreseen, these Christians pointed out. The same prophets had consistently lamented their people's blind eyes, stony hearts, and stiff necks. The Jews' rejection of the way that gentile Christians read these Jewish books, in brief, confirmed that the Christians actually had things right. Isaiah and Jeremiah had said so long ago.

Third, appealing to a model both pedagogical and historical, theologians spoke of progressive revelation: God's lessons to humanity,
unfolding in time, were attuned to the abilities of the students. Jews in
this view were infants, elementary learners. The advanced class, history
had revealed, had been reserved for the gentile church. This last argument, invoking this educational commonplace (beginners know less
than mature students do), corresponded nicely with the first one. Elementary students, understanding a text at its narrative, simplest level,
can grasp only its obvious, "bodily" meaning; advanced students,
trained in higher levels of interpretation, see past the obvious and into
the text's "spirit."

These talking points were not generated by orthodox Christian
theologians in an effort to describe actual Jewish contemporaries,
though they could be deployed in arguments with Jewish contemporaries. These interpretive positions are *topoi,* arguments intended to
persuade listeners of the speaker's superiority, while positioning his
opponent at a disadvantage. Such modes of argument were used
broadly, mutatis mutandis, in pagan and in Hellenistic Jewish
polemics as well. Skill in arguing, in using belligerent topoi to maxi-
mum strategic advantage—especially in courts of law—was the practical goal of Greco-Roman rhetorical education.

Arguments structured in these ways had appeared already in
Paul's letters and in the gospels. These first-century authors created
their own "rhetorical Jews," using the flesh/spirit dichotomy to disparage various opponents. Paul, for example, criticizes other Christian
Jews as being "fleshly" because they advocate circumcision for Christian pagans in Galatia: His own message, he insists, is the "spiritual"
one. (His letter to the Galatians is structured around this contrast,
whereby Paul/spirit/grace battles against circumcising opponents/
flesh/works.) The same rhetorical dichotomy could be mobilized
against Christian pagans who were tempted to listen to Paul's opposition. ("O foolish Galatians! . . . Having begun with the spirit, are you
now ending with the flesh?"; Galatians 3:1–3). The similar contrast of
"upper" and "lower" also worked well. Thus, in the fourth gospel,
John's Jesus squares off with non-Christian Jews. "You are from below," he says to his hostile auditors, "I am from above. You are of this
world [Greek: *cosmos*], I am not of this world" (John 8:23).

The rhetoric of prophecy/fulfillment depended on identifying or constructing congenial similarities between the older and the newer message, whereby the newer message provided the interpretive framework for the older scripture. When Paul twins Adam with Christ, for example, he uses this sort of argument: The first Adam was "a type of the one who was to come" (Greek *tupos;* Romans 5:14). The concept of graduated revelation/education, finally, with content suited to the abilities of the hearer, could blend nicely with this rhetoric's up/down, spirit/flesh dichotomies. Paul, for example, combines the two when chiding the argumentative Corinthians for being immature: "I fed you with milk, not with solid food, for you were not ready for it. And even yet you are not ready, for you are still in the flesh" (1 Corinthians 3:1-3).

The appeal to specifically biblical prophecy is everywhere in these Hellenistic Jewish documents. Paul invokes the principle ("Christ died for our sins *kata tas graphas,* according to the scriptures"; 1 Corinthians 15:3). The evangelists, structuring their respective presentations of the life and mission of Jesus upon this same conviction, demonstrate it through narrative. Mark's Jesus resigns himself to his arrest by saying simply, "Let the scriptures be fulfilled" (Mark 14:49). Matthew in particular, over sixty times in his gospel, explains events by saying that they were done specifically "in order to fulfill what was spoken by the prophets" (for example Matthew 1:23, on Mary's virginity; 2:14, on the flight to Egypt; 3:17, on the slaughter of the innocents, and so on). Luke's risen Christ "beginning with Moses and all the prophets . . . interpreted in all the scriptures the things concerning himself" (Luke 24:27; for the same idea, 24:44-47). John's Jesus, uncharacteristically curt, simply observes, "If you [Jews] believed Moses, you would believe me, for he wrote of me" (John 5:46).

Once Paul's letters and these gospels became scripture for the later gentile churches, all of these rhetorical topoi, ripe for reuse, were redeployed. The targets of choice might be "false insiders" (those other gentile Christians with a different message than the speaker's) as well as "the Jews" (the perennial intimate outsiders). By the fourth century, when the community claiming title to the Septuagint and to the New Testament found the emperor's favor, its double canon, its identity, and its theology were all securely interconnected by the tough ligaments of this polemical rhetoric.

This victorious fourth-century church designated itself both right thinking ("orthodox") and universal ("catholic"). Claiming that its teachings preserved traditions going directly back to Jesus and his original followers, this church pronounced itself "apostolic." Singularly empowered by Constantine's surprising decision in 312, this church propagated hostile caricatures of its defining "enemies"—pagans, surely; also other Christian communities ("heretics"); and also, with ever-increasing authority, Jews.

Unambiguous condemnations of paganism and of its invariable (rhetorical) accompaniments, fornication and idolatry, stood in both testaments. The gods and images originally targeted in the Jewish scriptures, of course, had been Canaanite deities. But once the condemnations of these ancient Semitic gods, thanks to the Septuagint, were available in Greek, they were easily redeployed against a newer pantheon, the urbane gods of Greco-Roman culture. Specifically in New Testament documents, moreover, intra-Christian diversity had also been strongly condemned. Paul had with sarcasm dismissed rival Christian missionaries as "super-apostles" (2 Corinthians 11:5); elsewhere, he cheerfully wished genital self-mutilation on his Christian competition (Galatians 5:12). Matthew's Jesus warns against non-Matthean Christians by calling them "false prophets," wolves in sheep's clothing. Matthew acknowledges that such people indeed pray to Jesus as well as work miracles, drive out demons, and prophesy in his name. They may think, therefore, that they follow Christ. Not so, teaches Matthew. On the last day, when it will be too late, these people will find themselves denied entrance to God's kingdom (Matthew 7:15–23). The author of the deutero-Pauline letter 1 Timothy consigns to Satan those Christians with whom he disagrees (1 Timothy 1:20). 2 Peter identifies Christians with beliefs different from his own as false prophets and false teachers: "they will secretly introduce destructive *haereseis*" (2 Peter 2:1). (This Greek word originally meant "opinion" or "school of thought"; by the fourth century, it means "heresy.") To the writer of the Johannine epistles, other Christians, quite simply, are "anti-Christ" (1 John 2:18–19; see also 2 John 7, said specifically of docetist Christians).[15]

But the question of the Jews was different and, in many ways, more complicated. In the earliest decades of the Christian movement, non-Christian Jews had posed a particular challenge to the new community's claims to correctly understand the meaning of God's promises to Israel. Paul himself was so baffled by his co-religionists' cool response to his message that he attributed their indifference or hostility to nothing less than the direct and providential intervention of God. God himself, Paul explained, was hardening Israel in order to allow the apostles more time to concentrate on turning the nations to the gospel. At a certain point—very soon, Paul thought—God would release Israel from their deafness and the whole world, Jew and Gentile, would be saved (see p. 62 above). In other words, while acknowledging the problem of his kinsmen's rejection of the gospel, Paul in his final letter also reveals a happy solution. God's prophets had foretold and described Israel's disobedience long ago: It was divinely imposed, merely temporary, and fated to be brief. God's steadfastness was the foundation of Paul's conviction. God had called Israel, and "the gifts and the call of God are irrevocable" (Romans 11:29).

By the second century, however, diverse gentile Christian communities regarded Jewish indifference to or contempt for the gospel as a permanent condition. In so doing, they rejected as heretical those other Christian communities, whether Jewish or gentile, that saw no conflict between Christ and the Law. To neutralize and to delegitimate the manifold diversity of these Jewish or Judaizing churches and to address the standing challenge of indifferent or hostile synagogues, these thinkers devised various arguments to explain why Jews were intrinsically incapable of seeing that Christians alone had correctly understood the Jewish scriptures. Carnal and proverbially stiff necked, the Jews had missed their opportunity (so went the argument) and failed to see that the promise of redemption had already passed from them to the gentile church. Or, for these same reasons, Jews (and those Christians who imitated them by keeping some of the practices associated with Jewish custom) were incapable of seeing in the Bible's god the clear repudiation of carnal Jewish practice. The true Christian, in brief, should have nothing to do with "the Jews." But this polarizing rhetoric did not describe a social reality so much as prescribe one. The absence of social clarity was what drove the either/or rhetoric of the argument.

Israel according to the flesh was *vetus Israel*, "old" Israel. The Christian (and gentile) church was *verus Israel*, "true" Israel. These sorts of arguments collectively comprise a theological temperament and a literary-rhetorical tradition that scholars label *adversus Iudaeos* or *contra Iudaeos*, "against the Jews." Arguments *adversus Iudaeos* served to confirm certain constructions of gentile Christian identity against many challengers: Jewish contemporaries, pagans sympathetic to Judaism, gentile Christian Judaizers (that is, gentile Christians who voluntarily assumed Jewish practices), and Jewish Christians (those Jews who both proclaimed Jesus and who lived according to their ancestral practices).

But the extreme variety of all of the competing gentile groups posed no less a threat to the developing sense of Christian identity. Just as only one community could be the true Israel, so too could only one community be the true church. The simple fact of confessional diversity compromised the claim to possessing revealed truth.

Gentile Christian contestants responded to their inherently competitive circumstances by waging rhetorical war on each other. Their ammunition of choice was those same polemics that they had developed and also continued to use against Judaism. In this context of erudite *intra-Christian* polemic, to call a gentile opponent a "Jew," to accuse him of thinking or acting in ways that this invective identified as "Jewish," was to condemn him for being "fleshly," "stiff necked," "stubborn," "malicious"—in short, for being deeply, intrinsically un-Christian; indeed, for being anti-Christian. As increasing numbers of well-educated Gentiles joined various Christian communities, the intensity of learned intra-Christian debate mounted. So did the anti-Jewish rhetoric of abuse, as these Christians "produced the 'Jews' that they needed" to attack their gentile Christian rivals. Eventually, in the course of the second, third, and fourth centuries, these theological arguments among different communities of gentile Christians elevated the *adversus Iudaeos* tradition into a defining aspect of orthodox Christian identity itself.[16]

4 ✦ PAGANS, JEWS, AND CHRISTIANS IN THE MEDITERRANEAN CITY

In Carthage they can say, "It is done by the pagans; it is done by the Jews." Here, whoever takes part is a Christian.

AUGUSTINE, *SERMO DENIS* 17:7 (ON THE POPULAR OBSERVANCE OF MUNICIPAL FESTIVALS IN 399 C.E.)

Key features of the *adversus Iudaeos* tradition, as we have just seen, formed as the rhetorical run-off of internal battles between well-educated gentile Christian intellectuals. But more goes into theology than just philosophy, and more goes into building the identity of a community than deciding whom to exclude. We can better understand the adversarial tradition of Christian anti-Judaism—and thus Augustine's singular challenges to it—by considering how it fit into its social context. What can the Christian rhetorical presentation of theological ideas about Jews and Judaism tell us about actual relations between Jews and Christians? Among different kinds of Christians? How did these scriptural communities relate to the pagan majority, and how did pagans relate to them? And how do social relations among all of these different ancient communities illumine, in turn, the ideas that we encounter in Christian polemics against "the Jews"?

Hostility between "Jews" and "Christians" already shapes those first-century documents that eventually made up the core of the later New Testament canon: Paul's letters and the gospels of Mark, Matthew, Luke, and John. Difficult to remember when reading these, however, is that most of the contestants presented in these writings are themselves Jews. When Paul claimed that he "violently persecuted the assembly (*ekklêsia*) of God and tried to destroy it" (Galatians 1:13), the recipients of his hostile attentions could *only* have been fellow

Jews. In Damascus, the probable location of his activity, Paul would certainly have had no authority, and no latitude, in "persecuting"— that is, prosecuting or disciplining—any non-Jews (that is, pagans). Elsewhere, when he speaks of receiving thirty-nine lashes, he again locates himself within the diaspora synagogue: This was a specifically Jewish judicial discipline (2 Corinthians 11:24).

These two data combine to give us a third: Both Paul and these others, whichever of them gave or got these punishments, all considered themselves and looked on each other as Jews. "Punishment implies inclusion." As for the Christian opponents frequently in the foreground of Paul's letters to his gentile communities, these too are Jews. ("Are they Hebrews? So am I! Are they Israelites? So am I! Are they descendants of Abraham? So am I! Are they servants of Christ? I am a better one"; 2 Corinthians 11:22–23.) These objects of Paul's ire appear to have been other Christian Jews who, like Paul himself, also worked to bring the gospel to the Gentiles.[1]

Paul's description of his own travails—imprisonments, beatings, Jewish juridical lashing, Roman beating with rods, stoning (2 Corinthians 11:23–27)—coheres well with the picture presented later in Acts (written probably c. 100). Early Christian apostles, Jews themselves, seem often to have met with hostility and rejection in the diaspora synagogues that provided the immediate context of their mixed urban missions. In the Gospel of Mark (written probably sometime after 70 C.E.), the author skillfully foreshadows the post-resurrection gentile mission in the course of telling his story. His Jesus works a single but spectacular healing in a pagan village (Mark 5); later, he agrees to perform an exorcism at the request of a pagan woman, and he subsequently teaches in pagan territory (Mark 7). Yet once in Jerusalem, Mark's Jesus "prophesies" that his followers would experience harsh receptions in the Diaspora: "They will deliver you up to councils; *and you will be beaten in synagogues,* and you will stand before governors and kings for my sake" (Mark 13:9). Mark's Jesus, in other words, seems still to envisage a Jewish Christian movement, because these synagogues mentioned in his warning would have no jurisdiction over gentile Christians.

The gospels depict intra-Jewish controversies sparked over typically Jewish concerns. What is the right way to worship the god of Israel? Which of his laws are the most important? What constitutes keeping his Sabbath? In light of his commandments, how is a person obligated to treat others: parents, spouses, children, and especially the poor? In the evangelists' stories, Jesus argues heatedly with other Jews about these questions. He debates with Pharisees, with Sadducees, with priests, with scribes, and with Jews of no party affiliation. They all quarrel about the Sabbath, about sacrifices, about fasting, praying, and giving charity properly. They quote scripture to each other and challenge each other's authority to interpret it. They exchange accusations of hypocrisy, impiety, and blasphemy.

The evangelists, in short, present a fairly typical portrait of Jewish interactions both in Jesus' day and in their own. All the noise, all the argument over scripture, all the fraternal name calling, is one of the most unmistakably Jewish things about the Jesus movement and about its earliest literature. Within a first-century intra-Jewish context, such arguments would and did sound like conflicting ideas about the right way to be Jewish. That right way would be the way urged by the writer of the text. The gospels, when we regard them as sectarian Jewish literature, deny any legitimacy to any construction of "Israel" or of the "people of God" or of "those from Above" at odds with their authors' own self-understanding. In this regard, they are much like the writings of that other near-contemporary Jewish sectarian community by the Dead Sea. (And compared to some of the things said in the Dead Sea Scrolls about Jerusalem's priests, the gospels in fact seem almost mild.) In the gospels, as in Paul's letters earlier, non-Christian understandings of Judaism are disallowed if not repudiated. And much of the rhetoric of rejection, at least in the gospels, is placed in the mouth of Jesus himself.[2]

Do the sectarian texts of these earliest Christians promote negative stereotypes about fellow Jews? Unquestionably. But that is what Jewish sectarian texts do, and that is what polemical rhetoric does. Further, all Jewish texts, beginning with Genesis, include warts-and-all presentations of some of their Jewish characters. In this sense, the gospels are no more intrinsically "anti-Jewish" than is the Bible itself. But again like the Bible itself, the gospels, once they drifted out of their communities of origin into a wider gentile world, were read as a standing indictment and perpetual condemnation of Jews and Judaism as such, rather than as a narrative exhortation to change from the wrong kind of Judaism to the right kind of Judaism (that is, to the author's kind of Judaism). Jewish sectarian rhetoric, shorn of its native context, eventually became anti-Jewish rhetoric.[3]

Two historical events particularly affected the composition and interpretation of the gospels. Unlike Paul's letters, which Paul dictated at mid-century, the gospels were composed *after* the Jewish war with Rome in 66-73 C.E. And like Paul's letters—and, also, eventually, like the Septuagint itself—the gospels' readership eventually became predominantly gentile. The arguments that the evangelists depict between Jesus and his Jewish contemporaries, the "predictions" of the Temple's destruction that they place in Jesus' mouth, their presentation of priestly complicity in Jesus' execution and their explicit linking of this complicity to the destruction of the Temple one generation after Jesus' death: All of these elements, once the gospels circulated outside of their communities of origin, made an enduring—and enduringly toxic—contribution to the arsenal of gentile Christian anti-Jewish invective.

The longest-lived and (eventually) the most toxic of these various accusations was the charge that "the Jews" killed Christ. Its roots trace back to New Testament texts. In Paul's letter to the Thessalonians the charge stands that "the Jews" killed Jesus (1 Thessalonians 2:14-16). Despite Jesus' indisputably Roman death, the evangelists place the onus for it on the Temple priesthood and on the people of Jerusalem. In the canonical gospels, Jesus himself names the chief priests as the culprits. The Gospel of Matthew, held by the early church to be an eyewitness account of these events, picks up these themes from Mark's gospel and amplifies them. "Jesus began to show his disciples that he must go to Jerusalem and suffer many things from the elders and the chief priests and the scribes, and be killed," Matthew teaches (16:21). Jesus' death specifically by crucifixion—a form of capital punishment exercised in Judea exclusively by Romans in Jesus' lifetime—is implied or explicitly "foretold" as occurring at the hand of Gentiles (Matthew 16:24; 20:19). But as Matthew's Jesus forthrightly teaches and as his Passion narrative dramatically proclaims, the priests and the Passover crowd were the ones truly to blame (Matthew 20:18; 26:1-27, 44).

Later gospel traditions further amplify this theme. Luke, uniquely, represents Pilate as declaring three times that Jesus is innocent. "I find no crime in this man," Pilate says to the chief priests and the assembled crowd (Luke 23:4). And again: "I did not find this man guilty of any of your charges against him" (Luke 23:14). And again: "I have found in him no crime deserving death" (Luke 23:22). Responsibility for Jesus' death shifts accordingly. John's Jesus, speaking with Pilate, makes the point even more plainly: "He who delivered me to you"—that is, Jerusalem's chief priest—"has the greater sin" (John 19:11).

Later Christians broadened the indictment to include Jews who were not present in Jerusalem at the time of Jesus' death. In the Acts of the Apostles (late first to early second century?), Peter addresses a crowd of Jewish pilgrims from the Diaspora who are gathered in the city for the holiday of Shavuot (Greek: Pentecost). "Men of Israel, hear these words: Jesus of Nazareth . . . *you crucified and killed*. . . . Let the whole house of Israel therefore know that God has made him both Lord and Christ, this Jesus *whom you crucified*" (Acts 2:22–23,36; emphasis mine). By the mid-second century, Justin Martyr taught that all Jews everywhere, in every generation since the crucifixion, were guilty of the crime of killing the Son of God (for example, *Dialogue with Trypho* 128). Another second-century Christian, Melito of Sardis, delivered an Easter homily retelling the story of the Exodus as a typology of Christ's crucifixion, while contrasting the Jews' joy in celebrating Passover with the sufferings of Christ. He builds to a dramatic crescendo: the accusation that the Jews—his contemporaries, clearly, as well as those presented in the gospels' narratives—are "god-killers," deicides:

> *He who hung the earth is hanging.*
> *He who fixed the heavens has been fixed.*
> *He who fastened the universe has been fastened to a tree.*
> *The Sovereign has been insulted.*
> *The god has been murdered.*
> *The King of Israel has been put to death*
> *by an Israelite right hand.*[4]

The rhetorical force of all these themes, further, was enhanced by another traumatic historical event: the Judean revolt against Rome led by Bar Kokhba in 132–135 C.E. The immediate causes of this rebellion are obscure. Its result was not: Hadrian crushed the revolt and (at least according to a Christian literary commonplace) banned Jews from Judea. The Romans now designated this territory by a political neologism, "Palestine" (a Latin form of "Philistine"), in a deliberate effort to denationalize Jewish/Judean territory. And, finally, Hadrian eradicated Jewish Jerusalem, erecting upon its ruins a new pagan city, Aelia Capitolina.

Gentile Christians viewed the earlier, first-century destruction of the Temple through the prism of this bloody second-century defeat. The twinned catastrophes of these two unsuccessful Judean revolts against Rome fused in Christian interpretive imagination with the gospels' post-70 "predictions" of the Temple's destruction and with their linkage of its destruction to Jesus' death. The Judean Jews' later military defeats served to confirm this Christian view that "the Jews" killed Jesus. Why else would God have permitted his own Temple to be destroyed? "You would never have dominated Judea," says Tertullian, speaking specifically about the Temple in his address to Rome, "if she had not transgressed to the utmost degree against Christ" (*Apology* 26.3, c. 200 C.E.). The Jews' greatest sin of all time, comments Origen a generation later, was their killing Jesus. After that, God abandoned them entirely (*Against Celsus* 4.32).

The Septuagint itself, replete with the ancient prophets' warnings about the first Temple's destruction and with laments about the Babylonian exile, provided its second-century gentile Christian readers with more ways to rhetorically magnify these Roman-period analogues. The aftermath of the wars against Rome was interpreted biblically, in light of the Septuagint's depiction of Judea in the sixth century B.C.E. under Babylon. Gentile Christian thinkers accordingly regarded Jewish contemporaries in the Diaspora from this perspective. These Jews, recall, had been settled voluntarily outside of the Land of Israel for centuries, in some places even before the unifying conquests of Alexander the Great. Jerusalem, their notional *metropolis* ("mother city"), was a distant reality compared to their *patria*, the cities of residence that they had viewed, for generations, as "home." In the eyes of gentile Christian theologians, however, this diaspora Jewish population had in effect just been driven out of Judea by the Romans after 70 C.E. into a punitive, divinely mandated, and long-foretold exile. They had no Temple left, no Jewish commonwealth; and after Hadrian, they could not even enter what had once been their capital city, Jerusalem. What else could such disaster measure, if not the depths of God's wrath? In short, by interpreting the whole sweep of biblical history from Cain to Caiaphas and beyond as the record of God's anger against the Jews, Christian theologians combined episodes in the Jewish Bible with these more recent disasters of the first and second centuries to produce a mass of mutually reinforcing arguments *adversus Iudaeos*.[5]

We see many of these arguments assembled in Justin, though they also appear frequently elsewhere. Contemporary Jews were in exile, Justin explained, deprived of their Temple and their commonwealth, as divine punishment for their role in the death of Christ (*Dialogue with Trypho* 16). God had tolerated the Temple service only as a bulwark against the perennial Jewish tendency toward idol worship (*Trypho* 32). The "old law" through Moses had been given to Jews in the first instance as a punishment for their stubbornness and obduracy (*Trypho* 11–14, 18, 21–22, 27, and frequently); what was not purely punitive was meant to be understood spiritually as pointing to Christ. But once Christ, the divine author of these figurations, finally appeared in the flesh, the Jews murdered him and rejected his teachings, just as they had done to the prophets before him.

By using the Romans to destroy the Temple, explained Justin, God had given the Jews yet one more opportunity to grasp what he had always truly wanted them to understand, namely, that the Law was actually about his Son. The Temple gone, no place for offerings remained, so that blood sacrifices (which God had never wanted anyway) were no longer possible. Surely the Jews would (finally!) realize now that Moses' law was never meant to be fulfilled in a "carnal," literal way (*Trypho* 18). Yet incredibly, stubbornly, the Jews persisted, circumcising fleshly foreskins rather than their hearts, observing the Sabbath carnally as a day of feasting and of physical repose. Having missed the

Christological meanings of the "old law," they now failed to understand that, through Christ and his church, a "new law" had been given (*Trypho* 11–12). No wonder the Jewish nation was broken, scattered, and powerless. A less stubborn, more philosophical people, sighed Justin, would have seen the light long ago and joined Justin's church.[6]

In real life, how traumatic for diaspora Jews was the loss of Jerusalem? In many ways, the wound was deep. The Temple and the city had long focused the pride and the piety of the wide-flung Jewish nation. Both had drawn Jews on pilgrimage throughout the Roman world and beyond. The Temple itself had been the beneficiary of an enormous volume of voluntary donations. Its sacrificial etiquette was seen as continuous since the days of Israel's wandering in the desert with the tabernacle: In this sense, these sacrifices had been part of Israel's worship even before coming into the Land. Descriptions of the ways that the altar functioned as the place for the praise, propitiation, and presence of the god of Israel wove throughout the better part of the Five Books of Moses and were thus proclaimed in community wherever Jews gathered on the Sabbath to hear their law. Praises of the Temple were enshrined in the psalms and in the prophets. The desire to rebuild it had fueled the hellish war under Bar Kokhba. Later rabbinic traditions preserved (and expanded upon, and occasionally invented) the details of its protocols. The day of its destruction, the ninth of Av (which usually falls in late summer), is still mourned and commemorated by a fast. In Jewish liturgies and benedictions from that day to this, prayers for its restoration and for the restoration of Jerusalem have assumed a prominent and permanent place.[7]

And yet, in practical day-to-day ways, how much of a difference could such a loss have made? For hundreds of years, the vast majority of Jews had lived outside of the Land of Israel. (East of the empire, Babylon was home to a large and even more ancient Jewish community whose residence traced back to the Babylonian exile of the sixth century B.C.E.) Generations of Jews spanning three to six centuries before its destruction had never experienced living in a Jewish commonwealth at all and had long ago accommodated themselves to this fact. Most of these Jews, for that matter, had never laid eyes on the Temple. They were already long accustomed to showing respect to their god without offerings and sacrifices, because such offerings in principle could be made only in Jerusalem. Instead, through the cycles of reading their scriptures, usually one day in seven on the Sabbath, they had heard and learned about such sacrifices. They could and did continue to do so long after the Temple ceased to exist.[8]

Through the public institution of the synagogue and the private institution of the family, in other words, Jews throughout the world had long since devised patterns of practice that honored their ancestral tradition in ways other than by making the offerings mandated by that tradition. Public reading of sacred stories, community support for the poor, a common calendar of Sabbath and holy days that (at least notionally) united Jews across vast distances, the domestic venue of so much of Jewish observance: Thanks to the unique literary medium of their tradition—that is, the Bible—Jews had long since detached the worship of their god from his original cultic site and learned how to live on the road.

Even after 70 C.E., then, and even after 135, Jewish life in the Diaspora went on much as it always had. (The half-shekel Temple tax continued as well, the funds now levied against all Jews and diverted by Rome to the Roman high god, Jupiter Capitolinus.) Roman government continued to respect the long-established ancestral practices of its Jewish subjects, as it customarily respected such practices of its other subject peoples. When Rome (perhaps in the late 120s) banned the practice of circumcision, Jews were exempted from the ban; slightly later, Antoninus Pius explicitly permitted circumcision to Jews, while banning it for non-Jews. Sometime between 196 and 211, the emperors Septimius Severus and Caracalla ruled that those Jews who served on town councils could exercise that office without performing "liturgies" (those rites and ceremonies incumbent upon a councilor) that might "offend against their religion." And finally, when in 212 the emperor Caracalla universalized Roman citizenship, Jews (as many others) who had been citizens of their own cities became, also, citizens of the city of Rome.[9]

The archaeological record for the entire Roman period, both in the Diaspora and in the Land of Israel, both before Constantine and well after him, also reveals that many Jewish communities continued to thrive. Synagogue buildings are refurbished and new ones built, occasionally on a grand scale. Wealthy pagans continue to support and to sponsor local Jewish activities; Jewish citizens continue to hold offices in municipal and imperial government; Jewish funerary artifacts and inscriptions attest to the continued rootedness and social integration of these communities in their diaspora setting. And as compendia of late Roman law codes (and the occasional comments of irate orthodox bishops) attest, the legitimacy of Jewish holy books, property, and practices continues to be asserted, and Jews continue to be citizens of their cities and of the empire, well after the empire itself was Christian. The rhetoric of the *adversus Iudaeos* tradition does not give us the measure of this social reality.[10]

♦♦♦

A TRAUMATIC HISTORICAL EVENT quite different from the failed Judean wars against Rome further stimulated the *adversus Iudaeos* tradition. Those traumatized, however, were not Jews but Christians—or, more specifically, *gentile* Christians. Beginning in the late first century and continuing thereafter, gentile Christians were vulnerable to acts of violence. They might be denounced before civic magistrates or condemned to capital punishments by imperial authorities. To be a (gentile) Christian was to risk harassment and imprisonment, perhaps juridical torture, and even execution.[11]

From the late-first to the mid-third century, the period before the imperial government became formally involved, these persecutions were random, sporadic, and local. The absolute number of Christians who suffered this abuse was probably not large. (Origen in 247 C.E. opined that "the number could easily be counted"; *Against Celsus* 3.8.) After 249, beginning with the emperor Decius, imperial initiatives attempted to enforce cultic conformity on the part of all Romans (except, again, Jewish Romans) in the effort to solicit divine protection for the empire. The Christian sense of persecution deepened as the numbers of Christians affected—whether they defied or complied with the government's initiative—increased.[12]

We are so accustomed to "knowing" that Rome persecuted ancient Christians that we can fail to see how odd, unprecedented, and anomalous such a persecution, in such a society, actually was. Pragmatic religious pluralism had long characterized ancient Mediterranean king-doms in general, the Roman Empire in particular. (No one wanted to have to deal with an angry god.) To understand the sources of this un-happy social innovation—the invention of religious persecution—we need to recall what concerned ancient peoples when they engaged in what we think of as "religious" activities. Ethnicity and antiquity; the standing obligations to one's own gods; the importance of communal cult acts, of showing and being seen to show respect; the premium placed on maintaining the *pax deorum,* the concordat between heaven and earth that guaranteed the well-being of city and empire: These are the considerations that mattered to them. Cult, the ancients assumed, made gods happy; and when gods were happy, humans flourished. Conversely, not receiving cult made gods unhappy; and when gods were unhappy, they made people unhappy.

The problem with gentile Christians, then, in the view of the pa-gan majority, was not that these people were "Christian," but that they were "gentile," or rather (renouncing the slipperiness of our English translations of *ethnos,* p. 34 above), that they were still "pagan." That is to say, the problem was that, whatever the new religious practices these people chose to assume, they were nonetheless, in the eyes of their neighbors, still obligated to their native religious practices too, and thus to their native gods. Gentile Christians became the objects of local resentments and anxieties precisely because they were deviant pa-gans, refusing to honor the gods upon whom their city's well-being de-pended. In consequence, when things went wrong—as things tend to do—gentile Christians were easily, readily blamed. As Tertullian fa-mously complained, "If the Tiber overflows to the walls, if the Nile does not rise to the fields; if the sky does not move or the earth does; if there is famine or plague, the cry goes up at once, 'The Christians to the lion!' " (*Apology* 40.2). Gentile Christians did not show their gods their due, and hence they incurred the resentful accusation of "athe-ism"—that is, of not honoring the gods (as opposed to the modern meaning of "not believing in God"). Divine anger would affect every-body. In brief, ancestral obligation, not particular beliefs—what people did, not what they thought—was what mattered.[13]

Popular fear of this strange new group fed also on rumor, which attributed terrible anti-social crimes to Christians: infanticide, cannibalism, incestuous sexual intercourse. Lurid accusations like these, as we have seen, conformed to stereotyped views of outsiders: Erudite ethnographies had habitually fastened similar descriptions on various foreign groups (see p. 26 above). Against Christians, such stories eventually lost their force as courts of law discredited and disproved them. (Christians, however, in their turn, continued to attribute these crimes to sectarian co-religionists.) Once a Christian stood before the magistrate, the matter instead turned on showing respect both for imperial authority and for the *mos Romanorum*, "the ancient customs of the Romans." Would the accused defer to the governor's request? Would he honor the emperor's image? Would she eat meat or sip wine offered to the gods? Many Christians complied; others refused. The stalwart might end their days in the arena, robed as characters from classical mythology, executed in spectacles recalling the stories of the same gods whom they had refused more conventionally to honor.[14]

The principals in these persecutions, both victims and victimizers, were Gentiles. The pagan context of their conflict—showing honor to the gods of majority culture—dominates the ancient accounts. Nonetheless, Christian writers found ways to implicate Jews in these incidents of pagan anti-Christian violence. In his *Dialogue with Trypho,* Justin accused the Jews of murderous harassment of Christians, extending back to the crucifixion itself: "Your hand was lifted high to do evil, for even when you had killed the Christ you did not repent, but you also hate and murder us" (*Trypho* 133). Tertullian characterized synagogues as "fountains of persecution" (*Scorpiace* 10). Origen suggested that Jews stood at the source of popular anti-Christian calumnies about ritual murder, cannibalism, and promiscuous sex (*Against Celsus* 6.27). And two important martyr stories, *Polycarp* (mid-second century) and *Pionios* (mid-third century), prominently featured villainous Jews as instigators of, agents in, or hostile witnesses to the sufferings of the martyrs.

Some historians incline to trust the historicity of these accounts of Jewish hostility, since the theme itself in martyr stories is generally so rare. Other historians hear in these accusations the strains of the *adversus Iudaeos* rhetoric transposed into a narrative key. The components of that rhetoric appear *in nuce* in Paul's letters and the gospels, when those authors complain that (other) Jews do not rightly interpret scripture. They achieve greater polemical force and coherence in the second century when, as we have seen, this rhetoric was applied in service to the problem of Christian biblical interpretation. Gentile Christian writers used it to make the case that their church, not the diaspora synagogue, best understood how to read Jewish scriptures. One of their proofs was that the Jews had never understood God's word. Not only did the Jews interpret scriptural passages as "fleshly" religious practices instead of as spiritual prescriptions, but they also never listened to their own prophets, as the prophetic texts themselves complained.

Christians also appropriated late Second Temple Jewish legends about the prophets. Embroidering on the canonical prophets' complaints about Israel's resistance to their message, these later legends related tales of the prophets' murders at the hands of their own recalcitrant people. Thus Isaiah ended his days sawn in half; Jeremiah died by stoning; Ezekiel was executed by "the ruler of the people Israel"; Micah, Amos, and Zechariah all perished violently (Amos after torture). These traditions, collected in the pseudepigraphic text *Lives of the Prophets,* enter Christian writings already in the first century. The Jews (or "Judeans") "killed both the Lord Jesus and the prophets," a problematic passage in Paul relates (1 Thessalonians 2:15). "O Jerusalem, Jerusalem, killing the prophets and stoning those who are sent to you!" laments Jesus in Matthew (23:37) and Luke (13:34). Matthew's Jesus, addressing crowds gathered at the Temple, adds:

> Woe to you, scribes and Pharisees, hypocrites! for you build
> the tombs of the prophets and adorn the monuments of the
> righteous, saying, "If we had lived in the days of our fathers, we
> would not have taken part with them in shedding the blood of
> the prophets." Thus you witness against yourselves, that you
> are sons of those who murdered the prophets. Fill up, then, the
> measure of your fathers. You serpents, you brood of vipers, how
> are you to escape sentence in Gehenna? Therefore I send you
> prophets and wise men and scribes, some of whom you will kill
> and crucify, and some you will scourge in your synagogues and

persecute from town to town, that upon you may come all the righteous blood shed on earth, from the blood of the innocent Abel to the blood of Zechariah son of Barachiah, whom you murdered between the sanctuary and the altar.

MATTHEW 23:29–35 (RSV)

This "trail of blood" motif, as Matthew deploys it, inculpates every generation of Jews since the second generation of humanity, associating the Jewish people with Cain. In this view, the Jews killed the prophets, and finally they killed even Christ himself, because they did not want to hear the prophets' message that the Law was really a coded form of the Gospel, its true referent Christ.[15]

Later Christians, writing apologies and martyr stories, applied this indictment even more broadly. They presented their own Jewish contemporaries as the current manifestation of this long line of persecutors that now stretched from the period of biblical Israel up to Jesus, thence to the generation of the apostles, and finally up to their own day. Paul's outburst in 1 Thessalonians, the various early Christian sermons preserved in Acts, the complaints of apologists and, eventually, some stories about the martyrs all deploy it. This "trail of blood" motif loomed large in Christian polemic, in other words, in part because the theme so supported constructions of Christian identity. Presenting non-Christian Jews as always and everywhere hostile to Christians (including those Septuagintal "Christians" like Moses and the prophets, whose complaints about Israel's obstinacy filled the pages of scripture), the younger community expressed its conviction that it was itself both the true Israel and the true church.[16]

Thus we read in the *Martyrdom of Polycarp* that "the whole crowd of Gentiles and Jews dwelling in Smyrna cried out in uncontrollable anger and with a great shout, 'This is the teacher of Asia, the father of the Christians, the destroyer of our gods, the one who teaches many neither to sacrifice nor to worship!' " (*Polycarp* 12.2). The "Jews" in this story speak of these gods as "ours": It is hard to imagine real Jews doing so. Also, as this sentence awkwardly attests, anti-Christian violence focused precisely on the issue of pagan public cult. Outside of the pages of this Christian literature, Jews' aligning themselves in this way with enraged pagan neighbors would have put themselves at risk. Though Jews were customarily excused from public cult, nonetheless (as we have seen) they occasionally earned the resentment of their neighbors for holding back from citywide acts of piety. In the volatile and violent context of these outpourings of civic anger against gentile Christians, then, it would have been at least incautious for Jews to make themselves so conspicuous. In front of the mob, they would have risked emphasizing their own degree of religious difference from the practices of majority culture precisely on this contested issue.

Martyr stories served as identity-confirming narratives for the Christian communities that preserved them. Reporting events as such was less the goal of this literature than was exhortation, the idealized presentation of Christian witness, and theological instruction. The gospels' passion narratives served as a literary and theological model of conduct for the presentation of the martyr, and those narratives of course had featured hostile, plotting Jews. The *adversus Iudaeos* tradition, constituted in no small way on the pattern of those narratives, also figured in this mix, which fact probably accounts for the prominence of hostile Jews in some of these later stories. That tradition set the terms for how "the Jews" were always and everywhere supposed to act toward Christians—that is, with unwavering malice and hostility. And thus they were depicted both in the complaints of Christian apologists such as Justin and Tertullian and in the narrative accounts of martyrs' deaths such as *Polycarp* and *Pionios*.[17]

Pedagogical and prescriptive, the *adversus Iudaeos* tradition also taught gentile Christians how they should act toward Jews. Why would Christians want to associate with the unrepentant murderers of their Lord? And, knowing as they did the true (that is, the spiritual and Christological) meaning of the Law, why would Christians want to involve themselves with the divinely repudiated practices of carnal Jewish ritual? Yet here, on precisely this point—gentile Christian interactions with Jews—we have rich evidence that gives us some measure of the gap between rhetoric and reality, between ideology and behavior, between what some Christians said and what other Christians actually did.

Christian writers—often the same ones most ideologically committed to separating Christianity from Judaism—frequently attest as well to the persistence of social behaviors that they otherwise insist are unthinkable and impossible. For the entire period from the late first century through the fourth, and arguably beyond, these literary sources complain about ongoing social intimacy between gentile Christians and Jews. Writers such as Ignatius (c. 100), Justin (c. 150), and Tertullian (c. 200) all voiced alarm at the tendency of gentile Christians to voluntarily assume Jewish practices. Both Origen in the third century and John Chrysostom in the late fourth century criticized members of their own congregations who worshiped and ate together with Jews in synagogues on the Sabbath and who then appeared at church on Sundays.

Chrysostom, Augustine's contemporary, particularly excoriated Antiochene gentile Christians for frequenting Jewish Sabbath services. In a series of sermons delivered beginning in 386 C.E., he complained that members of his congregation treated synagogues as holy places because those buildings contained scrolls of the Torah before which Christians would take oaths (*Discourses against Judaizing Christians* 1.3–5; 8.8). Worse: These Gentiles celebrated the autumn high holidays— Rosh Hashanah (1.5), Yom Kippur (1.2), Sukkot (7.1)—and even Passover with their Jewish neighbors (3.4). Worse yet: These Christians, ignoring the rulings of the Council of Nicea some sixty years earlier (325 C.E.), continued to celebrate Easter according to the Jewish date for Passover, precisely because it was the older custom, implicit in the gospels themselves (3.3–4). It was all more than Chrysostom could bear. "When have they [the Jews] celebrated the Pasch with us?" he demanded. "When have they celebrated the festivals of the martyrs with us?" (4.3). "If the Jewish rites are holy and venerable," he insisted, "then our way of life must be false" (1.6).[18]

In roughly the same period, imperially sponsored church councils, both in the Latin West and in the Greek East, repeatedly published canons the chief aim of which was to establish and enforce a separation of Christians, both clerical and lay, from Jews. The prohibitions reveal patterns of actual behavior. Some gentile Christians kept the Sabbath as their day of rest and worked on Sundays. They received festal gifts from Jews (and also from "heretics," that is, non-catholic

Christians). They accepted gifts of matzah at Passover and participated in Jewish worship. Christians co-celebrated Jewish fasts and
feasts, tended lamps in synagogues on Jewish feast days, and joined
with Jews (and, again, with heretics) in prayer. Christians and Jews
married each other, so that occasionally the Christian partner joined
the Jewish partner in his or her traditional practices. Archaeological
evidence reveals that Christians and Jews buried their dead together.
And the Jewish calendar—especially the date of Passover relative to
Easter—continued to influence Christian communal celebrations, the
pointed efforts of bishops and even of emperors notwithstanding.[19]

This is not to claim that "interfaith" relations in antiquity were
universally sunny: Beneath the smoke of hostile rhetoric, some genuine fires also burned. The stylized speech of these literary sources,
however, or their pointed ambiguity, makes clarity elusive. Celsus, a
pagan observer, noted in the late second century that Jews and Christians quarreled unendingly—though not as loudly and viciously, he
also notes, as different Christian groups quarreled with each other
(*Against Celsus* 3.1, on Jews and Christians; 5.63, on Christians who
"slander one another with dreadful and unspeakable words of
abuse . . . for they utterly detest each other"). Later, in the late fourth
century and on into the fifth century, reports of violence perpetrated
by Christians against Jewish persons and property begin to accrue, as
also against pagans and their holy sites and against Christian minorities ("heretics") and theirs. Descriptions of Jewish anti-Christian ag-
gression also appear in that same period. Beginning in the fourth
century and continuing thereafter, increasing acts of violence mar late
Roman Mediterranean urban culture. We shall consider some of these
episodes more closely toward the end of this study.[20]

But such violence is far from the whole picture. The gaps in our
data notwithstanding (for we invariably know less than we would like
to know), our very varied evidence for Jewish–Christian interactions,
its broad chronological spread (from the second to the seventh century and beyond), its wide geographical distribution (the Iberian
peninsula, Gaul, Italy, North Africa, Alexandria, Asia Minor, Palestine), and the rich variety of its media (stories, letters, sermons, imperial and ecclesiastical legislation, inscriptions, mosaics and other ar-

chaeological remains) also attest to centuries of friendly relations between these communities as well. These data too must surely be considered in any historical assessment of Christian reports of active
Jewish hostility, especially in the pre-Constantinian period. If Jews had
actually played—or even been commonly thought to have played—a
vigorous role in the pagan persecution of gentile Christians, then all
this other evidence of positive and long-lived social interactions between Christian Gentiles and Jews becomes extremely difficult to account for.

Pagan Gentiles continued to frequent synagogues also, and Christian writers complain about this as well. Tertullian in North Africa in
the third century and Cyril of Alexandria in the fifth century both
commented bitterly on the inconsistency of those pagans who worshiped both the god of Israel and their own deities. Commodian, a
third-century (or, perhaps, a fifth-century) North African Christian
criticized Jews for allowing such behavior on the part of sympathetic
pagans, whom he mocked as "half-Jews." "You ought to tell them," he
chides Jewish contemporaries, "whether it is right to worship the
gods." The archaeological evidence of gentile donations to Jewish projects and specifically to synagogues supports the picture that we can
cull from this literature: Late Roman pagans, like their Christian
counterparts, continued to find a place within Jewish communities.[21]

What Commodian *does* say, however, and what Chrysostom, even
in his most vituperative sermons, does *not* say hint in the direction of
an answer to the question of social context and *contra Iudaeos* invective.
As we have seen, scholars in the twentieth century conjectured that
synagogues ran actual missions to Gentiles, both pagan and Christian,
to persuade them to convert to Judaism, just as churches conducted
similar missions to Jews and to pagans. In this view, anti-Jewish invective measured the heat generated between these two communities by
their white-hot competition for the limited "convert" market. But
Commodian complains precisely that these North African synagogues
are *not* trying to convert interested pagans, while Chrysostom never
complains that Antiochene synagogues attempt to persuade interested
gentile Christians to "become" Jews, that is, to convert. In other words,
what makes the synagogue so dangerous—or at least so very aggravat-

ing—to many Christian bishops in the fourth century C.E. is precisely its continuing exercise of the practice that stretched back to the Hellenistic centuries B.C.E. Late Roman synagogues, like their earlier Hellenistic counterparts, received interested outsiders *without* trying to convert them. And that openness, precisely because it came without the demand for an exclusive commitment, is what accounts for the synagogue's continuing attraction.

A Gentile's participation in the community life of his Jewish neighbors, to whatever degree (casual and occasional presence, regular and committed interest, active philanthropy), was at his or her own discretion. That fact, and not the conjectured mutual missions, I suggest, is what explains all the pagan and Christian foot traffic through late Roman synagogues. That foot traffic in turn accounts in part for the increased levels of learned vituperation *adversus Iudaeos* in fourth-century Christian texts. And the lush tropes of this vituperation, in turn, combined with the explosion or exposure of "orthodox" Christian diversity in the wake of Constantine's efforts to create unity, made for its perfervid reuse in the intra-Christian quarrels of the imperial church.[22]

The exhortations of Christian leaders to their own flocks, urging the faithful to desist from attending municipal festivals, spectacles, and shows, make a related point. The structures of urban society and those activities characteristic of Mediterranean culture—education, government, recreation—were profoundly, intrinsically pagan. (Indeed, so important were these traditional festivals to urban life that later Christian emperors exasperated many of their own bishops by insisting that town councils continue to sponsor these activities.) Jews had long ago fitted themselves into the pagan city, encouraging outsiders' interest in and support for Jewish activities while participating in majority culture as they would. For gentile Christians, these urban structures (synagogues as well as baths and amphitheaters) and civic holidays were no less native than they were for Jews. And any male member of the curial class from whatever religious or ethnic group would have been educated within and would have reaped the benefits of a purely pagan curriculum. Despite traumatic episodes of earlier pagan hostility, then, and despite the vituperation heaped upon civic celebrations and entertainments by their own church leaders, Christians, like Jews, accommodated themselves to majority culture, evidently with much less difficulty than some of their leaders would have liked. That is because majority culture, in many ways, *was* their culture: All of these people were themselves Romans.[23]

◆◆◆

WHAT ACCOUNTS FOR the continuing socializing among members of these different groups? The answer lies in part with the strong and prevailing patterns of social and religious interaction that, by Augustine's time, had shaped life in the Mediterranean city for nearly a millennium. Celebrations of all sorts—processions, communal eating, urban and imperial feast days—were open and public. Particularly in the eastern empire, Jewish celebrations had long numbered among these. Indeed, so strong was this tradition of openness that the celebration of Christian worship, despite the regrets occasionally expressed by irate churchmen, might also be frequented by outsiders: pagans, heretics, and Jews (who would challenge the interpretation of Old Testament texts). Though orthodox theologians and bishops busily erected rhetorical fences (as did their Jewish counterparts, the rabbis), the situation on the ground evidently continued to be fluid. Within these late Roman avatars of Alexander's imported polis, then, and depending on whom you asked, it seems that no fences still made good neighbors.[24]

We are unprepared to look at the evidence this way because, first of all, good relations are not what we expect to see. We approach antiquity through the cultural memory of a millennium of violent Christian anti-Jewish hostility, from the massacres of the Crusades to the death camps of the last century. Our retrospect can prompt us to perceive Jews as segregated, perhaps even as self-segregated outsiders in their ancient societies, and perhaps to presuppose that the traditions of anti-Judaism so characteristic of late Roman Christian rhetoric translated, as it did in the later medieval and modern periods, into active and generalized anti-Semitism.

Similarly, cultural memory encourages our expectation that Christians, given the choice, would avoid pagan social activities. The memory of pagan anti-Christian persecutions—preserved, occasionally invented, and always scrupulously cultivated by the later church—makes ancient Christians' voluntary, indeed, insistent participation in and enjoyment of pagan urban culture seem deeply counterintuitive. Yet participate they did: These Christians, after all, were themselves Greeks and Romans (as, indeed, were their Jewish neighbors also). And we are so accustomed to seeing Constantine's conversion as the "triumph of the church"—for the very good reason that the vast majority of writings that survive from this period belong to church fathers who presented history in this way—that we easily lose sight of the huge population *extra ecclesiam* who in real life compromised and complicated the church's self-declared monopoly: myriad non-orthodox Christians (including Jewish Christians), Roman Jews, and throngs of pagans who probably continued to constitute the majority of the total population throughout the better part of the fourth century and perhaps beyond.

Orthodoxy's monopoly of the ancient literary sources obscures this messier social reality. Ideologues of separation, the church's bishops and theologians wrote treatises and delivered sermons that too often have been perceived as descriptions of actual Christian behavior, rather than the (perhaps wistful) prescriptions for behavior that the prelates would have preferred to see. When these men urged segregation on their balky congregations—to shun synagogues; to avoid Jewish, pagan, and heretical convocations; to spurn civic festivities with their contests and dramas and mime troupes enacting unsavory scenes from pagan mythology—they fought against centuries-old social patterns. Their theologically motivated effort to segregate the habitually mixing populations of Mediterranean cities was an evidently unwelcome innovation. The threats, complaints, and laments that fill their sermons, together with the echoes of their efforts that we find in church canons and in imperial legislation, all suggest that these efforts at separation met with frustration much more routinely than with success.[25]

Continuing positive interactions specifically between diaspora Jews and gentile Christians also had more particular contributing factors. One was the type of Christianity that had "triumphed" in the fourth century and beyond. Unlike many of its various rivals, the church backed by Constantine had laid very strong and direct claim to the Septuagint. Those scriptures enjoining and praising the fidelity of God to Israel and of Israel to God were, as the Old Testament, part of the church's own canon, read aloud whenever the community gathered for worship. What Christians heard in their own services in no small way coincided with what they heard if they went to the synagogue: the public reading, *in the vernacular*, of these same texts. In this way, the synagogue could not be alien to visitors from the church.[26]

True, the interpretation of the Old Testament was hotly contested, and that contest led directly to much of the vituperation and venom of *adversus Iudaeos* rhetoric. To make the Old Testament into a Christian book required strenuous efforts at reinterpretation, efforts that characterize the sermons and commentaries of this period. What people in church would have heard first, however, were the biblical stories themselves. Those scriptures that the church shared with the synagogue thus functioned as a bridge as well as a barrier between the two communities. And, ironically, some of the loudest and most articulate voices *adversus Iudaeos*—Justin's in the second century, Origen's in the third, Jerome's in the fourth—also relied upon specifically Jewish traditions of scriptural interpretation for their own work. Even these men learned from, and thus interacted with, contemporary Jewish scholars, the better to read and to understand their own Old Testament.[27]

The four canonical gospels could also encourage gentile Christian interest in contemporary Jewish practice. In these texts, also read regularly in community service, Jesus of Nazareth appeared as an observant Jew (Matthew 5:17-19), worshiping in synagogue on the Sabbath and keeping Passover and (according to John's gospel) the other great pilgrimage festivals to the Temple in Jerusalem. He recited the *Shema* (Mark 12:29) and wore the prayer fringes enjoined on Jewish males (*tzitziot* in Hebrew; *kraspeda* in the gospels' Greek; Mark 6:56). He gave instructions on how to pray in synagogue, how to keep fasts, and how to offer at the Temple (Matthew 5:23-24). He directed his followers on the proper dimensions for their phylacteries (Hebrew *tefillin*; Matthew 23:5). In community worship, first the gospel selection would be read aloud and then the sermon based on the gospel would follow. As the record of these sermons evince, the learned priest or bishop would frequently interpret these texts in ways that vilified Jews and Jewish practice. But, on the evidence of these churchmen's complaints, evidently the first impression on the listener was made, often, by the gospel stories themselves. Churchmen protested against their effect. "Christ was circumcised, therefore you should be circumcised," say Judaizing Christians, according to a fourth-century church father. "Christ lived according to the Law; therefore you should do the same" (Epiphanius, *The Panarion* 28.5,1). Many gentile Christians perceived Jewish practice as continuous from the Old Testament through the New Testament to what they saw in the activities of their contemporary Jewish neighbors. Some justified their own voluntary observance of these customs and festivals by pointing precisely to the example of Christ, whose practice they wanted to imitate. No less than the Old Testament, then, the New Testament itself could serve as a spur to Judaizing.[28]

The church, observed Augustine, was the bride of Christ; but the synagogue was his mother (*Against Faustus* 12.8; 22.39). His pithy remark touches on many of the reasons for the persistent ambivalence of catholic Christianity toward Jews and Judaism. True, church leaders routinely condemned Judaism along with paganism and with heresy, and their rhetoric *adversus Iudaeos* defined Jews in particular as the ultimate "other" against which to calibrate orthodox Christian belief and practice. It would be a mistake, however, in light of all this other evidence, to see their condemnations as a reliable measure of the actual separation of these communities or as an accurate index of a more general hostility. On the contrary: The vitality of habitual contacts, both social and religious, between Christians and Jews—as among Christians of all various sorts, Jews, and pagans—probably accounts for much of the shrillness and the obsessive repetitiveness of patristic invective.

Augustine himself certainly contributed his share to this invective. He too, no less than Justin or Origen or Jerome, decried Jewish "obduracy" and lamented Jewish "malice." Further, from the period of his own early schooling through to his productive years as a mature intellectual and a powerful bishop, Augustine moved entirely within a philosophical culture that valued the spiritual over the material, the eternal over the historical. Throughout his life, he thought within a range of theological cultures that in all their phases, whether heretical or orthodox, associated the Christian message with "the spirit" and the Christian construction of Judaism with "the flesh." And all of these various Christians looked to Paul as their premier authority for doing so.

Augustine, in short, was an unlikely revolutionary. Yet within the context of the *adversus Iudaeos* tradition, a revolution is precisely what he achieved.

PART TWO

THE PRODIGAL SON

Augustine the bishop had once been Augustine the heretic,
an active member for more than a decade in the church of
the Manichees.

Of all the aspects of Manichaeism that had attracted him,
Augustine later wrote, its solution to the problem of evil stood
foremost. Cosmic evil, said the Manichees, was the fault of the
Kingdom of Darkness, a force that was independent of and
co-eternal with the good Kingdom of Light and its god. Moral
evil—that is, sin—was the result of the victory of this other evil
entity within the good individual. Further, the Manichees
identified the god of the Old Testament, his creation, his law,
and his people as the historical expression of this Kingdom of
Darkness. And turning to the New Testament, they pointed
especially to the letters of the apostle Paul as their authority for
this view. Thus when Augustine, shifting allegiances, quit the
Manichees for the catholic church, more than his view of God
changed. His understanding of sin and of evil, his way of
reading the Bible, and his interpretation of the apostle Paul
had to change, too.

✦ ✦ ✦

5 ✦ THE HERETIC

Where does evil come from? Is God confined within a
bodily shape? Does he have fingernails and hair? And
can those men be considered righteous who had several
wives at the same time and who killed people and who
offered animals in sacrifice?

AUGUSTINE, CONFESSIONS 3.7,12

August 28, 392 C.E. At age thirty-seven, scarcely a year since his
forced ordination at Hippo and a scant five years since his baptism by
Ambrose back in Milan, Augustine faced the Manichaean teacher Fortunatus, his former colleague, in public debate. The municipal bath
was the only building large enough to hold the assembly gathered to
watch the event: not only crowds from both of the major Christian fac-
tions in Hippo but also those whom Fortunatus had been able to win
over to his own community. Perhaps some of the town's remaining pagans, intrigued, also attended; perhaps as well some of Hippo's Jews.
"Many people gathered," Augustine's biographer, Possidius, later commented (*Life* 6). "Some were truly interested, others merely curious."

The two men had known each other decades earlier, back in
Carthage, after Augustine had moved there in 371. Augustine had
come from Thagaste, an undistinguished town some 200 miles inland,
to complete the last phase of his education in rhetoric. He remained
in Carthage, on and off, for a dozen years, eventually enjoying local
notoriety as an aggressive apologist and spokesman for his church. In
time he left to pursue professional advancement in Rome. Some people later assumed that he had in fact been chased out by the proconsul. In 386, the imperial government had taken action against the
Manichaean community, driving them from the city; and by that
point, Augustine was well known in Carthage as a Manichee.[1]

✦✦✦

WHAT WAS THIS CHRISTIAN SECT that commanded Augustine's loyalty for over a decade? Born in Persian Mesopotamia during the previous century, Manichaeism began with the revelations that Mani, a visionary ascetic, received from his heavenly "twin." This celestial double explained to Mani that the entire universe and all life in it were the result of a momentous battle between eternally opposed principles, Good and Evil, Light and Darkness. Their antagonistic engagement continued still. Those who knew this mystery could aid the Kingdom of Light, undoing the damage wrought by this struggle by adopting revealed techniques of purification. Concerned to bring this message to the rest of humanity, Mani set about establishing the first self-consciously organized universal religion. He wrote down visions, prayers, and manuals of discipline, establishing an authoritative canon of holy books. He assembled loyal apostles and dispatched them to found churches. And, patronized by the emperor of Persia, he himself worked vigorously to disseminate his message. Eventually, however, angry Zoroastrian clergy alienated a succeeding monarch from Mani's enterprise. Mani was arrested, brought to the Persian court, imprisoned, and tortured. Around 276, he died a martyr's death.[2]

His movement, however, endured and flourished. In the East, via the Silk Road, Manichaeism eventually penetrated China; in the West, it traveled across the Syrian frontier into Palestine, Egypt, North Africa, and Rome, ultimately reaching Gaul and Spain. The extraordinary range of languages in which Manichaean texts are preserved—Arabic, Chinese, Coptic, Greek, Latin, Middle Persian, Parthian, Syriac (their chief original medium), Turkic, and several lesser-known Eastern tongues—gives the measure of the vigor and the vision of this extraordinary form of Christianity. Its founder, presenting himself, like Paul in the New Testament, as "the Apostle of Jesus Christ," felt charged to bring the good news of redemption, the final phase of Christian revelation, to all the nations. From the beginning, Mani's church was a mission church.

In the West, the Roman response was firm and harsh. Within twenty years of Mani's death, the pagan emperor Diocletian, on guard against "Persian" infiltrations, directed the proconsul of Africa to burn Manichaean leaders together with their books and to seize any property for the imperial treasury. Later Christian emperors treated Manichees no more kindly. In 372—around the time that the young Augustine became committed to the sect—Valentinian prohibited the group from meeting; in 382, Theodosius ordered those found living in community to be put to death.[3]

Unambiguously severe as this legislation was, its initial practical effects seem slight. As we know from Augustine, Fortunatus, and others, Roman Manichees continued to travel and to function in the open, proselytizing and debating. Manichees and their sympathizers could be found everywhere: in the army, among the wealthy in Rome itself, even within the clergy of the officially sanctioned church. It is true that in 386 a Spanish bishop, Priscillian, was brought up on charges of Manichaeism and magic, and he was subsequently executed by the state. The incident, however, caused something of a scandal. Local rivalries and factionalism seem to have had much more to do with Priscillian's demise than did the doctrinal irregularities of which he could conveniently and effectively be accused. But his death made a point: The possibility of prosecution was real. That fact seems to have been sufficient to discourage much active interest in Manichaeism on the part of the aristocracy: It was more prudent to commune with the church favored by the emperors. Effective persecution lay over the horizon, in the fifth and sixth centuries when, with the weakening of the Western Roman Empire, power pooled locally around the figure of the catholic bishop. Unlike the secular authorities, bishops stayed focused on the hunt for heretics.[4]

Mani's celestial twin had revealed to him that the ancient battle between Good and Evil continued in the condition of the current world. Hostage to the Kingdom of Darkness, particles of light—the actual substance of the divine—were trapped in matter, and permeated the physical cosmos. They collected and mingled in everything—stone, plants, animals, humans—and thus accounted for a universal condition of suffering. Collectively, these particles of captive godliness constituted the divine presence in the cosmos, "the suffering Jesus" or the "Cross of Light."

But through ascetic discipline, this revelation continued, the light could be redeemed. This conviction accounts for the Manichaean community's structure, ethics, and central ritual. Mani established a two-tier church. At its upper level was the spiritual elite, the "Elect": men and women who had taken vows of permanent celibacy, poverty, and extreme abstinence. Owning no property, mendicant, their vows required that they refrain from having anything whatever to do with acquiring even the few foodstuffs permitted them: bread, vegetables, fruits. Gathering and preparing such food invariably caused pain to the plants that were harvested. The Elect could not compromise their moral purity to such a degree.

The task of feeding the Elect thus fell to those in the church's second tier, the *auditores,* or "Hearers." These believers were not bound by such drastic vows. Once a day, both groups would gather together for a symbiotic assembly to commune for the single daily repast of the Elect. After shared psalms, worship, and the presentation of the meal, the auditors retired, and the Elect partook. Through their own digestion, they then "breathed out" and so liberated the light trapped in this sacred food. The freed particles of the Supreme Good, formerly dispersed, thus began their ascent, first collecting at the moon (whose phases evinced this process), then ascending to the sun, then passing, finally free, back to the Kingdom of Light, the realm of God the father of Jesus.[5]

Augustine had been raised in a much more conventionally Christian culture. "Salted" at birth as a catechumen, he had imbibed "the name of Christ," as he later put it, with his mother's milk (*Confessions* 1.11,17; 3.4,8). Catholic rituals, customs, and scriptures would have been familiar to him since childhood. Ironically, his catholic upbringing was precisely what prepared the way for Augustine's allegiance to Manichaeism.

Augustine had arrived in Carthage shortly after the death of his father (*Confessions* 3.4,7). With the financial support of a wealthy hometown patron, he plunged into a final cycle of study before launching himself into a remunerative legal career (3.3,6). He frequented theaters and prowled church services, looking for opportunities "to love and to be loved" (3.1,1; 3,5). In this way, aged eighteen, Augustine entered into a common-law marriage with a lower-class Christian girl, who bore his son, Adeodatus. And he pressed ahead with his legal studies, so that "the less honest I was, the more famous I would be" (3.3,6).

And then, abruptly, everything changed. Augustine encountered Cicero's *Hortensius*. He discovered philosophy.

> The book changed my feelings, altered my prayers to you, O Lord, and gave me a new purpose and ambition. Suddenly all the vanity I had hoped in I saw as worthless, and with incredibly intense desire I longed for immortal wisdom. . . . The book excited and inflamed me; in my ardor the only thing I found lacking was the name of Christ. . . . Any book which lacked this name, however well written or polished or true, could not entirely grip me.
>
> CONFESSIONS 3.4,8

Turning from Cicero, imbued with the residual piety of his upbringing, Augustine next went directly to what he thought would be the repository of Christian wisdom, namely the scriptures. His vague familiarity with them (previously, he would have *heard* these stories, not read them himself) did not prepare him for what he found. Older now, trained to study texts carefully and to appreciate beautiful prose, Augustine's new encounter unnerved him. He found reading the Bible intolerable.

One problem was, quite simply, the way that the words lay on the page. Anonymous translators had rendered the African Bible into clumsy Latin some centuries earlier, and its style was rough. It grated. ("It seemed unworthy in comparison with the dignity of Cicero"; *Confessions* 3.5,9.)

Worse, however, were its contents. Augustine's reading of the *Hortensius* had prompted him to regard the quest for God and quest for wisdom, ascetically and philosophically conceived, as essentially the same project. His Christian upbringing had prompted him to investigate the catholic scriptures, Old Testament and New, with this concern in mind. But the old Jewish narratives did not oblige his new sensibility. What did it mean, that God "made" man? And what did it mean, to be in God's image? And how was one to understand the unsavory lives of the patriarchs, with their multiple marriages and prolific progeny, their military engagements and their unending animal sacrifices? For that matter, why did God require such offerings? And the New Testament presented different but equally grave problems. Its Latin was no better than the Old Testament's, its contents no less troubling. The gospels disagreed both internally and with each other. Their problems began immediately with the birth narratives themselves. Matthew and Luke, each tracing Jesus' lineage, presented mutually incompatible genealogies.

Born and raised a Christian, Augustine knew that he wanted to remain a Christian. Newly awakened intellectually, he also knew that he could find few satisfactions in the *superstitio* of his mother's church. It was at this point that he encountered the Manichees. North Africa's Manichees offered a perfect solution to his quandary. They were Christian. ("The names of God the Father and of the Lord Jesus Christ and of the Holy Spirit . . . were always on their lips"; *Confessions* 3.4,10.) They had an enlightened attitude toward religious inquiry, disavowing—unlike the catholic church—arguments from authority. ("I fell among these people for no other reason," Augustine later claimed, "than that they declared that they would completely put aside the intimidations of authority and instead, by pure and simple rational effort, bring to God anyone willing to hear them out"; *Usefulness of Belief* 1,2.) The austerity of their Elect was impressive, while the ascetic commitments of the sect resonated effortlessly with Cicero's exhortation to flee bodily pleasures in order to free the mind for higher pursuits. And they read scripture both closely and critically, pointing out discrepancies (such as the differences between Matthew and Luke on Jesus' genealogy) and proposing rational explanations (in this instance, that the doctrine of Incarnation was both late and wrong; *Against Faustus* 3.1). Susceptible to their arguments, Augustine was impressed.[6]

The Manichees probably first engaged Augustine in the same way that Augustine later, as a Manichee himself, engaged catholic Christians: through debate. In that context, pointing out various problems with both testaments, the Manichees could press their prime theological principle. God, they firmly maintained, is wholly and solely good. From this they moved to a reasonable axiom: The good God cannot in any way be a source of evil. More: Evil had to be extremely powerful, or else God would obviously have overcome it. Thus, they concluded, evil must have an independent existence, necessarily quite apart from the good God. Evil actively resisted and defied God. Two opposed principles, they accordingly affirmed, not one supreme principle, accounted for the morally mixed universe and for man's difficult experience within it.

This dualist conviction informed both Manichaean ascetic discipline and their scriptural interpretation. The god of Genesis, they observed, had formed flesh, making humans "in his image." But human flesh clearly imposed urges and appetites on the individual that betrayed its fundamental moral orientation: The fleshly body was evil. Paul himself had taught as much. "I know that nothing good dwells within me, that is, in my flesh" (Romans 7:18). It was on this account that the Manichaean regimen, especially for the Elect, denied and disciplined the body. Only flesh purified through extreme austerity could serve to liberate light from matter, Good from Evil.

These premises entailed further conclusions, Christological, textual, and interpretive. Mani's Christ, the son of the high god, could have no direct involvement in evil flesh: Christ had only *seemed* to have flesh but was never truly in a fleshly body. The father of this docetic Christ, further, was not the god of the Old Testament. That deity, observed the Manichees, was clearly not a good god. Not only had he framed this flawed material universe and then, against common sense and experience, called it "good," but he himself behaved badly. Unstable, envious, needy, cruel: The Jews' god took pleasure in the blood of both men and beasts (*Morals of the Church* 10.16). Such a deity could not possibly be the father of Jesus and the god of Paul. Thus his Law had nothing to do with the gospel, and he as the god of the Law had nothing to do with the god of the gospel. Accordingly, then, the Old Testament had nothing to do either with the New Testament or with true Christianity.

For this position, the Manichees found an authoritative spokesman in the apostle Paul. After all, Paul had spoken in all his letters of the vital moral distinction between Law and gospel, works and grace, flesh and spirit, Jew and Gentile. Here the Manichees trod those theological pathways marked out in the mid-second century by Marcion's churches, which had long regarded Paul as the champion of "true"—that is, de-Judaized—Christianity. Indeed, their shared views of Paul seem to attest to actual contact and communication between the two communities. Nor was this resemblance lost on orthodox critics, who condemned Manichaean doctrine with polemics first honed against Marcion.[7]

Finally, all these positions—on the high god, on the docetic Christ, on the intrinsic evil of the flesh, on Paul's core message—converged on a precise polemical point. In articulating their own views, the Manichees repudiated Jews and Judaism. For this Christian church no less than for the others to which it opposed itself, "the Jews" served as a defining "Other." But what Jews, and which Judaism? That depended on the polemical project at hand. In their criticisms of the Old Testament and its morally unappealing deity, the Manichees disparaged ancient Jews from the patriarchs onward. Multiple marriages, fugitive couplings, busy procreation, a blood-drenched cult: Seen from the perspective of these austere ascetics, the religion of Israel was foolish, carnal, and indeed sacrilegious (*Usefulness of Belief* 6,13).

But contemporary society provided Roman Manichees with a closer, bigger, and much more important target for their anti-Jewish polemic: catholic Christians and their church. In the name of the gospel, the Manichees observed, Christians everywhere had freed themselves of circumcision, Sabbath observance, food taboos, and all the myriad fleshly things that the Jews' god demanded of his followers. Why on earth, then, retain the carnal Jewish book? If the church is the bride of Christ, she should be pure. But the catholic church had broken her vows. Unfaithful, she cherished letters and gifts (that is, these scriptures and their promises) from a lover who corrupted her chastity—namely, the god of the Jews.[8]

This god had seduced the catholic church with his vain pledges ("in his stone tablets he promises you gold and silver and abundance of food and the land of Canaan"). But the case was clear, the options mutually exclusive. One could accept the message either of the Old Testament (as the Jews had done and continued to do) or of the Gospel (as the Manichees had done). To accept both, as catholic Christians did, was a self-indicting admission of failure. "You receive both because you are only half-filled with each," observed Faustus, one of the Manichaean Elect and an old teacher of Augustine's. "But the one is not completed but corrupted by the other" (*Against Faustus* 15.1).

Not only were such "goods" as these—food, material security, land—low and unspiritual in themselves. They were self-evidently beyond the power of this god to deliver. His promises were false, his powers broken. Faustus pressed this point by alluding to the Jews' losses in their wars with Rome centuries earlier:

> This god is impoverished and needy. He cannot provide what he has promised. He cannot even give these things to the synagogue, his proper wife, who obeys him in all things like a maidservant. What chance is there of his delivering them to you, strangers to him who have proudly thrown off the yoke of his commandments? . . . Go ahead then. Stitch old cloth onto a new garment. Put new wine in old bottles. Serve two masters without pleasing either (Matthew 9:16–17). Make Christianity a hybrid monster, a centaur neither horse nor human. But, please, leave us to serve Christ only, content as his spouse with the immortal dowry that he has given us, in imitation of the Apostle Paul who said, "Our sufficiency is from God, who has made us able ministers of the New Testament" (2 Corinthians 3:5).
>
> AGAINST FAUSTUS 15.1

Catholic Christians, Faustus readily acknowledged, did not live according to Jewish Law. But in retaining the texts of Jewish Law, he complained, catholics still act and think as the Jews once had and still do. They, like the Jews, venerate the Old Testament, worship its god, and trust in his promises. The results were corrupting and carnal, for catholics interpreted even the Christian mysteries—the coming of Christ, his resurrection, the resurrection of believers, final redemption—in a fleshly manner. Catholics held that Christ had been born in a fleshly body and that he had died and been raised in this same fleshly body. Many believed that when the kingdom came, they too would be raised in the flesh, and that they would celebrate with a millennium of feasting together with Christ in the New Jerusalem. In the meantime, they regarded marriage as honorable and sexual procreation as its goal and purpose. And they not only permitted the consumption of wine and meat; they also feasted on such carnal foods over the graves of martyrs and in celebration of the dead. In brief, catholic Christians—misled and encouraged, no doubt, by their attachment to the Jews' books—were themselves mired in the flesh.[9]

By contrast, said the Manichees, their own holy books were untainted by association with Jewish scriptures, their Christianity untouched by such carnal sensibilities. Mani's Christ was docetic, seeming to have flesh but actually having none. The Elect through their stark self-discipline and their ritual meal "raised" Christ every day, restoring his scattered light back to the kingdom of his father. The light trapped in their own bodies and in the flesh of all other persons and things would eventually be liberated too: How could such a redemption be imagined as a "resurrection of the flesh"? In the meantime, even their auditors lived with restraint; if sexually active within marriage, they at least avoided procreation.[10]

The beliefs and activities of catholic Christians, they further asserted, had been unambiguously condemned by Paul the Apostle of Jesus Christ, and definitively superseded by the revelations of Mani the Apostle of Jesus Christ. Yet still the catholics refused to listen. In their continuing blindness to Manichaean truth, their promiscuous retention of the Jewish books, and their own obdurate fleshliness, catholic Christians were thus not merely "like" Jews. In all the ways that mattered most—in the interpretation and living out of Christian truth—these people *were* Jews. Thus Secundinus, a Roman auditor and former companion of Augustine's, mourned when he heard of his old friend's defection to the catholic church. "You have gone over," lamented Secundinus, "to the barbarous tribe of the Jews" (*Letter of Secundinus* 3).

"By their censures of the catholic faith," Augustine later observed, "and chiefly by their destructive criticism of the Old Testament, the Manichees affect the unlearned" (*Usefulness of Belief* 2,4). Their techniques were certainly effective on his eighteen-year-old self. The young Augustine was caught up in the power of their critique. ("It was as if some sharp intelligence were persuading me to consent"; *Confessions* 3.7,12.) And while his new church's condemnation of sexual activity and of procreation must have been awkward for the domestically attached new father, he knew that, as an auditor, he was excused. Further, his second-grade status within the sect also permitted Augustine to press on with his rhetorical education and his plans for a career. ("I remained in the grade they call 'hearers' so that I might not give up worldly hopes and duties," he later wrote; *Usefulness of Belief* 1,2.)

Finally, and no less important, if Augustine's continuing domestic sexual arrangement and his pursuit of professional success—both disparaged no less by the philosophical ideal than by his new church—caused him to feel anxious or compromised or guilty, he could find solace in a prime Manichaean ethical teaching. The individual replicated in miniature the cosmic battle between Good and Evil that raged throughout the entire world. His moral failings measured the strength of the forces of Darkness working within him—"the law of my members," as Paul had taught, "at war with the law of my mind" (Romans 7:23). For over a decade Augustine would believe that he himself did not sin but rather that some other, foreign, evil nature sinned within him. He took comfort in the thought (*Confessions* 5.10,18).

Meanwhile, he flourished, not least of all (as Augustine himself acknowledged) because his new community provided him with a theater for his growing rhetorical skills. "I was almost always noxiously victorious arguing against ignorant Christians who attempted to defend their faith. . . . [S]o I gained an enthusiasm for religious disputation, and from this, I daily grew to love the Manichees more and more" (*The Two Souls* 9.11). He proselytized, persuading others of his circle to join his new church (*Confessions* 4.1,1). And he was also sustained by the bond of membership in a small and intimate community. In Carthage, he could experience intimate daily contact with the Elect, together with other auditors providing alms and participating in their impressive liturgy. He had the solidarity and discipline of weekly Sunday fasts. And he could count on the social, moral, and material support of this small fraternity everywhere, whether in Africa or, years later, in Italy.[11]

♦♦♦

MANICHAEISM SUFFERS the fate of numbering among history's losers. After taking root and enduring in vastly varied and often hostile cultural settings for over a thousand years, it vanished. We make its acquaintance usually through the polemics and ridicule of its greatest Western critic, Augustine. Its own texts—many recovered only in the last century—can seem exotic and obscure because their message is so unfamiliar, and our own sympathies have been so contoured by its opponents. For all these reasons, we can have difficulty appreciating what it was about Manichaeism that compelled Augustine's ardent loyalty in Carthage, and indeed what kept him within this community long after his confidence wavered and his enthusiasm dimmed.[12]

Augustine himself singled out the Manichees' critique of the Old Testament as one of their most powerful weapons. Their way of reading these texts, especially Genesis, addressed two quite different though equally fundamental issues. The first concerned the complicated relation of gentile Christianity to Judaism. Here the Manichees cultivated ground already well worked by earlier Christian theologians. Like Valentinus, they saw in their own esoteric revelations an indictment both of the god of the Jewish Bible and of the people who so ignorantly worshiped him as the high god. Like Marcion, they especially esteemed the Apostle Paul, while holding that the text of his letters had been corrupted by hostile Judaizers. And like Justin Martyr, they enunciated their convictions about the correctness of their own religious behavior by constructing a thorough-going denunciation of Jewish practice both ancient and current. When the Manichees denounced Jewish practices as "carnal" or "blind" or intrinsically wrong-headed, they sounded much like their less exotic Christian counterparts.[13]

The other fundamental issue addressed by Manichaean readings of the Old Testament was the problem of conceiving god intellectually. Exploiting the many anthropomorphisms of the Bible, disallowing any scope for figural readings of Jewish texts, the Manichees easily ridiculed the idea of deity existing in man's image (hence their jibe about God's fingernails and hair in *Confessions* 3.7,12, cited on p. 105 above). And by insisting on physical resemblance as the meaning of "made in the image of God" (Genesis 1:26–28), the Manichees had an additional argument for decoupling the god of Genesis from the god of Jesus, Paul, and Mani. Humanity was just too physically various—different genders, different races—and the processes of sexual procreation too demeaning for God to have framed flesh at all, much less to have made it "in his own image."

> The question is not, Does God make man? but rather, What man does God make, and when, and how? For if God formed us according to his own image when we are fashioned in the womb—a belief that Gentiles [i.e., pagans], Jews, and you [catholics] all share—then God makes the 'old man,' producing him through lust and frenzy. This is hardly in keeping with divine nature. But if God forms us once we believe and we turn toward a better life . . . then God makes us 'new' men, producing us in honor and purity. This is the teaching that coheres with his sacred and venerable majesty. . . . The birth by which we are made male and female, Greeks and Jews, Scythians and barbarians, is not the birth through which God forms humanity. . . . Man is made by God not when he is divided into many, but when from many he becomes one. Diversity comes from the first birth, which is bodily. Oneness comes through second birth, discerning and indeed divine.
>
> *AGAINST FAUSTUS* 24.1[14]

Faustus argues his case here by summoning the dichotomies of John's gospel and Paul's letters—first birth and second (John 3.3-6), old nature and new (Ephesians 4:22-24), inner and outer man (2 Corinthians 4:16), spirit and flesh (Galatians 5:16-18). He also leans on commonplace contrasts that stem ultimately from Platonic philosophy. Thus when comparing the unity of baptism with the variety of physical birth (male and female, Greeks and Jews, Scythians and barbarians; Colossians 3:9-11; Galatians 3:28), he evokes the "one" and the "many." "Oneness" in Platonism codes supreme divinity; "multiplicity" codes lower levels of being. And when Faustus compares the sanctity of spiritual rebirth to "the humiliating process of ordinary generation" (accomplished, he remarks, through "intemperate frenzy, disgusting and shameful begetting, and the satisfaction of lust"), he characterizes this second birth as *intelligibile ac divina*.

I translated this Latin phrase as "discerning and divine." "Intelligible" as a type of Platonic shorthand would have indicated that this "second birth" relates to the mind, not to the flesh. The adjective modifies the noun *birth* in such a way that this birth relates to rational mental functions like understanding or thinking, as opposed to physical characteristics (sex, ethnicity, social status, and so on). In short, Faustus alludes here to the traditionally Platonic distinction between lower things apprehended through the senses (hence "sensible" reality) and higher things apprehended through the mind ("intelligible" reality).

In their native philosophical context, these terms expressed as well a contrast in modes of being, "immaterial" as opposed to "material." "Intelligible" in a classically Platonic sense denoted "spiritual," utterly incorporeal, without physical dimension. Intelligible realities—thoughts, for instance—have no extension in space. This aspect of the old Platonic definition of immateriality, however, Faustus would emphatically reject. "Intelligible" for him did *not* mean "without body." Rather, it indicated a moral orientation, not a mode of being: What was "intelligible" was "good." For the Manichees, there was no such thing as incorporeal reality. All being was embodied being. In other words, the Manichees were materialist. They thought of divinity—indeed, of all reality—as physical substance. "God" and "spirit" and "light" were very refined matter; "evil," "flesh," and "darkness" were grosser sorts of matter. But everything *was* matter.

Manichaeism in all its dimensions—its view of God and of Evil, its ideas about the universe and its origins, its concept of redemption, its ritual logic—relied fundamentally upon this principle that everything was matter of some sort. This commitment to materialism gave Manichaean thought tremendous coherence and explanatory power, especially when addressing the problem of evil. God and the human soul, they taught, were in reality of one substance. ("I thought that you, Lord God, were like a luminous body of immense size, and that I myself was a bit of that body"; *Confessions* 4.16,31.) Similarly, evil was "a kind of material substance with its own foul and misshapen mass" (5.10,20). Cosmic evil and moral evil were thus two instances of the same phenomenon: the incursion of the wicked, alien substance into the good. What made man good was God in him; what made man evil was Evil in him, represented especially in and by the intrinsic wickedness of his flesh. For this last reason especially, the Manichaean Christ was docetic, only "appearing" to have been embodied. He could not possibly be imagined as truly incarnate. Such an intimate combination of two substances as elevated as Divine Light and as base and corrupt as Evil Darkness would have compromised the very idea of Christ as God. "I was afraid to believe him incarnate," Augustine later wrote, "lest I had to believe him to be defiled by the flesh" (5.10,20).

Conceiving of good (thus God) and evil as particulate substantial realities meant, finally, that Augustine the Manichee had an explanation not only for the operation and effects of evil but also—perhaps even more important—for the origin of evil. Evil as an experience was curiously but compellingly de-personalized. When a person *did* evil (that is, when he sinned), in many ways the sin had little or nothing to do with him: Evil simply acted *through* him as a dark, invasive, and essentially alien nature. In this regard, human experience corresponded exactly to God's experience: He too, and his realm, had been invaded in precosmic times by this dark force. Evil was its own entity, totally independent of and co-eternal with God. Where had it come from? Why had it come? To such questions the Manichees responded: Evil simply *was*. Evil *always* was. Evil, like God, had no origin.

Thus despite their obvious resonances with earlier Valentinian and Marcionite systems of thought, these Manichaean views on divinity, cosmology, and evil were much more radical. Those earlier forms of Christianity had retained two of the prime ideas of Platonic paideia. Both rested on the concept of nonmaterial being, and both held to the principle that "being"—whether material or nonmaterial—was organized by hierarchical grades. These two ideas, incorporeality and order, enabled both Christian systems to retain their native pagan philosophical monotheism. For each, the high god presided in austere isolation at the very pinnacle of spiritual reality, while, on a plane of being far below, the Jewish demiurge busily and ignorantly organized matter. And this lower deity was himself contingent for his own existence (though he did not know this) on the distant Father.

Valentinus and Marcion's younger contemporary, Justin Martyr, was also a monotheist, his talk of Christ as "another god" notwithstanding (*Dialogue with Trypho* 56). He too subordinated the god who organized matter—for him, the pre-incarnate Christ—to the changeless, transcendent high god, just as "son" is subordinate to "father," and *logos* to *theos*. Justin accordingly shifted the role of cosmic antagonist, the opponent of Christ and of the high god his father, from the god of Genesis (whom Valentinus and Marcion had indicted) to the fallen angel Satan and his minions, whose status as rebels declared their subordinate rank. The graded hierarchies of all these Christian thinkers thus ensured the monotheism of their respective systems.

Manichaean materialism, by contrast, expressed a true dualism: God and the Prince of Darkness were each masters of different, unequal, but ontologically equivalent kingdoms. Both had existed from eternity. Such a radical dualism had the undeniable virtue of utterly insulating God from any responsibility for Evil. And, absent a concept of spirit, no principle of hierarchy could organize their relationship. If God in this materialist system were to be regarded as absolutely supreme, then he would have had to have created evil or to be somehow complicit in its operation—a thought, Augustine observes, that his piety simply forbade him to think.

Forced to choose between God's goodness and God's omnipotence, Augustine the Manichee relinquished divine omnipotence, and so preserved God's moral integrity: God does only good. And this conviction, coupled with his anthropomorphic understanding of the Old Testament's representation of God, required him to reject the Jewish scriptures, most especially the Book of Genesis, as well. "I felt it more reverent to believe that you were infinite in all respects but one, namely with respect to that mass of evil opposed to you, than to think that you were confined within the shape of the human body. I thought it better to believe that you had created no evil . . . than to believe that evil, as I understood it, came from you" (*Confessions* 5.10,20).

In the *Confessions,* writing with the clarity of retrospect, Augustine identified this philosophical idea ("I did not think that anything existed that was not material") as "the principal and almost sole cause of my inevitable error" (*Confessions* 5.10,19). He oversimplifies here. His attraction to and dependence on these materialist views was linked to and fueled by the urgency he felt in the face of the problem of evil. "I had no clear and explicit grasp of the cause of evil" (7.3,5). "I searched for the origin of evil, but in a flawed way; and I did not see the flaw in my search" (7.5,7). The god of more conventional forms of Christianity at the very least was willing to tolerate the operation of evil in his creation. But if he were all good and all powerful, whence this tolerance? By contrast, the Manichaean myth of the battle between two eternally opposed powers, imagined materially, firewalled their high god from any relationship, whether causal or contingent, with the independent dark force that he and his followers combated. In consequence, then, as Augustine's confidence in the Manichees' dualist and materialist explanations slowly eroded and finally, in Milan, gave way, their question, *Unde malum?* (Whence and why evil?), waxed increasingly acute.

So I came to Milan, to Ambrose, the bishop.
AUGUSTINE, *CONFESSIONS* 5.13,23

Whatever his mounting disquiet with his sect's theology, Augustine continued as a Manichee for as long as he remained in Carthage. Still chasing after professional advancement, he eventually quit his municipal professorship there in 383 and moved to Rome. Constantius, a wealthy *auditore,* received him, housed him, and provided for him when, on arrival, Augustine fell desperately ill (*Confessions* 5.9,16–10,18). Despite whatever doubts he might have had at this time (difficult to gauge, since retrospect and hostility shape his description of this period in the *Confessions*), Augustine continued to cultivate his Manichaean connections once he was in Italy. "I was in more intimate friendship with them than with others who were not in that heresy" (5.10,19).

His efforts paid off handsomely the following summer. The city of Milan, attempting to recruit a professor of rhetoric, had asked the Roman urban prefect Symmachus to make the appointment. Symmachus was an aristocrat and a pagan. Augustine's Manichaean network brought him to Symmachus' attention. Whatever Augustine's personal merit, the fact that he was a Christian heretic doubtless enhanced his application. Earlier in this same year, Symmachus had petitioned the Christian emperor Valentinian to permit the reinstitution of one of Rome's most venerable civic cults, centered on the Altar of Victory in the Senate. Milan's bishop, Ambrose, had objected vigorously and successfully, blocking this pagan effort. Sending a Manichee to occupy the Milanese municipal chair might well irritate the bishop—or so Symmachus probably hoped.[1]

During his unhappy period in Rome, and for a time after his arrival in Milan (the autumn of 384), Augustine once again read philosophy. This time it was the skepticism of the New Academy that caught his attention. "They taught that everything was a matter of doubt, and that understanding the truth lies beyond human capacity" (*Confessions* 5.9,17). As with his reading of the *Hortensius* over a decade earlier in Carthage, so once again with his study of these philosophers now: They too "were without Christ's saving name," and Augustine would not or could not commit to a non-Christian path. The absence of an established Manichaean community in Milan seems also to have accelerated his growing detachment from the sect. Nevertheless, his intellectual dependence on materialism continued, affecting his view of the world, of himself, and of the Bible. "If I had been able to conceive a spiritual substance, at once all their imagined inventions would have collapsed and my mind would have rejected them. But I could not" (5.14,24).

Desire for professional success, meanwhile, drove him onward. Augustine's advancement depended on his securing powerful patrons, and the confused political context of the thirteen-year-old boy-emperor's court made the search for such connections difficult and disheartening. Meanwhile, in the spring of 385, Monnica arrived from North Africa to assist (or direct) her son's efforts. Her presence, his disappointment with the Manichees, the gravitational pull of his childhood spent in Monnica's church, and his professional ambition together with a certain pragmatism (the ecclesiastical orientation of the court was well known) perhaps combined to propel Augustine to enroll as a catechumen in the catholic church. This tepid gesture committed him to no timetable for baptism (*Confessions* 5.14,24). Insecure, uncomfortably aware of his African accent, ardently ambitious, unexpectedly unmoored, Augustine drifted.[2]

By the late fourth century, the city of Rome was no longer the real capital of the Roman Empire. Military necessity required western emperors with their courts and their armies to reside in cities closer to the porous northern borders. Milan, just south of the Alps, was one of these garrison-capitals, replete with the wealth, the energy, and the talent that concentrations of political and military power can gather. In the mid-380s, it was also a cultural powerhouse, at the height of a renascence of Platonic studies. Erudite Milanese, both pagan and Christian, sponsored salons and reading groups dedicated to the study of Neoplatonic philosophy. Ambrose, the city's aristocratic bishop, enriched his sermons by borrowing not only from these late pagan works but also from philosophically sophisticated Greek patristic writings as well as from the exegeses of the Hellenistic Jew Philo of Alexandria. Floating between the reading groups and the church, Augustine thus received a double dose of late Platonism, the pagan stream through the salons, the Christianized stream through Ambrose.

Traditional Platonism had always emphasized the superiority of eternal to temporal, of spirit to matter, of mind to body, of the One to the many. In the third century C.E., Plotinus and his disciple Porphyry conformed the "upper-worldliness" of earlier Platonism to a new emphasis on "inner-worldliness." Like older Platonists, these Neoplatonists asserted the ontological reality of intellectual abstractions (Mind, Soul, Ideal Forms, and so on). But by conceiving such levels of being as arranged in an orderly hierarchy while insisting on a metaphysical linkage between the individual soul and these higher levels of the spiritual realm, Neoplatonists reconceptualized the way to know God: not only Look Up but also (indeed, especially) Look In. In short, these pagan philosophers developed a new language of introspection. The path to the One lay within the mind and thus the soul of the individual. By withdrawing from the distracting world of the senses, by training the mind in disciplined introspection, the philosopher could attain the happy life, defined as knowing God. The true goal of philosophy was the return of the soul to the divine One.[3]

Traditional Mediterranean piety had been the native matrix of Neoplatonism. Plotinus' and Porphyry's philosophical monotheism cohabited with their ancestral polytheism, and indeed most (not all) philosophers generally advocated piety toward the gods and their rites. Christian theologians had long availed themselves of Platonism in its various stages, while leaving its native paganism behind. And behind these Christian ventures stood the work of the Jewish philosopher Philo, whose first-century philosophical commentaries on the Septuagint had blazed the trail for later Christian theologians, who both preserved and appropriated his work.

Through Latin translations of the pagan writings and through

Ambrose's homilies—a creative mix of all of these sources, late pagan, Greek Christian, and Hellenistic Jewish—Augustine began his encounter with this great philosophical patrimony. In books six and seven of the *Confessions,* looking back some twelve years to this period, he vividly recounted the dramatic effects of this sudden immersion in Milan's cosmopolitan Christian culture. Listening to Ambrose, Augustine learned for the first time to think about the Old Testament allegorically or symbolically; *secundum spiritum,* with spiritual understanding. Biblical passages of seemingly intractable carnality, such as God's making man in his image, now yielded shining new truths. The divine "image" according to which God made Adam referred not to the body, Augustine now understood, but to the soul. God's image lay in the mind, whose intellectual processes, like the divinity whom they reflected, were utterly immaterial. Thought has no spatial extension; neither did the incorporeal God. Slowly, as Augustine assimilated Ambrose's sermons, Manichaean materialism began to fall away.

> I was delighted to hear Ambrose in his sermons to the people saying, as if he were enunciating a principle of exegesis: "The letter kills, but the spirit gives life" [2 Corinthians 3:6]. Those texts which, taken literally, seemed to contain perverse teachings, he would expound spiritually, drawing aside the mystical veil. . . . Fearing a precipitate plunge, I kept my heart from giving assent. . . . But from this time on I gave my preference to the catholic faith.
>
> CONFESSIONS 6.4,6–5,7

Scripture's humble style, which had offended his eighteen-year-old self, Augustine now saw as part of God's providential plan. Its seeming simplicity reached out to the uneducated many, while its obscurities enticed the interpretive skills of the learned few. "The absurdity which used to offend me in those books . . . I now understood to signify the profundity of their mysteries" (*Confessions* 6.5,8). Read in the light of Ambrosian allegory, the old Jewish texts revealed Christ and his church. The Manichees had it all wrong: The Old Testament, understood spiritually, really was a Christian book.

Pagan metaphysics, meanwhile, began to dissolve the seeming reasonableness of dualism as an explanation for the problem of evil. As he struggled to grasp the concept of nonmaterial being, Augustine was able to affirm other characteristics of the divine. The ancient features of philosophical paideia's high god—perfect, immaterial, immutable, radically stable—began to meld with those of the biblical deity. "With all my heart I believed you [God] to be incorruptible, free from injury, and unchangeable" (*Confessions* 7.1,1). To affirm God's immutability, however, was to deny the old Manichaean explanation for the origins of cosmic evil, namely, that an autonomous Kingdom of Darkness had invaded Light's domain and taken captive particles of the good, which now lay scattered within it. If God were immutable, he could not be subject to invasion. Where, then, did evil come from?

Late Platonists conceived this question completely differently from the ways that Augustine could, as he lingered in the twilight of his Manichaean phase. Wedded as he was to materialist views, Augustine thought of evil (as he thought of all other categories of being, including divinity) as some *thing*. But for the Platonist, evil, because a defect, was *no* thing. That is, evil did not actually exist, in the same way that darkness and silence do not "exist." Darkness is the absence of light. Silence is the absence of sound. Thus evil, too, is not a thing but a lack, namely, an absence of good. God is the fundamental cause of everything that is. He is not the cause of things that are not.

This way of framing the problem of evil had two applications, one cosmic, one moral. In terms of the cosmos, if aspects of the natural universe seemed corrupt, this very corruption measured an essential goodness because only what was good to start with could become less so. "Things which are liable to corruption are good" (*Confessions* 7.12,18). And looked at from a long enough perspective, imperfections that jar close up actually contribute to the beauty of the whole. (This last, "god's-eye" argument about evil and cosmic aesthetics can also be traced back to Plato.) In terms of morals, if the individual made a poor moral choice—in specifically biblical language, if he sinned—the cause of his sin was not his being overwhelmed by the material manifestation of a superior evil force. Rather, he sinned because of a poor use of his will, choosing to turn from a higher good (God being the highest good) to a lower good. *Why* an individual would choose a lesser good was a different question. Perhaps he lacked the intellectual training to perceive the higher good, or the self-discipline to regulate himself in order to choose it. In terms of the problem of ethical evil, however, the main point made by Neoplatonism was that the cause of sin lay within the self.

Thinking in this way enabled Augustine to absolve the biblical creator god of responsibility for evil. Indeed, to think of him as responsible for evil in any way was not only impious but patently absurd: No one, not even God, can "make" nothing (*Confessions* 7.13,19–20,26). Buoyed by his progress, Augustine then "seized the sacred writings of your Spirit and especially the writings of the apostle Paul." He saw in a new way that the two canons, Old and New, cohered both with each other and with his new philosophy. "I began reading and found that all the truth I had read in the Platonists was stated here [i.e., in the Bible] with the commendation of your grace" (7.21,27).

Neoplatonism also enabled Augustine to reconceive the moral status of matter. Though unquestionably inferior to spirit, matter in the Neoplatonist view could nonetheless be regarded as a product of the One, a sort of crust that formed at the outermost extremes of divinity, hovering on the cusp of nonbeing. Without compromise to himself and to his absolute goodness, then, God was the ultimate source of matter. As for ethical evil or sin, it could not be a consequence of man's being in the flesh. According to these philosophers, flesh did not cause sin because, metaphysically, it could not cause sin. Soul was "above" flesh in the hierarchy of being. What was "below" did not determine or control what was above it. Thus, though the flesh unquestionably importuned the soul through the senses, giving way to such promptings was never a foregone conclusion. Sin itself was a *decision*. And the decision to sin was made in the mind. In other words, sin was the prerogative of soul, not body. Flesh, for good and for ill, merely obeyed the mind's direction.

As he thought with these new concepts, Augustine felt the intellectual knots that had bound him for so long to Manichaeism loosen and come undone. His new convictions led him to embrace the teachings of Ambrose's church. At this point, he should have moved on to baptism. Instead, he lingered as a catechumen. Why?

Here a third consideration seems to have held Augustine back. He wanted baptism to come with a life-long commitment to celibacy. He was thirty-two years old.

In the late fourth century, when even most clergy were married, the church made no requirement of celibacy, and Augustine knew this:

> I was still strongly bound by the ties of woman. The Apostle did not forbid me to marry, though he exhorted me to something better and very much wished that all men were unattached, as he himself was (1 Corinthians 7:1–7). But I was weaker, and chose the softer option, and this single thing prevented me from deciding more firmly on others, so that I was weary and wasted with nagging anxieties.
>
> *CONFESSIONS* 8.1,2

Some of his later ecclesiastical opponents, criticizing Augustine for the ways that he linked his eventual teachings on original sin to human sexuality, accused him of never having really freed himself from Manichaeism. His scruples before his baptism might indeed seem like a residuum of the Manichaean ethic, which clearly had privileged sexual renunciation. But Augustine's metaphysics had changed, and his (albeit wavering) resolve now drew from the same source as his new metaphysics: philosophy. Ambrose presented such philosophy in Christian form, the return of the soul to God aided by commitment to holy celibacy. Cicero and Plotinus, the two pagan philosophers whose works had most affected Augustine, had both urged the man who would seek after wisdom to withdraw from the distractions of the senses. Renouncing sexual activity—a path that Plotinus himself had elected to follow—certainly went far toward meeting this goal.[4]

A variety of Christians, for a variety of reasons, had also taught the virtues of sexual renunciation. This ideal had roots going back to the foundational days of the movement. In the mid-first century of the common era, for example, in his letter to his gentile community at Corinth, Paul had given temperate instructions on sexual discipline within marriage. If one member of the couple wanted to abstain for a period, Paul had no objection, though he cautioned that extremes of abstinence might lead to sexual temptation. "Do not refuse each other except perhaps for a season, so that you might devote yourself to prayer; but come together again, lest Satan tempt you through lack of self-control." Nonetheless, Paul clearly regarded total abstinence as the higher path. "I say this by way of concession, not of command. I wish that all were as I myself am," that is to say, celibate (1 Corinthians 7:1–7).

Continuing on this theme, Paul reminded his community of the reason for his teachings. "In view of the impending distress, it is well for a person to remain as he is. . . . I mean, brethren, the appointed time has grown very short. . . . The form of this world is passing away" (1 Corinthians 7:25–31). Sexual renunciation better prepared the believer for the arrival of God's kingdom, as well as for enduring the travails that might precede it (the "impending distress" that Paul invokes here). Paul expected his generation to see these events.

Some decades later, the writer of the Gospel of Matthew attributed a similar teaching on celibacy to Jesus: "There are eunuchs who have been so from birth, and eunuchs who have been made eunuchs by men, *and there are eunuchs who have made themselves eunuchs for the sake of the kingdom of heaven.* He who is able to receive this, let him receive it" (Matthew 19:11–12). Whatever the marital status of the historical Jesus, later evangelists certainly presented him as single and thus celibate. Also, some members of a Judean community roughly contemporary with Jesus, the Essenes, had also renounced sexual activity. Common to all of these ancient Jews—the evangelist Matthew, the Essenes, Paul, Jesus—was their passionate belief that the Kingdom of God really was at hand. This apocalyptic conviction seems to have undergirded and informed their commitment to sexual celibacy.[5]

As time continued and as Christianity in its various forms settled into the broader world of Greco-Roman culture, these teachings also continued, and were continuously reinterpreted. Marcion's church read Paul as teaching against sexual activity as such, and so permitted baptism (thus full membership in the community) only to those who committed to celibacy. The vigor of his church ("spread throughout the whole world," as one of his orthodox critics, centuries later, grumbled) attests to how many people were willing to meet his standard. In the same period, Justin Martyr approvingly relates, a young Christian in Alexandria petitioned the governor for permission to be castrated

(Roman law prohibited the procedure): This man wanted to make himself one of heaven's eunuchs (*First Apology* 29). For pagan seers and sibyls no less than for Jewish prophets, abstaining from sex had long seemed an appropriate preparation for serving as a medium for divine spirit; Christian teachers and prophets who sought to be vessels of the Spirit endorsed such renunciation as well. In brief, many different theological commitments supported behaviors that, from the outside, all looked very similar. Eventually, from the second century onward, sexual renunciants (such as widows as well as married partners), virgins, and celibates—both male and female, both itinerant and resident—proliferated within very varied Christian communities. Asceticism, and sexual asceticism in particular, was practiced by Christians of all stripes—much to their mutual irritation.[6]

Two specific developments within this general culture of continence marked the ideal of celibacy in Augustine's place and time. The first is the early stirrings of organized communities of celibates, what will later become monasteries. In the East, charismatic individual ascetics, the anchorites of the Egyptian and the Syrian deserts, were collecting into communities. Pious tourists and temporary visitors from the West visited these people and places and circulated admiring stories back home. (Augustine speaks about the effect of hearing the story of St. Anthony's conversion to desert asceticism while he struggled to make his own commitment to celibacy back in Milan; *Confessions* 8.)

Second, and certainly no less important: In the later part of the fourth century, spurred especially by the politics and policies of the catholic Theodosius, Roman elites took a serious and prudent interest in aligning themselves with the emperor's church. To do so was simply a sensible first step toward advancing one's prospects in government service. These elites moved toward the church with their pagan aristocratic sensibilities intact, and these would have an important effect on western styles of communal celibacy.

Roman upper-crust sensibilities had long been shaped by reading and studying the great literature and philosophy of the classical past. Retirement from the world to improve the soul by reading elevating books that exercised the mind: This was the aristocratic ethic of *otium liberale* ("learned leisure"). Temperamentally and socially, such retreat was far removed from the charismatic wildness that marked much of Eastern desert monasticism: A country seat and a good classical library were the preserve of a very few. But *otium* is what Augustine longed for as he tried to imagine his way into Ambrose's church in the mid-380s. Thus when not worrying about marriage because of his sexual needs (*Confessions* 6.12,22), Augustine fretted because of his financial ones, and his paramount desire for a life of learned retirement. "It would be necessary to marry a wife with some money. . . . Many great men entirely worthy of imitation have combined the married state with a dedication to the study of wisdom" (6.11,19).

His situation was even more complicated than these practical musings indicate. In the mid-380s in Milan, Augustine perceived and believed that the catholicism to which he was now attracted was deeply compatible with the best intellectual and cultural traditions of philosophy. Intellectuals both pagan and Christian pored over Plotinus and Porphyry in Milanese reading salons. Ambrose preached that Christianity was not simply compatible with the best philosophy but that it *was* in fact the best, the truest philosophy. Ambrose's allegories operated by sharply contrasting, indeed by opposing, spirit to flesh, while maintaining that God, purely good, had made both. Through allegory, the bishop turned biblical patriarchal narratives into symbolic accounts of the soul's return to the divine. For the best and the brightest, the social and intellectual elites both of the salons and of the church, to be Christian was to pursue wisdom. And to pursue wisdom—linked as this quest was to these originally pagan forms of philosophy—meant to forswear sexual activity.[7]

Here Augustine's past experience as a Manichee probably did contribute directly to his current turmoil as a catechumen, though not in the ways that his later critics held. Throughout his entire time in that church, for more than a decade, Augustine had lived with the mother of his son, virtually married. His marital status had kept him relegated to the community's second tier as an auditor. He could neither ascend to the ranks of the Elect nor, consequently, could he gain access to the sect's canonical texts, which were restricted to the higher-ups. Now, more than ten years later, his new circles in Milan represented an even more pronounced elitism. Augustine could only recoil from what would seem like continuing as a second-class member of his chosen group, though now as a married catholic layman.[8]

Meanwhile, with Monnica's active involvement, he worked all fronts. His common-law wife, an impediment to his social ascent, was sent back to Africa. At the same time, he contracted an advantageous marriage to a catholic Milanese aristocrat, though he was forced to wait two years until the girl came of age. (She was probably around ten years old at the time.) Finally, as an interim arrangement, he took a mistress. This seemingly unremarkable development in fact mortified him deeply, because it publicly gave the lie to his philosophical pretensions. The only reason to take a mistress (as everyone knew) was for sex—an activity that the best and the brightest eschewed (*Confessions* 6.13,23–6.15,25).[9]

Living with such conflicts indefinitely was unbearable. Ultimately, Augustine found the inner strength to emerge from this exhausting impasse. By the end of the summer of 386, his study of "the books of the Platonists," his reading the letters of Paul, and his mounting dissatisfaction with his profession combined to enable him to make three decisions. He resolved to live a life of sexual continence. He resolved to receive baptism into the catholic church in Milan. And he resigned his professorship and thus his secular public life. These three decisions collectively define what tradition—and Augustine himself—designates his "conversion."

✦ ✦ ✦

THE ELABORATELY WRITTEN book eight of the *Confessions,* composed some eleven years after these events, provides a perspective on Augustine's life back in Milan that reflects his theological growth during that long interim. The writings that date from this period itself—the fall and winter of 386, after Augustine had resigned his professorship, before he received baptism on Easter 387—offer interesting contrasts to his more famous self-portrait. Thanks to the loan of a country estate from a wealthy colleague in Milan, Augustine temporarily realized his goal of living a life of *otium liberale.* Together with his mother, his brother, his teenage son, two adolescent students, and several scribes (*notarii*) to assist his literary efforts, Augustine passed the winter reading, teaching, and writing at Cassiciacum, in the foothills of the Alps. His goal was specifically Christian: to seek for God through contemplative asceticism by relying on faith, hope, and charity (*On Order* 2.8,25). The mode of his search, however, had a long and distinguished classical pedigree.

Augustine wrote four treatises over this winter, which he dedicated to learned and socially prominent gentlemen in his old reading groups back in Milan. In the first, *Against the Academics,* he provided a description of his decision to join the church. He reports that, trembling, he snatched up the writings of Paul, with the result that "philosophy's countenance, howsoever dim that light that was cast upon it, was revealed to me" (*Against the Academics* 2.2,6). (In his reprise of this scene in *Confessions* 8.11,27, he glimpses instead the face of Continence: The connotations, quite different, suggest the changes in Augustine's perspective on the event.) Augustine can readily express his own and his group's Christian piety in philosophical terms. He names secular education in the liberal arts and the subordination to mind of the body—the flesh, he says, is the soul's "dark prison" (*Against the Academics* 1.3,9) or "cave" (*Soliloquies* 1.14,24)—as pathways to the knowledge of God. True happiness rests solely in attaining such knowledge. Indeed, despite the vivid example of Monnica's unlettered piety, Augustine expresses some reservations about the degree of happiness possible for simple believers who "take no account of the liberal or fine arts" (*On Order* 2.9,26).

Augustine's theological positions changed, in some ways drastically, in the decades following his stay at Cassiciacum. Already when writing the *Confessions,* he lamented that the treatises composed during that liminal season between his conversion (July–August 386) and his baptism (April 387) still seemed to breathe "the spirit of the school of pride" (a reference to his former profession in rhetoric; *Confessions* 9.4,7). And near the end of his life, he gave these early writings a highly critical review in his *Retractations.* In that late work, he regrets that he had so highly praised the virtues of the philosophers and compared their work to the message of Christ (*Retractations* 1.3,2). But during his stay in Milan, it was precisely this combination of philosophy and scripture that had provided him, finally, with intellectually compelling answers to the challenges of Manichaean dualism, cosmology, and theodicy. In this period of retirement in 386, reading philosophy and scripture together, Augustine strengthened his grasp on his new way of thinking and undertook his lifelong project of reading deeply in Christian scriptures, both Old Testament and New. Scriptural and ecclesiastical language eventually grow more prominent in his writings, especially after his baptism and his return from Italy to Africa. His increasing concern with biblical interpretation signaled his moving the controversy with Manichaeism to the foreground of his work.

✦ ✦ ✦

AUGUSTINE CAME BACK to Africa almost two years after receiving baptism from Ambrose. Monnica's death and the disruptions of Roman power politics had delayed his return. Together with his son, Adeodatus, and his friend Alypius, he was greeted and warmly received by catholics in Carthage. Eventually, his small party made its way inland to Thagaste, their hometown. Augustine intended to live as a celibate layman on his family's land, approximating the experience of *otium* that he had left behind at Cassiciacum.[10]

Brief treatises continued to flow from him: on liberal arts (*Music*), on the soul (*The Soul's Immortality; The Soul's Greatness*), and an oblique treatment of the problem of evil, the first book of *Free Will*. Two frontal assaults on the Manichees also appeared: *Manichaean Morals*, a companion volume to *Morals of the Church*, written while still in Italy; and *On Genesis, against the Manichees*, in two books, completed once back in Africa. Though he had reversed sides in the six years since quitting Carthage for Rome, Augustine the rhetorician once again found his voice as a polemicist.

The companion volumes on catholic and Manichaean "morals" (that is, "ways" or "lifestyles") are a sharply worded reprise of many of the talking points made more suavely in the Cassiciacum writings. Augustine's polemical commentary on Genesis, by contrast, is noteworthy for several reasons. First, as an interpretation of the biblical creation account, the commentary is almost unrelievedly allegorical. The story of Adam and Eve, for example, Augustine notes, may be understood either "carnally" or "spiritually" (*Genesis against the Manichees* 1.19,30). The Manichees had erred by insisting that the story's meaning was "carnal," its idea of God anthropomorphic. Against such a reading, Augustine expands on the text's spiritual meaning, decoding "Adam" as the higher, rational part of the soul, "Eve" as the higher soul's helpmeet, the lower soul, and so on (2.11,15ff.). The commentary evinces the impact of listening to Ambrose's sermons back in Milan. This work sounds much more like Philo of Alexandria's first-century commentary on the same text than it does Augustine's own writings on Genesis that follow a few years later.

Noteworthy too is Augustine's use of another traditional interpretive trope. He correlates the seven days of the biblical week of creation to seven world-historical periods: the span from Adam to the second coming of Christ are history's six "working" days; the seventh "day" is the "Sabbath rest" of Christ and his saints. And he also correlates these periods to the seven ages of an individual's development, from infancy to old age, with the final stage also attesting to the "renewal" or "rebirth" of the "old man" in Christ (*Genesis against the Manichees* 1.22,35–1.25,43). This sort of macrocosm/microcosm framework, applying stages of salvation to both global and individual processes, will loom large when he turns his attention, a few years later, to a close reading of Paul's letter to the Romans. At that point, he will wring original theological insights out of his adaptation of this scheme.[11]

Finally, and most remarkably, this commentary hints at Augustine's—impatience? dissatisfaction?—with predominantly allegorical or figurative or "spiritual" approaches to scripture. In book one of *Genesis against the Manichees,* he interpreted God's activity both "historically" and "prophetically." (These are his terms.) But Augustine's "historical" understanding was also figurative. That is, he took Genesis as a description of God's actions in the past (hence the text's "historical" dimension); but the meaning of those past actions, he said, was "spiritual." Thus, as he states here, the "image of God" in man refers to man's soul, not to his physical appearance. And, relating the seven days of creation in Genesis to the stages of a universal salvation history, Augustine deems this cosmic "week" to be "prophetic" because its culmination—the seventh age of redemption, the cosmic Sabbath—lay off in the future.

Just at the beginning of book two, however, immediately before embarking on an equally figurative retelling of the story of Adam, Eve, and the serpent, Augustine interjects:

> History (*secundum historiam*) narrates past events; prophecy (*secundum prophetiam*) foretells future ones. Of course, if someone wanted to take literally (*secundum litteram*) everything recounted here—that is, to understand nothing whatever other than what the words themselves say (*non aliter intelligere quam littera sonat*)—and if he could do so while avoiding blasphemy and conforming to everything that catholic faith teaches, he should meet not with hostility, but rather with praise for being an excellent interpreter.
>
> GENESIS AGAINST THE MANICHEES 2.2,3

What did Augustine mean by reading the Bible in order to understand "nothing other than what the words say"? What does he mean by "according to the letter," which I translated above as "literally"? And how does such a reading relate to understanding events historically (*secundum historiam*, "according to history") or prophetically (*secundum prophetiam*, "according to prophecy")? At the end of his life, reviewing all his writings chronologically, Augustine evaluated this period of his work in his *Retractations*. Criticizing his own failed effort at interpreting Genesis "literally" that he had attempted in 393, four years after his commentary against the Manichees, he expanded on this expression *ad litteram*. He had wanted, said the aged Augustine, to understand Genesis *secundum historicam proprietatem:* "according to its historical character" (*Retractations* 1.18, on *Unfinished Literal Commentary on Genesis*).

This phrase implies something different from just a narrative of past events. Augustine had already designated that idea by the phrase "according to history," which I translated in the preceding paragraph as "historically." *Proprietas* indicates, rather, a particular quality or property of something. (Our English word *appropriate* catches something of its sense.) Further on, we will look at the way that Augustine thinks about interpreting texts, especially biblical texts, in some detail. For now, we may simply note that Augustine seems to be reaching for a distinction between a narrative about the past or set in the past (which he calls "history") and the significance or value (*proprietas*) of some sort of "simple" or "straightforward" reference to the past (*ad litteram* or *quam littera sonat*, "just what the words say").

Philosophical or allegorical or spiritual interpretation regarded the meaning of biblical passages from a timeless perspective, the perspective of eternity and thus of the divine. Historical, prophetic, and "literal" understandings of biblical texts, by contrast, place them in the temporal and thus within a human perspective. From his relative isolation in retirement at Thagaste, then, taking aim at the Manichees with rhetorical weapons as sharp as ever, and availing himself of the new interpretive armamentarium that he had acquired only recently, and at a distance, from Ambrose, Augustine began to embark on a new project: to think with the Bible—both its narrative and its content—*ad litteram*, in some particular way "historically," or "related to its setting in the past." Within a decade, one of the most original results of this effort will emerge: Augustine's teaching, against Faustus the Manichee, on Jews and Judaism.

◆◆◆

FOR AUGUSTINE, the period 390–391 was transitional personally as well as intellectually. At some point before the beginning of 391, he lost his son, Adeodatus. With him died Augustine's last reason for holding on to his family's property and his last public tie to his old relationship with his concubine and to his former, pre-catholic life.

Perhaps this great change sharpened Augustine's resolve in a new way. He was determined to found a celibate male community dedicated to Christian learning. In the spring of 391, Augustine left Thagaste and journeyed to the coast, to Hippo. He was looking for a place to establish his community, and he wanted to recruit an acquaintance there to join his enterprise.

He journeyed advisedly. Augustine was now a big fish in a small pond: The trained orator, the man with a past both as a former Manichee and as a secular success in the imperial court, was now a vociferous champion of catholic Christianity. Churches with leadership vacancies frequently drafted talented men into ecclesiastical life. This was how Ambrose, who at the time was not yet even baptized, had ended his government service to become bishop of Milan (374 C.E.).

Augustine, still a layman, preferred a life of intellectual retreat. Hippo had no vacancy: Its bishop, Valerius, though old, was in good health. Augustine thought that he was safe. He miscalculated. With Augustine present at mass, Valerius suddenly addressed his congregation on the urgent need to "find and ordain a priest for the city." Thus prompted, the people seized Augustine and propelled him forward to the bishop's seat. As he wept, they demanded his ordination; and Valerius, acquiescing, welcomed the coerced newcomer into the clergy (*Life* 4).[12]

Valerius' community was a beleaguered minority in Hippo, overshadowed by a larger, better established, and sometimes hostile Christian church. Catholics in North Africa had been divided and feuding for almost a century by the time of Augustine's forced ordination. The trouble had begun during the last of the pagan imperial persecutions, back in the year 303: Some clergy had complied with the government's orders and had handed over Christian holy books to be burned. Other clergy had defied the order and were jailed or died in prison or were even martyred.

A new day dawned shortly thereafter, in 312, when Constantine, becoming sole ruler of the western empire, declared himself the patron of the church. But by that point North Africa's church was divided, its clergy riven with dissent as the stalwart accused the pliant of collaboration and betrayal. The confessors, who had stood firm in the time of persecution, regarded their compromised brethren as *traditores* ("traitors"), who had "handed over" the sacred scriptures for destruction. In consequence, the stalwarts challenged the legitimacy of *traditor* sacraments. How could a cleric be a conduit of the Holy Spirit when through his conduct he had sinned against the Spirit by betraying Christ? The integrity of the sacraments was at stake. Those baptized by traitorous clergy, the confessors insisted, would have to be baptized again.[13]

Those of the confessing church were in the majority. They called the "treasonous" clergy "Caecilianists," after the name of one of their bishops. The Caecilianists returned the favor and called the confessors "Donatists," after Donatus, one of their bishops. Both sides wasted no time in taking advantage of Constantine's new mood, and they asked him to adjudicate. The emperor convened a committee of overseas bishops to examine the African case. These foreign bishops, disliking the idea of rebaptism and fighting their own fights against local purists, found in favor of the Caecilianists. At a stroke, the Caecilianists became the "catholics," that is, the representatives of a universal (*catholica*) communion. The confessors became the "Donatists," followers of Donatus (said their enemies), not followers of Christ.

Over the course of the fourth century, periods of mutual hostility and even violence between the two communities alternated with periods of relative calm. By Augustine's day, these North African Christians had settled into an unquiet modus vivendi. Virtually identical in terms of doctrine, calendar, creed, liturgy, and canon, these people kept the same holidays and venerated the same martyrs. Donatists and catholics alike saw in their respective communities the "church of the martyrs," which they celebrated through public readings of the martyrs' stories and enthusiastic *laetitiae,* celebrations with food, drink, and dance held in cemeteries over holy tombs. Many believers in both communities, clerical and lay, affirmed the ancient Christian hope for the approaching End of the Age, with its attendant expectation of bodily resurrection and a thousand-year reign of the saints with Christ on earth. When Faustus the Manichee complained of the carnality of those churches that revered the Old Testament, he had beliefs and behavior such as these in mind.

Catholics and Donatists also shared a common conservative biblical culture, marked by the sort of interpretations that elicited Manichaean scorn for their *superstitio.* (This attachment to biblical stories was one of the reasons that Western Manichaean missionaries had developed close critical readings of both testaments, and one of the reasons that this critique, as Augustine noted, was so successful.) The biblical culture common to both sides in turn explains why, despite their differences, the two North African communities were united in their loathing of the Manichees. Both churches greatly emphasized the importance of ecclesiastical sacraments, especially baptism—to the point, in the case of the Donatists, of requiring *re*baptism. Both celebrated martyrdom and venerated relics, the bodily remains of the martyred dead. Both strongly defined redemption in terms of physical resurrection. Both drew deeply from the Old Testament for their ideas about God and community. They could regard only with hostility and contempt a group claiming to be Christian that looked upon baptism as superfluous, physical resurrection as ridiculous, and the Old Testament itself as repulsive and intrinsically irreligious. The Manichees for their part returned their contempt. Repudiating the Old Testament, championing a dualist reading of the letters of Paul, advocating the coherence and rationalism of their own system against the *superstitio* and "Jewish carnality" of their orthodox competition, the Manichees remained a thorn in the side of both Donatists and catholics.

Augustine had entered the church through Ambrose in Milan. When he returned to Africa, he identified with the Caecilianists, whose local minority status was offset by their wider recognition abroad, which the Donatists lacked. Initially, however, while living in relative seclusion in Thagaste, he could remain aloof from this factional tension. And by this point, he was somewhat culturally removed from both groups. Before his ordination and after, Augustine's writings evince a philosophical sophistication that was foreign to the concerns and traditions of both North African churches. The intellectual culture of cosmopolitan Italian catholicism that had so captivated Augustine back in Milan was of little local consequence.

Donatism, meanwhile, the home church of North Africa, dominated Hippo. By inducting Augustine into their clergy, Valerius' congregation acclaimed its champion. They had little hope of appreciating Augustine's erudite catholicism, and probably less interest. It was his rhetorical presence that they valued: He would be there to preach, to debate, and to build up. Valerius cushioned the blow to Augustine's aspirations for intellectual retreat by giving him a garden near the church where he could establish his celibate male community. And so in this way—precipitously, definitively—Augustine was wrenched out of his new life and put back into a version of his old one. Public life had found him again.

This abrupt change in Augustine's personal circumstances did not correspond to an equally abrupt change in his thought. The broad outlines of his intellectual program remained the same before ordination and after. The several brief works that he produced or completed in this period of the early 390s—*The Usefulness of Belief; Two Souls, against the Manichees;* book one and the earlier sections of book two of *Free Will; Faith and the Creed; Sermon on the Mount*—demonstrate his increasing familiarity and facility with biblical texts and with the traditions of his church. But they also evince his continuing preoccupation with and allegiance to some of the cardinal points of late Platonic philosophy.

For instance, when preaching in 393, Augustine criticized pagan philosophers as well as Manichees for disparaging the ideas of incarnation and resurrection. Both groups were wrong, he said, to regard the human body as somehow polluting. Yet he himself could not quite endorse a positive valuation of flesh. The redeemed body, he asserted, quoting the church's creed, will indeed rise. But raised "body" is one thing and raised "flesh" something else. The raised body, Augustine explains, "will be no longer flesh and blood." Rather, it will be "simply body . . . changed to an angelic thing," the "spiritual body" that Paul had spoken of in 1 Corinthians 15, now made suitable to celestial habitation (*Faith and the Creed* 4,10; 6,13; 10,24). His position here on this issue was closer to those which he would eventually identify as dangerously inadequate (such as Origen's) than to his own later positions on the religiously positive value of flesh itself. In the *Retractations,* decades later, he repented what he had taught here (1,17).[14]

Augustine likewise continued to grapple with the problem of evil, specifically ethical evil, that is, sin. His metaphysical definition of sin had remained constant since Cassiciacum: Sin occurred when the individual turned away from eternal good to a temporal good. (So he had stated in book one of *Free Will,* written in 388 back in Italy [1.16,34–35]; so he repeated in book two, composed sometime after his ordination in Hippo [2.20,54].) He also continued to assert that agents willed freely, otherwise they could be neither virtuous nor derelict. If someone does good deeds because he cannot do otherwise, it is not to his credit; neither can someone compelled to do evil deserve censure.

The ways in which Augustine framed this issue began to shift, however. While still in Italy, he had fretted about God's indirect responsibility for human sin: After all, when God had given free will to humans, he certainly knew that they would misuse it (*Free Will* 1.2,4). Once back in Africa, however, Augustine's defense of the will's freedom became increasingly oblique, his questions (and answers) seemingly motivated less by the question of human merit as such and more by the question of divine justice. Thus, in 392, Augustine observed that God would not be just in punishing sinners unless sinners had the choice not to sin. But the biblical God *is* just, and he *does* punish sin. It follows, then, that when someone sins he must do so of his own free choice. Therefore, he concluded, the will is free (*Against Fortunatus* 15; 20). In other words, Augustine's defense of human freedom seems motivated less by a desire to assert something intrinsic about human beings and more by his desire to defend his idea of a just god. As his study of the Bible became more profound, his arguments about the relationship between divine justice and human freedom grew increasingly complex. Soon, this complexity would also contribute to his innovative teaching on Jews and Judaism.

In the meantime, curiously, Augustine's presence as priest in Hippo created an opportunity for catholic and Donatist cooperation. In August of 392 he was approached by a delegation drawn from both communities. Distressed by "the plague of Manichaeism [which] had taken hold of both citizens and visitors in great numbers," this group requested that Augustine publicly debate the Manichaean priest, Fortunatus, whom they blamed for the sect's local successes (*Life* 6). Augustine consented, and on the 28th and 29th of August he confronted his former colleague in the baths of Sossius, to debate the respective virtues of catholic and Manichaean positions on the origin and nature of evil.[15]

✦ ✦ ✦

"I NOW THINK an error what I previously thought was true." With this opening statement, Augustine challenged his former colleague. "Whether I am right, I hope to hear from you." "Describe this error," responded Fortunatus. In this way, before Hippo's gathered crowds, their public confrontation began.

Augustine opened by attacking the Manichees' doctrine of God. Their belief in a primordial battle between Good and Evil, he argued, compromised the idea of divine omnipotence: An all-powerful god could never be under threat of hostile invasion, nor could an inviolable god suffer injury. Fortunatus countered by asserting the moral incorruptibility of God, meaning that no evil could ever proceed from him ("Not darkness, not demons, not Satan"). He thereby implied (since these evil entities had to originate from somewhere) that only a dualist explanation could account for evil without compromising the moral goodness and, therefore, the very definition of God. Only the Son, said Fortunatus, came forth from the Father, to effect the salvation of souls. And then, significantly, Fortunatus fortified his position by quoting from the New Testament, in this instance specifically from the Gospel of John. "I am the way, the truth, and the door [*sic*]. . . . No one can come to the Father except by me" (John 14:6). "He who has seen me has seen the Father also" (John 14:9). "Whosoever believes in me shall not taste death forever, but has passed from death to life, and shall not come to judgment" (John 5:24; *Against Fortunatus* 1–3).

By citing scripture and by being the first to do so, Fortunatus had seized the rhetorical high ground. He also established a pattern that would continue for the duration of the first day of their debate. Augustine, criticizing Manichaean doctrine, was the only contestant to actually describe it. Fortunatus, citing New Testament texts—the Gospel of Matthew, the Gospel of John, and especially the letters of Paul—made his case by invoking material familiar to all the assorted Christian members of their audience. He thus had the added advantage of presenting the position that he represented (but did not actually describe) as rooted in those Christian texts that the majority of the audience considered canonical. Augustine, by contrast, argued deductively or philosophically. Simply by invoking verses from the New Testament, then, Fortunatus unsettled Augustine's case, making his own position seem to be sanctioned by scripture.

Finally, well along into their contest, Augustine saw a way to use the Bible to his own advantage. "Our audience wanted us to discuss the question whether two contrary natures exist by using rational argument. But since you keep taking refuge in scripture, I will engage you on that field." He then cited the first line of Paul's letter to the Romans, where Paul proclaimed that Jesus was "descended from David according to the flesh" (Romans 1:3). The Manichees, Augustine knew perfectly well, held that fleshly bodies were the product of evil forces. Their Christ was docetic: He had not really assumed flesh, but had only seemed to. By invoking Romans 1:3, Augustine hoped to create daylight, publicly, between Fortunatus' Manichaeism and Paul's authority.

But Fortunatus was prepared, and he responded readily. Christ was born of a virgin, he reminded his audience, and so fleshly descent from David—that is, through the paternal line—was irrelevant. Besides, he continued, "that which is born of the spirit is spirit, while flesh comes from flesh," alluding to the Gospel of John 3:6. Capping his response, Fortunatus then quoted Paul: "Flesh and blood shall not inherit the kingdom of God, neither shall corruption inherit incorruption" (1 Corinthians 15:50; *Against Fortunatus* 19).

The first day of debate abruptly broke off here. In an aside, the shorthand scribe recording events noted that "the audience erupted at this point" and dissolved into scattered pockets of argument. Fortunatus, this scribe continued, then said that "the Word of God had been fettered in the race of darkness." At that point, concluded the *notarius,* the crowd actually broke up the proceedings because they were so horrified by Fortunatus' remark.

These were Augustine's scribes, and it was Augustine who later put into circulation this transcript of the debate. By the end of the second day, as we will shortly see, Augustine did indeed back Fortunatus into a corner, and the Manichee did leave Hippo. In light of all this, many historians have simply assumed that this occasion was the unmitigated success that Augustine claimed it was.[16]

Following the debate as it unfolds in the transcript, however, this conclusion is less than clear. Augustine had been aggressive and lawyerly: scolding Fortunatus (*Against Fortunatus* 3), complaining repeatedly that he responded to all of Fortunatus' questions while Fortunatus answered none of his (5, 7, 8, 10), even implying darkly that Manichaean morals might indeed be (albeit secretly) as profligate as popular rumor held (2–3). These complaints tell us more about Augustine's rhetorical training than they do about the actual comportment of Fortunatus and of his sect: Handbooks on rhetoric advised speakers to make exactly such accusations in order to discredit opponents in oral argument. Also—highly trained, highly skilled, and highly professional orator that he was—Augustine doubtless projected confidence and conviction when he spoke.

But Fortunatus, the transcript reveals, had retained control of their dialogue. He persistently frustrated Augustine's attempts to induce him to declare Manichaean theology by the simple expedient of quoting supportive New Testament texts instead. And quotation was itself a shrewd strategy, enabling him to make statements of seemingly unimpeachable orthodoxy. It would be curious, then, if at this juncture, having already deflected Augustine's Christological gambit by quoting Paul against "flesh and blood," Fortunatus had then volunteered his sect's teachings on the dispersed and suffering Christ. Nor does that Manichaean teaching follow easily from his last recorded remark. Perhaps, instead, Augustine's sympathizers in the crowd really did break up the meeting in order to give him time to regroup. The evidence of the first day's transcript cannot help us to decide.

The best reason to think that Augustine had not done well on the first day of the debate, however, and the best reason to suspect that even Augustine knew that he had not done well, is what happened on the second day.

This time Fortunatus opened. He made a simple statement of principle: God is all good; nothing he makes is evil; the evil things of this world thus have a source other than God, because evil things are foreign to him. Augustine responded by concurring with Fortunatus' theological point: God is all good; nothing he makes is evil. Then he moved into his familiar argument on free will as the origin of and explanation for evil, which he defined as sin.

> Evil originates in the voluntary sin of the soul, to which God gave free will. If God had not given free will, he could not judge justly, whether to punish or to reward. There would be no point to the divine instruction that we should repent our sins, nor any point to God's forgiving our sins through our Lord Jesus Christ. Why not? Because unless someone sins of his own free will, he does not sin at all.
>
> *AGAINST FORTUNATUS* 20

Fortunatus then answered Augustine with a query very similar to the one that Augustine himself had put four years previously in book one of *Free Will:* If God gave the soul free will, is he not at least implicated in human sin? If free will, which is the reason why man sins, was given by God, then "he would participate in my fault, because he would be the author of my fault." Fortunatus framed his response in Pauline language about "sin dwelling within us" (cf. Romans 7:17). Augustine, undeterred, simply repeated his prior remark: Neither sin and thus just punishment nor merit and just reward is possible without free will.

At this point, abruptly, a fusillade of allusions and quotations from the Gospel of John, the Gospel of Matthew, and especially from the letters of Paul burst from Fortunatus. All of these texts supported his two main points: There is much more to evil than simply the evil that men do ("Apart from our bodies, evil things dwell in the whole world," *Against Fortunatus* 21); and men do evil because this larger, cosmic, contrary nature, alive in the flesh, compels them to do evil. Romans 8:7: "The mind of the flesh is hostile to God." Galatians 5:17: "The flesh lusts against the spirit and the spirit against the flesh." Romans 7:23–25: "I see another law in my members, warring against the law of my mind and leading me captive to sin and death. Miserable man! Who will deliver me from this body of death?" (*Against Fortunatus* 21).

Augustine then responded to Fortunatus. What he said, however, represents a fresh departure from his earlier remarks. Abruptly, surprisingly, Augustine qualified his earlier description of the will's freedom through an ad hominem appeal to common experience. And as he did so, he too invoked scripture, alluding to Paul (sin and death comes through one man—that is, Adam; Romans 5:12) and thus, through Paul, to Genesis:

> That man who was first formed [Adam] could exercise his will in
> complete freedom. He was made so that absolutely nothing could
> resist his will, as long as he subjected himself to God's command.
> But after he freely chose to sin, we who descend from him were
> plunged into binding constraints (*nos in necessitatem praecipitati*

sumus). If you reflect for a moment, you'll see the truth of what
I say. Today, before we start sinning, we have it in our power
to do or not to do as we want. We've formed no habit. But
once, through the exercise of our freedom, we start to sin,
the pernicious sweetness and pleasure of sinning overwhelms
the soul. Tangled up in and by its own habits, the soul cannot
triumph over the obstacles that it has made for itself through
its own sins. Many people, for example, do not want to swear,
but their tongue has become so habituated to swearing that they
just cannot stop themselves. . . . Do you want to see for yourself
whether what I say is true? Just try not swearing: you'll feel the
force of habit for sure. . . . *This* is what "wars against the soul":
habit, formed in the flesh. *This* is the "mind of the flesh" that
cannot be subject to God's law.

AGAINST FORTUNATUS 22

Because of Adam's sin, Augustine argues here, humanity is currently so constituted that will is in fact *not* as free as Adam's had originally been. This is not an argument about original sin: That signature
teaching of Augustine's is still many years off in the future. But it is an
argument about diminished capacity. People now have a type of will,
Augustine says, that is different from what Adam's had originally
been: Now, because sin is habit forming, habit undermines the will's
free operation. Individuals still choose to sin freely, in the sense that
nothing outside of themselves compels them to sin. But once they sin
(as they invariably do), they sin thereafter with progressive ease. And
when they finally decide that they want to stop sinning, they discover
that they have great difficulty. The will's effectiveness—what we would
call "will power"—has become compromised through habitual sinning. Its debility is an effect and a consequence of Adam's fall.

Fortunatus resisted Augustine's argument. He protested that Augustine reduced the scope of cosmic evil to the relatively small scale of
human wrongdoing. Earlier, Fortunatus had alluded to Matthew (15:13
and 3:10, on good and bad trees, good and bad fruit), and he had very
effectively quoted Paul in support of the idea of cosmic evil. Now he
continued to press this point. "The same apostle said that we struggle

not only against flesh and blood, but also against principalities and powers, spirits of wickedness, and the force of the kingdom of darkness" (*Against Fortunatus* 23, referring to Ephesians 5:12).

But Augustine was now in control of their encounter. He simply ignored Fortunatus' challenge while continuing to badger his opponent with his own statements about the nature of God—the same points with which he had opened the debate (*Against Fortunatus* 1). If God is truly all-powerful and incorruptible, Augustine insisted, then no Kingdom of Darkness could ever have invaded the divine sphere and somehow carried off the "divine sparks" of soul supposedly now trapped in flesh. Finally, though still unconvinced, Fortunatus acknowledged that he could not defend his views on evil's origin given Augustine's insistence on divine omnipotence. He conceded the debate (*Against Fortunatus* 37; note that Fortunatus' starting point, God's goodness, was simply buried by Augustine's onslaught). Augustine's biographer Possidius closes his report of this incident by relating that Fortunatus left Hippo shortly thereafter and never returned (*Life* 6).

◆ ◆ ◆

WHAT CAN WE LEARN from what happened here? The transcript of this debate, first of all, reveals surprising areas of agreement between all three of these North African Christian communities, areas that Augustine's own prior descriptions of Manichaeism had not disclosed. Fortunatus, for example, was just as inclined as his more orthodox hearers to see God the father of Christ as "an avenger of evil" (*ultor malorum*; *Against Fortunatus* 20)—a surprisingly "Old Testament" characterization of the deity for a communicant of a sect that rejected the Old Testament.

Furthermore, Fortunatus both upheld and appealed to "the authority of evangelical faith" and "the authority of scripture" (*Against Fortunatus* 20). For Manichees, the New Testament was more like orthodoxy's apocrypha: It was not itself canonical, and thus in this sense it was not authoritative. The Manichaean canon had been self-consciously authored by Mani himself precisely to avoid the disorders of other churches, in which the founding figure (such as Jesus), having composed no writings of his own, had left confusion and corrupted secondhand traditions in his wake. Further, as we saw earlier, Manichaean missionaries prided themselves on *not* arguing from authority. As Augustine noted, they prized their ability to argue by appeal to "reason alone," and they disparaged catholics for relying on authority to excess. (See, for example, *Usefulness of Belief* 1,2, quoted on p. 110 above). In the course of this debate, however, whether for strategic reasons or out of genuine conviction, Fortunatus appealed conspicuously and continuously to scripture, and he drew attention to this fact. "I cannot demonstrate that I believe rightly unless I confirm my belief by scripture's authority" (*Against Fortunatus* 20).

Another area of surprising commonality, this time between Fortunatus and Augustine, is in their respective definitions of God. Both contestants declare their belief in a supreme deity who is incorruptible, immutable, intangible, all good, radically transcendent, and so on. (For Augustine's statement, see *Against Fortunatus* 1; for Fortunatus' statement, see 3. Both reprise this definition at the beginning of the second day; see 19–20.) Each criticizes the other for insufficiently applying the principles of this definition to the rest of his theology, but neither challenges the definition itself.

This god was originally the god of philosophical paideia. Introduced into the Septuagint by Hellenized Jews, baptized into contesting churches in the mid-second century by a wide variety of Christian intellectuals, this god had never been native to the narratives of the Old Testament, which portrayed Israel's god as a character who acted and spoke and felt and did. But the well-educated within all of these scriptural communities perceived no awkwardness, so unselfconsciously did they read their sacred texts in terms of the categories of meaning bequeathed them by their (fundamentally Hellenistic) education.

Fortunatus' allegiance to this concept of deity also gives the measure of how western his branch of Manichaeism had become, despite its historic origins in Persian Mesopotamia. The old Greek philosophical idea of an immutable high god still provided the plumb line for all intellectually respectable theological discussion, at least within Rome's empire. Hence Augustine's opening salvo the first day of their debate: He attacked the Manichees' conceptualization of the high god not for its heretical features—on the contrary, their god was eminently respectable and religiously recognizable—but for its philosophical incoherence. The Manichaean myth of a primordial battle between good and evil, he insisted, in effect made their god insufficiently unchanging (*Against Fortunatus* 1–2).

Fortunatus, of course, denied his accusation. But by refusing to continue their dispute on this point—the impassibility of the high god—Fortunatus also reveals how much more attuned to the biblical culture of the average North African Christian audience he was than Augustine. The whole time that Augustine had been in Italy, acquiring his cosmopolitan panache and his sophisticated philosophy, Fortunatus had been at work proselytizing North Africans. The subtext of Augustine's initial attack—Manichees are bad philosophers because their myth violates the (philosophical) idea of divine impassibility—mattered much less to their audience, Fortunatus apparently knew, than did establishing a position on the authority of the gospels and of Paul. On the second day, when Augustine outflanked his opponent, he did so by appealing not to New Testament texts (Fortunatus had found too much ammunition there already) but to the North African Everyman and the common experience of compulsive swearing.

In support of docetic Christology, the impossibility of physical resurrection and the essential antipathy of flesh and spirit—all core Manichaean teachings—Fortunatus had little difficulty marshaling impressive authority from Paul's letters. Indeed, the entire debate, as one historian has noted, seems to have turned on the interpretation of certain Pauline texts. And when, on day two, Augustine pressed him to explain why God permitted the soul to suffer the hardships of this life if nothing had compelled him to do so, Fortunatus replied with Paul's defense of divine prerogative in Romans 9:20: "O man, who are you to answer back to God? Shall the thing made say to its creator, 'Why did you make me like this?' " This verse, as we will see, would have a long future in Augustine's own writings once he developed his mature understanding of Paul on election and grace and accordingly had to defend the justice of his own god.[17]

Even though Augustine was the undisputed winner of this debate, Fortunatus had touched on a true weak spot in Augustine's defense of the freedom of the will. Free will, the Manichee had insisted, does not and cannot in and of itself account for sin. Here Fortunatus drew as much on traditions that can be traced back to Greek philosophical ethics as he did on passages in Paul's letters (such as Romans chapter 7) that could be taken to imply or describe inner conflict in ways that obliged Manichaeism. Free will in philosophical thought had never been imagined as a neutral capacity to choose between good and evil. The truly free will in this system always inclines to the good.[18]

For Fortunatus, then, the fact that people do sin was evidence that the will was not truly free, because no truly free will would sin. It followed, therefore, for him as for the Manichees generally, that the soul sinned involuntarily, compelled by some force foreign to its self to do what it did not want to do. He thus defended his view with a lengthy catena of statements from Paul on the hostility of flesh to God or to spirit, drawing especially on the letter to the Romans, wherein the apostle himself seemed to mourn that he could not do the good that he wanted to do, and that he found himself doing the evil that he did not want to do, because of his entanglement in flesh (Romans 7:19-20; *Against Fortunatus* 21). The agent in this compulsion, urged Fortunatus, working through flesh, was Evil itself, the coercive force of the Kingdom of Darkness.

Augustine, at the turning point of their debate, took a position on the exercise of free will that was both like and unlike Fortunatus'. In one way, he essentially conceded Fortunatus' point. He too said that human will currently was not *exactly* free. But—and here is where they differ crucially—for Augustine, what compelled the will to err was not exterior to the self. On the contrary, the source of this miserable compulsion *was* the self. Human souls, bound to mortal flesh (the "law in my members," as Paul had said, Romans 7:23) easily form bad habits. Bad habits facilitate bad choices and thus inhibit the will's free exercise.

Habit, its effects on the will, the burden of mortality in consequence of Adam's sin: All of these discrete elements of his response to Fortunatus had appeared already in Augustine's writings well before their debate. Back in Cassiciacum, Augustine had considered the ways that *consuetudo* ("habit," "custom") acted on the soul (*Against the Aca-*

demics 3.6,13, written during the winter of 385–386). Mortal flesh clearly made the soul more susceptible to sin, he observed, and the flesh was also susceptible "because of the most just law of God, on account of ancient sin," that is, the sin of Adam (*Morals of the Church* 22,40; written in Rome in 388). And earlier, in 392, he had drawn connections between life in the fleshly body, habit, and sin (*Two Souls, against the Manichees* 10,13; 14,23).

But Augustine, when he had first voiced such ideas, had also contended that "whoever wishes to live rightly and honorably . . . attains his object with perfect ease. In order to attain it, he has only to will it" (*Free Will* 1.13,29; in 388). And some eight months before this confrontation with Fortunatus, he asserted that, since wisdom impedes the soul's sinning, "the wise man alone does not sin" (*Usefulness of Belief* 12,27; in 391–392).

It was the specific context of his debate with Fortunatus that altered the significance of these various elements. Augustine had begun his defense of free will in this debate by arguing deductively: If a just god punishes sin then the will must be free, if wrong-doing is not willed freely then transgression is not sin, and so on. As their debate progressed, however, other emphases emerged, until finally the question hovering over both contestants was the moral character of an omnipotent god who (because he could not be coerced) would either permit or induce the souls of his own creatures to suffer (*Against Fortunatus* 17;20).

By linking moral choice both to Adam's fall and to the individual's psychological and moral development, Augustine had, de facto, reduced the free operation of the will. These two historical events—one distant (Adam's sin), one proximate (one's own sins)—necessarily impinged on individual choice. Mortality, the punishment of Adam's sin, was forever after inherited along with the flesh itself. "We are born of earth, and we shall all go into the earth on account of the sin of the first man" (*Against Fortunatus* 22). For everyone after Adam, then, the soul is connected with the sort of flesh (that is, mortal flesh) that facilitates the formation of habit.

Habit—feelings and actions with a past—in turn creates a compulsive emotional pathway that exerts immediate influence on moral decision making. In this way, a person's previous wrong choices combine and collude to compromise his or her freedom in the present. The result is conflict and ethical paralysis. People want to do something but find that they cannot do it, or they do not want to do something but find themselves doing it anyway. (Hence Augustine's apposite evocation, on this point, of the difficulty in trying not to swear.) The Pauline verses that Fortunatus adduced did indeed bespeak intense conflict. "The mind of the flesh is hostile to God; it is not subject to the law of God nor can it be" (Romans 8:7). "The flesh lusts against the spirit and the spirit against the flesh" (Galatians 5:17). But this conflict, insisted Augustine, attested not to two contrary natures at war, pitting body against soul, but to a single soul caught between its present desires and the habitual pull of its own emotional past.[19]

The debate with Fortunatus sharpened a number of issues for Augustine. Evoking Adam as he suddenly did on the second day of their debate, Augustine did more than introduce into this context his earlier idea that habit mitigated ethical freedom. By framing his response explicitly in terms of Adam's fall, he introduced a biblical and, at the same moment, a historical perspective. The prior question ("How does habit affect will?") ceded to the more fundamental question: *Why* are humans so constituted that habit affects will? By framing this question with the biblical story of Adam's fall, the problem of ethical evil became, more clearly, the question of the justice of God. Augustine remained committed to his fundamental principles: To be justly punishable, sin had to be utterly voluntary; to be justly rewarded, so did virtue. Thus if "Adam" and "habit" implied that human agents, though now functioning with diminished capacity, were still culpable, then their condition had to be compatible with the justice of the judging god who was the ultimate source of that condition.

After his debate, and despite his new duties as priest, Augustine pressed ahead both with his study of scripture and with his writing campaign against the Manichees. In *Faith and the Creed* (393), he again counterpoised the effects of habit to the Manichaean doctrine of two natures when considering the problem of sin, reclaiming two favorite Pauline verses from these opponents, Romans 7:25 ("With my mind I serve the law of God, but with my flesh the law of sin") and Ephesians

2:3 ("We were by nature children of wrath"; *Faith and the Creed* 10,23). Committed to the interpretive principle that the Psalms referred to Christ—another way to assert the essential Christianity of the Old Testament—he began a continuous commentary on all of them, producing interpretations of the first thirty-two psalms by 395.

But the premier texts and issues contested by catholics and Manichees were Paul's letters, the gospels, and the moral status of material creation as presented in Genesis. Augustine again began to work on these directly. In 393, he attempted another anti-Manichaean commentary on Genesis, this time not allegorical but *ad litteram.* He soon abandoned the project. ("My inexperience collapsed under the weight of so heavy a load," he recalled decades later in his review of this work; *Retractations* 1.[18]17.) The so-called antitheses from the Sermon on the Mount ("You have heard it said. . . . But I say"; Matthew 5:21–22, for example) had long served the Manichees as evangelical support for their rejection of the Old Testament. Against them, in *The Lord's Sermon on the Mount* (394), Augustine argued in defense of the basic harmony of Old and New Testaments. And then, shortly thereafter, he began a new cycle of work. Plunging into a concentrated study of the Manichees' favorite apostle, Augustine again took up the letters of Paul.

What did Saul want but to attack, seize, bind and slay
Christians? What a fierce, savage, blind will was that!
Yet he was thrown prostrate by one word from on high,
and a vision came to him whereby his mind and will
were turned from their fierceness and set on the right
way towards faith.

AUGUSTINE, *TO SIMPLICIANUS* I.2,22

Augustine's first serious encounter with Paul had occurred in Carthage, when he was a Manichee. The Paul whom he met at that time was unencumbered by any positive relationship with the Old Testament and thus with Judaism. The Manichees had explained away all affirmative references to Jewish scriptures, law, or practices in Paul's letters with their theory of textual corruptions. Anything else that contradicted what the Manichees thought Paul should have said—such as his claim that Christ was descended from David according to the flesh (Romans 1:3)—they accounted for by holding that Paul's own thought itself had developed, so that some of his statements were more sound than others. More positively, the Manichees readily fastened on Paul's habitual use of binary opposites—flesh/spirit, Law/grace, sin/righteousness—to build a firm base for coherent and compelling dualist interpretations of their own. And Paul himself, though his letters were formally outside of the Manichaean canon, was esteemed by North African Manichees as a foundational authority.[1]

This Manichaean Paul had been Augustine's own companion during the whole period of his intellectual coming-of-age, from his nineteenth year until he was well past thirty. His close reading of the books of the Platonists in Milan then introduced him not only to a new way of conceiving God, matter, and the problem of evil, but also to a new apostle. At that heady moment, Augustine enthusiastically discovered and remained convinced that Paul expressed (though more perfectly because Paul was Christian) the same wisdom as did the Neoplatonists. Through Paul's letters, Augustine glimpsed the face of philosophy (*Against the Academics* 2.2,6). In Paul's description of the visible things of creation making known the invisible God, Augustine heard the summons to the soul to retreat from temporal things and to return to the realm of the eternal (Romans 1:20; *True Religion* 52,101).

Neoplatonism would remain forever fundamental to Augustine's thought. Beginning in the mid-390s, however, challenged publicly as he had been by Fortunatus' adept appeals to the Pauline epistles in the course of their debate, Augustine shifted strategies in his campaign against the Manichees. The erudite treatises appropriate to his gentlemanly audience in Italy and to his continued life of retirement back in Thagaste would no longer do. He was now a churchman, responsible to and for a congregation, and to a wider church established in the Bible belt of Latin Christianity.

Augustine worked to be able to express his understanding of Paul in a more scriptural idiom. As he learned how to do so, his earlier, more philosophically framed arguments and vocabulary ceded to the narrative structure and to the inherent drama of biblical salvation history. Taking the issues that the Manichees had set—the origin of evil, the status of the Law, the character of the Old Testament's god, the role of the will and the flesh in both sin and salvation—Augustine began an intensive project of exegesis. His goal was to interpret Paul's letters in such a way that he could defend the goodness of the created order and of the Old Testament (and thus the goodness of its god) while using Paul's own words in defense of the freedom of the will.

The summer of 394 marked the beginning of Augustine's staccato production of works on Paul. *Notes on Romans* preserved a transcript of answers that he had given in discussion with fellow clergy at Carthage. Later, back in Hippo, he completed a commentary on Galatians but abandoned a more ambitious work on Romans, the *Unfinished Commentary*. (He left off this project, he later explained, because he was so "discouraged by the magnitude and labor of this task"; *Retractations*

1.23[22],1). Chapters 7 through 9 of Romans in particular offered the Manichees strong support for their views on dualism, cosmic evil, and moral determinism. Paul spoke there of the Law and sinful passions working death through the flesh (Romans 7:5), of all of creation groaning while it awaited redemption (Romans 8:22), of the Old Testament's god controlling human actions (Romans 9:13–18). Addressing these difficult verses in passing in his *Notes on Romans,* Augustine considered them again shortly thereafter in greater detail (questions 66, 67, and 68 in his volume of collected essays, *On Various Questions*). Finally, capping this period and in a sense (as we shall see) transforming it, he returned to Romans 7 through 9 yet again in 396 for his *Answers to Simplicianus.*

Augustine's goal throughout this protracted effort was to construct from Paul an argument against the Manichees that was both scriptural and, by his definition (which we are still trying to grasp), "historical." Having already tried and failed in his attempt to understand Genesis "according to its historical character" (*Retractations* 1.[18]17, remarking on the *Unfinished Literal Commentary*), he now discovered that Paul's letters were no easier to interpret with this concern in mind. He petitioned the famous Jerome in Bethlehem to send him translated biblical commentaries of the great Greek fathers (*Letter* 28.2,2), and he attempted to consult whatever Latin authorities he could. All of these data—his fitful literary production, his search for authoritative guides, his dissatisfaction with his own repeated efforts to interpret these texts—attest to a more fundamental problem. In the mid-390s, Augustine was struggling with his own uncertainty about how to read the Bible.[2]

Help came to him from an unlikely quarter. Once again, the charged anti-Manichaean sentiment of both catholics and Donatists served to bring members of these two mutually alienated North African communities together. Back in 392, the desire to frustrate the missionary success of the Manichee Fortunatus had precipitated a cross-congregational coalition of Hippo's Donatists and catholics, who united to ask Augustine to intervene. Two years later, Augustine himself effected a similar initiative. His efforts resulted in a generative intellectual coalition between himself and the work of an elder contemporary, one of the most original and important Latin theologians of the fourth century: the Donatist layman Tyconius.

Tyconius is one of the most elusive figures of late Latin Christianity. A highly original and independent thinker, he had insisted—against the perfectionist principles of his own Donatist community—that in the age before the End, the church must remain a "mixed body" containing both sinner and saint. Censured for taking this position by a Donatist council in the mid-380s, Tyconius nonetheless remained loyal to his church. He died sometime before Augustine encountered his writings. (There is no evidence that the two ever actually met.) Perhaps his reputation as a dissident Donatist was what initially commended his work to Augustine's attention. Though his dispute with the Manichees preoccupied Augustine throughout the 390s, he was already engaged in anti-Donatist polemics as well. In that contest, he readily made many of Tyconius' arguments his own.[3]

But Augustine found much more in Tyconius than just a quarry for arguments against Donatist separatism. Tyconius pointed the way for him to reconceptualize his reading of the double canon of scripture. In his handbook of biblical interpretation, *The Book of Rules*, Tyconius had identified seven compositional principles governing scriptural prose that, once understood, he claimed, could serve as "keys or windows to the secrets of the Law." By "Law" Tyconius intended much more than just the Five Books of Moses or the traditions of Jewish practice. For him, Law indicated the entire Bible, the New Testament as well as the Old, which taken together constituted "a vast forest of prophecy" (*Book of Rules* prologue). This perspective on scripture reversed the usual terms of Christian interpretation, enabling Tyconius to read the gospel in light of the Law, not just the Law in light of the gospel. And this mode of reading in turn enabled Tyconius— and through him, Augustine—to understand Paul's letters in a new way.[4]

Tyconius' originality emerges most clearly when we compare him with his fellow biblical interpreters. Christian writers had long relied on philosophical and typological allegory when commenting on the Bible. Spiritual allegory provided a way to draw metaphysical truths from scriptural narrative and Christian meanings from originally Jewish texts. In more classically allegorizing writings, especially those originating from Alexandria—Philo's commentaries (mutatis mutandis), Origen's, or those later works by Ambrose (and the young Augustine) that borrowed from this tradition—characters, images, and incidents in biblical narrative were frequently matched to timeless moral or metaphysical truths. Thus, famously, in Genesis 3, Adam stood for the higher intelligence of the soul, the serpent for the distracting world of the senses, and so on (see p. 48 above). Such allegorical interpretations were, in this sense, strongly "vertical."

More "horizontal" allegories—temporally oriented interpretations that sought to demonstrate that Christianity was the fulfillment of Judaism or that episodes in the gospels revealed the true meaning of incidents in the Septuagint—worked by identifying correspondences between events, images, personages, or numbers across the Old Testament/New Testament divide. This sort of typological allegory often established a relative inferiority of the Septuagint prototype to its later Christian correlate. In the New Testament's Epistle to the Hebrews, for example, the earthly temple in Jerusalem represents an inferior copy of the heavenly tabernacle, the Jerusalem priesthood is an inferior anticipation of the eternal priesthood of Christ, the sacrifices at the earthly altar imitate only imperfectly the perfect sacrifice of Christ, and so on (Hebrews 8:5; 9:11-28). This sort of typological reading reinforced the proof from prophecy: the Old Testament prototype imperfectly presented and predicted, its New Testament correlate completed and perfected.

Justin Martyr's *Dialogue with Trypho* stands as a monument to this kind of interpretation. When he drew correspondences between the Septuagint's references to "wood" or "tree" and the Christian proclamation of Christ's cross, for example, Justin not only identified a common figure or type shared between the text and the later tradition. He also made a point about meaning and discernment: The earlier images found their deepest and truest significance when understood as prophetic foreshadowings of Christ's crucifixion (*Trypho* 86; 90-91). Melito of Sardis (as we have seen; p. 83 above) transmuted the entire biblical story of Passover into an intricate typological code for Christ's Passion. Melito assumes that the events described in Exodus had occurred in the past. But the ultimate historical significance of these events, he firmly believed, could be grasped only when they were understood by appeal to the Christian message. In other words, the present, not the past, set the terms for interpretation.[5]

Tyconius too relied on typology to unpack the "mystical rules . . . of the whole Law" (*Book of Rules,* prologue). But where other theologians had used such interpretation to build various analogies between the (inferior) Old Testament and the (superior) New Testament, Tyconius used typology to argue for the two testaments' theological concinnity, and even their identity. A single divine initiative of redemption, he urged, bound the two testaments together. Abraham, Moses, David, Paul, the contemporary believer: All shared and share the same faith. "The Spirit, the faith, and the grace given by Christ have always been the same." Before his incarnation, Christ gave grace to the righteous within Israel; after his incarnation, he made the same grace available to all peoples. "By his coming, Christ bestowed these gifts upon the whole race, having removed the veil that was covering the Law." Tyconius alludes here to Paul's words about Moses' face, veiled when he descended Sinai (2 Corinthians 3:13-17; Exodus 34:33-35). In so doing, Tyconius makes a further point, namely, that the Law itself perdures, continuous from the era of the Old Testament past to the era of the New, in the present. Christ, he said, had taken the Law, originally revealed solely to Israel, and made it available to all peoples. In other words, the difference between these two historically distinct dispensations was only one of "measure" (*modo*), not of kind (*genere; Book of Rules* 3,9). The *same* Law was given, the first time to Israel, the second time to the nations.[6]

By so defining his terms, Tyconius established the biblical identity of those within the present-day church: They stood in the spiritual line of Abraham, continuous from Isaac down to contemporary times. ("This line has never been broken," he asserts; *Book of Rules* 3,2). But by this same argument Tyconius also established the historical identity of Israel. The significance of the righteous within Israel was not that they foreshadowed or represented types or figures of the future church. Rather, it was their historical integrity as witnesses to faith that anchored the church in the Israelite past, creating a continuous community of the redeemed (3,9).

Commenting on this salvation history, Tyconius raised a crucial question. If God had predestined the saved by his promise to Abraham (they were Abraham's line "according to the spirit"), why then had he later, in Moses' day, given the Law at all (*Book of Rules* 3,4)? What did the Law have to do with a redemption that, long before, had already been securely promised? And how could the Law confer any continuing benefit now that Christ had come?

Tyconius untangled these questions in his handbook's Rule 3, "On the Promises and the Law." Turning precisely to those two letters in which Paul had seemed most harsh in his assessment of the Law, Galatians and Romans, Tyconius urged that the Law had always played a crucial role, and indeed that it continues to play a positive role in this divine process of salvation. The Law was nothing less, he said, than God's instrument through which he led the pious, in both biblical eras, to faith.

How so? God, said Tyconius, knew that he had given a Law that no one could possibly fulfill. And God also knew that people would know this as well. The truly pious individual, however, would realize that God would never leave humanity in such a desperate situation without a remedy.

> The thinking person who realizes that humanity cannot possibly
> fulfill the Law . . . and yet who fails to understand that there is a
> life-giving remedy [namely, faith], is nothing less than perverse
> and blasphemous. It is simply not possible that the good God,
> knowing that the Law could not be fulfilled, would have provided
> no other access to life. . . . Faith cannot tolerate such a thought,
> or even allow it . . . for faith knows that the Lord is good and just.
>
> BOOK OF RULES 3,8

This conviction about God's moral character, this confidence both in divine justice and in divine mercy, said Tyconius, defined pious faith. Such an affirmation was itself the faithful response to the fear and frustration caused by a person's invariably disheartening failures with the Law. To make demands of his creatures that he already knew they could not meet would be perverse. But God was not perverse. God was both good and just. The pious, affirming their faith (that is, their confidence) in God's goodness, were and are accordingly moved to turn toward God and to implore his help. Harkening to them, God gives such people the grace to do out of love what they had tried, and failed, to do out of fear, namely, to be truly righteous under the Law. In other words, like a harsh school-slave sternly delivering young students to their master, "the Law . . . drove people toward faith" (*Book of Rules* 3,8; an allusion to Galatians 3:24: "The Law was our *paidagôgos* until Christ came"). "For the righteous, the Law does not work wrath, but rather it exercises their faith" (*Book of Rules* 3,19). *Lex fidei demonstratrix:* "The Law points the way to faith" (3,9).

God, of course, had always foreseen the faith of his elect. That was the basis on which, observed Tyconius, he had made his promise to Abraham. And since divine foreknowledge is perfect and inerrant, God's promise of salvation, like his knowledge of who would be saved, was absolutely secure. What then of those instances in scripture that speak as if the promise were contingent or conditional (as, for example, at Isaiah 1:19: *"if* you obey me and are willing")? In such places, Tyconius explained, God was actually addressing those who were within the community of the saved but not of it. That is, God uses such language when addressing "the impious and sinners" (*Book of Rules* 3,18; Tyconius' insistence that Israel and, subsequently, the church had always been a mixed body of sinners and saints is what had earned him the censure of his own Donatist community). Why would God say *"if* you hear me" when he inerrantly knew (even before he made the individuals in question) the identity of those who would hear him (3,18)? Clearly, said Tyconius, in such places, God must be addressing the sinners.

Divine foreknowledge, Tyconius further insists, does not *cause* the foreseen faith of the saved. Rather, such faith was their own accomplishment, achieved through their own free will. This faith precedes their reception of the grace that enables them to fulfill the Law out of love (*Book of Rules* 3,16–20). That grace, however, is purely a gift. Therefore, Tyconius concludes, the faithful give glory to God precisely for this grace, knowing that "we have nothing that we did not first receive" (3,11; an allusion to Paul in 1 Corinthians 4:7: "What do we have that we did not first receive?").

Tyconius' reading of Paul integrated the Law in a very positive way into the process of salvation. He thus provided Augustine with an-other strong argument against the Manichees' rejection of the Old Testament and their demeaning assessment of the Old Testament's god. Furthermore, by insisting that divine election rested on God's foreknowledge of freely chosen faith, Tyconius suggested to Augustine a reading of Paul against Manichaean determinism that acknowledged and indeed depended on human moral autonomy. And finally, by in-sisting that the dynamics of Law and faith, will and grace were con-stant across nations, times, and individuals, from Abraham to Jacob to David to the apostles and on into the present life of the church, Tyco-nius disclosed in the entire double canon of scripture a continuous and consistent record of God's saving acts in history.

Tyconius' *Book of Rules* helped Augustine to find a way out of the impasse that he had come to in his own struggle to make sense of Paul's letters. Adopting and adapting his arguments, Augustine in 394 began to work directly on Romans. Cautiously commenting on Ro-mans 3.20 ("No flesh will be justified before him [God] by the Law, for through the Law comes knowledge of sin"), Augustine warned, "Such statements must be read with great care, so that the apostle seems nei-ther to condemn the Law nor to take away the free exercise of human will" (*Notes on Romans* 13–18.1) To this end, Augustine applied to Paul's epistle a fourfold scheme of salvation history: prior to the Law (*ante legem*), under the Law (*sub lege*), under grace (*sub gratia*), and in peace (*in pace*).[7]

> *Ante legem* we pursue fleshly concupiscence; *sub lege* we are pulled
> by it; *sub gratia* we neither pursue nor are pulled by it; *in pace* there
> is no concupiscence of the flesh.... Thus [under grace] we still
> have desires, but since we do not obey them, we do not allow sin
> to reign in us. These desires arise from the mortality of the flesh,
> which we bear from the first sin of the first man, whence we are
> born fleshly [*carnaliter*: by this, Augustine intends a moral quality
> of the soul as well as a physical quality of the body]. They will
> not cease save at the resurrection of the body, when we will have
> merited that transformation promised to us. Then there will be
> perfect peace, when we are established in the fourth stage.
>
> NOTES ON ROMANS 13–18.2, 10

As we have seen Augustine do earlier, correlating seven world ages with biblical time periods and with the stages of an individual life (*Genesis against the Manichees;* see p. 135 above), so he does again with this fourfold model here. Universal history is framed by biblical terminals, humanity before Israel ("prior to the Law") to one edge, the Second Coming ("in peace") to the other. The incarnation thus stands at and as the hinge of history, turning humanity's pathway from God's revelation to Israel ("under the Law") to God's revelation in Christ ("under grace"). But, again like Tyconius, Augustine also holds that the process of salvation is both linear and interior. The individual repeats in miniature what all humanity lives communally, sharing the same beginning and end points: Adam at one end; eschatological transformation in Christ at the other.

Augustine had already experimented with such a fourfold periodization of time at some point prior to *Notes on Romans,* in the course commenting on Jesus' feeding of the crowd of 5,000 (John 6:9–13; cf. Matthew 14:15–21). The five barley loaves that Jesus blessed on that occasion, Augustine explained in question 61 of his *On Various Questions,* stand for the Five Books of Moses. These five loaves/books nourished this Jewish crowd because they were not yet spiritual but still "carnal," that is, they still were living according to the five senses, and so on (question 61.1). The notice in Matthew 14:16 that this crowd had been following Jesus for three days then prompted Augustine to remark that the full span of human history divides into three time periods (*tempora*), which he designated *ante legem, sub lege,* and *sub gratia.* A fourth time, he continued here, refers to the eschatological peace of the heavenly Jerusalem (question 61.7). This correlates to the fourth stage (*in pace*), which he later speaks of in *Notes on Romans.*

This earlier essay on the miracle of the loaves and fishes seems primarily a typological exercise in biblical number symbolism, wherein Augustine spins correlations between numerals, quantities, and events in the Old Testament and the New with dizzying ease. Ancient Christians loved and valued this sort of interpretation: Its ingenuity delighted them, its flexibility helped them to establish the ways in which the "true" and "deeper" meaning of Old Testament figures was revealed in the New. (Pagans and Jews in antiquity valued and savored this numerological and symbolic style of reading no less, when they applied it for their own reasons to their own texts.) Thus, as Augustine continues to comment on Jesus' miraculous feeding of the crowds, he notes that the twelve baskets of leftovers after the meal correspond to the twelve apostles (question 61.3), that a second crowd fed with seven loaves refers to the seven gifts of the Holy Spirit (question 61.4), that the two fish relate to the two offices that the Old Law designated through anointing—namely those of priest and prophet (question 61.4), and so on. In brief, the idea of the three (or four) periods as Augustine first formulates it in question 61 is less about time and history—despite his use of the term "time periods" (*tempora*)—than it is about associating numbers and symbols across the Old Testament/New Testament divide.

Once Augustine turned to Romans, however, the scheme of the four stages (*gradus*) helped him to read more closely and to think more creatively about the interpretive challenges of that letter, especially those of Romans 7 and 9. At this slightly later point, the scheme provided a dynamic scaffolding for his thoughts on the relationship between Law and grace, election and free will, and thus for his developing ideas on the process of conversion.

This was so because, when applied not only historically and communally but also biographically and, therefore, individually, this four-stage scheme heightened the drama of salvation. History's turning point, the coming of Christ, moved humanity from "under the Law" to "under grace." But this transition became much more acute and dramatic when configured individually. A single person's spiritual development also pivoted upon the crucial move from stage two to stage three. This change was less a transition or a process that an event: the moment of conversion. How does an individual move from condemnation to redemption?

This dramatic, individualized story orients Augustine's reading in *Notes on Romans*. He saw in Romans 7:15–16 a description of the moral torque suffered by the person constituted under the Law: "I do not want to do what I do; but what I hate, this I do. If, moreover, I do what I do not want to do, I agree that the Law is good." "One must take care," Augustine cautions, "lest he think that these words deny free will, for it is not so" (*Notes on Romans* 44.1). The key to effecting this transition from Law (which can only instruct the sinner on what he *should* do, but cannot help him to do it) to grace (which enables the man to do as he knows he should) lies precisely, says Augustine, in the free exercise of that individual's will. Insufficient to prevent him from sinning, man's free will does suffice to prompt him to turn in faith to Christ in order to implore divine aid. "Through his free will man has a means to believe in the Liberator and to receive grace so that . . . he might cease to sin" (44.3). Receiving grace on account of his faith that Christ will help him, man then moves *sub gratia*. The motor of this movement is the will.

But Paul's letter to the Romans contained passages extremely difficult to reconcile with a strong view of man's moral freedom. What about God's choice of Jacob over Esau, before either had been born? This episode, Augustine admits, "moves some people to think that the apostle Paul has done away with the freedom of the will" (*Notes on Romans* 60.2; Romans 9:11–13). What about Pharaoh: How much free choice did he have, once God hardened his heart? (*Notes on Romans* 62.1–7; Romans 9:17). And how just was God whether in hating Esau or in punishing Pharaoh, if the unborn Esau had done nothing yet and the hardened Pharaoh had had no free choice?

Here Augustine of necessity must complicate his original presentation. Man, he suddenly notes, cannot actually will at all—not even to ask Christ for help—unless God has called him first. Clearly, neither Esau nor Pharaoh willed rightly. Did that imply that God had not called them? But if God condemned them when he alone had decided *not* to call them, he would be unjust, essentially punishing these men for the consequences of his own divine decision. In his effort to follow Paul closely, Augustine seems to have painted himself into a corner.

Just preceding this juncture, Augustine had adduced a line from the Gospel of Matthew and a key argument from Tyconius' *Book of Rules*. "Many are called, but few are chosen" (*Notes on Romans* 55.1–2; Matthew 22:14). God *justly* distinguishes between those whom he (merely) calls and those whom he (actually) chooses, Augustine now explains, according to his inerrant foreknowledge, "by which he knows the character even of the unborn" (*Notes on Romans* 60.4). Foreknowing the movements of the human heart, God graciously calls the elect, who at this point still languish as sinners in stage two, *sub lege*. They want not to sin but they are unable to stop sinning. God calls to this group "according to his purpose," specifically, his purpose of election (55.5). The elect, receiving this call, then respond autonomously—just as God had foreseen they would—with a "good will." Their good will then prompts them, still *sub lege,* to turn in faith to Christ for help. At this point they receive grace again, a second time, through the Holy Spirit, which enables them to do good works. They can thus fulfill the Law through love. Once this occurs, the elect finally stand *sub gratia,* in the third stage, able not to sin.

This is a fatiguing amount of qualification: Augustine in effect has introduced a double loop into his argument. An entire back-and-forth cycle of divine foreknowledge and human predisposition now prefaces the sinner's calling out to Christ for help. Why so complicated?

Augustine was trying to accommodate his idea of free will and election to yet another difficult Pauline passage in Romans 9. Right after Paul had declared that God loved Jacob but hated Esau when both were still in the womb, he had continued:

> What then shall we say? Is there injustice on God's part? God
> forbid! For he says to Moses, "I will have mercy on whom I will
> [already] have had mercy, and I will show him compassion upon
> whom I will [already] have had compassion" (Exodus 33:19). So
> it depends not on man's willing or running, but on God's mercy.
> For the scripture says to Pharaoh, "I have raised you up for this
> very purpose of showing my power in you, so that my name may
> be proclaimed in all the earth" (Exodus 9:13). So he has mercy on
> whomever he will and he hardens whomever he will.
>
> ROMANS 9:14–18

The sequence of tenses in Augustine's Latin text—a future ("I will have mercy") and a future perfect, that is, a future form of a past tense ("I will have had mercy")—informs the double loop of his interpretation here. The past action ("I will have had mercy"), Augustine explains, occurred when God graciously called out, the first time, to these people even though they were still sinners. He called them "according to his purpose," because he knew absolutely and inerrantly that they would freely respond to his call with the "good will" of faith. Augustine, borrowing from Tyconius for this idea, thus concludes *fidem elegit in praescientia*, "[God] chooses faith through his foreknowledge" (*Notes on Romans* 60.11). The future action ("I will have mercy") then follows.

> "I will have mercy," he says, "on whom I will have had mercy." God was merciful to us the first time when he called us when we were still sinners. "On whom I will have had mercy," he says, "so that I called him," and still "I will have mercy on him" yet again once the man has believed. Yet how does God show mercy this second time? He gives to the believing seeker the Holy Spirit.
>
> *NOTES ON ROMANS 61.2–3*

Paul's line in Romans 9:16—"It [that is, election] depends not on man's willing or running but on God's mercy"—had risked making God seem arbitrary and human moral effort seem otiose. But God *is* just, Augustine insists, because he *does* distinguish between sinners, and he does so on account of his foreknowledge of their future merits.

God also does so because, to be just, he must do so. "If he does not choose according to merit," says Augustine, "it is not election, for all are equal prior to merit, and no choice can be made between absolutely equal things" (*Notes on Romans* 60.8). A person's foreknown "good will" that occasions God's call is thus the completely independent moral accomplishment of the elect. By preserving this thin sliver of human initiative—the elected sinner's response to God's call—Augustine likewise preserved God's justice. Augustine's "reconstruction" of this divine–human interaction, when the person hovers on the cusp of the transition from Law to grace, stage two to stage three, provided a morally coherent explanation of and reason for divine discrimination. God saves the elect because they deserve to be saved. They deserve to be saved because they freely will their faith, which God perfectly foreknows. This freely willed faith is what distinguishes the saved from the reprobate. *Fides inchoat meritum.* Faith, concludes Augustine, initiates the distinction of merit (62.9).

✦✦✦

AUGUSTINE'S SOLUTION to the problem of human freedom and divine election in his *Notes on Romans* was, as we have just seen, complex. It was also fragile, and he seemed to know this. When he undertook a formal commentary on the letter, its prospective scale discouraged him, and he quit. Meanwhile, staying within the basic framework proposed in *Notes on Romans,* he continued filling in details—and generating more and more of them—in shorter studies of these difficult passages.

In question 66, again investigating Romans 7, he sketched his four stages (identified this time as *actiones,* "proceedings"), once more affirming the Law's essential goodness despite its entanglement in sin and death. This constellation of issues—sin, death, the Law—brought him back to Adam and to the consequences of Adam's disobedience for the rest of the race.

Conscious, as ever, of the use that the Manichees had made of this chapter of Paul's, Augustine was especially sensitive to several problems with his own description of Adam's sin and humanity's subsequent sinfulness. He did not want to associate sin excessively with flesh: That would play too much into the Manichees' dualist materialism and moral determinism. (Paul's own language, of course, did not make this effort any easier for him.) It must be the will, an aspect of soul, that plays the crucial part in sinning. But Augustine also did not want to sound too much as if a damaged soul, on the analogy of the fleshly body, were somehow inherited from Adam: That too might play too much into Manichaean materialism. Souls must be purely spirit, and spirit is not like matter, nor does it behave like matter: It is not inherited, passed on from one generation to the next in the way that flesh is. And finally there was the more general problem of holding divine justice to at least as high a standard as human justice. No human judge could justly punish one person for the crime of another. How then could God justly punish those yet unborn for the sin of a distant ancestor?

Augustine attempts to square these circles in question 66.3 by introducing the concept of human "nature" and by associating this nature with Adam in a particular way. After Adam's fall, he says, every later person was born with a body that was mortal and with a nature that was "carnal." Humanity suffered this condition because in Adam *natura nostra peccavit* ("our nature sinned"). Here Augustine has to distinguish carefully between *caro*, "flesh," and *qualitas carnalis*, "carnal character." Flesh is a material substratum, created good by the good God. Carnal character is a negative moral quality and descriptive primarily of the sinner's soul, which after Adam easily inclines toward sin, forming bad habits. When a person is constituted in stage three, *sub gratia*, his flesh is still mortal, but his soul, through grace, has been released from its carnal character. In this way, he can be said to have "died to sin" (question 66.1–2; 6).

Natura nostra, the vague "human nature," appears primarily in this context to deflect the threat to God's justice posed by his punishing all humanity for Adam's transgression. Augustine reasons that all humanity—the "we" of the Latin *nostra*, "our"—must somehow have participated in Adam's sin: That way, his sin was "our" sin, and "we" sinned when he sinned. Because Adam was the primal parent (of Eve also, according to Genesis 2, as well as of all later generations), all humanity, argues Augustine, was somehow, actually, historically, really "in" him.[8]

Humans, in this view, live a sort of double life, one distant and aggregate, one proximate and individual. Everyone already existed in Adam (the distant historical mode), and each exists individually as a discrete person (the proximate historical mode). This distant/proximate structure, invoked already by Augustine back in 392 in his debate with Fortunatus to explain why souls sin (*Against Fortunatus* 22; see pp. 146–147 above) is summed up by the word *nature* here. In its distant, collective aspect, nature safeguards divine justice. All were present in Eden; therefore, all are justly punished. Forensic necessity required that Augustine assert the historical or real or actual aspect of that distant collective life: The entire race, in this view, truly was present "in" Adam. And this historical realism in turn gives the measure of how far Augustine's thinking on Genesis had changed since 388–389, when

"Adam" had served primarily as a symbol for "mind" (*Genesis against the Manichees* 1.19,30).

Augustine's thinking on human moral autonomy also became more complex during this same period. *Free Will*, a treatise started in Rome and completed back in North Africa, changes noticeably in style, tone, and substance between book one (begun in 388) and book three (finished in 395). In the course of his work on Romans, as we have seen, Augustine had had to assert repeatedly that Paul nowhere impugned man's moral autonomy. Having defended free choice in these Pauline writings only obliquely, Augustine now applied himself directly to the issue by resuming this long-interrupted work.

Augustine had originally conceived and written *Free Will* as a philosophical dialogue between himself and Evodius, one of his former students. In book one, a synopsis of the views held at Cassiciacum, Augustine had been unblushingly optimistic about the effectiveness of human will. He repeated his usual argument on the necessity of uncoerced choice: Man sins because he wants to sin, or else God would not be just in punishing sinners. Why does man make bad moral choices? Because he strays from learning (*disciplina*). "Hence to do evil is nothing but to stray from education" (*Free Will* 1.1,2). But when man wills rightly, in accordance with divine law, he accrues merit (1.14,30), and ultimately achieves the happy life. "Whoever wishes to live rightly and honorably," Augustine concluded, "and prefers that to all transient goods, attains his object with perfect ease. To reach it, he has only to will it" (1.13,29).

Sometime after his ordination as priest at Hippo in 391 but before his elevation as bishop in 396, Augustine wrote books two and three (*Retractations* 1.9[8],1). His discussion from the midway point of book two probably dates toward the end of that period. Near the conclusion of book two, where Augustine struggled to understand the root reason why an uncoerced will would turn from what is good, the optimism of his earlier chapters fades considerably; and Evodius, his quondam partner in the dialogue, virtually disappears. In what becomes a somber monologue, Augustine now presents a picture of man *in via*, "on the road" in this life, at risk of wandering off the path into darkness because of his weakness (*Free Will* 2.16,41). The sense of foreboding continues to build in book three. Man sins, Augustine explains there, because his loves are misordered. Carnal custom (*consuetudo*) deflects his control of his desires and affections. The penal condition of ignorance and difficulty—Adam's patrimony—retards man's progress (3.7,23; 18,52).

These themes are not new. Augustine had sounded all of them in his earlier notes on Paul. There, however, they had been woven into the essentially optimistic pattern of salvation history. In book three of *Free Will*, these elements are static; or, rather, they pile on top of each other as Augustine builds his description of the sheer extremity of man's situation. Mortality and habit weigh man down; his own sins compound the inherited penalties of ignorance and difficulty. He moves in a situation of acute danger, through intense darkness, trying to keep his gaze riveted on the bright, distant light of Christ while the night presses in on all sides and the Devil hovers near to hand (*Free Will* 3.20,55-56; 3.24,71-25,76). Fear of hell, rather than adherence to education, keeps him on the right road. "If any suggestion springing from a desire for the inferior should deflect our purpose," Augustine concludes, "eternal damnation and the torments of the Devil will recall us to the true path" (3.25,76). The lambent certainties of Milan, Cassiciacum, and Rome seem long gone.

◆ ◆ ◆

THE YOUNG AUGUSTINE had come to Carthage back in 371 originally to pursue a career in law. Had he continued on that course, he would have spent his intellectual gifts crafting verbally brilliant arguments and mastering the intricacies of late Roman litigation. Instead, after discovering philosophy via Cicero, he gave himself over to "the pursuit of wisdom" while turning to the study of rhetoric. Later, in Milan, his rounds of teaching as a municipal professor were punctuated by command performances—more verbal pyrotechnics—before the imperial court, lauding its programs and policies and praising the emperor. Like his forsaken career, his chosen one also relied upon ceaseless efforts to cultivate useful connections and powerful patrons. Between times, Augustine attempted to launch himself as a cultured writer, conceiving treatises on learned topics (rhetoric, aesthetics, liberal arts).

Talented, ambitious—or as he memorably put it, "all hot for money, honors, marriage" (*Confessions* 6.6,9)—Augustine aimed ultimately to secure a post in the imperial government. His life, with all his hopes and all his fears, was relentlessly public.

Once he resigned his post and committed himself to baptism, celibacy, and Christian *otium liberale* in the fall and winter of 386-387, Augustine probably thought that he had left all that behind. His unexpected conscription into Hippo's clergy after nearly four years of such retirement came as a shock. As he assumed his new duties, he would have found himself once again performing in public, teaching classes (for catechumens), exploring and explaining the meaning of texts (in sermons to congregations and in smaller seminars to fellow clergy), delivering formal and polished addresses (to elevated ecclesiastical assemblies), and establishing networks with powerful and more established men (the more senior bishops of his own province, and especially with Aurelius, bishop of Carthage). Between times, Augustine launched himself as a Christian "public intellectual," composing commentaries on the Bible and learned polemical pieces against the enemies of his church. Part of the shock of his transition in 391 would have stemmed from his necessary adjustment from a contemplative literary retirement to the rough-and-tumble of North African church life. But part would have been the shock of the familiar: A different version of his old life had found him again.[9]

A voice from his past, from the quiet life that ordination had wrested from him, came to Augustine in a letter that he received sometime in 396. A decade earlier, exhausted by his ambitions and exhilarated by his tandem study of Neoplatonism and Christian scripture, Augustine had sought the guidance of Simplicianus, a senior priest in Milan. "I wanted to consult with him about my problems," Augustine later wrote of this moment in the *Confessions,* "so that he might suggest a way fitted to someone in my troubled state whereby I could learn to walk in your [God's] way" (*Confessions* 8.1,1). Simplicianus had Augustine's measure. He related the story of the conversion and baptism of the Roman rhetor Marius Victorinus, whose translations of pagan Platonists Augustine had been reading. Augustine in turn (though perhaps only retrospectively) had Simplicianus' measure. "As soon as your servant Simplicianus told me this story of Victorinus, I was on fire to imitate him—which was, indeed, why Simplicianus had told me" (8.5,10).

Simplicianus more recently had encountered some of Augustine's works of biblical interpretation, and he now wrote with questions, some on Old Testament texts, some on the perennially thorny passages in Romans 7 and 9. His letter does not survive, but Augustine's affectionate response does. Admitting freely that he has toiled over these verses and had great difficulty with them, Augustine shouldered Simplicianus' request to consider them yet again (*Letter* 37.2–3). Shortly thereafter, Augustine produced the first work of his episcopacy, *To Simplicianus*.

Question 1 of that treatise, which treats Romans 7:7–25, essentially recapitulated the major points of *Notes on Romans* 28–38 and of question 66, though without directly mentioning the four stages of salvation history. Augustine's comments here conform to his earlier descriptions of man's condition *sub lege* and *sub gratia*. He affirms the goodness of the Law against the Manichees (*To Simplicianus* 1.1,16). He explains man's carnality by appeal to Adam's sin (*peccatum originale* here—not "original sin" in the later Augustinian sense but rather "the first sin" or "the sin from man's origins"; 1.1,10–11). And he repeats his assertion that the movement from sin to grace depends on man's freely willed faith (1.1,6; 11; 14).[10]

Question 2 returned Augustine to Romans 9:10–29, Paul's discussion of God's sovereign will acting in history. Regretting the passage's obscurity, Augustine summarized the purpose of Paul's entire letter, which he said he would take as his guide: No man should glory in the works of the Law, because good works are done only through faith, received by grace. Faith depends on first receiving God's call; no one can believe who has not first been called (*To Simplicianus* 1.2,2).

If this is so, then how can God justly elect only some people and not others? The case of Jacob and Esau, once again, put the question most acutely: Neither had been born, so neither had yet done anything to merit either fate. The problem of Jacob's prenatal election and Esau's prenatal rejection thus called into question the justice of

God. "How can election be just—indeed, how can there be any sort of choice at all—when there is no difference?" (*To Simplicianus* 1.2,4).

Thus far Augustine was on familiar ground. This is precisely the point in his prior discussions of Romans 9 where he had applied his adaptation of Tyconius' solution: God elects on the basis of his foreknowledge of man's [future] good will, and the faithful respond to his call (Notes on Romans 60.4; 11; *On Various Questions* 68.4). This appeal to divine foreknowledge preserved a space for human initiative in the process of redemption, thereby protecting as well the moral coherence of God's choices. But upon reaching this same point when responding to Simplicianus, Augustine—suddenly, surprisingly, unequivocally—rejects foreknowledge and dismantles the solution to the problem of election that he had so painstakingly worked out such a short time before. "If election is by foreknowledge, and God foreknew Jacob's faith, how would you prove that he did not elect him for his works? . . . Before Jacob and Esau were born they had neither faith nor works. . . . We still have to inquire, then, why that choice was made" (*To Simplicianus* 1.2,5).

This is a good moment to step back from Augustine's argument and instead to imagine Augustine as he was in the process of framing it. Augustine of course was not "writing" his response to Simplicianus. He was dictating it. (Writing in antiquity was a specialized technology. Ancient "writers" usually dictated to scribes, reviewing and polishing their product later, before putting it into circulation.) The circumstances of this kind of composition are readily apparent in *To Simplicianus,* one of the most vivid, and vividly oral, of all of Augustine's works. From this point on, once he has ruled out divine foreknowledge when considering Jacob and Esau, his tone seems to alternate between excitement and urgency as he boxes himself into various interpretive corners and fights his way back out again. Kinetic, repetitious, fatiguingly dialectical: *To Simplicianus* enables us to overhear Augustine as he (literally) thinks out loud. We witness, by following him, the birth of an idea.

Augustine's decision to rule out divine foreknowledge as a factor in the process of election threw all of the interlocking Pauline issues into crisis. Absent foreknowledge of the twins' future characters and choices, on what grounds did God or could God discriminate between them fairly? Augustine still insists that *something* has to distinguish those whom God loves from those whom God hates: "No one is elected unless he is different from him who is rejected" (*To Simplicianus* 1.2,6). But Augustine cannot now say what that difference might be.

What prompted Augustine to put himself, and his interpretation of Romans, into such difficulty? After all, he had argued not that long ago that unless humans freely distinguished themselves morally from each other, God's action whether to reward or to punish could not be just. That position had been his first line of defense against Manichaean determinism. "He who sins, sins by free will," he had insisted to Fortunatus. "He has done no evil who has done nothing of his own will" (*Against Fortunatus* 17). And shortly thereafter, working specifically on Romans, Augustine had introduced his cumbersome double loop of divine-human interaction: God foreknows man's "good will" and calls the elect "according to his intention" (*propositio*); man, harkening to God's call, turns freely to supplicate Christ and thus receives grace in order to cease sinning (*Notes on Romans* 55:1–5; see p. 167 above). The point, again, was to safeguard human moral autonomy—no matter how drastically reduced—as a way to safeguard God's justice.

Now, however, Augustine sees these issues differently. His earlier interpretation seemed to him to imply, unacceptably, that the predisposition of human will actually determined God's *proposito,* his intention. But man's freedom—even in the tiny, circumscribed arena of man's future good will—could not be permitted in any way to determine the action of God. To preserve divine sovereignty, Augustine now decided, the initiative of conversion must lie utterly outside the individual. God himself determines not only who receives the ability *sub gratia* to fulfill the Law ("will power") but also, prior to this moment and in a sense creating it, God determines who will be predisposed to receive his call ("good will").

> The good will does not precede God's call, but God's call precedes
> even the good will. The fact that we have a good will at all is
> rightly attributed to God, who calls us. . . . So the sentence, "It is

not him who wills or him who runs but God who has mercy"
cannot be taken simply to mean that we cannot attain what we
wish without the aid of God. Rather, without his first calling us,
we cannot even will.

TO SIMPLICIANUS 1.2.12

Restat ergo voluntates eliguntur. Man's very will, concludes Augustine, is itself chosen by God. Man does absolutely nothing on his own
to merit salvation. Divine decision, not human disposition, determines the difference between the saved and the damned. The initiative
of salvation rests exclusively and entirely with God.

What then of God's justice? According to what standard does God
make these choices? Why love Jacob, why hate Esau, if absolutely nothing distinguishes them? In the face of such absolute divine prerogative, can humans understand God's justice at all? Indeed, on any
normal understanding of the word, can God be said to be "just"?

A short eighteen months or so earlier, in 394–395, working slowly
through the opening verses of Romans, Augustine had asked this
same question (*Unfinished Commentary on Romans* 9:1). At that point, he
had argued that divine justice transcended human justice because
God's mercy so transcended human mercy. God, argued Augustine in
this earlier commentary, sent out the Holy Spirit everywhere to ad-
monish people to repentance, so that sinners would repent and thus
be saved. In light of God's great forbearance and the superabundance
of his grace, what then could possibly be the sin against the Holy
Spirit that Christ said could never be forgiven (Matthew 12:32; *Unfinished Commentary on Romans* 14.2)? After a long review of great sinners,
all of whom—even David the adulterer, even Paul the persecutor—had
received forgiveness once they repented, Augustine had concluded
that the one unforgivable sin was despair: "continuing in wickedness
and maliciousness with despair of the kindness and mercy (*indulgentia*)
of God." If one despairs of being forgiven, she has no motivation to repent. If she does not repent, she cannot reform, and so she will continue to sin. To be driven by this hopeless despair, said Augustine, is to
profoundly misunderstand the amplitude of divine mercy, thus the divine generosity that abides with divine justice. Despair is tantamount

to resisting "the grace and peace of God," which is nothing other than the Spirit itself (*Unfinished Commentary on Romans* 22.3–4).

But in 394, when he wrote those words, Augustine had held that human initiative played some role in man's decision to repent or not to repent. By 396, such initiative has disappeared: God's purposes, Augustine now believed, could never be contingent upon man's decision. Having excluded faith as a grounds for merit, having attributed man's good will itself to God's action, having obscured any means to discern between one person and another, Augustine moved to redefine the only variable left in his equation: the nature of God's call.

If some people responded to God's call and others did not, then the only explanation consistent with God's absolute sovereignty, Augustine now argued, was that he did not call everyone in the same way. Those whom he elects he calls *congruenter,* "effectively" or "appropriately," so that they will follow. Those whom he rejects he calls differently, so that they do not follow. The proof is tautological. If God had chosen these people, he would have called them effectively, so that they would have followed. Since they did not follow, although they must have been called (a nod, here, to Matthew 22:14, "Many are called, but few are chosen"), God must have called them, but not *congruenter.* God's absolute authority is thus preserved because the initiative of salvation rests exclusively with him. "God has mercy on no man in vain" (*To Simplicianus* 1.2,13).[11]

In short, God's decision whether to have mercy or to withhold it is absolutely and entirely his alone, unaffected by any independent predisposition or merit on man's part. But how can God make such determinations justly? At this point, Augustine turns to Paul's image of the divine potter and the human pots.

> You will say to me then, "Why then does God still find fault? For who can resist his will?" But who are you, O man, to answer back to God? Will the molded thing say to its molder, "Why have you made me like this?" Has the potter no right over the clay, to make out of the same lump [*consparsio*] one vessel for beauty and another for menial use? What if God, desiring to show his wrath and to make known his power, has endured with much patience

the vessels of wrath made for destruction, in order to make
known the riches of his glory for the vessels of mercy, which he
has prepared beforehand for glory, even us whom he has called,
not only from the Jews but also from the Gentiles?

ROMANS 9:19-24

The Latin term here for this lump of clay, the *consparsio* from
which God fashions humanity (Romans 9.21), had caught Augustine's
eye years before, in 394. At that point, he had associated the term with
man's condition *sub lege,* "under the Law," when man did not want to
sin but could not avoid it. Using *massa,* a synonym for *consparsio,* Augustine had then continued with a simile. "As long as you are a molded
thing, says Paul, and you are like this 'lump of clay' (*massa luti*) . . . it be-
hooves you . . . not to answer back to God" (*Notes on Romans* 62.19). In
other words, within this earlier commentary, the lump of clay (*massa
luti*) was a symbol. It stood for the carnal aspects of human moral character, man's earthly self, the "man of clay" (*homo luti*), which the believer had to renounce before he could investigate spiritual things
(*Notes on Romans* 62.17–23).

At some point shortly thereafter, in his next pass at Romans 9, the
lump of clay (*massa luti*) as his synonym for Paul's *consparsio* suddenly
became a "lump of sin" (*massa peccati*), and its significance became
more concrete, more historical, and more historicized. Invoking Adam
and fallen human nature (*natura nostra,* which "sinned in paradise"),
Augustine asserted that all humanity was formed from this same
lump of sin. Because of their origins in this sinful mass, people can
have no merit unless and until they turn from their earthly orientation. *Noli esse lutum:* literally, "do not want to be clay"; instead, become
children of God (*On Various Questions* 68.3). Still, Augustine had insisted then, when God does choose between people, even though all
humans originate from this single sinful mass, he does so on the basis of what they deserve (*meritis*), "for God's will cannot be unjust . . .
and there must be some differences between them." Such merits are
discernible, however, only to God. To other people, they are *occultissimi,*
"most hidden" (question 68.4).

Now, reviewing these verses again for Simplicianus, Augustine makes more extreme his own earlier appeal to the divine discernment of hidden merit in defense of God's justice. He returns here to his idea of the *massa peccati*. Because of the sin in the garden, he repeats, all humanity shares in Adam's offense against God and all are made from this same sinful clay. Everyone, he concludes, is born deserving only condemnation.

Nevertheless, Augustine insists, God's judgments are just—but *not* because God measures the differences in what people deserve (merits in both the negative and the positive sense), no matter how hidden these might be. (Previously, he had insisted that measuring merit was the only fair way to judge; *Notes on Romans* 60.8; also question 68.4, cited just above.) He now interprets the effects of humanity's origins in the *massa peccati* to mean that no one is capable of having any sort of positive merit whatsoever. God's justice has been preserved, rather, because in light of humanity's universal sinfulness, God has condemned absolutely everybody. "Sinful humanity must pay a debt of punishment to the supreme divine justice" (*To Simplicianus* 1.2,16). If God has condemned all humanity, and condemned all humanity rightly, argues Augustine (after all, everyone sinned "in Adam"), then no one can impute any unrighteousness to him. Indeed, the ubiquity of this condemnation displays God's rigorous fairness, his irreproachable justice. By leaving a man to his deserved condemnation, Augustine adds, God does not choose to do him harm; he simply declines to do him good (1.2,15–18).

Of course, then, God "hated" Esau—though not the man, Augustine explains carefully. God hates none of his creatures, "but he hates Esau the sinner" (*To Simplicianus* 1.2,18). Formed from the *massa peccati*, Esau was born condemned. Indeed, like all Adam's progeny, Esau was already condemned when still in the womb. In light of his new construction of the penalty for Adam's sin (universally and fairly imposed by God), Augustine has shifted the challenge to God's justice. The question is not, How is God just in condemning someone? Rather, in light of his scrupulously just condemnation of absolutely everybody, the question becomes, How is God righteous in *redeeming* anyone? How could God justly choose to show mercy to Jacob?

At this point, Augustine turns once again to Paul's image of the potter with his lump of clay. He understands this image as a historically descriptive metaphor for humanity's actual condition, the *massa peccati*, the "lump of sin." All humanity is shaped from this same single mass. But God is absolutely free to decide how to use this mass, shaping the clay of humanity to whatever vessels he wants, making some as vessels "of wrath" meant for destruction, some others as vessels "of mercy." God is the potter. He owes man no explanation. And if man does not like this, Augustine answers, quoting Paul, *"O homo tu quis es qui respondeas Deo?* Who are you, O man, to answer back to God?" (Romans 9:21; *To Simplicianus* I.2,18).

This same verse, defending the absoluteness of divine prerogative by alluding to Paul's image of the pot challenging the potter, had been invoked years earlier, in 392, in the course of Augustine's public debate with Fortunatus (see p. 150 above). There, however, it had been the Manichee who had quoted this passage. In a brief span of time, a mere four years, Augustine had thought himself into a position on the human condition and the problem of evil that was no less severe than Fortunatus' had been. And his appeal to Romans 9:20 in *To Simplicianus* signaled, as definitively as had Fortunatus' appeal to the same verse years earlier, that Augustine had run out of explanations in defense of his view of God. Man simply cannot understand God's justice, Augustine now insists. All he can do, if he would be pious, is aver (because God must be just) that God is just. Piety forbids him to question why God does what he does. Who is man anyway, that God should explain his reasons to him?

In the months between his answer in question 68 and his answer in *To Simplicianus*, a change had occurred in what Augustine was content to regard as unknowable. Earlier, he had held that human merits, whether positive or negative, were "most hidden" (*occultissimi*; question 68.4). Now, he emphasizes that divine justice, God's standard of fairness, is what is "most hidden" (*occultissima*) and furthest removed (*remotissima*) from human understanding:

"O man, who are you to answer back to God?" A man talks back to God when he is displeased that God finds fault with sinners, as if God compelled any man to sin when he simply does not bestow his justifying mercy on some sinners. For that reason, he is said to "harden" some sinners—not because he drives them to sin but because he does not have mercy upon them. God decides whom to withhold mercy from according to a standard of fairness which is most hidden and far removed from the power of human understanding. "Inscrutable are his judgments, and his ways past finding out" (Romans 11:33). He finds fault with sinners justly, because he does not compel them to sin. Justly also he has mercy on some.

TO SIMPLICIANUS 1.2,16

Augustine, in short, had abandoned any thought of understanding God, or of clearly perceiving God, as an exemplar of justice. God's justice could be affirmed only by faith.

✦✦✦

WHAT ACCOUNTS FOR this landslide in Augustine's thought? Scholars have proposed a number of causes, whether literary, environmental, or psychological. Perhaps some other commentary on Romans had radically reoriented Augustine's reading of Paul's letter. Or perhaps this great change was the cumulative effect of his own reading and rereading of Paul. Or perhaps the difficult working conditions of his new position in the church had worn him down. Or perhaps he had become disillusioned with the life that he thought he had won back in Milan: "Very possibly, it could not bear the terrific weight of his own expectations of it."[12]

A certain *tristesse* lingers over many of these reconstructions. And indeed it is very difficult for most modern Western readers to look at Augustine's new understanding of Paul without seeing in it some sort of register of despair. Standing as we do to this side of the eighteenth century, our cultural instincts have largely been formed and nurtured by the presumptions of Renaissance humanism and of Enlightenment moral autonomy. A theology that insists that humans are completely (and "justly"!) powerless; that wholeness totally depends upon factors absolutely beyond one's own influence, much less control;

that God is endlessly punitive and in all cases morally opaque: Such a theology can seem to us to inventory nothing other than the loss of hope, the profound disillusionment, the growing melancholy of the theologian.

The sheer energy and self-confidence that mark Augustine's life and work in the period immediately following his formulation of this new reading of Paul, however, overwhelm any diagnosis of discouragement or despondency that the conclusion of *To Simplicianus* can so easily prompt. If Augustine's creativity and productivity may be taken as evidence of his morale, then he was at his most tentative and insecure during the *earlier,* "optimistic" phase of his priesthood, when he still argued in defense of man's moral freedom and God's ethical transparency. Abandoned commentaries, unfinished treatises, postponed books, transcripts of private lectures, small essays: It did not add up to much. Only *after* 396 did he become the man—and the author—whom Western culture knows as Augustine.

The period of his early priesthood had marked out a six-year-long Jabbok for Augustine, a time when he wrestled with powerful angels: the texts of his Bible; his view of the relation between the testaments; his post-Manichaean, post-Milanese beliefs about divine justice and human freedom; his understanding—affected deeply by his study of pagan Neoplatonists—of the ways that time relates to eternity, that history relates to scripture, and that the human being (mind, soul, and body) relates to God. With astounding courage and sheer acuity, he rethought absolutely everything that he had come into this phase of his life with. Even those earlier convictions that he did keep were transformed by the new perspective that he finally achieved in the early years of his episcopacy.

Small wonder, then, that Augustine limped through this period of his early priesthood. But unlike the biblical Jacob (Genesis 32), he did not limp thereafter. On the contrary: *To Simplicianus* marked the beginning of a lifetime of sustained and self-confident creativity. The astonishing and astonishingly original *Confessions* (c. 397–401). Thirty-three authoritative books against Latin Manichaeism, *Against Faustus* (a *grande opus,* as he called it; c. 398–400). A master work on the strength of which alone he would have been established as one of the greatest Latin fathers, *Literal Interpretation of Genesis* (c. 401–414). *On the Trinity,* yet another master work (c. 399–419). And crowning it all, his *magnum opus et arduum,* "a huge and difficult work," *City of God* (c. 413–427). Add to this an enormous body of sermons, letters, and lesser treatises. Five million words in all, only a fraction of which written before 396. This productivity was the equivalent, one of Augustine's biographers has calculated, of publishing a modern three-hundred-page print book every year for forty years.[13]

A straightforward construction of divine justice and of human freedom both fall victim to Augustine's agitated dialectic in *To Simplicianus.* But we will miss what Augustine has accomplished if we allow the gloom that can settle over us as we read his conclusion in that work to shape our historical understanding of Augustine's life and thought at this transitional moment. What happened by 396 was that Augustine had finally found a way to understand his Bible coherently. Exegetically in his response to Simplicianus, philosophically and (in a sense) autobiographically in the great masterpiece that followed, his *Confessions,* Augustine resolved a foundational dilemma of ancient biblical theology. He brought the timeless, unchanging high god of philosophical paideia and the active, engaged chief personality of the Jewish Bible together into a single coherent whole. And the actions within time of this timeless god, he insisted, were always just, whether humans understood his justice or not: This conviction constituted *fides,* "faith." By the first years of his episcopacy, in other words, Augustine had achieved a new understanding of God. That idea nourished him for the rest of his life.

Understanding God and understanding how to read the Bible was for Augustine one and the same project. To grasp his theology, we need to grasp his interpretations of scripture. The trajectory of his earlier work through Genesis and through Paul was oriented by his effort to conceive of a way to read scripture *ad litteram,* "according to its 'historical' character," *quam littera sonat,* plainly, "according to just what the words say" (as he wrote back in 388–389; *On Genesis, against the Manichees* 2.2,3; we will consider what he meant by this shortly). He finally began to achieve this new understanding in part by thinking specifically about Paul—not only the Paul of Pauline theology, the champion of grace, but also the Paul of salvation history, the embodiment of dramatic conversion, the man singularly chosen by God to effect history's transition from *sub lege* to *sub gratia*. Paul the persecutor. Paul the convert. Paul the apostle to the Gentiles. And most surprising (as we shall see), Paul the Jew, who valued the Law and kept it according to Jewish tradition not only before his conversion but also thereafter. Paul *ad litteram*.

How did Augustine find this Paul? The scriptural canon helped him. As a late-fourth-century catholic bishop, Augustine had many more sources to draw on when constructing his picture of the historical Paul than most academic historians do now. Modern critical scholarship on New Testament texts has identified only seven letters as indisputably Pauline: 1 Thessalonians, Philemon, Philippians, 1 and 2 Corinthians, Galatians, and Romans. Scholars contest the status of 2 Thessalonians, of Ephesians, and of Colossians. (I number among those who think that these letters, which read like sermons, were written by later followers of Paul, not by Paul himself.) Firm consensus sees 1 and 2 Timothy and Titus (the so-called pastoral epistles) as later, pseudonymous writings in an evolving Pauline tradition. Paul's authorship of Hebrews was challenged already in antiquity; again, modern consensus regards it as an anonymous Christian sermon, not as a genuine letter of Paul's. As for Acts, its chronology conflicts with that of Paul's own letters, and its biographical details about Paul often sit uncomfortably with what autobiographical information we have from Paul himself. Historians use Acts for Paul with caution.[14]

Spared the educational advantages of modern scholars, Augustine could and did use all of this material when constructing the Paul of late Latin theological tradition, whom he naturally assumed to be the Paul of history as well. Thus, in the 390s, we see him beginning to think about Paul's life as well as about Paul's work, to think with Paul's biography as well as with Paul's theology. His view of the one intimately informs his interpretation of the other. And his new ways of thinking about and with Paul in turn inform both his maturing approach to the Bible more generally and (as we will shortly see) his novel ideas on Torah, Jews, and Judaism in particular.

Controversy always sharpened Augustine's thinking. His recurring engagement with the Manichees over Genesis and especially over Paul had led directly to his interpretive breakthrough when reading Romans in 396. Another controversy, unfolding in this same period but with a quite different sparring partner, also clarified his thinking on these larger issues of biblical narrative and its historical *proprietas*. This time, his antagonist was not a Manichee but a fellow catholic, the formidable Jerome; the contested Pauline text not Romans but Galatians; the contested theological question not the justice of God but the historical reliability of scripture.

In the second chapter of his letter to the Galatian churches, Paul famously described two earlier moments of controversy involving gentile believers: a plenum meeting in Jerusalem to discuss whether gentile Christians should convert to Judaism (Galatians 2:1-10) and a later falling-out in Antioch between Peter and Paul over Jewish and gentile Christians' eating together (Galations 2:11-14). Centuries later, orthodox commentators struggled to make sense of the second episode. Their presumption that Jesus himself had taught against Judaism made their task more difficult. How could Peter, who had followed Jesus during his lifetime and thus heard him repudiate Jewish practices (so went the orthodox understanding) possibly be concerned decades later about a point of Jewish Law? The great Origen in the early third century framed an elegant answer, which Jerome in the following century appropriated for his own comments on Galatians. Of course Peter knew that Christ had overthrown the Law, this interpretive tradition urged. The argument with Paul had actually been a pretense enacted for the edification of their audience. Consequently, both Paul's rebuke to Peter and Paul's later report of this rebuke in Galatians were feigned as well.[15]

Working on his own Pauline commentaries in 394-395, Augustine had written to the elder Jerome appealing for translations of Greek patristic authorities. In the same communication, however, he signaled his disapproval of Jerome's understanding of Galatians 2 (*Letter* 28.3, 3-5). To ascribe this sort of polite deceit to scripture, Augustine protested, would only undermine its authority. And to undermine the authority of scripture would open the door to

Manichaean claims that these biblical texts were corrupt. Reiterating his view in a sermon from the same period, Augustine emphasized his main interpretive point: Paul's text must be read straightforwardly, as the accurate report of a true disagreement. "Otherwise," as he later continued to Jerome, "the Holy Scripture, which has been given to preserve the faith of generations to come, would be wholly undermined and thrown into doubt, if the validity of lying were once admitted" (*Letter* 40.4,5).[16]

This issue of the historical and moral integrity of scripture informs Augustine's approach to the fourth-century Pauline canon as well. He uses these texts not only to construct his four-stage model of salvation history, but also to *reconstruct* the historical Paul, both preconversion and postconversion. From his brief works on Romans and Galatians in 394–395 through to the *Ad Simplicianum* in 396, Augustine had continuously regarded Paul as a premier historical example of how God moves a person from *sub lege* to *sub gratia*. For him, Paul's biography modeled Christian conversion, while Paul's theology articulated its principles. Augustine's views on Paul's life affected his view on Paul's "work"—that is, on Paul's teachings on grace, free will, and divine justice, as Augustine understood them—and his views on Paul's work affected his idea of Paul's life. When these views shift, they shift in tandem.

It is his view of the historical Paul that finally defeats Augustine's earlier ideas on free will, grace, and conversion. Paul's personal history as Augustine began to imagine it could not accommodate Augustine's earlier understanding of how the saved individual moves from "under the Law" to "under grace." The Paul of canonical tradition, Augustine noted, described his former self as a blasphemer and a persecutor (1 Timothy 1:13), a foolish, impious, and hateful man enslaved to various pleasures (Titus 3:3; *Unfinished Commentary on Romans* 21.6), and as a zealous, violent Pharisee (1 Corinthians 15:9; Galatians 1:13; *Commentary on Galatians* 7.1-4). Augustine further enriched Paul's "first-person" depiction with the before-and-after portraiture of Acts, wherein Paul looms large both as a recalcitrant persecutor before his conversion and as a committed apostle thereafter (Acts 8:3; 9:1-4; *Unfinished Commentary on Romans* 15.5-6; question 66.6).[17]

In *Notes on Romans,* Augustine had argued that the sinner's transition from Law to grace depended upon God's foreknowledge of the individual's good will—that is, of the person's desire, while still a sinner, to call on Christ for help to stop sinning. This good will was the autonomous attribute of the individual, foreknown by God. But the more that Augustine thought *ad litteram* with the New Testament's traditions about Paul's preconversion self—including what he took to be Paul's own remarks about his preconversion self—the less his "historical Paul" obliged Augustine's earlier model. No New Testament text gave Augustine reason to think that at any point prior to his transformation on his way to Damascus, Saul had called on Christ for help (cf. *Notes on Romans* 61–62). On the contrary: A ruthless persecutor and, indeed, a murderer, Saul had liked his work (Acts 8:3; 9:1–4). Yet God—mysteriously, ineluctably, even violently—had redeemed Saul from the error of his ways, without Saul's having done the least thing to deserve such redemption, indeed without Saul's having evinced a scintilla of desire to be so redeemed.

Thus, at the finale of book one of his response to Simplicianus, Augustine dramatically closed his exhausting examination of the dynamics of will and grace by invoking Paul at the very moment of his conversion.

> What did Saul want but to attack, seize, blind and slay Christians? What a fierce, savage, blind will was that! Yet he was thrown prostrate by one word from on high, and a vision came to him whereby his mind and will were turned from their fierceness and set on the right way towards faith so that, suddenly, from a marvelous persecutor of the Gospel a more marvelous preacher was made. What then shall we say? . . . "Is there unrighteousness with God? God forbid!"
>
> ROMANS 9:16; *TO SIMPLICIANUS* 1.2,22

In terms of any kind of foregoing merit, Saul's redemption was inexplicable. Obdurate, violent, proud, he had done nothing to deserve God's mercy. Yet God had called him anyway. For Augustine, then, Saul was a premier historical illustration of God's sovereign will, an irreducible example of the absolute freedom of the divine pre-rogative. What else could Paul (and Augustine) do but offer humble praise for God's graciousness in the face of his divine inscrutability? "For his judgments are unsearchable, and his ways past finding out" (Romans 11:33; *To Simplicianus* 1.2,22).

*Who but you, O God, have spread over us a canopy of
authority in your divine scriptures? For "the sky will be
rolled up like a scroll" which is now "stretched over us
like a skin [parchment] covering" (Isaiah 34:4; Psalm
103.2). Your divine scriptures have a more exalted
authority now that the mortals through whom you
dispensed them have met their mortal end. You know,
Lord, you know how you clothed human beings with
skins when by their sin they became mortal (Genesis
3:21). So too did you give us the canopy of your scriptures to serve "like a skin covering," all your words
fitted together in agreement to give us shelter.*

AUGUSTINE, *CONFESSIONS* 13.15,16

Paul's letters and Acts had provided Augustine with key components of his new vision of salvation history in 396. Around this same
time, while working on these ideas about the correspondence between
scriptural texts, historical events, and biblical interpretation, Augustine also began working at a more fundamental level on the correspondence between language and meaning. Inspired in part by the
Book of Rules, Tyconius' handbook of scriptural exegesis, Augustine
embarked on his own guide to the interpretation of the Bible. His formal education as a master of rhetoric gave him command of all manner of theories and rules and verbal sensitivities and techniques of
argumentation and interpretation when approaching or creating a
text. In *De doctrina Christiana,* or *Christian Teaching,* Augustine applied
this vast erudition to the task of reading God's book.[1]

The very fact of human language, Augustine had long held, was
charged with religious significance. The ways that he thought about

language were bound up with his vision of history and with his views on the theological meaning of man's existence in time. Back in 388–389, commenting on Genesis, Augustine had attributed the complexities and rigors of communication to the first sin. Man's current dependence on language, and the sheer difficulty of finding meaning in and through ambiguous signs—whether those signs be events, numbers, the spoken word, or even the text of scripture itself—were both the symptom and the consequence of the great sin that marked the beginning of history. Interpretation and its attendant difficulties witnessed to the price paid by the entire species for the fall (*Genesis against the Manichees* 2.4,5–5,6). From that point onward, meaning could only be mediated. When God cast Adam from Eden, he exiled him into the dislocated consciousness caused by living in time.[2]

Reflecting formally in *Christian Teaching* on the problem of interpretation—the consequence of mediated meaning—Augustine focused more precisely on an immediate source of these difficulties: the problem of distinguishing between different kinds of signs (*signa*; singular *signum*). Signs are indicators that refer to things other than themselves. Some signs are natural, with no intentionality. ("Where there's smoke"—a natural sign, lacking intention—"there's fire.") But the signs that matter for the rhetorician are *signa data*, "given" or "intentional" signs, of which the premier example is human language. Intention informs human speech; understanding language requires interpretation. And linguistic signs themselves fall into two categories: signs that point to specific things or to an immediate interpretive context (*signa propria*, "proper" or "self-referring" or "literal" signs), and signs that refer to things or ideas outside of their immediate context to something else (*signa translata*, "referred-away" or metaphorical signs).

At issue between these two sorts of *signa* is their interpretive points of reference. *Signa propria* are, in a sense, reflexive. The key to interpreting them properly is found within the context that they occupy. If such a sign occurs in a biblical story, this means that the key to understanding it lies within that same story. And, since the Bible often narrates accounts of things that occurred in the past (*secundum historicam*), then understanding that story *ad litteram* or *secundum historicam proprietatis* means that its interpretive frame of reference must also lie "in the past."

A single word in a passage can function both ways, as Augustine illustrates with a passage from 1 Corinthians 9:4–9. Paul wrote:

> Do we not have the right to our food and drink? . . . Who serves as a soldier at his own expense? Who plants a vineyard without eating of its fruit? . . . Do I say this on human authority? Does not the Law say the same? For it is written in the Law of Moses, "You shall not muzzle an ox when it treads out the grain" [Deuteronomy 25:4].

Paul in this passage had argued that the Christian community should support the person who worked to bring them the gospel (see p. 58 above). To clinch his argument, he cited a law from the last of the Five Books of Moses, Deuteronomy, on how to treat animals. "Is it for oxen that God is concerned?" (1 Corinthians 9:10). The person who understood *ox* as a *signum proprium* within the context of Deuteronomy would think, "Well, yes." A person with spiritual insight, however, would realize that in this instance *ox* also functioned as a *signum translatum,* referring away from the sign *ox* to the apostle (*Christian Teaching* 2.10,15).

The Bible is a special instance of *signa data* because of its unique double authorship: the timeless, eternal God who is its source and the historically and linguistically contingent humans who were its medium (*Christian Teaching* 2.2,3). To this constitutive complexity of scripture the widely variable quality of biblical translations and manuscripts add yet more layers of interpretive difficulty. And infinitely compounding all of these problems is the Bible's literary style itself. Its seeming simplicity concealed rich profundities; mysteries lay encoded in images, figures, and especially in numbers. Nothing was superfluous; everything needed to be understood. But how?[3]

Augustine took as his interpretive North Star the double injunction in scripture to love God and neighbor (cf. Matthew 22:36–40). "Scripture enjoins nothing but love (*caritas*), and censures nothing but lust (*cupiditas*). . . . By 'love' I mean the impulse of one's mind to enjoy God on his own account and to enjoy oneself and one's neighbor on account of God" (*Christian Teaching* 3.10,16; Augustine had introduced this idea back in 1.33,37). Such an orientation, he insists, ensures that the reader will interpret according to the received teaching of the church ("for [scripture] asserts nothing except the catholic faith, in time past, time present, and future"). And such an orientation aids the reader in discerning whether to interpret an ambiguous *signum* figuratively (that is, in a metaphorical sense, as referring to something other than itself) or specifically (*proprie*, meaning within the time frame of the biblical story itself, thus "historically"; 3.10,14).

Correct discernment of ambiguous signs is crucially important because of the twin dangers in scriptural interpretation: understanding figurative expressions literally, and understanding literal expressions figuratively (*Christian Teaching* 3.10,14).

The Jews, said Augustine, particularly err in the first way, understanding metaphorical phrases *ad litteram* and so attending solely to the "carnal" or this-worldly aspects of biblical *signa*. Jews thus interpret the Sabbath—a *signum translatum* actually directing the understanding mind toward those "higher" realities revealed in and through Christ—as if it were a *signum proprium,* a sign pointing exclusively to a self-referring meaning (that is, to the this-worldly Sabbath rest, one day out of seven). Accordingly, Jews fail to "raise the mind's eye above physical creation in order to absorb eternal light," and so remain confined by their "fleshly" practices and impoverished understanding in "a miserable kind of spiritual servitude" (*Christian Teaching* 3.5,9).

So far, Augustine has said nothing about Jewish readings of scripture and about Jewish religious practices that had not been said during the preceding centuries of the evolving *adversus Iudaeos* tradition. His next statements thus mark an interesting departure. Turning from this familiar critique, he suddenly offers a novel endorsement. "The form that this slavery took in the Jewish people," Augustine continues, "was very different from the experience of other nations" (*Christian Teaching* 3.6,10). Most Jews may have missed the spiritual meaning (that is, the Christian meaning) of their own tradition, mistaking scripture's *signa translata* for *signa propria;* but even in this enslavement they directed their worship to the one true God, who was the author and source of these precepts. Thus by "doing" the Law, despite not understanding its higher meanings, the Jews conformed to the divine will. The Jews were the only nation before the coming of Christ to worship the true God without resorting to images.

The Law, enacted in this way, served the Jews in the way that a pedagogue serves young children, usefully directing them through discipline so that they get to school. Thus those Jews of Jesus' generation who joined the earliest apostolic community in Jerusalem, precisely because of their former life of slavery under the Law, were already "close to being spiritual." Habituated by Jewish religious practices, they were propelled to great spiritual heights once they believed. Selling all of their possessions and giving the proceeds to the apostles, they dedicated themselves wholly to God (Acts 4:32–35; *Christian Teaching* 3.6,10). No gentile church of this first generation attained a spiritual level as lofty as the church of Jerusalem did, Augustine continues, precisely because the Gentiles lacked what the Jews uniquely had, namely, God's Law.[4]

The "signs" to which Jews were enslaved—that is, the precepts of the Law, mediated by the Bible—were "useful" because authored by God himself. But the Gentiles before the coming of Christ were slaves to "useless signs" of which they themselves were author. Slavery to the divinely authored Law led to true worship of the true god; slavery to signs of human authorship, to "the pollution of a horde of fictitious gods" (*Christian Teaching* 3.8,12). Nor were all Jews who lived according to the Law slaves to the Law. Those who were "spiritual" among them, despite living in the era of slavery before Christ came, were free. These people—the patriarchs, the prophets, and others—had indeed lived the Law according to Jewish practice; but they also glimpsed its higher significance. In consequence, it was through these people—and thus uniquely through Israel—that the Holy Spirit gave to humanity the support and comfort of the scriptures (3.9,13).[5]

This mention of the patriarchs moves Augustine to emphasize the importance of considering context, both cultural and historical (even as a modern reader would identify such terms), when construing scripture.

> People generally regard as culpable only such actions as men of
> their own time and place tend to blame and condemn, and they
> regard as commendable and praiseworthy only such actions as are

acceptable within the conventions of their own society. And so
it happens that if Scripture enjoins something that varies from
the practices of its readers, or if it censures something that their
practice does not, they consider the passage to have a figurative
meaning. . . . We must pay careful attention to the conduct appropriate to different places, times, and persons, lest we make rash
imputations of wickedness.

CHRISTIAN TEACHING 3.10,15–12,20

Surveying the wide variety of social practices, which alter di-
achronically within the same culture (he gives the example of changes
in Roman dress) and synchronically across different ethnic groups
(*gentes*), Augustine distinguishes between culture-specific custom and
timeless moral instruction. In the latter category fall such teachings
as, "Do not do to another what you would not wish to be done to yourself" (Tobit 4:16). He then turns to the moral instruction offered by
time-bound exemplars, the patriarchs and the other heroes, such as
David and Solomon, presented in the Old Testament. Despite multiple marriages, he claims, the patriarchs of old practiced chastity,
"looking only to the procreation of children in the sexual act" (*Christian Teaching* 3.18,27). The husbands in Corinth, to whom Paul permitted marital intercourse as a curb to lust, evidently could not be chaste
with a single wife (1 Corinthians 7:2). And when scripture relates "the
sins of great men," it is to denounce them, not to endorse them.
Therefore, concludes Augustine, "even if it is possible to observe or
trace a prefiguration of future events in them, one should nevertheless
take up the literal meaning of their deeds," reflecting humbly on one's
own sins in contemplating theirs (*Christian Teaching* 3.23,33). Neither
ethical awkwardness nor figurative significance should deflect the in-
terpreter from the effort to read such passages as historically descriptive as well.

Without due consideration of historical context and of "specific"
meaning (*proprietas*), Augustine concludes, the *signa* of scripture will be
misconstrued. This interpretive point in defense of the morals and
mores of Old Testament heroes leaves him poised to argue against one
of the Manichees' traditional criticisms of the catholic canon. Some of
their most effective polemic targeted the behavior of Old Testament

patriarchs and kings, whose many marriages offended their ascetic sensibilities. (On the evidence of the young Augustine, the sensibilities of thinking catholic Christians were offended as well; *Confessions* 3.7,12–13.)

Instead, surprisingly, Augustine broke off *Christian Teaching* at this point, about halfway through book three. It lay fallow for almost three decades. Augustine recovered his unfinished work only as he was arranging and commenting on his own writings in the last years of his life (c. 426–427; *Retractations* 2.4,1). At that point, he finally completed book three and added book four, picking up composition where he had left off, on knowing when to read for literal or figurative meanings. Perhaps in 396, on the cusp of an energetic campaign against the Donatist churches, his dependence here on the handbook of the Donatist Tyconius made continuing this project too awkward. (Once he resumed book three in 426, he moved explicitly into a lengthy consideration of Tyconius' *Book of Rules*. By then, however, the Donatists had been safely outmaneuvered.) Or perhaps his attention and energy were absorbed by the ambitious preaching program in the spring and summer of 397 that he undertook in Carthage.[6]

Whatever his immediate reason for leaving *Christian Teaching* to one side, Augustine went on over the course of the next few years to develop his new interpretive insights into texts and time and his new theological insights into divine justice and human freedom in two very different but related writings. The later and longer work was his *Against Faustus* (c. 398–400). Unfurling in thirty-three books, this treatise was at once a massive refutation of Latin Manichaeism and at the same time an utterly novel defense of the religious legitimacy of Judaism. We will look at *Against Faustus* closely and at length very shortly.

The earlier and greater work—arguably the greatest book that Augustine ever produced, and certainly one of the masterpieces of Western letters—was the *Confessions*.

♦♦♦

THE *CONFESSIONS* APPEARS like a starburst in the late 390s. A brilliant and profoundly original work of creative theology, its thirteen books combine biblical interpretation, late Platonism, and anti-Manichaean polemic with haunting autobiographical meditation. This examination of his past life, which begins in book one and shapes Augustine's narrative through the close of book nine, is the stylistic hallmark of the *Confessions*. It is what makes the *Confessions* so unusual in its own period, so perduringly valuable to Augustine's later biographers, and so seemingly accessible to his modern readers.

In the works on Paul that had absorbed him in the several years immediately preceding the *Confessions,* Augustine had constructed an idea of conversion as a clear and precise movement from "under the Law" (*sub lege*) to "under grace" (*sub gratia*). Unlike the more traditional seven-stage model of salvation history and of personal growth, in which the transition seemed more gradual and the stages more evolutionary, Augustine's four-stage model, linked now to Paul's letters, presented salvation with dramatic precision. The coming of Christ stood at the center of world history, abruptly defining the change from Law to grace; and the same dramatic transition shaped an individual life, marking the measure of personal redemption (see p. 165 above). Further, laboring again to interpret Romans 9 through 11 in his tortuous response to Simplicianus, Augustine had made this charged moment, the turning of the will to God by God, definitive both of Paul's own conversion and of Paul's theology itself. Small surprise then that the story of his own life in the *Confessions*—assembled with constant reference to Paul—seems dramatically driven toward the narrative crescendo of his own conversion, unforgettably described in book eight.[7]

Reading Augustine's *Confessions* this way—that is, as primarily a story about his own conversion—in turn highlights a strong theme in its first seven books. These become the discordant overture to book eight's final, soaring harmonies. Augustine's past life emerges as a tale of missteps and false starts, a sequence of erroneous conversions initiated, most often, by powerful encounters with books. Virgil's *Aeneid* charges the child Augustine's imagination, but his growing mastery of classical literature only sweeps him into the "torrents of human custom" (*Confessions* 1.16,25). The young Augustine, in Carthage, then dedicates himself to the quest for wisdom, precipitated by his powerful encounter with Cicero's *Hortensius*. This resolve propels him first to the Bible (which he, "swollen with pride," finds intolerably crude; 3.5,9), and then to the Manichees (who never let him near their own books, and who lie to him, he says in retrospect, about the books of the church; 3.6,10–11). Star charts and horoscopes lead him toward astrology (4.3,4; cf. 5.3,6–5,9); the writings of the New Academy, to the edge of philosophical skepticism (5.14,25). Finally, the books of the Platonists (7.9,13), together with his rereading of Paul's letters (7.21,27), liberate him from his captivity to Manichaean materialism. By the end of book seven, Augustine's intellectual conversion is complete. However, despite his new convictions, he still lingers as a catechumen. The problem with proceeding to baptism, says Augustine, was his sexual need (8.1,2).

Successive waves of conversion stories, each bearing a message of heroic renunciation, now break over Augustine. First, Simplicianus relates how the great Roman orator Marius Victorinus, relinquishing his pride, came to baptism. (Augustine "burns to follow" his example, *Confessions* 8:2,3–5,10). Next, his friend Ponticianus speaks to him about Saint Anthony's call to the Egyptian desert and about a community of male celibates directed by Ambrose who live just outside Milan (8.6,14). Finally, Ponticianus relates his personal knowledge of two affianced couples in Trier who resolved to quit the world and, committing themselves to celibacy, dedicate their lives to God (8.6,15).

Augustine's wrenching self-portrait of inner conflict dominates the rest of book eight. He finds himself trapped by the memory of his former delights. Those pleasures that he had once loved—though he wants to love them no longer—had forged a chain of habit in his soul, binding his will to its own disorder. Panting, weeping, throwing himself prostrate, Augustine agonizes over his own indecision, his divided will, the paralyzing paradox of wanting and not wanting the same thing at the same time. "I prayed in my great unworthiness, *da mihi castitatem et continentiam domine sed noli modo:* grant me chastity and continence, O Lord; but not yet" (*Confessions* 8.7,17). Back in 388, two years after he had resolved to join the church, Augustine had written that one could attain the righteous life "with perfect ease," since to do so required merely an act of will (*Free Will* 1.13,29, quoted on p. 171 above). Now, speaking of the moral torque caused by the divergence between thinking and loving, between knowing and wanting, his new view of the will is much more complex. What moves people, thought Augustine in the late 390s, is not what they know but what they want. Accordingly, he presents his conversion of 386 in new perspective:

> Many years had flowed by—a dozen or more—since I at nineteen had read Cicero's *Hortensius* . . . and yet still I was postponing giving up this world's happiness. . . . I was frantic in mind, in a frenzy of indignation at myself for not going over to your Law and to your covenant, O my God, where all my bones cried out that I should be. . . . The way was not by ship or by chariot or by foot; it was not as far as I had gone when I went from the house to the place where we now sat. For I had only had to will to go in order not merely to go, but also to arrive; I had only to will to go— but powerfully and whole-heartedly, not turning and twisting a half-wounded will this way and that. . . . What is the source of this monstrousness? Where is its root? Might the answer not lie in the mysterious punishment that has come upon all humanity, the deep hidden damage within the children of Adam?
>
> CONFESSIONS 8.7,17–9,21

Suddenly, the chanting of an unknown child reaches the irresolute, exhausted Augustine. *Tolle, lege:* "Pick up and read!" Remembering the story of Anthony, how he had been called to the desert by his chance hearing of Matthew's gospel ("Go, sell all you have, give to the poor . . . and come, follow me"; Matthew 19:21), Augustine decides that this voice, too, is a divine command. He snatches up the book that he had left lying in the garden, a volume of Paul's letters, and lets his eye fall on whatever verse awaits him on the opened page. "Not in rioting and drunkenness," Romans 13:13–14 instructs him, "not in chambering and wantonness, not in strife and rivalries; but put on the Lord Jesus Christ and make no provision for the flesh and its desires." "I neither wished nor needed to read further," Augustine concludes. "At once . . . a light of relief from all anxiety flooded my heart, and all the shadows of doubt disappeared." His way clear, his resolve firm, he confidently gives himself over to his new future (*Confessions* 8.12,29–30).

If only Augustine had ended the *Confessions* on this note! The rising action of its first seven books could stand as the kinetic buildup to the emotionally extravagant climax in book eight. And its following book, which relates Augustine's baptism, a religious vision that he shared with his mother, and Monnica's death, could then close the whole as its decorous diminuendo.

But instead, Augustine continued. Once book nine concludes the narrative section of the *Confessions,* fully 40 percent of its eighty thousand words still remain. Augustine abruptly shifts his focus from his past (c. 387, when the "autobiographical" section ends in Italy) to his present (c. 397, when the bishop of Hippo mediates on the question of how to know God). Book ten contemplates memory; book eleven, the nature of time; book twelve, spiritual and material creation; book thirteen, revelation, redemption, eternity. These incandescent final books retrospectively alter any simple reading of the earlier, narrative ones. The problem with regarding the *Confessions* primarily as autobiography, then, is the way that such a reading risks losing a view of the work as a whole. When Augustine wrote his masterpiece, he clearly had more than an exploration of his personal past in mind.

Augustine himself saw the *Confessions* as falling into two uneven halves: the first ten books (including the tenth, on the nature of memory) oriented around himself (*"de me"*), the last three around Genesis 1:1 ("In the beginning God created the heavens and the earth"; *Retractations* 2.6,1). Throughout, he interwove biblical fragments and images from Genesis, Paul, and especially Psalms together with allusions to the works of the pagan Neoplatonists Plotinus and Porphyry. And he cast the whole in the form of a prayer to the omniscient god who already knew everything that Augustine relates to him. (Within the conceit of this presentation, the reader is only obliquely involved.) Whatever else it is, then—elegiac, intricate, acute, intense—the *Confessions* is also very odd. Both the structure and the content of this book frustrate any single attempt to define it.

However, renouncing the temptation to psychologize the *Confessions* as Augustine's "true confessions"—that is, as an intimate narration of his personal past, a candid review of former sins and current regrets—is surely a step in the right direction. To do so is not easy, given modern fashions of reading. And Augustine's persistent recourse to a rich vocabulary of (especially sexual) transgression—earthly yearnings (*concupiscentia carnalis*), shameful lusts (*flagitia*), illicit congress (*fornicatio*), passionate desire (*appetitus, libido*), sin (*peccatum*), sin (*facinus*), sin (*iniquitas*)—feeds a prurient modern preoccupation. (Let the reader beware: *Fornicatio* is also how Augustine categorized his theft of pears at the age of twelve; *Confessions* 2.6,14.) It might help to remember too, despite the habitual locution "Augustine wrote," that Augustine did not "write." The thoughts that seem to throb across the centuries did not pour out of him and onto the page in a torrent of tormented introspection during some dark night of the soul. Augustine performed the *Confessions,* declaiming its beautiful phrasing always in the presence of at least one or two other people, the skilled *notarii* taking shorthand dictation. What moderns take to be intimate self-portraiture is often the product of their own presentism, overstimulated by Augustine's rhetorical artistry.

Reading the *Confessions* as autobiography leaves too much of it unaccounted for. We cannot get a satisfactory answer to the question, "What are the last four books doing here?" But there is a single constant focus. One unique character figures prominently in all thirteen of these books, and his textual presence unites the whole: the god of the Bible. If we see the *Confessions* not as religious autobiography but as very original theology, if we turn our attention away from Augustine and toward his ideas about God, we can allow its coherence to emerge. Such a reading enables an answer to the old interpretive question, which then gets turned on its head. The question to the *Confessions* is no longer: Why, when presenting his introspective autobiography, did Augustine write the last four books as he did? but rather: Why, when presenting his views on God, did Augustine write the first nine books at all?

◆ ◆ ◆

IN THE PERIOD since his sudden ordination in 391, and more specifically since his public debate with Fortunatus in 392, Augustine had struggled to frame his ideas on God, creation, and the process of redemption through his reading of the Bible. By 396–397, his efforts had led him to three insights that particularly concern us here. First, he saw that understanding scripture required not only a "spiritual" reading (that is, one that grasped the manifold meanings available through enigmas, types, numbers, and other symbols) but also a "literal" or "historical" reading (one that took the past described in the text as an important interpretive context—in his own terms, a reading *ad litteram* and *proprie*). Second, Augustine understood Paul's personal history as illumining and articulating a Pauline theology of grace. And third, he held that the difficulties attendant on interpretation of all sorts, in secular matters no less than sacred ones, define fallen humanity's condition in time. These three convictions converge in Augustine's *Confessions*. They set its central inquiry: How can fallen man know God?

This is the question that opens Augustine's book. The problem is itself paradoxical: How can you look for something unless you already know what you're looking for? So too Augustine asks how to call on God in order to know him if he is calling on God in order to know him. "Grant me, Lord, to know and to understand which comes first, to call upon you or to praise you? And does knowing you precede calling upon you? But who calls on you who does not know you?" (*Confessions* 1.1,1). When he moves from the retrospect of books one through nine into the present, Augustine uses this question to frame his inquiry into mind and memory (two key components of the search). Thus book ten opens with a prayer to God: "Let me know you, You who know me. Let me know you even as I am known" (*Confessions* 10.1,1); and it closes with a line from Psalm 21: "They shall praise the Lord who seek him" (10.43,70).

By the end of book thirteen, the answers to Augustine's petition have accumulated. God has provided humanity with many means of knowing him: physical creation (*Confessions* 13.28,43; 33,48); scripture (13.15,16; 29, 44; 34,48); the church (13.23,33; 34,48); his divine Son, "who is the mediator between You the One and us the many" (11.29,39, with deliberate reference to the Platonic contrast). But it is especially the mind itself, which in the beginning God made according to his own image and likeness, that provides a royal road back to God (Genesis 1:26-27; cf. *Confessions* 13.34,49). By turning inward—the clarion call of late Platonism—a person can find God because God is there, "deeper in me than I am in me" (3.6,11).[8]

God is within the self. Why, then, is knowing God, finding God so difficult? Augustine answers that sin has ruptured the human self and thus, also, the relationship between the self and God. For the human race, and thus for each individual person, sin has torn apart the soul by rupturing how it loves, tearing apart will and affect, thought and feeling. (This is the topic particularly explored, in a sense demonstrated, in books one through nine, Augustine's historical narration of his own divided self.) And sin has ruptured the relationship between the individual and God by plunging the person into the dislocated dimension of time. The human experience of time, Augustine explains, delineates the crucial differences between the human mind, which is God's image in man, and God himself.

God is outside of time. He knows everything perfectly and (an aspect of this quality of knowing) he knows everything all at once, in "the simultaneity of eternity" (*Confessions* 13.7,9). Further, no gap whatever divides divine knowing from divine willing and divine doing. This divine seamlessness of thought, will, and deed accounts for the way that God created the world without compromising his unchangeable perfection. Everything, including time itself, "occurred" simultaneously. Before creation there was no "time"; therefore, strictly speaking, there is no "before creation." With astonishingly few arguments and with an amazing ease of reference—Genesis to Plotinus and back again—Augustine neatly dispatched one of the defining difficulties of biblical theology. The timeless, changeless deity of philosophical paideia and the engaged, active deity of biblical narrative have, in his formulation, truly made their peace with each other, and melded into a single, coherent concept of God.[9]

Fallen humanity, however, has an utterly different experience of self and of time. People know incompletely, they will ineffectively, they do imperfectly. This abiding condition of imperfection reflects the quality of human consciousness, which is itself distended in time. To understand this distension and its consequences is to understand the effects of living in time. Augustine admits that he cannot say what time is, but he gives a dizzying description of *how* time is (*Confessions* 11.14,17). Time, he says, functions psychologically; that is, its effects are experienced within the soul. "It is in you, my mind, that I measure time" (11.27,36). And how is time measured? By its flow, its constant movement from the future into the present and thence to the past.

Considering the mind's effort to measure time's flow, Augustine notes that only time's middle term, *present,* designates something that actually exists. The future does not yet exist; the past no longer exists. Only the present "is." Thus the present alone is what the soul at any given moment actually experiences. But what is "the present"? What is "a moment"?

> Not even one day is entirely present. All the hours of the day add up to twenty-four. The first of them has the others in the future, the last has them in the past. . . . A single hour is itself constituted of fugitive moments. . . . If we can think of some bit of time which cannot be divided into even the smallest instantaneous moment, that alone is what we call "present." And this time flies by so quickly from the future into the past that it is an interval of no duration. Any duration is divisible into past and future. A present moment takes up no time.
>
> CONFESSIONS 11.15,20

The present itself is thus constantly receding and inherently ungraspable. It exists between two huge planes of nonbeing that spread out infinitely in either direction: the past (which has no existence, since it no longer is) and the future (which has no existence, since it is yet to be). Yet all of a person's consciousness, her entire ability to know and to understand, is circumscribed by and limited to this infinitely tiny, perpetually transient moment. Human consciousness drifts awash in this sea of nonbeing.

"I am scattered in times whose order I do not understand," Augustine laments. "The storms of incoherent events rend my thoughts, the inmost entrails of my soul" (*Confessions* 11.30,40). Experience—by definition, solely in the present—constantly runs between the fingers of the soul like sand. How, then, can humans know anything? How can meaning be distilled from this ceaseless flow of atomized experience? How, indeed, can the mind *grasp* anything?

Augustine begins to frame an answer by thinking about language. Language, like experience, is also intrinsically tangled up in time: it too depends on the linear passage from being (present) to nonbeing (past). Consonants and vowels alternate to create phonemes, words follow words, nouns verbs. Both in its smallest units (consonants and vowels) and in its larger ones (sentences and more), language works by having a beginning, a middle, and an end. (Like all ancient people, Augustine thinks of words and texts orally, in terms of their being spoken and heard; *Confessions* 11.6,8-11,13). Time shapes language, and language shapes time.

It is only thanks to memory, however, that humans can manage to wring meaning from language. Memory, says Augustine, is that part of the soul that processes both language and experience. We cannot know the meaning of a word, or of a sentence or of a speech, until its end is reached. Only at that point do we remember the whole, and we then interpret what these units of sound convey. Thus, if *language is intrinsically narrative*—syllables, words, stanzas, speeches all have a beginning, a middle, and an end—*understanding is intrinsically retrospective.* Meaning emerges and can only emerge through the act of recollection. We owe to the integrative function of memory the fact that we can think and know at all.[10]

But meaning is never immediately present: It is always and necessarily mediated through the images, signs, and words that memory reflects upon. Thus, just as time is not the same as the units that we measure it by, so also meaning is not the same as those words that we use in our effort to convey meaning, or in those words from which memory attempts to wring meaning. Meaning, for humans, is always a retrospective and imperfect achievement.

This tenuousness of significance obtains even in the case of inspired words, that is, scripture. God's Word, the Son, exists co-eternal with him, spoken "in the simultaneity of eternity." But in the gospel, "the Word speaks through the flesh" (*Confessions* 11.7,9); and once written, God's word is incarnate in contingent human language. The written, historical word can sustain a diversity of truths. The validity of these truths cannot be limited by the historically contingent intentions of their original authors. Nor can all of scripture's meanings ever be known at once (12.23,32–30,41). And, of course, scripture can also be misunderstood and misinterpreted (cf. 6.4,5–5,8). Yet despite its condition of contingency in language, the Bible nonetheless mediates the knowledge of God. It is the divinely constructed bridge between eternity and time.

Scripture thus stands between humanity and God as "a solid firmament of authority . . . like a skin stretched above us." It exists because of Adam's fall and because of God's providential response to his fall. "You know, Lord, how you clothed men with skins when by sin they became mortal (Genesis 3:21); so you have stretched out the firmament of your book like a skin, that is, your words . . . which you have placed over us by the ministry of mortal men" (*Confessions* 13.15,16). "To instruct the unbelieving people You produced from physical matter sacraments and visible miracles and the sounds of the words of your book" (13.34,49). And whatever other truths scripture communicates, it commences with and most straightforwardly asserts that in the beginning the eternal changeless God made the invisible and the visible universe (11.31,41; 12.2,2). The true God is the creator God, who made all things and called them good. This is an assertion *ad litteram.*

But since scripture (necessarily) describes God in language, it also measures the difference between God and humanity. God, in eternity, knows all things simultaneously, as do the angels who dwell in the "heaven of heavens," the "intellectual, nonmaterial heaven where the intelligence's knowing . . . is not partial, not in an enigma, not through a glass, but complete total openness, face to face . . . concurrent, without any temporal successiveness" (*Confessions* 12.13,16). Man, trapped in time, can no longer know God (or anything else) in this way. Nor will he again know God in this way until his transformation at the end of time (11.29,39; 13.15,18). Thus, in the only passage of his entire book in which Augustine "stops" speaking and God himself "speaks," Augustine imagines God's saying to him,

What is said in Scripture is said by me. Yet it is said to those who exist in time, while time does not affect my own Word, which

exists as my equal in eternity. What you see by the Spirit's action
I also see, just as what you say by the Spirit's action, I also say.
But you see in temporal sequence and I see outside of time, you
speak in temporal sequence and I speak outside of time [*non ego
temporaliter dico*].

CONFESSIONS 13.29,44

Augustine's great exploration of memory in book ten of the *Confessions* is thus his anthropological companion piece to the philosophy of time that he sets out in book eleven. Memory's premier role, as we have just seen, is cognitive: It is the site of necessary intellectual processes, the way by which a person meaningfully locates himself within time. But memory also has negative effects. It is the site within the soul most marked by the habits of the heart, what Augustine elsewhere calls the soul's "weight": *amor meus pondus meus* (*Confessions* 13.9,10). This idea mingles with Augustine's vivid appropriation of late Platonism and his no less vivid recourse to the language of Psalms, wherein the seat of knowledge is so often the "heart." For all these reasons, "knowing" for Augustine is never solely a function of cognition. Knowing immediately implies loving. Man seeks truth because man loves truth, and his love directs his path. Love is the motor of the will.

But in consequence of the Fall, Augustine asserts, a person's will is divided and ineffectual, his loves misdirected. Augustine understands Romans 7 as the scriptural manifesto of this condition. Exactly in the place where the Manichees had read proof of external coercion, of the good soul's struggle against the incursions of the forces of evil, Augustine saw the thrashing around of the will divided against itself. Human will is indeed "free," but only in the sense that nothing outside of itself forces its self to sin. Wounded by sin, the will fights against itself. It knows one thing and wants something else; it thinks one thing and feels something else. "I do not understand my own actions . . . I do not do what I want, but I do the very thing that I hate. . . . I can will what is right, but I cannot do it. For I do not do the good that I want, but the evil I do not want is what I do" (Romans 7:15–20).[11]

Understanding these verses in Romans 7 as descriptive of humanity's punishment and of the universal human condition after Adam's sin (which Augustine invokes immediately in the fourth and fifth lines

of the first book; *Confessions* 1.1,1), Augustine demonstrates their veracity (that is, the veracity of his current interpretation of them) by describing his own past in their terms. Power, praise, sexual satisfaction,
wealth: Augustine/Everyman pursues these goals because he loves
them, but they can never bring him true happiness. Unaided by grace,
fallen human love is compulsive, uncontrollable, disordered, deplet-
ing. Only the love of God—which can be given only by God—heals and
sustains. The love of God alone is true happiness.

So essential is love to human motivation that God uses it to effect
salvation: He redeems the fallen individual by reorienting what and
how the person loves, enabling the person to love him. Only by the
grace of God, says Augustine, can the person come to love what is
good, rather than simply what he wants. Thus he presents the story of
his own past, building to the tumultuous account in book eight, when
he finally can praise God for "converting me to yourself" (*Confessions*
8.12,30). But the purpose of Augustine's entire story, beginning from
book one, is to provide a narrative demonstration both of his current
theological convictions and of the mode of his realization of these: be-
latedly, retrospectively, in time. The event in the garden so dramatically rendered indeed occurred back in 386, in Milan; but Augustine
could not possibly have described it as he does in book eight without
the theological development of the intervening ten years.[12]

In that decade, Augustine's understanding of Paul's theology had
developed together with his understanding of Paul's biography. Coupled with his conviction that scripture preserved a reliable record of
past events (the position that had led to his argument with Jerome
over the apostles' level of Jewish observance), Augustine in his response to Simplicianus produced a portrait of Paul *ad litteram*. And
seeing in Paul a model by which to understand his own past, coupled
with his conviction that all understanding is intrinsically retrospective, Augustine produced the Augustine *ad litteram* of the *Confessions*.
The purpose of that construction, of the "historical" Augustine, is to
illustrate his current understanding of the ways that the timeless God
saves his fallen creature, trapped in time.

Augustine emphasizes the retrospective nature of this description
of his past, of his Augustine *ad litteram*. His constant refrain in the ear-

lier "autobiographical" books is that he did not understand, while living it, his own experience. "I did not know what you were doing with me," he notes to God (*Confessions* 3.4,8, on reading *Hortensius*). "Very secretly, you were putting a check on me" (4.14,23, on his oratorical ambitions). "Where was I, when I was seeking You? You were there before me, but I had departed from myself. I could not even find myself, much less you" (5.2,2, on his quest for wisdom in Carthage). "Gradually, though I did not realize it, I was drawing closer" (5.13,23, on listening to Ambrose).

The double time frame of these first nine books, the past and the present, demonstrates Augustine's point about epistemology, how we know what we (think we) know. Retrospect mediates meaning. But Augustine's double time frame also provides scope for his literary artistry: It is this device that gives his story its great poignancy. We watch as the young Augustine lives his life utterly innocent of the future, while we overhear the older Augustine of 397 confiding his new insights on his old life to his silent and all-knowing God. The deeper and truer significance of all of these past events—going to school, stealing pears, reading Cicero, joining the Manichees, quitting Africa for Italy, listening to Ambrose—was available to Augustine, Augustine claims, only long afterward, once his memory had done its work.

Retrospect is necessary for Augustine's reader, also. Not until reaching the complex final books of the *Confessions* can the reader understand the strategy of Augustine's autobiographical narrative in books one to nine. Rather than beginning with the abstractions laid out in his closing books, Augustine opens with a narrative application of these abstractions. He offers his life story in such a way that the reader is persuaded of the truth of the theological principles that shape it long before she encounters those principles as such. Augustine's story is a concealed form of his theology; his theology is the revealed form of his story.

In the *Confessions,* Augustine applied the principles of his maturing theology to two poles of historical reality: to his individual life (books one to ten) and to the creation and eventual completion of the universe (books eleven to thirteen). Shortly thereafter, again using Manichaeism as a foil, Augustine began to apply his ideas to a median time, the span of biblical history described in the unified canon of the Old and New Testaments. More *ad litteram* constructs emerged from this exercise: the god who chose Israel and who revealed his Law to them; the Jewish people, among whom were Jesus, Paul, and the other apostles; the society of Jews and Gentiles that had formed the context of the earliest mission and had become the foundation of the church. Thinking with the Bible in the new ways that his work in the 390s had enabled, Augustine in his next major writing, *Against Faustus,* elaborated a defense of divine justice and human freedom on the new terrain marked off in his response to Simplicianus. In so doing, he produced as well something all but unprecedented within his tradition: a Christian affirmation of Jews and Judaism.

PART THREE

GOD AND ISRAEL

Christian anti-Jewish invective expresses ideas about Judaism. But no less, Christian anti-Jewish invective expresses ideas about Christianity.

When Augustine left Manichaeism for catholic Christianity, he embraced a new concept of God. He achieved a new understanding of the sources of and reasons for evil. And he embraced a much larger Bible, one that included the Old Testament along with the New. Surprisingly familiar, however, was his new church's understanding of Judaism. In this one realm, catholics and Manichees seemed curiously agreed. Both churches decried the carnality of Jewish practices. Both churches condemned the obtuseness of Jewish biblical interpretation. And both churches held that the Jewish cult of animal sacrifices in Jerusalem linked Jewish worship to idolatry. Challenged by a thoughtful Manichaean missionary on the unseemly Jewishness of the scriptures and doctrines of catholic Christianity, Augustine answered with a brilliant and novel defense. He reimagined the relationship of God and Israel, and thus he reimagined as well the relationship of his church, past and present, to the Jews.

❖ ❖ ❖

*Do I believe the gospel? you ask me. My obedience to its
commands shows that I do. . . . I have left my father, my
mother, my wife and my children and all else that the
gospel requires; and yet you ask me if I believe in the
gospel. . . . The gospel is nothing other than the preaching
and the precepts of Christ. I have parted with all gold
and silver. I no longer carry money in my purse. I am
content with daily food, neither caring nor concerned
about how I shall eat tomorrow, or how I will be clothed;
and yet you ask me if I believe in the gospel. . . . You see
me poor and meek; a peacemaker, pure in heart; mourn-
ing, hungering, thirsting, and bearing persecutions and
enmity for righteousness' sake. And still you doubt my
belief in the gospel?*
FAUSTUS, QUOTED BY AUGUSTINE, *AGAINST FAUSTUS* 5.1

Faustus was an elder contemporary of Augustine's and, like Augustine, he was North African. Their paths had crossed briefly in
Carthage, back in late 382 C.E. when Augustine was still a Manichaean
auditor and a municipal professor of rhetoric, and Faustus an itinerant *electus* and bishop. Book five of the *Confessions* tells the story of
their encounter. Augustine had grown agitated by the discrepancies
that he noted between texts of scientific astronomy and those pious
explanations of celestial phenomena retailed by the Manichees. Once
Faustus arrived, other Manichees assured him, he would answer all of
Augustine's questions. Things went otherwise. Faustus disappointed
Augustine, who soon realized from conversation that Faustus' liberal
arts education was too thin for him to truly engage the issues that
Augustine had found so unsettling. Ultimately, each man went his

own way, Augustine off to Italy (in 383), Faustus remaining in North Africa.

In 386, caught up in the imperially sponsored purge of Manichees in Carthage, Faustus was exiled to a bleak island in the Mediterranean. During the year or so that he spent there, he composed his *Capitula,* the work that provides the scaffolding for Augustine's later response, *Against Faustus.*

Manichaeism alone, Faustus urged in his *Capitula,* was the purest form of Christianity. By this he meant that his was the only church utterly untainted by the Judaizing that, in the Manichaean view, characterized and thus compromised catholic Christianity. To help his fellow Manichaean missionaries make this case, Faustus designed and clearly organized his presentation in the *Capitula* to serve as a collection of talking points and arguments for use against catholic disputants (*Against Faustus* 1.2). Faustus opened each unit by repeating a catholic challenge to Manichaeism. "Do I believe the gospel?" (2.1). "Do I believe in the incarnation?" (3.1). "Do I believe the Old Testament?" (4.1). "Why do I not believe the prophets?" (12.1). His responses to all of these set-piece questions together made up a comprehensive challenge both to traditions of catholic biblical interpretation and to defining points of catholic doctrine: creation, the incarnation and fleshly resurrection of Christ, the bodily resurrection of the redeemed at the end of time, and so on. More fundamentally, the *Capitula* called into question the very concept of orthodoxy's double canon, Old Testament and New.

Many of the points adduced by Faustus against catholic understandings of Christ, of scripture, and particularly of Paul's letters had been rehearsed much earlier by the mid-second-century theologian Marcion. Marcion, like Faustus, had emphatically disallowed any Christian value to Jewish scriptures. The Jewish god was a bad god; the Jewish laws were bad laws, fleshly in conception (obedience to them promised material rewards, such as progeny, long life, and an earthly kingdom) and fleshly in execution (male circumcision, physical rest on the Sabbath, and so on). But the true god had nothing to do with flesh, and neither did his son, the Savior: The Christology of both Marcionites and Manichees was docetic. Those places in Paul's letters that seemed to teach that Christ had a fleshly body or that spoke positively of the Jews' books or practices or laws, said the members of both groups, were self-evidently the corruptions of Judaizing copyists, or (so the Manichees) mistakes that Paul corrected elsewhere in his writings.

We cannot pursue this comparison in any detail, because Marcion's writings did not survive imperial orthodoxy's censure. With Faustus' work we have better luck. Augustine presented his arguments against Faustus as if the two men had been engaged in active debate, quoting first from Faustus' text, then giving his rebuttal "as if Faustus had stated his opinions himself, and I had replied to him" (*Against Faustus* I.I; we will look at the reason for Augustine's presenting his views in this way shortly). In consequence, we have most, if perhaps not all, of Faustus' *Capitula*.

As we saw in the transcript of Augustine's actual dispute with Fortunatus, so we see again in this ersatz transcript here: Only Augustine refers to and relates any specifically Manichaean teachings. For his part, Faustus never mentioned any, but instead made his case entirely by appeals to the writings important to catholic Christians. His various arguments about how to read scripture all unite around a single premise, namely, that the (Jewish) Law has nothing whatsoever to do with (true, Christian) revelation. For Faustus, the source of this premise lay in the revelations of Mani as preserved in the canonical writings of his own church. Nonetheless, he insistently focused on catholic scriptures alone and astutely emphasized those places within and between Paul's letters and the gospels on the topic of the Law that appeared at least inconsistent where not flat-out contradictory. Faustus thus created the vivid impression that the mutual antagonism between Law and gospel emerged naturally, indeed inevitably, from the New Testament texts themselves.

Faustus' arguments reveal not only his impressive command of New Testament writings but also his coherent and critical approach to interpreting them. For example, he gave Paul's epistles priority over the gospels as a source of Christian instruction, both because they were firsthand documents and because Paul himself had authenticated them with his own signature. ("I, Paul, write this greeting in my own hand"; I Corinthians 16:21. "See with what big letters I write to you in my own hand"; Galatians 6:11. Several deutero-Pauline epistles, of course, use this same form of authentication.)

But what about those places where Paul seemed to contradict not only himself but also Manichaean revelation as well? In Faustus' view, only those statements that agreed with Mani's could be true. Accordingly, such difficulties could be resolved in one of two ways. If two mutually exclusive statements truly seemed authentically Pauline, then together they testified to the progress that the apostle himself had made in understanding the (true) gospel. For example, Paul's view that Jesus was a fleshly descendant of King David (Romans 1:3) had obviously ceded later to his more enlightened understanding in 2 Corinthians 5:16: "From now on we know no one from a human point of view." (Thus the RSV translation. The Latin, however, which mirrors Paul's Greek, for "human point of view" says simply *secundum carnem*: literally, "according to the flesh.") "Even though we once knew Christ from a human point of view"—again, *secundum carnem*—"we know him that way no longer" (*Against Faustus* 11.1). Intractable clashes between statements in Paul's texts and the principles of Manichaean doctrine witnessed to the later corruptions of anonymous Judaizers. For example, developing his comparison of the two passages from Romans and 2 Corinthians just cited, Faustus reasons: "If the earlier verse [in Romans] is Paul's, then he later corrected himself [in 2 Corinthians]. And if you don't like the idea that Paul ever wrote anything requiring correction, that's fine too. In that case, this verse [in Romans] is not his" (*Against Faustus* 11.1).[1]

Faustus demonstrated equal argumentative agility when he considered canonical gospel texts. Unlike Paul's letters, he notes, the gospels' accounts are secondhand: they only speak *about* Jesus but make no claim to be *by* Jesus. The purported sayings *of* Jesus tendered by the evangelists scarcely offset the secondhand quality of their material. This is so because, even when more than one gospel reports a saying attributed to Jesus, the different contexts for the saying provided by each undermine the authority of what both report. Matthew and Luke, for example, each depict Jesus' curing a centurion's servant. Only Matthew, however, connects this episode with the saying "Many will come from the East and come from the West to sit at the table with Abraham, Isaac and Jacob; but the children of the kingdom will be cast into the outer darkness." Luke's parallel scene lacks this saying entirely (compare Matthew 8:11 and Luke 7:9). Further, these two parallel scenes diverge descriptively. Matthew's centurion petitions Jesus directly; Luke's centurion, by contrast, asks Jewish elders to present this request on his behalf. And finally, even though Luke also relates Jesus' saying about the table of Abraham, the context that he places it in does not correspond to Matthew's at all. Rather than working a cure, as in Matthew, Luke's Jesus gives a sermon (Luke 13:24–29). "Given how uncertain we must be about the [historical] context of this saying," observes Faustus, "there's no reason *not* to question whether Jesus ever said it at all" (*Against Faustus* 33.2–3).

What about the authority possessed by these texts as products of Jesus' own apostles (as catholic tradition understood the Gospels of Matthew and John to be) or of the apostles' intimate followers ("Mark" in Peter's case, "Luke" in Paul's)? On this point, too, Faustus responds after careful deliberation. The catholics' attribution of the first canonical gospel to the apostle Matthew the former tax collector is undermined, Faustus points out, by the very language of the text itself. After Jesus calls Matthew, the gospel continues, "and he got up and followed him" (Matthew 9:9). Who writes like this about himself? asks Faustus. If Matthew the quondam tax collector-turned-apostle had truly authored this gospel himself, should he not have written, "He called *me,* and *I* got up and *I* followed him"? This text, Faustus accordingly concludes, was written not by the historical Matthew, but by some later, anonymous author writing in Matthew's name (*Against Faustus* 17:1).

Surveying all four gospels, analyzing in detail their various similarities and their evident differences, Faustus concludes that some unknown men of a later generation—not the original apostles, surely, and even more certainly not Christ himself—were the actual source of many of the evangelical traditions. These later, anonymous authors, he held, had presented their own views under the names of the original apostles or those of their followers precisely to appropriate an authority that they otherwise would have lacked. But in fact, urges Faustus, the gospels "are so filled with discrepancies in their stories and with errors in their teachings that they cannot be made to agree either within themselves or between each other" (*Against Faustus* 32.2). Accordingly, he concluded, Manichees were free to sort through these garbled stories, receiving as divine teachings only what cohered with Mani's revelations.

In so doing, observed Faustus, the Manichees were only exercising the same sort of discretion with New Testament texts as the catholics did with Old Testament texts. "You sip so daintily from the Old Testament," he taunted, "that your lips are scarcely wet!" (*Against Faustus* 32.7). His mocking observation made a point. Catholic Christians manifestly felt free to honor whatever they found useful in the Old Testament and to utterly disregard the rest; so too Manichaean Christians felt free to respect whatever they found useful in the New Testament, selecting whatever supported their faith while "rejecting the rest as inconsistent with the majesty of Christ the Lord and of God his father" (32.2). The uneven quality of the gospels themselves, Faustus continued, makes such prudence the measure of piety: Too much of the catholic Bible related material that was simply insulting to truly Christian understandings of divinity. "It is for good reason that we always bring critical discernment to bear on these scriptures, which are so discordant and diverse. By considering everything, and by comparing some verses to others, we weigh carefully whether a saying could actually have been pronounced by Christ. For your predecessors have attributed many sayings to the Lord that clash with his teachings, even though they appear under his name." But now, finally, the evangelists' hodgepodge of blunders and falsehoods stood exposed for what it truly was: a sorry mix of rumor and opinion passed on pseudonymously by *nescio quibus . . . semi-Iudaeis,* "obscure half-Jews" (33.3).

This last accusation comes at the close of Faustus' remarks (at least, as Augustine has edited them). Its message provides an important pathway back into the body of Faustus' treatise. Faustus had mounted his criticisms of catholic scripture with great force and clarity, revealing in the process his comfortable familiarity with the texts of Paul's letters and of the gospels. Yet the total number of books within the *Capitula* dedicated specifically to problems with New Testament writings is relatively small: only five (namely, book eleven and books thirty to thirty-three), from a given total of thirty-three. By contrast, assorted criticisms of pagan, Jewish, and catholic monotheism as opposed to Manichaean dualism merit four books. Arguments attacking the very idea of divine incarnation—the catholic doctrine that Faustus especially assaults—required another nine. But fully fourteen books—by far the greatest concentration of Faustus' efforts—are given over to a thorough-going and detailed critique of the themes, commandments, personages, and practices that stand in the Old Testament. In short, to quote Faustus' own admirably succinct summary, "We [Manichees] are enemies not of the Law, but of Judaism" (*Against Faustus* 22.2).

Once again, Faustus offered many of the same criticisms of Judaism that Marcion had made centuries earlier. The character of the Jews' god was frightfully un-godlike. He was ignorant (not knowing where Adam was, he had had to call out to him; Genesis 3:9). He was jealous and vengeful (as he repeatedly described himself; for example, Exodus 20:5, and frequently elsewhere). He was bloodthirsty, emotionally unstable, and prone to violence. Faustus warmed to his topic:

> These books [of the Law] . . . portray a god so ignorant of the
> future that he gave Adam a command without knowing that
> he would break it. . . . Envy made him fear that a human being
> might eat of the tree of life and live forever. Later, he was greedy
> for blood and fat from all kinds of sacrifices, and jealous if these
> were offered to anyone other than himself. At times his enemies
> infuriated him, at other times, his friends. Sometimes he
> destroyed thousands of men over little; at other times, over
> nothing. And he threatened to come with a sword and to
> spare no one, whether the righteous or the wicked.
>
> AGAINST FAUSTUS 22.4

Such a morally impaired deity, Faustus continued, was well matched with the sort of heroes—patriarchs, kings, and prophets—who peopled the pages of Israel's sacred scripture:

> We [Manichees] are not the ones who wrote that Abraham,
> enflamed by his frantic craving for children, did not fully trust
> God's promise that Sara his wife would conceive. And then—even

more shamefully, because he did so with his wife's knowledge—he
rolled around with a mistress (Genesis 16:2–4). And later—in fact,
on two different occasions—he most disreputably marketed his
own marriage, out of avarice and greed selling Sara into pros-
titution to two different kings, Abimelech and Pharaoh,
duplicitously claiming that his wife was his own sister, because
she was very beautiful (Genesis 20:2; 12:13). And what about Lot,
Abraham's brother [sic], who lay with his own two daughters
once he escaped Sodom (Genesis 19:33–35)? . . . And Isaac who,
imitating his father, passed off his wife Rebecca as his sister, so
that he could shamefully benefit from her (Genesis 26:7)? . . . And
Jacob, Isaac's son, who had four wives and who rutted around like
a goat among them (Genesis 29–30)? . . . And Judah, *his* son, who
slept with his own daughter-in-law Tamar (Genesis 38)? . . . And
David, who seduced the wife of his own soldier Uriah, while
arranging for him to be killed in battle (2 Samuel 11:4,15)? . . .
Solomon, with his three hundred wives and seven hundred
concubines (1 Kings 11:1–3)? . . . The prophet Hosea, who married
a prostitute (Hosea 1:2–3)? . . . Moses, who committed murder
(Exodus 2:12)? . . .

Either these stories are false, or the crimes that they relate are
real. Choose whichever option you please. Both are detestable.

AGAINST FAUSTUS 22.5

◆ ◆ ◆

FAUSTUS DELIVERED THESE DESCRIPTIONS with energy and *élan*. And
the sheer number of his examples also helped him to make his point.
Still, these sorts of accusations, and even the ways in which he made
them, were not original to him. Faustus' broadsides against Jewish traditions and practices had roots regressing nearly half a millennium,
through the works of those second-century gentile Christian thinkers
who had repudiated the Septuagint, all the way back to pagan critics
of the Hellenistic synagogue. And his criticisms of anthropomorphic
deity and of the blood sacrifices mandated by traditional cult had an
even longer (and also, finally, pagan) pedigree, originating in the de-

bates between different schools of philosophy in the Hellenistic period.[2]

The long rehearsal of these arguments in Mediterranean learned culture entailed as well their equally long-lived and continually rehearsed counterarguments. This rhetorical arsenal, well stocked and exceedingly stable, remained constant long after the *dramatis personae* original to the arguments had changed. Carneades, for example, a pagan Platonist of the second century B.C.E., had attacked Homer's unseemly deities while ridiculing their Stoic defenders; later, Hellenistic Jews and, later still, Christian apologists availed themselves of his arguments, but used them against paganism itself. Pagan intellectuals had long derided circumcision, Sabbath rest, and other Jewish practices; Christians (whether Jews or Gentiles) striving against each other as well as against non-Christian Jews over interpretations of the Septuagint, picked up the same themes. Hellenistic Jews had long defended (and constructed) the greater antiquity and thus the greater prestige of Moses, the Law, and the prophets against similar claims made by pagan Greeks in defense of their poets and philosophers; later, Christian apologists appropriated these Jewish arguments for their own antipagan campaigns.[3]

Finally, many of the particular ways in which Faustus framed his dismissive remarks about catholic texts as such—that they were internally inconsistent and mutually contradictory, for example, or that, if they really meant what Faustus' (catholic) opponents thought they meant, they would have had to have been written in a different way, or that only two possible ways of interpreting Old Testament stories existed and either was disastrous for his opponents' case—were second nature to any of Faustus' well-educated contemporaries, and to Augustine in particular. Such techniques of argumentation had been Augustine's stock in trade in his earlier life: As a professor of rhetoric, he would have drilled them into his own students. Thus, even though Faustus and Augustine are the spokesmen for two very different types of Christianity, they each build their respective arguments against the other by using exactly the same tools, namely, the adversarial conventions of Greco-Roman rhetorical culture.[4]

Two distinct yet related social settings had sustained the longevity of these methods of argumentation in the Greco-Roman world: the institutions of secondary education (Hellenistic gymnasia earlier; Roman-era schools later) and the chambers of municipal governments (whether city councils or courts of law). During the seven-plus centuries that stretched between Alexander the Great and Augustine, the learned and the literate (for the most part, the sons of the social/political elite) were taught how to present a persuasive case for or against some proposition by orally rehearsing traditional arguments and their coordinating traditional counterarguments. Handbooks on grammar, style, and presentation, equipped with exercises to illustrate and exemplify this contentious verbal thrust and parry, both embodied and enabled the extraordinary stability of the rhetorical curriculum. The goal of such an education was "to train rhetoricians who could argue for the meaning of a text that a given situation required, by means of a set of standard *topoi* for either case." In other words, this education focused not so much on how to interpret a text—texts were ambiguous, and could carry many meanings—but rather on *how to conduct an argument* about how to interpret a text.[5]

Public disputes propelled this pedagogic model. Those trained in rhetoric imagined, practiced, and performed interpretive argument as an *agôn*, a trial or contest or competition. (The original home of this word was Greek athletics.) From courts of law and city senates to disputes between educated opponents over literature or philosophy, this contentious way of framing discussions about meaning, together with its repertoire of stock challenges and defenses, passed easily and naturally into Christian literary production. Theological treatises on biblical interpretation thus imitated and evoked courtroom argument, and sometimes courtroom drama as well. When Augustine framed his response to Faustus as if the two men had actually been disputing with each other, he situated his counterarguments within the familiar mode of rhetorical and forensic competition. Among its many benefits, this style of presentation—a virtual debate rather than an actual one—netted its author two undeniable advantages: He shaped the discussion, and he had the last word.[6]

Scope for creative talent rested with an individual's ingenuity in deploying the matériel of this culture of contention. Ingenuity, testified Augustine, as well as eloquence Faustus had in abundance (*eloquio suavis, ingenio callidus; Against Faustus* 1.1). "When he came to Carthage," Augustine recalled in the *Confessions*, "I found him gracious and pleasant with words. . . . and I was delighted by the feeling and the force that he brought to his discourse, and by the fitting language which flowed with facility to clothe his ideas. . . . Every day he practiced delivery of a discourse, and so acquired a verbal facility which was made even more agreeable and attractive by the controlled use of his mind and by a certain natural grace" (*Confessions* 5.6,10–11). Augustine's fellow clergymen certainly felt the force of Faustus' talent: When a copy of Faustus' work "against correct Christian faith and catholic truth" came into their hands, they urged Augustine to respond (*Against Faustus* 1.1). In terms of ingenuity and eloquence, of course, Augustine was more than Faustus' match. Nevertheless, his response to Faustus—arduous and belabored, for all its flashes of fierce originality—betrays how much hard thinking Augustine needed to do to answer Faustus' challenge.

What made Faustus so dangerous—dangerous enough to call forth the massive counterattack that Augustine mounted—was not his re-using the centuries-old criticisms of earlier Christian heretics or his deploying the derogations of their common culture's rhetorical arsenal. What made Faustus so dangerous was the way that he built his case by appealing to so many of the anti-Jewish attitudes and traditions of interpretation that the Manichees held in common with Augustine's own church.

❖❖❖

TERTULLIAN OF CARTHAGE, one of the champions of Latin Christianity, well illustrates some of the sources of Augustine's predicament. Tertullian had flourished in the decades to either side of the turn of the third century. A brilliant stylist, outstandingly argumentative even within an argumentative rhetorical culture, Tertullian was a controversialist who relished his work. He waged verbal war unceasingly against whomever and whatever he viewed as an enemy of his church: pagans, Jews, and heretics (the usual unholy trinity for combative theologians); Christians unduly attracted to philosophy (which the well-educated Tertullian himself used freely when shaping his own arguments); various feminine vanities (cosmetics, coiffures, jewelry); moral laxity of any sort (not wanting to fast, for example; or not wanting, in time of persecution, to die). He finally wandered off into schism, joining a community—designated "Montanist" by other Christians—whose rigor and zeal matched his own. So fundamental to subsequent Latin Christianity was the considerable body of Tertullian's works, however, that his writings survived, highly valued by later generations of North African catholics who chose to overlook his schismatic lapse.[7]

Among Tertullian's many treatises was his massive polemic against the mid-second-century Christian theologian Marcion (introduced on p. 67 above). In this work, Tertullian did not quote his opponent when refuting him in the way that Origen would later quote Celsus and as Augustine would later quote Faustus. But he did say enough for us to reconstruct much of Marcion's thought, for which, ironically, *Against Marcion* remains one of the best surviving sources. Marcion had established his theology by compiling the *Antitheses,* a collection of quotations from Paul's letters and a version of Luke's gospel juxtaposed to select passages from the Septuagint. (This format itself attests to the Greco-Roman schoolroom, with its fondness for epitomes and excerpts rather than whole texts.) The contrasts between his selections from these two sets of sources enabled Marcion to articulate his profound conviction that the gospel of Christ and of Paul his apostle could in no way be reconciled with the god, the laws, and the behaviors depicted in Jewish scripture.

Some fifty years later, insisting on the sanctity, the morality, and the innate Christian significance of Jewish scripture, Tertullian vigorously rebutted Marcion's position. His strategy was simple. Wherever Marcion had identified a conflict between the Law and the gospel, between the Old Testament and the New Testament, Tertullian deflected Marcion's criticism away from the Jewish god and the Jewish texts and onto the Jews themselves: their behaviors, their practices, their ancient sins, their more recent military disasters.

No less ingeniously, Tertullian also accused his two quite different polemical targets of committing the exact same interpretive error, "for from the Jew the heretic has accepted guidance" (*Against Marcion* 3.7,1). Marcion and the Jews, Tertullian insisted, stood united in a fellowship of ignorance. Both read the biblical texts without the requisite spiritual understanding. Accordingly, both failed to realize that the Law and the prophets had long ago foretold the incarnate Christ of Tertullian's faith, whose life and death, resurrection and second coming, perfectly conformed to the messianic pronouncements of Israel's scriptures. Further, Tertullian's linking of Marcion and the Jews, absurd as actual description, was extremely shrewd as invective. On the one hand, this strategy allowed Tertullian to affirm, to appropriate, and even to amplify Marcion's disparaging remarks about those Jews and that Judaism that their equally hostile reading of the Jewish scriptures had created. And on the other hand, this same strategy enabled Tertullian—at the same moment and by the very same arguments—to assert, against Marcion, the Christian authority of the Jewish books. The more Marcion criticized the Jewish god, the more Tertullian reclaimed that god for his own Christianity by repudiating God's recalcitrant ancient followers. In the end, Marcion ceded first place as the target of Tertullian's rhetoric, for Tertullian had identified Judaism as the source of Marcion's error. "Let the heretic now give up borrowing poison from the Jew!" (*Against Marcion* 3.8,1). As much as he rails against Marcion in *Against Marcion,* in brief, Tertullian rails against Jews and Judaism even more.

In so doing, Tertullian presented himself as simply and piously repeating the repudiation of the Jews that he (like Marcion) read not only in the gospels and in Paul's letters but also (unlike Marcion) in the Jewish scriptures themselves. (To make this case, Tertullian availed himself of arguments that appeared earlier in Justin's *Dialogue with Trypho;* see p. 70 above.) The Law given to Israel was indeed harsh and punitive, he said, and this was so because Israel needed harsh punishment. Through such laws God sought to chastise and discipline the reprobate nation. "This Law was not laid down because of its author's hardness"—as Marcion wrongly had claimed—"but ... [in order] to tame the people's hardness" (*Against Marcion* 2.19,1). And Jewish law as such—that is, the Law as interpreted by Jews—had no intrinsic significance for Christianity, Tertullian said, again agreeing in principle with

Marcion. (He does hint, however, at the Law's figurative or prophetic significance, which secured its spiritual value for Christianity. "I say nothing of the Law's secret and sacred meanings"; "I say nothing of the figurative sense of that healing"; 3.19,2; 22,1.) Thus Jesus and the heroic first generation of the church, correctly understanding scripture, explicitly repudiated fleshly Jewish practices. Jesus had defied the Jewish understanding of the Sabbath (4.12,1); his apostles had turned aside from "Judaism itself" (*ipso Iudaismo*; 3.22,3); and Paul, composing Galatians, wrote "the primary letter against Judaism," abolishing the "ancient law" even as God himself had done (5.2,1).

Yet still the Jews persisted. By continuing in their fleshly observances—even after the resurrection of Christ, whom their own prophets had said they would murder; even after the punitive destruction of their city and their Temple, the only place where they could enact most of their wrong-headed ancestral practices; even after being driven out of their native land in punishment for their rejection of God's son—the Jews confirmed all the reasons why God had given them the Law to begin with. They were stiff-necked, stubborn, belligerent, utterly unrepentant. Accordingly, concluded Tertullian, Israel was punished forever with exile. Indeed, their permanent displacement had been instigated by Christ himself, who in the Psalms had demanded of his Father, "Scatter them in your might" (Psalm 59:12; *Against Marcion* 3.23,1–4).

For all their theological differences, then, Marcion and Tertullian also exhibit striking similarities. Both employ the same rhetoric of argumentation to present their respective theological positions (insisting, for instance, that only two ways of reading the Septuagint exist, the wrong way and their way). Both complain that their Christian opposition errs when interpreting contested texts—Luke's gospel, Paul's letters, and the Septuagint—by failing to construe them with spiritual understanding. And both articulate and refine their respective positions by appealing to demeaning images of Jews and Judaism, the better to accuse their Christian opponent of reading, behaving, and consequently erring like "the Jews."

But the "Jews" of their arguments are a construct: They are "rhetorical Jews," not historical Jews. The image of Jews used in these polemics did not derive from these authors' observing and then describing their Jewish contemporaries, but from their deploying literary-rhetorical techniques in disputes over sacred texts. (For that matter, Paul and the evangelists had similarly generated their own rhetorical Jews in order to express their convictions about "true" or "correct" Judaism, for them oriented around their various convictions about Christ; pp. 38–40 above.) Put differently: *The "Jews" of such intra-Christian writings,* whether those of formative first-century authors (eventually gathered in the New Testament) or those of their later theological avatars (such as Valentinus, Marcion, Justin, Tertullian, Origen, Faustus, and, with a difference, as we shall see, Augustine) *are first of all a rhetorical strategy.* They are conjured in order to assist their authors in positioning themselves advantageously within the *agôn* of intra-Christian theological dispute, which for Paul and the evangelists had been an intra-Jewish dispute as well.[8]

✦✦✦

THE TROPE OF Jewish blood offerings well illustrates the bookishness that shapes the "Jews" of so much of ancient intra-Christian polemic. Marcion, for example, had disparaged this people and their god for their mutual and unseemly interest in such sacrifices, on conspicuous display throughout the Five Books of Moses. Both Christ and his apostle Paul, said Marcion, had renounced not only these sacrifices but also all of the other fleshly Jewish practices that went with them—food laws, circumcision, fasts and feasts, the Sabbath, and so on. (Marcion was aided in this interpretation, remember, by purging his copies of the gospel and of Paul's letters of any positive reference to Jewish tradition; p. 67 above.) The god who had commanded such carnal practices, Marcion urged, was accordingly to be abandoned along with these practices themselves. After all, Christians had been given a new revelation in order to live *secundum spiritum,* according to the spirit, not *secundum carnem,* according to the flesh (*Against Marcion* 2.18,2–3 on the Law; 5.2,1–3 on Paul's principled anti-Judaism).

Tertullian, though he repudiated Marcion, also agreed with him, and he even amplified Marcion's anti-Jewish critique. He ascribed different motives, however, to the god who had commanded the cult.

Mandates of sacrifice appear in the Jewish Bible, Tertullian explained, because of the desires of the Jewish people themselves, *not* because of the desires of their god. God through his Son had given Israel such elaborate ritual protocols for good reason, namely, to distract them from their perennial tendency to make and to adore idols (*Against Marcion* 2.18,3). So too with the Jewish food laws: undisciplined eating had stimulated Israel's febrile lust for idols in the past, "for *the people had eaten and drunk, and risen up to play*"—the notorious incident of the Golden Calf (Exodus 32:6; cf. Paul's use of this incident against the Corinthians' former idol worship, 1 Corinthians 10:6–14; p. 59 above). All the prohibitions and conditions about acceptable foods were likewise part of God's effort to instill in the Jews some ethic of self-restraint. (Without success, Tertullian notes, for while the wandering Jews ate manna, "the bread of angels," in the desert, they also "hankered after the cucumbers and pumpkins of Egypt"; *Against Marcion* 2.18,2–3).

But God did not care about such trivialities in themselves. And he certainly had no need of blood offerings, as he had plainly declared through his prophets: "What to me is the multitude of your sacrifices?" (Isaiah 1:11). Thus, Tertullian concludes, "we should appreciate that great care by which, when this people inclined to idolatry and transgression, God sought to attach Israel to his own worship by commanding for himself, *as if* he needed them, rituals similar to those of this world [that is, of pagans]. He did so precisely to divert this people from the sin of making idols" (*Against Marcion* 2.18,3).

Like Marcion, in other words, Tertullian also saw blood offerings as intrinsically wrong worship. Jews, like pagans, they both held, were attached to blood sacrifices. And this was because Jews, like pagans, were drawn to the worship of idols. But unlike Marcion, Tertullian distinguished between the Jews and their god, and consequently between the Jewish god and the pagan gods. Those "troublesome scrupulosities" about cult that in Marcion's view had made Israel's god seem like a bad god had actually been given by the good God for a good purpose, though to a bad people, Israel (*Against Marcion* 2.18,3; 4.31,3–7).

All the time, energy, and ingenuity that both Marcion and Tertullian expend in their quarrel about the purposes, sources, and significance of Jewish sacrifices, however, can distract us from a simple fact: Neither of these Christian combatants had ever seen a Jew offering sacrifices.

This was so for two reasons, each of which derives from the same peculiarity of Roman-era Judaism. For centuries, Jews had largely restricted their cultic activity to the Temple in Jerusalem. After 70 C.E., when Rome destroyed the Temple, even those Jews who lived near Jerusalem ceased to make offerings. The *idea* of sacrifice, variously reinterpreted and memorialized, continued to live on. Prayers, said some authorities, or charity or other pious acts, might now take the place of offerings. Or study of the biblical rules of sacrifice might acceptably substitute for the once-performed act. A penitent heart was the acceptable sacrifice that effected atonement, and so on. The actual performance of Jewish sacrifice, however—by Marcion's day and, accordingly, by Tertullian's—had long ceased.[9]

But in the cities of the Mediterranean Diaspora—the only places where Marcion (who ultimately lived in Rome) or Tertullian (who lived in Carthage) would have encountered actual Jews—*no Jews had ever offered sacrifices in any case.* Before 70 C.E., when and if diaspora Jews chose to close the distance between their home cities and the Temple, they went on pilgrimage. Otherwise, their voluntary contribution of the half-shekel/two-drachma "Temple tax" enabled their long-distance inclusion in the atonement accomplished through the cult, while they remained at home. Further, the place where Jews would congregate as a community in these diaspora cities, often called a *proseuchê* ("prayer house"; see p. 20 above), makes the same point: Unlike the temples of majority culture, Jewish gathering places contained no altars. Synagogues/prayer houses were not sites of sacrifice.[10]

Why, then, did so many educated Christians aim all this rhetorical firepower at a Jewish practice that had long ago ceased in Jerusalem and that locally had never existed at all? There were many reasons. To focus on sacrifice enabled these critics to draw on the rich arsenal of arguments originally supplied by the Academy, the Platonic tradition that had criticized anthropomorphic deities, their cults, and their (Stoic) defenders. In other words, tried-and-true rhetorical ammunition on this general topic lay ready to hand. Also, and again by drawing on originally Platonic notions to use against Jewish sacrifice, Christian thinkers could place themselves meaningfully within Mediterranean antiquity's metaphysical universe, wherein an immaterial Idea was always better, both morally and spiritually, than its temporal, material enactment. (It had been on this basis that some first-century Hellenistic Jews, interpreting Torah allegorically to understand its "inner" or "spiritual" meanings, had left off actually performing the biblical commandments. Philo had rejected their behavioral inferences, but accepted their interpretive priorities; *Migration of Abraham* 16.89–91; p. 49 above.) And finally, by insisting on the centrality, indeed the absolute necessity, of blood sacrifices for Judaism, Christians could make the polemical point that the Temple's destruction had made the *practice* of Judaism itself definitively impossible. According to the Jewish scriptures, argued these Christians, Jews could not "literally" fulfill any of the Law's ordinances on offerings. By extension, then, Jewish efforts to keep other commandments "literally"—the food laws, circumcision, Sabbaths and various holidays—should cease as well.[11]

Further, in the liturgical universe of the churches, readings culled from the Septuagint and even from the gospels continued to conjure the narrative presence of Jewish offerings, while in the real world of the Greco-Roman city, the gods of the majority actually did receive cult: This happenstance passively underscored their similarity. Imperial efforts to mandate cult—Decius' in the mid-third century, Diocletian's in the early years of the fourth century—also reinforced for Christians the idea that sacrifices were tantamount to "paganism" (p. 88 above). Constantine and his heirs only strengthened this association by isolating sacrifices as that pagan practice most offensive to them ("worthless" or "empty" in the language of the *Theodosian Code* 16.10,2, prohibiting such offerings in 341). While adoration of the imperial image, and urban celebrations of the emperor and his family, continue long after 312, animal offerings dropped out of this liturgy.

Finally, God's evident sanction of the Roman destruction of the Temple and thus his sanction of Jewish cult aligned the facts of history with the principles of Christian polemic: "fleshly" interpretations were wrong, and animal sacrifice offensive and objectionable. Christian arguments against sacrifice also drew the sting from jibes (whether made by pagans or by those Christians who disputed the Christian relevance of Jewish sacred texts) that the Jews' god had been "taken captive" along with his people (so Minucius Felix in a second-century Christian apology, *The Octavius,* 10.4; so similarly Faustus, two centuries later, *Against Faustus* 15.1). Rome's gods had not defeated Israel's god; rather (as the *contra Iudaeos* tradition made clear), God had never wanted a sacrificial cult to begin with, so he used the Romans, finally, to end it. All of these factors—the social and cultural experience of life in the Greco-Roman city; the pagan imperial efforts to mandate universal blood offerings; biblical depictions of sacrifice; the philosophical view that "higher" worship was spiritual, not material—combined to create, to support, and to strengthen this polemical association of blood sacrifice, idols, and Judaism.

Small wonder, then, that in 361 C.E., when Constantine's nephew, the emperor Julian, renounced the Christianity of his childhood for the worship of the traditional gods, he also decided to rebuild the Temple in Jerusalem. Julian knew that Christian apology had long associated Judaism with paganism precisely on account of this issue of sacrificial cult. While flamboyantly reestablishing pagan sacrificial rituals, he accordingly decided to reestablish the Jewish cult too. "The Jews agree with the Gentiles," he noted, "except that they believe in only one god. That is indeed peculiar to them and strange to us, since all the rest we have in a manner in common with them: temples, sanctuaries, altars, purifications, and certain precepts" (*Against the Galileans* 306B). And a rebuilt Temple, Julian knew, would embarrass the church, which had made so much apologetic use out of its destruction (see p. 85 above). Julian died in 363, too soon to effect much of his program, and his plans to restore the Jews' temple came to naught. But his efforts only enhanced the power of this old and provocative conflation of blood sacrifice, idolatry, and Judaism.

Some twenty-plus years after Julian's death, these two great rivers of Christian anti-Judaism, the heterodox and the orthodox, coursed together through Faustus' *Capitula.* Marcion and Mani stood at the source of the former tradition. At the headwaters of the other, specifically in North Africa, stood Tertullian, whose deployment of anti-Jewish invective—whether to rebuff Jewish ridicule of Christianity (*On*

Spectacles 30.5–6), to undermine Judaism (*Against the Jews*), or to rebut Christian competitors (*Against Marcion*)—recurred throughout his numerous works. His mid-third-century theological heir, Cyprian, the great bishop of Carthage, in his turn compiled an influential anthology of biblical proof texts to aid preachers in mounting such arguments. The first book of these testimonia, *To Quirinius,* offered quotations from scripture selected to show that "the Jews, as foretold, have departed from God and lost his favor . . . while the Christians have succeeded to their place" (*To Quirinius* 1.5). Familiar talking points shaped Cyprian's headings: that the Jews worshiped idols, that they murdered the prophets, that they would lose Jerusalem, that spiritual circumcision supersedes fleshly circumcision, that baptism alone washes away the blood of Christ staining the Jewish people, and so on. *To Quirinius* was frequently mined by later generations of catholic polemicists and preachers. And so great was Cyprian's influence that numerous later polemical writings—*Against the Jews, On Mount Sinai and Mount Zion, On the Unbelief of the Jews, On Calculating the Date of Easter*— borrowed authority by circulating under his name. Thus while Faustus owed his negative assessment of New Testament texts and of the heroic figures of Israel's past to traditions specific to his own community, much of his critique of Jews and Judaism simply echoed what generations of more orthodox North Africans had already heard in their own churches.[12]

Faustus' clever appeals to and manipulations of these two traditions of anti-Jewish invective, together with his own argumentative ingenuity, clearly unnerved Augustine's colleagues. Insisting that behavior and doctrine gave the true measure of a person's religious commitments, Faustus urged that North African Christians, at the end of the day, differed little from North African pagans. Shared customs, a common calendar, and similar commitments to the idea of a single high god, he opined, all underscored their essential similarity. And since Jews (as catholic tradition had long claimed) were really much like pagans—their traditions of sacrifice as well as (in the Manichaean view) their commitment to a single god both pointed in this direction—all three groups, seemingly different, actually constituted a single community. In terms of theology and praxis, Faustus asserted, only the Manichees truly stood apart. "In our belief and our worship," he explained,

> we resemble neither the pagans. . . . nor the Jews. Nor, properly
> speaking, are we in schism from you catholics. True, both you and
> we acknowledge and worship Christ. But our belief and worship
> are different from yours, and in schism, little distinguishes the
> newer group from the original. . . . It's from the pagans, rather,
> that you've taken the teaching of a single divine principle as the
> source of all things. You've changed their sacrifices into your love-
> feasts, their idols into your martyrs (whom you pray to like they
> pray to idols!). Like the pagans, you appease the dead with wine
> and feasts. You keep gentile holidays—the first of each month, the
> January new year, the summer solstice. And your way of living has
> remained just like theirs. Plainly, *you* are in schism from them!
> Your sole distinction is where you hold your meetings. In that
> regard, you simply imitated the Jews, who separated from
> Gentiles but who, in fact, are also just like them. True, Jews have
> no idols. But they used temples and sacrifices and altars and
> priests, and a whole round of sacrificial ceremonies exactly like
> the gentile ones, though even more superstitious. And Jews, like
> the pagans and like you, also hold to a single divine principle. In
> short, both you and the Jews are mere break-away groups from
> the pagans: your meetings may be separate, but your beliefs and
> practices are virtually the same. . . . In fact, only two truly distinct
> groups exist: you Gentiles, and we Manichees.
>
> AGAINST FAUSTUS 20.3–4

But when he so chose, Faustus could easily turn these arguments around, and taunt catholics with their resemblance to Manichees. Once again, he urged that behavior gave the true measure of belief (a point that Faustus also made about his own Christianity; *Against Faustus* 5.1, quoted on p. 213 above). "I reject circumcision as disgusting; so do you. . . . I reject sacrifice as idolatry; so do you. . . . Both of us regard Passover and Sukkot as useless and needless. . . . Both of us despise and deride the various laws against mixing types of cloth, or species of animals. . . . You cannot blame me for rejecting the Old Testament, because you reject it as much as I do. . . . You deceitfully praise with your lips what you hate in your heart. I'm just not deceitful, that's all" (*Against Faustus* 6.1). "Your Christianity, just like mine, is based on the belief that Christ came to destroy the Law and the prophets. You prove this by what you do, though you deny it with what you say" (18.1).

Catholics, he said, hypocritically clung to the Old Testament while despising everything that it enjoined and represented. Manichees, more honest, forthrightly rejected these unsavory Jewish books. But a core of common convictions actually united the two Christian communities, Faustus suavely suggested, despite the catholics' unwillingness to acknowledge this fact. The bond shared by Manichees and catholics was their principled and mutual contempt for the teachings and the practices of Judaism.

Faustus the Manichee blasphemed against the law and the prophets, against God who is their source, and against the incarnation of Christ. He convicted all these by appeal to the New Testament, the texts of which, he also claimed, had been corrupted. Against him I wrote a huge work.

AUGUSTINE, *RETRACTATIONS* 2.7,1

Earlier catholic authorities may have provided Faustus with valuable sources for much of his anti-Jewish rhetoric, but they also provided Augustine with a ready model for rebutting him. Augustine could have done what we have already seen Justin and Tertullian do: deflect criticism from the Jewish scriptures by training it instead on the Jewish people. And Augustine also could have deflected Faustus' criticisms of orthodox doctrine by berating his opponent's ability to think "spiritually." This latter tactic had the added advantage of enabling the speaker to identify his "unspiritual" Christian opponent with the unspiritual Jews, whose putative carnality, stubbornness, and spite inured them, like him, to the truth of sound and spiritual doctrine. By using such arguments, Tertullian had reviled Marcion for his "Jewish" errors, and Faustus had equated catholic practice and belief with Judaism.

But the scripted back-and-forth of this *adversus Iudaeos* rhetoric evidently did not tempt Augustine. Enabled, perhaps impelled by all his hard thinking in the 390s—on the figure and the theology of the apostle Paul, on Tyconius and his views on the positive correspondence of Law and Gospel, on divine justice and human freedom, on understanding the Bible *ad litteram* as well as *secundum spiritum*—Augustine had begun to think about God, time, and scripture in new ways. And these new ideas, in turn, spurred him to rethink received ideas about Christianity's relationship with Judaism, and about Judaism itself, both past and present.

Contributing to this effort, too, was the latest round in his ongoing conflict with Jerome over Paul's letter to the Galatians. Back in 394, at work on his own Pauline commentaries, Augustine had challenged Jerome's interpretation of the quarrel between Peter and Paul as Paul related it in Galatians 2:11–14 (above, p. 186). At issue between these two apostles was whether gentile Christians needed to convert to Judaism in order to regularize their status within the Christian movement. Jerome, following an established interpretive tradition, had asserted that their quarrel had been a pretense enacted for the edification of the community. Peter and Paul should be understood, he explained, on the analogy of "two orators in a court of law whose dispute is not real but simulated for the sake of their respective clients." Both men knew, said Jerome, that Christ had abrogated the Law.

Augustine had objected strenuously. How could Jerome maintain that Paul had deceived not only his and Peter's listeners by pretending to quarrel but also the untold generations of later hearers of the New Testament by deliberately providing a false account of this same event (*Letter* 28.3,4–5)? At stake, Augustine felt, was not only the authority of biblical interpretation but ultimately the truthfulness of the biblical text and, therefore, the authority of scripture itself.[1]

Three years passed, all without response from Jerome. (It turned out that this letter went missing. Jerome finally read it only years later, once Augustine made and sent a fresh copy.) Thus around 397—that is, approximately as he worked on *Confessions* and shortly before reading and responding to Faustus' *Capitula*—Augustine again wrote to Jerome. In this later communication, he reiterated his earlier points while adding a further challenge to the older man's interpretation. What would have been wrong *in any case,* Augustine now asked, if these Christian apostles, Peter and Paul, were still living according to the Law's commands? "After all, Paul was a Jew," Augustine observes. Thus he, as Peter also, would have maintained his people's traditional practices even after becoming a Christian. Indeed, they would have had no reason not to (*Letter* 40.4,4).

Augustine grounded his assumption that these two Christian apostles had continued to live Jewish lives in part on his reading of 1 Corinthians 9:20, where Paul had said "I have become to the Jews like a Jew, in order that I may gain the Jews." Paul did not mean by this that he hypocritically dissembled, Augustine insisted, merely acting "like a Jew" in order to gain Jewish members for the church. That sort of reading ran down the same slippery slope as did Jerome's on Galatians 2, and Augustine would have none of it. He further reasoned that, if Paul's words were taken to imply that he only mimed respectful piety when enacting the Law, then the rest of his statement ("to those outside the Law I became as one outside the Law"; 1 Corinthians 9:22) might likewise be taken as meaning that he had also (albeit insincerely) worshiped idols in order to win Gentiles.

> If Paul had observed those *sacramenta* [this is Augustine's term for Jewish rites] because he pretended that he was a Jew in order to gain the Jews, why did he not also offer sacrifice with the Gentiles since he became like someone without the Law for those who were without the Law, in order that he might gain them, too? But instead, he acted as someone who was a Jew by birth, and he said all these things not so that he might deceitfully pretend to be what he was not, but because he thought that he might mercifully help these people in that way.
>
> AUGUSTINE TO JEROME, *LETTER* 40.4,6

Therefore, concluded Augustine, this passage in 1 Corinthians attested to the Apostle's compassion as well as to his integrity. Becoming "like a Jew" and "like a Gentile" did not mean *pretending* to be either a Jew or a Gentile. Rather, it indicated Paul's act of imaginative identification with Jews and Gentiles. Paul showed the sort of compassion to these people (be they Gentile or Jew) that he, were he in their situation—that is, not yet in Christ—would have wanted them to show to him. But his display of Christian compassion, Augustine firmly insisted, did not call into question Paul's sincerity in honoring Jewish observance (*Letter* 40.4,6).

Further, continued Augustine, Paul clearly understood that the problem with the Law—and thus with Peter's fear of the "circumcision party," which had led him to advocate Jewish practices for gentile Christians in Antioch (Galatians 2:14)—was *not* the Law itself, nor even those ritual practices (*sacramenta*) surrounding its observance. Augustine had long held that these had their source in the divine will and were, therefore, good (*Christian Teaching* 3.6,10; p. 193 above). The problem was a false belief *about* the Law, namely, that it was necessary for salvation. Of course, in the period before Christ came, the Law indeed had been necessary for salvation. (Otherwise, notes Augustine, "the Maccabees would have become martyrs for the Law without purpose or benefit"; an allusion to 2 Maccabees 7.) But once Christ had come, died, and been raised, the profoundest meaning of Israel's sacred signs and enactments had been made clear. The Law pointed to Christ himself (*Letter* 40.4,6).

Peter of course had also known that the Law was no longer necessary for salvation. Under pressure from the "circumcisers," however, he had urged gentile Christians in Antioch to take on Jewish ancestral practices, beginning with circumcision. To do this, Augustine assumed, Peter would have to have acted *as if* he had thought that those practices were still necessary for salvation. How else could he have hoped to persuade these Gentiles to take on such a burden? This was the "pretense" or "hypocrisy" (*simulatio*) for which Paul had reprimanded him, as the apostle later recounted in Galatians 2 (*Letter* 40.4,5). Further, Augustine continued, when Paul himself renounced the "evil" (*malum*) to which other Jews adhered, when he regarded "as loss and rubbish" the prerogatives of Jewishness that he himself had formerly valued (Philippians 3:8), he had in mind precisely those errors of interpretation and belief *about* the Law that non-Christian Jews still lived in.

But Paul certainly never derogated the Law as such, Augustine insisted. And the indictment that Paul rendered in Philippians surely did not encompass the "ceremonies of the Law when those were observed because they were the customs of the fathers. For that [legitimate] reason, Paul himself still observed them—again, not because they were necessary for salvation, as some of the Jews thought, nor to enact a false pretense, something for which he had rebuked Peter" (*Let-*

ter 40.4,6). Thus, he urged, at issue in Antioch, pure and simple, was whether *gentile* believers needed to keep Jewish law in order to be saved in Christ. They did not. Peter's action had been truly mistaken, and Paul had truly corrected him. With exemplary humility, Peter had accepted this public reprimand; and Paul accurately reported the incident, the record of which was authoritatively preserved in the church's scriptures. Later readers should interpret Paul's letter accordingly, concluded Augustine, as a straightforward and reliable report of an actual event.[2]

These letters to Jerome about Galatians, dating as they do from 394–395 (*Letter* 28) and c. 397 (*Letter* 40), suggestively frame this intense period of amazing creativity in Augustine's life. *To Simplicianus, Christian Teaching,* and *Confessions,* each in its own way, had asked the question how the timeless God works through time to effect the salvation of his creatures. In *Simplicianus,* Augustine had looked at an individual life—Paul's—against the biblical backdrop of election that arced from Genesis to the New Testament (and which continued, much more obscurely, into the confusions of the present day). In *Christian Teaching,* he had considered the ways that the Bible—its texts, its words, its story—referred the reader to God's timeless truth despite the provisional qualities of its own witness: various languages, variable manuscripts, multiple translations, the basic puzzle of how words work. And in the *Confessions,* Augustine explored man's exile in time, the consequence of Adam's sin, and the ways that mind, love, and will seek God within the punitive, disorienting distension of this life, a condition that Augustine dramatically described by narrating his own life story. But *Confessions* also held out the consolation of divine mercy, exploring the myriad ways in which God's grace, incarnate in history— through the Bible, through the church, and most especially through the Son—works to close this gap between his creature and himself, until time would be dissolved in eternity.

These great themes, when looked at within the context provided by *Letters* 28 and 40, converge on a particular point: the role of the Law in the history of salvation. Why had God given it? What did it have to do with redemption in Christ? Why should the Law still be part of Christian scripture at all? Indeed, what did the whole prehistory of Israel have to do with the church, whether in the generation of the church's founding or now, in the years of its triumph? Thus when Faustus' *Capitula* came into his hands—nine of its thirty-three books aimed against the very idea of incarnation; fourteen of its thirty-three books specifically attacking the Old Testament, the people of Israel, and contemporary Jewish practice—Augustine, for his own reasons no less that for the sake of his unnerved brethren, was challenged to respond.

Faustus himself, in addition, posed a very particular challenge. The threat lay not in his mastery of the specifically Manichaean critique of catholic doctrine and scripture: Augustine, as a member of that same community for over a decade himself, knew those arguments inside out. On dangerous display throughout the *Capitula,* however, was Faustus' equal mastery of the various interlocking themes and arguments well known to North African catholics, especially through preaching: the polemics *adversus Iudaeos* of their own tradition. Thanks to Faustus' ingenuity, these familiar, biblically based critiques ricocheted off of their original rhetorical targets back onto the church that had launched them. It was Faustus' deft appropriation of this catholic critique of Judaism that made him so dangerous. And it was Augustine's defensive confrontation with Faustus and, via Faustus, with traditional catholic anti-Judaism, that combined with the new directions in his own thought to propel the vigorous originality of his lengthy riposte, *Against Faustus.*

◆ ◆ ◆

TYPOLOGY SERVED AUGUSTINE as his weapon of choice against Faustus. As strategies go, this one may hardly seem very original. After all, as soon as we have evidence of the Christian movement—that is to say, with Paul's letters—we also have examples of this mode of reading. By constructing theological correspondences between figures and events in the Jewish Bible and in the life of Christ and of his church, Paul had transformed the episode of the Golden Calf into a warning about the perils of idolatry issued to his own community of Corinthian Gentiles. So too, about a century later, Melito had decoded the Exodus story as a typological prophecy of Christ's passion. And Justin Martyr, around the year 150 C.E., had rendered the entire Septuagint into a vast collection of coordinated images that precisely foretold through their biblical avatars the events, beliefs, and doctrines of Justin's own community.

To the degree that it was "prophetic," such a strategy of reading was intrinsically "historical"; that is, it articulated a revelation that was disclosed in time. Prophetic typology created a mesh of interpretive connections between the biblical past and the Christian present and/or future whereby the later, Christian datum became the point of reference for understanding the deeper meaning or spiritual significance of the earlier, Old Testament exemplum (*figura*) or type (*tupos*). As such, typological readings of scripture had long served as reliable ammunition in the arsenal of arguments *contra Iudaeos*. In that polemical context, "Jews" often coded the sorts of misunderstandings and misinterpretations risked by a reader who did not share the same point of reference as the author.

Augustine himself, against Faustus, effortlessly conjured such prophetic correspondences in defense of the double canon of catholic scripture. *Christus igitur sonant haec omnia*, he asserts: "The Bible everywhere speaks of Christ" (*Against Faustus* 22.94). Thus, as Noah saved his family by water and wood, and so did Christ save humanity through baptism and crucifixion (12.14). The variety of animals saved in the ark resonates with the variety of nations saved in the church (12.15). The waters came seven days after Noah boarded the ark; Christians hope for salvation in the cosmic "seventh day," the Sabbath rest of the saints. Abraham left his country and kindred; so Christ left his as his message went out to the Gentiles. Isaac carried the wood for his sacrifice, Christ for his. Christ recalls the angel at Jabbok, the stone under Jacob's head; the evangelists, the angels ascending and descending the ladder (12.26). The correspondences go on and on (and on, especially in books twelve and thirteen, on Old Testament prophecy).

But by this point in time and for his own reasons, Augustine had been struggling for years to understand the Bible *ad litteram* and *quam littera sonat* and *proprie*, and thus we see him asserting here against Faustus regarding both testaments what he had asserted against Jerome regarding Galatians. Its symbolic richness notwithstanding, insists Augustine, scripture also and always reliably "reports things that were done" (*facta narratur; Against Faustus* 12.7; see p. 187 above). History for Augustine is a theological category, not a secular one. Augustine "does history" by interpreting biblical texts according to the doctrines of his church, not by doing research. What makes his biblical theology "historical" in his own view is his emphasis on taking the "past" conveyed in the biblical story as the interpretive framework for the meanings that he offers. Reading scripture *ad litteram* to Augustine meant that he interpreted the Bible's figuratively meaningful texts "with reference to the past," as well as to the (Christian) future.

The Bible for Augustine, in other words, was not only a peculiar physical incarnation of the word of God. Nor was it solely an infinite treasury of Jewish types and figures whose deepest meanings lay off in the Christian future. The Bible also contained meanings about events and ideas whose interpretive point of reference lay within the time frame of its own narrative, thus at a point in the past. In the analytical language of *Christian Teaching,* the meanings of biblical *signa* ("signs"), while frequently *translata* ("figurative" or "referring away"), were also *propria* ("literal" or "referring back"), that is, to the story's own narrative framing; *Christian Teaching* 2.10,15). The Bible offered accounts of *gesta,* things that happened in the way that the text itself relates (Augustine asserted *contra* Jerome) at that particular moment in the history of salvation. Thus, if the Old Testament depicted God as giving the Law to Israel and as praising Israel for keeping the Law, an understanding of these texts *littera sonat* ("as the words say") will assert that the text "means" what it says.

Augustine's *ad litteram* reading of the Old Testament—as also of the New Testament—provided him with texts that praised the Law, that rejoiced in the giving of the Law, and that pronounced the Law and its observances good. Many elements of traditional Christian teaching, both orthodox and heterodox, accordingly had to shift within this mode of reading. The old antagonistic contrast between Law and gospel, for example, was undermined. Law and gospel are neither opposites nor alternatives. Whether publicly or privately, globally or individually, Law and gospel stand together as two historically specific modes of a single divine initiative of redemption. This conviction, attained in part through his study of Tyconius, undergirded Augustine's four stages of salvation history: *ante legem* (before the Law), *sub lege* (under the Law), *sub gratia* (under grace), and *in pace* (eschatological peace; p. 163 above). God had given the Law to Israel to lead to faith. Providential, not punitive, the Law was a benefit and a privilege (*Against Faustus* 12.3). While many of its precepts, "appropriate rather than good in themselves" were due to the proverbially stony Jewish heart (18.4), the Law itself endures forever, because it refers in its entirety, whether directly or indirectly, to Christ (12.4 and 12.7, and frequently).

This scriptural Christ—"not the Christ produced by the Manichees, but the Christ of the Hebrew prophets"—had removed the veil obscuring the ultimate meaning of the Law. Through his incarnation and crucifixion and bodily resurrection, Christ had revealed that the Law, which had foretold all these events, referred to himself. In this way, the Law *was* the gospel. "The *same* Law that was given to Moses became grace and truth in Jesus Christ" (*Against Faustus* 22.6, recalling the Gospel of John 1:17). Accordingly, "the Apostle himself... when praising and commending Israel's privileges, specifically mentions the giving of the Law. If the Law had been bad, the Apostle would not have praised the Jews for having it" (*Against Faustus* 12.3; a reference to Romans 9:4).

Augustine's Christological interpretation of the Law, thus far, might seem interesting but not particularly innovative: After all, Justin Martyr, tirelessly decoding the Septuagint for Trypho, had also asserted that the problem with the Law was the Jews' interpretations of it, and not the Law itself (see p. 70 above). But when conjoined with his commitment to reading the Old Testament *ad litteram* and *proprie* as also meaningful within its own frame of reference, Augustine's typology becomes radically innovative. This orientation enabled him to assert not only that the Law itself was good, but also, and much more boldly, that *the Jewish understanding of the Law as enacted by Israel and as described in the Bible was also good.* Ancient Jewish *behavior*, asserted Augustine, with all its purification rituals and blood offerings and food restrictions and pilgrimage holidays and codes of conduct for the Sabbath, was also praiseworthy. Scripture commends Israel for their loyalty to the Law. A plain understanding of the text leads to the conclusion that traditional Jewish practice truly conformed to divine intention.

This simple assertion was revolutionary. It stood centuries of traditional anti-Jewish polemic, both orthodox and heterodox, on its head. The Jews' "literal-mindedness" in observing the Law had long provided Christian critics with absolute proof of Israel's turpitude: As their own worst enemy (so went the argument), the Jews through their insistent loyalty to fleshly ancestral practices indicted themselves. Instead of understanding the Law "spiritually," Jews had understood "carnally" and thus remained enmeshed in the fleshly "works of the Law." Their rules about food were small-minded and arbitrary; their sacrificial protocols mimicked those of idol worship, to which Jews were in any case strongly inclined. Circumcision was at once repulsive and laughable; Sabbath behavior deeply antisocial. Of all the bad and offensive things about Judaism, pronounced the *adversus Iudaeos* tradition, fleshly Jewish *practice* was the very worst of all.

Augustine argued exactly the opposite. "The Jews were right to keep all these things"—immersions and seasons and *most* especially (and radically), he asserts, blood sacrifices and fleshly circumcision. The Jews had *not* erred in their mode of observing the Law and enacting its mandates "in a fleshly way," *secundum carnem,* rather than *secundum spiritum,* "according to the spirit." On the contrary, they had done just what God had commanded them to do (*Against Faustus* 12.9, and frequently). Despite the plenitude of spiritual meanings available in scripture (and Augustine could effortlessly conjure Christological references from any Old Testament text), God, he maintained, did not speak only in allegories when he gave Israel his Law. In the time before Christ came, the Law also prescribed behavior. Laws about permissible and forbidden foods, whatever their symbolic aspect, also instructed the people about what they should and should not eat. Laws about the Sabbath, whatever they contained prophetically, really did prescribe and prohibit certain activities when they were given. God, in brief, had charged Israel with more than preserving the divine word of the Law in the text of his book. He had charged them as well with *enacting the commands of that same Law in the flesh, within historical time.* And precisely because these ancient Jews performed the Law *secundum carnem,* "the lives of these men as well as their words were prophetic" (*Against Faustus* 4.2). No less than did Jewish scripture, then, Jewish rites and Jewish behavior—God's word interpreted *proprie*—also served as *signa translata,* signifying divine truths.

A special group within Israel—patriarchs, prophets, holy women and men—enlightened by divine revelation, had understood the ultimate Christological significance of the Law. Their people by and large did not possess this divine knowledge. Yet through their enactment of these mandated observances, *both* groups of Jews had foretold Christ. The heroes of Israel, "not only in their speech, but also in their lives," were prophets; and by enacting the word of God, so too the entire Jewish nation was "one great prophet" (*Against Faustus* 13.15). "Through those men whose hearts were enlightened by the wisdom of God, we may seek out the prophecy of the coming of Christ and his church *not only in what they said but also in what they did;* and the same is true of the body of the whole people. All this accords with what the Apostle said, that 'these things were done as examples (*figurae*) for us' " (1 Corinthians 10:6; *Against Faustus* 22.24).

For Augustine, then, the semiotics of prophecy encompasses deeds as well as words, "for material symbolic acts (*corporalia sacramenta*) are nothing other than visible speech (*verba visibilia*)." This likening of physical actions to language in turn provides Augustine with a way to explain why and how the divine truth signified through *sacramenta* can remain the same, even though the sacraments themselves, those ritual acts communicating this truth, clearly changed. (The church celebrates the eucharist, for example; it does not sacrifice animals.) Ever since the Fall, Augustine had long held, language and indeed all human communication had been intrinsically time bound, its meanings necessarily and ambiguously mediated by signs. Syllables and words, to be sounded, had to unwind in time; their coherence and significance were the accomplishment of memory. Language is intrinsically narrative; interpretation—thus meaning—is intrinsically retrospective.

Augustine had worked out these difficult concepts about language and time, reference and meaning, especially in *Christian Teaching* and in the final four books of the *Confessions*. But now, against Faustus, he easily evoked them to explain how the Bible is the temporal embodiment of eternal truth, and thus how ancient Jewish rites and current Christian rites both indicate the same changeless truth, even though their outward forms, time bound and transient, diverge. He focuses on a particular part of speech to make his point. Verbs, he notes, in the effort to relate modes of action and being, communicate the *idea* of time's flow through distinctions of tense.

> With spoken language, the form of the verb changes in terms of letters and syllables according to its tense: "done" indicates past action, "to be done" indicates future action. Why then, likewise, should those symbols which declare the death and resurrection of Christ not differ from those older symbols which only predicted these things? We perceive a difference in the sound and the form of words if they indicate past or future: "has suffered" and "about to suffer," "has risen" and "about to rise." So too with material symbolic acts, a form of visible speech which, though sacred, is also changeable and transitory. For while God is eternal, the water of baptism—in fact, every corporeal aspect of rite—is transitory. And the very word "God," which must be pronounced in the consecration, is only a sound which passes away in a moment. *The actions and sounds pass away . . . but the spiritual gift that they communicate is eternal.*
>
> AGAINST FAUSTUS 19.15

Some of the behaviors that God demanded of Israel—Sabbath rest, avoidance of certain foods—might oblige Augustine's reinterpretation, serving as a kind of enacted allegory of Christian truth. But the *adversus Iudaeos* traditions, both orthodox and heterodox, had particularly rebuked Jews on account of blood sacrifices. How, in any circumstance, could a rite so blatantly pagan, so obviously bound up with the worship of images, so intrinsically fleshly, have ever been appropriate to the worship of the true god?

These sacrificial protocols, many Christians held, were worse than merely "pagan": They were actually demonic. One esteemed source of this view was, once again, the mid-second-century theologian Justin

Martyr. Modifying a tradition drawn originally from the Hellenistic synagogue, Justin had identified the gods of the nations (*daimones* in the language of Psalm 95.5 LXX) with the demonic progeny sprung from an act of primeval divine-human miscegenation, when fallen angels, "the sons of God," had intercourse with "the daughters of men" (Genesis 6:1-4). Their demonic offspring, Justin said, seduced or persuaded pagan nations to worship them or their images with blood offerings. Once Israel also fell into idolatry, worshiping the Golden Calf, God instituted a mass of intricate rules of sacrifice governing his own worship. He did so for the "ungrateful and unrighteous nation," explained Justin, "as an accommodation, enjoining them to offer sacrifices as if to his name, so that you would not serve idols." But even this prophylactic distraction did not work: As the prophets later complained, Israel continued to worship demons and even sometimes to sacrifice their own children to them. These same prophets therefore reminded the unruly people that God himself had no use for sacrifices—in fact, he despised them (*Dialogue with Trypho* 19 and 22, citing Amos 5:18 ff. and Jeremiah 7:21 ff.). Faustus simply echoed Justin (probably via Tertullian) when he dismissed Jewish laws of sacrifice as "pure paganism." But he extended the target of Justin's polemic by characterizing the blood-loving Jewish deity as "a demon, for he is not God" (*Against Faustus* 16.1; 18.2).[3]

Augustine's commitment to *ad litteram* reading turned this long-lived polemical tradition, also, on its head. His argument with Jerome on Galatians had sharpened his commitment to the principle that biblical texts did not dissemble, nor would they ever portray divine dissembling: God did not act "as if" when giving his Law. Against Faustus, he made the same point, referring to that biblical passage wherein Jesus himself ordered the leper whom he had just healed to submit to a priest and "give the offering, as Moses commanded" (Matthew 8:4). But why would God—who through the prophets repeatedly disavowed any need for offerings—nonetheless still require them? The only reason God could have had, Augustine concludes, was pedagogical: God had wanted "to teach us something that would be good for us to know, which was suitably symbolized by these offerings" (*Against Faustus* 6.5).

If God chose sacrifices as his instrument of instruction, then any resemblance between Jewish offerings and pagan ones must be strictly superficial. The two cultic protocols only looked similar, Augustine explained, and this was not because the Jews had imitated pagans but rather because pagans, prompted by the offspring of fallen angels, had imitated the Jews. These demonic beings "whose chief sins are pride and falseness" foreknew that God would institute such worship in Israel for himself. Maliciously, they prompted their gentile followers to worship images with *sacrilega imitamenta* ("impious imitations") of true worship. Therefore, Augustine concludes, rather than indexing a Jewish tendency toward idolatry, blood sacrifices in fact attest to a demonic imitation of the divine, which these fallen creatures then foisted on benighted Gentiles (*Against Faustus* 20.18). "Thus the nature of sacrifice as due solely to God appears not only when the true God righteously claims it, but even when a false god arrogantly demands it" (22.17). In further support of his argument, Augustine reasons "historically." Pointing to Genesis 4:4, he observes that blood sacrifice had been designated proper and pleasing worship as early as humanity's second generation, when God had accepted Abel's offering of firstborn sheep. In other words, urges Augustine, pagan practices, when seen from the right vantage, actually confirm the correctness of *Israel's* blood offerings.

What then of the infamous episode of the Golden Calf, the prime biblical example in *adversus Iudaeos* traditions of Israel's intrinsic religious instability and of their abiding attraction to idols? Augustine carefully reviews the story. With Moses missing on the mountain, the people forced Aaron to make the Calf, which they worshiped with sacrifices. Once Moses returned, he burned the Calf utterly, ground what remained into powder, scattered that powder on the water, and then made the people drink (Exodus 32:1–20).

Audaciously, Augustine recasts these events by training his attention on a seemingly incidental narrative detail. It made sense, he said, for Moses to destroy the Golden Calf, "but why should he have made them *drink* it?" The seeming anomaly of Moses' action fuels Augustine's conviction that the text itself beckons him to a richer level of meaning. "Who can help but feel excited at the prospect of understanding what this action prophetically signified?" Tacking vertiginously between Exodus, scattered New Testaments verses, and Psalms, Augustine triumphantly produces his answer. The Calf, understood prophetically, he says, represents *gentile* pagan communities (a nod here to the "likenesses of four-footed beasts" that Paul mentions when excoriating pagan society; Romans 1:23). That is the community scorched by the Lord Christ ("I am come to set fire to the earth"; Luke 12:49). When the Gentiles thus have their idolatry burned out of them (losing the "form" of the Calf) and are humbled ("ground," in the language of the Exodus story), they are then "sprinkled in the water" and *imbibed by Israel,*

> that is, *by the preachers of the gospel.* In this way, through baptism, these former pagans are admitted into these Israelites' bodies, that is, into the body of Christ, which is the church. . . . So this calf [representing idolatrous society], by the fire of zeal, the keen penetration of the word, and the water of baptism, rather than swallowing the people [Israel], was instead by them swallowed.
>
> AGAINST FAUSTUS 22.93

Augustine does not contest the historicity of this incident: The Jews in the desert really did worship the Calf, some of them really were slaughtered in punishment, and Moses really did rebuke the whole people (*Against Faustus* 22.79). But the prophetic significance of the Bible's report of this incident, he insists, lies less with Israel's condemnation because of idol worship and more with the gentile nations' redemption, through Israel (from whom sprang the first generation of apostles), from idol worship. And *that,* concludes Augustine, should stop the mouths of the heretics and the blasphemers!

Still—even granting for the moment that God might have commanded sacrifices in a first-order way, because for pedagogical reasons he really did want this sort of worship, and even granting for the moment that Israel had pleased God in a first-order way when worshiping him through sacrifices—the question remains: *Why* blood sacrifices in particular? Indeed, why blood sacrifices at all?

On this specific question, the argumentative advantage of Augustine's Christological typology becomes clear. *Only* blood sacrifices would serve, he says, because only blood sacrifices correspond typologically to the true sacrifice of true flesh and true blood that they represent and prophesy: the passion of the incarnate Son. Augustine sounds this theme repeatedly throughout his lengthy rebuttal of Faustus' critique. All of the Old Testament, but particularly the laws regarding offerings, he asserts, are typological references to Christ's redemptive death. "These [Jewish] sacrifices typified what we now rejoice in, for we can be purified only by blood, and we can be reconciled with God only by blood. The fulfillment of these types is in Christ, through whose blood we are both purified and redeemed. . . . Whatever kind of sacrifice you name, I will show you that it prophesies Christ" (*Against Faustus* 18.6). "In the sacrifices, we recognize the mysteries of revelation, by which things prophesied were foreshadowed. These things were our examples, and in many different ways they all pointed ahead to the one true sacrifice, which we through our rites now commemorate. Now that this sacrifice has been revealed and has been offered . . . sacrifice is no longer binding as an act of worship, though it retains its symbolic authority" (*Against Faustus* 6.5). "God, using certain types, prefigured the true sacrifice" (*Against Faustus* 22.21). The Jews, then, had never been at fault when making blood offerings to God: He had commanded and they had obeyed, thus perfectly prophesying the Son's coming in the flesh and his dying in the flesh (12.9; 14.6, and frequently). Through this defense of blood sacrifice, Augustine defends, against Faustus, the incarnation of Christ. But the reverse is no less true: Defending the incarnation, Augustine also defends Jewish blood sacrifices.

What then of that salvation uniquely wrought by Christ's coming in the flesh: his redemption *of* the flesh, proleptically accomplished and historically instantiated by his own fleshly resurrection? Here Augustine, improbably, seizes upon that most reviled and ridiculed of Jewish religious observances, male circumcision.

Pagan culture had long derided Jewish circumcision as bizarre and repulsive. Imperial law restricted its practice explicitly to Jews; Roman comedy mocked it with the joke-name "Apella." (The Latin *a-pella* corresponded to *sine pelle,* "without [fore]skin," thus, a Jew.) In his *Dialogue with Trypho,* Justin Martyr put these negative associations to more polemical use: Circumcision was God's way, said Justin, of singling Jews out for the special punishments that they so well deserved in light of their role in the death of Christ. "Fleshly circumcision," Justin explains to Trypho, "was given for a sign, to separate you from other nations and from us [gentile Christians], and so that you would suffer what you now suffer." (Justin evidently indicates those measures taken by Rome after the Bar Kokhba Revolt of 132–135 C.E., when he sets his dialogue.) "Your land is desolate, your cities burned, strangers eat your fruit, and none of you can go up to Jerusalem. You are marked off from other men by your circumcision alone." In light of the Jews' consistently dismal record—after all, they have killed Christ, murdered the prophets before him, and rejected not only Christians and Christianity, but also God himself—such punishment, Justin observed, is fully justified (*Trypho* 16).

But even in and of itself, Justin further argued, physical circumcision made little sense as a "sign of righteousness." (The phrase comes from Paul, Romans 4:11.) After all, none of the generations between Adam and Abraham had been circumcised, though just men lived during that period (*Dialogue with Trypho* 19); and women, incapable of circumcision, are nonetheless capable of being righteous (23). Therefore, Justin concludes, the "circumcision" that registers as a "sign of righteousness" is not physical but spiritual, the circumcision of the heart (18, and frequently). God had never intended that the Jews should "literally" practice fleshly circumcision, and their doing so simply attested to their enduring inability to think and to act *kata pneuma,* "in a spiritual way." Indeed, the Jews' insistent fleshly enactment of God's spiritual command simply revealed Judaism for what it was: the unintelligent anti-type of Christianity.

Faustus too had little good to say about circumcision; but unlike Justin, he used what he viewed as its intrinsic offensiveness to mock the Jews' god as well as the Jews' rites—and, by extension, to ridicule the religious ideas of catholics also. Circumcision is an "obscene distinction" (*Against Faustus* 19.4), a "disgusting mark" given by the Jewish god to the Jews, evidently for purposes of mutual recognition (25.1). This way, Faustus speculates, when in the company of other gods, the Jews' god can know when he is being addressed: He hears his summons as "the god of Abraham, and Isaac, and Jacob." This invocation of the first three generations of circumcised Israel identifies the finite god of their particular tribe. Moving beyond these broadsides, Faustus next rehearses many of the same points that Justin had made: Circumcision is antisocial, marking Jews off from all other people; and it is nonsensical, since the Jews' own books relate the lives of men in the generations before Abraham who were also righteous. No matter, concludes Faustus. The main point is that catholic Christians are *not* circumcised. Therefore, they have no right to call upon the god of the circumcised who had commanded circumcision (*Against Faustus* 25.1).

Cleverly, Faustus united the general cultural aversion to actual circumcision and the catholic traditions deriding Jewish circumcision to form the thin edge of his polemical wedge. With these combined arguments he drove a divide between catholics and their Old Testament and between Jesus and his "native" Jewish environment as presented in the gospels. "I reject circumcision as disgusting," he forthrightly acknowledges, "and if I am not mistaken, so do you." His observation about their mutual revulsion toward circumcision leads into a much longer list of the many Jewish practices that Manichees and catholics alike abhor in principle and ignore in practice. By these means he comes to his main point: In retaining these Jewish books as part of their own canon, catholics are guilty of rank hypocrisy (*Against Faustus* 6.1; also 16.2–8).

Further, by keeping the Jews' books, Faustus repeatedly asserts, catholics betray Christ, who himself always strove against Judaism. Christ came to "destroy" circumcision, as well as Sabbath, sacrifices, and all the other works of the Law (*Against Faustus* 17.1–2). "Your Christianity, like mine, is based on the belief that Christ came to destroy the Law and the prophets," he claims, noting that Christ himself never observed the Sabbath and never taught that it should be observed (18.2). And, of course, Christ reviled circumcision: Why else would he have said that the proselyte who received circumcision became a child of hell twice over (*Against Faustus* 16.6; Matthew 23:15)? In sum, the religion of Moses differed utterly from the religion of Christ; and the Jews, strongly attached to Moses, rejected Christ because Christ rejected Moses (*Against Faustus* 16.6). What then of Christ's statement that he came not to destroy the Law, but to fulfill it (Matthew 5:17)? Either the saying itself is spurious, answered Faustus (*Against Faustus* 18.3), or else Jesus made it under duress, to pacify the Jews who raged against him exactly "because he trampled upon their ancient institutions. . . . For everyone knows that the Jews were always ready to attack Christ" (19.2). The true followers of Christ, in brief, are those who most completely reject the Judaism that Christ himself rejected. These true followers, obviously, were not the catholics, but the Manichees.

As he had done with other Jewish practices, so also Augustine does with the circumcision of the flesh: Dismantling the Manichaean critique, he affirms the excellence of circumcision *secundum carnem* not only against Faustus but also against the traditions of his own church. And, again, he does so by interpreting (and thus radically rehabilitating) the historical Jewish *sacramentum* as a typological prophecy of Christ. Precisely by virtue of its very fleshliness, insists Augustine, and indeed by virtue of its precise location in the male sexual organ, carnal circumcision symbolized the central redemptive miracle of Christianity itself: the transformation of the redeemed at the resurrection of the dead. Physical circumcision prophesies the "putting off" of that mortal nature that is conveyed from generation to generation *by* generation. Christ achieved this putting off of humanity's mortal nature by "putting off" his own genuine mortality through the resurrection of his own flesh. Do the Manichees balk at this idea? asks Augustine. (No doubt, some of his fellow catholics did as well.) That was their problem.

> To God, all things are pure. It is mere prurient absurdity, then, to find fault with God's putting on the organ of human generation the sign of human *re*generation. . . . If you ask, as you often do, whether God could not come up with some other way of sealing the righteousness of faith, we respond: Why not this way? If all things are pure to the pure, by how much more are all things pure to God? . . . Try not to blush, then, when someone asks whether your god had nothing better to do than to entangle part of his nature with these sexual organs that you revile so much. The subject is delicate, on account of that penal corruption that now

attends human procreation. These things involve the modesty of
the chaste, the passions of the impure, and the justice of God.

AGAINST FAUSTUS 6.3

Continuing in this line, Augustine observes that Christ rose on
the day after the Sabbath, which is to say, on a Sunday. Since the Sabbath is the seventh day of the week, that first Easter Sunday was in effect the eighth day of the week of the Passion. For this reason, too, the
Old Testament's command to circumcise on the eighth day typologically prophesied both Christ's resurrection and also that redemptive
miracle that his own resurrection represented and made possible, "the
eradication of that mortality which comes from our carnal generation," the sign and the punishment of Adam's fall. Christ's resurrection looks ahead to the general resurrection on the "Sabbath without
end," when the body of the saint will rise. This risen body will be
changed, not substantially (it will still be flesh), but morally, "so that
it is no longer corruptible and mortal." Quoting Paul in 1 Corinthians
15, Augustine concludes, "To put on immortality, the body puts off
mortality. *This* is the mystery of circumcision, which according to the
Law took place on the eighth day; and on the eighth day, the Lord's
day, its true meaning was fulfilled by the Lord" (*Against Faustus* 16.29; so
too 19.9). Had the Jews understood God's command to circumcise *secundum spiritum* without performing it *secundum carnem* (as the
framers of the classical *adversus Iudaeos* tradition would have wished),
neither they nor the Law that they were privileged to carry would have
prefigured the fundamental *mysterium* of Christianity itself: the redemption of the flesh through Christ's coming in the flesh, dying in
the flesh, and being raised in the flesh. Israel's performing circumcision in the flesh *secundum carnem*—and indeed, their performance of all
of the commandments *secundum carnem*—had been, precisely, the
point of God's giving them his Law.

This praise of Israel for their fleshly obedience moves Augustine to
a striking revision of his own earlier views on Jesus' attitude toward
and actions regarding the Law. In his early commentary on Galatians,
Augustine had argued that Christ had alienated the Jews because he
did not fulfill some of the Law's commands *ad litteram*. (The term can

be read both to mean "to the letter" as in "very scrupulously," and it can also mean something like "actually"; *On Galatians* 22.1.) And as recently as his work in *Christian Teaching,* Augustine had sounded much like Faustus: Jesus had alienated his Jewish contemporaries, he wrote there, by his flagrant disrespect for Jewish law. When Jesus came, he "disregarded these signs . . . and refused to follow these practices as the Jews observed them" (*Christian Teaching* 3.6,10). Now, a scant three years or so later, Augustine sees his "historical Jesus" quite differently. "Christ never tried to turn Israel away from their god," he insists, "but rather, he charged them with being turned away. . . . He not only never broke one of God's commands himself, but he found fault with those around him who did, . . . [for] it was God himself who gave these commandments through Moses" (*Against Faustus* 16.24). So vigilant was Christ in keeping the Law's commands *as the Jews traditionally had understood and enacted them* that he remained in the tomb, his body "resting from all its works" during the Sabbath. For this reason he rose again only "on the eighth day," once the Sabbath had passed (16.29).

As for condemning the proselyte of the Pharisees as a "two-fold child of hell" (Matthew 23:15), explains Augustine, Christ spoke not against circumcision, and certainly not against conversion to Judaism, but rather against the proselyte's imitating his teachers the Pharisees, who themselves were unfaithful to the Law (*Against Faustus* 16.29–30). The reason for hostility between the Pharisees and Jesus, he concludes, was that the *Pharisees* did not keep the Law, while Jesus did (16:32). And those Jews who did not believe in Christ rejected him for this same reason, namely, "because they did not observe even those precepts that Moses had taught plainly" (*aperte;* 16.32, drawing on Matthew 23:23–24). Finally, he notes, Faustus' polarized reading of the gospels exaggerates Jewish hostility. "Many Jews who were part of fleshly Israel have believed in the Gospel," observes Augustine, naming as obvious examples the apostles themselves, the thousands mentioned in Acts, and those in the "churches of Judea" referred to by Paul (Galatians 1:22). "And many Jews who are part of fleshly Israel will eventually believe as well." In Christ the cornerstone, members of both groups, Jews and Gentiles, have been joined (*Against Faustus* 22.89, an allusion to Ephesians 2:11–22).

Earlier theologians had of course also noted that the gospels portrayed Jesus as honoring Jewish law. The great Origen of Alexandria explained this seeming oddity by arguing that Jesus had revealed the true, spiritual meaning of Torah to his apostles only *after* his resurrection. During his lifetime, Jesus, like his apostles, had kept the Law "literally" (*Against Celsus* 2.2). In this way, Origen was able to reconcile the reports in the gospels and in Acts that Jesus and his apostles observed Jewish law with the church's conviction that the true meaning of the Law was "spiritual," not "literal." (Origen, remember, was the ultimate source for Jerome's interpretation of the apostles' conflict in Galatians 2 as a "useful lie." That fight occurred too long after Jesus' resurrection for Origen to reasonably hold that Peter was still loyal to the Law.) One of the prime accomplishments of Jesus' mission, Origin further opined, was "to introduce to mankind a doctrine which did away with the customs of the Jews while reverencing their prophets" (*Against Celsus* I.29).

Augustine's argument was both broader and much more original than Origen's, and it enabled his imputing a practical Jewishness to the ancient church utterly without ambivalence. To the position that Jesus and his apostles, most especially Paul, had at any point condemned the Jewish observances of the Law—a view shared by most strains of gentile Christianities on the sliding scale of "orthodox" to "heterodox"—Augustine objected strenuously. Not only had Jesus himself always remained a Law-observant Jew, he insisted, but so had the original apostles and so, always, had Paul. And they remained observant well after the resurrection—in fact, said Augustine, the Law was honored through traditional Jewish practice for the duration of the founding generation of the church, which is to say, for as long as the Temple stood. Those other Jews whom these apostles proselytized also continued to keep the Law; and some—like Timothy, who had a gentile father but a Jewish mother (Acts 16:1–5)—even chose to receive circumcision out of respect for those other Christian Jews who still valued "the old sacraments." No reason not to do so, Augustine asserted; and for the peace of the church, such sensitivity was actually a good thing. This first Jewish-Christian generation understood that their beloved ordinances had pointed forward to and found their fulfillment in Christ; and giving up such practices, after a lifetime of honoring them, would have been disorienting and difficult (*Against Faustus* 19.16). So too would forcing observance on Gentiles have been, because they had not been brought up in these customs. Paul had rightly reprimanded Peter, insisted Augustine, on precisely this point.

But beyond tradition, he urged, a profound pastoral and theological reason for continuing to live by Jewish custom had guided these apostles: It was crucially important that their gentile congregations see that they kept the Law. These Gentiles, turning to Christ, had been instructed both that they had to abandon their old gods and that they were not to assume Jewish practices. But keeping the Law was not at all like worshiping idols, and the reasons for not worshiping idols had nothing in common with the reasons for Christian Gentiles' not living like Jews. Therefore, concluded Augustine, this unique Jewish generation, the font of the church, ceased their *actio prophetica* only gradually, "lest by compulsory abandonment it should seem to be condemned [as pagan practice was] rather than brought to a close" (*terminata; Against Faustus* 19.17). Furthermore, Augustine added, the gentile Christians of this first generation actually chose to Judaize, voluntarily assuming some Jewish dietary customs in order to accommodate the sensitivities of Jewish Christians "for the sake of the Cornerstone, who makes both one in himself" (*Against Faustus* 32:12; Acts 15:29 on dietary disciplines; Ephesians 2:11–22 on Christ's uniting Gentiles and Jews into one "building").

Augustine's understanding of Jesus' own Jewish observance not only explained how Jesus served as the church's cornerstone. It also affected and was affected by Augustine's understanding of history, of historical narrative, and of the interpretation of scripture *ad litteram*. The past itself, he observes, no longer exists. "The past is gone, and the truth of what is past lies in our own judgment, not in the past event itself" (*Against Faustus* 26.5. This observation neatly recapitulates his richer discussion in book eleven of the *Confessions*). If we must assess whether the report of a past event is true, our judgment will necessarily depend upon the authority of the sources mediating our knowledge. The reason Christians believe that Jesus was born of a virgin and that he died on a cross, Augustine asserts, is "because it is so written in the gospel." The gospel's authority reflects and is reflected by the authority of the church. While the gospel is history of a special sort—

unlike secular histories, it reports and reveals the will and the actions of God—it is, nonetheless, still a textual account of the past, though a divinely authorized one. Therefore, concludes Augustine, "we believe both that Christ really was born and that he truly died because the Gospel is truth. . . . And we can affirm with confidence that what happened in the past (*factum*) was nothing other than what Gospel truth teaches" (*Against Faustus* 26.7).[4]

Thus, as the gospels themselves relate, Jesus was a pious Jew, as were his parents before him; he was circumcised in the flesh on the eighth day, and his parents brought an offering for him in the Temple according to the practices of their time (*Against Faustus* 32.18 and 22; Luke 2:21–24,41). An *ad litteram* reading asserts the historicity of these narrated events. But even more fundamentally, an *ad litteram* reading as a principle of biblical interpretation, Augustine insists, reinforces sound doctrine. Interpreting the Bible in this way serves as a bulwark against heresy—most precisely, says Augustine, against the heresy of Faustus' docetic Christ:

> When the Gospel says that Jesus slept, Jesus really did sleep
> (Matthew 7:24). When the Gospel says that Jesus was hungry,
> he really was hungry (Matthew 4:2). When it claims that he
> was thirsty (John 19:28) or sorrowful (Matthew 26:37) or glad
> or whatever else—all of these claims are true just as they
> were reported (*narrata*) and none of these states was feigned.
> Jesus actually experienced all these emotions and conditions,
> undergoing them not out of a natural necessity, as we do, but
> rather through the effective exercise of his will, according to his
> divine power. For men feel anger or sorrow or weariness or hunger
> or thirst involuntarily, but Christ felt them voluntarily. Men are
> born without any act of their own will, and we suffer against our
> own will. But Christ was born by an act of his own will, and he
> suffered as an act of his own will. Nonetheless, his experience of
> these states was no less real for being voluntary. And they were
> faithfully and accurately written down, so that whoever believes in
> Christ's gospel is not deluded with lies, but instructed with truth.
>
> *AGAINST FAUSTUS* 26.8

Confronting Faustus, Augustine brilliantly integrated his defense of catholic dogma and scripture with a startlingly original and positive apologetic for ancient Jewish practice. Both the generations between Abraham and Jesus and the foundational generation of Jesus and his apostles, he argued, witnessed to catholic truth precisely by living according to the Jewish interpretation of Jewish law.

But what about Augustine's own Jewish contemporaries, and current Jewish practice? At what point had being a Jew who lived like a Jew turned from an asset to a liability? Did present-day Israel *secundum carnem*—that perduring community of unbelievers—have any positive relation or relevance to the community of Christ? These questions in their mid-first-century form had hung over Paul as he pondered the nature of God's promises and the election and destiny of his "kinsmen according to the flesh." Especially in his letter to the community at Rome, he had contemplated the ultimate destiny of his people while working out his view of the dynamics of grace, faith, and election. Three and a half centuries later, in a social context unknown and unknowable to Paul, these questions in their post-Constantinian form hung over Augustine as, reading Romans, he defended his god, his Bible, and his view of revelation and history against Faustus. Had the word of God failed (Romans 9:6)? Had God rejected his people (Romans 11:1)? Had they stumbled so as to fall (Romans 11:11)? Had God, after all, changed his mind about choosing Israel to receive his gifts and his call (Romans 11:29)?

> *"Then God said to Cain, 'What have you done? The*
> *voice of your brother's blood is crying out to me from*
> *the earth!'* " *Thus from the sacred scriptures does*
> *God's voice accuse the Jews.*
> AUGUSTINE, *AGAINST FAUSTUS* 12.10

In the course of his vigorous defense of catholic canon and doctrine against Faustus, Augustine produced, as well, a startlingly novel apology for traditional Jewish practice. But the same historical periodization that, according to his argument, commended the "fleshly" *sacramenta* both of the ancient Jews of the Old Testament and of the apostolic generation of the New Testament would seem necessarily to lead him to condemn these practices in the present. Fulfilling the commands of the Law *secundum carnem,* he claimed, had witnessed to Christian truth only for that period before their ultimate meaning was revealed through Christ's resurrection. Continuing in the Law *secundum carnem* had witnessed to the Law's abiding sanctity only for that period of the foundation of the church, when the new community of Jews and Gentiles first joined together. With the church now established, however, the Christological significance of Old Testament figures revealed, and the vast majority of Christians Gentile, what point could there possibly be to Jewish practice? What further positive significance could these old prefigurations of Christian truth still hold?

Before working toward Augustine's answer to these questions, it might be well to pause for a moment to recall what we are looking at and what we are looking for. Theological argument in late antiquity, when conducted at the level that we examine it here, occurred in and through highly constructed rhetoric. The author of *Against Faustus* was one of the most brilliant ecclesiastical rhetoricians of his period, or of any other. The goal of theological dispute—as of any forensic contest—was to dismantle and discredit the opponent's position while promoting one's own, often through appeal to inherited modes of argumentation (see p. 221 above). We will search our sources in vain, or we will misinterpret them, if we read them to discern how their authors "really felt" or what they "really thought" about a given topic or person or group of people. Those foci of modern interest are not on immediate display in ancient literature. Nor will we get an undistorted view of what real people were actually doing by depending simply on the rhetorical presentation of certain ancient people—be they Jews, pagans, heretics, women, martyrs, emperors, virgins, bishops, monks, or soldiers—for our picture. Finding ancient people in these sources, or reconstructing ancient people in part by appeal to these sources, takes work.

I say this to put Augustine's argument about Jews in *Against Faustus* in context. The position that he assumes vis-à-vis his Manichaean opponent on "the Jewish question" cannot help but make him seem (by the measure of modern civil society) the more attractive of the two figures. But Augustine was as capable of bitter anti-Jewish invective as were any of his fourth-century peers. His remarks about contemporary gentile Christians who Judaize, his comments to Jerome about contemporary Jewish practice, and his sermons on the gospels' passion narratives, as we will shortly see, leave little doubt of that. If we regard Augustine's theological teachings about Jews as evidence for what he really thought or really felt about Jewish contemporaries, we will come away with the impression of a man riddled with deep inconsistencies, emotional conflicts, unresolved anger, and so on.

But his theological writings do not yield evidence to help us with such questions. What Augustine, in sermons or in treatises or in letters, said about Jews (or "Jews")—and, for that matter, what he said about other communities, persons, places, and ideas—often depended on what he needed to say in order to get his argument where he wanted it to go. In his response to Faustus, Augustine's defense of the flesh, of Jewish cult, and of Jesus' or Paul's or Peter's Jewish practice, does not give us evidence about what Augustine "really thought" or "really felt" about his actual Jewish neighbors and about local late-fourth-century Judaism. What it does provide us with, in abundance, is evidence of his self-confident creativity when arguing against a theological opponent.

In his treatment of "contemporary Jews" and of "contemporary Judaism" as theological categories, Augustine's creativity continues. His position on this topic once again contrasts in surprising and positive ways with that of the older *adversus Iudaeos* tradition. Occasional strains of that older tradition nevertheless still sound. Thus, despite the ways that his new argument relies on typologies that correlate fleshly sacrifices with a fleshly Christ (that is, with a Christ who was truly incarnate), Augustine can still lapse into the old language that demeans Jewish offerings. "God is not greedy for blood and fat," he "tells" Faustus, "but by requiring from a fleshly people sacrifices suited to their character [that is, sacrifices that were also fleshly], he by certain types prefigured the true sacrifice" (*Against Faustus* 22.21). Elsewhere in the same treatise, he states that these blood sacrifices were well suited to "a perverse people" (18.6). In another place, Jesus' Jewish contemporaries fume with "rage and hostility" (22.36). It is as if, when Augustine is not consciously developing his own argument, Faustus' stock questions and criticisms—Why would a spiritual god ask for sacrifices of flesh? Why did the Jews so emphatically reject God's own son?—elicit from him stock *adversus Iudaeos* rejoinders. But the general utility of this older catholic tradition, for this specific project, had been compromised: The astute Faustus had co-opted too much of it in his *Capitula*.

On the evidence of the other works that he had undertaken in the second half of the 390s, however, Augustine's thinking about biblical texts and textual interpretation, and his thinking about *how* to think about the past, had already moved off in new directions, directions that diverged from the salient points of the old *adversus Iudaeos* invective. We can see this most clearly by watching how Augustine, in the course of countering Faustus, focuses on two episodes—one biblical, one historical—around which the earlier anti-Jewish tradition had built particularly caustic condemnations: the story of Cain and the "exile" of the Jews after the war with Rome in 70 C.E. Drawing on his positive evaluation of ancient Jewish practice, arguing by appeal to the historical typologies that so strongly shape this entire refutation, Augustine framed a strategic characterization of contemporary Jewry against Faustus. To do so, he began where the Bible began: with Genesis.

All of Genesis, Augustine asserts, "in its most minute details prophesies Christ and his church" (*Against Faustus* 12.8). He proceeds to demonstrate how this is the case by reinterpreting Genesis through ingenious typologies, linking every story from the creation of humanity in Genesis 1:26 through to Jacob's benedictions in Genesis 49 to historical incidents and theological truths relating to Christ and his church. Beginning with the seven days of creation, Augustine reviews the course of salvation history as seven stages or ages. In the last "day," the current "sixth age," he states, the image of God within man is, through the church, being renewed (*Against Faustus* 12.7; he had used the same device in his earliest commentary, *Genesis against the Manichees*, p. 135 above; he evoked it again in *Confessions* 13). God's creation of man and then of man's "wife" from his side, Augustine continues (sliding from Genesis 1 to Genesis 2) recalls also the creation of the church, Christ's bride, made from his side "by the sacrament of his blood." (This image refers both to the eucharist as the blood of Christ and to the passion narrative in John's gospel, in which a Roman soldier spears the side of Jesus' corpse, "and at once blood and water came out"; John 19:34). From this point on throughout the rest of book twelve, the ideas of *flesh* and *blood,* variously defined, contrasted, or conjoined, weave throughout Augustine's presentation.

Augustine moves next to a marital metaphor. Just as a man leaves his father and mother to cleave to his wife, to become "one flesh" with her (Genesis 2:22–24), so also Christ "left his mother the Synagogue, stuck as she was in a fleshly way (*carnaliter,* an adverb: "fleshily stuck") to the Old Testament, to cling to the church, his holy bride, so that in the peace of the New Testament they might be one flesh" (*Against Faustus* 12:8, with a nod toward Ephesians 5:32, on the "mystery" of the church as Christ's bride).

This association of the Old Testament with flesh in a negative sense and of the New Testament with flesh in a positive sense (the chaste flesh of the church, of whose body Christ is the head) leads Augustine (skipping over the Fall!) directly to a comparison of the primeval brothers in Genesis 4. The transition is tricky, because Abel, the "good brother"—and a type, as we will shortly see, of Christ—is the one who deals in "flesh": he makes blood offerings to God, sacrificing firstborn sheep. Cain, by contrast, offers produce. Augustine finesses the interpretive awkwardness by associating Cain and his "fruit of the earth" with "earth" itself, the source of his produce (*ex terrae*, "from the earth"). *Earth* and *earthly* are implicitly "bad" in this comparison, in order to do what Augustine needs them to do for his exegesis. Their moral value, however, changes shortly.

God rejects Cain's offering. Abel's offering of sheep God accepts. Because Augustine associates Abel's offering with the New Testament's "faithful praise of God," he correlates these sheep with the church's worship, characterized by *innocentia* ("harmlessness" or "blamelessness"). Cain's vegetable offerings, by contrast, resonate with the earthly or earth-bound works (*terrena opera*) of the Old Testament. Just as God preferred Abel's "blameless" worship to Cain's "earthly" worship, so does he value the New Testament's service over that of the Old Testament (*Against Faustus* 12.9).

Suddenly, in the midst of this awkwardly constructed but nonetheless boilerplate comparison wherein "Jews = earth bound = bad," Augustine interrupts himself. *"Earlier, the Jews had done these things rightly"*—that is, these *terrena opera*—"but they were unfaithful in not distinguishing the period of the Old Testament from the period, once Christ appeared, of the New Testament." Augustine proceeds with his typology only after he has defended Jewish blood offerings yet one more time. (Remember, he had invoked Abel's sacrificing of animals to justify the Jews' cult against accusations that it smacked of paganism; p. 248 above.) Abel is a figure for Christ, he says, and Cain a figure for the Jews. Weaving together lines from Psalms, Matthew, and John, Augustine then moves to his next point: Abel, the younger brother, is killed by Cain, the elder brother; so also is Christ, the head of the "younger" people (that is, the Gentiles) "killed by the elder people, the Jews" (*Against Faustus* 12.9).

Malice, jealousy, uncontrolled rage: biblical commentators, whether Jewish or Christian, had long associated such negative emotions with the figure of Cain. But the tale of Cain and Abel is only the first of a rich series of stories about rival siblings in Genesis in which the younger son supplants the elder son. When looking to this theme to express the divine chosenness of their own community, interpreters had many other, more narratively developed unhappy brothers to choose from: Isaac and Ishmael, Jacob and Esau, Joseph and Jacob's other sons. Patristic writers before Augustine who had interpreted Genesis 4 most often presented Abel as a type for the church and Cain as a type for the synagogue and thus for the Jews. Such typologies tended to emphasize the difference between God's reception of the brothers' respective offerings. God, said these Christian commentators, clearly preferred the church to the synagogue.[1]

Augustine, when arguing with Faustus, also presents the story of Cain and Abel as a story of God's preference for Christian rites over Jewish ones; but he develops other, newer ideas as well. "Cain" for Augustine serves less as a symbol signaling the unsuitableness of current Jewish worship (though it is that, too) and more as a *tupos* explaining two striking characteristics unique to the Jewish people as now constituted: their persistent religious or ethnic or national identity (different ways of noting the same thing) and their ubiquity. No foreign ruler whether pagan or Christian, Augustine remarks, has ever succeeded in forcing the Jews to relinquish their ancestral practices and their sacred Law (*Against Faustus* 12.13; quoted on p. 16 above); and the Jews have persisted in remaining a distinct people despite being scattered everywhere, a minority deprived of their own commonwealth (12.12). Augustine attributes these two singular facts of Jewish existence to God himself. If it is God who scatters the Jews to punish them for the death of his Son, it is also God who protects the Jews, and God who has ensured that other nations know that it is he who protects them. Protects them how? (And from what?) God, explains Augustine, has placed upon the Jewish people the "mark of Cain" (12.12–13).

This description of Jewish nationhood has very broad application, which we can best see by following Augustine step by step as he develops it. "God asks Cain where his brother is," states Augustine, quickly noting (since Manichees saw this question as indicating the Jewish god's ignorance) that God, of course, knew the answer, but that he spoke to Cain in the same way that a presiding judge in court asks the criminal to acknowledge his crime (*Against Faustus* 12.10). Cain replies that he does not know Abel's whereabouts and that he is not his brother's keeper. On this point, Augustine jumps from Genesis 4:9 directly into the present: "And what answer do the Jews give us up to this very day when, with God's own voice—that is, with the sacred scriptures—we interrogate them about Christ, other than claiming that they do not know the Christ of whom we speak? Cain only pretended not to know where Abel was; but the Jews, in denying Christ, are themselves deceived." If only the Jews had been willing to keep the Christian faith, he comments, they might indeed have been Christ's "keeper." Augustine then continues with the lines quoted at the beginning of this chapter: God's own voice, through scripture, accuses the Jews of shedding Christ's blood (12.10).

Only now does Augustine, in citing Genesis 4:10 ("The voice of your brother's blood cries to me from the earth!"), come to his first main point: that the Jews' murder of Christ founded the church. Bypassing the opportunity to develop a charge deicide, he instead uses Abel's murder to expand on an elaborate sacramental metaphor. "The blood of Christ has a loud voice on the earth, when all the nations of the earth, receiving his blood"—again the eucharistic image—"respond, 'Amen!' *This* is the voice of Christ's blood, the voice of the faithful who have been redeemed by his blood" (*Against Faustus* 12:10). God then curses Cain "from the earth, which has opened its mouth to receive your brother's blood from your hand." The earth, God tells him, will no longer give its yield to Cain; he will live "groaning and trembling" on the earth (Genesis 4:11–12). Augustine proceeds to transmute these verses in Genesis into yet more images of the eucharist and of the church. (Because Augustine personifies the church as a female character here, I will put the first letter in upper case, since *Church* functions as the figure's personal name.)

Thus the unbelieving people of the Jews are cursed "from the earth," which is to say, from the Church. In the confession of sins, the Church has opened her mouth to receive the blood of Christ poured out for the remission of sins. That blood was poured out by the hand of the persecutor who chose not to be *sub gratia* but *sub lege*. And so the Church issues the curse, that is, the Church understands and declaims that curse spoken by the apostle Paul when he says, "Those who are under the works of the Law are under the curse of the Law" (Galatians 3:10).

AGAINST FAUSTUS 12.11

By framing the Jews' status as their choice to remain *sub lege* rather than, through Christ, to move *sub gratia,* Augustine is of course repeating Paul's vocabulary. But he now thinks with this vocabulary in terms of the four stages of salvation history that he had mapped out some time earlier in his *Notes on Romans:* before the Law, under the Law, under grace, and in peace (p. 163 above). History has surged to a new stage; Christ, the turning point of history, has brought fallen humanity from under the Law to under grace. Yet those Jews who chose not to follow Christ have refused to advance. Their lives are out of joint with the times.

Augustine continues to develop these ideas with a thick mix of metaphors for Christ, the church, and the Jews. God cursed Cain, saying that Cain will till the earth but he will gain no advantage from it. But wait; isn't the church the "earth" that drank in Christ's blood? How do Jews "till" the church? Augustine catches himself: "We need not understand 'the earth that Cain must till' as the same earth that opened its mouth to receive the blood that he shed." What "earth," then, is this?

The Church acknowledges and declares that the Jewish people are cursed "from the earth" because, even after killing Christ ["Abel" in this imagery] they still continue to "till the earth"; that is, they try to wrest a sustaining yield from earthly circumcision, earthly Sabbaths, earthly unleavened bread, earthly Passover. But everyone knows that this earthly tilling conceals the sustaining yield of Christ's grace, which the Jews do not receive as long as they continue in their impiety and unbelief, as the New Testament reveals.

AGAINST FAUSTUS 12.11

Earth in this passage now symbolizes scripture, which the Jews continue to till (or "work," *operatur*) without benefit. "Tilling the earth" in an "earthly" way equates to enacting (thus to understanding) the commandments of the Old Testament in a "fleshly" way. This idea of right and wrong interpretations of scripture immediately puts Augustine in mind of that classic Pauline image for Jewish textual misunderstanding, the veil that obscures the deep meanings of the Law (2 Corinthians 3:13–18). This obscuring veil, says Augustine, lies over the minds of unbelieving Jews whenever they read the Old Testament. It is removed only by Christ who, he says, taking a quick swipe at the Manichees, "does not do away with the reading of the Old Testament, but with the veil that hides its *virtus*," the strength or sustaining power that it can yield when read the correct way. How does Christ accomplish this unveiling? Augustine jumps to the Passion narrative: When Christ dies on the cross, the curtain of the Temple tears in two (Matthew 27:51). Christ's passion reveals the "mysteries of the rites" (*secreta sacramentorum*) that had been hidden within the Temple/the Old Testament/Judaism. Christ's passion gives this revelation to the faithful who go to him, "mouths open in confession in order to drink his blood" (*Against Faustus* 12.11.)

Having wended his way (in very few lines) from murder and plowing through God's curse, Christ's crucifixion, veils and Temple curtains, textual interpretation, the eucharist, and the church, Augustine comes back, once again, to Cain. The Jewish people, he says, like Cain, continue to till the earth (now a metaphor for scripture) by observing the Law in an earthly way, which is to say, in a fleshly way (*carnaliter*). In consequence, the earth/scripture will not yield its *virtus* to them, because the Jews do not recognize that scripture's *virtus* is, precisely, the grace of Christ. Then, another association: "So, too, was Christ's own flesh 'the earth' from which, by crucifying him, the Jews produced our salvation, because he died for our sins" (*Against Faustus* 12.11). That is, the Jews "sowed" Christ, but they did not harvest him. Jewish unbelief and impiety prevent them from garnering the fruits of their toil. They killed Christ but, because of their unbelief, they gained no benefit from the result of his death, which is to say, the power of his resurrection. The risen Christ did not appear to those who had crucified him,

Augustine concludes, just as Cain was not allowed to see the fruit of his labors.

I have taken more than 1,600 words to explicate (most of, not all of) the thick mass of images that Augustine took some 480 words to present. Within this mass lurks a crucial question: the problem of human moral agency, which immediately brings in tow the problem of divine justice. Why is it that the Jews do not understand the message that they themselves transport and embody? Why do they not accept the grace that God, through Christ, offers them? Augustine so far has touched on this question only lightly. At one point he explains the Jews' failure by saying that they were too proud of their "works of the Law," alluding to Paul in Romans 3. Excessively pleased with their own righteousness, the Jews could not humbly acknowledge their own sins. Thus their offerings to God have not been accepted; and so they seethe, inflamed with rage, against the humble one (Abel/Christ) whose offering God accepts (*Against Faustus* 12.9). Shortly later, Augustine speaks another way: The Jews do not follow Christ because they do not want to follow Christ. They are *nolentis,* "unwilling" to be *sub gratia* (12.11). Yet in the final lines of this same chapter, the Jews are prevented from understanding the Christological significance of scripture by God's own curse. Till as they might, they cannot get the earth to give them its yield. "As God said, 'You will till the earth, but it will no longer yield to you its *virtus.*'" And what is this *virtus,* this power that Jews cannot benefit from? The power of Christ's resurrection, that Christ who was "crucified in weakness, but who lives by the *virtus,* the power of God," citing Paul (2 Corinthians 13:4).

So is Jewish pride or disinclination or incomprehension the cause of their blindness or its effect? As he considers the prophets of the Old Testament in books twelve and thirteen and argues for their immediate significance for the church, Augustine will try to frame a morally coherent answer to this question. It is a version of that same question that had driven him in his younger years first to the Manichees and then away from them; a version of that question that his period in Milan with "the books of the Platonists" had helped him to reframe; a version of that question that came to dominate his response to Simplicianus and that will reemerge to dominate his controversy with Pelagius. How does the idea of an all-good and all-powerful god cohere with the problem of evil? How does a just god justly punish human wrong-doing, if the ability to do good is solely his own gift? How does divine justice relate to human freedom? Or—its iteration in this particular passage of *Against Faustus*—how can God justly condemn Israel for not believing in his Son, if the source of that unbelief is God himself? As he works through book twelve to book thirteen, Augustine will present his answer.

✦✦✦

MEANWHILE, IN BOOK TWELVE, Augustine continues to interpret God's curse. Not only will the earth no longer yield its *virtus* to Cain but he will "live groaning and trembling on the earth" (Genesis 4:12). "Here no one can fail to see that wherever the Jews are scattered, they groan and tremble," Augustine comments, correlating Cain's ancient fate with the current fate of the Jews. "They groan for the loss of their kingdom, and they tremble in fear at the vastly superior number of Christians." But Cain, he notes, immediately complains to God after hearing this curse. He seems more anxious about being driven from his fields and about bodily death than he is about his impending separation from God. (Cain will be "hidden from God's face"; Genesis 4:14; *Against Faustus* 12.12.)

In Cain's complaint, too, Augustine sees the Jews. Cain worries about the death of his flesh because his thinking is fleshly (*carnaliter*). That mode of thinking, ironically, is what death truly is, notes Augustine, quoting Paul: "To be carnally minded is death" (Romans 8:6). "But Cain, not understanding this, groans at being sent from his kingdom [*sic*], and trembles at the prospect of bodily death." Cain regrets the loss of his fields, when he is about to lose his former intimacy with God. And Cain fears fleshly death, when what's really at issue—and really much more terrible—is his spiritual death. But Augustine's odd word choice for Cain's fields points to the parallel that he constructs throughout this passage. Cain's groaning *amisso regno*, "at being sent from his *kingdom*," in consequence of killing Abel conjures the fate of the Jews in 70 C.E., the notional beginning of the second exile, in consequence of their killing Christ.

Suddenly, God interrupts Cain's anxious complaining:

What does God say? "Not so! Anyone who kills Cain will be undone by vengeance seven-fold." It's as if God had said, "It will not be as you say. The impious race (*genus*) of the carnal Jews will never die a bodily death. Whosoever would destroy them in this way will unloose a vengeance seven-fold, that is, he will bear away from them the seven-fold vengeance which I have wrapped around the Jewish people [to protect them] on account of their guilt in murdering Christ." Thus, the Jewish people will never perish, for the whole length of the seven days of time. They make visible to the Christian faithful the subjection that they merited because they, in the pride of their kingdom, put the Lord to death. And so "the Lord God placed a mark upon Cain, lest anyone coming upon him should kill him" (Genesis 4:15).

AGAINST FAUSTUS 12.12–12.13

The "mark of Cain," in colloquial English, often serves as a phrase synonymous with a "mark of shame." Neither in the biblical story itself nor in Augustine's reuse of it, however, does the phrase work that way. True, the one who bears it is a murderer. But the point of the sign is not to shame its bearer, but to warn anyone who comes upon him that the murderer stands under the protection of God. What is this *signum,* the protecting mark that God puts on the Jews? It is *signum legis suae,* the sign of their Law, "which distinguishes them from all other nations and peoples." But what does this mean? Though every other people subjugated by Rome adopted the ceremonies of Roman worship, observes Augustine, the Jews alone, whether under pagan kings or Christian ones, have "never lost the sign of their law," meaning that they have never stopped observing their ancestral practices. Augustine deems this fact *revera multum mirabile,* "a wonder to be greatly respected" or "a miracle to be greatly in awe of."

This God-given sign, his Law, is enacted by Jews everywhere. It in turn explains why no emperor or king who has Jews living within his dominion "kills them." Augustine specifically explains what he means by "killing" Jews: "that is, no monarch *forces them to cease being Jews,* marked by the sign of their own religious observances, and by those same observances set apart from the rest of the community of nations" (*Against Faustus* 12:13). Sabbath, circumcision, food laws, and so on: No monarch coerces Jews to stop keeping their Law *secundum carnem*. Jews, living in every corner of the empire, bereft of their own kingdom, "terrified" by the vastly superior number of Christians, do worry about this fleshly sort of loss, the separation from the performance of their ancestral customs, Augustine implies. Like Cain with his fleshly thinking (Genesis 4:14, just explored), the Jews never realize that, precisely on account of their own fleshly thinking about their Law, they have cut themselves off from the eternal life promised by Christ's resurrection (*Against Faustus* 12.12).

✦✦✦

THIS IS ANOTHER good place to pause. As we have just seen, Augustine has described Jews as "terrified" (*tremens timore*, "trembling in fear") because of the vast Christian majority, to whom they live "in subjection"; and he has also observed that kings do not "kill" Jews. Some historians—notwithstanding Augustine's explicitly metaphorical use of the phrase "killing Jews"—have taken this passage in *Against Faustus*, and other similar passages in later writings of his, to express Augustine's concerns about the Jews' actual physical safety. Other historians have understood his description of Jews as "living in subjection" to the Christian majority to frame some sort of "policy": In a Christian society, they say, Augustine thought that Jews should live in servitude. And still others, finally, hold that Augustine's theological argument about the reasons for Jewish existence had a happy effect on imperial law, influencing Christian emperors so that they decide to protect Jewish religious prerogatives.[2]

But Augustine does not write in a society where the lives of Jews are under threat; nor is late-fourth-century North Africa the same sort of culture that much later medieval and early modern Europe will be. In that later time and place, Jews will be forced to wear special clothing and eventually to live in special quarters ("ghettos"). They will be socially disenfranchised, and from time to time they will fall victim to searing Christian violence. But in Augustine's world, Jews are Roman citizens. They sit on city councils. They own land. And the legal precedent for assurances regarding their ancestral customs stretch back for centuries before the ascent of Christianity. To the degree that participation in local politics and access to local power, to education, and to courts of law reflect society as a system, late-fourth-century Jews are still part of "the system." We will see an instance illustrating this, directly involving Augustine, shortly (p. 312 below).

Augustine's depictions of Jews "groaning and sighing" are drawn not from contemporary Jewish life but from the biblical language of the story of Cain as he finds it in his text of Genesis. He imputes to the Jews a "fear of death"—which he specifically and immediately describes as a metaphorical death: fear of being forcibly separated from their customs, *not* fear of being actually murdered—because he builds an analogy between the biblical mark of the trembling, fearful Cain (which protected the primal fratricide) and the typological mark of the "Jewish" Cain (which protects the Christological fratricides). Their "subjection to the vastly superior number of Christians" refers to the "loss of their kingdom," which means that all Jews must now live within Christian kingdoms (*Against Faustus* 12.12). *But Jews suffer no actual servitude within the societies of those kingdoms, nor does Augustine say that they should.* Their *metaphorical* servitude to Christians, as we will shortly see, is a product of Augustine's theological imagination, and it concerns their loyal relationship with their own holy books (see p. 320 below). In short, and once again, Augustine's Jews are rhetorical Jews, not historical Jews. On offer in *Against Faustus* is theological argument, not social or historical description.

Augustine's rhetoric may line up with social reality, however, at one specific point: the issue of religious coercion. Exactly in the period during which he wrote this treatise, some Christians did attempt to forcibly separate others from their habitual religious customs. Who are the coerced? *Against Faustus* was written c. 398–400. It appeared well before Augustine and his colleagues began actively to prosecute a policy of Christian religious conformity by bringing pressure to bear on the Donatists. That local effort—a brilliant orchestration of imperial power, coercive legislation, and ecclesiastical authority—does not get under way substantially before 405. But in 399, North African *pagans* felt the force of their Christian emperor's zeal exactly in these years. In 399, the Western emperor Honorius sent imperial agents to Africa with orders to close down pagan shrines, to dismantle temples, and to destroy the images of the gods. (Honorius' edict is preserved in the *Theodosian Code* 16.10,18.)

Violent riots between pagans and Christians ensued. When the dust settled, some images were gone and some sanctuaries ruined; many others remained. But the initiative clearly exhilarated Augustine, who saw in the emperor's effort the realization of ancient promises in Psalms, Jeremiah, and Isaiah, which prophesied that one day the nations would destroy their idols. Thus, in *Against Faustus,* rehearsing an argument between a pagan, Faustus, and himself, Augustine states that the pagan would not hesitate to accept the authority of Hebrew scriptures, their foreignness notwithstanding, because "we can prove the reliability (*fides*) of the Hebrew prophets from the fulfillment of their prophecies." He then quotes from Psalm 2 and Psalm 72, which speak of Israel's broad dominion ("to the ends of the earth"). Historical Israel never attained such reach, continues Augustine, and current fleshly Israel is without their kingdom. The prophecy, then, must speak to the hegemony of "spiritual Israel," that is, to the hegemony of the Christian empire. The pagan also would be persuaded, Augustine asserts, because "he would see the idols of the nations perishing from the earth, as predicted by the prophet Jeremiah" (*Against Faustus* 13.7). Quoting Isaiah, he continues: " 'In that day, a man shall cast away his idols of gold and silver. . . .' Has this man perhaps hidden his idols? Or perhaps he knows someone . . . who has done this out of fear of the Lord who, through the stern prohibition of the kings . . . who serve him and bow down to him . . . now shakes the earth" (13.9; this "prohibition" is Honorius' legislation). And finally, Augustine concludes, the very antiquity of the Jews' books, so copiously filled with prophecies that now exactly fit the times, would further impress the pagan because the Jewish books provided completely independent witness to the claims of the church (13.9–10; for "public and undeniable proofs" of splendid Christian triumphs, 22.76).[3]

How does Augustine's Christian triumphalism vis-à-vis pagans relate to his theological argument about Jews in *Against Faustus*? His point was not to suggest that, in some real way, Jews were in any danger of becoming the next imperial target. They were not. From the days of Constantine, the earliest and readiest targets of imperially sanctioned Christian violence had always been other Christians. And even though now (in the late 390s), with the innovations of the Theodosian era, emperors stood on the cusp of persecuting pagans, no one seems either to have expected or conceived any such initiatives' being aimed at Jewish populations. Augustine's construction of the "mark of Cain" in *Against Faustus* is not an argument against some supposed Christian violence but a theological restatement of how things generally were for Jews in any case.

The Jews' abiding allegiance to their scriptures and customs, Augustine continues, is by heaven's decree their divine safeguard. Their ancestral practices themselves constitute the mark of Cain whereby God signals to the rest of humanity his continuing connection to and protection of the Jewish religion and thus his continuing desire that the Jews always exist as a people. Any monarch who might try to force Jews to stop living as Jews, he asserts, in effect strives against God, who is doubly the source of their practices: the first time by giving them the Law through Moses at Sinai, the second time by "sealing" them in their ancient observance of the Law at the time of their exile in 70 C.E. In other words, according to Augustine, the Jews are in a completely different category from pagans (the source of whose religion is demons) and from heretics (the source of whose error is their own pride). Jewish law together with the *catholica* share the same source, namely, God himself. For this reason, disputing Faustus' argument that pagans, Jews, and catholics are all essentially the same, and only the Manichees are different (*Against Faustus* 20.3–4, cited on p. 233 above), Augustine maintains the opposite. Jews and catholics, he insists, stand together in one religious community, over against all others. True, the Jews, like the Manichees, do not realize (though catholic Christians do) that the Law fundamentally refers to Christ. Nonetheless, "if we divide all who have a religion into those who worship the one God and those who worship many gods, by this distinction . . . the Manichees must be classed along with the pagans, and we belong with the Jews" (20.10).

Though Augustine, in another passage, identifies the Manichees and "all others who stubbornly persist in various errors, resisting the truth" with Cain, and thus with the Jews (they all leave the presence of

God and inhabit the land of Nod, "that is, the land of fleshly distur-
bance"; cf. Genesis 4:16; *Against Faustus* 12.13), he has made a powerful
argument against the Manichaean view of Jews and Judaism and thus
against the Manichaean view that the Old Testament is unsuitable to
Christianity. By appeal to fleshly Israel's continuous and continuing
existence as evidence of God's own continuing protection, Augustine
has by extension asserted the divine source of his own church, which
claims Israel's history and Israel's books as its own. The patriarchs of
Israel, and indeed the entire Old Testament nation, are for Augustine
simply "our fathers" (*patres nostri; Against Faustus* 20.22).

✦ ✦ ✦

THESE THEMES about exile and identity combine to form the second
main point of Augustine's argument in books twelve and thirteen: the
positive role that contemporary Jews, virtually despite themselves,
continue to play for the church. Divine providence had arranged history, claims Augustine, such that the Jews, whenever they wish to reject or defy Christianity, actually promote it. By killing Christ, the Jews
brought about the founding of the church and the redemption of the
Gentiles (*Against Faustus* 12.11). And by clinging to their Law and thus
spurning the gospel while they wander in the punishment of exile, Augustine asserts, the Jews still perform a unique, and uniquely valuable,
service to the church. Scattered all throughout the empire, the whole
people exist as a *scriniaria,* a "guardian of the books for the sake of the
church, bearing the Law and the Prophets, and testifying to the doctrine of the church, so that we honor in the sacrament what they dis-
close in the letter" (12.23). Preceding Christian tradition had seen the
consequences of the Jews' war with Rome as exclusively punitive. Augustine, reimagining those traditions through his creative interpretation of Genesis 4, turned both the exile of the Jews after 70 C.E. and
their abiding religious distinctiveness into something that the church
should regard as positive and even providential. Once Christianity
moved out into the Diaspora, Augustine claims, God sent the Jews out
there too, so that they would continue their unique historical mission
as witnesses to the message of the incarnate Son.

The ready identifiability of their customs, the antiquity of their nation and of their sacred texts, their extreme attachment to those texts, and, finally, their widespread dispersion: On account of all these factors, Jews everywhere serve to authenticate, even to vindicate, Christian beliefs. "From the Jewish manuscripts we prove that these [prophecies] were not written by us to suit the event, but were long ago published and preserved by the Jewish nation" (*Against Faustus* 13.10; also 15.11). And the Jews' rejection of the Christian interpretation of their prophecies only serves to strengthen the church's claims:

> It is a great confirmation of our faith that such important
> testimony is borne by enemies. The believing Gentiles cannot
> suppose that these testimonies to Christ are recent forgeries,
> for they are found in books held sacred for so many ages by
> those who crucified Christ, books still venerated by those who
> blaspheme him. . . . The unbelief of the Jews has been made of
> signal benefit to us, so that those who do not receive these truths
> in their heart . . . nonetheless carry in their hands, for our benefit,
> the writings in which these truths are contained. The unbelief
> of the Jews increases rather than lessens the authority of these
> books, for their blindness is itself foretold in them. They testify
> to the truth by their not understanding it.
>
> *AGAINST FAUSTUS* 16.21

The Jews *as* Jews, concludes Augustine, are thus the servants of the church.

✦ ✦ ✦

THE VERY CLARITY of these scriptural prophecies of Jewish unbelief, however, and their unambiguous confirmation, raised once again for Augustine that same cluster of questions that had dogged him earlier, during his prolonged struggle with Paul's letter to the Romans. If the sin of unbelief is mandated by heaven—as was the case with Esau, hated by God while still in the womb (Romans 9:11–13); as was the case with Pharaoh, whose heart God hardened (Romans 9:17–18); and as is the case with anyone whom God chooses to shape as a "vessel of wrath made for destruction" (Romans 9:22)—how then is God just in punishing the sinner? If all are equally, hopelessly sinful before the reception of grace—the conclusion wrought by Augustine's understanding of human solidarity "in Adam"—then how does God with any justice decide between sinners? And what does God's "election" of Israel mean if salvation, going to the Gentiles, has passed Israel by?

In *To Simplicianus*, written two years or so before he began his response to Faustus' *Capitula*, Augustine had closed his examination of Romans 9 with a dramatic consideration of the conversion of Paul. Paul (as Augustine imagined him) had been a blasphemer and a sensualist, a hateful and violent persecutor of the church. God had called him nonetheless. Wrenched into a new life *sub gratia*, chosen according to some standard of justice that was both utterly secret (*occultissima*) and incomprehensible (*inscrutibilia*), Paul exemplified for Augustine God's radical freedom to save whomever he would. And, of course, God also had the absolute freedom *not* to save, as well. How did he arrive at his decisions? Impossible to know. The pious could only affirm God's justice as a principle of faith. "Is there unrighteousness with God? God forbid!" (Romans 9:14; *To Simplicianus* 1.2,22). God owes explanations to no one.

Augustine opens *Against Faustus* on this same note. Why was someone as intelligent and well-spoken as Faustus left in such great error? Why does God so often choose to help, instead, the slow and the feeble? Divine mercy makes its decisions, says Augustine, according to its secret or hidden standard of fairness (*occulta aequitate*; *Against Faustus* 1.1). And human moral decision, he continues, "in accord with the just judgment of God," operates without constraint (2.5). Augustine similarly conjures this unconstrained will in book twelve, as we have seen, when explaining the Jewish resistance to God's grace. The Jews were not saved because they had not wanted to be saved: They were *nolentis*, "unwilling" (12.11). Elsewhere, against Manichaean views on evil, he repeats a sentence that he had been using against them since his very earliest writings, back in Italy: "The origin of sin is in the will" (22.22).

Our familiarity with Augustine's previous work on this question of human moral freedom, however, should caution us against being beguiled by his word choice here. Throughout his life as a catholic Christian, Augustine would hold that human will was "free." But in that arc of his work that we can trace from his debate with Fortunatus to his *Notes on Romans* through to the *Confessions,* his definition of the scope of the will's freedom had changed. *Free* comes to mean, for him, "not subject to any exterior force." The sentence on the "unconstrained" exercise of the will just alluded to, for example, stands in a passage where Augustine speaks against astral influences on human destiny. Though no corresponding Latin word appears in his text, "without *external* constraint" better translates his meaning (*Against Faustus* 2.5).

But will operated with extreme internal constraints. The will as now constituted—as Augustine argued brilliantly when explicating Romans 9 to Simplicianus; as he demonstrated brilliantly in his narration of his own past in the first eight books of the *Confessions*—is undermined by its own self. Conflicted, ineffectual, this will is indeed "free"—no star or demon or external power compels it—but it is free only to sin. Absent grace, the best that a person can do is to *want* not to sin, though he cannot *not* sin. (This idea of inner conflict fueled Augustine's newer interpretation of Romans 7:15–16: "I do not do what I wish to do, but what I hate, this I do.") This enervating condition is the just penalty visited on the whole family of man, because of the sin committed by the whole family of man, back when all were "in Adam."

Augustine's comments on Faustus in *Against Faustus* 1.1, then, and his remark on the Jews in 12.11, both come down to the same thing: Neither party had embraced true Christianity because neither had been enabled by God to do so. Or, as Augustine says in book nine, using Paul's image of the olive tree (Romans 11:16–26): The unbelieving Jews have been broken off from the trunk of the good olive, "that is, from the holy Hebrew stock," while Faustus, a Gentile, "remains in the bitterness of the wild olive" (*Against Faustus* 9.2). But it is God's hand—rendered unobtrusive, perhaps, thanks to the passive voice of the verb—that does this pruning.

Augustine especially invokes God's "mysterious and hidden justice" throughout books twelve and thirteen, where he discusses the fate of the Jews from the perspective of biblical prophecy. In a dense cento of verses culled from the gospels, Isaiah, Daniel, and Psalms, Augustine reviews the patent prophecies of Christ's passion and resurrection. Because Jews know this Old Testament's literature intimately, he says, "we can argue with them from actual events" (even though, as he himself claims here, Jews are divinely prevented from understanding; *Against Faustus* 12.44). The expectation of the Gentiles' turning to the God of Israel in the messianic age stands in their own sacred writings, says Augustine; that great conversion, achieved through the church, has been most manifestly realized. And the Jews' own history, since the crucifixion of Christ, only reinforces the church's views. Their temple gone, their sacrifices no more, the priestly and kingly anointing ceased: All had happened exactly as their own holy books had foretold.

> That symbolic anointing could not stop until the coming of Christ, who was prefigured by this ritual. For among all of their anointed ones the Jews always searched for their redeemer, the one who was to save them. But *they were blinded by the secret justice of God*. Thinking only of the messiah's power, they failed to understand his weakness, through which he died for us.
>
> AGAINST FAUSTUS 12.44

Excaecati occulta iustitia Dei. Why then can Jews not understand the clear meaning of their own writings, to which they have always been so loyally attached? Because God has blinded them. Why did he do that? We cannot know why: His reasons and the standards of fairness that he uses are "hidden" or "secret" or "obscure" (*occulta*). All that piety can do is affirm that this secret standard must be just, because it is God who uses it.

Augustine on this point sounds very much like Paul, whose letter to the Romans guides him in his own thinking. Paul too had marveled at his kinsmen's unbelief, and he too had attributed their "hardening" to divine initiative. God "hardens whomever he chooses" (Romans 9:18). The elect within Israel understand, but "the rest were hardened"—that is, by God (Romans 11:7). Israel's hardening is a "mystery" (Romans 11:25).

But Paul had written within a time frame that was utterly different from Augustine's. He was convinced that he and his generation stood poised on the cusp of cosmic change, when the god of Israel would ac-

complish the definitive defeat of evil through the imminent return
from heaven of his Son. Paul held this conviction both early and late.
He affirms it in the first letter that we have from him ("We who are
alive, who are left until the [second] coming of the Lord, will not precede those who have died"; 1 Thessalonians 4:15) and he repeats it in his
final one ("Salvation is nearer to us than when we first believed"; Romans 13:11). And history, Paul asserted, would never end with God
breaking his promises to Israel. In Paul's scenario, Israel had been hardened both temporarily and providentially. God wanted the gospel (so
Paul reasons) to go from the "remnant" within Israel (among whom,
says Paul, he himself stands) thence to the Gentiles. The greater part of
Israel would understand only once the Gentiles' "full number" had
been gathered in (Romans 11:25).

God ensured that the gospel would spread according to this pattern of reception by making Israel, for the (brief) time being, deaf and
blind to his message of redemption (Romans 11:8). In other words, according to Paul, God's hardening of Israel was strategic, not punitive.
And it was only temporary. As history rushes to its conclusion, and as
the "full number" of Gentiles comes to Christ, God will cease hardening "part of Israel. . . . And so all Israel will be saved" (Romans 11:26). In
the end, God has mercy on all (Romans 11:32).[4]

Augustine believed firmly that Judaism was essentially, uniquely,
congruent with Christianity. His defense of actual Jewish practice,
both ancient and contemporary, and his insistence that Jesus, Paul,
and the entire first generation of the church had honored the Law and
kept it—and that their gentile counterparts, to the church's benefit,
had adopted some of its precepts—enunciated this belief. So too did
his historicizing typologies, by which he bound both testaments together. His outlook on the abiding sanctity and value of the Law aligns
him in many ways with Paul.

But his perspective, inevitably, is very different. By Augustine's
lifetime, long centuries stood between Christ's resurrection and his
anticipated second coming. Augustine does not share Paul's sense of
an impending ending, with all the clarity that such a conviction can
bring. And he knows something that Paul did not know: that Jewish
Jerusalem, and its Temple, had been destroyed.

The simple passage of time between Paul's period and his own thus required Augustine to reinterpret the significance of the Jews' rejection of the gospel. In his view, this rejection occurs in two distinct phases: first, in the past, with their crucifixion of Jesus, and, second, from that point up to the present, with their continued resistance to the message of the church. And, unlike Paul, Augustine had to make sense of the destruction of the Temple. For him as for the tradition that he stands in, the "death" of the Jews' temple and of their kingdom was the divine penalty exacted for their role in the death of Jesus.

Their own prophets, Augustine repeats, had foreseen that the Jews would kill Christ, that they would not even recognize who he was. (For this reason, Augustine later commented, Jesus had prayed, "Father, forgive them. They do not know what they do" [Luke 23:34; *Faith in Things Unseen* 6.9]. He makes the same point here, alluding to Paul, in *Against Faustus* 13.11, quoted just below.) Seeing contemporary Jewish communities all throughout the empire as the effect of a punitive exile, the transgenerational consequence of "fratricide," facilitated the church's rereading of the Septuagint whereby all these disparate, more recent events could be worked back into the grand pattern of biblical salvation history. All of those prophetic texts that spoke of displacement, loss, and exile under Assyria and Babylon could now be reused to make religious sense of Jerusalem's destruction by Rome and of the Jews' current, wide dispersion. The prophets' words about forgiveness, about the restored and eternal house of David, and about the turning of the Gentiles to the god of Israel could all be referred to the church. "The kings of the earth are now happily subdued by Christ," Augustine enthuses in 399. "All the nations serve him. . . . The hearts of the faithful are confirmed by seeing these ancient predictions now fulfilled" (*Against Faustus* 13.7).

The Jews, by rebuffing the gospel, had certainly given the church ample time and opportunity to go to the Gentiles. Why then was Israel still hardened? Why still blind? And why should they be held accountable if (according to this reading of the prophetic script) it were God himself who had prevented their receiving Christ back in the days of Pilate, and God who prevented it still? Augustine puts these questions into the mouth of an imaginary interlocutor:

Some person might be moved to ask why the Jews, in whose books we find all of these prophecies (which we know have been realized), do not join with us in the communion of the Gospel. But once he was shown that their continuing unbelief had also been foreseen, he would only trust these books that much more. For who is so foolish that he does not see that the Jews do not believe, who so lacking in judgment that he pretends not to see this? Who, indeed, can doubt that the prophet Isaiah spoke precisely about the unbelieving Jews when he said, "The ox knows its owner, the ass its master's stable; but Israel has not known me, my people have not understood me" (Isaiah 1:3)? And elsewhere, as the Apostle reminds us, "All day long I have stretched out my hands to an unbelieving, contrary people" (Isaiah 65:2; Romans 10:21). And especially where he says, "God has given them a spirit of remorse, and eyes so that they do not see, and ears so that they neither hear nor understand" (Isaiah 6:10; Romans 11:8). There are many similar passages.

But what if this person then goes on to ask, *In what way have the Jews sinned, if God was the one who blinded them so that they did not know Christ?*

AGAINST FAUSTUS 13.11

In defense of divine justice, Augustine again invokes divine inscrutability:

If he asks such a question, we would attempt to instruct this naive man, teaching him that the penalty of this blindness that afflicts the Jews is indeed fair, since it is a *punishment for their secret sins, which are known only to God*. And we would demonstrate that both the Apostle and the prophets have spoken about precisely this sort of situation, that is, about the judgment of *secret* sins. "For this reason," Paul says, "God gave them up to the lusts of their own hearts, and to an immoral mind, so that they would act in ways that were not fitting" (Romans 1:24). In saying this, Paul wishes to teach that public, obvious sins occur as the penalty for *prior, hidden sins.* Lest I go on too long, I would then simply point to the prophet Jeremiah. Jeremiah teaches, "He is a man. Who should know him?" But lest the Jews use their not recognizing Christ as an excuse—for if they had known, says the Apostle, "they would not have crucified the Lord of glory" (1 Corinthians 2:8)—the prophet immediately goes on to show that the Jews' not recognizing Christ was itself *the just penalty for something else, something that they had secretly earned.* And so Jeremiah continues, "I, the Lord, search the heart, I try its reins, so that I might give to each one as he deserves, according to the fruit of his deeds" (Jeremiah 17:10).

AGAINST FAUSTUS 13.11[5]

Secret sins known only to God (*occultos peccatis Deo cognitis*). A continuing penalty merited by other, prior, hidden sins (*quorumdam occultorum*). Punishments secretly earned (*occulti meriti*). For Augustine, unlike for Paul, God's hardening of Israel was punitive, not strategic; abiding, not temporary. History was not rushing to a conclusion. The unbelief of the Jews was not a momentary anomaly, useful to the gentile mission though in itself hard to explain. To the late Roman bishop, the Jews' unbelief was a standing condition, an *obduratio*, a hardening long ago foreseen. The only explanation for this state of affairs that honored God's moral character was to hold that the Jews must have sinned in some way that scripture had not recorded, thus in some way that even the most careful reader could not know. But in what way? God knows, answers Augustine. *Only* God knows.

A few years earlier, when coming to the end of *To Simplicianus,* Augustine had pondered "the hardening of the ungodly," the way that God justly decides to leave sinners to their sins. And yet, mercifully but mysteriously, God sometimes chooses to give to some of these sinners the gift of his grace. At this point, Augustine had again recalled Paul's rebuff to the person who might protest that God, in choosing some, was unfair to all. When considering the obscurity of God's judgments, Augustine urged, one should always hear Paul's challenge in Romans 9:20—"Who are you, O man, to answer back to God?"—like a "recurring refrain." "If God's punishment of the ungodly were not just, then his decision to spare a sinner could not be considered a gift. But his punishment *is* just. God is not unrighteous when he punishes." Everyone is sinful. No one is righteous. God would have been perfectly just if he had turned his back on everyone after Adam. But instead—graciously; inexplicably—God calls some sinners to salvation. When and where God does decide to show mercy, then, Augustine concluded, the only appropriate response is to praise God, not to question him (*To Simplicianus* 1.2,18).

It was on this point that Augustine had turned to consider God's selective salvation explicitly in terms of Jews and Gentiles.

> "Us also he has called, not only from the Jews, but also from the Gentiles" (Romans 9:24). Paul speaks here of the vessels of mercy, which God has prepared for glory. He did not call all of the Jews, but only some of them. Nor did he call all of the Gentiles, but only some of them. For a single mass of sinful and impious humanity has come from Adam, to which single lump, absent the grace of God, both Jews and Gentiles belong. If the potter out of this single lump of clay makes one vessel for honor, another for dishonor, then it is clear that God, too, has made from the Jews some vessels for honor and some for dishonor; and he has done the same from the Gentiles. It follows, then, that all humanity must be understood as coming from this single lump.
>
> TO SIMPLICIANUS 1.2,19

This resolution to the mystery of salvation, presented with such urgent conviction in *To Simplicianus*, backlights Augustine's consideration of the same themes when he argues against Faustus. Romans 9:21, the potter's clay, makes no formal appearance; but the figure of Adam, the anguish of the sinner's divided will, and the solution proffered by the *massa damnata* recur throughout this treatise. So too does Augustine's insistence that among the redeemed some Jews will number, since "many Jews, part of fleshly Israel, have believed in Christ, and many of them will, in the future, come to believe in Christ" (*Against Faustus* 22.89). The Jews as a people, however, by divine will, would continue to exist until the end of time (12.12).

What happens to them then? In this treatise Augustine does not say. The one instance here where he quotes Romans 11:26, "All Israel shall be saved," he lets Paul's statement pass without comment (*Against Faustus* 10.2). Elsewhere, when citing Paul, he conjures the pots made from this "single lump," Paul's "vessels of mercy" (Romans 9:23–26). Augustine here varies the definition of the term *Israel*. Sometimes Israel refers to "fleshly" Israel, he says; at other times, to "true" Israel, the community of the redeemed, constituted both from fleshly Israel and from those Gentiles who, as the seed of Abraham, are also heir to the promises of salvation (*Against Faustus* 22.89; Galatians 3:29). Whoever believes rightly, however, whether Jew or Gentile, whether now or eventually, is enabled to do so only by the mercy of God.

Defending the Old Testament against Faustus' arguments, Augustine's appeal to divine inscrutability and to humanity's secret sins provided him as well with a way to make moral sense out of difficult biblical passages. Why, when David ordered a census of his nation, did God reprimand his pride by "lessening the number that he could boast of"—in other words, by killing seventy thousand other people in order to teach a lesson to the king? God in his *occulto iudicio,* his "secret judgment," explained Augustine, had determined that these particular seventy thousand did not deserve to live (*Against Faustus* 22.66; 2 Samuel 24). Why did God forgive David but withhold forgiveness from Saul, when both had acknowledged their respective sins with exactly the same words, in exactly the same way? "The words sounded the same to human ears; the divine eye saw a difference in their hearts" (*Against Faustus* 22.67; 1 Samuel 15:24; 2 Samuel 12:13). When virtually the whole people sinned in the desert with the Golden Calf, why did Moses spare most, but cut three thousand down? Because God, "in his deep and hidden judgment" (*alta et secreto iudicio*) had decided that those particular Israelites merited immediate punishment (*Against Faustus* 22.79; Exodus 32:27–28). Such events stand in scripture, Augustine tirelessly repeats, as *figurae* ("examples") to give Christians opportunity to absorb both the lesson and the warning.

✦✦✦

AUGUSTINE TOOK THIRTY-THREE BOOKS to thrash out his response to Faustus' challenge. Of these, book twenty-two, with its ninety-eight chapters, is the longest. It begins with one of Faustus' most rhetorically lush and scripturally fortified attacks on the Old Testament. These books, said the Manichee, "contain shocking calumnies against God himself" (*Against Faustus* 22.4). The sex lives of the patriarchs were scandalous; that of Israel's kings, even worse (22.5). Moses himself shed blood in violence, as did his god, to a dreadful degree (22.5 and 4). In book twenty-two, Faustus declares himself, plain and simple, the enemy of Judaism (22.2; see p. 219 above).

Augustine returns a barrage of overwhelming force: insults to his opponent's ability to read and to reason (*Against Faustus* 22.7,22,32); arguments directed to a pagan straw man (22.14-19); thoughts on the principles of just war (22.74-75); lectures on the necessarily metaphorical quality of language that imputes emotion to God (22.18,21); observations on the importance of considering historical context when assessing the behavior of ancient actors (22.23-24, 79); and numberless typologies, many extremely imaginative even by the measure of the day. (David's lust for the bathing Bathsheba, for example, "a heinous crime" historically, becomes a typological prophecy of Christ, "the desire of the nations, who loved the Church when she washed herself on the roof, that is, when she cleansed herself of the pollutions of the world"; 22.87.) Amid all this pulsing verbiage, however, comes a surprising respite: a brief meditation on good and evil, right and wrong, the opacity of personal experience, the moral opacity of God. If theological treatises were musical compositions, we would recognize in this passage the same chords that had shaped Augustine's response to Simplicianus, the same chords that had sounded in his long prayer to God, the *Confessions*.

Human acts of justice or injustice must be voluntary. Absent this moral authority, neither just rewards nor just penalties can exist—and no sensible person thinks that. But a man's ignorance or weakness can prevent him from knowing what he ought to do, or from doing what he wants to do. This condition is the consequence of the secret penal arrangements and inscrutable judgments of God, "in whom there is no injustice" (Romans 9:14). God's faithful word thus tells us about Adam's sin; and scripture truthfully relates that "in Adam all die," and that "through him sin entered the world, and through sin, death" (Romans 5:12). How well we know from our own experience that, because of this punishment, the body corrupts and troubles the soul, and "by means of this dwelling of clay, greatly burdens the thinking mind" (Wisdom of Solomon 9:15). How well we know that we can be delivered from God's just sentence only by the grace of his mercy. And so, groaning, the Apostle cries out, "Wretched man that I am! Who will deliver me from this body of death? The grace of God through Jesus Christ, our Lord" (Romans 7:24–25). This much we know. The reasons why God distributes his judgments and his mercy as he does, however, so that one person is like this and the other like that, are hidden; but, nevertheless, they are just. . . . Within the judgment of God and the movements of the human will lies the secret reason why the same prosperity helps one person, but ruins another, or why adversity will undo one person, but strengthen someone else. What a trial is the entire life of man upon this earth! (Job 7:1). . . . But it remains true, nevertheless, that whatever good befalls us comes to us through God's good favor, and whatever bad befalls us comes to us through his just judgment.

AGAINST FAUSTUS 22.78

These thoughts provide the larger theological context for Augustine's extraordinary argument, against Faustus, in defense of Judaism, and for his even more extraordinary argument in defense of the Jewish praxis of Judaism. The pivotal texts for his arguments came from Paul's letters. When reading Paul to extricate him from the interpretations of the Manichees, Augustine thought with Paul's basic, Jewish division of humanity: Israel and the nations. And like Paul, he asserted Israel's historic prerogatives, thereby echoing much of the mood and the matter of Paul's praises of Israel in Romans 9:4–5. No other nation was like Israel. Only Israel had received God's revelation. Only Israel had worshiped God alone, utterly without images. Only Israel had safeguarded, both in word and in deed, those divine mysteries that had pointed ahead to the incarnation and resurrection of God's son, and that pointed ahead still to his redemption of humanity. By crucifying Christ, Israel had helped to bring salvation to the nations. By denying Christ, and thus by continuing in their ancestral understanding of the Law, Israel performed the fulfillment of their own prophecies of exile, and thereby continued to assist in bringing the gospel to the nations. Wandering everywhere, always bearing their books, "tilling the ground" of their earthly understanding of the Law: Israel, all unknowing, was the servant of the church. No less after their rejection of Jesus than before, Israel *secundum carnem* witnessed to God's redemptive acts in history. In this sense and for these reasons, Augustine could agree with Paul's statement, though not with his meaning: "The gifts and the call of God are irrevocable" (Romans 11:29).

But when reading Paul to understand the relationship between soul and body, between willing and wanting, between the individual sinner and God, Augustine dissolves this distinction in favor of another, also derived from Paul. Jews and Gentiles descend equally from Adam; both, back in Eden, had been equally "in Adam." For this reason, the biblical dichotomy, "Jews" and "Gentiles," gives way for Augustine to another, more fundamental dichotomy: "vessels of honor" and "vessels of dishonor," the saved and the damned. As regards salvation, Jews were no better and no worse off than was the rest of humanity's *massa damnata*. Jews too were trapped in the penal condition of ignorance and difficulty that marked all human experience after the Fall. Jews too languished *sub lege,* not wanting to sin but not able, of their own will, not to sin. Whether God chose to leave them there or to bring some from among them *sub gratia,* to himself, he would do so, for them as for anyone, for inscrutable reasons, but justly.

12 ✦ "SLAY THEM NOT . . ."

*The Jews who killed him, who refused to believe in him
and who refused to believe that he had to die and to rise
again, suffered an even more wretched devastation at
the hands of the Romans. Utterly uprooted from their
kingdom . . . they were dispersed the whole world over—
indeed, there is no part of the earth where they are not
found. Thus by the evidence of their own scriptures
they bear witness for us that we have not fabricated the
prophecies about Christ. . . . A prophecy precisely on
this point occurs in the Book of Psalms, which they also
read. . . . "Slay them not" it says, "lest at some time
they forget your Law. Scatter them by your might"
(Psalm 59:12).*

AUGUSTINE, CITY OF GOD 18.46

When Augustine first began to enunciate his thoughts on the
original apostles' keeping Jewish Law, he had written to Jerome, challenging the older man's views on Paul and Peter's confrontation in Antioch (*Letter* 28; p. 186 above). He took that occasion to voice, as well, his reservations about Jerome's great project, a fresh Latin translation of the Old Testament based on Hebrew (thus, Jewish) manuscripts rather than on the traditional Septuagint text. The Greek texts, Augustine pointed out, enjoyed the authority of tradition, and the authenticating miracle of their origin (*Letter* 28.2,2). This letter, entrusted to a colleague in the winter of 394–395, did not reach Jerome.

Augustine followed with a longer letter toward the end of 397 (*Letter* 40). In this second letter, as we have seen, Augustine again raised the issues that had prompted his prior one: the reasons for Paul and Peter's falling out; the status of Paul's report of their argument in

Galatians 2; the necessary truthfulness of biblical narrative, which in turn supports the Bible's authority and that of the church. Augustine also defended once more his view that Paul and Peter, as apostles of the risen Christ, would have continued to live as observant Jews (p. 237 above). And, finally, Augustine suggested to Jerome that the latter formally disavow the erroneous opinions on display in his commentary on Galatians (40.4,7).

Letter 40, unbeknown to Augustine, also wandered. Sometime in 403, still awaiting a response to his questions, Augustine sent copies of his two prior letters, as well as a third, new one, which was both briefer and more urgent than the others (*Letter* 71.1,2). He was anxious, yet again, about the potential for Jerome's scholarship to undermine the authority of the Bible and of the church. At issue this time was not one of Jerome's biblical commentaries, but Jerome's new translation of the Bible itself. In North Africa, this new Latin Old Testament was already, and literally, wreaking havoc.

The quality of the older Latin versions, based on the Septuagint, was uneven and unlovely; but by now, sanctioned by more than two centuries of use in community worship, those versions were traditional, beloved, and deeply familiar. For this reason, when the bishop of Oea (modern Tripoli) introduced Jerome's recent rendering into his community's service, Augustine worriedly related, the congregation nearly rioted. (At issue, perhaps, was the identity of the vine under which the prophet Jonah had rested—a "gourd" so the traditional version or an "ivy" so Jerome; *Letter* 75.7,22; Jonah 4:6.) Those familiar with the Greek claimed that Jerome's new version was incorrect. The poor bishop was compelled to ask local Jews to adjudicate. "Whether out of ignorance or malice," Augustine continued, "they claimed that the Greek and the older Latin said what the Hebrew books said too."[1]

Jerome's work on the gospels, Augustine soothingly continued, was truly wonderful, and "for it we offer God no small thanks. There is almost no problem in any of the passages when we compare it with the Greek original." Why, then, Augustine wondered, did Jerome's translation from the Hebrew differ so markedly from the Septuagint? That older version, Augustine noted, had been the text of choice for the apostles themselves, and "it has no small authority" (*Letter* 71.4,6).

Also, he asked, why leave people in such an awkward situation? Readers could easily check Jerome's work against the Greek, but no such ease of access obtained for Hebrew manuscripts: How then could Jerome's translation be vindicated? (71.2,4). Beneath the courtesy, Augustine's meaning was clear: Jerome's efforts risked a pastoral crisis for the Latin church. "I beg you, in the Lord," concluded Augustine, "do not delay in answering all these questions" (71.4,6).[2]

For better and for worse, Augustine's prayer was soon answered. Already irritated by the unsynchronized epistolary traffic between them—shorter communications had volleyed between the two men before Augustine finally re-sent copies of his first two, long letters together with his query triggered by events in Oea—Jerome responded in high dudgeon and fired off a long and heated reply. Some of the sound and fury of his missive was simply his indignation at Augustine's criticisms, which the famously self-regarding Jerome experienced as an attack. In defense of his reading of Galatians, Jerome proclaimed, his weaponry would be Christ (fortified, however, by a solid wall of Greek patristic authorities, which he knew Augustine could not read; *Letter* 75.2,2–11).

But much of the roar of Jerome's response came from traditional *adversus Iudaeos* rhetoric, now mobilized by Jerome against Augustine himself. Augustine's position on Jewish Christians' having kept the Law, he darkly observed, was a heresy like that of the "Ebionites." This group, "though they believed in Christ, were condemned by our fathers *for the sole reason* that they mixed the ceremonies of the Law with the gospel of Christ and professed the new teaching without giving up the old."[3]

Jerome went on, conjuring a similar contemporary community of Jewish-Christians "found throughout all the synagogues of the East," the heresy of the Minaei (a Latinized form of the Hebrew *minim*, "sectarians"). Even the current Jewish authorities, he said, condemn them. (Jerome designates these authorities "Pharisees," though in the fifth century no Pharisees exist. His word choice, rather, reveals the degree to which the vocabulary of the New Testament could reinforce hostile late Roman Christian rhetoric against both Jews and heretics: Contemporary enemies, thus transformed, became as well the canonical enemies of Christ.) These Jewish Minaei, also known as "Nazareans" (a nod, obviously, to Jesus' hometown of Nazareth), hold much the same faith as do orthodox gentile Christians, Jerome continued. They believe that Jesus was the messiah, that he was also the son of God, and that he was born of the Virgin Mary, suffered under Pontius Pilate, and rose from the dead—all points of doctrine articulated in the church's own creeds.

Not good enough, warns Jerome: The Nazareans' orthodoxy is nullified by their continued Jewish practice. "Insofar as they want to be both Jews and Christians, they are neither Jews nor Christians." Such people can never be accepted into the church, Jerome declares, and not only because their practices, despite their beliefs, make them heretics. Rather, their very example was dangerous; indeed, they themselves are dangerous. "If we were required to accept the [Christian] Jews with their legal observances, and if it becomes permissible for them to observe in the churches of Christ what they practiced in the synagogues of Satan—I am going to say what I think—they will not become Christians, but they will make us Jews!" (*Letter* 75.4,13).

Jerome's assault ran on and on. He scolded Augustine for the "heretical" implications of his views; he heroically warned against the contagions of Jewish practices. ("I shall proclaim frankly, even if the whole world shouts against me, that the ceremonies of the Jews are dangerous and deadly for Christians and that whatever Christian keeps them, Jew or Gentile, has gone down into the Devil's pit!"; *Letter* 75.4,14.) As for those Jews in Oea who challenged the aptness of Jerome's new translation—"your Jews," as he calls them—clearly they either did not know Hebrew, or else they lied: no surprise, huffed Jerome, because it was well known that Jews willingly corrupted even the Hebrew text of Scripture just to spite Christians (75.6,20–22).

✦✦✦

SOMEWHERE BENEATH all this overheated rhetoric burned Jerome's desire to bully Augustine into some version of the awkward position that he himself was in. Before moving to Bethlehem from Rome in the late 380s, Jerome had undertaken to produce a new Latin translation of the Bible. In the West, neither the New Testament nor the Old Testament had ever had a single authoritative Latin version, and a miserable multiplicity of local traditions was the result. (Augustine himself had noted the vast number and variable quality of Western translations in *Christian Teaching*: "In the early days of the faith, any person who got hold of a Greek manuscript and who thought of himself as skilled in both languages went ahead with his own Latin translation"; *Christian Teaching* 2.11,16.) Jerome's efforts to produce a standard text began with the gospels, and this new version was received with relatively little controversy. Once he began work on the Old Testament, however, Jerome decided to bypass the Septuagint, and instead to work up a fresh translation based on the original Hebrew.

By this point, those forms of gentile Christianity that had laid claim to the Septuagint had a long and ambivalent relationship with its Hebrew foundations. On the one hand, Hebrew, and originary Jewishness, authenticated "orthodox" tradition: The very architecture of the double canon, Old and New Testaments, declared this idea. By the second century, some gentile Christians reinforced the authority of the Gospel of Matthew—attributed by tradition to one of the original twelve apostles—by claiming that it had been composed first in "Hebrew" for preaching to Jewish Christians and translated only later into Greek. From the fourth century onward, with the imperial development of a Christian Holy Land in the Galilee and in what was once Judea, legends grew about miraculous retrievals of sacred relics: the shirt that Mary wore while nursing Jesus, pieces of the true cross, the bones of St. Stephen. Such stories often featured a "wise Jew" who, combining local knowledge with biblical authority, established the authenticity of the sacred object or place. (Frequently, their mission completed, such "Jews" end the tale by converting to the church.) *Verus Israel*, "true Israel" (that is, the "true" church) was supported by the olive trunk of the *veritas hebraica*, Hebrew (but also Jewish) truth.[4]

Yet gentile Christians had also long been aware of unnerving differences between the Greek and the Hebrew texts of the Jewish scriptures. Justin Martyr, in his *Dialogue with Trypho*, discussed at length the reading of Isaiah 7:14: *parthenos* or "virgin" in the Greek, *aalmah* or "young girl" in the Hebrew. He complained to Trypho about "Jewish teachers" who maintained that the Greek *neanis,* "young girl," would better capture the meaning of the original text (*Trypho* 43; 66–67). At other points, Justin accused Jews of suppressing Christological references in the Greek biblical text by editing them out. (Trypho responded that this "seems incredible"; *Trypho* 72–73. These Christian "references" had actually been edited in.) Christian interpolations into Old Testament texts had become notorious enough by the late fourth century that Manichees, publicly disputing with less exotic Christians, could score cheap points by alluding to the subject. ("Shall we take another favorite passage of yours: 'They shall see their life hanging, and shall not believe their life'? You insert the words 'on a tree,' which are not in the original"; Deuteronomy 28.66; *Against Faustus* 16.5. Augustine does not rebut Faustus on this particular point.) Finally, in the 230s, the great Christian scholar Origen, then living in Caesarea on the coast of modern-day Israel, determined to sort out a stable version of the Septuagint. This project involved him in research in Hebrew language and in the Hebrew text of the Bible, thus with local Jewish scholars as well. Origen's work, in this sense, paved the way for Jerome's.[5]

But in terms of temperament if not of talent, Jerome was no Origen; and compared with the politics of theological dispute in the third century, those of the late-fourth-century church, thanks to imperial patronage, were much more fraught. And even though Jerome the monk was a trilingual biblical scholar—a public image that he vigorously cultivated through steady streams of letters, commentaries, and translations of various texts both Greek and Hebrew—he was also a fierce controversialist, a good hater, and a dogged fighter. In the public arena of fourth- to fifth-century pan-Mediterranean theological brawling, however, he got as good as he gave. By so advertising his Jewish expertise, he had handed his enemies a powerful weapon. Jerome's advertisements for himself—stories dropped about his nighttime Hebrew tutorials with Jewish teachers, about his consultations on biblical interpretation with local Jews, and about his ready familiarity with Hebrew names and places—could be and were used against him. To express Christian truth, claimed his enemies, Jerome had relied inappropriately, even dangerously, on Jewish knowledge.[6]

Augustine's letters thus presented Jerome with a golden opportunity to display his own bona fides, his principled awareness as a good Christian of the contaminating dangers of Jews and of Judaism. Unhesitatingly, he accused the younger man of Judaizing, just as his enemies had done to him. Using the time-honored script of *adversus Iudaeos* tradition, invoking other unacceptable mixes of Jewish practice and Christian doctrine—the Ebionites, the Minaei, the Nazareans—Jerome categorized Augustine's proposals as heretically "mixed" as well. True Christianity could give no scope to those who were both Jew and Christian at the same time. And Jerome's alarmist, there-goes-the-neighborhood argument (absent sufficient hostility to Judaism, he warns, the next thing to happen will be Christians who Judaize or, still worse, who convert to Judaism) served to caution Augustine even more vividly of the dire consequences of thinking as he did—and thus of disagreeing with Jerome (*Letter* 75.4,13–14).

But Augustine had already withstood this sort of barrage at close range once before. Faustus, in his *Capitula,* had employed exactly the same rhetoric, drawn from the same tradition, as did Jerome in his epistle. They had even deployed some of the same tropes. Musing on the dangerous consequences of inadequately identifying and excising covert Jewish incursions into Christian truth, Faustus had spoken of his own previous spiritual endangerment. Back when he, as a pagan, had thought of converting to Christianity, Faustus recounted, he had initially contacted the wrong sort of people, people who had the wrong sorts of texts. These people may not have thought of themselves as Jews, he continued, but they esteemed the Law and the prophets as Christian scripture, and they uncritically adhered to questionable gospel texts. Recalling his difficulties with Jesus' saying in Matthew 5:17 ("Do not think that I have come to abolish the Law and the prophets; I have come not to abolish but to fulfill them"), Faustus told how

I, like you, from reading this verse without sufficient consideration, had almost resolved to become a Jew. And rightly so,
for if Christ came not to destroy the Law but to fulfill it, and if
a vessel, to be fully filled, must not be empty but rather partially

filled to start with, I concluded that no one other than a Jew
could possibly become a Christian. That was the way to be nearly
filled with the Law and the prophets, so that then coming to
Christ would fill the person to his capacity. . . . It seemed then
that I, as a Gentile, could get nothing by coming to Christ, for I
brought nothing that could be filled up from his additions. What
is required in order to be partially filled? Sabbaths, circumcision,
sacrifices, new moons, immersions for purification, the Feast of
Unleavened Bread, distinctions of food, drink and clothes, and
other things too numerous to specify. . . . With Christ, as the Son
of God, seeming to say that he had come not to destroy these
things but to fulfill them, what was to prevent me from becoming
a Jew?

AGAINST FAUSTUS 16.5[7]

This is Faustus' version of the there-goes-the-neighborhood argument, used with such flourish by Jerome. And their dire warning
shared the same *sous-texte,* Faustus with orthodox North African
Christians in view, Jerome thinking mainly of Augustine: Just because
the audience for this cautionary tale did not know that they or he had
slid down the slippery slope of heretical Judaizing did not mean that
such was not, in fact, the case. The worrying example of other wayward
faux-Christian communities, such as the near-proverbial Nazareans,
lay ready to hand. (Faustus, like Jerome, also invokes them, and to the
same end. "Such people practice circumcision, they keep the Sabbath,
they shun swine's meat and other things like that, all according to the
Law. And yet they still claim to be Christians!"; *Against Faustus* 19.3). Finally, both the Manichee and the monk lamented loudly that such Judaizing, even if un-self-aware, polluted the sacred memory of those
foundational figures holy to the true church. "Beware of making Jesus
into a liar, and of making yourself into a Jew, by obligating yourself to
fulfill the Law just because Christ did not destroy it!" (*Against Faustus*
19.3). "How well you succeed in defending Paul! He did not pretend to
hold the Jews' error; he actually did hold it. . . . What an original sense
of mercy the Apostle demonstrates! While he wanted to turn Jews into
Christians, he made himself into a Jew. . . . How pathetic, how de-

plorable are those who, on account of their own belligerence and their love for the abolished Law, make a Jew out of the Apostle of Christ!" (*Letter* 75.4,17).

✦ ✦ ✦

AUGUSTINE RESPONDED to Jerome's bullying in *Letter* 82 (c. 405). It is a miniature masterpiece of careful and creative biblical interpretation combined with moral exhortation and quiet authority—a striking contrast to Jerome's preceding scholar-as-diva performance. In this letter, Augustine repeats, with clarity and conviction, many of the important points made earlier and less elegantly in his commentary on Galatians, in his treatise *About Lying,* and in his baggy, prolix rejoinder to Faustus. He begins from a position of experience, warning Jerome of the dangers of imputing the "useful lie" to Paul, Peter, and the scene described in Galatians:

> The Manichees claim, when they cannot twist the lucid teachings
> of the holy scriptures to some other meaning, that very many
> passages in these same scriptures must be false. . . . And yet even
> they do not attribute this falsity to the apostles who wrote them
> [as Jerome's reading did], but rather to persons unknown who
> later corrupted the manuscripts. . . . Does not your holy wisdom
> understand how great an opportunity would lie open to their
> malice were we to say that the apostles' letters had been falsified
> not by others, but by themselves?
>
> LETTER 82.2,6

And then, with appeals to the Law and the prophets, referring to the gospels, Paul's letters, and Acts, Augustine calmly rehearses once more the assertions that had given Jerome his excuse for accusing Augustine of Judaizing. Unfazed, training his sights on the incident at Antioch, Augustine repeats Paul's avowal: "As for what I am writing to you, look, before God, I do not lie!" (Galatians 1:20; *Letter* 82.2,7).

Paul had always and everywhere vigorously denied that Gentiles should observe the Law like the Jews, said Augustine; but scripture abounds with instances where Paul himself, as a Jew who was a Christian, kept the Law. "When Paul circumcised Timothy, or fulfilled his Nazirite vow at Cenchreae, or when he . . . undertook the celebrations of those rites [at the Temple], . . . he did this so that he would not be thought to condemn, like the Gentiles' idolatry, those rites that God had commanded in earlier times, fittingly, to foreshadow things to come" (Acts 16:3, 18:18, 21:26; *Letter* 82.2,8). Those Christians of Judea who were zealous for the Law had accused Paul of preaching against it to diaspora Jews; but that accusation was false, and Paul's sacrificing in the Temple proved it so. "At that time, the [Christian] Jews were not to be kept from those rites as if they were wicked, and the Gentiles were not to be forced to those rites as if they were necessary" (*Letter* 82.2,9). (After all, he notes shortly later, "it was God who commanded people to practice circumcision, but Satan who convinced them to worship idols," 82.2,12.) Finally, harking back to his argument that historical and social context had to be considered when interpreting the Bible, Augustine observes that the commands of the Law should not be regarded as something bad just because they cannot make people good, a transformation that only God's grace through Christ can do. "They are *not* bad, because they were commanded by God as appropriate to those times and persons" (82.2,14). That "appropriate time" included, emphatically, "the time of the presence of the Lord in the flesh, and during the apostolic generation" (82.2,15).

Augustine courteously thanks Jerome for his concern in cautioning him against the ideas of "the heretics who, while they wanted to be both Jews and Christians, were neither Jews nor Christians"—the much maligned, much-invoked Ebionites and Nazareans. "You were so kind to warn me," he deadpans, "with the greatest good will to avoid their opinion, though in fact I had never thought to do otherwise" (*Letter* 82.2,15). But that case has no bearing at all, he insists, on the sincerity of Paul's Jewish practice. Or was Jerome saying that Paul and all the other observant Jewish Christians of his generation were right to keep the Law, but only if they did so as a pretense? If so, continues Augustine, then "we are slipping not into the heresy of Ebion or of those commonly called Nazareans, but into some new heresy that is even more destructive, since it arises not from error, but from an aim and a desire to deceive" (82.2,16). (Besides, he adds, a person motivated to take on Jewish practices chiefly by a love of deceit would have to be crazy: *insanire*.) He closes this part of his response to Jerome by summoning a powerful Roman image of piety, dignity, and filial affection: the respect due to the body of a deceased parent.

> Once the faith that had been announced by these observances
> and fulfilled by the death and resurrection of the Lord had finally
> come, it was as if the vitality drained out of their celebration. And
> yet, like the bodies of the deceased, they had to be borne to their
> burial, not with feigned respect but with genuine piety, neither
> abandoned immediately nor cast off to the abuse of their enemies
> as if to a dog's fangs.

This image of burial implied closure, however, as well as affection and respect.

> Now, however, if any Christian—even if he is a Jew—wishes to
> celebrate these observances once again, that would be like
> disturbing ashes already at rest; not like once again piously
> accompanying the body to its resting place, but rather like
> wickedly violating its tomb.
>
> LETTER 82.2,16

So no, Augustine says, a Jew who converts to Christianity now, or any Gentile who is a Christian, is not at liberty to reengage these old *sacramenta;* and he refers Jerome to his earlier writing *Against Faustus* where, he says, he had already opined as much (*Letter* 82.2,17; *Against Faustus* 19.17). And, Augustine continues, "I absolutely agree with your statement that any Christian who observes these, be he from the Jews or from the Gentiles, whether deceitfully or sincerely, has plunged into the Devil's pit" (*Letter* 82.2,18). Yet he immediately turns back to the period of the gospels (could he be needling Jerome?) and insists on the sincere piety of Jesus' own Jewish observance. Jesus himself had been circumcised—not as a pretense (*fallaciter*) by his parents or because he was then too young to defend himself. He sent the cured leper to the priest "as Moses commanded." He worshiped in the Temple on the great Jewish feast days. Jesus, like Paul and like Peter and like James and like all of his other apostles, had lived his life as a pious and Law-observant Jew (82.2,19).

As he begins to wind down his response, Augustine turns yet once again to the fight between Peter and Paul in Antioch and to Paul's account of it in Galatians 2. Asserting once again that Paul acted deceitfully neither during this argument nor in his later account of it, Augustine considers the figure of Peter. Back in 394–395, when writing his own commentary on Galatians, Augustine had praised Peter's exemplary humility in sustaining correction from a junior colleague in public—the harder role by far, Augustine noted at the time, than to be the one correcting a colleague in public (On Galatians 2:11,15). Now, ten years later, Augustine dwells on Peter's humility and the value of his example, "for he offered to those who would come after him a rarer and holier model of behavior than did Paul. For Peter offered them an example that they should not decline to receive correction even from younger men. . . . Thus in Paul we praise righteous freedom and in Peter, holy humility" (Letter 82.2,22). Jerome, Augustine's senior, was a careful reader of texts. We can assume that he caught Augustine's drift.

Augustine takes another ten chapters to finish this communication. He is studiously courteous, occasionally tongue-in-cheek. He admiringly notes all of the Greek authorities—"six or seven, as I recall"—whom Jerome had cited, admitting frankly that he had read none of them; though he does mention, in passing, that Jerome had also, elsewhere, criticized or denounced four of these—"including Origen, whom you had earlier praised most marvelously"—so that of this group only three remained standing (Letter 82.3,23). Augustine continues by admitting that his interpretation of Galatians, thus his views on Jewish law, are his own. But he is not alone: "The apostle Paul comes to my rescue." Citations to innumerable authorities, he implies (is he needling Jerome again?), mean less than does being loyal to canonical scriptures, to being certain that none was written to deceive, and, of course, to having Paul on one's side (82.3,24).

Can Augustine and Jerome be friends? Augustine puts the question, asking whether truly Christian friendships can occur in a context where the witticism of the pagan author Terrence—" 'Flattery begets friends, but truth gives birth to hatred' obtains more than does the saying of the church, 'Wounds from a friend are more trustworthy than are the willing kisses of an enemy' " (Proverbs 27:6; *Letter* 82.3,31). He apologizes for the way that his earlier letter had wandered in Rome, creating such a stir that Jerome thought that Augustine had written and circulated a book attacking him. He promises to do better, and begs that Jerome will always correct him when he needs to be corrected. A passing acknowledgment of the differences in their ecclesiastical rank ("to be a bishop"—Augustine's office—"is greater than being a priest") gives way to a soothing courtesy ("Augustine is still less than Jerome in many ways") and to one last reference to the "correct" interpretation of the incident at Antioch and the relevance of Peter's example for Jerome ("although, one should not reject or disdain correction, even from someone inferior"), and then, finally, Augustine is done (82.4,33). Well, almost. Those conspiratorial Jews whom Jerome had mentioned, the ones who covertly alter biblical texts whether Hebrew or Greek to spite Jerome: "Would you be so good as to point out what Jews ever did this?" (82.5,34; Jerome had complained in *Letter* 75.6,20–21).

✦✦✦

WITH THESE LETTERS, we have begun to move out onto different terrain in terms of our evidence for retrieving what Augustine writes about Jews and Judaism. First, beginning shortly after the turn of the century, we lose the Manichees as a prime focus of Augustine's attention. Perhaps he no longer felt them to be a serious challenge to the North African church; perhaps, if they ever had been such a threat (doubtful, I think), they no longer were. Or perhaps Augustine decided that by now he had argued and written enough to establish his own bona fides as an ex-Manichee. With this diminution, however, his remarks on Jews and Judaism, both positive and negative, scatter into different rhetorical and theological contexts, and thus they often do different duty.

Second, the old accepted chronology of Augustine's letters and sermons, because of spectacular finds of previously unknown manu-

scripts in the last decades of the twentieth century, has been strained
to bursting. The entire enormous project of going over all of this corpus, and of integrating it with a chronology for his treatises, must begin again. With Augustine's major writings, the situation is not nearly
so severe. Thanks to the *Retractations* (the catalogue of his own works
that Augustine composed toward the end of his life), and thanks to
the meshing of various sorts of references internal to his works together with well-known external dates, the gross chronology of those
works—or, at the very least, their sequence—is fairly secure. With his
letters and his sermons, however—writings of his not included in the
Retractations—we lose this security.

Another reason for some of the uncertainty on dates and sequence
is the scope and size of the major writing projects that Augustine, after *Against Faustus,* begins to undertake. According to the older
chronology (we do not have a newer one), Augustine started his important work on the Trinity in 399; he finishes sometime in 419. His
Literal Commentary on Genesis, begun in 401, is not completed until 414.
The sermons on the Gospel of John, which we'll consider shortly, take
the decade between 407 and 417, according to some scholars; others
prefer 412–420. The *Sermons on the Psalms* (all one hundred and fifty of
them) also range across years, from 392 to 418. *City of God,* finally, gets
under way three years after the "fall" of the city of Rome in 410; Augustine concludes it in 426. In short, his big projects occupy zones of
time. They lack precise dates of composition.[8]

Shorter treatises also appear regularly all throughout these years,
and Augustine produces an astonishing stream of letters and other
sermons as well. Where we have chronological scaffolding provided by
the *Retractations,* or where we can find an echo from a datable work of
a particular set of themes or associations in another, undated one, we
can still have a reasonably good sense of where we are. But in pursuit
of our specific topic, we will have to consider works whose period of
composition is very uncertain. Augustine's sermon *Against the Jews,* for
example, not mentioned in the *Retractations,* has been assigned variously to 418–419, to 425, and to 429. Another relevant writing that
probably began life as a sermon, *Faith in Things Unseen,* used to be dated
early (c. 400); currently, it is dated late (420–425). And in one madden-

ing incident of near-synchrony, a letter to Augustine from an episcopal colleague in Italy, Paulinus, coincides approximately with the date when Augustine would have composed his two sermons on Psalm 59.[9]

In those two homilies, Augustine referred a line specifically to the Jewish people. "Slay them not, lest my people forget. Scatter them in your might" (Psalm 59:12). This quotation from Psalm 59, understood as directed to contemporary Jews, will eventually become the signature statement of Augustine's so-called witness doctrine. But was this usage original to him? Paulinus had also "thought with Jews" when reading this psalm, framing his ideas with questions gleaned from Paul's letter to the Romans. In *Letter* 121 (currently dated between 410 and 415) he wrote to Augustine with questions about his interpretation of these texts. Was Paulinus the one who, in his letter to Augustine, first drew this connection between Psalm 59:12 and the Jews? And thus was Paulinus the one who first suggested this reading to Augustine? Or did Augustine, composing his sermon on this psalm sometime in the same period, come to this idea independently, so that when he received Paulinus' questions, he already had his answers (*Letter* 149, written perhaps late in 416)? We will look more closely at their correspondence shortly.

This use of Psalm 59:12, in either case, reprises the same cluster of themes that Augustine in *Against Faustus* had attached to the figure of Cain. Augustine's exposition of this line from Psalms, like his exposition of the figure of Cain in Genesis 4, combines the ideas of punitive wandering and of divine protection, both for the benefit of the church, mediated in some fashion on account of and by the Jewish understanding of the Law. Before continuing our pursuit of Augustine's positive usage of these ideas of Jews and Judaism, however, we should consider also his very different statements about Jews, made as he gave sermons on a different biblical text, the Gospel of John.

John's gospel, the bane of modern interfaith dialogue, contains some of the harshest language about Jesus' Jewish contemporaries of any writing in the New Testament. Most of these statements come out of the mouth of its main character. John structures his story around high-contrast polarities: light/darkness, above/below, God/Satan, spirit/flesh, sight/blindness, knowledge/ignorance. Jesus and his fol-

lowers belong to and embody the positive cluster. "The Jews" throughout John's story are their opponents. John's Jesus tells them forthrightly, "You are from below, I am from above. You are of this world, I
am not of this world" (John 8:23). John's Jesus represents the only way
to know God the Father; since the Jews do not know who he is, they
clearly do not know the Father either, though they insist that they do
("We have one father, God himself"; John 8:41). They oppose Jesus and
try to kill him (John 7:1, 7:19, 10:31, 11:53). They are not "of God"; far
from it. As Jesus tells them, "You are of your father the devil" (John
8:44). And even though the Romans must, in the end, make some appearance in and around the crucifixion, they are not the villains of the
piece. As John's Jesus consoles Pilate, who resists proceeding with the
execution, he tells him that "the one who handed me over to you"—
that is, the Jewish high priest—"is guilty of the greater sin" (John 19:11).

Augustine takes this gospel's highly hostile representation of Jews
and, in the course of creating his sermons, usually makes it worse. One
scholar, analyzing this material in a recent close study, has noted that
60 of the 124 sermons contain "appreciable anti-Jewish material, and
between fifteen and seventeen are extensively or completely taken up
with it." The tone and tenor of John's gospel obviously make their own
contribution. But much of Augustine's hostile characterization, so
readily obliged by this particular gospel, contrasts sharply with prominent features of his own earlier work. Here he repeats many of the
standard tropes of *contra Iudaeos* invective, even if those speak against
the arguments that we have watched him develop so arduously elsewhere. For example, when arguing with Manichees, Augustine had understood Jewish blood sacrifices as God's prime teaching device to
prophesy his incarnate Son. When presenting his sermons on John's
gospel, Jewish sacrifices become the same old same old: "You know
that the sacrifices were given to that people because they were so
fleshly, their hearts so stony, in order to keep them from falling into
idolatry" (*Sermons on the Gospel of John* 10.4): This line could have come
(and in a sense, had come) from Tertullian's *Against Marcion*. Carnal
people, carnal promises, stony hearts, an ever-present proclivity
toward idol worship: Augustine's Johannine Jews seem a different tribe
from the one encountered in *Against Faustus*.[10]

As we have seen him do in earlier writings, so here: Augustine easily segues from the "scriptural Jews" of the passage that he explicates
to contemporary "rhetorical Jews," modern instantiations of the various vices and sins that he sees in, or reads into, the gospel story. From
time to time—a standard move in ancient rhetoric—he addresses these
Jews directly. ("Is the living temple of God to be laid low by your
blows?" [*Sermons on John* 93.4]; "Have you become so hardened, false Israelites?" [114.40].) Sometimes we can catch a glimpse of his actual
fifth-century Jewish neighbors, passing their Sabbaths by dancing on
their balconies, when he criticizes the Jews' "fleshly," unspiritual day
of rest. ("God forbid . . . that we call that kind of thing 'observing the
Sabbath'!" *Sermons on John* 3.19. We'll return to dancing Jews in a moment.) Often where the biblical text has "Pharisees" or "priests," Augustine is happy to substitute "Jews." When he is not itemizing Jewish
sinfulness ("malice," "evil," "perversity," "hatefulness"), he laments
Jewish spite, envy, and arrogance. Jesus' death, for Augustine as for
John's gospel, occurs less through the specific agency of Jerusalem's
priests or leaders than through the generalized agency of "the Jewish
people." And in twenty-three of the places where he thus inculpates
the whole people, the gospel text that he comments on has no connection to Jesus' death at all.

Some of the themes from Augustine's more "positive" theology of
Judaism do make their appearance in these homilies, but they are the
somber ones. The scattering of the Jews post-70 C.E., for example, here
as in patristic commentary generally, is the punishment for their role
in Jesus' death. But Augustine adds to this idea his signature positive
gloss: More than merely punitive, the Jews' exile is also providential,
because everywhere that Jews go, they bring their books with them.
Thus, and despite their hostility, they serve everywhere to authenticate
Christian claims, because their exile, the penalty for the crime of
killing Christ, was foretold by their own prophets (e.g., *Sermons on John*
35.7). Augustine also repeats his solution to the mystery of salvation:
Jews do not believe because Jews do not want to believe. But he also
maintains that Jews do not believe because they cannot believe: God
has blinded them. On what basis? And how fairly? "God blinds and he
hardens by abandoning, by not helping. He does this *occulto iustitio,* by

a hidden judgment." Once again, Augustine's God is both merciful and just, but never at the same time to the same individual. In human experience, God is *either* merciful *or* he is just. "There cannot be injustice with God. Thus, when he helps, he acts mercifully; and when he does not help, he acts justly" (53.6).

What sense can we make of these differences between the Augustine of *Sermons on John* and the Augustine of *Against Faustus*? Their contrast gives us, first of all, some measure of the force and the flexibility of Augustine's rhetoric and some appreciation for the way that different contexts and different audiences affect both what he says and how he says it. Against Faustus, Augustine defends catholic canon and dogma—the Christian relevance of the Jewish scriptures, the work of redemption achieved by the incarnate Christ. Before his own congregations, he exploits the stark contrasts of the fourth gospel as one of the ways to communicate the doctrinal principles that he sees in John: Christ's divinity and his humility; the absolute difference between right and wrong understandings of the Law and thus of grace ("the Jews" of course represent the wrong understanding); the sharp distinctions between carnal and spiritual, between the synagogue and the church. His rhetoric, in both instances, illumines for us not Augustine's "feelings" about or dealings with real Jews, but his construction and use of various kinds of "Jews" in service to whatever teaching that, at a given moment, he wants to drive home.

+++

TO INSIST on the rhetorical quality of these "Jews" in Augustine's works is *not* to say that real Jews were not a normal part of the North African landscape. Jews had lived in North Africa for centuries, and Carthage probably held the largest Jewish settlement outside of Rome in the Western Diaspora. Nor is it to say, because Augustine uses "rhetorical Jews," that Augustine had limited contacts with actual Jews. Except for the accident of a single letter, recently discovered, we have no evidence of contacts, and we also have no evidence for lack of contacts. What we do have is no clear evidence. Did Augustine deal frequently with actual Jews? Infrequently? Almost never? Not at all? Absent evidence, how can we know?

Three questions need to be considered before attempting any re-construction of Augustine's personal interactions with his Jewish con-temporaries. First, where are these Jews? Second, what in Augustine's works provides us with any information about these Jews? Third, where and how would Augustine most likely have encountered these Jews?

Augustine in his student years had lived in Carthage (something that he will continue to do, irregularly, as bishop of Hippo), and later in Italy: in Rome, in Milan, in Cassiciacum, and (briefly) in Ostia, Rome's port city. Rome, Milan, and Ostia certainly had significant Jewish populations (Rome's was enormous); but Augustine makes no mention of Jews when he writes about his sojourn in those places (such as *Confessions* book 5 or book 9). If we want to catch glimpses of real Jews in his works, then, we need to look to Carthage, to Hippo, and to other North African towns. (We have bumped into the Jews of Oea already, p. 291 above.)

How many Jews did North Africa hold? Out of what total popula-tion? As usual with ancient demography, numbers elude us. There is no way to know, in part because there is no way to be secure in the in-terpretation of inscriptions, grave finds, and other such material evi-dence. Also, given a gentile Christian population as steeped in biblical culture as North Africa's was, clarity on the ethnic/religious prove-nance of an artifact—Latin-speaking Jews? Gentile Judaizers? Regular church-going Gentiles?—can be difficult to come by. (Absent familiar-ity with the culture of the seventeenth-century Massachusetts Bay Colony, an archaeologist from some distant future, armed only with her own knowledge of the Bible, might conjecture from all the Heph-zibahs and Calebs and Abigails and Ezras on colonial grave markers that New England had been settled by English-speaking diaspora Jews.)[11]

Jews, Jewish, Judaism, synagogue, Israel: These words and their cog-nates appear countless times in Augustine's writings, as in the writ-ings of most patristic authors. Given the historical development of orthodox Christian identity, this is not surprising. (And very fre-quently—though not always—these writers' Jews are "Jews in the head.") Sometimes Augustine mentions something only incidentally that might, perhaps, attest to proximity and observation. In *Against*

Faustus, he notes that Jews neither cook on the Sabbath nor pick fruit from a field on that day. Taunting Faustus in this same passage, he suggests, "It would be good if you would rest at home—and not just one day a week, like the Jews, but every day" (*Against Faustus* 6.4). He mentions as common knowledge that Jews chant psalms in daily worship (*On Psalms* 148.17: The hymns of Christians are better). Jews celebrate Sukkot for a week, he remarks elsewhere, for which they build booths (*Sermon* 133.1). Jewish men spend Shabbat in the theater (*On Psalms* 50.1), while the women dance on their balconies. (This dancing he found very irritating, and he complains about it in a number of sermons and writings: *Sermon* 9.3,3; *On Psalms* 32.2,1,6; 91.2.) Jews butcher a lamb for Passover: Once, Augustine had thought of this practice as offering a "sacrifice." Later, he corrects himself and rightly identifies the practice as simply part of the preparation for the commemorative Passover meal (*Genesis against the Manichees* 1.23,40; *Retractations* 1.9,2).

Jews can serve as positive moral exemplars as well as negative ones, and they sometimes do double-duty within the same sermon. Augustine brings up Jewish behavior to a listening congregation in order to upbraid them, a not-even-the-Jews-do-this technique. Not even the Jews or the laborers attended an imperially sponsored theater festival in the town of Simittu, so the men of Bulla Regia should stop availing themselves of actors, prostitutes, and theatrical entertainments. (Confusingly, he then cites Carthage as a place of dubious morality, precisely because it is full of Jews; *Sermon S. Denis* 17.7–9; quoted on p. 79 above.) Not even the Jews exchange small gifts of money on the (pagan) January New Year: Neither should his Christians (*Sermon* 196.4). Whether these Jews are actual or exemplary (thus Jews or "Jews") is hard to tell. Augustine seems aware that not all Jews are committed to the same level of religious observance, and he mentions this to his congregation when speaking on the parable of the prodigal son (*Sermon* 112A.13): This observation may attest to actual familiarity. And, finally, Jews—real ones, we must assume—can serve as consultants, to help Christians to better understand the meaning of Hebrew words, whether in the Old Testament (as at Oea) or in the New (as for the transliterated *rasha,* "wicked man," of Matthew 5:22; *The Lord's Sermon on the Mount* 1.9,23).

Jews, we can safely assume, really did live in Augustine's neighborhoods. He pointed to them; he described them; he expected his audience to know whom he meant. But where might he have actually interacted with Jews? In three places, primarily. First, there were the public municipal spaces (baths, forum, theater, circus, schools, market, and so on). How much time would Augustine the bishop have spent in such places? Probably not much. Augustine the student in Carthage and, later, Augustine the professor of rhetoric (both in Carthage and later in Milan), probably much more. After Monnica dies, he mentions specifically going to the baths at Ostia (*Confessions* 9.12,32). Later, back in Africa, inter-Christian contests that he participated in, whether against Manichees or against Donatists, took place in the baths, which offered some of the largest enclosed spaces in any Roman city. Did Augustine encounter Jews in these public spaces? He makes no mention. Given patterns of urban living in Roman late antiquity, we must infer that he most probably did, because it would be incredible if he did not. And given his silence on the subject, we can also infer that such encounters as he did have in these venues were inconsequential.

The second place where Augustine might have encountered and interacted with Jewish contemporaries was in Christian basilicas. We know from varied evidence—some of it, the remarks of irritated churchmen—that Jews (and heretics and pagans) might choose to listen to a sermon. And canon 84 from the Fourth Council of Carthage, in 436, forbade bishops to debar these outsiders from services (see p. 399, n. 24, below).

If we look to Augustine's sermons, do they evince the presence of Jews? Yes and no. He will "address" Jews in his sermons, but this is a common rhetorical device to infuse drama into presentation. We cannot infer from his rhetoric that real Jews were in the room. Speaking at length about the identity of the "true Israel" against the Jewish claim, Augustine says to his congregation, "It may be well to address them, briefly, *as if* they were present"; and from that point on he narrates a disputation between "the Jews" and himself (*Sermon against the Jews* 7.9). What Augustine says about Jews is his sermons can range from mildly positive (especially when he complains to his congregation about how badly catholics are acting) to hardly inviting to down-

right insulting. "Open your eyes, Jews! The sun is shining over here"—
that is, in the church, though the Jews are lost in shadows (*Sermon*
136.3). Augustine will also exhort his congregation to "look at" or to
"hear" Jews, whether contemporary ones or biblical/textual ones: another dramatizing device. "Look at the masses of Jews right now! See
how that nation is uprooted, scattered throughout the whole world.
Look at the [olive tree's] branches, broken and cut away" (*Sermons on
John* 16.3). "See how the Jews wish to kill him!" (*Sermons on John* 51.8).
This sort of rhetorical address in a sermon cannot with any security
present us with (so to speak) the Jew in the pew.

A glance at the subject index under *Jew* or *Judaism* in any volume
of Augustine's sermons reveals the familiar themes of *adversus Iudaeos*
invective: Jews are blind, hard-hearted, fleshly, stubborn, and prideful;
they murdered Christ; they are exiles; they carry the church's books;
they are saved only by conversion. Would late-fourth- to early-fifth-
century North African Jews care to listen to this? I can only guess, but
I would guess not. But perhaps Jews went to hear him on Christmas?
In a sermon for that day preached in Hippo, Augustine says to his congregation, "You are all Christians. By the grace of God, the city is
Christian. There are only two sorts of people here, Christians and
Jews" (*Sermon* 196.4). Is "here" the basilica, and thus the congregation
before him? Or is "here" Hippo, and thus the larger population of the
town? With most scholars, I think "town." On the other hand, Augustine was one of the greatest verbal performers of his day within a
culture where such performances were savored, appreciated, and recre-
ationally enjoyed. Might Jews in Hippo, or in Carthage, or in some
other city, drop by to hear him speak? Considering the patterns of urban living in Roman late antiquity, again, I think that we must infer
that some Jews sometimes listened to him in his basilica because,
again, it would be incredible if they did not. But inference is not evidence.

Finally, local Jews and local Christians may have been in social
contact with each other in ways that prompted Christians to Judaize—
that is, to adopt, as Christians, some of the customs of the Jews. As a
pastor, then, Augustine would have been indirectly in contact with
Jews through Judaizing members of his own congregation. Augustine

does occasionally mention that Christians Judaize. "If anyone, even a catechumen, is caught observing the Sabbath according to Jewish custom," he noted somewhat gloomily in 395, "the whole church is in an uproar" (*On Galatians* 35.5; the source of Augustine's gloom was his congregations' open reliance on astrology, which he thought much worse than Judaizing). In a later letter, he responds to a Bishop Ascellicus who was troubled by a local Christian's success in encouraging others to Judaize (*Letter* 196.4,16). Was the Old Testament itself, heard in church services, the inspiration for such Judaizing? Or was its source, instead, the local synagogue? I assume the former, because we have no preaching from Augustine (or others of his colleagues) complaining to his congregation, as Chrysostom did to his, that members of the church frequented Jewish gatherings. To conclude: Though he frequently mentions "Jews" and speaks variously both about them and "to" them, Augustine's sermons in themselves provide no clear evidence that Jews were either actually present in his audience or even indirectly involved with it.[12]

The third place where Augustine could have encountered Jews and interacted with them was in his *secretarium* where, in his capacity as bishop, he arbitrated lawsuits. "When called upon whether by Christians or by members of any other sect," his biographer Possidius recorded, "Augustine heard their cases with care and deliberation." He passed much of his time in his audience hall, "missing the mid-day meal, sometimes even fasting all day" (Possidius again, *Life* 19.3). Every work day, every work week, he spent his daylight hours listening to the arguments of plaintiffs and respondents. Then as now, most of these cases revolved around money and real estate: taxes, bequests, debt, property disputes. Tiresome, confounding complexities, he called them (*perplexitates; On the Work of Monks* 37).[13]

This is where we—and Augustine—meet Licinius.

Licinius was a local landowner with an awkward real estate problem: One of Augustine's colleagues, a Bishop Victor, had defrauded Licinius of a piece of property. Licinius had purchased this property from its former owners, who in their turn had purchased it at some point prior from Licinius' mother. Licinius evidently had come to Augustine with documentation, and Augustine, examining his dossier of tablets, was satisfied that they established ownership. "But what he went on to say in his complaint," Augustine wrote to Victor, "is quite incredible":

> He claims that Your Holiness then bought all of this parcel from the same old woman, his mother, and that you chased him off the property, even though he owned it in full right! And when he brought his complaint to you, *you* told him, "I bought it. If your mother was wrong to sell it to me, take her to court. Don't ask me for anything because I don't owe you anything."
>
> LETTER *8.1

If he's lying, Augustine tells Victor, write right back. But, he continues diplomatically, "if, because you do not know the law, you thought that you could answer him like that, Your Charity should know that a person in legal possession of a property cannot legally be evicted from it. And his mother had no right to sell her son's land to you, even if some part of it still belonged to her." The son, Augustine warns Victor, has a solid case, and he certainly was not about to sue his own mother. He would rather go after the man who had invaded his property—"the position," Augustine adds with some delicacy, "in which I wish Your Fraternity did not find himself." Victor should restore his property to Licinius immediately, and then try to collect from his mother. "And even if she refuses to give back to you the price that you paid to her, this man must in no case be deprived of his property. He must get it back. Justice is on his side; the laws cry out in his favor." Remember what Paul teaches, Augustine concludes, quoting 1 Corinthians 10:32: "Give no offense to the Jews or the Greeks, nor to the church of God"—the likely consequence if Victor, refusing to cooperate now, pushes Licinius to pursue the case before the episcopal court (*Letter *8.1*)[14]

Augustine probably had more in mind than just the bishop's court when he concluded his letter with this quotation from Paul. We would not know that, however, had he not added a single word to Licinius' name back in the letter's first line: *Iudaeus Linicius.* Licinius the Jew.

This letter is undated and undatable. We do not know where Licinius' land was, nor Victor's church, except that both, presumably, were convenient to Hippo. What we could guess from the first paragraph of this letter is what its second paragraph goes on to reveal: Licinius and his mother have a troubled relationship. (Augustine got to the bottom of that, too, and in his second paragraph he gave Victor some practical advice about restoring peace in their household; *Letter* *8.2.) As a clue to social relations between Jews and Christians in late-fourth- to early-fifth-century North Africa, however, what is most valuable about this brief, precious document is what it holds in common with *The Hound of the Baskervilles:* Nobody barks.

Licinius the Jew asks Augustine the bishop to intervene on his behalf in a property dispute between himself and one of Augustine's own colleagues, another bishop. Both men—and, after he received this letter, also Bishop Victor—understood that if Licinius could not get satisfaction through these negotiations, he would take his claim, together with his documentation, to the *episcopalis audientia,* yet another ecclesiastical gathering. Augustine, extremely familiar with Roman law, unhesitatingly takes Licinius' side in the affair. And also, with studied finesse, he slaps Victor's fingers. This letter, this entire episode, testifies not only to Augustine's sense of justice but also to Licinius' unselfconscious expectation of justice. And this episode also testifies to Augustine's (and perhaps to Victor's) acknowledgment that, were Licinius to take the matter to the bishop's court, Bishop Victor would lose. All the principals in this case knew themselves to be members of the same society, ruled by the same law. The single most striking thing about this episode—which is the *only* clearly attested instance we have of a substantial encounter between Augustine and a Jew—is that Licinius' being Jewish seems not to have mattered in the least. If Augustine had neglected to add "Iudaeus" to this note, historians would have interpreted *Letter* *8 as evidence of just another property dispute—which is exactly what it is. And that fact in turn gives us a glimpse at the gap between rhetoric and reality in Augustine's Africa.

◆ ◆ ◆

LET'S RETURN TO THE RHETORIC—or, rather, to the theology—of Judaism that Augustine had achieved by circa 400. His thoughts on Jews and Judaism were a small piece of his much larger, astonishingly rich spiritual and intellectual achievement of the late 390s. In *To Simplicianus,* he had come to an understanding of grace, sin, and free will that enabled him to affirm, in a new way, the justice and mercy of God. In *Christian Teaching,* he explored how signs convey meaning; and in so doing, he came to a new appreciation of the unique sanctity of Israel's Law. And in *Confessions,* he integrated the insights of these two preceding works into a theory of knowing. How does the fallen human, trapped in time, know the timeless God? Because God graciously reveals himself in various ways in time, not least of all through the Bible. The Bible, Old Testament and New Testament together, is both God's word and salvation's history. It refers in its entirety to God's Word, Jesus Christ.

Augustine had thought through these ideas against the claims of Manichaeism. Given his personal past, he could hardly have done otherwise. He formulated his theology of Judaism just as or after finishing these earlier important works, and the insights that he gained through them inform his arguments in *Against Faustus.* But the single most important factor contributing to his novel views on Jews and Judaism—the factor that gave his teaching its coherence, its scope, its power, and its sheer originality—was that Augustine had Faustus' *Capitula* to work against.

In the *Capitula,* Faustus had attacked the creator god. He renounced flesh, both humanity's and Christ's. He repudiated the Old Testament and the "Jewish" parts of the New Testament. Augustine the ex-Manichee knew these arguments well; and by this point (398? 400? shortly later?), he had already written numerous times against them. *Manichaean Morals, Genesis against the Manichees, Free Will,* any of his comments on scripture, whether in formal writings or in collections of essays: Virtually all of his earlier works up to and including the *Confessions* put his anti-Manichaean polemic on display. But Faustus challenged Augustine at a deeper level. He too was creative and clever and talented and original. We see this most clearly in the ways that he adapted the arguments of orthodox traditions *adversus Iudaeos* to deploy them together with those of the older Manichaean arsenal. In consequence, Faustus' *Capitula* also had great coherence, scope, power, and originality. It summoned the same from Augustine.

What are the salient elements of Augustine's new teaching?

1. *God chose Israel, he gave them his Law as a benefit and as a privilege, and Israel genuinely received it, all according to divine will.* Augustine's commitment to these ideas shapes his understanding both of the way that God works through history, and of the way that the Bible relates how he did and does so, beginning with creation itself. Within this interpretive framework, Israel *secundum carnem* appears as a prime incarnation of God's will in history and as the privileged recipient of God's law. These positions entail a certain theory of reading as well as a general theological orientation toward the god who creates. For Augustine, the images and events described in the Bible, when understood *translata* (in their "referred" or metaphorical sense), point beyond the historical moment narrated by the biblical text to future truths about Christ and his church. Figural interpretation of scripture is, of course, fairly traditional. But to discern scripture's figured, prophesied truths correctly, Augustine insists, these same texts must *also* be understood *proprie* (in a "self-referring" way) and *ad litteram* ("historically")—that is, as meaningfully framed by the historical period in which their own narratives are set. For example, the story of the Golden Calf, understood *proprie*, describes an event both that truly occurred *and* that was never a deal breaker: God's intimacy with Israel, as the biblical story immediately goes on to relate, continues and develops well beyond this point in Exodus. (Orthodox traditions *contra Iudaeos* had long insisted otherwise.) Understood prophetically or figuratively, as *signa translata*, Exodus 32 even in its smallest details reveals the future redemption of the Gentiles, the realization of Israel's unique mission (see p. 249 above). In brief, when interpreting the Old Testament, Augustine did not need to posit an anti-Jewish past to account for the Christian future.

2. *Traditional Jewish praxis—Sabbath, immersions, holidays, food laws, and most especially blood sacrifices and fleshly circumcision—truly and appropriately fulfilled God's command.* This is the single brightest star in

the constellation of his original ideas in Augustine's theology of Judaism. Against the grain of late Roman Neoplatonic philosophy, he emphasized the value, even the necessity, of seeing history as vital to revelation and of seeing flesh as vital to spirit. Thus, against the prior catholic traditions *adversus Iudaeos,* which had emphatically denounced "fleshly" Jewish practices, Augustine asserted that such practices had been and still were absolutely fundamental to orthodox Christianity precisely because they were and are "fleshly."

Praxis, the "traditions of the fathers" as Paul calls it (Galatians 1:14), is where Judaism is at its most emphatically, distinctly, ethnically, carnally Jewish. Without this, said Augustine, you cannot have Christianity; because without this, you cannot have the incarnate Christ. Against Manichaean Docetism, of course, Augustine as others had long taught that Christ truly had a human body. Here, however, he affirms much more than that. *Christ is God at his most emphatically, distinctly, ethnically, carnally Jewish.* Christ, Augustine insisted, was God in a male *Jewish* body, which was necessary for the perfect fulfillment of the Law. And the Law had to be—could only be—fulfilled *secundum carnem,* because redemption is not just the redemption of the soul but the redemption of the whole person, body and soul together. Thus, in his Jewish flesh, Christ piously and perfectly kept all of Israel's commandments, from the circumcision that he received on the eighth day of his human, Jewish life up to leaving his tomb on the third day after his death, when he rose in the flesh only once the Sabbath was over. Historical Jewish practice, understood in this positive way, not only enables a robustly "plain" reading of the Old Testament and of the New, Augustine maintains; it actually safeguards catholic doctrine.

3. *Jesus, the original apostles, the churches of Judea, and Paul all kept the commandments piously and sincerely, according to the traditions of their fathers.* Here too, Augustine's teaching was original, though doubtless the clarity and force with which he expressed it owed much to the attacks of Jerome. Against Jerome's reading of Paul and Peter's fight in Galatians, Augustine emphasized that scrip-

ture does not lie, and thus that a desire to deceive can never be attributed to its authors. Thus against Jerome's louder, more hostile, classically *adversus Iudaeos* understanding of Christian identity—no one can be both a Jew and a Christian at the same time but only one or the other—Augustine affirmed the contrary. Pointing both to Jesus and to the disciples, he insisted that the entire founding generation of the church was both Jew and Christian at the same time. Had they not been, he further argued, they would have compromised their mission to the Gentiles, by confusing them about the profound difference between the Law (which, though God-given, they did not need to keep) and their false gods (whose cults they could not, under any circumstances, continue to keep). And even the Gentiles of this first Christian generation had Judaized, he said, assuming some of the practices of their Jewish brethren, in this way also living as both Jews and Christians at the same time. In these ways, according to Augustine, Christian identity is bound historically as well as textually to Jewish identity.

4. *God and the Jews, and thus the church and the Jews, maintain an abiding relationship. This relationship is founded upon their shared biblical text and is especially communicated in that text by the figure of Cain.* The image of Cain typologically reveals the "future"—which for Augustine means the present—of Israel *secundum carnem*. Both Cain and the Jews are fratricides. Like Cain, whom God exiled in punishment for the crime of killing Abel, the Jews too are in exile, driven from their kingdom for the crime of killing Christ. Like Cain, who worried about his own fleshly death, so the Jews now worry about their "fleshly" death, that is, *not* their physical death but their ethnic/religious "death" as a separate people with their own inherited traditions of worship. With the resounding success of the gentile mission, Augustine taught, observing the Law *secundum carnem* is no longer appropriate to the times. Yet nonetheless, God has providentially arranged things, bringing good out of bad, by having the Jews' stubborn Jewishness—of which he himself is author—benefit the church. The very visible evidence both of their exile and of their Judaism, the ubiquity of their presence and thus the

ubiquity of their books, publicly confirms the Christian understanding of these books, which long ago exactly foretold their current condition. "They have eyes that would not see" (Romans 11:8;
Isaiah 29:10): Fleshly Israel is blind to the truth of the gospel. "Let
their backs be bent down forever" (Romans 11:9; Psalm 69:23):
Since they cultivate the Law in an earthly way, their eyes are turned
not to heaven, but to the earth (*On Psalms* 58.2,7–8). Toiling in (unknowing) servitude to the Christians, the Jews actually carry their
books for the church. Jews as Jews, Augustine asserted through
this argument, were not a challenge to Christian identity but a
witness to it and a support for it, confirming in their allegiance to
their scriptures the validity of the Christian claim.

5. *God protects the Jews as he had protected Cain. He has placed his mark
upon them, protecting their special identity by protecting their ancestral
practices; and these ancestral practices are themselves God's "mark."*
Without the visibility of their ancestral practices to identify them,
Jews could not be of service to the church. The prophecies of their
exile and of their blindness would not be so plainly manifest; their
dependence on and identification with their books would be neither so strong nor so well known; pagan skepticism of Christian
claims could not be so readily allayed. Any ruler (even a Christian
ruler) who would try to "kill" Jews—that is, who might attempt to
separate them forcibly from their divinely mandated observances—calls God's curse down upon himself. Thus, despite the
fact that individual Jews had always joined the church and would
always join the church, concludes Augustine, the Jews as a people
apart, marked by their unique and uniquely God-given practices,
will continue to exist until the close of the age.

◆◆◆

BUT IN *AGAINST FAUSTUS,* Cain is not the one who goes into exile carrying
a load of books. That job goes to Ham, the middle son of Noah. In another intricate typological reading, Augustine coordinates almost
every detail of Genesis 9:20–27, the story of Noah's drunkenness, with
the future history of the ancient church. This time, the drunk Noah,
supine and naked, is the stand-in for Christ in his mortality. Of the

three brothers, Ham is the one who "sees his father's nakedness," that is, he is those Jews who consent to Jesus' death. Ham runs out to tell his two brothers about their father's nakedness; so also the Jews tell "Shem" (who stands for Jewish Christians) and "Japhet" (who stands for Greek Christians) about Christ's "nakedness" (that is, about his death). By broadcasting Christ's mortality to Christians both Jewish and gentile, the Jews/Ham likewise broadcast the Bible's deepest meaning, "for what was hidden in the prophets was disclosed by the Jews." Noah cursed Ham, saying that he would be a slave to his brothers (*servus,* Genesis 9:25–27). The Jews, by disclosing what the prophets really meant—the prophets all spoke of a crucified and risen messiah, though the Jews never understood this—are thus the slaves of their (Christian) brothers, "cursed" because they still live under the Law (Galatians 3:10; *Against Faustus* 12:11). But this servitude is of a very particular kind. The whole nation (*gens*), carrying the Law and the prophets, is a librarian who ports a chest full of books (*scriniaria,* feminine of *scriniarius* because of the feminine *gens; Against Faustus* 12.23).

From Cain to Ham to slaves to servile book caretakers. Out of this congested set of images and episodes Augustine constructs his idea of the Jews as wandering book slaves who witness to Christian truth. The *wandering* part and the part about *obvious Jewish identity* (conveyed to outsiders by visible, physical behaviors) come from Genesis 4: Cain, the exiled, divinely marked, divinely protected fratricide. The *slave serving the church* comes from Noah's curse to Ham, who becomes a slave to his brothers in Genesis 9. The *books* refer to scripture, the (misunderstood) script for the Jews' visible practices, whose deepest meanings had to await the messiah's crucifixion and resurrection before they could be (retrospectively) understood by others.

But the Law and the prophets speak not only about Christ. They also speak about his church. They declare the *freedom of the church:* Christians are no longer obligated to keep the Law according to the letter. For this reason, Augustine teaches, the Jews carry their books around *ad testimonium adsertionis ecclesiae,* "to testify to the *adsertio* of the church." This is another dense knot of associations. An *adsertio* is a formal declaration of freedom, a public, legal act by which a slave becomes a freedman. The Law and the prophets, borne by the slave-Jews, testify to the divine manumission of the church. Freed by Christ from bondage to the Law, Christians honor through the church's rites (*sacramenta*) what the Jews announced in the letter (*per litteram; Against Faustus* 12.23-24). And by not understanding this truth, the Jews further display their witness to this truth, because their own books had foreseen that the Jews would not understand (*Against Faustus* 16.21). In short, the main theme of Paul's letter to the Galatians—exactly what Paul had corrected Peter about; exactly what Augustine had corrected Jerome about—is the Gentiles' freedom from the Law in Christ. This declaration of freedom in the gospel provides Augustine with his scaffold for all of his other ideas here. Assembling these discrete biblical elements into a unified image, he produces this historically rooted *figura* of the Jewish people as key to understanding Christian faith. Augustine is the ultimate theological *bricoleur*.

But he was also a former professor. It is not surprising then that Augustine also knew a lot of ways to say "people who are responsible for books." "The Jews serve us, as if they were our *capsarii* carrying *codices* for us to study," he says in his sermon on Psalm 40. But this *capsarius* moves within Genesis 4: He is also "Cain the elder brother, who killed his younger brother, and so received the mark that no one should kill him, that is, so that he remains that people"—the Jewish people. When skeptical pagans question Christians, Christians can summon the Jews' books. "Thus has God arranged all things, ordered all things for our salvation" (*On Psalms* 40.14,7). "The Jews, scattered throughout the world, are like the custodians of our books" (*Sermon* 5.5). "The Jew carries the codex . . . they have become our librarian" (*On Psalms* 56.9,1). Book custodian (*custos librorum*), librarian (*bibliothecarius, librarius*), guardian of the book cask (*scriniarius, capsarius*). The Law and the prophets universally speak about Christ; the Jews, reading wrongly, unwittingly carry these books that they think are theirs but that actually belong to the church. In this way, the Jews help the church to spread the gospel.[15]

This set of associations—Jews, exiles, books, testimony—is the verbal core of what scholars designate Augustine's "doctrine of Jewish witness." Historians (myself among them) have termed this Augustinian teaching original and distinctive, as indeed it is. When we place his teaching within its native historical context, however, second- through fifth-century Christian rhetoric, what is striking, indeed surprising, is how traditional many elements of his "witness doctrine" actually look.

That Jews are punished for their rejection of Christ by the loss of their kingdom is an idea that goes back to the gospels themselves. Luke's Jesus all but names Rome as he weeps over Jerusalem and the consequences of the Jews' coming denial of him. "Indeed the days will come upon you when your enemies will set up ramparts and surround you and hem you in on every side. And they will crush you to the ground, you and your children; and leave no stone upon another" (Luke 19:43–44). John's gospel actually does name Rome when the chief priests and Pharisees assemble to plot Jesus' death. "If we let him go on like this, everybody will believe in him, and the Romans will come and destroy our holy place"—that is, the Temple—"and our nation" (John 11:48).

Using the destruction of Jerusalem and the "exile" of the people to confirm Christianity is common to *all* patristic commentary. Origen even chides Josephus for omitting from his *Jewish War* the "real cause" behind these events: Josephus "ought to have said that the plot against Jesus was the reason why these catastrophes came upon the people" (*Against Celsus* 1.47). Their role in Christ's death, Origen observes, is the reason why the Jews are "scattered all over the earth" (*Against Celsus* 2.34). Augustine creatively uses the figure of Cain to represent the Jewish people post-70; but *what* Cain typifies recapitulates many of these traditional ideas about guilt, punishment, and exile. Put differently: Augustine's interpretation of the "mark of Cain" to mean current Jewish practice and to indicate the divine means and sign of their continuing preservation, is emphatically original. His understanding of the causes of the Jewish defeat in 70, and of the Jews' subsequent exile, typified for him by "Cain," is not.

Those gentile communities who lay claim to the Septuagint saw the gospels' prophecies of exile under Rome through the proximate lens of the Bar Kokhba revolt in 132–135 C.E. and through the distant lens of the classical prophets: Isaiah, Jeremiah, Ezekiel, and Daniel (p. 84 above). Tertullian, explaining the exile as the prophesied consequence of the crucifixion, actually quotes Psalm 59:12, "Scatter them with your might" (*Against Marcion* 3.23). Indeed, so clearly did the prophets foresee both the Jews' murder of Jesus and their subsequent punitive exile that gentile Christian theologians proclaim their own incredulity at the Jews' incredulity. Again, Augustine condenses in pithy, nicely balanced phrases these ideas about the Jews' blind witness to their own prophets' prophesies of this blindness, but he is not the first to think them.

That Jews are particularly connected to and represented by their holy books is also an early and prominent theme in Christian writing. So too is the conviction that these books alone authenticate "true" Christianity. The roots of these ideas also trace back to first-century writings. Paul had declared himself to be "set apart for the gospel of God which he promised beforehand in the holy scriptures" (Romans 1:2). Luke's risen Christ "beginning with Moses and all the prophets interpreted to them the things about himself in all the scriptures" (Luke 24:27). Historically, this conviction on the part of these earliest authors is unremarkable, since they themselves were Jews (or in Luke's case, perhaps, a very textually Judaized Gentile). But their statements, preserved in the Christian canon, helped to establish the deference paid to Jewish books and even to the "Jewish" language, Hebrew, long after the ethnicity and culture of orthodox Christianity had changed.[16]

The effects of this deference are especially evident in the biblical culture of Western Manichaeism. To make headway as missionaries, Latin-speaking Manichees worked up an impressive expertise in Jewish texts. They may not have liked them, but they knew them, and they developed careful criticisms of them. Those parts of the *Capitula* that remain in the twelfth, the thirteenth, and the twenty-second books of *Against Faustus* give the measure of this deference. The clarity and force of Faustus' innumerable arguments against the Jewish people, their practices, and their books presents a reverse image of the clarity and force with which orthodox Christians thought "Jews" when they thought "scripture." A wandering, exiled, broken people with such revolting religious customs and with such dreadful holy books—no true Christian would want any part of that, urged Faustus. Wandering Cain with the eternally visible mark of the divine Law; servile Ham with his heavy *scrinium*, toiling beneath the chest that holds the Law and the prophets so that Christians can shake their finger at skeptical pagans (especially in light of the "prophetic" events of the temples' closures in 399)—true Christians everywhere are happy to have such a slave to carry such books, answered Augustine. In short, Augustine's association of Israel *secundum carnem* with their scriptures is not in itself an original idea; nor is his assertion that their exile, their books, and their example verify Christian claims. Rather, it is the power of his style, the sheer élan of his rhetoric in coordinating all of these disparate ideas around the figure of Cain that makes Augustine's image of the Jew-as-book-slave so outstandingly vivid. His servile Jewish *scriniarius,* eternally marked by his ancient books and his own sacred practices, is Augustine's rhetorically pungent reprise of many different traditional Christian ideas.

✦✦✦

ONCE HE DISCOVERED PSALM 59, Augustine was moved to reprise these ideas yet again. This discovery perhaps occurred at some point between 410 and 415, when he was pressing forward in his long-term project of composing sermons on the entire book of Psalms. He shaped his interpretation of verse 12—"Slay them not, lest my people forget; scatter them with your might"—by appealing exactly to those same arguments that he had advanced in *Against Faustus.* "What does it mean, 'to be killed'?" Augustine asks here. And he answers, "It is to forget the Law of the Lord." (The language of the psalm dictates his use here of *forget.* Against Faustus, he had emphasized the agency of others, namely monarchs who might try to coerce/"kill" the Jews by disrupting their practices.) Because of their unique customs, Augustine continues, the Jews have survived as a people despite the loss of their kingdom. They are marked like Cain (again he refers to Genesis 4:15); and the sign marking them is their Law, which is to say, their traditional practices. Augustine specifies some of these here: circumcision, Sabbath, slaughtering a lamb for Passover, and eating unleavened bread (*On Psalms* 59.1,21; the same point with practices unspecified, *Against Faustus* 12.13).

At the end of his first sermon on Psalm 59 and again in the course of his second one, Augustine comments further on the significance of

"Scatter them." Once more, he describes the exiled Jews' carrying their books, this time referring to Paul's letter to the Romans. Here Augustine conceptualizes the ultimate fate of the Jews with another favorite image, the olive tree in Romans 11 (some branches remain on the trunk; others are broken off, thus "scattered"). And he also refers to the vessels of mercy and of wrath shaped by God the potter in Romans 9:21 (*On Psalms* 59.1,21–22; 59.2,22; so also *Against Faustus* 21.3. All three texts use these same Pauline verses). Behind these two sermons on Psalm 59 stand his ideas on the mystery of salvation as he had formulated them, thinking particularly with Romans, when writing to Simplicianus. God had chosen Paul mysteriously, despite Saul's murderous behavior. "How had he deserved it? It is not for us to say" (*On Psalms* 59.1,12). Salvation, he repeats, is not universal, and it depends entirely on God's election. The true Israel, "Israel according to the spirit," will comprise *some* Jews and *some* Gentiles, inexplicably chosen by God out of the sinful mass of humanity, the "lump of clay" in Romans 9:21 (*On Psalms* 59.2,2; see further, 59.2,6–7).

Sometime during this same period, Augustine received a substantial epistle from his friend and fellow bishop Paulinus of Nola. Shaky chronology prevents us from knowing which came first, Augustine's sermons or Paulinus' letter. Addressing Augustine as the "blessed teacher of Israel," Paulinus asked about the interpretation of a variety of verses both from the New Testament and from Psalms (*Letter* 121.1,2). The meaning of Psalm 59:12 especially exercised him. This psalm should be understood, Paulinus observes, as the voice of the Son speaking to the Father. *Scattering* clearly refers to the Jews, who lost their temple and their kingdom and were exiled for their part in the crucifixion of Christ. But why would Christ plead "lest they forget your Law"? If God has repudiated the Jews, "what good does it do them," asks Paulinus, "not to forget the Law?" After all, "what does their remembering and meditating on the Law contribute to their salvation, which is acquired solely by faith?" (*Letter* 121.1,7).

Turning to Romans, Paulinus continues to think about the salvation of the Jews. "As regards the Gospel," Paul had said about his kinsmen, Israel *secundum carnem*, "they are enemies, because of you [Gentiles]; but as regards election, they are beloved, because of the forefathers" (Romans 11:28). What good does being "beloved by God" do for the Jews, Paulinus asks, if they are damned outright for being the enemies of Christ? Behind this question stands a more fundamental one: Why did God configure salvation as a zero-sum competition between Gentiles and Jews in the first place? Does Paul's statement not imply that the Gentiles would not have believed unless the Jews, first, had not believed? "How was God . . . incapable of acquiring both peoples, rather than having only one or the other?" Paulinus asks. "If the Jews are beloved of God, how will they perish? And if they do not believe in Christ, how will they not perish?" (*Letter* 121.2,11).

Augustine responded to Paulinus several years later and at length. (An earlier reply, which we no longer have, had evidently gone missing; *Letter* 149.1,2.) As with *Letter* 82 to Jerome, so also with *Letter* 149 to Paulinus: Augustine uses his correspondence as a way to summarize and to condense earlier, more diffuse teachings. This time, his topics are the Jewish people, Jewish law, God's justice and mercy, and final salvation. He begins from his interpretive set point: Whenever any psalm mentions the Jews' "scattering," it refers to events in the year 70, after "they were defeated and wiped out in a terrible war" (*Letter* 149.1,3). Turning more specifically to Psalm 59.12, Augustine reiterates his earlier argument against Faustus, and again makes Genesis 4:15, the "mark of Cain," the pivot of his exegesis (*Letter* 149.1,9; *Against Faustus* 12.13). The Jews' books prove to skeptical pagans that the church did not invent Christ. Christ had been foretold long ago "in the manuscripts of our enemies." And, again, he notes that Jews are nowhere "killed," meaning that they practice their religious customs freely. In so doing, they unwittingly render a service of witness to Christ and to his church:

> *Do not kill them,* lest this people's name be extinguished; *so that they may not forget your Law,* something that might have happened if, compelled to follow gentile rites and sacrifices, they would not have retained the name of their own religion. In scripture they are symbolized as Cain, upon whom God placed his mark, so that no one would kill him. Then, as if the psalmist had been asked what

should be done with this people . . . so that they might serve to testify to truth, he immediately added *Scatter them with your might* to the first sentence, *Do not kill them so that they do not forget your Law.* For if the Jews lived in only one place on the earth, they could not by their testimony assist in the preaching of the gospel, which causes the earth throughout the world to bear fruit. For this reason, then, the text states *scatter them with your might,* so that through their Law, which they do not forget, they might be witnesses everywhere to him whom they denied and persecuted and killed. That Law foretold the one whom the Jews do not follow. But it does not do the Jews themselves any good not to forget the Law. It is one thing to hold the Law in the memory, quite another to hold it in mind and deed.

LETTER 149.1,9

Augustine next considers those passages that Paulinus had singled out in Paul's letters. Puzzling over Romans and the unequal fates of Gentiles and Jews, Paulinus felt that "Paul's" statement in 1 Timothy only compounded the problem. "God wants all people to be saved and to come to the knowledge of truth" (1 Timothy 2:4). Why then, Paulinus asked, if he wants to save all people, has God acted as if he could save only one people or the other, only the Gentiles and not also the Jews (*Letter* 121.2,11)?

Augustine dispatches this difficulty by quoting the next sentence of this deutero-Pauline epistle: "For there is one God, and one mediator between God and humanity, the human Jesus Christ" (1 Timothy 2:5). These two sentences stand in this sequence, he explains, so that the reader would understand the phrase "God wants all people to be saved" to mean "saved in Christ," the unique mediator between God and man (*Letter* 149.2,18). This idea of delimited redemption moves Augustine easily to Romans and to the restatement of his understanding of redemption that he had worked out in the late 390s. "Hence, do not let the words of the same apostle about the Jews alarm you," he counsels Paulinus, "namely, 'In terms of the gospel they are enemies on your account, but in terms of election, they are beloved, on account of the forefathers' " (Romans 11:28). God's ways are unsearchable, his judgments inscrutable (Romans 11:33). The pious can only trust in his wisdom and his justice; they cannot understand his reasons. Why does it please God to make so many people who he foreknows will remain reprobate? Because he makes good use of evil for the benefit of the good, asserts Augustine. To human minds, however, his plan is concealed (*in abdito*).

It is at this point that Augustine confronts, and so reinterprets, Paul's statement about the ultimate redemption of all Israel: "I do not want you to be ignorant of this mystery, brothers and sisters. For blindness has come upon a part of Israel, until the fullness of the Gentiles has entered, and so *all Israel will be saved*" (Romans 11:25). Paul limits Israel's blindness to only "a part," notes Augustine, because some Jews had indeed received the gospel. Similarly, the "fullness of the Gentiles" refers not to all Gentiles, but only to that fraction of the Gentiles "who have been called according to God's plan": Only they are predestined to election. Accordingly, he continues, *"all Israel" that is saved does not and cannot mean all of "Israel according to the flesh"—that is, the Jews.* What does Paul mean, then? "Israel according to the spirit," Augustine concludes; *verus Israel,* "true Israel," the Israel of God. This "Israel" designates the community of the redeemed, which is composed of those particular Jews and those designated Gentiles whom God, in his inscrutable wisdom, chose to save. Likewise when Paul quotes Isaiah 59:20, "I shall take away their sins," the apostle speaks "not to the sins of all the Jews, but only to the sins of those Jews who were chosen" (*Letter* 149.2,19).[17]

"This is the point," continues Augustine to Paulinus, "at which Paul adds the words that you set forth to be investigated: 'They are enemies in terms of the gospel on your account' " (Romans 11:28; *Letter* 149.2,20). Christian salvation had depended on Christ's being slain, an act that only enemies could commit. "Here is an example of how God uses evil for the improvement of the good." The second clause of Paul's statement, "they are beloved in terms of election on account of the forefathers," must therefore refer to a different subject, Augustine explains, not to "the Jews" who were the subject of the first clause. The true subject of the latter clause, the identity of God's "beloved," Augustine concludes, are those who were predestined "according to the election that was hidden in the foreknowledge of God" (*Letter* 149.2,20).

Augustine concludes by deftly synopsizing this view of Romans, achieved so laboriously when he had commented on these same verses, years ago, to Simplicianus. Proceeding to Romans 11:29—"The gifts and the call of God are irrevocable"—Augustine again modifies Paul by understanding "calling" in light of Matthew's teaching on how few are chosen, even though many are called (Matthew 22:14; *Letter* 149.2,21). The only call that is irrevocable, he says, is the one that goes out "according to God's plan," which summons those whom he already predestined and infallibly foreknew. But if the initiative for salvation rests entirely with God, how then does he come *justly* to his decision about whom to save and whom to leave? By what criteria does he judge? God alone knows, answers Augustine. Piety affirms that, while God's reasons may be hidden (*occulta*), they can never be unjust. "Is there injustice with God? God forbid!" (Romans 9:14; *Letter* 149.2,22). To Paulinus' more fundamental question—not whether God could have saved the Jews, but why he chose not to—Augustine answers that there is no answer. But not many Gentiles are chosen, either. All are equally children of Adam, and thus many from each people are condemned justly, though some from each people are mercifully saved.

At some point after this exchange with Paulinus, Augustine again turned to Psalm 59:12. We have two undated sermons from him that appeal to this special verse, one titled *Faith in Things Unseen*, the other, *Sermon against the Jews*. *Faith in Things Unseen* 6.9 offers a condensed presentation of now-familiar ideas: the Jews' exile, their books, their practices, their service to the church. Jews read their books, Augustine says, but because of God's *occulto justoque iudicio*, his "hidden just judgment," they do not understand them. Why has God thus judged the Jews? For *occultioribus causis*, "rather obscure reasons." Augustine refers to Psalm 68:22–24, on the Jews' blind eyes and bent backs, quoted by Paul in Romans 11:10. And he then deploys Psalm 59:12, "Slay them not," in his now-usual way. By never forgetting the Law, the dispersed Jews serve the church. "In their hearts they are our enemy; in their books, our witness." What is striking about this passage in the sermon is not its content, but its economy of expression. Augustine has thought out this argument so well and mobilized its supporting scriptural citations so often that he can convey it, when he wants, in very few words.

In his *Sermon against the Jews,* Augustine moves at a more leisured pace. His topic is not Jews as such, but rather the true claimants to the identity of Israel. He begins by invoking Paul's olive tree and its broken branches (Romans 11:17-18), then he taunts Jews for reading what they do not truly understand. (Augustine mentions here that Jews "chant" the prophets, perhaps evidence for his knowledge of actual Jewish liturgical practices; *Against the Jews* 1.2.) The fallen Temple and the continuing exile are pressed into their usual service, and various Temple sacrifices, once explicated, reveal the blood and flesh of the incarnate Christ—no accident, since Christ came to fulfill the Law, not to destroy it (*Against the Jews* 2.3-5). Augustine next decodes several psalms in similar fashion (Psalms 44, 68, 79, 49, 45; *Against the Jews* 2.3-6.8). Thereafter, he enacts a debate between himself and "the Jews, as if they were present" (*Against the Jews* 7.9 and passim).

Only at this point does Augustine cite Psalm 59:12. He uses it to rebuke the Jews for their continuing exile and for their witless service to the church. ("Mindful" of the Law, the Jews never realize that what they carry is actually a covenant for the Gentiles, to whom they unknowingly minister; *Against the Jews* 7.9.) In this way, the older brother (Esau/the Jews) now serves the younger brother (Jacob/the Gentiles). Quoting Isaiah 53:8, Augustine then declaims: "This is said about Christ, whom you, *in your parents,* led to death" (*Against the Jews* 7.10). Jews are ignorant, blind, and deaf (7.10-8.11); they build destruction (8.11). By turning the Gentiles to God, the church has proved that she, not the Jews, is the true "house of Jacob," she is "the fruitful olive tree" (9.12-10.15; Psalm 51:10). "Proclaim these divine testimonies to the Jews, with great love for them," Augustine exhorts his congregation, and so brings his performance to a close.[18]

These clusters of scriptural citations and allusions, the continual reference to Paul's letter to the Romans, the wandering Jews with their Law and their books: We have seen all of this before. But something is different here. What is most interesting about these two sermons, what they hold in common with each other and what distinguishes them from Augustine's prior works on Jews and Judaism is not something that they have, but something that they lack. Cain, Augustine's premier biblical figure for the Jews, is suddenly strangely absent. What happened to Cain? Where did he go? Why? To find him, we must look in *City of God.*

✦✦✦

CULT MAKES GODS HAPPY. Happy gods make for happy humans. And of course the opposite is also true: absent cult, gods grow angry. When gods are angry, humans pay.

This traditional understanding of political and social relations between heaven and earth was as strong in the early fifth century C.E. as it had been during the lifetime of Alexander the Great in the late fourth century B.C.E. When a marauding army of Goths humiliated the city of Rome in 410, impatient pagans lost no time in pointing to the real culprits: the misguided and zealous Christians, who had closed public altars and withdrawn public monies from the old cults. Under those gods, the city and the empire had flourished. Now that Rome had deserted her gods, her gods had deserted Rome.

It was in response to this pagan challenge that Augustine began his final master work, *City of God.* He labored on a huge scale: twenty-two books, written across thirteen years. *City of God* began as a reconsideration of Roman history. Its first ten books review how Rome had had her downs as well as her ups under the old gods, and how what had passed for Roman virtue was in service to Roman lust for power, *libido dominandi.* But the true subject of Augustine's *magnum opus et arduum,* this "huge, difficult work," as he described it, was his monumental consideration of the entire course of salvation history, from Genesis through to final redemption. And in composing this vast project, Augustine produced as well a symphonic reprise of his own work, repeating and reinterpreting the master themes of a lifetime of vital theological reflection.

In *City of God,* Augustine's commitment to the centrality of the Bible as God's revelation, both textually and temporally, remained as firm and as clear as ever. But the two decades or so that intervened between his completing *Against Faustus* and his composing the second half of *City of God* had seen important changes in Augustine's position on many key problems. Three in particular affect, and were affected by, the ways that he thought about Christianity's relationship with Jews and with Judaism. They are (1) the relationship of flesh to spirit, body to soul; (2) the relationship between biblical texts and historical time, thus between language and meaning; and (3) the relationship of prophecy to history, and thus of God's will to contemporary events. To conclude our work on his broader theology—the context for his innovative and important teachings on Jews and Judaism—we must follow the development of his thinking on these more fundamental issues. By this somewhat circuitous route, we will find our way back to Cain.

Spirit and Flesh

We have already seen how Augustine, in the years between his priesthood and his becoming bishop, had changed his mind on the question of human salvation, moving from maintaining the resurrection of "body" to the resurrection of "flesh" (p. 141 above). This was a distinction with a great difference—the difference, in Augustine's lifetime, between orthodoxy and heresy. More precisely, distinctions of ideas about salvation, spirit, and flesh measured the difference between the ways that the great third-century theologian Origen had been able to think about redemption (and thus about divine justice) and the ways that his fifth-century counterparts were able to think about Origen.

In the intellectual freedom of third-century Christianity, Origen had read Genesis as describing God's ordering of two different realms of creation. God's primary creation, "made" before time, was eternal and spiritual, the native home of all rational beings. God's secondary creation he made out of nothing (*creatio ex nihilo*). This latter creation was the temporal realm of the material cosmos. Fallen rational beings, in order to learn from mistakes that they had made in the spiritual cosmos, lived for a while in this lower cosmos. In eternity, these rational beings had had "spiritual bodies." (This was Origen's reuse of Paul's term for the type of bodies that Christians would have at Christ's Second Coming, the *soma pneumatikon;* 1 Corinthians 15:44; p. 68 above.) In time or in history, they lived for a while in fleshly bodies, whose source was also the good and gracious God. At the end of time, all souls, even Satan's, would understand the error of their ways, repent of the sins committed both before they had had material bodies and afterward, and freely choose to turn, with love, to God. At that point, flesh and matter, their purpose as a moral learning tool for the soul now completed, would sink back into the nothingness from which they had come.[19]

This way of imagining salvation seems exotic, but that is because Origen and his work represent the road not taken by later Christian theology, much of which was shaped in reaction against him. In its own day, Origen's theology powerfully responded to the problem of evil, which in monotheistic systems with an all-good, all-powerful god becomes as well the problem of divine justice. By positing that rational beings had a life (and thus made moral choices) well before they ever appeared in fleshly bodies, Origen was able to dissolve the ethical problem posed by the wild diversity of human conditions in this life. Why would a just and loving god permit a baby to be born blind? Because of some sin committed by its soul prior to its life in its fleshly body. Divine providence had determined that exactly *that* sort of body could best instruct *that* particular soul, in order to begin that soul's process of freely choosing to turn back to God. How could a just god "love Jacob" but "hate Esau" when both were still in the womb? That was the Bible's way of hinting at Origin's system: God "hated" not Esau, of course, but only Esau's sin, whatever it was that Esau's soul had done wrong before God sent it into Esau's body. God was the infinitely effective, infinitely resourceful, infinitely patient lover of souls, swaying considerate scales. No soul would be lost forever. Origen's interpretation of biblical salvation history, by emphasizing the free will of the individual rational being, thus also emphasized the universality, thus the absolute fairness, of God's love. His God, within this system, providentially arranged the material universe so that each and every soul, his creatures whom he loved, would eventually freely will to turn back to him, to love him. Eventually all are saved.

Origen's legacy proved controversial. Exactly in the period when Augustine came into his intellectual maturity as a catholic churchman, the late 390s and the early 400s, the controversy burst upon—and blew apart—the pan-Mediterranean community of orthodox theologians. Here Augustine's inability to read Greek probably protected him: Dependent on Latin translations of Origen's works, he could not really join in the international epistolary fray. But when a younger contemporary in Rome, Pelagius, later defended an idea of human moral freedom that was much closer to Origen's than to Augustine's, Augustine convulsed Latin Christianity with tireless polemics against "Pelagianism" and endless defenses of his own ideas of divine predestination. As usual, argument sharpened his thinking, but it also provoked him to extremes.

These extremes seem particularly evident in Augustine's final formulation of his ideas about divine justice and human freedom. Many of his theological positions, taken in the course of the Pelagian controversy, sound diametrically opposed to those of Origen. Where Origen held that all would be saved, Augustine held that all should be damned. Where Origen held that every rational being has free will, Augustine held that, absent grace, human will was free only to sin. For both biblical theologians, God's two great attributes are justice and mercy. But Origen's god expresses these attributes simultaneously and universally: To each soul, he is both just and merciful. Augustine's god expresses these attributes serially and selectively: To each soul, God is *either* just *or* merciful, and those who receive mercy are in the minority. For Augustine, even babies, if unbaptized, go to hell, and the greater part of humanity is justly predestined to damnation. For Origen, even Satan will at last be redeemed, for God desires the salvation of all his creatures.[20]

This sharp contrast between Augustine and Origen paralleled the sharp contrast between Augustine and those two great pagan contemporaries of Origen's, Plotinus and Porphyry, whose works had affected him so powerfully back in Milan (p. 126 above). The issues dividing them are nowhere greater than in their respective views on the relation of bodily flesh to soul. For Origen as for these pagan Neoplatonists, something about the fleshly body was intractably "other." They identified "self" with "soul." Flesh was not-self, simply the soul's inconvenient vehicle while it sojourned in time. With the Manichees, of course, the contrast between Augustine's ultimate position and their own was even sharper, their view of the struggle between self and flesh more drastic. Mani had taught that the flesh was entirely the work of the force of darkness: not just other but also evil. The body was not the temporary habitation of the good self, but its prison. And for all of these thinkers, the progress of the soul or (in Manichaean-Pauline vocabulary) "the inner man" toward God was measured by its freedom from the flesh.

Augustine radically reconceived this body/soul dichotomy. Living with and working through all of these preceding positions—first as a young man with the Manichees; later in Milan as a reader of pagan Neoplatonic philosophy and a hearer, via Ambrose, of Origen—he ultimately came to define human nature quite differently. The first important steps toward this redefinition had come in the mid-390s, as he worked to pry Paul's letters away from Manichaean interpretations. By understanding "spirit" and "flesh" not as substances but as moral categories, Augustine de-materialized evil. Bodily flesh does not cause the sins of the flesh: Sin's origin lies in the defective will of the "fleshly soul," which burdened the entire species after Adam. Once the soul, through grace, is no longer "fleshly" (that is, inclined toward sin), the fleshly body will become "spiritual," that is, morally oriented toward God and the good (p. 170 above).

This way of conceiving spirit and flesh in turn helped Augustine to pry the Old Testament away from Manichaean interpretation. When fleshly bodies engaged in fleshly activities, Augustine maintained, that behavior was not necessarily "fleshly," that is, sinful. The problem with sexual activity, for instance, was not that it engaged fleshly bodies but that it involved both soul and body in that great index of the sinful state, pleasure. Pleasure was sin's bait. It anesthetized the will. Pleasure operated involuntarily both in the soul (which, once it started sinning, rapidly became habituated) and in the body. In short, people sin not because they like sin, but because they like pleasure. People, in fact, could even hate sin but, because of pleasure, still find themselves repeatedly sinning anyway: That was precisely the predicament of the person *sub lege*, "under the Law," before he moved *sub gratia*, "under grace." This was the awful conflict that Augustine's Paul had explained by saying, "The evil that I do not want to do, I do. . . . Wretched man that I am! Who will deliver me from this body of death?" (Romans 7:19,24). This was the wrenching misery, at peak before his conversion, that had moved Augustine to pray, "Oh Lord, give me chastity and continence—but not yet!" (*Confessions* 8.7,17). And this was the obvious truth that Augustine, with some irritation, threw at Faustus: "If there were no pleasure in what is unlawful," he snapped, "no one would sin!" (*Against Faustus* 22.28).

The *only* redeeming thing about conjugal intercourse, said Augustine, despite the risk of pleasure, was the opportunity that it presented for procreation. The Manichees had all of this exactly upside down: In their vicious insistence that flesh in itself was evil, they even permitted sexual activity to their *auditores* provided that the couple practice contraception (p. 115 above). "You would have thought better of Mary had she ceased being a virgin without becoming a mother, instead of becoming a mother without ceasing to be a virgin!" (*Against Faustus* 30.6). No wonder, then, that the Manichees displayed so extremely the invariable consequence of doctrinal perversity: They misread the Bible. With the Old Testament, they completely missed the fact that the patriarchs had conjugal intercourse not because it gave them pleasure, but because it gave them children (*Against Faustus* 22.48). The narrative's seemingly incidental details—which bad readers invariably miss— revealed the obvious truth of Augustine's position. When Leah (who was neither beloved nor beautiful) traded her mandrake roots with the beloved, beautiful Rachel in exchange for Jacob's sexual services, what happened (Genesis 30:14–17)? Nothing! What more proof did Faustus need?

> Once he discovered his wives' agreement, Jacob suddenly and
> unexpectedly had to turn from the beautiful wife to the plain one.
> Did he go white with anger? Or dark with melancholy? Did he try
> to wheedle his way with flattery, so that he could return to the
> prior arrangements with Rachel, and satisfy his own desires?
> No! . . . Seeing that his wives were concerned about the pro-
> duction of children—the same result that he himself sought
> from conjugal union—he thought it best to yield to their
> decision. . . . This control over the appetites, and this desire to
> beget children, Faustus would have been intelligent enough to

see and to approve, had his detestable sect not so corrupted his character and his talents. That is what led him to find fault with everything in Scripture. That is what taught him to condemn the procreation of children as the greatest crime, whereas it is the entire point of marriage.

AGAINST FAUSTUS 22.50

In his great commentary on Genesis *ad litteram,* written during the years between completing *Against Faustus* and starting *City of God,* Augustine further explored the implications of God's having created fleshly bodies "in the beginning." Why would God have made the fleshly, gendered bodies of Adam and Eve, he asked, if not precisely for the purpose of sexual procreation (*Literal Interpretation of Genesis* 3.21,33; 9.3,5–11,19)? In Paradise, before sin, the individual fleshly body of each primal parent had been harmoniously and sinlessly united with its soul. Therefore, in Paradise, intercourse, orgasm, and conception could all have occurred at will, without pleasure; and childbirth would have been without pain (9.10,16–18). Once the primal pair sinned, however, all this became impossible. Two enormous punishments interrupted the harmonious soul/body relationship: sexual pleasure and death. After the sin in the garden, both for Adam and Eve and for every generation thereafter, procreation had to wait for the "stirrings of lust": involuntary, thus shame-producing, carnal appetite (9.30.40–41). And of course, ever since Adam and Eve, each soul was torn, unwilling and unhappy, from its native home, the fleshly body, by death (9.32,42).

When Augustine again takes up these issues in *City of God,* he speaks not only of what physical sex in the garden should have been like had Adam and Eve not sinned so soon (book fifteen) but also of what beatitude at the end of time would be like, when the souls of the saints are reunited with their fleshly bodies. As Christ had ascended in his risen flesh, so too would the saints, restored to their bodies, rise to heaven (book twenty-two). There they would experience that greatest possible joy: the unmediated knowledge of God. No more words. No more symbols. No more books. No more interpretation. In eternity, no more time. This happy ending—the ultimate marriage of the Bible's history of salvation and the metaphysics of Neoplatonism—drives Augustine to the edge of vibrating paradox, because he insists that the saints will have this knowledge in the flesh. But how can physical bodies see that which has absolutely no body of any sort, namely God the father? "The saints will see God *in* the body; but whether they will see through the eyes of the body, in the same way that we now see the sun, moon, stars, sea and earth and all the things on the earth—that is no easy question" (*City of God* 22.29). Jesus' saying in the Gospel of Matthew might imply bodily vision: "Blessed are the pure in heart, for they shall see God" (Matthew 5:8), but Paul's saying, "we shall see God face to face" certainly does *not* imply that God has a face (1 Corinthians 13:12). Whatever and however, Augustine concludes. The one certainty is that the saints will rest eternally, body and soul, with God (*City of God* 22.30).

Augustine's arguments in *Against Faustus* in defense of Jews and Judaism—God's choice and approval of Israel *secundum carnem;* the positive significance especially of blood sacrifices and of circumcision; the traditional, fleshly Judaism of Jesus and of his apostles, including Paul—are all discrete points within this much larger, even more intellectually ambitious undertaking: to retrieve and to defend the positive theological status of the flesh. The values native to late Platonism fought against his project. So did traditional Christian rhetoric, especially traditional *contra Iudaeos* rhetoric, as Faustus so amply demonstrated in his *Capitula*. Within that discourse, flesh was too often bad and defective and dangerous; flesh was too "Jewish." But the orthodox doctrines of Creation, Augustine insisted, and of Incarnation and of Resurrection compelled the effort.

This effort served many of Augustine's projects, both exegetical and theological. It gave him a way to bind the Old Testament and the New Testament together into a single grand narrative of salvation. It steadied his attempts to devise a theory of reading, one whose frame of reference was human time, thus historical time. It enabled him, within a very small period of years (perhaps months), to reverse his earlier understandings of how Jesus and the Pharisees had each observed Torah (p. 255 above). It supported him, against Jerome, in his reading of Galatians and in his understanding of the profound Jewishness of the church's founding generation, Jews and Gentiles both

(p. 299 above). And it even provided him with a way to regard contemporary Jewish observance as God-given, as God-protected, and as good for the church. By wanting to value "flesh" positively, Augustine came to value "Jew" and "Judaism" positively. His stunningly original teaching on Jews and Judaism was one of the strongest, brightest threads in this intricate pattern of mutually supporting associations that he wove to construct his entire theology.

Texts and Time

Sin made human flesh mortal, thus "narrative": the life of fallen man as she now moves through time has a beginning, a middle, and an end. And sin made human knowing "narrative," dependent upon sequence and memory to achieve an inexact apprehension mediated through signs, be those signs actions or words. We have seen how Augustine grappled with these ideas, whether he thought about texts (*Christian Teaching*) or about the soul, sin, and time (*Confessions,* especially books ten to thirteen) or about the prophecies enacted by ancient Jewish ritual (*Against Faustus*). When he writes book eighteen of *City of God,* however (sometime around 425?), these ideas creatively recombined. His rich appreciation of the fact of language itself as a sign and an effect of Adam's fall helped Augustine to achieve a startlingly new and simple solution to an old and complex problem: the relation of the Hebrew text of the Bible to that of the Septuagint.

Augustine's ideas about Adam's fall into time and thus into language had the effect of radically relativizing the value of *any* linguistic record of God's word. God was beyond and outside of time. For this reason, even the original Hebrew of the Bible was already a sort of "translation" from the timelessness of the divine realm into the historical realm of the linguistic and thus of the human. Any language, even the Bible's original language, attests to the primal dislocation of consciousness suffered by the species after Eden. The Bible truly did mediate knowledge of God, Augustine said; but that knowledge, because it was mediated, was always and already compromised by the necessary uncertainties of interpretation.

God's Spirit, Augustine nonetheless asserted, is the "author" of scripture in both its Hebrew and its Greek recensions. For this reason, the Septuagint takes precedence over any other Greek rendering, divinely authorized as it was through the miracle of the seventy-two authors' inspired translation. In those many places where its Greek differs undeniably from its Hebrew, Augustine thus concluded, this difference is also due to the Holy Spirit, and vice versa: Anything in the Hebrew that is not in the Greek "is something which the Spirit of God decided to say not through the translators but through the prophets." There are no mistranslations, only a plenitude of meanings, divinely intended for different audiences: to the Jew first (primarily through the Hebrew) and also to the Greek (for whose ultimate benefit, maintained Augustine, the Septuagint was made). Seen from this point of view, Ptolemy's translators, those legendary Jewish sages sent from Jerusalem to render the Hebrew Bible into Greek, had served as prophets to the gentile church (*City of God* 18.42–43).

History and Revelation

What happens when the temporal narrative of history lines up with the prophetic narrative of the Bible? Can the action of God be discerned in contemporary events?

On this question Augustine sustained a profound change of mind. In *Against Faustus,* and in many other writings of approximately the same period, Augustine had voiced his excited conviction that the world, through the agency of the empire, was living through a long-foretold moment in the history of salvation: the Gentiles' destruction of their own false gods. The surprise of government-orchestrated antipagan coercion, put in place by the emperor Honorius, spurred Augustine to pronounce excitedly that ancient altars were being destroyed *secundum propheticam veritatem* ("according to prophetic truth"). Prophets in Israel's ancient scriptures had spoken of the Gentiles' destroying their idols and abandoning their false gods as an apocalyptic act, achieved at the end of time, when God would reveal himself in glory and establish his kingdom (p. 35 above). Now, in 399, the closing of pagan temples in Carthage confirmed for Augustine that the empire's government, within the quotidian, enacted God's will. Recent events should convince any pagan of the truth of the church, Augustine declared, once he was shown the ancient script for this destruction, namely, the books of the Jews. Such a man would see

> these same kings of the earth now happily subdued by Christ . . . and he would hear the words of the psalm in which this was predicted so long ago: "All the kings of the earth shall bow down to him; all the nations shall serve him" (Psalm 72:10). . . . And reading what was said in this psalm about Christ and about his Church, he would find that what was foretold there is fulfilled now. . . . He would see the idols of the nations perishing from the earth, and he would find that Jeremiah had predicted this. . . . "In that day," said Isaiah, "a man shall throw away his abominations of gold and of silver" (Isaiah 2:20).
>
> *AGAINST FAUSTUS* 13.7

It was for this very purpose, Augustine continued, that God, through Rome, had sent Israel with their books into exile. Otherwise, Christians would have reason to fear that pagans would accuse them of having forged such prophecies "once the events that they describe were already occurring, . . ."

> were it not for the Jews. Widely dispersed and widely marked, they are Cain, who received his sign so that no one would kill him; they are Ham, the slave of his brothers, bearing those books for his brothers' instruction. From these same books we prove that these things were not written by us to fit the times. They were published long ago in the Jews' kingdom, and preserved as prophecies; and now they are made manifest and fulfilled . . . "for these things happened to them as an example, but they were written down for us, in whom the end of the ages has come" (1 Corinthians 10:11).
>
> *AGAINST FAUSTUS* 13.10

Caught up in the moment, Augustine identified God's purposes with Rome's policies. But unlike these ancient prophets (and unlike many of his contemporary co-religionists), Augustine was not thinking apocalyptically. The church's triumph did not signal the end of time, but a special quality of the times—ideas that Tyconius' work had helped him to think (p. 424, n. 21, below). Further, Augustine's division of time into the "cosmic week" calmed Paul's apocalyptic pronouncement in 1 Corinthians considerably. By definition, the "sixth age" of the universe had already begun with the coming of Christ. It would end only with his Second Coming. How long would this current period between his first and second advents last? That was unknowable and unknown: All that could be asserted with certainty was that the last age had already commenced (*Against Faustus* 12.14). In the indefinite meanwhile, however, believers could savor the gospel's triumph, indeed its vindication. "We have seen Christian emperors, who have put all their confidence in Christ, gaining splendid victories over ungodly enemies who hoped in idols and the worship of demons" (*Against Faustus* 22.76).

When voicing these views, Augustine sounds much like an earlier bishop, Constantine's contemporary and "biographer," Eusebius of Caesarea. Eusebius had lived at an equally heady moment, when after 312 C.E. the church became the startled recipient of Constantine's largesse. Stopping anti-Christian persecution, Constantine threw himself into his new role as the patron of the church, endowing basilicas, underwriting episcopal expenses, convening councils, commissioning copies of Bibles. Commenting on Constantine's elaborate (and expensive, and ambitious) program of public building in Jerusalem, Eusebius rhapsodized that it seemed as if "the glory of the God of Israel" had returned to its ancient seat. "Perhaps *this* is the new and second Jerusalem announced in the prophetic oracles" (*Life of Constantine* 3.33).

As Augustine would later do, Eusebius framed contemporary events by using and reinterpreting formerly apocalyptic prophecies. And this prophetic perspective netted Eusebius two advantages. First, it enhanced the prestige of his patron, promoting in biblical accents the belief that the supreme ruler on earth enjoyed very close relations with the supreme ruler in heaven. Such a view of the ruler's special status, regarded skeptically in modern democracies when elected officials make similar claims, was deeply traditional to Roman political culture. What was new after 312 was not these claims' being made for the emperor but the identity of the cultural institution making these claims: the church and her bishops, which now took their place in this chorus of praise alongside the more traditional panegyrists, oracles, city councilors, and Roman senators. Second, by appropriating apocalyptic prophecies for such present-day, nonapocalyptic events, Eusebius also challenged those Christians who still clung to now-outmoded (and perhaps embarrassing) apocalyptic views. Politics had recast prophecy. See, Eusebius could say, the prophets spoke not about the end of time, but about our time, now; and the glorious ruler whom they foresaw was not the Christ of the Apocalypse, but our patron, the emperor of Rome.[21]

Augustine's "Eusebian" rhetoric, stimulated similarly by imperial initiatives, also had practical advantages. An empire that supported the catholic church against her pagan enemies—and that would soon support Augustine's church against her schismatic rivals, the Donatists—certainly seemed from within this perspective of realized prophecy to have God on its side. Indeed, during the decade that followed this imperial action in Carthage, while his church vigorously encouraged the Donatists to "return" to the *catholica* with a well-coordinated plan of state coercion and ecclesiastical persuasion, Augustine robed his church's resort to violence in the mantle of biblical precedent. The Donatists complained that coercion was un-Christian: "With whom did Christ ever use force? Whom does he compel?" Augustine readily produced Christian models. "See, they have the apostle Paul. Let them acknowledge in him Christ's first using force, and afterwards teaching, first striking and afterwards consoling. . . . Why then should the church not force her lost children to return?" (*Letter* 185.6,22, written c. 417; Augustine had already pointed to Paul's "conversion" as a New Testament example of divine coercion in *Against Faustus* 22.70). Christ, too, in the parable of the great banquet, had ordered his servants to "compel" tarrying invitees to join the feast. The divine take-home message was clear: "Disobedience meets with coercion" (Luke 14:23; *Letter* 185.6,24). To Donatists, the coercion of the Christian Roman Empire looked and felt very much like the earlier coercion of the pagan Roman Empire. Augustine was unimpressed. Both Pharaoh and Moses had "coerced" Israel, but their reasons and their goals could not have been more different, though their means, to an outsider, might look the same.[22]

His defense of the Old Testament against Faustus had equipped Augustine very well to defend religious coercion against the Donatists. Just because two actors seem to behave the same way, he had also insisted against the Manichee, shared external resemblances cannot establish a common internal morality. Both pagan and Jewish sacrifices looked alike, but they had absolutely different origins and absolutely different ends (*Against Faustus* 20.18; 22.17). All wars look the same, but people's motivations differ, so that some wars are just while others are not (22.74). Multiple wives might seem the measure of sexual profligacy, but the patriarchs had many wives "not for the love of pleasure" but for the purpose of chastely begetting children (22.48). Only God could see into people's hearts. Thus when events occurred that seemed, to the external viewer, inexplicable or unjust—the slaughter of some thousands but not others, when all had worshiped the Golden Calf; the choice of David over Saul, when each had acknowledged his sin with exactly the same words in exactly the same way; the choice of unborn Jacob over unborn Esau, when neither could have done anything whether good or bad—faith's only choice was to affirm God's justice. The reason for God's choices, however, remained to humans *occultissima*. That was why the affirmation of God's justice was, precisely, an affirmation of faith.

For Augustine, the fall of Rome in 410 began to close the window of prophetic transparency that Honorius' action in 399 had thrown open. In his mature theology, the hiddenness that so obscured God's justice seeped increasingly into many other dimensions of life. The triumphant clarity of the Theodosian age cedes, in *City of God,* to abiding ambiguity. The church in the age before the End is no communion of saints but an imperfect *corpus permixtum* containing a good share of sinners as well. (Tyconius had given him this idea early on; and initially, Augustine had used it to critique the Donatists. Later, he will use it simply to describe the church.) The empire, neither demonic before 312 nor holy thereafter, lacked any absolute religious significance. And events whether positive (such as the universal proclamation of the gospel) or negative (famine, earthquake, or the fall of Rome) were eschatologically opaque: They could not be matched with scriptural prophecy to indicate anything of the divine plan. However certain in their faith, Christians could never be certain of their circumstances. For the period of time that stood outside the biblical canon, history's patterns and the ultimate significance of events, like God's standards of justice, were *occultissimi* as well.[23]

Augustine unrolled this somber vision in the twenty-two books of his *City of God*. The whole was united by his pursuit of a single theme: the history of love. Ever since Cain and Abel, he said, all humanity has been divided between two great cities, according to the orientation of their love. Those who love carnal, lower things (and, most insidious of all, themselves) belong to the *civitas terrena*, the "earthly city," Babylon. Those who love God belong to the heavenly city, Jerusalem above, the city of God. Augustine's argument takes these two cities of apocalyptic tradition, Jerusalem and Babylon, and transmutes them into two opposed moral communities existing together, indefinitely mixed, within time. Wandering in the exile of history, humanity has been separated from its distant, heavenly homeland by the first sin of the first man, Adam; by the weight of original sin, which afflicts every generation thereafter, disordering human love and, therefore, human society; by the vast river of time, flowing on into a future of unknowable duration. The citizens of God's city live in this world as pilgrims and as strangers; *peregrini*, "resident aliens." The home that they yearn for, the glorious city promised to them and, through Christ, won for them, lies beyond history's horizon.[24]

It is to tell this tale of two cities that Augustine, late in life, sacrifices his elaborately developed typology of Cain as a figure for the exiled Jews. He does so in part because Genesis 4:17 so well obliges his new idea. After murdering Abel, Cain "went away from God's face," settled east of Eden, and proceeded to "build a city." Another city, Rome, Augustine immediately remarks, was also founded after fratricide, when Romulus killed Remus. Both Roman brothers were citizens of the earthly city, contending for power and glory. No such struggle for sovereignty explains the history of the primal brothers, however, "for Abel did not aim at power in the city which his brother was founding. But Cain felt the diabolical envy that the wicked feel for the good simply because they are good, while they themselves are evil." The struggle between Romulus and Remus demonstrated how citizens of the earthly city strive against each other. The fight between Cain and Abel, by contrast, "displayed the hostility between the two cities themselves, the city of God and the city of men" (*City of God* 15.5).

Augustine goes on to ponder the motivations of the good and of the wicked, minutely analyzing the language of Genesis 4 to understand how Cain's sullenness, caused by God's accepting Abel's offering but not his, led him first to envy, then to rage, and finally to violence (*City of God* 15.7). The well-worn verses from Romans 9 preface this investigation, as Augustine reminds himself and his readers of God's decisions when distinguishing "the vessels of wrath from the vessels of mercy by a deeply hidden yet just dispensation known only to himself" (*City of God* 15.6). God had warned Cain to master the sin that lurked in wait for him, but Cain did not do so (Genesis 4:7). His jealousy only grew stronger, until at last he murdered his brother. "Such was the man who founded the earthly city," Augustine concludes. (The line of the heavenly city is established on earth by the slaughtered Abel's replacement, Seth; Genesis 4:25; *City of God* 15.15). But before Augustine proceeds to the rest of Genesis, he mentions— almost in passing—one last thing about Cain. "He also symbolizes the Jews by whom Christ was slain, that shepherd of the human flock who was prefigured by Abel, the shepherd of the flock of sheep. But this is a matter of prophetic allegory, so I will not explain it here. Besides, I recall that I said something on this point in my book *Against Faustus*" (*City of God* 15.7).

Cain's role as the founder of the earthly city placed him solidly at the earliest part of biblical and universal history, and Augustine wanted to leave him there. *City of God,* following the sequence of biblical books as it does, has a strong narrative line, one that typology, with its energetic back-and-forth between the testaments, risked muddying. But the main reason why Augustine released Cain from service as a figure for "the Jews" was because in *City of God* he had recast the moral and emotional quality of "wandering" and of "exile." Back in the glory days at the turn of the fourth to the fifth century, the new initiatives of the blooming Christian kingdom made an apposite contrast to the

Jews' humiliating loss, centuries earlier, of their own kingdom. Augustine's rhetoric had emphasized that contrast. At that point, and for a long while thereafter, Cain the exiled fratricide aptly symbolized both the Jews' crime and their permanent punishment. And Augustine's deeply original interpretation of the mark of Cain that protected Cain in his exile adroitly communicated the rich mix of ideas that Augustine associated with his theological construction of Jewish law and Jewish practice: divine origins, distinctiveness, visibility, a form of public pedagogy. Even after his discovery of Psalm 59.12, Augustine's interpretive center of gravity remained Genesis 4:15: Both in his two earlier sermons and in his letter to Paulinus, he elucidated the psalm by referring, explicitly, to Cain (pp. 324–327 above).

Cain drops out when Augustine quotes Psalm 59.12 only in his two later, undated sermons; and I think that this is so because Augustine delivered them only after he had conceived and become committed to his vision in *City of God.* The great theme of that work is wandering. The longing for home and the acute sense of displacement defines the experience and the identity of the Christian and not, as in so many of Augustine's earlier writings, the experience and the identity of the "Jew." Cain the fratricidal wanderer would have confused this plaintive and morally positive image of Augustine's wandering citizen-saint sojourning in time, far from his heavenly home. Thus Cain, resolutely earth-bound, becomes the first to build a city; and the city that he founds is the *civitas terrena,* "the earthly city, which longs for earthly joys" (*City of God* 15.15).[25]

Accordingly, when in book eighteen of *City of God* Augustine finally takes up the birth and death of Jesus, and thus the fate of the Jews, Cain makes no appearance. But all of Augustine's earlier ideas that he had developed against Faustus are there: the missing kingdom, the visible practices, the permanent blindness, the unwitting servitude, the ancient testimony, the divine immunity to ethnic death, the broadest possible dispersion of Jews and their books to aid and to amplify the broadest possible dissemination of the gospel. Everything *but* Cain reappears in book eighteen. In his absence, Augustine hangs all of these ideas, originally generated from his reading of Genesis, from the hook of Psalm 59.12.

The Jews who killed him and who refused to believe in him . . . were dispersed all over the whole world . . . and thus by the evidence of their own scriptures they bear witness for us that we have not fabricated the prophecies about Christ. . . . It follows that when the Jews do not believe in our scriptures, their own scriptures are fulfilled in them, while they read with blind eyes. . . . It is in order to give this testimony, which in spite of themselves they supply for our benefit by their possession and preservation of those books, that they are dispersed among all nations, wherever the Christian church spreads. . . . In fact there is a prophecy given before the event on this very point in the book of Psalms, which they also read. "As for my God, his mercy will go before me; my God has shown me this in the case of my enemies. Do not slay them, lest at some time they forget your Law; scatter them by your might" (Psalm 59:11-12). God has thus shown to the church the grace of his mercy in the case of her enemies the Jews, since, as the apostle says, "their failure means salvation for the Gentiles" (Romans 11:11). And this is his reason for forbearing to "slay" them—that is, for not putting an end to their existence as Jews, although they have been conquered and oppressed by the Romans: it is for fear that they might forget the Law of God and thus fail to give convincing testimony on this point. . . . Thus it was not enough for the Psalmist to say "Do not slay them . . ." without adding, "Scatter them." For if they lived with that testimony of the Scriptures only in their own land, and not everywhere, then the Church, which is everywhere, would not have them available among all the nations as witnesses to the prophecies given beforehand about Christ.

CITY OF GOD 18.46

❖ ❖ ❖

AUGUSTINE THE MASTER OF RHETORIC had a knack for finding and deploying good proof texts. And his identifying such proof texts—a pithy scriptural sound bite condensing a much larger complex of theological ideas—often came considerably after he conceived and developed the ideas that they served to sum up. It was in the late 390s, when he wrote *To Simplicianus* and immediately thereafter, *Confessions,* that Augustine first reimagined the relation of divine grace and human will so that the initiative of salvation rested solely and entirely with God: God turns the sinner toward himself (see p. 188 above). Only later, after 411, did he discover Proverbs 8:35. "The will is prepared by the Lord." He used it repeatedly thereafter. His belief that all humanity was in some real way "in Adam," voiced at the turning point of his debate with Fortunatus back in 392, later spurred Augustine's conceptualization of original sin when he squared off against the idea of free will promulgated by Pelagius. Eventually, Romans 5:12 ("Adam . . . in whom all sinned") would serve as his slogan for this teaching, but the verse itself had played no conspicuous role at either formative stage of his thinking about sin and Adam, whether early (against Fortunatus) or late (against Pelagius).[26]

These observations should provide some purchase when we assess Augustine's use of "Slay them not." Within his own lifetime and thus within the contemporary context of his own works, Psalm 59:12 never had this status as a major proof text in his arsenal. He had come to it too late, well after he had already coordinated all of those biblical, theological, and historical ideas about the Jews and their continuing role in the Christian commonwealth around the figure of Cain. By the time that he found Psalm 59, he did not need it; when he did use it, he usually used it together with Genesis 4. Only within the specific context of the latter half of *City of God* did Augustine finally relinquish Cain as a type of the Jews. His much larger idea of the heavenly pilgrim's earthly exile demanded it. His other two sermons—also late and, within Augustine's own lifetime, relatively unimportant—reflect this decision that the much grander *City of God* had dictated. Thus it was only when Augustine presented his theological "Jews" there, and never in any of his earlier writings, that Psalm 59.12 assumed its standalone posture.

In later Christian tradition, and even more frequently in modern scholarship, Psalm 59.12 does loom large as *the* Augustinian proof text about Jews and Judaism. This is so, in both instances, for the same reason: precisely because of its placement in *City of God.* That work is one of the abiding masterpieces of late Latin theology, and it went on to exert a huge and formative influence on Western medieval culture. When later Christians during the Middle Ages wanted to summon Augustine's authority for a statement that they wanted to make about Jews, Psalm 59.12 as presented in *City of God* stood ready to hand.

But this verse will not help us if we want to understand the birth and development of Augustine's theology of Jews and Judaism on its own terms, within his own lifetime, and within the specific context, social and intellectual, of late Latin Christianity in Roman antiquity. For that project—how Augustine thought about Jews and Judaism, not how later Christians thought about Augustine on the Jews—*Against Faustus* is the essential text. It is the text in which all of his most original ideas on this topic come together most fully and for the first time. In its citations of Faustus' *Capitula,* it provides us with a rare and valuable look at another community of late Latin Christians, North Africa's Manichees, against whose moral concerns and textual practices Augustine pitched so much of his maturing theology, including his radically innovative theology of Judaism. It acquaints us in unexpected ways with the issues at stake—textual, ethical, doctrinal, ritual, social, political—when late-fourth-century Christians imagined and constructed their contesting identities. It affords us a clear look at how these contesting Christians used "Jews" and the *adversus Iudaeos* rhetoric when they fought with each other. And finally (though only occasionally), it even provides fleeting glimpses of late-fourth-century North African Jews.

For all of the important differences in presentation, themes, and goals between *Against Faustus* and *City of God,* however, Augustine concluded that longer, later work on the same point and with the same Pauline image that he had used more than two decades earlier against the Manichee. Yet once again, his thinking about grace and Law, about divine justice and human freedom, returned him to the *massa damnata,* the divine potter's clay that he had derived so long ago from chapter nine of Paul's letter to the Romans. The image condensed so many of Augustine's theological points of principle: the solidarity of the race in Adam, the mysteriousness of God's judgments, the absoluteness of divine prerogative, the necessity of faith's affirmation of God's justice, no matter how hidden that justice may be. As a metaphor for humanity, this image of the *massa* ultimately overrode the significance, even the utility, of the terms "Jew" and "Gentile" within Augustine's thought. After Adam's sin, he wrote,

> the whole of mankind is a condemned lump, for he who committed the first sin was punished, and along with him all the stock which had its roots in him. The result is that there is no escape for anyone from this justly deserved punishment, except by merciful and undeserved grace. Humanity is divided between those in whom the power of merciful grace is demonstrated, and those in whom is shown the might of just retribution. Neither of these could be displayed in respect of all mankind, for if all had remained condemned . . . then God's merciful grace would not have been seen . . . and if all had been transferred from darkness to light, then the truth of God's vengeance would not have been made evident. *Many more are condemned by vengeance than are released by mercy.*
>
> CITY OF GOD 21.12

Augustine's idea of eternity, with its Neoplatonic embellishments and its raised fleshly bodies, is peculiarly Christian. Within that context, the defining distinction is between the saved few and the damned many: "Jew" and "Gentile" disappeared. But when considering not eternity but history (both past and present), Augustine thought as people within ancient Mediterranean culture had always thought: Humans are defined by the gods that they worship. Restated in biblical idiom, this idea defines the difference between Israel and the nations; the difference, before Christianity, between Gentiles and Jews. And here, as he argued against Faustus, Christians and Jews formed one community over against pagans and heretics, because (true) Christians, like Jews, worshiped the One God (p. 276 above).

Thus against Jerome no less than against Faustus, Augustine insisted that Jews were not a challenge to Christianity but a witness to it. In their allegiance to their ancestral practices, he asserted, the Jews unknowingly confirmed the church's claim to their scriptures. (Their having these texts in Hebrew conferred no advantage; and when reading and living by a book—by God's book—interpretation is all.) Augustine's "witness doctrine," in short, fundamentally addressed questions of theology and identity internal to his own community.

Augustine had little reason to think that his ideas on this topic would some day, in their turn, be interpreted "literally." He lived in a society governed by Roman law, wherein Jews were still citizens. All this changes as European society alters in the wake of the western Roman Empire's demise. Nevertheless, because of Augustine's tremendous authority, his "witness doctrine," mediated through *City of God,* became part of that erudite tradition through which patristic learning shaped Western Christian thought. In the changed social context of medieval Christendom, Augustine's invocation of Psalm 59, interpreted literally, ultimately would safeguard Jewish lives. But that is a story of another time, for another time.

EPILOGUE

All things are foreknown, and man has free choice.
PIRKEI AVOT (ETHICS OF THE FATHERS) 3,15

Where Augustine's thought is most characteristically "Augustinian"—in his approach to biblical interpretation, and to interpretation more generally; in his ideas about the flesh, and about its relation to spirit; in his thoughts on the nature of time, and of history, to eternity; in his understanding of sin, and of the mystery of salvation; in his views on the incarnation and resurrection of Christ—we find him thinking with "Jews." The ways that he depended on "Jews" as a fundamental element in his broader theology enabled him, indeed perhaps compelled him, to play the stunning variations that he did on the themes of the older *contra Iudaeos* tradition. But are rhetoric and theology, important though these are, all that he finally leaves us with? Can we move beyond the rhetoric to see a measure of social reality? Is there any way to know how Augustine thought and felt, not about rhetorical "Jews," but about his actual Jewish contemporaries?

As we have already seen, what Augustine says about theological and rhetorical Jews, whether positive or negative, cannot be read as direct evidence to help us settle this question (see pp. 261–307 above). What can and does help us, however, is something that he does *not* say. But to appreciate the meaning of this significant silence, we must first situate it, albeit briefly, within its significant context: three episodes of violent religious repression that occurred during the middle years of Augustine's episcopacy. The first was the imperially sponsored coercion of North African pagans. The second was the duress inflicted on Donatist Christians by church and state acting in concert. And the third—for which we have unnervingly excellent primary testimony—was the forced conversion to catholic Christianity of the 540 Jewish residents of Magona, one of two cities on the island of Minorca.

✦✦✦

WE RETURN TO THE YEAR 399 and to the religious coercion of pagans (p. 340 above). The emperor's initiative, directed against the great temple of Juno Caelestis in Carthage, served to inspire acts of Christian vandalism elsewhere in North Africa. Bad feeling simmered and urban violence irregularly erupted for years thereafter, and outraged pagans sometimes pushed back hard. (Sixty Christians were killed in Sufes, payback for their destruction of the town's statue of Hercules; *Letter* 50.) And yet, as we have seen, Augustine trumpets this moment as if it were an unmitigated victory for the church. He musters Old Testament authorities, draping current events in prophetic glory. He boasts to enemies and to friends alike—Faustus on the one hand; his congregation at Hippo on the other (*Against Faustus* 13.7–10; *Sermon* 22.4)—that God's ancient promises were being fulfilled in their own day. Even the violence on both sides, even the loss of life, did not disturb his confident conviction that these acts of religious repression were profoundly *right*. About the religious coercion of pagans, in brief, Augustine evinces not the slightest qualm.[1]

It was the Donatists, however, who presented the single gravest challenge to the local hegemony of catholic Christianity, a challenge more pointed than that of any other community in North Africa. They had the numbers on the ground and were present in force in the cities and in the many small towns of Roman Africa's hinterlands. Their clerical hierarchy duplicated that of the imperial church, to which they offered a specifically African alternative. Further, they could appeal to that traditional heroic standard of spiritual excellence: stalwart perseverance in time of persecution, whether the persecuting empire be pagan or Christian. The catholic hierarchy had to move against this formidable rival. But they had to do so carefully—especially once they allied with imperial force—lest they seem to be the aggressors, and so reinforce the Donatists' self-presentation as the church of the martyrs (and thus as the "true" church).[2]

The imperial church prosecuted its case thoroughly and with consummate political skill, and Augustine himself took a very active role in these proceedings. Already in 393, he worked with Aurelius, bishop of Carthage, to coordinate a vigorous program of anti-Donatist "public relations": preaching and teaching on the one hand, writing letters of collegial courtesy to Donatist bishops and circulating invitations to public debate on the other. Once the emperor Honorius stepped into the fray, however, he changed the local calculus of power. In 405, the emperor posted his Edict of Unity to Carthage. From that time on, through the application of prejudicial laws, Donatists were actively encouraged to rejoin the "true" church. Catholic clergy, meanwhile, assumed control of the Donatist churches, both the buildings and the congregations; Donatist bishops had the options of submission, arrest, or exile. The noncompliant, finally, would thenceforth be regarded as heretics, and thus subject to the same legal disabilities as heretics. The first, diplomatic stage of the campaign was over.[3]

As with African pagans, so with these African Christians: Some complied, others grudgingly acquiesced. A radical fringe drawn from those who resisted, however, pushed back violently, destroying catholic churches and occasionally mutilating and even murdering catholic clergy. The catholic church responded with the power of the catholic state; more bloodshed, including executions, resulted. Both communities slowly settled down into a situation of erratically waged civil war. Finally, in 410, Honorius posted another order: "We abolish the new superstition and we command that the regulations in regard to catholic law be preserved unimpaired and inviolate" (*Theodosian Code* 16.11.3). Summoned to Carthage the following year, 285 Donatist bishops confronted 286 Catholic bishops to plead their case before an appointed imperial officer, himself a loyal catholic. The conclusion was never in doubt: The officer found in favor of the catholics. This latest turn of the screw increased the pressure of hostile law on Donatist laymen as well as on clergy. Armed resistance in the countryside persisted, sometimes transmuting into defiant suicides: In one effort to persuade an imperial agent to desist, the Donatist bishop of Timgad, together with his entire congregation, even threatened to burn their basilica down around themselves.[4]

The repression of the Donatists signaled the catholic clergy's unambivalent embrace of the coercive power that Honorius had so suddenly made available to them. Both as a tireless strategist and as a committed anti-Donatist campaigner, Augustine actively availed himself of this unprecedented opportunity. But he went much further, framing a theological justification for the use of force that intimately linked his long-held views on sin and vitiated human will to the pastoral obligations of the church. Already against Faustus, Augustine had argued that a coercive action in itself could be neither good nor bad: Its moral quality cohered with the intentions of its agent. Force applied out of love and toward a good end could never be morally wrong. God himself had set the example, whether when disciplining Israel for their own salvation or when wresting Paul away from the Pharisees and claiming him for the church. How, then, could the church countenance doing any less now for the wayward Donatists, especially since the means to effect such discipline, thanks to the emperor, lay so ready to hand?

Communion was no guarantee of salvation, as Augustine himself was the first to admit. The *catholica,* no community of saints, existed as a diverse collectivity that included many sinners as well. (This idea of the church as a *corpus permixtum* had come to Augustine from his great Donatist mentor, Tyconius; p. 158 above.) Inside the church, however, salvation was at least a possibility, while outside the church there could be no salvation. This distinction between salvation's necessary and sufficient conditions mirrored for Augustine the distinction between the church's divinely mandated responsibilities and God's sovereign, and secret, decisions about election. In sum, Augustine is even harder on nonconforming Christians than he was on pagans. He suffered no misgivings about the application of force in the one instance; in the other, he actually urged coercive action. To rebuke religiously errant Christians, if necessary by force, was a clear and sacred duty. The conscientious pastor, like the conscientious father, *must* apply such "discipline" for the ultimate well-being of his charge. In brief, Augustine insisted, the church coerces heretics for the heretics' own good.[5]

Untroubled equanimity in the face of the religious repression of pagans, urgent advocacy for the use of force to "persuade" fellow

Christians. The pattern of such hostilities followed the broad lines of sacred violence described in the Bible, which Augustine saw as prescribed by the Bible. In the church's Old Testament, God had explicitly condemned the worship of idols, commanding Israel to extirpate such practices from the Land; in the church's New Testament, Paul had full-heartedly repeated this condemnation. And God was no less intolerant of deviant practices on the part of his people: His designated scriptural spokesmen—holy men, priests, kings, and prophets—unceasingly repudiated cultic diversity within Israel, just as Paul, the evangelists' Jesus, and the authors of other New Testament texts repudiated diversities of practice and belief within the early church. If Christian monarchs brought the coercive power of the Christian state against pagans and against heretics, those external and internal enemies of Christian truth, they did God's work: Augustine found innumerable scriptural precedents for such initiatives. But where in scripture did God advocate the repression of Judaism itself? And how did Augustine regard the forced conversions of Jews?

✦✦✦

EVIDENCE BESPEAKING RELATIONS between late Roman Christians and Jews in the fourth and fifth centuries is as startlingly inconsistent for the entire empire, eastern and western, as it is for the island of Minorca in 418 C.E. On the one hand, reports begin to accrue from various corners of the Roman world describing the seizure or destruction of synagogues and the forced expulsion or baptism of Jewish communities. On the other hand, contemporary Jews do not act as if they feel marginalized: They maintain enormous and exquisite community structures in the heart of Roman cities; they mock Jesus (thus Christianity) openly, to the point of provoking urban riots; and in one eastern city, Laodicea, they even physically abuse a local archdeacon.

The language and the substance of imperial law also pull in at least two directions. In the *Theodosian Code*, rhetorical humiliation of this "nefarious" and "un-Roman sect," and occasional hostile legislation aimed particularly at converts to Judaism, sit cheek by jowl with imperial orders to respect Jewish persons, places, and privileges and with imperial assertions of Judaism's continuing legitimacy. Finally, the social and political prominence of some late Roman Jews, and the Jewish inscriptions that publicly proclaim the names of converts, suggest that the laws against Jews' holding high office or against gentile (more specifically, Christian) conversions to Judaism do not reflect widespread initiatives.[6]

Most of our relevant evidence specifically for Minorca comes from an encyclical letter written by its bishop, Severus; and it provides, in miniature, a similarly complex picture. Much of this complexity is embodied in the figure of Theodorus, the island's preeminent citizen and a former *defensor civitatis* ("protector of the city," thus Magona's premier magistrate). Emperors had established this office back in the 360s. The defensor was charged with expediting local legal cases and with ensuring some measure of justice to the poor. In 409, the emperors added a further refinement: Holders of such office, they decreed, had to be men "imbued with the sacred mysteries of orthodox religion"—in other words, catholic Christians (*Code of Justinian* 1.55.8).

At some point during the decade between the establishment of this last law and the religious violence of 418, by consent of the city councilors together with the major local landholders and the bishop, Theodorus had served Magona as its defensor. By then, noted Severus, Theodorus had "already fulfilled all the [other] duties of the town council." In 417–418, the incumbent defensor was his kinsman, Caecilianus, a *vir honestus* and *praecipuus* ("a preeminent man of rank"; *Letter of Severus on the Conversion of the Jews* 19.6). Through the interlocking links of marriage, social status, land, and wealth, their family's connections extended far, perhaps to the highest levels of the imperial government.

But these two men also held high office within another community: their synagogue. Distinguished for his learning as well as for his prestige and his largesse, Theodorus was also the leader of his ethnic/religious community, its *pater pateron* ("father of fathers") as well as its *doctor legis* ("teacher of the Law"; *Letter of Severus* 6.2). The younger Caecilianus ranked as a *pater Iudaeorum* ("father of the Jews," 19.8). Jews, in brief, seem to have been the predominant group both socially and politically in Magona, perhaps on Minorca in toto. And the wealthiest and most powerful man on the island, a learned and honored patron respected and relied on by Christian and Jew alike, was himself a Jew (*Letter of Severus* 6.1).[7]

Severus, the bishop of Minorca's other city, Jamona, ranked well below this distinguished Jewish gentry in terms of social status and (thus) education. (To compose his encyclical letter, he enlisted the services of a gentleman ghost writer, Consentius, who provides us with a direct link to Augustine; *Letter* *12.13.) But in the late summer of 416, around the time that Severus assumed episcopal office, the island's Christian community unexpectedly acquired a new and different patron: the first martyr of the church, St. Stephen (Acts 6–7; *Letter of Severus* 4.1). During the previous winter, in December 415, Christian clergy near Jerusalem had discovered human remains and identified them as Stephen's. Authenticated almost instantaneously by the miraculous cure of scores of the afflicted faithful, the greater portion of Stephen's relics were moved to Jerusalem. A lesser portion, thanks to a peripatetic monk, traveled first to North Africa and then to Minorca, where they were deposited in a church outside of Magona.

As Severus tells the story, Stephen's presence instantaneously altered the customarily warm relations between Christians and Jews:

> Immediately, our complacency (*tepor*) heated up, as did our hearts which, as Scripture says, "burned in the way" (Luke 24:32). At one moment, zeal for the faith fired us; at another moment, the hope of saving a multitude spurred us on. In the end, even the obligation of greeting one another was broken off. Our old habit of easy acquaintance was disrupted and—out of love for eternal salvation—the harmful visibility of our long-standing affection turned into temporary hatred. In every public place, we battled against the Jews over the Law; in every household, we fought for the faith.
>
> LETTER OF SEVERUS 4.4–5.2[8]

Severus exaggerates here: This "immediate" change of atmosphere took him more than a year and a half of patient anti-Jewish preaching to effect. But once he finally roused his flock to action, events did move quickly. In February 418, their hostility honed, Christians from both cities, with Severus at their head, converged on Magona's Jews. Initially demanding a public disputation, they next insisted on inspecting the synagogue, which was rumored to hold stockpiled weapons. (The existence of such a rumor, and its evident credibility, themselves index the success of Severus' preaching; in the event, however, no weapons were found; *Letter of Severus* 8.4–5.) Then, suddenly—though in retrospect, he says, providentially—Severus lost control of his people.

> Before we reached the synagogue, certain Jewish women (by God's arrangement, I suppose) acted recklessly and, doubtless to rouse our people from their gentleness, began to throw huge stones down on us from a higher spot. Although these stones (marvelous to relate) rained down like hail on top of the closely packed crowd, not one of our people was harmed or even touched by a direct hit. But at this point, the terrible Lion [Christ] momentarily took away the mildness from his lambs. While I protested in vain, they all snatched up stones and, neglecting the warning of their shepherd [Severus]—for they were united in a single plan, more from zeal for Christ than from anger—they decided that the wolves [Jews] had to be repulsed by horns. (In fact, no one could doubt that they did this with the approval of him who alone is the True and Good Shepherd.) . . . [T]he Jews retreated, and we gained control of the synagogue. . . . Fire consumed the synagogue itself and all its ornaments, except for its books and its silver. The sacred books we removed and retained, so that they would not suffer any harm among the Jews; but the silver we returned to them, so that they would not complain about any theft on our part, or any loss on theirs.
>
> Thus, while the Jews stood there, stupefied by the loss of their synagogue, we set off for the church to the chanting of hymns, giving thanks to the Author of our victory.
>
> *LETTER OF SEVERUS* 13.3–14.1

Neglecting to mention who started the fire, Severus passed on to a review of the many dreams, portents, prodigies, and miracles that followed this day of destruction. In the end, he relates, faced with the choice of conversion or exile, the demoralized Jewish community in its entirety agreed to accept baptism, consenting as well to assume the expense of raising a new basilica where once their synagogue had stood (*Letter of Severus* 30.2). Concluding on a note of enthused exhortation, Severus urged his fellow bishops to "take up Christ's zeal against the Jews . . . for the sake of their eternal salvation." Severus hoped that his exemplary (and utterly illegal) action would serve as a "spark" whereby "the whole earth might be ablaze with the flame of love," thus consuming the Jewish "forest of unbelief" (31.2–4).

Augustine, we now know, was directed toward these events by Consentius, the man whose literary culture had enabled Severus to craft his account. At some point shortly after these forced conversions, sometime in the year 419, Consentius had written to Augustine, partly about the virtues of using force (and subterfuge) against heretics (*Letter* *11), and partly about his role in shaping Severus' letter on "Stephen's" conversion of Minorca's Jews (*Letter* *12). A hard pragmatism underlay Consentius' words: The church, he believed, should avail itself of coercion, because coercion worked.[9]

When did Augustine receive Consentius' letters? And what effect, if any, did they have on his own position regarding contemporary Jews? The chronology of Augustine's letters, sermons, and later writings, now uncertain, makes precision impossible here. I have suggested in this study that his two sermons on Psalm 59 ("Slay them not") and his letter from Paulinus about the salvation of the Jews were all written at about the same time, between the years 410 to 415; we cannot know in what sequence (*On the Psalms* 59.1 and 2; *Letter* 121). After Augustine's first response to Paulinus went missing, his second response eventually followed at some indeterminate point after their first round of correspondence (*Letter* 149). How long after? As late as c. 419? Before or after Augustine had received these recently found letters from Consentius? I do not know; and until the huge effort of a complete revision of Augustinian chronology is successfully completed, I do not see how we could tell.

But certainly, by the time that he heard from Consentius, Augustine had already witnessed the advantages to the *catholica* that the us-ages of coercion could bring. Why not extend such salutary "discipline" to the Jews? If we can judge from an event that occurred c. 425 in Uzalis, another North African town, local Christians might well have endorsed such an action. When Severus' letter was read aloud there, the enthusiastic congregation was moved to applaud "the marvelous deeds of the glorious Stephen, accomplished on that island [Minorca] through the presence of his relics, for the salvation of all of those Jews who believed" (*The Miracles of Saint Stephen* 1.2). Support for such a campaign was further stimulated by Christian fears and hopes about the coming apocalypse, which waxed in the wake of Rome's fall in 410. According to one reading of Paul's letter to the Romans, the Jews at last would embrace Christianity at the End of the Age, once Christ returned. (In an utterly different religious and cultural moment, the historical Paul himself had asserted a cognate conviction.) Indeed, Bishop Severus had conjured this belief at the conclusion of his letter. Exhorting his fellow bishops to be "zealous" in order to save Jewish souls, he cited Paul in support: "Perhaps that time predicted by the Apostle has now indeed come, so that with the 'fullness of the Gentiles' having come in, 'all Israel will be saved' " (Romans 11:25–26; *Letter of Severus* 31.3). And finally, Augustine's own theological rationale in defense of religious coercion—that the loving effort to save Donatist souls, otherwise lost, not only justified the use of force, but morally obligated the Christian leaders of both church and state to use such force—could easily have been extended to embrace the Jews as well.[10]

But Augustine never moved in the slightest degree in this direction. His embrace of the coercive power of the state against pagans, his advocacy of that force against Donatist Christians, and his voluble defense of his position on this question of force, could not contrast more sharply with his position on Jewish contemporaries. In contrast to what he *does* say in favor of repressing "false religion" and of disciplining "false" Christians, we have what he does *not* say to or about those catholics who would coerce Jews. He never praises Consentius. He never praises Severus. So far as we know, he never read Severus' letter aloud to his congregation in Hippo, as his fellow bishop had read it to the church in Uzalis. Augustine, too, had dedicated a chapel to Stephen in Hippo, where the saintly dust also made miracles. When

Augustine reviewed the details of these miracles, he dwelt upon the saint's healings, exorcisms, and acts of charity: No *contra Iudaeos* theme sounds (*City of God* 22.8). Stephen, for Augustine, inspired no missionary effort directed at Hippo's Jews.

Severus' justification for coercing the Jews of Magona sounded very like Augustine's justification for coercing the Donatists of North Africa: By compelling these intimate outsiders in, bishops could help them to take an essential step toward their ultimate redemption. But for the full course of his long episcopate, Augustine never advocated extending such muscular pastoral care to current Jewish communities. If, according to Augustine, Jews represented a theologically unique community vis-à-vis pagans and heretics, then in this period of late Roman religious repression, that theological significance translated for Augustine into social significance as well. Jews, uniquely, were a *ceterarum gentium communione discreti*, "a community set apart from the other nations" (*Against Faustus* 12.13), and the agent of their separation was God himself. Pagans and heretics thus were the church's responsibility; the Jewish community, God's.

Here, then, we come again to the positive evidence that helps us with our question. What Augustine *did* say about Jews, both early (*Against Faustus*) and late (*City of God*), remained consistent from 399 C.E. through to 425 C.E. and beyond. His lifting up of the divine injunction not to "kill" Jews *always* stood in his teachings as a metaphor for the divinely willed freedom of current Jewish practice. He initially generated this understanding from the mark of Cain/God's protection of fratricidal Israel in Genesis 4.13–15 (*Against Faustus*, c. 399–401). A decade and more thereafter, he combined this reading of Genesis and this understanding of Cain's mark/Jewish practice with the words of David/the voice of Christ in Psalm 59 (his two sermons and his first, lost response to Paulinus's letter, c. 410–415, on the one hand; his extant response to Paulinus, *Letter* 149, c. 415–420, on the other). Once he conceived of *City of God* and reconceived exile as the *Christian* historical experience par excellence, he rested his teaching on God's protection of Jewish practice on Psalm 59, standing alone (*City of God* 18.46, c. 425; also *Sermon against the Jews* and *Faith in Things Unseen*). No one should forcibly separate Jews from Judaism, Augustine taught, whether he saw such an attempt in the pages of 1 Maccabees or in the letter of an episcopal colleague. To do so, he insisted, was to contravene God's will.

Augustine never conceived his teaching about Jewish religious prerogative as a juridical injunction. It always served as a theological argument about the value of "fleshly," historical Jewish practice as a prophecy of an incarnate, historical, Jewish Jesus. So too with Augustine's invocation of Psalm 69.22 by way of Romans 11:10: "Bend down their backs always." This verse was always a metaphor for the spiritual consequences of "earthly" (thus "Jewish") biblical hermeneutics; it was never a prescription for gentile Christian social practice. So too with Augustine's understanding of Israel's exile after 70 C.E.: The "scattering" of fleshly Israel was never solely a divine punishment for the Jews, but it was always, also, a providential divine gift to the nations, or more precisely to the church, to aid in her mission to turn the nations from their idols and demons to the true god, Israel's god. Augustine's arguments, and his motives, were theological. But the idea that drew all of them together, the idea of Israel and thus of the Jews, was for Augustine explicitly social and historical as well.

Israel's books are the church's books, taught Augustine, because the church's books are Israel's books, while the New Testament proclaims to the nations the fulfillment of God's promise of redemption to "Israel." But the identity of the redeemed Israel, the "all Israel" that Paul prophesied would be saved (Romans 11:25–26), never meant all of fleshly Israel. On this point especially, for Augustine, the Jews as a people embodied the paradox of divine justice and human freedom, the mystery of God's election. Many are called, few are chosen, and yet the will is free. God in his unerring justice condemns because of secret sins, known only to himself. He grants salvation purely as a gift, mysteriously, to the chosen few. Thus redeemed Israel, Augustine insisted, was always and only the community of the elect, that tiny minority removed from the *massa damnata* of Jews and Gentiles both. Only those mysteriously chosen few comprise the citizenry of Jerusalem Above, the city of God.

Finally, I have argued in this book that Augustine's teaching on Jews and Judaism had the power and clarity that it did in no small way because of the power and the clarity of the anti-catholic arguments assembled by Faustus in his *Capitula*. In that work, Faustus adroitly used both testaments to defend Latin Manichaean points of principle—on the sources of evil, on the theological status of gendered flesh, on the nature of salvation, and on the docetic Christ. It was Faustus, with his reading of Genesis and especially of Paul the apostle, who created the opportunity for the multitude of Augustine's intellectual trajectories in the late 390s to intersect. Thanks to Faustus, and to Manichaean biblical interpretation, Augustine was inspired to bring these intellectual trajectories together precisely on the point of his theological construct of the "Jew."

But this Augustinian "Jew" was never simply an abstract biblical *tupos* figuring catholic doctrinal truths. The idea always pointed to socially rooted actors on the stage of Christian history, the Bible's master narrative interpreted *ad litteram,* the history of God's salvation of the flesh. Augustine's "Jew" expressed the continuing positive theological significance of Judaism as an incarnate, historical community; and that community *in principle* stretched continuously from the pages of the Bible (with all its mystical heights and depths) to the synagogues of the late Roman Empire. Thanks again in no small way to Latin Manichaeism and in particular to its gifted spokesman, Faustus, Augustine was able to conceive and to construct a catholic theology that drove Neoplatonism's metaphysics back into history, and history—human time—back into biblical interpretation.

But with the closing of the canon, Augustine taught, the clarity of divine intention and action in history had dimmed. Postbiblical history had begun with Rome's destruction of the Second Temple; it would end only with the Second Coming of Christ. During the indefinite meanwhile, Augustine insisted, fleshly Israel—the "exiles" of 70 C.E.; his Jewish contemporaries; Jews thereafter—would remain history's Pole star, a continuing quotidian revelation of God's will shining in the darkness of secular time.[11]

The better we understand Augustine's theology of Jews and Judaism, the better we understand the interplay of all these great themes in his work. And the more clearly we see the theological continuity in Augustine's thought between "Jews" as a *signum* and Jews as an actual historical community, the better we see the theological principle so fundamental to Augustine the former Manichee and to Augustine the former philosophical enthusiast. Augustine asserted that flesh and spirit, time and eternity, creation and redemption, "belong" together. They had been joined together by the god of the Bible. They were embodied and enacted by that god's son. And they were revealed to humanity through the books, the traditions, and the historical existence of Israel—that point in his vision where "Jews" and Jews meet.

ACKNOWLEDGMENTS

Augustine and I met in 1971, at Wellesley College, in a seminar on heresy, crusade, and inquisition. I had volunteered to lead the second week's discussion, which focused on something called "the Donatist controversy." "You might want to have a look at a new book by Peter Brown," suggested my wonderful professor, Eleanor McLaughlin. The rest, as they say, is history.

The idea for the present study came to me in, of all places, Jerusalem. The occasion was the 1993 World Congress of Jewish Studies. My topic was anti-Judaism in the formation of Christian identity. My angle into the topic was the commentaries on Paul's letter to the Romans that Augustine, as a new churchman, had written in the mid-390s. In the frenzied final minutes of packing for that trip, I thought to throw the old, clunky translation of *Against Faustus* into my suitcase, along with a photocopy of Dave Efroymson's important essay, "The Patristic Connection." In that article, Efroymson had demonstrated that the luminaries of ancient proto-orthodox tradition—Justin, Tertullian, Irenaeus, Origen—had exercised their most virulently anti-Jewish rhetoric not against Jews but, curiously, against other, "heretical" Christians. Augustine, I knew, had written *Contra Faustum,* his monumental repudiation of North African Manichaean Christianity, only a few years after completing the early Pauline commentaries. Guided by Efroymson's insights, I thought that I would bolster my presentation of Augustine's anti-Jewish remarks in his smaller Pauline works by mining *Against Faustus* for even stronger ones. Once in Jerusalem, however, editing and re-editing my paper for the morning panel, I did not get to *Against Faustus* until sometime after midnight. I decided at that point just to skim some chapters, cull a few choice anti-Jewish remarks, and then get some sleep.

It never happened. Instead, energized by my own astonishment, I did not and could not stop reading. Augustine, I saw, had indeed attacked Manichaean Christianity when he attacked Faustus. But he never repudiated Judaism to do so. On the contrary: He defended Judaism and even praised it, while defending and praising, as well, the traditional practices of contemporary Jews. He even insisted that the Jews had no less a protector than God himself, who would punish whatever monarch, pagan or Christian, who attempted to impede their observances. In brief, in *Against Faustus*—at the very last moment, and purely by accident—I found the opposite of what I had expected to find. I remember staring out the window of the Mishkenot Sha'ananim at daybreak, watching the walls of the Old City glow gold, as I struggled to frame the thought dawning in my own mind: Between 394-395 (when he wrote his commentaries on Paul) and 399-400 (when he began *Against Faustus*), Augustine had come to a view of Jews and of Judaism that differed dramatically not only from his own prior teachings but also from the prevailing traditions of his church.

Augustine and the Jews had its beginnings in my manic twenty minutes on that morning panel, now fifteen years ago; and I recall with gratitude the generosity of my listeners, who tracked my ideas, shared my excitement, and encouraged me to press on. From that time to this, I have benefited greatly from the support of many friends and colleagues. Special thanks, first, to Ora Limor, David Satran, and Guy Stroumsa, who invited me to attend the 1993 WCJS, and again to David and Guy for supporting my application to Hebrew University as Lady Davis Visiting Professor. Jeremy Cohen encouraged me to expand upon my ideas in an international seminar on Jews and medieval Christianity held in Wolfenbüttel; the late Keith Hopkins, inviting me to the King's College Research Centre, gave me a chance to pull them together. I am especially grateful to Ben Isaac and Jonathan Price for welcoming me into Tel Aviv University's energetic community of classicists, historians, and religionists; and to Shlomo Biederman, Gidi Bohak, Menachem Fisch, and Itamar Gruenwald, for facilitating my formal association there as a Sackler Visiting Professor. An invitation to lecture at the Thirteenth Oxford International Conference on Patristic Studies provided me with a wonderful opportunity, before an ideal audience, to share some of the results of my early research. Elaine Pagels, at an especially bleak moment, offered kindness and good counsel. In Paris, for Archipel 33, Gérard Mordillat and Jérôme Prieur coaxed me to think out loud about the big picture: Roman Mediterranean culture and ancient Christianity's place within it. In the pages of *The New Republic,* Leon Wieseltier provided me with similar scope, while doing me (and future readers of this book) the great service of pruning and chastening my prose: Shock eventually yielded to gratitude. Conversations back in Jerusalem with Brouria Bitton-Ashkelony and with Israel Yuval quickened my imagination and broadened my field of vision; while my dear friend Oded Irshai—bibliographic hunter-gatherer *extraordinaire*—has sustained me in all seasons with endless streams of great ideas and inspired insights. To all these scholars, my warmest thanks.

I was able to begin a new cycle of research in 2001, for which I am indebted to my then-chairman, John Clayton, who enthusiastically endorsed my request for leave; to my then-provost, Dennis Berkey, who approved it; and to the National Endowment for the Humanities, for the grant that supported me while I worked. Texans, when they die, John once explained to me, have small need of heaven: Given the choice, they go, instead, to Texas—and Texas, indeed, is where John now lies. I miss his quick intelligence, his wisdom, and his humor. In peace his sleep, and may his memory be for a blessing.

Early into my first draft, I appealed for criticism to three colleagues whose work has set the bar for my own: Liz Clark, Robert Markus, and Margaret Mitchell. All three responded with gracious goodwill and acute suggestions, and I appreciate greatly the time that they took from their own projects in order to help me with mine. Margie in particular exceeded all reasonable expectations, sending back almost twenty single-spaced pages of comments, corrections, and challenges: My readers, no less than I, have benefited greatly from her broad and deep erudition and her energetic generosity. Jim O'Donnell and I have been exchanging correspondence on issues Augustinian since before the advent of e-mail. As I worked my way through this project, he poked and prodded whatever ideas I sent his way, to my edification. Glen Bowersock and Ramsey MacMullen each read and commented on an earlier avatar of Part I of this study, saving me from various errors large and small, and pushing me to think harder about those points on which we differed. Lynn Cohick and Andrew Jacobs, co-chairs of the Early Jewish-Christian Relations Group of the Society of Biblical Literature, patiently awaited the arrival of my manuscript for some three years running before I could finally oblige. At the 2007 meeting in San Diego, the panel of scholars that they convened to discuss *Augustine and the Jews*—Philip Rousseau, Jeffrey Trumbower, Tina Shepardson, and Ra'anan Boustan—inspired and enabled me to make several important eleventh-hour revisions and additions. Ra'anan's sharp and insightful comments, indeed, prompted the final form of my epilogue. My deep thanks to everyone.

When Sandy Dijkstra, my indefatigable literary agent, brought my book proposal to Trace Murphy, my editor at Doubleday, I thought that I would have the project done within two years. As the semesters flowed by and (to my disbelief) one year gave way to the next, I apologized and agonized and noisily lamented. They expressed only patience with me and confidence in the book. Thank you, Sandy, for all your encouragement; thank you, Trace, for your quiet and unfailing kindness. Thanks, too, to my dear friends—working moms all—for their steadfast assurances that, some day, my three daughters would no longer be teenagers and that my book would eventually be finished: Susan Black, Esther Chazon, Lucy Kerman, Ross Kraemer, Amy-Jill Levine, Renee Melammed, Sari Miller, Mara Plekss, Adele Reinhartz, Shifra Sharlin, Susan Thistlethwaite, Leslie Valas, Eleni Zachariou. And finally, for their assistance to me in the course of this project, my thanks to special helpers in the religion department of Boston University: Karen Nardella, the department's administrative assistant; Brenda Gardenour; and graduate students Mireille Bishay and Roddy Knowles. Special thanks to Cristine Hutchinson-Jones for emergency indexing.

Two standing debts, appropriately acknowledged here. The first is to my doctoral advisor, John Gager. My own work, and the work of the dozens of students that John through the program at Princeton has produced, share a family resemblance, inherited from him: a commitment to understanding ancient Christians not in contrast to their contemporaries, whether pagan or (especially) Jewish, but in active and organic contact with them. *Augustine and the Jews* is a late product of John's instruction. Behind John stands a prime source of this commitment: his own teacher, Krister Stendahl. Krister has served as mentor to many of us in the field of ancient Jewish-Christian relations. His seminal 1963 article, "Paul and the Introspective Conscience of the West," continues to exert a salubrious effect on modern scholarship; and much of my own work, both on Paul and on Augustine, can be seen as an extended footnote to his insights in that luminous essay. John, Krister: thank you.

Indebted as I am to all of these colleagues, friends, and teachers, I owe still more to my husband, Alfred I. Tauber. Together we have ridden out the heavy storms of the past eleven years, buoyed by our love for each other, steadied by hope and by the ballast of sheer stubbornness. I dedicate this book to you, Zev, with deepest respect, admiration, and love.

TIME LINE

354	Augustine born in Thagaste, North Africa
360–363	Emperor Julian converts from Christianity to paganism; plans to rebuild Jewish temple in Jerusalem
379–395	Reign of Theodosius I; legislation against paganism
395	Honorius, emperor of western Roman Empire; Arcadius, emperor of eastern Roman Empire
396	Augustine becomes bishop of Hippo
399	Honorius orders closing of pagan temples in Carthage
404	Eruption of pan-Mediterranean controversy over Origen's theology
405	Legislative noose tightens around Donatist Christians (Edict of Unity)
410	"Fall" of Rome to the Visigoth Alaric, an Arian Christian
411	Council of Carthage rules against Donatists
418	Forced conversion of Jews on Minorca
429	Arian Vandals invade North Africa
430	Augustine dies in Hippo

CHRONOLOGY OF AUGUSTINE'S
LIFE AND WORK

354	Born in Thagaste, North Africa
366-369	Grammatical education in Madauros
370-373	Higher studies in Carthage; begins relationship with common-law wife; birth of son Adeodatus; reads Cicero's *Hortensius,* resolves to pursue Wisdom; joins the Manichees as an *auditor* ("hearer")
373-374	Returns to Thagaste to teach
374-383	Teaches rhetoric in Carthage
383-384	Leaves Carthage for Rome; stays within Manichaean network
384	Assumes post in rhetoric in Milan
386	Reads Neoplatonic texts in translation (late winter/ spring?); decides to join catholic church (= the conversion scene in *Confessions* 8; August); resigns post in Milan; retreats to Cassiciacum; writes early dialogues (autumn)
387	Baptism at Easter by Ambrose in Milan; leaves Milan to return to Africa via Rome; death of Monnica (August)
388-389	*Free Will*, book one; *On Genesis, against the Manichees*; returns to Thagaste; death of Adeodatus. *Manichaean Morals*; *Morals of the Church*
391	Inducted into clergy at Hippo; *Usefulness of Belief*
392	Begins sermons/commentary on Psalms; completes first thirty-two psalms by 395 (*Sermons on Psalms*); debates Fortunatus the Manichee (August); circulates *Against Fortunatus*
393	Speaks before bishops' council in Hippo (*True Religion*); question 61 of *Answers to Various Questions*; *Unfinished Literal Commentary on Genesis*
394-395	Studies the exegetical work of Donatist theologian Tyconius, esp. *Book of Rules;* lectures on Paul in Carthage (*Notes on Romans*); writes early Pauline commentaries (*On Galatians*; *Unfinished Commentary on Romans*); writes to Jerome about Galatians (*Letter* 28); *On Lying*

395–396	*Questions* 66–68 of *Answers to Various Questions* (metaphorical use of *massa*); *Letter* 41 to Aurelius, mentioning Tyconius' *Book of Rules* (?); finishes books two and three of *Free Will*
396	Becomes sole bishop of Hippo; reads Romans again; *Answer to Simplicianus* (historical use of *massa*)
397	Anti-Donatist preaching campaign; begins *On Christian Doctrine*, interrupting composition in book three; begins *Confessions*; writes *Letter* 40 to Jerome
398–399	Begins *Against Faustus*; Honorius closes temples in Carthage
401	Begins *Literal Commentary on Genesis*; completes by 414
403	*Letter* 71 to Jerome
404	*Letter* 75 from Jerome
405	Emperor Honorius takes more steps against Donatists, *Edict of Unity*; *Letter* 82 to Jerome
410	"Fall" of Rome to Visigoths. Begins sermons on the Gospel of John, completed between 417 and 420
410–415?	Paulinus writes to Augustine asking about salvation of Jews and the meaning of Psalm 59 (*Letter* 121); Augustine composes two sermons on Psalm 59 (*On Psalm 59*), explicating it in terms of Genesis 4 and the mark of Cain; Augustine's first letter responding to Paulinus goes missing
411–420?	*Sermons on the Gospel of John*
411	Council of Carthage against Donatists. Augustine attacks the theology of Pelagius; begins *City of God*
414–420?	Second letter to Paulinus, on salvation of Jews, how to understand Romans, Genesis 4 on the mark of Cain, and Psalm 59 together (*Letter* 149)
418	Forced conversion of Jews on Minorca
419	*Letters* *12 from Consentius, referring to incident on Minorca
426	Completes *City of God*; writes *Sermon against the Jews* and *Faith in Things Unseen*: All three use Psalm 59 without reference to Genesis 4
427–428	Resumes and completes *Christian Teaching*; writes *Retractations*
430	Vandals besiege Hippo; death of Augustine (August 28)

NOTES

PROLOGUE

1. *Sefer Zekhirah* (Book of Remembrance) cited in S. Eidelberg, *The Jews and the Crusaders*, 121–22. See also D. Berger, "The Attitude of St. Bernard of Clairvaux to the Jews," 89–108.

2. S. Simonsohn, *The Apostolic See and the Jews*, traces the effects of Augustine's witness doctrine on medieval papal policies toward Jews; J. Cohen, *Living Letters of the Law*, surveys the later theological transmutations of Augustine's teaching during the European Middle Ages.

3. "If the Judaism of the Diaspora in this period did produce any literature, it has been entirely lost" (F. Millar, "Jews of the Graeco-Roman Diaspora," 110). Possible exceptions to this observation are the fresh renderings of Jewish scriptures into Greek produced by Aquila, Symmachus, and Theodotion, three Jewish translators working over the course of the second century C.E. These newer versions provide an oblique glimpse both at the Jewish perception that Christians had appropriated the Septuagint and at the fact that Jewish communities in the western Diaspora continued to rely on a translated biblical text. A compelling explanation for the sudden literary silence of the western Jewish Diaspora has thus far evaded historians. For an analysis of two late Latin texts, possibly Jewish, see L. Rutgers on *Collatio legum Mosaïcum et Romanarum* (a comparison of Roman and Mosaic law) and *Letter of Annas to Seneca* (on superiority of the knowledge of God to the worship of idols) in "Jewish Literary Production in the Diaspora in Late Antiquity," *Hidden Heritage of Diaspora Judaism*, 235–284. For the glimmers of Jewish anti-Christian polemic in the late second century and the much later invective in the Babylonian Talmud see n. 7 below.

4. A crucially important second-century text embodying this dynamic—a pagan taking gentile Christians to task for deviating from Jewish custom—is Celsus' *On True Teaching*, preserved by and rebutted in Origen's *Against Celsus*. Harnack's position as the starting point of this particular interpretive debate is well known. The history that I give here and in the following paragraph has been rehearsed concisely, and with copious references, in W. Horbury, *Jews and Christians in Conflict and Controversy*, 14–25 and 200–206; M. Taylor, *Anti-Judaism and Early Christian Identity*; J. Carleton Paget, "Anti-Judaism and Early Christian Identity"; and A. Jacobs, *Remains of the Jews*, 201–206. Taylor offers an analytic typology of different kinds of Christian anti-Jewish rhetoric, and she particularly criticizes Marcel Simon and W. H. C. Frend for their own

post-Harnack theories: Both men claimed that real, often hostile encounters with actual Jews stood behind the *contra Iudaeos* rhetoric. Taylor proposes, instead, that gentile Christianity's need to distinguish and to differentiate itself from its Jewish matrix made its traditions *contra Iudaeos* a standing necessity for the construction of its identity, whatever the contact or lack of contact with Jews. Horbury dissents from Taylor, and he postulates missionary competitiveness as the stimulus for these Christian traditions. (Tertullian's treatise *contra Iudaeos*, for example, seems to Horbury to supply "a fuller picture of Jewish-Christian missionary rivalry, in competition for the same potential non-Jewish adherents"; *Jews and Christians*, 140.) Carleton Paget and Jacobs offer rounded considerations of both arguments; I propose another reconstruction in Part I of the present study.

5. "Or are they such slaves to habit," Simon continued, "that they will go on producing a type of literature that has lost, centuries earlier, its justification and purpose?" (*Verus Israel*, 140).

6. Blumenkranz understood Augustine's *Tractatus* as a statement of the bishop's desire to convert Jews (*Judenpredigt* passim); his specifically exegetical argument is found on pages 110–181, presented in summary form on pages 210–212. He repeats these points discursively in a later essay, "*Augustin et les Juifs, Augustin et le Judaïsme*," 226 and 230 (problematic Jewish presence), 227 (Jewish missionary efforts), and 233, 235–236 ("missionary" counterarguments). Simon construed the phenomenon of Gentiles' voluntarily Judaizing and even converting to Judaism as evidence *eo ipso* of Jewish missionary endeavor. I argue briefly against this idea of competitive missions in "*Excaecati Occulta Iustitia Dei*" 320–324, at length in "Christian Anti-Judaism," and in the present book. Behind the work of Blumenkranz and Simon stands the still-valuable study of Christian sources from the texts of the New Testament to late imperial legislation: J. Parkes, *The Conflict of the Church and the Synagogue* (originally published in 1934). Parkes also posited Jewish missionary activity to account for Christian anti-Jewish invective.

7. Jews never produced an *adversus Christianos* literature comparable to the vast Christian *adversus Iudaeos* literature (though the pagan Celsus [see n. 4] repeats some Jewish calumnies about Jesus' parentage). A greater familiarity with both families of sources, however, has enabled recent scholarship to detect echoes of Jewish anti-Christian rhetoric both in ancient Christian sources and in later, Babylonian rabbinic texts. For the former, see especially W. Horbury, "Tertullian on the Jews"; for the latter, see most recently, P. Schäfer, *Jesus in the Talmud*. On intra-Jewish concerns about *minut* ("sectarianism") and the identification of such *minum* (sectarians) as "Christians," see D. Boyarin, *Dying for God*.

8. "Harnack was right in recognizing the internal importance of exegesis *adversus Iudaeos* for Christian education," Horbury has suggested, "but wrong in supposing that significant contact between Jews and Christians had ceased" (*Jews and Christians*, 202). Seeking a "medial position" between current maximalists in the Blumenkranz-Simon stream (for whom invective plus conversions signal vigorously competitive Jewish and Christian missions) and minimalists (among whom I number, and for whom Jewish–Christian contacts, controversy, and conversions do not evince competing missions), J. Carleton Paget has proposed a theory of mitigated missions—that is, although not all Jews in all places sought converts, perhaps some Jews in some places did ("Jewish

Proselytism," 102). What this more modest proposal gains in plausibility, however, it loses in explanatory power: Occasional missionary efforts in discrete localities cannot account for the ubiquity and the extreme hostility of Christian *contra Iudaeos* rhetoric. In the course of the present study, I propose an alternative explanation.

9. Syriac traditions of anti-Jewish polemic have been comprehensively studied by C. Shepardson, *Anti-Judaism and Christian Orthodoxy*. She notes how contemporary Jewish communities, the attractions of synagogue rituals and of Jewish holidays, and intra-Christian anxieties about doctrinal deviance all contributed to the sound and the fury. No comparable study yet exists for Coptic tradition; see, however, S. Shoemaker's essay " 'Let Us Go Burn Her Body,' " which notes the ways that evolving legends of the death of the Virgin Mary were privileged sites for expansions of *contra Iudaeos*.

CHAPTER I: GODS AND THEIR HUMANS

1. The premier source for Augustine's life remains his own work of retrospective theology, *The Confessions* (hereafter cited in notes as *Conf.*). Augustine's father, Patricius, who formally affiliated with the church only toward the end of his life (*Conf.* 9.9,22), has frequently been identified as pagan (see, e.g., H. Chadwick, *Augustine,* 10; S. Lancel, *Saint Augustine,* 9, apparently in view of Patricius' eleventh-hour baptism). This seems unlikely to me. Infant baptism, while a strong local custom in North Africa, was hardly universal (Augustine himself was not baptized as a child; *Conf.* 1.11,17). Men with public careers often postponed it (as did Augustine, with his mother's active cooperation and approval. Patricius, as a public figure in Thagaste, a member of the local curia, may have made the same decision). And the household was itself extremely Christian: Monnica was energetically pious; and Augustine, who describes "our whole household, except my father" as believers, notes that his father impeded his children's Christian upbringing in no way (*Conf.* 1.11,17). Finally, and most simply, Augustine describes his childhood Christianity as "implanted in me as a boy by my parents" (*parentibus meis, The Usefulness of Belief* 1.2). On his parents' struggles to fund his education, see *Conf.* 2.3,5–6.

   Augustine describes his fascination with Virgil and his regret that his difficulty learning Greek prevented him from equally enjoying Homer in *Conf.* 1.13,20–23). His lack of Greek had lifelong repercussions, and Peter Brown rightly calls Augustine's failure "a momentous casualty of the Late Roman educational system: he will become the only Latin philosopher in antiquity to be virtually ignorant of Greek," *Augustine of Hippo,* 36.

   To the degree that education required facility with classical Greek and Latin texts, to that degree it was "pagan." This did not prevent Christians (or Jews, for that matter) from serving both as students and, in some cases, as teachers in Mediterranean schools. H.-I. Marrou provides a comprehensive survey of the ancient curriculum from its stirrings in pre-classical Greece to its transformations in Byzantium and in early medieval Europe in *The History of Education in Antiquity.*

2. For a very good general introduction to Hellenism, see F. W. Walbank, *The Hellenistic World.* Archaeological evidence in particular measures the diffusion of Hellenism's visual vocabulary; for beautiful images of these material re-

mains as well as sharp historical analysis, see J. Elsner, *Imperial Rome and Christian Triumph.* "Hellenism was a language in which peoples of the most diverse kind could participate.... [Its] thought, mythology, and images ... constituted an extraordinarily flexible medium of both cultural and linguistic expression" (G. W. Bowersock, *Hellenism in Late Antiquity,* 7). Hellenism's supple cohesion both enabled and was supported by the political (thus religious) and social organization of the city, on which, see A. M. H. Jones' magisterial study, *The Greek City from Alexander to Justinian.* Greek was long the language of Christians in Western churches (and, notably, in Rome itself) because of the numbers of immigrants who came from the East; learned Latin Christians could compose in Greek because of their bilingual education.

3. For a description both learned and lively of the congested universe of Mediterranean divine–human interactions see esp. R. Lane Fox, *Pagans and Christians,* 11–261. For an orientation in cultic etiquette, including purity rules, offerings, prayers, banqueting, and procession, see W. Burkett, *Greek Religion.* "Anyone wishing to ascend into the podium," advises a first-century inscription from Tunisia, erected near an area sacred to Asclepius, the god of healing, "should abstain for three days from women, pork, beans, the barber, and the city baths, and he should not enter wearing shoes" (R. MacMullen and E. N. Lane, *Sourcebook,* 37). Jewish sacrificial cult was concentrated in Jerusalem, and the rules for sacrifice and purity appear throughout four of the Five Books of Moses (Exodus, Leviticus, Numbers, and Deuteronomy). E. P. Sanders, *Judaism: Practice and Belief, 63 BCE–66 CE,* situates these Jewish purity rules in their cultic context of late Second Temple Judaism, while drawing attention to the ways that these practices were a particular expression of more general, recognizably Mediterranean patterns of regulating proximity to the divine. On the Christian fear of demons lurking around public altars, see most recently A. Y. Reed, "The Trickery of the Fallen Angels and the Demonic Mimesis of the Divine."

4. Ancient philosophy presents a closer analogue to modern religion than ancient "religion" does. Individual philosophical schools emphasized personal assent and intellectual allegiance to particular propositions (hence the "doctrines" of Platonism or of Stoicism), and a decision to identify with such a school entailed making commitments to distinctive behaviors and/or dress and/or diet as well. For these reasons, Hellenistic authors frequently identified Jews as a nation of philosophers: see M. Stern, *Greek and Roman Authors on Jews and Judaism,* vol. 1, for copious examples. Pagan intellectuals converting to some form of Christianity also spoke of their decision on the analogy of joining a philosophical school; thus, for example, Justin Martyr in the opening chapters of his *Dialogue with Trypho.*

5. I. Malkin, *Ancient Perceptions of Greek Ethnicity,* assembles a splendid group of essays on Greekness and ideas of ethnicity, many of which consider this famous passage from Herodotus 8. On Hellenistic Jewish adaptations of these ideas, see the essay by E. Gruen in Malkin's collection, "Jewish Perspectives on Greek Culture and Ethnicity." On the *Ioudaismos/Hellenismos* distinction in the passage from 2 Maccabees, see the commentary by J. A. Goldstein in *II Maccabees,* 192. G. W. Bowersock deftly draws out the vicissitudes of this vocabulary of ethnicity and religion and its later permutations in Christian Greek texts, wherein *ethnikos* ("ethnic") becomes the standard word for "pa-

gan." This usage "suggests at one and the same time the local character of pagan cults . . . and the role of Greek culture in sustaining those cults" (*Hellenism in Late Antiquity*, 10–11). For more on Paul's positive orientation toward the Jerusalem temple, see S. Stowers, *A Rereading of Romans*, 130–131.

6. C. P. Jones, *Kinship Diplomacy in the Ancient World*, reveals how ancient parties to treaties discovered that they were "cousins." The Jewish god did not leave behind offspring as the Greek gods did, so Jews in the Hellenistic age constructed kinship lines and thus diplomatic relations through heroic patriarchs instead. In this way, for example, they became "related to" the Spartans: The divine Heracles, in the distant past, had evidently married a granddaughter of Abraham. "After reading a certain document," announces a Spartan king to the Jewish high priest, "we have found that Jews and Lacedaemonians [Spartans] are of one family [*genos*], and share a connection with Abraham." This text (a Hellenistic Jewish fabrication) is reported both by Josephus (*Antiquities* 12.226; late first century C.E.) and in 1 Macc. 12.21 (mid-first century B.C.E.). For discussion, see Jones, *Kinship Diplomacy*, 72–80; and Gruen, "Jewish Perspectives on Greek Culture," 361–364.

7. The claim is frequently found that Christianity, as a religion of conversion, "separated religious belief and practice from *Romanitas*, cult from culture," and thus invented what we mean by "religion" in the modern sense as a category independent of a particular ethnic group. Thus, for example, D. Boyarin, "Semantic Differences," 71–72 (the source of this quotation). But some ancient Christians seem to have seen things differently. They are the ones who "are gathered into the one race [*genos*] of the saved people," said the second-century church father Clement of Alexandria (*Miscellanies* 6.42.2). Christians, preached Polycarp (mid-second century) are "the race [*genos*] of the righteous" (*Martyrdom of Polycarp* 14.1). D. K. Buell has underscored the ways in which early Christian writers use precisely these ancient concepts of race/*genos* to articulate their communal identity; see "Rethinking the Relevance of Race for Early Christian Self-Definition," "Race and Universalism in Early Christianity," and *Why This New Race*. On Paul in particular, see C. J. Hodge, *If Sons, Then Heirs*.

8. For pagans, see e.g., R. Turcan, *The Gods of Ancient Rome* and *The Cults of the Roman Empire*. M. Beard et al. discuss *evocatio*, whereby "the gods of the enemy could be seduced" (*Religions of Rome*, I:34). More frequently, war was imagined as a clash between deities as well as between their peoples, as Homer, Jewish scriptures, and later Christian ones amply attest. Bowersock traces the long lives of deities whose local characteristics were preserved despite, and eventually because of, their "translation" into Greek, in *Hellenism in Late Antiquity*, e.g., 18 (Arsû/Ares, an Arab god), 25 (Aiôn/Osiris). Note too, in the case of Jewish/Spartan kinship diplomacy explored in n. 6 above, that the Jews who construct their family connection to Sparta deal straightforwardly with the historical existence of Heracles.

9. Modern scholars can have a hard time seeing all the other gods mentioned in the Bible, and they often project the constructs of modern monotheism, whether Jewish or Christian, onto their ancient ancestors, interpreting away (or simply not noting) the unselfconscious references to the real existence of foreign gods in the sacred texts of each tradition. Ancients (whether pagan, Jewish, or Christian) did not confuse "gods" with their man-made images,

and neither should we. In the view of the pagan majority, gods could inhabit their statues from time to time, just as they visited their altars and other sanctuaries. Cult images in this way were sanctified by the divine presence. (The ability to tell when a god tenanted his statue was the mark of the elevated sensibility of a holy man; see e.g., Bowersock on Heraiscus in *Hellenism in Antiquity,* 25.) But pagans too distinguished between their gods and the images of their gods.

10. Athenagoras, a late-second-century Christian apologist, makes both of these points nicely in the very beginning of his work in defense of Christianity, addressed ostensibly to the emperors Marcus Aurelius and his son, Commodus. "In your empire," Athenagoras observes, "different nations have different customs and laws, and no one is hindered by law or by fear of punishment from following his ancestral customs, no matter how ridiculous these may be" (*Legatio* 1). Similarly, the pagan Celsus, also in the late second century, points out that Jews "observe a worship which may be very peculiar but it is at least traditional. In this respect they behave like the rest of mankind, because each nation follows its particular customs" (*Against Celsus* 5.25).

11. On the intertwining of municipal government, imperial government, sacrificial cult, and priesthoods, see Jones, *The Greek City,* 227–235; and the more recent essays assembled in M. Beard and J. North, eds., *Pagan Priests.* The early-third-century church father Tertullian particularly inveighed against Christians' frequenting the theater, the baths, and the competitions: These were tainted with the images and worship of pagan deities. A similar discussion of the pitfalls of living with idols appears in the near-contemporary rabbinic tractate *Avodah Zarah,* its Hebrew title an exact match for Tertullian's treatise *On Idolatry.* On the evidence, most gentile Christians, most diaspora Jews, and some among the rabbinic Jewish subculture in Palestine all made their peace with this level of engagement with "idolatry." On this last point, see especially Y. Eliav, "The Roman Bath as a Jewish Institution."

    In 425, the emperor Theodosius II tried to prohibit not only Christians but also Jews and pagans from attending theater and horse races on Sundays and Christian holy days: Evidently, members of all three groups were there (*Codex of Theodosius* 15.5.5; A. Linder, *The Jews in Imperial Roman Legislation,* no. 50, 301–304). This drawing of the battle lines between the high-minded and the majority continued into the sixth century. The Syriac Christian Jacob of Serûg repeats the nonchalant response of Christians with whom he pleads to cease attending plays and pantomimes: "It is a game, not paganism. What do you lose if I laugh? The dancing of that place cheers me up, ... I am baptized just as you are," *Homilies on the Spectacles of the Theatre,* cited in Bowersock, *Hellenism,* 38. In Christian North Africa, Augustine experienced similar frustrations a century earlier. Markus illumines the abiding interpenetration—or synonymy—of religious and civic life, and Augustine's pragmatic acquiescence to this social fact, in *The End of Ancient Christianity,* 107–123.

12. The surveys of Hellenistic and of Roman religion mentioned earlier all have discussions on the cult of the ruler. J. Elsner's *Imperial Rome and Christian Triumph* offers an especially fine discussion on how the emperor's image, ubiquitously displayed, was itself thought to have numinous power and, like ancient temples, was considered a place of asylum (this was true well into the Christian period, 53–87). On the emperor's image and ancient politics and

piety, see further K. Hopkins, "Divine Emperors." See also H. Drake, *Constantine and the Bishops,* who nicely notes the religio-political messages encoded on coins, "antiquity's sound bites." S. Price, *Rituals and Power,* insists on a difference between the ways that the gods were worshiped and the ways that honor was shown to the emperor ("Language sometimes assimilated the emperor to a god, but ritual held back," 213); I. Gradel, *Emperor Worship and Roman Religion,* discounts any such distinction. And what went up sometimes came down: Through *damnatio memoriae,* a repudiated emperor like Nero or Domitian, once safely dead, could be celestially demoted.

To oppose the emperor was to commit sacrilege: This held true even after Constantine's conversion; see Jones, *Later Roman Empire,* 1:93, who also comments on Constantine's personal approval of theatrical competitions and gladiatorial games dedicated to him, under supervision of an imperial priest. Bowersock, "The Imperial Cult," 181, notes that the fifth-century church historian Philostorgius complains, in *Church History* 2.16, of Christians in Constantinople who pray to a statue of Constantine "as to a god." See too Bowersock's later essay "Polytheism and Monotheism in Arabia and the Three Palestines." R. MacMullen surveys the continuing cult of the emperor after Constantine in *Christianity and Paganism,* 34–39. Constantine's "object was to obtain the support of the supreme ruler of the universe . . . in the defence and administration of his realm. . . . The basic conception was Roman rather than Christian. Constantine wished to maintain the *pax deorum* as his predecessors had done, but he looked to a new divinity and for new procedures to maintain it"; J. H. W. G. Liebeschuetz, *Continuity and Change in Roman Religion,* 292.

CHAPTER 2: GODS AND THE ONE GOD

1. My discussion here is much indebted to the recent work of J. Barclay, *Jews in the Western Mediterranean Diaspora;* and E. Gruen, *Heritage and Hellenism* and *Diaspora.* A very full survey of the relevant primary material is available in E. Schürer-Vermes et al., *History of the Jewish People in the Age of Jesus Christ.* A convenient and extremely well organized compendium of translated primary sources for this Jewish population (including inscriptions and papyrus texts as well as excerpts from literary ones) is now available in M. Williams, *Jews among the Greeks and Romans.*

On Jews as Hellenistic colonists, Josephus reports that the Seleucid king Antiochus the Great (223–187 B.C.E.) settled 2,000 Babylonian Jewish families in Asia Minor to garrison his colonies there (*Antiquities* 12:147–153); similarly, a Ptolemaic king settled Jews in outposts of his territories (*Against Apion* 4:44).

"So populous are the Jews," wrote Philo in his essay *Flaccus,* "that no one country can hold them, and therefore they settle in very many of the most prosperous countries in Europe and in Asia, both in the islands and on the mainland; and while they hold the Holy City where stands the sacred Temple of the most high God [Jerusalem] to be their mother city [*metropolis*], yet those cities which are theirs by inheritance from their fathers and grandfathers, and ancestors even further back, are in each case accounted by them to be their fatherland [*patria*] in which they were born and reared" (*Flaccus* 46).

For the Jewish communities of Asia Minor, see too W. Ameling, "Die jüdischen Gemeinden im antiken Kleinasien" and, following him, Gruen's further thoughts on *apoikia* ("colonies"), *metropolis,* and *patria*—vocabulary drawn from Philo and Josephus—in *Diaspora,* 242. Roman Jews in the early fifth century C.E. were no less attached to their hometowns in the Diaspora than their earlier, Hellenistic counterparts had been. When in 418 C.E. the Jews of Magona were faced with the choice of exile or conversion to Christianity, one of them observed that "whoever does not abandon his fatherland [*patria*—that is, the island of Minorca] will not be able to retain the faith of his fathers [*fides patrum*]," *Letter on the Conversion of the Jews* 18:19; hereafter *Letter of Severus.*

Jewish apocalyptic texts—those writings that pronounce the conviction that the god of Israel was about to intervene in history, overcome evil once for all, and establish his kingdom—also abound in this period from roughly 200 B.C.E. to 200 C.E. Since many of these texts modeled themselves on older biblical prophecies that speak about the redemption from Babylon, they also used the imagery or literary framing of "exile," as later Christian writers, polemically, will also do (see p. 84 above). By the sixth century and later, drawing again on this same biblical imagery, rabbis in Babylon will do the same, speaking of Rome as initiating the second exile. In reality, however, Jewish populations had been settled in the West for centuries before the Roman destruction of Jerusalem in 70 C.E.

2. Showing courtesy toward pagan gods, Philo remarked, ensured peace between Israel and the nations, "for reviling each other's gods always causes war" (*Questions and Answers on Exodus* 2.5, commenting on Exod. 22:28 LXX). He goes on to add that this verse of Scripture urges Jews to respect pagan rulers who are "of the same seed as the gods" (ibid. 2.6). See further P. van der Horst, " 'Thou shalt not revile the Gods.' " Not all Hellenized Jews were so polite, or politic; see, e.g., Wisdom of Solomon 13–15; similarly, Paul in Romans 1:18–35; and frequently elsewhere, discussed on p. 37f.

3. Outsiders' opinions on Jews, their religious culture, and their practices are gathered, translated, and commented on in Menachem Stern's great collection, *Greek and Latin Authors on Jews and Judaism.* The various concessions made to Jews of the first century in various cities—permission to assemble on their own holidays, to observe the Sabbath or other ancestral traditions, to collect monies to be sent to the Temple in Jerusalem—are conveniently assembled in M. Pucci ben Zeev, *Jewish Rights in the Roman World,* 374–377, 471–482 (on Jews and the imperial cult).

4. For the text and translation of Moschos' inscription, see Schürer-Vermes, *History of the Jewish People* 3:65. Niketas of Jerusalem contributed 100 drachmas to subvene a Dionysiac festival around 150 B.C.E. (ibid. 3:25). Herod's building program of pagan (especially imperial) temples is discussed in ibid. 1:304–311; see Josephus, *Antiquities* 16.136–149, who also mentions Herod's paying for the imperial liturgies as well. On Herod's sponsorship of the Olympic games, see *Antiquities* 16.149; on his insistence that his sister's suitor follow Jewish practices, see *Antiquities* 16.225. Herod is the king whom people love to hate; a more appreciative view of his life can be found in P. Richardson, *Herod.*

"To the Most High God, the Almighty, the Blessed. . . . Pothos, son of Strabo, dedicated in the prayer-house, according to his vow, his house-bred slave Chrysa, on condition that she be unharmed and unmolested by any of his heirs under Zeus, Gaia, and Helios," reads a manumission inscription from the Bosporus, mid-first century C.E. The Jewish god dominates its invocation; Greek gods cluster at its close. What is the ethnicity, then, of the donor? Is Pothos a god-fearing pagan or an ancient Jew? For a tour through the most recent arguments, see I. Levenskaya, *The Book of Acts in Its Diaspora Setting*, 111–116 (with the full text of the inscription on p. 239); she concludes that Pothos was a god-fearing pagan; also L. Levine, *The Ancient Synagogue*, 113–123; he concludes (on p. 114) that Pothos was a Jew. Those who wonder why it should be so difficult to make the identification will appreciate two articles by R. Kraemer: "On the meaning of the Term 'Jew' in Graeco-Roman Inscriptions," and "Jewish Tuna and Christian Fish." For the two Jewish inscriptions to the Jewish god placed in the Egyptian temple of Pan, see Levinskaya, *Acts in Its Diaspora Setting*, 94–95.

5. M. Williams, *Jews Among the Greeks and Romans*, 107–131, assembles translations of the ancient primary evidence for Jews as ephebes, citizens of pagan cities, members of town councils, officers in gentile armies. Going to the gymnasium and being a member of the ephebate meant that one was a member of the citizen body. The first-century C.E. inscriptions listing the ephebes' names in Cyrene (Jesus son of Antiphilos and Eleazar son of Eleazar) are dedicated to the gods of the gymnasium, Hermes and Heracles, as Barclay notes in *Jews in the Western Mediterranean Diaspora*, 235 (see too 326–331 on Jewish participation in civic life). In Judea itself, the question of how much Greek culture was too much remained hotly disputed; see, e.g., 1 Maccabees 1–2.

"To the eternal god," opens an inscription dedicating a synagogue "for the salvation of our lord Severus A[lexander], the pious, felicitous emperor, an[d of Julia Mamaea] the empress, mother of the emperor, does Cosimos the chief of the customs station, the flautist, and the head officer of the synagogue of the Jews, gladly fulfill his vow." Levine, *The Ancient Synagogue*, 276, discusses this and other inscriptions dedicating synagogues to emperors.

6. Pagan donor inscriptions have received a tremendous amount of attention, in part because they relate to the question of gentile "god-fearers," those pagans who voluntarily assumed some aspects of Jewish practice while continuing in their own native cults as well. J. Reynolds and R. Tannenbaum first published and discussed the Aphrodisias inscription in their 1987 monograph *Jews and God-Fearers at Aphrodisias*. The third-century date that they originally assigned to the inscription has been challenged, and scholars now contemplate dates well into the Christian period (as, e.g., A. Chaniotis, "The Jews of Aphrodisias," 209–242). A later date raises the intriguing possibility that some of the non-Jewish donors might have been Christians as well as pagans. Pagan god-fearing was a "wide and loose category" (Levinskaya, *Acts in Its Diaspora Setting*, 79), not a technical designation for a clearly demarcated or defined group (such as *proselytos* would be for "convert"). Levine, *Ancient Synagogue*, collects, describes, and discusses all of this material.

7. Sometimes in our texts, "Judaizing," like "god-fearing," seems to indicate simply the adoption by non-Jews of some Jewish practices. At other times, however, the word seems to mean something like "converting to Judaism" (or, perhaps, pretending to) as in the Greek version of Esther 8:17. Paul in Galatians 2:14 complains that Peter wants to compel gentile Christians in Antioch

"to Judaize": there the issue seems to be food. For a clear discussion of this murky topic, see S. Cohen, *The Beginnings of Jewishness,* 175–197.

8. See M. Goodman, "The Pilgrimage Economy of Jerusalem in the Second Temple Period." Sanders provides a clear account of the vast wealth held by the Temple treasury, *Judaism: Practice and Belief,* 83 (with values on gold talents translated into U.S. dollars at the rate of $400/ounce) as well as a calculus of the donations from the two-drachma or half-shekel Temple tax paid by every adult Jewish male. "This was not a large sum: approximately two days' pay for a day labourer, a man at the bottom of the pay scale. That it was paid is one of the things about first-century Judaism that is most certain," 156. On these donations, see further Pucci ben Zeev, *Jewish Rights in the Roman World,* 468–471.

9. Accusations of sexual misconduct, such as we see here in Wisdom of Solomon and in Paul, were a reliable and near-universal rhetorical trope of such ancient polemic, on which now see J. Knust, *Abandoned to Lust.* On the rebellion in the Diaspora, dated to either 115/117 C.E. or 116/117 C.E., very little is known. Relevant sources from inscriptions, papyri, and literature are assembled and assessed in M. Pucci ben Zeev, *Diaspora Judaism in Turmoil.* The Jews' deliberate destruction of pagan holy sites hints at a possible religious factor fueling the revolt: The destruction of idols had long been associated with the messianic age (*Diaspora Judaism,* 129–133). For Augustine's allusion to such prophecies when the emperor Honorius, in 399 C.E., closed pagan temples in Carthage, see pp. 273–274 above.

10. Ben Isaac provides an exhaustive survey of the building blocks of inter-ethnic hatreds in *The Invention of Racism in Classical Antiquity;* for Jews in particular, see 440–491. He notes that "Christian activity is responsible for the preservation of a good deal of ancient source-material on Jews that is not available for other ethnic groups in antiquity," 441. The city of Rome occasionally expelled foreigners, among whom Jews, in the late Republic and early empire; for varying analyses of the purposes and the effects of these expulsions, compare the volumes by Gruen, Lampe, and Barclay.

11. Nicely observed by G. Bohak, "The Ibis and the Jewish Question," 43, whose article reviews some of the truly scurrilous things that Greco-Roman writers said about Egyptians. Insults directed specifically against Jews are collected, organized, and analyzed by P. Schäfer, *Judeophobia;* see also L. Feldman, *Jew and Gentile in the Ancient World,* who sorts hostile remarks according to popular prejudice (107–122) and learned prejudice (123–176).

12. On the religious dimensions of Roman adoptions, see M. Beard, *Pagan Priests,* 38. Paul uses the language of adoption as a metaphor for the way that Gentiles, through Christ's baptism, enter into God's promises to Israel: they "receive the adoption of sons" (Gal. 4:5 RSV); "and if sons then heirs" (Rom. 8:14–17). On the language of political alliances to describe Gentiles' "becoming" Jews, see Cohen, *The Beginnings of Jewishness,* 125–139, 156–174.

Domitian's motivations in acting against Flavius Clemens, Domitilla, and others are obscure. Their being god-fearers, as opposed to converts to Judaism, might have been enough to give Domitian an excuse: Aristocrats had elevated civic obligations and served as priests, and Roman elites were particularly exercised by "pollution" from foreign cults. P. Lampe, *From Paul to Valentinus,* 198–205, speculates that the couple were Christians, not Jews; on this issue, I incline to trust Dio rather than the later version of Eusebius, *History of the Church* 3.18.4. Lampe errs in stating that the couple, as Jewish "sympathizers" (as opposed to "converts"), "cannot likewise religiously worship the emperor, and their loyalty is suspected" (204). Sympathizers—another term for the catch-all "god-fearers"—remained pagans, and nothing prohibited them from continuing in their native cults.

13. "Some who have had a father who reveres the Sabbath," complained the Roman satirist Juvenal, "worship nothing but the clouds and the divinity of the heavens, and see no difference between eating swine's flesh (from which their father had abstained) and that of a man. In time, they take to circumcision. Having been inclined to flout Roman law, they learn, follow and respect Jewish law, and all that Moses handed down in his secret book: forbidding [Jews] to give directions to anyone who does not cherish the same rites, leading only those who are [also] circumcised to the fountain that they are looking for. For all of this behavior the father was to blame, who gave up every seventh day to idleness, separating it utterly from the concerns of daily life" (*Satires* 14.96–106). M. Stern analyzes this and others of Juvenal's poetic insults to Jews in *Greek and Latin Authors on Jews and Judaism*, 2:94–107. The offense to ancestral custom also bothered the philosopher Celsus (late second century C.E.). "If the Jews maintained their own law, we should not find fault with them, but rather with those who have abandoned their own traditions and professed those of the Jews" (*Against Celsus* 5.41).

14. Paul gives the number of this earliest group of witnesses as "almost five hundred brethren" (1 Cor. 15:5–6); Acts 1:15, if it indicates the same assembly, claims a smaller number, "about one hundred and twenty."

15. For a survey of this balky literature and an examination of its themes, see G. Nickelburg, *Jewish Literature between the Bible and the Mishnah;* much more briefly, see P. Fredriksen, *From Jesus to Christ*, 77–78, 81–86. Sanders considers these biblical passages along with diaspora writings and relevant rabbinic material with explicit reference to the question of the apocalyptic inclusion of Gentiles in *Jesus and Judaism*, 212–221.

16. Was Jesus himself a prophet of the kingdom or its messiah? These two identifiers seesaw back and forth in the Gospel of John. "He cannot be the Messiah, can he?" asks the Samaritan woman (John 4:29 NRSV). "Can it be that the authorities really know that this is the Messiah?" asks a crowd in Jerusalem (John 7:26). Later, some in the crowd pronounce, "This really is the prophet," while others claim, "This is the Messiah" (John 7:40–41). The evangelist prefers the much more elevated title of divine Son, but the echo of this older dispute in his gospel is interesting. For a short introduction to the historical Jesus as apocalyptic prophet, see E. P. Sanders, *The Historical Figure of Jesus;* for a lucid statement of historical principles guiding the latest quest for the historical Jesus, see J. Meier, *A Marginal Jew*, vol. 1. For the ways that charismatic elements in Paul's letters c. 50 C.E.—pronouncements about the coming kingdom; perfectionist ethics; works of power like healings, exorcisms, and discerning between spirits—help us to identify these same elements in the earliest strata of traditions about Jesus, see P. Fredriksen, *Jesus of Nazareth, King of the Jews*, 74–153.

17. Paul's most sustained description of his hostile initial response to the Jesus movement in the Diaspora comes in Gal. 1:13–15, which is followed by his

sketch of his relations with the earlier apostles back in Jerusalem, and his call to be an emissary to pagans (Gal. 1:16–2:10). Other Jews in the movement also worked to induct pagans: Paul addresses his letter to a (mostly pagan? entirely pagan?) Christian community at Rome, where he has yet to visit (Rom. 15:23). This positive pagan response to the gospel caused controversy and consternation for Jews both inside and outside the new movement.

18. Many Jewish traditions articulate these two poles of opinion, with many views falling between the two extremes. The Dead Sea Scrolls express the most exclusivist extreme, anticipating redemption solely for members of the sect; some rabbinic texts, and the later rabbinic tradition, anticipate the redemption both of Israel and of the nations. For an ordered and ample overview of this material, see E. P. Sanders, *Paul and Palestinian Judaism.* Mishnah Sanhedrin 10, a late-second or early-third-century text, seems to want to split the difference: "All Israel has a place in the world to come," it asserts, while immediately going on to list the [Jewish] exceptions ("And these shall have no place . . .").

19. "The universalist passages in Old Testament prophecy, most signally Second Isaiah's prediction that all nations will eventually worship God alone, stop short of making Jews of all mankind," notes Thomas Braun, "The Jews in the Late Roman Empire," 157. For a more thorough review of these texts, see P. Fredriksen, "Judaism, the Circumcision of Gentiles, and Apocalyptic Hope," 544–548. By the mid-second century, hostile gentile Christians were familiar enough with this Jewish eschatological theme—namely, that when God (or his messiah) establishes his kingdom, the nations will stop worshiping idols and will enter the kingdom without converting to Judaism—that they invoked it to assert that, by the Jews' own standards, Jesus must have been the messiah. See, e.g., Justin, *Dialogue with Trypho* 122–123; and Tertullian, *Against Marcion* 3.20–21.

20. On synagogues as the first port of call for these missionaries, see, e.g., Acts 13:5 ("When they arrived at Salamis, they proclaimed the word of God in the synagogues of the Jews"). Paul preaches in the synagogue of Pisidian Antioch, attracting Jews, proselytes (i.e., converts to Judaism), and god-fearing pagans, but is driven from town by his host community; Acts 13:14–51. (A similar story, ending again with the apostles run out of town, is set in Iconium; Acts 14:1–7.) Paul is stoned in Lystra (Acts 14:19), brought before town magistrates by irate pagans in Philippi and beaten with rods (Acts 16:19–22), and is accused before the city authorities in Thessalonica (Acts 17:1–9) and before the Roman proconsul in Corinth (Acts 18:12–17). In Ephesus, the gospel ignites an urban riot by enraged pagans seeking to protect the local cult of the goddess Artemis (Acts 19:23–41). For Paul's own description of his woes, inflicted variously by Jews, Greeks, and Romans, see 2 Corinthians 4:8–9; 6:4–5; and 11:24–26.

CHAPTER 3: PAIDEIA: PAGAN, JEWISH, CHRISTIAN

1. Philosophers were not the only genre of pagan monotheists. Asia Minor was the cradle of the cult of *Theos Hypsistos* ("the highest god"), a popular third-century C.E. pagan form of monotheism. This cult was also aniconic, worshiping the highest god through solar piety, lamps, and hymns. Fourth-century

Christian heresy-hunters complained that this community mimicked the church. Inscriptions and sites belonging to these worshipers have been found in areas that also held synagogues, which might mean that their cult had been stimulated by contact with Jews. For pagan monotheism both "high" and "low," see most recently the essays gathered in P. Athanassiadi and M. Frede, *Pagan Monotheism in Late Antiquity,* especially the essay by S. Mitchell, "The Cult of *Theos Hypsitos.*"

2. Hellenistic Platonists "had disputed whether Matter was an inert, formless and hence ethically neutral entity," writes R. T. Wallis, "or an active principle of evil." The great pagan Neoplatonist Plotinus, he continues, "characteristically offers a paradoxical combination of both views. Since goodness consists in form, he argues, it is precisely Matter's lack of any form whatever that proves its identity with Absolute Evil. . . . Plotinus, however, is no dualist; his Matter is not an independently existing principle, but the point at which the outflow of reality from the One fades away into utter darkness. Matter's evil is thus not a positive force . . . [but rather] an utter sterility, or 'poverty,' which communicates its own deficiency to the bodies based on it, and thus becomes the source of all the sensible world's imperfections, including . . . the wickedness of individual souls" (*Neoplatonism,* 49–50, with many references to Plotinus' *Enneads*).

3. A. D. Nock, in his edition of the pagan Sallustius' essay on theology and cosmology, provides a tour through the metaphysics of this idea of the universe and introduces its many intermediaries. For the ways that this cosmic architecture and its implications affected Jewish and, later, Christian theology, see H. Chadwick, *Early Christian Thought and the Classical Tradition;* see also A. Scott, *Origen and the Life of the Stars,* 53–172.

4. Peter Struck's recent study *The Birth of the Symbol* provides a wonderfully rich entry into the complex interpretive world of ancient Greek enigma, mystery, symbol, and allegory. (All those terms function as synonyms in these exercises in ancient interpretation.) Such literary efforts could be made only by a literate and educated elite, but this way of thinking symbolically and allegorically had a trickle-down effect into the more general population through religious ritual practice and holy space. Struck's examination of a mural found in Hera's temple on the island of Samos (third century B.C.E.?) deftly makes this point. "In this mural, Hera is depicted as fellating Zeus, and we are told . . . that Chrysippus [a first-century Stoic philosopher] interpreted the painting allegorically: it portrayed matter receiving the *spermatikoi logoi* of the divine." He continues that later Christian writers found this interpretation implausible and the painting itself scandalous, and they took Chrysippus' interpretation as evidence that he too was embarrassed by the temple's art. Struck continues, "It is most doubtful that the artist was attempting to shock; this simply would not make sense at the largest and most important (and expensive) center of active worship of the Greeks' highest-ranking goddess. If the drawing were offensive, embarrassing, or sacrilegious in the eyes of the priests or the worshipers, we can safely assume that it would not have lasted a minute on the wall. What did the artist, the priests, and the worshipers see when they looked at this image?" After making the case for a more widely diffused understanding of what historians identify as Stoic allegory when they encounter it in texts, Struck concludes, "Do Chrysippus's readings

make sense ... or is he, out of some assumed embarrassment, passing off a hermeneutical whopper? The former seems to me much more likely" (280–282).

5. Three recent lively and learned appreciations of the ways that Hellenistic Jews admired and appropriated Greek learned culture may be found in E. Gruen's *Diaspora* and *Heritage and Hellenism*, and in J. Barclay's *Jews in the Western Mediterranean Diaspora*.

6. For a pagan statement of the same interpretive principle, see Sallustius, *Concerning the Gods and the Universe*, 3: "That the myths are divine can be seen by those who have used them—inspired poets, the best philosophers, and the gods themselves in oracles.... But why do they contain stories of adultery, robbery, father-binding, and all the other absurdity? Is it not perhaps a thing worthy of admiration, done so that by means of the visible absurdity, the soul may immediately feel that the words are veils, and believe the Truth to be a mystery?"

   Later Christian writers were no more ready than their pagan and Jewish counterparts had been to extend the courtesy of allegorical reading to the myths of outsiders; meanwhile, of course, such "spiritual" understandings were de rigueur for Christian textual interpretation. The less learned within one's own community, for this reason, could pose no less a challenge than hostile outsiders. Thus Origen of Alexandria, in the early third century: "Simpler Christians ... believe such things of the Creator as would not be believed of the most savage and unjust of men.... The reason that they make impious or ignorant assertions about God is simply this: that scripture is not understood in its spiritual sense, but is interpreted according to the bare letter" (*On First Principles* 4.2,1).

7. "The earliest 'Christian' texts," notes historian Judith Lieu, "... are irreducibly 'Jewish.' This is so both because they are so thoroughly indebted to the Scriptural tradition (the LXX), and because they rely on contemporary patterns of Jewish interpretation and thought. Written in Greek, they belong to the Hellenistic Diaspora. Indeed, it is partly for this reason that these writings do not belong themselves to a distinctive Christian *theology* so much as to its sources" (in P. Fredriksen and J. Lieu, "Rival Traditions," 89).

8. The observation is H. Chadwick's "Oracles of the End," 125, whence these references to Plutarch and to Porphyry. J. Rives offers a brief and lucid discussion of pagan ideas on demons in *Religion in the Roman Empire*, 20. Pagan demons might be either good or wicked; in later Jewish and Christian usage, they are almost always wicked. Because of his ethnic particularity and his appetite for blood sacrifices, the Jews' god, opined Faustus the Manichee, was clearly a "demon" (*Against Faustus* 18.2). See further M. Frede, "Monotheism and Pagan Philosophy in Later Antiquity," 41–79.

9. Ancient pagans took seriously the idea that gods might appear in the likeness of human beings. Josephus relates the story of a Roman matron and her husband who were deceived by a conniving suitor and a deceitful priest. With her husband's permission, the woman went into the god's sanctuary where the suitor, impersonating the god, sexually violated her: "she was at his service all night, supposing that he was the god" (*Antiquities* 18.66–80). According to Acts, after Paul worked a spectacular cure in Lystra, the watching crowd cried out, "The gods have come down to us in human form!" and attempt to sac-

rifice oxen to Paul (whom they identify as Hermes) and to Barnabus ("Zeus") (Acts 14:8-18). On the Syrian divinity "Theandrites" (*theos* means "god," *aner* means "man"), see Bowersock, *Hellenism in Late Antiquity,* 18.

10. On the religious and scientific significance of this idea of the cosmos, "which later antiquity inherited from Aristotle and the Hellenistic astronomers," see E. R. Dodds, *Pagan and Christian in an Age of Anxiety,* 6-14. The ubiquity of the zodiac, attested in pagan, Jewish, and Christian material culture, reveals the religious ecumenism of this view of the universe and of its architecture. For a clear pagan statement on the universe's relation to the single high god, see Sallustius, *Concerning the Gods and the Universe.* In the late fourth century, the Manichee Faustus identified such monotheism—the "belief in a single principle" that stands as the source of this cosmos—as a way of thinking about the world that was common to pagans, Jews, and catholic Christians (*Against Faustus* 20.3-4).

11. Lampe gives a thorough review of these theologians' levels of education in *Paul to Valentinus,* 241-256 (Marcion), 257-284 (Justin), 292-318 (Valentinians). He observes that, of the three, Marcion seems to have had the least amount of "higher" education specifically in philosophy. But to the degree that Marcion attempted (on the evidence, successfully) to build a rational and consistent theological system based on close readings of received texts (in his case most especially the letters of Paul) together with a mode of life consistent with such a theology, Marcion was engaged in what contemporaries would certainly identify as a philosophical enterprise.

12. The Valentinian Ptolemy introduces some rules for how to read Moses' books correctly in *Letter to Flora* (preserved in Epiphanius, *Panarion* 33.3-7). Until the middle of the last century, scholars had to rely mainly on the hostile descriptions of his Christian opponents for knowledge of Valentinus' work. With the 1948 discovery of the Nag Hammadi library in Egypt, this situation improved significantly. Many of the rescued codices contained Coptic translations of earlier, Greek writings from Valentinus and his school. For translations of these, see *The Nag Hammadi Library,* ed. James M. Robinson.

13. The quest for the historical Marcion is hampered by later orthodoxy's success in destroying his writings. Marcion's positions can be gleaned, cautiously, from Tertullian, *Against Marcion.* In his edition of that work, E. Evans distills some of Marcion's teachings, *Tertullian Adversus Marcionem,* 1:ix-xvi, and 2:642-646. The fourth-century Syriac polemics of Ephrem amplify our earlier Latin sources; see his *Prose Refutations* (which also revile Marcion's third-century theological heir, Mani). On Marcionite anti-Judaism and the western patristic response to it, the fundamental essay remains D. Efroymson, "The Patristic Connection"; important also is J. Lieu's *Image and Reality,* 261-270.

14. "The gospels could not possibly be either more or less in number than they are," taught Irenaeus, bishop of Lyon, taking aim, respectively, at Valentinians (who had too many gospels) and Marcionites (who, with only one gospel, had too few). Irenaeus explained why this was so. "Since there are four zones of the world in which we live, and four principal winds, the church . . . fittingly has four pillars, everywhere breathing out incorruption and revivifying men. From this it is clear that the Logos, the artificer of all things, he who sits upon the cherubim and sustains all things . . . gave us the gospel in fourfold form, though held together by one Spirit. . . . for the cherubim have four

faces, and their faces are images of the activity of the Son of God. . . . [And] the gospels, in which Christ is enthroned, are like these" (*Against Heresies* 11,8).

15. The ferocity of this family quarrel only got worse as time passed. By the late second century, a bemused pagan observer noted that Christians "slander one another with dreadful and unspeakable abuse. And they would not make even the least concession to reach agreement, for they utterly detest each other," reported by Origen (*Against Celsus* 5.63). Origen does not deny the truth of Celsus' description but observes that such intersectarian bitterness also characterizes pagan philosophers and pagan medical doctors. All of these parties, of course, would be arguing with each other by using the rhetorical wrestling holds that they had learned in the schools.

16. "A Christian author might identify a fellow Christian as a 'Jew' if it suited his argument," notes J. Knust. "Alternatively, an author might invent a fictional, or loosely historical, 'Jew' for the purposes of self-definition and identity creation. This was especially the case in heresiological literature, which accused target Christians of being either 'too Jewish' or 'too Greek' " ("Early Christian Re-Writing," 492; the quotation in the text above is from p. 493). Knust's essay traces the extreme plasticity, both textual and interpretive, of the story of Jesus and the adulterous woman, which floats in different manuscript traditions of Luke and of John. By the fourth century, interpretations of this particular story had become distinctly anti-Jewish.

   Knust's essay draws on a seminal article by David Brakke, which analyzed the ways that Athanasius' rhetorical alchemy turned local Christians opposing Athanasius on the date of Easter into enemy "Jews" ("Jewish Flesh and Christian Spirit in Athanasius of Alexandria"). Brakke nicely breaks down the "constructed Judaism" of this intra-Christian/anti-Jewish rhetoric into binary opposites (see his chart, 478).

CHAPTER 4: PAGANS, JEWS, AND CHRISTIANS IN THE MEDITERRANEAN CITY

1. The quotation in this paragraph is from Sanders, who goes on to note, "If Paul had considered that he had withdrawn from Judaism, he would not have attended synagogue. If the members of the synagogue had considered him an outsider, they would not have punished him" (*Paul, the Law, and the Jewish People*, 192).

   Scholars habitually describe Paul's evangelizing activity as his "mission to the Gentiles," but this phrase obscures that mission's abiding synagogue context. First, the density of scriptural references in his letters broadcasts Paul's presumption that his gentile recipients had the "biblical literacy" to understand them and thus him: Such Gentiles could be found only in the penumbra of synagogue. Second, the floggings that Paul both gave and got presuppose a synagogue context; see P. Fredriksen, "Paul and Augustine," 8–14, and "Judaism, the Circumcision of Gentiles, and Apocalyptic Hope," 548–550. (Acts dramatically but implausibly transforms such community disciplines, perceived by recipients as "persecutions," into "executions.")

   Whence the violence of the diaspora synagogues' response to the early Christian message? Some scholars conjecture theological offense. Ancient Christians proclaimed a crucified man as the messiah; Jews, so goes the argument, on the strength of Deuteronomy 21:23 ("cursed of God is every man hanged on a tree"), took offense at the idea of a cursed messiah. Others conjecture legal offense. The Torah would be canceled in the days of the messiah; therefore, Jews feared that the proclamation of Jesus as messiah would induce a general defection on the part of Jews from the Law. (This last theory particularly runs aground on the point that Jesus' earliest apostles obviously thought that he was the messiah, and yet—as the argument over kosher food in Antioch demonstrated [Gal. 2:1–15]—Jesus' earliest apostles also continued to live according to Jewish tradition.) Or perhaps these diaspora Jews were exercised by the Gentiles' claim that they, too, were now, in Christ, also members of the people of God. (This last conjecture, currently enjoying a vogue among New Testament scholars, in essence repeats the accusations of ancient Christian rhetoric—namely, that Jews did not want to share salvation with Gentiles.)

More sensible that any and all of these earlier speculations is Martin Goodman's proposal in his essay "The Persecution of Paul by Diaspora Jews." Goodman observes that, although "there might have been all sorts of theological reasons for Jewish hostility to early Christians, theology alone can never explain the risks taken by synagogue authorities in imposing violent discipline on Christian Jews such as Paul" (187). Instead, he suggests, practical concerns about the social consequences of the Christian proclamation *for pagans* motivated synagogue authorities. "The problem for Paul's fellow Jews lay in the hostile reaction to the conversion of gentiles to Christianity to be expected from unconverted *gentiles,* in particular the civic and Roman authorities, and the possibility that, because Paul portrayed himself as a Jew, they as Jews might be blamed for his behavior" (384). "The political factor which impelled diaspora Jewish leaders to persecute [Paul] was the need to lead a quiet life untroubled by the hostility of pagan neighbors resentful that a Jew should try to lure them away from the ancestral worship on which, in their eyes, their security depended" (387). My discussion here expands on Goodman's insight.

2. "The Wicked Priest was called by the name of truth when he first arose," claims the scroll's commentary on the prophet Habakkuk. "But when he ruled over Israel, his heart became proud, and he forsook God . . . he robbed and amassed riches . . . heaping sinful iniquity upon himself. And he lived in the ways of abominations, amidst every unclean defilement" (*Pesher Habakkuk* 8.8–13). Not even Caiaphas, in the gospels, got such bad press. For more bashing of the Jerusalem priests, see too *Damascus Document* in G. Vermes, *Dead Sea Scrolls in English.*

3. Origen, in the early third century C.E., commented on the quarrelsomeness and factiousness of late Second Temple Judaism. "There was in Judaism a factor which caused sects to begin, which was the variety of the interpretations of the writings of Moses and the sayings of the prophets" (*Against Celsus* 3.12). On the ways that Jewish sectarian writings can transmute into gentile anti-Jewish writings, see John Marshall, "Apocalypticism and Anti-Semitism."

4. The accusation of Jewish culpability for Jesus' death appears in an early source, Paul's letter 1 Thess. 2:14–16. The passage, however, is of disputed authenticity, because it ill accords with what Paul has to say in his other letters about Jesus' death, and it so conforms to recognizably post-70 polemical

themes. For a concise review of these problems, see B. Pearson, "1 Thessalonians 2:13-16." On the growth of this tradition of Jewish culpability in the gospels themselves, see P. Fredriksen, *From Jesus to Christ*, 107-126; for the later iterations of this theme of Jews as Christ-killers, see R. Wilken, *John Chrysostom and the Jews*, 125-126. Both N. de Lange, *Origen and the Jews*, 78-79, and J. Lieu, *Image and Reality*, 281-282, discuss the ways that the twinned defeats of 70 and of 135 reverberate in later Christian tradition.

5. Trypho, the Jewish interlocutor in Justin's famous dialogue, literally represents this idea. Though Justin presents Trypho as a Hellenistic Jew (well-read philosophically, oriented to the Septuagint as his biblical text, fluent in Greek, and so on), he casts his interlocutor as "a refugee from the recent wars," that is, the Bar Kokhba rebellion in 132-135 C.E. (*Trypho* 1). This Christian assertion that the Roman conquest of Jerusalem in 70 C.E. and the destruction of the Temple inaugurated the "second exile" masks two important historical realities: the antiquity of the Jewish settlements in the western Diaspora, and the continuity of Jewish settlement in the Land of Israel. The later rabbinic traditions that emanate from the Land of Israel evince no such consciousness of exile, for the good reason that the Galilean rabbis were still "at home." In short, the idea of the year 70 as the start of a second exile was originally Christian. *Jewish* traditions of a second exile had to wait to be framed by later, Babylonian rabbis. See the rich essay by I. Yuval, "The Myth of the Jewish Exile from the Land of Israel."

6. Krauss and Horbury, *The Jewish-Christian Controversy*, offer a lucid overview of the various elements of this invective tradition as well as a presentation of the various Christian authors who amplify and transmit it. Horbury's excellent collection of essays, *Jews and Christians in Contact and Controversy*, scrupulously analyzes these texts and traditions with attention to both families of sources, Jewish and Christian; and he demonstrates that some of these sources evince real social contacts among the various groups. (Horbury takes these contacts as evidence of "Jewish-Christian missionary rivalry," e.g., 140; I do not.)

7. In the Jewish liturgical calendar, 9 Av is set aside as the date on which both temples, Solomon's and Herod's, were destroyed. Josephus, an eyewitness to the Roman siege of the city, provides an unforgettable account of the Temple's destruction in Book 6 of *Jewish War*. For the "fated day" of the Temple's destruction, "the day on which, of old, it had been burned down by the king of Bablyon," *Jewish War* 6.250. E. P. Sanders gauges the emotional and financial links between diaspora Jews and Jerusalem's temple by reconstructing patterns of donations (*Jewish Law from Jesus to the Mishnah*, 283-308). For a thoughtful appraisal of the role of the Temple as a holy site before 70 C.E. and as a site of memory in later Christian and Jewish traditions, see Eliav, *God's Mountain*.

8. We have no way of knowing whether diaspora Jews improvised sacrificial offerings where they were, as they improvised various purification rituals (on which, Sanders, *Jewish Law*, 255-271). Egyptian Jews made offerings at the Jewish temple in Leontopolis, which functioned from roughly 160 B.C.E. to 73 C.E. Jews in the Diaspora continued to slaughter lambs for the Passover meal, an activity that outside observers occasionally mistook as offering sacrifices, as Augustine did in *Genesis, against the Manichees* 1.23,40 (corrected in *Retractations* 1.9,2).

9. Before 212 C.E., individual Jews might be Roman citizens (as Paul is portrayed in Acts 22:25); after 212, the privilege was extended to the entire free population of the empire. For permission to Jewish parents to circumcise, see *Digest* 48.8.11; on Jews as members of city councils, see *Digest* 50.2.3.3; full discussion in Linder, *Jews in Roman Imperial Legislation,* 99–106.

10. For the archaeological evidence of the flourishing synagogue culture of fourth-century Palestine, see G. Stemberger, *Jews and Christians in the Holy Land,* 121–160. The famous synagogue at Sardis in Asia Minor stood at the heart of the ancient city, integrated architecturally into the same structure that held the gymnasium. The Jewish community there throve "right up to the Persian destruction of the city in 616" (L. I. Levine, "Jewish Archaeology in Late Antiquity," 535); for Levine's whole survey of materials both in the Diaspora and in the Land of Israel for this period, see 519–555. This same volume of the *Cambridge History of Judaism* also includes valuable essays on the Jewish communities of Italy (L. Rutgers, "The Jews of Italy," 492–508) and of Spain (where bleaker circumstances prevailed in the wake of the fifth-century barbarian conquests; S. Bradbury, "The Jews of Spain," 508–518), as well as an authoritative consideration by A. Linder, "The Legal Status of the Jews in the Roman Empire," 128–173.

11. Ancient Christian chronographers liked to break up pre-Christian Roman history into ten persecutions, beginning the count with Nero, the emperor (along with Caligula) whom everybody loves to hate. Historically, that represents a confusion: As the earliest reports of Nero's action explain, Roman Christians stood accused of arson, not of Christianity. Nero's action, in other words, was a diversionary criminal prosecution, not a religiously motivated persecution. If we can trust the traditions about Peter and Paul that date their martyrdoms to this event, then Jewish as well as gentile Christians were arrested and put to death—more evidence that the issue was social scapegoating rather than religious persecution. Late New Testament texts, such as the Epistle to the Hebrews, the letters of Peter, and (perhaps) Revelation seem written in or to communities in time of persecution, hence my vagueness in locating such activity sometime in the late first century. See also Lieu's remark, quoted in the following note.

12. "It is not always easy to distinguish here between the real consequences of actual persecution and the creation of a mental world where persecution and conflict is the norm; hence the disparity between some scholarly estimates of the extent of actual persecution before 250 C.E. and its brooding presence in much Christian literature"; J. Lieu, *Image and Reality,* 282.

13. "We also are a religious people," protests the Roman proconsul Saturninus in 180 C.E. to Christians arraigned before him in Carthage (*Scillitan Martyrs* 3). In his efforts to have them agree to swear by the genius of the emperor, Saturninus repeatedly solicits their cooperation. ("Cease to be of this persuasion," 7; "Have no part in this folly!" 8; "You wish no time for consideration?" 11; "You have a reprieve of thirty days. Think it over," 13). "Will you offer sacrifice?" asks the proconsul Quintillian of Pionius in Smyrna (c. 250 C.E.). "No," answers Pionius. "I am a catholic presbyter." Quintillian: "Offer sacrifice." Pionius: "No." Quintillian: "Do you pay heed to the air? Then sacrifice to the air!" (*Martyrdom of Pionius* 19). Fear of heaven spurred these efforts; "the best that humans could hope for," David Potter remarks, "was that they could

keep the gods in a good mood" ("Roman Religion," 134). On the sporadic and local nature of pre-Decian sacrificial initiatives and their source in traditional piety, see T. D. Barnes, "Legislation against the Christians"; on the theme of sacrificing to the emperor, F. Millar, "The Imperial Cult and the Persecutions." Christians who were Jews escaped this pressure to conform to the practices of the majority, because as Jews their exemption from such cult was ancient, traditional, and long acknowledged by majority culture.

14. Pliny, a provincial governor, reports to the emperor Trajan in the early second century that the Christians tried before him had confessed to meeting together "to take food, but [only] ordinary and harmless food" (Letter 10.96). Particularly after the mid-third century, when imperial initiatives cast a wider and finer net, the main problem faced by churches was how to deal with the significant numbers of those who had lapsed, whether clergy or lay, whether by flight or by outright apostasy. On prisoners' executions staged as tableaux drawn from mythology, see K. Coleman, "Fatal Charades."

15. For a brief introduction and a new English translation of *The Lives of the Prophets,* see D. Hare in Charlesworth, *Pseudepigrapha* 2.379–400. Hare discusses the Christian appropriation of these traditions further in *The Theme of the Jewish Persecution of Christians,* 137–141. On the poor fit of this theme within Paul's letters, see B. Pearson, "1 Thessalonians 2:13–16." Rosemary Ruether explores the ways that this idea of the Jews' murder of their own prophets fed into early theological constructions of the role of Christ in *Faith and Fratricide.* Finally, Judith Lieu has done fundamental work tracing the impact of this tradition on later Christian apologies and martyr stories; see esp. *Image and Reality.*

16. The Montanists, for example, were a millenarian, charismatic Christian sect that originated in second-century Phrygia. They enjoyed a reputation as stalwart martyrs and as inspired prophets among their admirers; to their Christian opponents, they were frauds. The trope of "persecution by Jews" served as the acid test for true Christianity. Thus "Anonymous," a source preserved by Eusebius, responded to the Montanists' challenge to "orthodox" identity and scriptural practices: "They used to dub us 'slayers of the prophets,' because we did not receive *their* prophets. . . . [But] is there a single one of these followers of Montanus . . . who was persecuted by Jews or killed by lawless men? Or were any of them seized and crucified for the sake of the Name? Or were any of the[ir] women ever 'scourged in the synagogues' of the Jews, or stoned?" (*History of the Church* 5.16,12). The passage resonates with references to Matthew 23:31–37.

17. Still valuable is Parkes' discussion and survey of these martyr stories in *The Conflict of the Church and the Synagogue,* 109–150. For a review of this issue with fuller notes, see P. Fredriksen and O. Irshai, "Christian Anti-Judaism," 993–997.

18. "Few things are more important to religious life than the calendar and the celebrations of festivals on the proper dates. . . . This is why the debate over the date of Easter in the early Church was not simply a minor dispute over calendar. It was a dispute about religious and communal identity. . . . Conflicting religious ideas may be able to coexist alongside of one another, and often do, but religious practices, by their very nature, force a choice. . . . If

churches were empty because the Jews were celebrating their high holidays, this suggested that the Jewish way was more authentic. If Christians used the Jewish calendar to set the date of a Christian festival, this could only mean that the Jews had the true calendar. In such a setting there was no middle ground," R. Wilken, *John Chrysostom and the Jews,* 77–78.

Rome, like Antioch, also had a large and well-established Jewish community, whose observance of Yom Kippur may have stimulated the creation of an autumn Christian counterfast, Ember Day; see D. Stökl Ben Ezra, "Whose Fast Is It?"

19. The Council of Elvira in the early 300s condemned Christians' marrying Jews (canon 16), asking Jews to bless fields (c. 49), accepting Jewish hospitality (c. 50), and having sexual relations with Jews (c. 78). Toward the end of that century, the Council of Laodecia prohibited Christians from resting on the Sabbath and working on Sundays (c. 29), from receiving gifts from Jews and from heretics (c. 37), and specifically from accepting gifts of matzah from Jews (c. 38). Nor, ruled the bishops, should Christians share in Jewish fasts and feasts or tend lamps in synagogues on festal days or pray together with heretics and Jews (*Apostolic Canons,* c. 69, 70, 63). Linder collects and analyzes this legislation in *Jews in the Legal Sources of the Early Middle Ages.*

20. The theme of non-Christian Jews forcing Christian Jews out of synagogue communities appears already in the late first century, retrojected back into the lifetime of Jesus. In the Gospel of John, the parents of a blind man cured by Jesus avoid answering the hostile queries of "the Jews," "for the Jews had already agreed that if anyone should confess [Jesus] to be the Christ, he was to be put out of the synagogue" (John 9:23). Later second-century gentile Christian authors complain of Jews' cursing Christ, or cursing Christians, in their synagogues. Whether a "benediction against heretics" even existed in this period, and whether the heretics (Hebrew: *minim*) so targeted were other Jews, Jewish Christians, or all Christians, has become a tangled question. For a very full discussion of the modern bibliography as well as the historical question, see W. Horbury, "The Benediction of the *Minim* and Early Jewish-Christian Controversy"; see also the important article by R. Kimelman, "*Birkat ha-Minim* and the Lack of Evidence for an Anti-Christian Jewish Prayer in Late Antiquity." Horbury has also established that Tertullian, in late-second-century Carthage, knew of Jewish stories mocking Jesus' resurrection that appear in early medieval Jewish texts (see "Tertullian on the Jews"). For an analysis of fourth- and fifth-century violence, and the seizure or destruction of property, see the excellent essays in vol. 13 of *Cambridge Ancient History: The Late Empire,* A.D. *337–425,* especially the chapter by Peter Brown, "Christianization and Religious Conflict"; also MacMullen, *Christianity and Paganism.*

21. Some pagans keep the Sabbath and Passover, yet worship at traditional altars, Tertullian, *To the Nations* 1.13.3–4; men in Phoenicia and Palestine, calling themselves god-fearers, consistently follow neither Jewish nor pagan customs, Cyril, *On Worship in Spirit and Truth* 3.92.3; some men live between both ways, "half-Jews" who rush from synagogue to pagan shrine. The Jews ought to tell them that it is wrong to worship the gods, Commodian, *Instructions* 37.1–10. On donor inscriptions by Gentiles (thus perhaps Christians) in the late Roman synagogue, see p. 19 above. Fergus Millar remarks on the "revolutionary

implications" of re-dating the Jewish inscription from Aphrodisias, with its list of gentile god-fearers, that, together with the synagogue material from Sardis, "offers the occasion for a complete reevaluation of the place of Judaism in the religious map of the Late Roman Christian empire in the East.... As soon as we read this document, not as a product of the period when both Christian and Jewish communities lived as tolerated or threatened minorities in an essentially pagan world, but as reflecting the first stage of Christian dominance, it appears in a wholly new light. What is not clear, of course, is whether the 52 gentile 'God-fearers' had come from paganism or Christianity.... But on any construction, it offers a sudden glimpse of religious fluidity in the fourth century, and of an attractive power of Judaism, for which earlier documentary evidence had not prepared us," "Christian Emperors, Christian Church and Jews of the Diaspora in the Greek East," 17–18. On patterns of Late Roman urban piety more generally, Liebeschultz, *Continuity and Change;* and Markus, *The End of Ancient Christianity.*

22. Millar implies the same, when speculating about the religious orientation of the god-fearers in Aphrodisias, "Jews of the Diaspora in the Greek East," p. 18, "[I]t was the conversion of *Christians* to Judaism which contemporary Emperors, at least primarily, sought to ban, and which was subject to penalties on the individual concerned." Millar cites the several places in the *Theodosian Code* specifying these penalties and gives references to discussions of them in Linder, *Jews in Roman Imperial Legislation.* Conversion more than god-fearing itself had lain at the heart of pagan Roman complaints about Jews also, pp. 26–28 above; see also P. Fredriksen and O. Irshai, "Christian Anti-Judaism," pp. 987–990. And, as Millar himself goes on to note, again on the evidence from Aphrodisias, neither the Jews nor the three converts to Judaism, named as such on the second face of the inscription (from the fifth century), seem very concerned about these penalties, since the inscription itself attests to a certain level of advertisement of these conversions or, at the least, to the absence of any effort to conceal them. Millar concludes, "[T]he over-all effect of the re-dating is to suggest the need for a radical reconsideration of the place of Judaism in the predominantly Christian Greek empire" (pp. 19–20).

23. "When by our statutory law we forbade the practice of sacrilegious rites," stated the emperor Honorius in 399, "we were not giving our authority for the abolition of the festivals which bring the citizens together for their communal pleasure. In consequence we decree that, according to the ancient customs, these forms of entertainment should be available to the people, although without any sacrifices or illegal superstition," *Theodosian Code* 16.10.7.

"The Christian emperors ... continued to safeguard what they saw as the traditional amusements of their subjects.... In 399 they rounded off a series of enactments by formally prohibiting the abolition by local authorities of the [urban] festivities on the pretext of their association with the 'profane rites' which had accompanied them and were now prohibited" (Markus, *End of Ancient Christianity,* 108 f., with numerous citations to legislation in the *Theodosian Code*). See too Millar, "Jews of the Diaspora in the Greek East." T. Braun looks at the relationship between the great Antiochene pagan orator and the Jewish patriarch and *vir clarissimus* Gamaliel VI, who sent his son to study rhetoric under Libanius ("The Jews in the Late Roman Empire," 160). Braun also notes that rabbis had similar problems with their own communities as bishops did with theirs: "Rabbi Meir ruled against Jews going to theatres or races because the entertainments there were in honour of idols. The Antiochene Jews whom Chrysostom reviled for backing dancers and 'being wounded for charioteers' were ignorant or heedless of this ruling. . . . Rabbi Nathan conceded that Jews might attend gladiatorial shows if they shouted to spare the life of the loser" (170). Braun cites in support *j Avodah Zarah* 1:7B and Chrysostom's *Discourses against Judaizing Christians* 1.4.

24. This "mixing" even extended to allowing pagans, heretics, and Jews, should they so choose, to listen to church services. Some bishops found their presence unnerving, or so the language of a canon from the Fourth Council of Carthage implies: "A bishop may not prohibit anyone—whether a pagan, a heretic, or a Jew—from entering into the church and hearing the word of God; and they may stay until the catechumens are sent out"—that is, until the consecration of the eucharist (c. 84, promulgated in 436 C.E.; Mansi 3, col. 958). Proclus, a fifth-century archbishop of Constantinople, alludes to the Jewish presence (whether actual or rhetorical) at service in his Homily 2. "A Jewish person standing here," he complains, ". . . .after the congregation has been sent home, will stand outside and mock our words, saying as follows; 'Why do you, Christians, come up with these innovations, and boast of matters that cannot be proved? Did God ever appear on earth? Never, except in the time of Moses'" (quoted in J. Barkhuizen, "Proclus of Constantinople," 194). Later, in a fine frenzy of ecumenical frustration, Proclus preached:

> Let therefore the pagans be killed!
> Let the Jews be destroyed!
> Let the Samaritans be ashamed!
> Let the Manichaeans be dispersed!
> Let heretics be destroyed,
> And all the enemies of the immaculate, catholic, apostolic church!
>
> HOMILY 15, quoted in J. Barkhuizen,
> "Proclus of Constantinople," 193

25. Some bishops were less doctrinaire than others. Peter Brown tells the story of a deflected demonstration against the Olympic Games instituted in the city of Chalcedon in 434–435 C.E. Monks arriving to protest were turned away by the city's bishop: "Are you determined to die, even if no one wishes to make a martyr of you? As you are a monk, go sit in your cell and keep quiet. This is my affair" (*Authority and the Sacred*, 51, citing Callinicus, *Life of Hypatius* 33).

26. On Greek as the Jewish liturgical language in the West, see Bradbury, *Severus of Minorca*, 32; also Millar, "The Jews of the Graeco-Roman Diaspora" and "Christian Emperors, Christian Church, and the Jews of the Diaspora." Wilken notes, "In Greek-speaking cities, even in Palestine, the Jews prayed in Greek (*jSotah* 7.1; 21b) and used Greek as the language of instruction" (*John Chrysostom and the Jews*, 57). During the events around the forced conversion of Jews on Minorca, both communities, Christians and Jews, spontaneously took up the joint chanting of Psalms: Presumably the language there was

Latin (*Letter of Severus* 13.1–2). I assume that Commodian's "half-Jew" (*medius iudaeus*), the North African pagan who dashes between traditional altars and the synagogue, would most likely have been listening to Latin too (above, n. 21).

27. On Christian writers' availing themselves of Jewish learning whether directly (Origen, Jerome) or indirectly (as does Augustine, via Jerome), see A. Kasemar, "The Evaluation of the Narrative Aggada"; and the older discussions in de Lange, *Origen and the Jews;* and in Wilken, *John Chrysostom and the Jews.* The Old Testament itself could always inspire pious Christians to Judaize. This seems to be the case with one Aptus, a North African Christian who began urging his co-religionists to avoid certain meats and to assume other ancient Jewish practices; see Augustine, *Letter* 196 to Asellicus.

28. "It is because they are Christians," observes Wilken, "that the Judaizers are drawn to the Jews, and it is as Christians that they justify their actions. . . . [T]hey sanctioned their observance of the Law by appealing to the example of Jesus, who as a Jew had kept the Law." He brings as examples Origen (*Commentary on Matthew* 79), Epiphanius (*Against Heresies* 28.5.1), and Chrysostom (*Discourses against Judaizing Christians* 3.4), who all mention Christians' justifying their Jewish practice by following the example of Jesus himself, *John Chrysostom and the Jews,* 93.

CHAPTER 5: THE HERETIC

1. Disputes had long provided entertainment in antiquity, from the Hellenistic age up through the late Roman period. They offered those trained in rhetorical-philosophical culture the opportunity to demonstrate their skills, and listeners appreciated a good show of verbal fireworks. Augustine's reputation as a talented orator precipitated his forced ordination at Hippo in 391. The aged bishop there, Valerius, was a native Greek speaker. He announced at Sunday eucharist his intentions of finding a younger and more verbally agile man to serve as priest; the crowd caught the hint, seized the visiting Augustine, and refused to release him until he acquiesced (*Life* 4). See also p. 138 above. On Jews residing in Hippo, see, e.g., *Sermon* 196.4, and p. 310 above.

   Western Manichees used public disputes as a means to missionize, a style well suited to the young Augustine's temperament and training. While an *auditor* of the sect in Carthage, he cheerfully exercised his skills in this new forum (*On the Two Souls against the Manichees* 9.11. For the rumor that he had been exiled from Carthage because of his sectarian affiliation, see *Answer to Petilian* 3.25,30. Augustine had in fact left for Rome in 383, three years before the proconsul's purge.

2. An account of the latter part of Mani's life is preserved in an extraordinary Greek codex discovered in 1969. The most recent brief biography is available in the excellent collection edited by I. Gardner and S. Lieu, *Manichaean Texts from the Roman Empire,* 3–8. A virtual one-volume introduction to ancient Manichaeism, this work also gives clear summaries of Manichaean teachings and practices; a wide-ranging assortment of various revelations, prayers, and psalms; Roman anti-Manichaean legislation; and excerpts from hostile contemporaries, such as the older Augustine. Papyri discoveries in Egypt in the last several decades (of which Gardner and Lieu take account) have greatly en-

riched scholarly resources. Older, still-valuable studies include H. C. Puech, *Le Manichéisme;* F. Decret, *Mani et la tradition manichéenne;* and M. Tardieu, *Le Manichéisme.* For an analysis of the movement that focuses on ritual rather than doctrine, see J. BeDuhn, *The Manichaean Body in Discipline and Ritual.*

3. P. Brown surveys this legislation and its effects in "The Diffusion of Manichaeism in the Roman Empire." Gardner and Lieu, *Manichaean Texts,* 145–150, provide select translations of some of these laws. Augustine acknowledged but belittled the state persecution of Manichees: His former teacher, Faustus, denounced as a Manichee before the proconsul by catholic Christians, "was only banished to an island, which can hardly be called a punishment at all" (*Against Faustus,* 5.8); and he notes that these Manichees were released by a public decree of amnesty.

4. "When it came to the enforcement of . . . imperial orders against dissident Christian groups, it will have been the local Catholic bishops who stood in the front line," observes D. Hunt. "The evidence of local communities points to the Catholic bishop as the figure most identified with state 'persecution': only with his active participation could these laws take effect" ("The Church as a Public Institution," 274). See also P. Brown, "The Diffusion of Manichaeism in the Roman Empire"; and J. O'Meara, *The Young Augustine,* 103. On the discovery of a Manichaean missionary sheltering in the catholic hierarchy, Gardner and Lieu, *Manichaean Texts* 143. On Priscillian and the ways that his enemies presented him, see V. Burrus, *The Making of a Heretic.*

5. "According to your sacrilegious nonsense, Christ is not only mingled with heaven and all the stars," thundered Augustine the bishop c. 399 C.E., "but he is conjoined and compounded with the earth and everything born of it, no longer *your* savior, but needing to be saved by you, by your chewing and belching. This impious fantasy leads your auditors to bring you food, so that by your teeth and bellies you can liberate Christ, who is bound up in it" (*Against Faustus* 2.5). The etiquette of dismissing the non-initiate members before the sacred meal has obvious parallels with less exotic Christian practices: catholic catechumens also had to retire before the eucharist.

   The strictures binding auditors permitted them to marry but discouraged procreation (births prolonged the entrapment of light), and they could still live in the world and own property (as, indeed, the young Augustine did). Bringing alms to the Elect was a daily discipline, as were the community's prayers, which were augmented by weekly fasts on Sunday. The efforts of the Elect whom they sustained, meanwhile, counted toward their merit too, so that in their next cycle of life, an auditor might be reincarnated as an Elect—or perhaps, Augustine much later observed with contempt, "if they possess greater merit, they shall enter into melons or cucumbers or some other food for you [the Elect] to chew, to be purified through your digestion" (*Against Faustus* 5.10).

6. Both Augustine (*The Happy Life* 4) and the Manichees (*The Usefulness of Belief* 1.2) characterized the catholic Christianity of his youth as *superstitio.* The Manichaean claim to superior rationality obviously appealed to the young Augustine, and he alludes to it often; see e.g., *The Happy Life* 1,4; *Morals of the Church* 2,3; *Usefulness of Belief* 1,2; *Conf.* 3.6,10; and *Against Faustus* 20.3. The intense asceticism of the Elect clearly impressed him at the time also, though in his later anti-Manichaean tracts, whether through insinuation or outright

insult, he suggests that they were secretly profligate; see *Morals of the Church* 1.2 ("they make a great show of chastity and of notable abstinence"); *Morals of the Manichees* 20.74; later, and more scurrilous, *About Heresies* 46.9-10. On his unnerving realization that the genealogies related in the gospels of Matthew and of Luke do not correspond, see *Sermon* 51.5-6. Faustus had had similar problems with these discrepancies (*Against Faustus* 3.1).

7. On the similarities (and differences) between Marcion's and Mani's views on New Testament texts, especially the Pauline letters, see Tardieu, "Les principes de l'exégèse manichéenne," 142-144.

8. "Remember that the promise of Canaan in the Old Testament is made to the Jews, that is, to the circumcised, who offer sacrifice, and abstain from swine's flesh, and from other animals which Moses pronounced unclean, and who observe Sabbaths, and the Feast of Unleavened Bread [Passover], and other things of the same kind which the Old Testament's author enjoined," observed Faustus. "Christians have not adopted these observances, and no one keeps them. If we will not take the inheritance, we should surrender the documents" (*Against Faustus* 4.1; see also 6.1).

9. North African Christians, both the catholic minority and the Donatist majority, were given to energetic millenarian convictions. A specifically African chronographical tradition had identified the zone of time corresponding to 400-500 C.E. as the 6,000th year since the creation of the universe and thus the period to expect the Second Coming of Christ and the resurrection of the saints. Both churches, further, were much given to feasting with food and drink at the graves of the holy dead, a custom that greatly embarrassed Hippo's new, cosmopolitan priest. ("Fleshly gorging," *carnalis ingurgitatio*, Augustine complained; *Letter* 29.11). On the feasts for the dead, see especially F. van der Meer, *Augustine the Bishop*, 498-525; see also P. Brown, *The Cult of the Saints*. On North African millenarianism, see P. Fredriksen, "Apocalypse and Redemption in Early Christianity." On contesting Jewish and Christian understandings of final redemption and how these affected both biblical interpretation and attitudes toward Jerusalem and the Land of Israel, see R. Wilken, *The Land called Holy*.

   Faustus' jibe about the evident paganism of these Christian convictions and practices hit home: "The [pagan] sacrifices you changed into love-feasts, the idols into martyrs, whom you pray to as pagans do to idols. You appease the ghosts of the dead with food and wine. You keep the same holidays as the pagans do, the new year in January, the mid-summer and mid-winter feasts. In your way of living you have made no change at all" (*Against Faustus* 20.4). Augustine worked hard to wean his congregation in Hippo away from such festivities, and his effort traumatized both parties (*Letter* 22.2-8).

10. Since Augustine and his common-law wife had only one child together in the course of their relationship, during most of which time he had been an *auditor*, it seems probable that they practiced contraception according to the rhythm method, then commended by his church but condemned by hers. Augustine hints at this in *Conf.* 4.2,2.

11. Augustine's efforts as a Manichee to proselytize do not seem to have extended to the two women in his life, his mother, Monnica, and his unnamed wife. When Augustine returned home to Thagaste for what turned out to be a brief stint of teaching grammar, his mother initially refused to have the young

Manichee under her roof or at her table (*Conf.* 3.9,19; she eventually relented). His Carthaginian spouse he encountered in his pre-Manichaean days, at a catholic service (*Conf.* 3.3,5). When, fifteen years later, he sent her back to Africa from Milan so that their relationship would not impede his ambitions for a more socially advantageous match, "she left vowing never to know a man again" (*Conf.* 6.15,25). P. Brown comments, "In all probability she had been a good catholic throughout her life with Augustine," *Augustine of Hippo*, 89; on the social status of their union, 61–63. Augustine enjoyed and took advantage of the support of the Manichaean network in Italy (*Conf.* 5.10,18; 13,23). On the sexual and alimentary regimen of auditors, see further BeDuhn, *Manichaean Body*, 56–73.

12. Augustine describes his mounting disenchantment in Book 5 of the *Confessions*. Manichaean astral traditions did not square with the physical sciences (*Conf.* 5.2,3–3,9). Though they insisted that New Testament texts had been corrupted by Judaizers, they could never produce uncorrupted copies (5.6,21). Faustus, the much-anticipated Manichaean bishop, proved to be a disappointment (5.4,10–13).

13. Faustus points to contempt for Jews and Judaism as common ground between catholics and Manichees: "I reject circumcision as disgusting, and so do you. I reject observing Sabbath as superfluous; you do, too. I reject sacrifice as idolatry; you do too. . . . We both look upon the weeks of Passover and Sukkot as unnecessary and useless," and he goes on to ridicule other biblical legislation as "things which we both despise and laugh at" (*Against Faustus* 6.1). Augustine reports that the Manichees "asserted that the scriptures of the New Testament had been tampered with by persons unknown, who wanted to insert the Jews' law into the Christian faith," but that their persuasiveness on this point suffered by their inability to produce any uncorrupted copies (*Conf.* 5.11,21).

14. "Gentiles" in Faustus' remark refers to "pagans." Greco-Roman culture was unabashedly anthropomorphic in depicting deity. In this way, Faustus universalizes the error against which Mani taught: Everyone, he says, pagans, Jews, and catholic Christians, wrongly construed the relation of divinity and humanity. This passage of *Against Faustus* is filled with references to the Gospel of John and to the Pauline letters, thus making the case that in rejecting Manichaeism, catholics reject both the gospel and the teaching of Paul.

CHAPTER 6: THE SOJOURNER

1. Describing the struggle between Symmachus and Ambrose over Rome's Altar of Victory, Peter Brown comments, "Smarting under so dramatic a snub to the traditional religion, Symmachus may well have been glad to ensure that a man such as Augustine, known to him as a member of a violently anti-Catholic sect, would be in a position to speak before the Emperor," *Augustine of Hippo*, 70. Augustine's position as Milan's professor of rhetoric meant that he had to deliver speeches praising the emperor to the emperor. ("How unhappy I was . . . on the day when I was preparing to deliver a panegyric on the emperor! In the course of it I would tell numerous lies, and for my mendacity would win the good opinion of people who knew it to be untrue"; *Conf.* 6.6,9). Neil McLynn points out as well that political circumstances had con-

spired to minimize competition for this post—something else that worked to Augustine's advantage, offsetting his lack of important, established local patrons (*Ambrose of Milan*, 169–170).

2. "Valentinian's court lacked a single focus," McLynn notes. (Small surprise, in view of the emperor's age.) "Augustine's afternoons were consigned to the arduous and frustrating search for reliable patrons. His difficulties well reflect the shifting, elusive balance of power in Milan. It is perhaps not surprising that he was increasingly drawn to, and eventually captured by, one of the city's few solid and reliable institutions: the church of Bishop Ambrose," *Ambrose of Milan*, 170; see too *Conf.* 6.11,18. Augustine's position as the city's rhetor would have made him extremely conscious of his foreign accent (*On Order* 2.17,45).

3. The "vast ordered cosmos" of the Neoplatonists, observes R. Markus, had its source in "the transcendent One, beyond speech and beyond thought, which communicated itself to beings below it in the infinitely ordered hierarchy down to the lowest levels of the system. The universe was pictured as a sort of cascade of divine light descending from its transcendent origin, dissipating itself gradually in multiplicity, limitation, and ultimately the darkness of non-being. The descending self-communication of the One constitutes a cosmic hierarchy which provides the soul with the route for its ascent. To liberate itself from the realm of darkness and multiplicity the soul needs to retrace the universal order, ascending from its place of exile, from its dissipation among material things and multiplicity, to its goal and its true home," *Conversion and Disenchantment in Augustine's Spiritual Career*, 14–15.

   P. Brown provides a lucid overview of the specifically Christian aspects of Milanese Neoplatonism, *Augustine of Hippo*, 88–100.

4. "That sexual relations have value only for procreation had been implicit in Plato and was common ground for most moralists of late Antiquity. And the *Symposium*'s doctrine that the sexual energy is more profitably directed towards the Ideal world provided a strong incentive to total celibacy," Wallis, *Neoplatonism*, 9. His whole first chapter on "the effects of the new otherworldliness" (11) provides a valuable context for understanding the philosophical lineaments of Augustine's dilemma.

5. A.-J. Levine analyzes these early Christian traditions on sexual renunciation in their apocalyptic context in "The Earth Moved." On possible connections between Jesus' instructions on sexual celibacy and what we find in Paul's letters, see P. Fredriksen, *Jesus of Nazareth, King of the Jews*, 98–101.

6. P. Brown's *Body and Society* presents a picture gallery of these various Christian behaviors; Dodds has a wonderful sense for the competitive asceticism of the desert fathers, *Pagan and Christian*, 33 and nn. 2–4. R. Lane Fox, in his chapter "Living Like Angels," puts the various Christian practices, the ideal and the real, within the broader social context of marriage laws, medical writings, penitential practices, church canons, and apocryphal apostolic acta, *Pagans and Christians*, 336–374.

7. Ambrose was a patron of Christian virgins, but he was also, very practically, in the thick of arranging and sanctioning upper-class Christian marriages in Milan; see McLynn, *Ambrose of Milan*, 258–259. "Sexual renunciation was

never a central, or even an explicit, part of Ambrose's call to baptism. It was a preoccupation that Augustine had brought with him to Milan and that conditioned his understanding of the bishop's preaching" (ibid., 223). B. Stock notes the twin sources of this "preoccupation" from Augustine's past: "Cicero and Mani represented different sorts of influence on Augustine, but they had one meeting-point—and orientation in the direction of the ascetic life," *Augustine the Reader,* 43.

8. Stock shrewdly observes how frustrated Augustine must have been as a "second-class" Manichee back in Carthage. "The canonical texts were known only to the higher ranks of the hierarchy.... Even within the intimacy of the group, the *auditores* had little or no direct access to the canonical books.... For the nine years of his apprenticeship, while his interpretive abilities grew in leaps and bounds, Augustine was not given free access to the sacred texts of his chosen faith, nor was he encouraged to read them critically," *Augustine the Reader,* 46.

9. "The ideal of philosophical retirement was as stringent as any call to the monastic life: it would mean breaking off his career, his marriage, all forms of sexual relations" (Brown, *Augustine of Hippo,* 106).

10. S. Lancel, citing Augustine's biographer Possidius, holds that Augustine relinquished his personal property "to the church community of his native town" once he returned to Thagaste (*Saint Augustine,* 130). J. O'Donnell reconstructs this period very differently: "As long as Adeodatus was alive Augustine was no cleric, and showed no signs of clerical ambitions for his son.... The career change that Augustine undertook at that moment—abandoning Milan for Thagaste—was an ordinary sort of failure and retirement.... Augustine did not sell all he had, give to the poor, and follow Jesus. He quit his job, went home, and lived very comfortably. Very little really changed, apart from Augustine's sleeping arrangements and the venue of his quite ordinary rustication" (*Augustine,* 58,61).

    Also, Augustine's continuing literary production implies that he either owned trained slaves or had the money to hire scribes: *Notarii* were expensive, and Augustine could not have produced his treatises without them.

11. Classical culture had long drawn this correspondence between the seven stages or ages of the world and the developmental stages of the individual. Christian thinkers added another dimension, coordinating the phases of creation/salvation history distilled from the Bible to the spiritual trajectory of the individual believer. Hints of this temporal scaffolding will appear in the *Confessions* (on which, see J. O'Donnell, *Confessions* 2:52–53 and 135–136). Augustine appeals to it most explicitly in *True Religion* 26.49. Two classic explorations of this theme in early Christian writings are A. Luneau, *L'histoire du salut,* and G. Ladner, *The Idea of Reform,* 222–238. Also valuable are Markus' comments in *Saeculum,* 17–21.

12. Augustine gives these details in *Sermon 355,* preached toward the end of his life. His mockery of the Manichee Faustus for being "merely" exiled as opposed to murdered gives an oblique measure of the regret Augustine may still have felt about this turn in the direction of his life. Faustus was "only banished to an island, which can hardly be called a punishment at all, for it is what God's servants do of their own accord every day

when they wish to retire from the tumult of the world" (*Against Faustus* 5.8).

13. Relations between these two, unequal branches of the North African church were complicated by the fact that both could make a reasoned and reasonable appeal to the teachings of the great Carthaginian bishop and martyr Cyprian (d. 258). In the roiled atmosphere after the Decian persecution, Cyprian had presided over an episcopal council that ruled that the sacraments of heretics were invalid and that those baptized by heretics had to be rebaptized into the true church. He also insisted on the primacy of the bishop of Rome—a principal that he disregarded when he needed to. The two contesting wings of the church after Diocletian's persecution of 303 split this theological heritage down the middle, the Donatists emphasizing the necessity of rebaptism, the catholics the sovereignty of the bishop. See Markus, *Saeculum*, 108–115.

14. Raised, and therefore "saved," the body became a theological problem only eventually, in the course of the late second to early third century. Those theologians (like Valentinus and Marcion) whose Genesis described the activities of a hostile *kosmokrator,* whose Christ was docetic, and whose redemption was noncosmic, ahistorical, and spiritual, could take the "spiritual body" of 1 Corinthians 15:42–50 to mean that redemption was purely spiritual and that the raised body was something like what Augustine described it to be in *Faith and the Creed.* Their Christian opposition (such as Justin and Irenaeus), in insisting that Christ was incarnate and salvation terrestrial (in Jerusalem, in fact), also held that raised bodies would be fleshly. The latter view effortlessly lent itself to an active millenarianism that calculated the date of the Second Coming—a tradition that had a particularly strong theological pedigree in North Africa. (One of Augustine's contemporaries, the bishop Hilarianus, announced in 397 C.E. that the year 6000 since creation—thus, the return of the risen Christ—was a scant century off; *On the Passage of Time* 1.55–74.) Millenarianism, especially after Constantine, was renounced in its turn (in part for being "too Jewish"); and theologians with intellectual commitments to Platonism, such as Origen and, later, Augustine, accordingly interpreted the "spiritual body" as made of spirit. See pp. 330–333 above for Augustine's change of mind on this question; on the issue more generally, P. Fredriksen, "Apocalypticism" in Fitzgerald, *Augustine through the Ages*, pp. 49–53.

15. *Life* 6. The topic of the debate is nowhere spelled out. Fortunatus wanted Augustine, as a former Manichee, to publicly repudiate rumors of Manichaean sexual misbehavior. "The matter that we are considering today is the way that we live, our mode of behavior. We are mistreated because of [sexual] crimes that are falsely attributed to us. Therefore let the good people gathered here today hear from you whether these scurrilous accusations are true or false" (*Against Fortunatus* 1–2). Augustine manages to imply that the charges *could* be true, since he had been only an *auditor,* and thus not privy to the meetings of the Elect. He then moves the debate to a focus on "faith," by which he meant doctrine (*Against Fortunatus* 3).

16. An exception is F. Decret, who conjectures that some of Augustine's supporters in the crowd, sensing that he was not acquitting himself well, deliberately interrupted the debate at this point to relieve him (*Aspects du*

manichéisme dans l'Afrique romaine, 48 f). Or perhaps the catholic and Donatist listeners—the vast majority of the audience—were genuinely upset by the specific Pauline verse quoted by Fortunatus. In light of the vivid belief in bodily resurrection that so marked African Christianity, 1 Corinthians 15:50 would be a difficult verse for them to hear.

17. W. H. C. Frend observed that this debate was a contest in how to interpret Paul in "The Gnostic-Manichaean Tradition in North Africa," 21. Against incarnation, Fortunatus cites Phil. 2:5–8 (Paul's verses on Christ appearing in the likeness of man and in the form of a slave; *Against Fortunatus* 7); against both incarnation and, by extension, physical resurrection, he cites 1 Cor. 15:50 ("flesh and blood cannot inherit the Kingdom"; *Against Fortunatus* 19); as well as Gal. 5:14 (crucifying the world to the self and vice versa) and 5:17 ("the desires of the flesh are against the spirit and the desires of the spirit are against the flesh"; *Against Fortunatus* 21).

18. In one construal of Greek moral philosophy, choice assumed knowledge, and choosing the bad rather than the good implied ignorance. Once a person knew good from bad (so goes the assumption), he would love the good and choose it. In short: What you know directs what you love and thus how you choose. Origen's theology is a monument to this way of construing free choice. Augustine also emphasized the erotic aspect of knowing in the Platonic tradition, to which he adds his conviction as a Christian that, after Adam, all human loves are "disordered." Disordered love negatively affects will and choice. People chose according to what they love, not what they know; and they often chose while knowing that their choice is "bad," because their love pulls them more strongly in one direction than their knowledge of good can pull from the other direction. Augustine takes Paul to describe the same quandary in Romans 7:7–25 ("I do not do what I want to do, but the thing that I hate, this I do. Wretched man!" v. 15). He speaks about the bad effects of disordered libido early, in a writing begun while he was still in Italy. He holds there that "the soul is dominated by lust," though by "clinging to wisdom," one can break these bonds (*Free Will* 1.11,22). Later, starting with his reply to Simplicianus, he will insist that even wisdom does not help. Left to their own devices, people cannot love the good unless God's grace enables them. In the *Confessions,* Augustine narrates the turmoil of his life before baptism in light of this newer idea.

19. "The soul would need no healing if it had not infected itself by its own sinning. . . . Thus the pull of fleshly desire is the soul's own pull against the self, a disease from which it needs to be healed, not a foreign power from which it needs to be set free" (W. Babcock, "Augustine and the Spirituality of Desire," 192).

CHAPTER 7: THE CONVERT

1. *"Apostolum accipis?" "Et maxime!"* ("Do you acknowledge the authority of Paul the Apostle?" "Absolutely!"; *Against Faustus* 9.1). For an analysis of the ways that North African Manichaeism based itself on Paul's letters, see F. Decret, "Utilisation des épîtres de Paul chez les Manichéens d'Afrique"; for Paul's effect on techniques of scriptural interpretation, Tardieu, "L'exégèse manichéenne."

2. "It is conventional to think that 391 marked an important turning point, with formal affiliation to the ecclesiastical hierarchy through ordination. That moment brought a real shock to Augustine and opened a difficult and frustrating period in his life, when one literary project after another fell to pieces in his hands as a desperate writer's block settled on him," notes O'Donnell of this series of small studies, *Confessions* 1:xlii.

3. Though no major anti-Donatist treatises date from this period, Augustine was already in diplomatic communication with his Donatist counterpart in Hippo (*Letter* 23); and by 394, he had composed a rhyming popular song "Against the Donatists," as street-level propoganda (*Retractations* 1.20[19]). E. Plumer, in *Galatians*, 249–252, gives a quick overview of Augustine's anti-Donatist activities in the early to mid-390s; Brown, in *Augustine of Hippo*, chap. 20, energetically narrates Augustine's early initiatives and their consequences. M. Tilley, in *The Bible in Christian North Africa*, 113–129, places Tyconius within his Donatist context.

4. Part of the freshness of Tyconius' approach was due to his deriving his exegetical rules primarily from the biblical text itself. No statement about divine impassibility, for example, or about the prerogatives of the rational soul commences or controls his discussion, which is remarkably indifferent to and independent of non-African exegetical traditions. Tyconius' framing of the entire Bible within the categories of "Law" and "prophecy" emphasized, rather, his concern to understand how God's purposes unfold in time. Up until recently, scholars had dated Augustine's first contact with Tyconius no earlier than 396—two years later than the date that my discussion here assumes. That later date rests on Augustine's *Letter* 41 from 396 or 397, wherein he specifically mentions reading and thinking about Tyconius' work. The similarities of their readings of Paul, however, appear in the works of 394 (Fredriksen, "Augustine and Israel"). P.-M. Hombert has now established the earlier date as the period of Augustine's first encounters with Tyconius' work, *Gloria gratiae*, 85–90; see too Lancel, *Saint Augustine*, 179.

5. Augustine's efforts to frame interpretation *ad litteram* and *proprie* will reverse the direction of these earlier theologians' efforts: For him, in a special sense, the past, not the present, must set the terms for interpretation *ad litteram*.

   "The historicity of the event behind the text is not at issue for Melito. . . . The reality (*alêtheia;* "truth") lies in the fulfillment [of the prophecy], not in an event whose occurrence in the past is its principal feature. . . . If you could prove that the scriptures were fulfilled, then you had demonstrated both the truth of the claimed fulfillment and the reliability of the supposed scriptural predictions. In a culture where the government consulted the Sibylline Books [a collection of pagan oracles], this was more effective than we might suppose," F. Young, "Typology," 35–36. She expands on these points in her later, fuller study, *Biblical Exegesis and the Formation of Christian Culture*, 119–139 (on reference and cross-reference) and 186–213 (on types of typology).

   "Biblical language determined theology," observes K. Froehlich, "and . . . theological presuppositions shaped the reading of the Bible. It was in the hermeneutical circle of biblical text, tradition and interpretation that Christian theology as a whole took shape" (*Biblical Interpretation in the Early Church*, 1). His introduction lucidly surveys issues and major writers from the first through fourth centuries.

6. Once he constructs his theology of Judaism, Augustine will keep this Tyconian idea of "measure" or "way" (*modus*) and type (*genus*), but alter it. For Tyconius, the contrast is between Israel's having the Law in the Old Testament, and Christ's bringing the Law to the nations in the New Testament. For Augustine, God reveals the Law to Israel in the Old Testament, and Israel—as represented by the apostles in a first-order way and as represented by fleshly Israel, exiled after 70 C.E., in a second-order way—brings knowledge of the Law, now fulfilled in Christ, to the nations.

7. "Although Augustine was severe toward this [Tyconius' work on Paul in his *Book of Rules*] in the evening of his life . . . there is no doubt that it was helpful to him in the period of his first Pauline exegeses," comments Lancel. "These initial meditations on St. Paul, with Tyconius as his guide, were now steering him toward the transformation of his own theology of grace," *Saint Augustine*, 179–180.

8. On this idea of universal guilt for a transpersonal sin and the way that it conjures the idea of a "double life" (corporately in Adam, individually for each person), see especially J. Rist, *Augustine*, 92–147, on soul, body, and personal identity. Rist notes, "Augustine says that [Adam] was 'one man' and also the whole human race (*totus genus humanum*). That is an allegory perhaps, and of course Adam does represent each and every one of us allegorically. But in Augustine's time Adam cannot be a merely allegorical figure. And the transmission of sin to us is not an allegory, not just a symbol of our similarity to Adam . . . but an historical fact. The historical Adam is 'the whole human race' of which we are all members" (126).

9. Right after his surprise ordination, Augustine petitioned Valerius for time off to study scripture before assuming his new responsibilities (*Letter* 21). O'Donnell speculates reasonably that Augustine might have sent this letter from Thagaste, having fled back there shortly after the event, in part impelled by dread, in part drawn back to the idea of a life in retirement. In either case, Augustine would have had to settle affairs with his property there before his move (*Augustine*, 25).

10. Augustine frames his classic teaching on original sin in the course of arguing against Pelagius, after 410. Then he will state that all people after Adam have inherited not only Adam's penalty (mortal flesh and the type of soul that forms bad habits easily once it starts sinning) but also Adam's guilt. For this reason, he will argue, even babies who are not baptized are, on this account, condemned. See P. Fredriksen, "Beyond the Body/Soul Dichotomy"; see also p. 423, n. 20, below.

11. Augustine seems to configure the relation of divine and human wills as a zero-sum game: As God's sovereignty, in his view, increases, humanity's moral autonomy correspondingly decreases. Only a brief time earlier, Augustine had referred to that passage of Acts that described Saul's participation in Stephen's stoning (Acts 6:8–7:60). Speaking of Paul's postconversion regret of this moment, Augustine comments, "he later reproached himself regretfully for that incident when he was filled with that same Spirit which he had first foolishly resisted" (*Unfinished Commentary on Romans* 15.6). By 396, such human "resistance" to a divine overture is theologically unthinkable. "The effectiveness of God's mercy cannot be in the power of man to frustrate" (*To Simplicianus* 1.2,13).

12. Brown, *Augustine of Hippo,* 150; and see his entire chapter "The Lost Future," 146–157, for an elegiac consideration of the intangible environmental factors affecting Augustine; see too Lancel's lucid analysis of Augustine's theological arguments in *Saint Augustine,* 186–203 (a chapter dedicated precisely to this transitional period). Markus speaks of Augustine's "intellectual landslide" in *Conversion and Disenchantment,* 23; for his discussion of the 390s, see 14–23. In Fredriksen, "Beyond the Body/Soul Dichotomy," 99–102, I evaluate possible sources that may have prompted Augustine's new views in *To Simplicianus.*

   C. Harrison, in *Rethinking Augustine's Early Theology,* has recently argued that Augustine's position in *Notes on Romans* is something that he only "briefly entertained," and that his stronger statement in *To Simplicianus* was his "returning to what he had always, deep down, believed" (Harrison, 151); *Romans* is an anomaly and *Simplicianus* a return (ibid., 163). For the reasons that I lay out in my narrative here, I cannot find Harrison's argument persuasive. Augustine in his *Retractations* also points to his essay to Simplicianus as representing a turning point in his understanding of the relationship of grace to free will. "When answering this question, I made a great effort to defend the free choice of the will; but the grace of God prevailed" (*Retractations* 2.28,1).

13. "Augustine was always busy with words. The five million or so that we have from him were all written in the last forty-three years of his nearly seventy-six years of life, and by far the majority during his thirty-four years as bishop of Hippo. The average is approximately that of a 300-page printed book every year for almost forty years," O'Donnell, *Augustine,* 136 f.

14. Paul presents his earliest arena of activity as Damascus and claims not to have been known "by face" to the Christians of Judea (Galatians 1:15–22); Acts starts Paul off in Jerusalem, which is in Judea, where he is already a notorious persecutor (Acts 7:58; 8:3). In that same passage in Galatians, Paul insists that after receiving his call, he did not go to Jerusalem to speak with the earlier apostles for a period of at least eighteen months, perhaps longer; Acts has him going directly back to Jerusalem after a very brief stint in Damascus (Acts 9:20–30). See P. Fredriksen, "Paul and Augustine: Conversion Narratives . . .", 3–20, for full discussion with bibliography.

15. To complicate matters, the Neoplatonist Porphyry, a sharp critic of Christianity, had lighted on exactly this passage to disparage Peter (who, he said, was guilty of error) and Paul (who was guilty of impudence, in rebuking his senior) as well as the church more generally (because its leaders disagreed among themselves). Jerome's reconstruction of events, borrowing from Origen, sought to discredit Porphyry's critique (*Commentary on Galatians,* preface to book one). For two lively reviews of this quarrel, see E. Plumer, *Augustine's Commentary on Galatians,* 41–53, and O'Donnell, *Augustine,* 92–96.

16. The correspondence between Augustine and Jerome proceeds unevenly throughout the 390s and into the early years of the fifth century (*Letter* 28 in 394–395; *Letter* 40 in 397; *Letter* 71 in, perhaps, 403; *Letter* 75 [Jerome] in 403 or 404; and *Letter* 82, the last of this volley, c. 405). Plumer, *Augustine's Commentary on Galatians,* 47–53, gives a good summary of this correspondence. O'Donnell notes that "Jerome needed both men to be on the right side, but Augustine needed the written text to be truthful" (*Augustine,* 93). On the relevance of this dispute to the Donatist controversy, with which Augustine was simultaneously involved, see R. Cole-Turner, "Anti-Heretical Issues."

17. Allusions to Paul's conversion suddenly appear and cluster in these works in the 390s; see G. LeRoy, "Ac 9,4b dans la prédiction de Saint Augustin," esp. the chart on 17–21.

CHAPTER 8: THE BIBLICAL THEOLOGIAN

1. Behind or beside Tyconius stood the ultimate model of Latin rhetorical performance and analysis, Cicero; see O'Donnell's remarks in *Augustine*, 29. Augustine had reflected on techniques of biblical interpretation in a brief, earlier tractate, *Usefulness of Belief* (c. 391). There he formally introduced terms for analyzing the fourfold sense of the Old Testament: historical (what has been written or done in the past), aetiological (for what reason), analogical (which establishes correspondences between the two testaments), and allegorical (which gives the spiritual sense; *Usefulness of Belief* 3,5). This slim treatise, with its combination of rhetorical analysis, autobiographical retrospect, and anti-Manichaean polemic, anticipates the compositional elements of the *Confessions*. Ultimately, however, his argument in the earlier treatise turns less on exegesis and more on the ways that belief necessarily depends on authority.

2. "Reading and writing," notes Brian Stock, "were among the labours imposed on the first couple as a result of their disobedience in the garden of Eden. They were the consequences of human curiosity and pride. Before the fall, there was no need of such cumbersome instruments of communication. God spoke to Adam and Eve directly, as he did to the Hebrew prophets, or he made his will known without the use of language. Reading and writing arose in time and were to disappear at the end of time, when the soul would be restored to unity with God," *Augustine the Reader*, 15–16.

3. Latin readers, in addition, stood at one linguistic remove from the New Testament, which was written originally in Greek, and at two removes from the Old Testament, translated from a Greek translation of the original Hebrew. And, as Augustine well knew, the Latin translations were numerous, their quality variable. For all these reasons, knowledge of languages helped enormously when interpreting biblical texts (*Christian Teaching* 2.11,16).

4. Augustine drew this image of the Law as a harsh school-slave of immature students from Gal. 3:24, where Paul said, "The Law was our school-slave until Christ came." Tyconius, in *Book of Rules* 3,8, had used Paul's verse similarly (see p. 162 above). Gal. 3:24 RSV gives "custodian" for Paul's *paidagogos*, which the NRSV changes, without improvement, to "disciplinarian." This confuses car pool with class time. A pedagogue was the slave who led the child to school, ensuring that he got to his teacher; he did not himself give instruction. It is interesting that both Tyconius and Augustine had combined Gal. 3:24 with 2 Cor. 3:14, on Christ's removing "the veil" that had obscured the Law (Tyconius in *Book of Rules* 3,9; Augustine in *Usefulness of Belief* 3,9). For both, the combined verses made the point that Christ's coming had done away not with the Law but with the difficulties in understanding and living according to the Law, which had kept the Law restricted to Israel. This verse from 2 Corinthians makes no such appearance in *Christian Teaching*, though it will return a few years later, against the Manichees, in *Against Faustus*.

5. *Usefulness of Belief* 3,9 had also mentioned "useful servitude" to the Law, but

without making the positive points about Jewish observance that Augustine makes here. Tyconius had insisted that Abraham and others were righteous under the Law.

6. See Lancel, *Saint Augustine,* 192–197, on the sermons of 397. J. O'Donnell, *Augustine,* 141, speculates on the awkwardness that Augustine might have felt in being so dependent on Tyconius. "As I have already written repeatedly, I await learning what you think of Tyconius' seven rules or keys" (*Letter* 41,2 Augustine to Bishop Aurelius of Carthage).

7. Paul may be invoked in the rhetorically powerful position at the end of the opening passage of *Conf.* 1.1,1, where Augustine praises God for the gift of his faith, implanted "by the humanity of your Son, and by the ministry of your preacher." Augustine had closed *To Simplicianus* with this same image of Paul as God's chosen preacher (1.2,22). Book eight, which features the dramatic conversion in the garden in Milan, is built on a scaffolding of Pauline reminiscences from Romans; see O'Donnell's commentary, *Confessions* 3:3–71, and his remarks in *Augustine,* 73–80 and (on the historicity of this scene) 348 n. 132.

8. G. Wills accomplishes an extraordinarily simple and lucid description of Augustine's complex thought on this topic in *Saint Augustine,* 88–99.

9. Book eleven in particular is a dense mix of references to Genesis and to Plotinus. On Christ as the timeless Beginning, see *Conf.* 11.4,6–9,11. On time coming into existence only with Creation, see *Conf.* 11.8,12; on the old saw about God preparing hell for people who ask what he was doing before he made the world, see *Conf.* 11.12,14. "You have made time yourself" (*Conf.* 11.13,15). "You are unchangeably eternal," Augustine says to God, "the truly eternal Creator of minds. Just as you knew heaven and earth in the beginning without that bringing any variation into your knowing, so you made heaven and earth in the beginning without that meaning a tension between past and future in your activity," *Conf.* 11.31,41.

10. O'Donnell, on this point, defers to R. M. Pirsig's *Zen and the Art of Motorcycle Maintenance,* 247: "The past exists only in our memories, the future only in our plans. The present is our only reality. The tree that you are aware of intellectually, because of that small time lag, is always in the past and therefore is always unreal" (*Confessions* 3:175).

11. In Romans 7, Paul's "I" is not Paul. It is the rhetorical ego of *prosopopeia* ("speech in character"), whereby the speaker speaks in the persona of someone else, thereby dramatizing his presentation. In his *Notes on Romans,* Augustine understood Paul in Romans 7:14–20 as employing this device: Paul "describes a man who is under the Law, before he has received grace" (*Notes on Romans* 44.1–46.6). Much later, in the closing years of his campaign against the defenders of Pelagius, he will interpret Paul's rhetorical *I* biographically and insist that Paul speaks of his own torment here. Augustine's personally conflicted apostle (constructed in part by his taking deutero-Pauline letters and Acts as descriptive of Paul) was not the Paul of history, who had a very robust sense of self. Krister Stendahl's article famously made this case ("Paul and the Introspective Conscience of the West"); for the details of Augustine's theological transformation of Paul, with full bibliography, see P. Fredriksen, "Paul and Augustine: Conversion Narratives," and "Beyond the Body/Soul Dichotomy."

12. "You [God] were converting me to yourself" (*Conf.* 8.12,30), echoes Augustine's description of Paul's conversion, when he commented on Romans: "If

those things which delight us serve to turn us to God, this is due not to us, but to him" (*To Simplicianus* 1.2,21).

CHAPTER 9: THE WAR OF WORDS

1. Modern New Testament scholarship places Romans chronologically last in the sequence of Paul's extant letters. Faustus' argument for Paul's gradual improvement required a different chronological sequence.

   The Manichees' commitment to Mani as the final revealer and apostle of Christ, together with their theory of textual corruptions in Paul's letters and the gospels, put them in a position of greater scriptural independence vis-à-vis their Christian opponents than Marcion had been vis-à-vis his. At mid-second century, Marcion conceived the idea of a New Testament canon: No definitive collection(s) preceded him. The *Apostolicon*, his edited collection of Paul's letters, reflects this formative period, when Marcion could both name his selection and produce "corrected" versions of their contents.

   Marcion proposed Galatians, 1 and 2 Corinthians, Romans, 1 and 2 Thessalonians, "Laodiceans" (i.e., Ephesians), Colossians, and Philippians. He excluded 1 and 2 Timothy, Titus, and Hebrews. (Evans reconstructs this collection in *Tertullian Adversus Marcionem* 2:644–646.) Marcion, in other words, could shape his version of a closed canon, but he necessarily held many of the Pauline letters themselves, albeit edited, in common with his opponents. And his attitude toward these texts was more urgent than that of the later Manichees, because by the logic of his own theology, both Paul's letters and Luke's gospel, now expurgated (or, as he saw it, restored to their original versions) were necessarily inerrant and totally authoritative.

   By Mani's period and later, however, the catholic New Testament canon was well established. But, having a different historical point of origin for the final or perfect revelation (namely, Mani) and having a different set of canonical texts (namely, those exclusive to Manichaeism), the Manichees were much less invested in orthodoxy's New Testament. For them, these scriptures functioned as apocrypha: relevant to Christianity, yes; but certainly not in themselves authoritative. Accordingly, though Manichees had to consider the entire New Testament collection when debating catholics, the texts themselves were under no pressure to conform to Manichaean revelation. Faustus' nonchalant comments cited in *Against Faustus* 11.1—that either Paul eventually corrected himself or else later Judaizers corrupted his texts and that the catholics' decision on this question was a matter of indifference to him—well reflect his church's greater independence from orthodoxy's texts.

2. Homer's gods, their behaviors, and their cults fueled centuries of argument between pagan Stoic and Platonic philosophers. "The Homeric gods and the whole pantheon could be so discreetly allegorized," notes Henry Chadwick, "as to make it possible for a philosophical mind to continue to worship according to the traditions of his fathers without . . . an undue number of mental reservations. On the other hand the Academy, the successors of Plato . . . developed almost into a professional opposition to all Stoic doctrines and, in particular, to the Stoic defence of the traditional cultus," *Contra Celsum*, x; see also n. 3 following.

3. These standard arguments, yoked to their standard counterarguments, perdured so unchangingly and functioned so adaptively that modern historians can reconstruct the details of much earlier verbal wrestling holds by availing themselves of polemical or apologetic works from much later periods. A famous analogue to Augustine's *Against Faustus,* for example, is the mid-third-century "virtual" disputation by Origen of Alexandria, *Against Celsus.* Celsus, a late-second-century pagan philosopher, had written a critique of Christianity called *On True Doctrine.* In that earlier work, Celsus argued that Christianity was philosophically muddled and intrinsically impious. Sometimes Celsus expresses his views in his own persona, criticizing "barbarian" Judaism together with Christianity; at other times, he presents arguments in the persona of a Jew disparaging Christianity (and in so doing, relates some genuinely Jewish anti-Christian traditions that show up, much later, in the Talmud, e.g., *Against Celsus* 1.32). Origen, several generations later, responds to both genres of criticism.

   "In truth," observes Chadwick in his edition of this work, "the Stoa and the Academy [i.e., Stoic and Platonic philosophers, respectively] had provided arguments and counter-arguments on a wide range of subjects, with the result that we frequently find that where Celsus shows affinity with the Academy, Origen has only to fall back on the traditional refutation provided by the Stoics, and vice versa. . . . Partly in consequence of this continual reference to the debates of the Hellenistic philosophical schools, the *Contra Celsum* is of high interest not merely to the historian of the Christian church but also to the student of Hellenistic philosophy. In respect of some Stoic doctrines, it has been observed that they were first made intelligible by Origen's comments," *Contra Celsum,* x–xi. Further, Origen parries Celsus' criticisms of Judaism (and thus, to some extent, of Christianity) by referring to the apologetic traditions of Hellenistic Jewish writers (such as Philo) against paganism. This (almost three-way) fight makes *Against Celsus* a gold mine for traditions of learned invective.

4. The "forensic, schoolroom approach to the treatment of textual evidence," notes Margaret Mitchell, operated fully among and between well-educated churchmen arguing over interpretation of the Bible. Courtroom language and tactics framed exegetical debates as contesting theologians used "stereotypical characterizations of 'literal' and 'allegorical' readings that were recommended in rhetorical training, as means of substantiating their own case and denigrating that of their opponent" ("Patristic Rhetoric on Allegory," 421; Faustus evidently knew his Cicero, see ibid., 419). His days as a rhetorician superbly prepared Augustine for his work as a theologian and controversialist.

5. See Mitchell, "Patristic Rhetoric," 416. Rabbinic modes of textual interpretation were no less affected by this (originally pagan and Greek) rhetorical environment; on which see esp. P. Alexander, " 'Quid Athenis et Hierosolymis?' "

6. Thus too in the mid-second century, Justin Martyr literarily controlled his encounter with "Trypho the Jew" in his *Dialogue with Trypho;* so too, about eighty years later, Origen presented his arguments against Celsus as if theirs had been a living disputation. "The rhetorical education was the backbone of ancient culture," observes Robert Wilken, "and every intellectual pursuit be-

trayed its influence—the writing of history, philosophy, poetry, theological polemics, biblical commentaries, and, eventually, preaching" (*John Chrysostom and the Jews,* 97; see Wilken's whole discussion in chap. 4, 95–127).

7. Cyprian of Carthage, the mid-third-century bishop of the church that Tertullian purportedly had quit, was said never to pass a day "without reading Tertullian. He frequently said to his secretary, 'Hand me the master,' meaning Tertullian" (So Jerome [Augustine's contemporary], *On Famous Men* 53). Tertullian served as a Latin conduit for much of Justin Martyr's earlier *adversus Iudaeos* arguments in *Dialogue with Trypho* (D. Efroymson, "The Patristic Connection," 100–108).

8. Tertullian, attacking Marcion, particularly revels in the martial language of the *agôn*: "So much for skirmishing: from this point I take up the real battle, fighting hand to hand." From this image he moves directly into an analysis of the "form" and "character" of biblical prose; of the frames of reference particular to "prophetic diction"; and of the abundance of "enigmas, allegories and parables," which of course must be "understood otherwise from the way that they are written" (*Against Marcion* 3.5,1–3; cf. 3.17,2–3, where he expounds on the types and figures through which the Bible codes its mystery [*sacramentum*]. In short, this sort of theological polemic reads like a sportscast mixed in with various grammar lessons, literary criticism, and passing insults to "the Jews."

9. For example, the Jewish text *Avot de-Rabbi Natan* 4.5 relates this story about a conversation between two figures from the period of the Temple's destruction in 70 C.E.: "Once, as Rabbi Jochanan ben Zakkai was coming forth from Jerusalem, Rabbi Joshua followed after him and beheld the Temple in ruins. 'Woe unto us,' cried Rabbi Joshua, 'that this, the place where Israel atoned for its sins, has been destroyed!' But Rabbi Jochanan said to him, 'My son, do not grieve. We have another atonement as effective as this was. What is it? It is acts of loving kindness, as it is said, "I desire mercy and not sacrifice"'(Hosea 6:6)."

10. Centuries before the Hellenistic and Roman empires, when Persia ruled supreme, Jews living in the garrison town of Elephantini on the Nile made offerings in a temple to their god, but by our period that temple was long gone. (Schäfer, *Judeophobia,* relates the historical circumstances of this ancient temple to later traditions of Egyptian anti-Judaism.) The temple in Leontopolis, also in Egypt, was destroyed by the Romans in the wake of the First Revolt (66–73 C.E.). For most of the Hellenistic and all of the Roman period, Jews established no alternate sites of such worship. Mosaics in later Roman-era synagogues present motifs that recall Temple sacrifices and imagery, evidently in an effort to re-create Temple space, thus associating through images and liturgy the synagogue's rituals with those of the Temple. Contemporary church ornamentation used similar motifs to make the counterclaim—namely that Christianity, not Judaism, was the true heir to and incarnation of the sacral traditions preserved in the Old Testament. J. Magness, "Heaven on Earth," provides a fascinating tour of this Christian/Jewish competition, conducted at the level of art and architecture. Theological polemic *against* Jewish cult obviously did not devalue the prestige and power of Temple imagery when the church wished to claim it for itself.

11. "To the Jews arguments of this sort must have appeared fantastic," notes Robert Wilken. "Judaism did not need the city of Jerusalem or the temple to legitimate the observance of the law. Long before the temple was destroyed, for example, Jews had been celebrating Passover outside the city of Jerusalem and in cities throughout the Mediterranean world. . . . [W]ithin Judaism, the destruction of the temple never assumed the theological importance it did in Christianity, and the religious crisis provoked by the loss of Jerusalem was resolved long before the fourth century. There is no trace in Jewish sources that Jews thought the loss of the temple invalidated the observance of the Law" (*John Chrysostom and the Jews*, 151).

    For the prominent place that the Temple's destruction assumed in later Christian anti-Jewish rhetoric, especially within intra-Christian battles over the date of Easter vis-à-vis Passover, now see C. Shepardson, "Paschal Politics."

12. On these works attributed to Cyprian see John Gager, who hears in them "clear echoes of public debate and persistent Jewish criticism" (*The Origins of Anti-Semitism*, 154). William Horbury places them in the context of both intercommunity and intracommunity conflicts in *Jews and Christians in Contact and Controversy*, 180–199, on pseudo-Cyprian's *Against the Jews* in the context of specifically North African *adverus Iudaeos* writings. For a brief survey of the themes and contents of this North African tradition (which includes the contributions of Commodian and Lactantius), see B. Blumenkranz, *Judenpredigt*, 9–43; see also Krauss and Horbury, *Jewish-Christian Controversy*, 13–26 (an analytic survey of themes *adversus Iudaeos*) and 29–43 (a prosopography of Christian anti-Jewish writers).

CHAPTER 10: THE REDEMPTION OF THE FLESH

1. In this initial letter of 394, Augustine cautions that Jerome's theory of the "useful lie" undermines interpretation: "I think that it is extremely dangerous to entertain the idea that the Sacred Books contain any lie anywhere; that is, the idea that the men who composed and wrote the Scriptures may have lied in their own books. . . . If we allow into that supreme authority even a single 'useful' lie, nothing will remain of those books because, whenever anyone finds something in them difficult to do or to believe, he will appeal to this same idea and attribute the passage to the plan or purpose of a lying author" (*Letter* 28.3,3).

    The quotation about the "two orators" comes from Eric Plumer's summary of this dispute (*Augustine's Commentary on Galatians*, 46); it is a close paraphrase of Jerome's point in his Galatians commentary 2:11–13. Still fighting this fight ten years later, Augustine remarks anent this point of Jerome's that he fears less for the apostles if their positions are compared with those of pagan philosophers than he does for the apostles' being compared to "lawyers of the court, when they lie during the trials of others" (*Letter* 82.2,13).

2. "Otherwise," continued Augustine, again taking aim at the argument in Jerome's commentary, "the Holy Scripture, which had been given to preserve the faith of generations to come, would be wholly undermined and thrown into doubt, if the validity of lying were even once admitted" (*Letter*

40.4,5). Augustine's understanding of Paul and Peter's dispute was first articulated in his own commentary, written together with his two early efforts on Romans, in 394–395. He repeated these same points in another treatise that dates from the same period, *About Lying*. In his Galatians commentary, Augustine had also addressed the issue of Paul's circumcising the Christian Timothy, whose mother was Jewish (Acts 16:1–30). Paul "did so to avoid scandalizing his own people. He did not act hypocritically (*simulans*) in any way, but rather he acted out of that indifference with which he says: 'Circumcision is nothing, and uncircumcision is nothing' " (1 Cor. 7:19; *Commentary on Galatians* 41.6). For a spirited account of this controversy from Jerome's vantage, and of the dangers involved in walking the fine line between invoking Judaism to understand Christianity and being perceived as actually Judaizing, see A. Jacobs, *Remains of the Jews*, 57–100, esp. 89–99 (Augustine and Jerome).

3. Justin's creative adaptation of this Jewish tradition did double duty, denouncing not only pagans for their idolatrous cult but also Jews for having had a cult at all. "Within Justin's schema of salvation-history the Jewish relationship with God is distinguished by their exceptional hard-heartedness," notes A. Reed. "Despite God's repeated attempts to guide them towards his will, the Jews respond with chronic, willful disobedience. . . . All of the traditional emblems of Jewish chosenness are here transformed into signs of this nation's exceptional waywardness" ("The Trickery of the Fallen Angels," 155). Reed notes also a distinctly North African line of descent from Justin's argument in the works of Tertullian, Cyprian, and Commodian (ibid., 144).

4. In an earlier treatise, *On the Usefulness of Belief*, Augustine had argued that, while knowledge rests on reason, belief necessarily depends on authority; and he went on to praise the authority of the *catholica*. Such appeals to authority recur frequently throughout his response to Faustus, e.g., *Against Faustus* 13.5 ("The authority of our books, confirmed by the agreement of so many nations, is supported by the succession of apostles, bishops, and councils"), and 11.2 ("The outstanding witness of the catholic church is supported by a succession of bishops from the original seats of the apostles up to the present time").

CHAPTER 11: THE MARK OF CAIN

1. Jon Levenson, *The Death and Resurrection of the Beloved Son,* explores the ways that both groups of interpreters shape this theme of sibling rivalry. Christian comment on Cain as the typological murderer of Christ, notes Lisa Unterseher, is surprisingly scant, whereas this reading of Genesis 4 will be the key exegetical framing for Augustine's "theology of Judaism" ("The Mark of Cain and the Jews"). Her chap. 3 gives a useful survey of pre-Augustinian exegesis on this passage.

2. On Augustine's putative desire that Jews should live a "miserable survival," "oppressed into servitude," see, for example, Jeremy Cohen, *Living Letters of the Law,* 28 and 35; on his teaching as "policy," see 37–65 passim. Cohen also characterizes *Against Faustus* as concerned primarily with the physical protection of Jews (ibid., 39). Marcel Simon asserts that Jews' existing "in misery was a Christian theological desideratum which affected Roman law" (*Verus*

Israel, 227). Legal historian A. M. Rabello states that the specific Christian theological requirement that Jews survive "led to changes in civil law" ("The Legal Condition of the Jews in the Roman Empire," 696). The first mistake—that is, that Augustine thinks that Jews should live in misery—seems to rest on a misreading. Augustine *does* say that Jews should live "with their backs bent down forever." But that is a line from Psalm 69, quoted by Paul in Rom. 11:8. Where Augustine does repeat this line, as in his sermon of Psalm 59, he refers it not to the Jews' social condition, but to their habitual hermeneutical posture: They read the Bible in an earthly way, not in a spiritual way. The second mistake—that Christian theology prompted imperial policy's protection of Jews—attributes to Augustine a prestige and an influence that he certainly did not have in his own lifetime; it wrongly assumes that late Roman Jews lived under a general threat of violence; and it ignores the chronology of Roman legal precedent, which antedates Augustine's lifetime by centuries.

3. Describing the swirl of violence that followed in the wake of Honorius' order, Brown writes, "Augustine and his colleagues stood at the center of this storm. In Carthage, he would preach to great crowds amid cheers of 'Down with the Roman gods!' It is the first time that we see him, a peace-loving man, intensely sensitive to violence, thoroughly caught up in the excitement which his own passionate certainty had done so much to provoke," *Augustine of Hippo,* 231. In his chap. 20, which contains this passage, Brown describes the two cresting waves of anti-Donatist and anti-pagan coercion in North Africa (ibid., 226-232). Markus gives a piercing analysis of Augustine's theology of history during the heady days of the 390s and early 400s (*Saeculum,* 30–42).

4. Did Paul mean *all Israel* when he said "all Israel"? Or did he intend by that phrase only that part of Israel that he (and God) considered truly to be Israel? The commentaries written on this question are varied and endless. I take a maximalist view here; other scholars do not. For a comparison of the two religious thinkers on exactly this point, see P. Fredriksen, "Paul and Augustine: Conversion Narratives, Orthodox Traditions, and the Retrospective Self." A conviction similar to Paul's was voiced by other Jews almost two centuries later. Mishnah Sanhedrin 10.1 proclaims, "All Israel has a place in the world to come"—and then proceeds immediately to list the exceptions ("And these shall have no place . . .").

5. The first chapter of Romans is Paul's indictment of pagan culture. It is a classic passage of Hellenistic Jewish rhetoric, a "sin list" of the moral consequences of gentile idol worship. Augustine's reuse of Rom. 1:24 here puts it in a prophetic context, whereby Paul's dark allusion to pagan sexual misconduct serves to justify the divine condemnation of all Israel, except for that part called by grace—like the apostles; like Paul; like whoever in future generations converts to the true church—who represent the chosen remnant (Rom. 9:6-24; 11:6).

CHAPTER 12: "SLAY THEM NOT . . ."

1. F. van der Meer nicely observes that Latin Christian art had reinforced the imagery of the older Latin translation. "We know well what was behind this

[the near-riot in Oea]. For nearly two hundred years Christians in the west had seen a certain picture on graves, sarcophagi, church walls, and innumerable other places. It was the little slender figure of the prophet [Jonah] stretched out naked and fast asleep under the *cucurbita* with the hanging gourds: one arm was nearly always over his head and his legs were crossed, and the whole manner of presentation suggested an Endymion who has somehow wandered off into the pages of the Bible," *Augustine the Bishop,* 341; for photographs of sculptures of the heroically nude prophet, buff and beardless, ibid., after p. 296).

2. Augustine was hard pressed to come up with a justification for Jerome's project of translation from the Hebrew. If the Western churches adopted Jerome's version, they would be out of synch with the churches of the East, which clung to the Septuagint; and whenever someone challenged Jerome's text, it would be easily shown not to agree with the traditional Greek, which could be produced and was a language that many people (not Augustine, though!) were comfortably familiar with. "But if anyone is upset by something unfamiliar in the translation from the Hebrew, and he raises the charge of falsification, he will rarely or never have access to the Hebrew texts by which your translation might be defended. But even if one did have access, who would tolerate the condemnation of so many Latin and Greek authorities? And in addition, even the Hebrews, when consulted, might offer a different response, . . . and who would be the judge?" (*Letter* 70.2,4).

   S. Lancel synopsizes the problems that Augustine's lack of Greek caused for his work on the Trinity (*Saint Augustine,* 377–380). For the most recent word on Augustine's knowledge of Greek, see O'Donnell, *Augustine,* 126.

3. Orthodox writers who specialized in describing and denouncing heretics usually provide a much clearer view of their own concerns than of the practices, beliefs, and occasionally even of the existence, of those other Christians whom they condemn. In the mid-second century, for example, Justin remarks on the existence of Jews who hold Christian beliefs but who still live according to the Law. Such people, he continues, sometimes prevail upon gentile Christians to Judaize as well. Justin thinks that members of both groups will be saved, though he acknowledges that other Christians do not share his views (*Dialogue with Trypho,* 47). By the end of that same century, Irenaeus condemned a similar group as "heretics." These people, he said, still practice circumcision; live according to Jewish tradition; and insist that Jesus was fully and normally human, albeit also the messiah who was crucified and raised. Irenaeus labels such heretics "Ebionites" (*Against Heresies* 1.26,2; 3.21,1; 5.1,3).

   The word *Ebionite* is related to a Hebrew word *evioni 'im* ("the poor"), a self-designation, perhaps, of the ancient community in Jerusalem. (Paul in his letters mentions collecting from his diaspora assemblies to give to "the poor back in Jerusalem"; Rom. 15:26; also Gal. 2:10.) Accustomed to naming heretical sects after their ostensible founder (Valentinus founded the Valentinians, Marcion founded the Marcionites, and so on), heresiologists eventually buried this Hebrew connection to "the poor" beneath their conviction that the sect had been established by that notorious heresiarch, Ebion. By the late fourth century, these heresiological discussions have a Talmudic quality: Are these heresies actual groups? Or are they categories—that is, abstract boundary markers, a theoretical assemblage of various notions of what would make a group unacceptable to orthodoxy? See especially H. I. Newman's article, "Jerome's Judaizers," for a thoughtful review of the arguments and the evidence.

4. The "potential for misunderstanding and inter-religious strife" is intrinsic to such efforts at self-definition, by which a hostile caricature of the "other" group provides the building blocks of one's own identity. A. Jacobs observes that, in antiquity, "such confrontation and argumentation was not the unfortunate consequence of the Christian appropriation of a superlative Jewish voice, but rather the goal of this attempt to construct a theological self out of the haunting difference of the other" ("A Jew's Jew," 258–286; on "originary Jewishness," 261). Eusebius reports the story about the originally Hebrew Gospel of Matthew (*The History of the Church* 3.24,5). Of course, the gospels and Paul's letters, with their occasional outcroppings of Hebrew and Aramaic, make the same point. On the authenticating Jews of Christian relic legends, see G. Stemberger, *Jews and Christians in the Holy Land,* 58–59; O. Limor, "Christian Sacred Space and the Jew." Finally, Robert Wilken offers a panoramic view of the Christianization of Jewish sites in Roman Palestine in *Land Called Holy.*

5. Isaiah 7:14 LXX and its relation to the Hebrew text long remained a sore spot. Origen gives a (faulty) philological defense of translating *'aalmah* as "virgin" on the basis of other texts in Deuteronomy, and then makes a more commonsense argument: "What kind of sign would it be if a 'young girl' rather than a 'virgin' bore a son?" (*Against Celsus* 1.34–35; so similarly Tertullian, *Against Marcion* 3.13). On this particular passage, see A. Kamesar, "The Virgin of Isaiah 7:14." Scholars have established that Christians and Jews communicated, quarreled, and learned from each other while interpreting their respective Bibles: see in particular the works of A. Kamesar, N. de Lange (for Origen), J. Lieu, W. Horbury, A. Salvensen, and M. Hirshman. Rabbinic sources for their part evince familiarity with Christian concerns. *Tanhuma Va-yera* 6, a late commentary, relates: "Moses requested that the Mishnah be written down, too [that is, as the Torah was written]. But the Holy One, blessed be he, foresaw that in the days to come the nations of the world would translate the Torah and read it in Greek and say, 'We are Israel.' " (Thanks to my colleague Jesper Svartvik for bringing this text to my attention.) See also W. Horbury's discussion of the story reported in the Babylonian Talmud about Abbahu, a fourth-century rabbi in Caesarea: Because they live cheek by jowl with *minim* in the Land of Israel, Jews there study the Bible closely, says Abbahu, whereas Babylonian Jews, absent *minim,* do not (bAvodah Zarah 4a; Horbury, "Jews and Christians," 204–205).

6. A. Jacobs provides a sharp and lively analysis of the battle between Jerome and his nemesis Rufinus over Origen, Hebrew language, and Judaizing in *Remains of the Jews,* 71–90; on Augustine and Jerome, see 90–100.

7. "I give unceasing thanks to my teacher," said Faustus at the start of book sixteen, "who prevented me from falling into this error, so that I am still a Christian." And he concludes, "The wise teaching of Mani rescued me from danger" (*Against Faustus* 16.1 and 5).

8. The sequence of Augustine's formal writings can be gleaned with relative se-

curity from his review of these in the *Retractations*. Augustine offered that work in part as a critical consideration of his own theological development, not as a chronological record of it, though he does state his intention to review his works in the order in which he composed them (*Retractations*, prologue 3). The particular dates assigned to these writings are less secure, the (vaguely canonical) chronology more wobbly since P.-M. Hombert published *Nouvelles recherches de chronologie augustinienne* in 2000. The dating of sermons and letters, in light of the new discoveries of twenty years ago, now has to be entirely reviewed: a huge undertaking. My narrative here depends on the relative sequence or the clustering of Augustine's works, not their absolute dating; and some dates—like Honorius' orders in 399, or the Gothic sack of Rome in 410—do provide external set points by which to get our bearings. The major biographies of Augustine usually include a chronology. Brown's *Augustine of Hippo*, though now dated, usefully attempts to coordinate dates in broader late Roman history with events in Augustine's life and with the appearance of his works; see the more recent, Lancel, *St. Augustine*, 531–536, with considerable discussion in the body of the book. For the older dating of the sermons and letters, see A. Fitzgerald, *Augustine through the Ages*, s.v. "Sermones" and "Epistulae," with clear charts. These dates, as the ones given for individual writings in this last reference work, are less certain than its articles sometimes have them appear.

9. *Against the Jews* has usually been dated to the last five years of Augustine's life. Lancel, tying the sermon's themes in with the points that Augustine makes in *Letter* 196 to Asellicus, suggests instead the years 418–419. I see no way of settling the question; but the sermon must date to some time after the composition of *Letter* 121 to Paulinus of Nola.

10. This paragraph and the next relies on D. Efroymson's careful examination and analysis ("Whose Jews?"; the quotation is from p. 198).

11. "The Jews of Roman North Africa," notes Karen Stern, "figure strangely in the historical record—attestations of their presence in Africa are simultaneously frequent and scarce. Christian authors commonly announce that African towns teem with Jews, who are their distinct rivals and antitheses . . . [but] in contrast, only sporadic discoveries of Jewish archaeological materials have attested to the settlement of Jews in North Africa during the late antique period" ("Inscribing Devotion and Death in Context," 1). Stern goes on to reread the record of the material remains. Older sources on this question of the distribution of Jews in Roman North Africa include J. W. Hirschberg, *History of the Jews in North Africa* (with a map indicating Jewish settlement, 1:22), and Y. Le Bohec, "Inscriptions juives et judaïsantes de l'Afrique romaine," reviewing archaeological data. Still valuable also is T. Barnes, *Tertullian*, s.v. "Jews," updated by W. Horbury's essays on Tertullian collected in *Jews and Christians in Contact and Controversy*. More recent studies include Lancel, *Saint Augustine*, 356 and 519 n. 24; J. B. Rives, *Religion and Authority in Roman Carthage*, 214–223, with a clear discussion of the inscriptional material; J.-M. Lassère, *Ubique Populus*, on various North African settlements; and two essays by C. Setzer, "Jews, Jewish Christians and Judaizers in North Africa" and "Jews in Carthage and Western North Africa, 70–235 C.E."

12. Rhetorical techniques—speaking in the voice of a second author or character, conjuring an opponent by directly addressing him or them, enacting a debate

or diatribe—enlivened Christian sermons. There are now many fine studies on this topic. On Augustine's oral presentation of Paul, see T. Martin, *"Vox Pauli."* More broadly, looking at these techniques as learned "ventriloquism," Jacobs, "A Jew's Jew"; and M. Mitchell, "Patristic Rhetoric on Allegory," and her ample examination, more specifically, of Chrysostom, Augustine's contemporary, *The Heavenly Trumpet.* The text of *Sermon* 196.4 seems unarguably to indicate the Jewish population of Hippo (*Christiana est civitas, duo genera hominum hic sunt . . .*). So, for example, see F. van der Meer, *Augustine the Bishop,* 77; T. Raveaux, "Augustinus über den jüdischen Sabbat seiner Zeit," 215; and B. Blumenkranz, *Judenpredigt,* 60 n. 2.

13. Of all the innovations that Constantine's act of patronage brought to both church and state, his decision in 318 to empower bishops to serve as a type of alternative judiciary was one of the most consequential (*Theodosian Code* 1.27,1). Lancel has an excellent chapter on the legal, social, and financial intricacies and burdens that Augustine's role as clerical magistrate involved him in (*Saint Augustine,* 259–270). On Constantine's agenda in so empowering bishops, and his desire to find a way around the clogged and corrupt mechanisms of imperial governance in the early fourth century, see esp. Drake, *Constantine and the Bishops,* 315–346.

14. *Letter* *8 comes from a cache of twenty-nine of Augustine's letters that were discovered by Johannes Divjak and published in 1981. The edition of the *Bibliothèque augustinienne* vol. 46B has a clear translation and valuable notes. For discussion of this particular letter, see H. Castritius, "The Jews of North Africa at the time of Augustine of Hippo," and, by the same author, generously annotated, " 'Seid weder den Juden noch den Heiden noch der Gemeinde Gottes ein Ärgernis.' "

15. References in Augustine's works to Jews as the keepers of the holy books have recently been collected and analyzed in an excellent essay by G. Folliet, "Iudaei tamquam capsarii nostri sunt," 443–450. Folliet, using the unusual word *capsarius* as a tracer, follows the reception of this idea in post-Roman and later medieval works (ibid., 450–457). Already by the late sixth century, we find an addition to Augustine's original idea that in hindsight seems ominous. Commenting on Psalm 59, Cassiodorus opined that perhaps the Jews are dispersed so that by study (presumably of the books that they carry) "they might be roused [or "provoked"] to convert" (*Exposition on the Psalms* 58:12; Folliet, "Capsarii nostri sunt," 451). Augustine himself never suggested such a thing; for him, God has "disenabled" most Jews from such understanding.

16. "The patristic comments attest to a clear and widespread Christian inclination to recognize the Jewish norm of biblical literature, and therewith the position of the Jews as hereditary custodians of scripture," Horbury, "Jews and Christians on the Bible," 211. In this connection Horbury cites F. C. Burkitt's observation that "the Church was singularly willing to accept the verdict of Jewish scholarship, even at the cost of abandoning famous proof-texts" (217).

17. Some scholars insist, against his own clear statements to the contrary, that Augustine anticipated the salvation of all the Jews at the end of time. Thus, for example, Michael Signer in his article "Jews and Judaism," in *Augustine through the Ages,* 472; most recently, J. Cohen, "The Mystery of Israel's Salvation," 276. In the same essay, Cohen labors over Origen's reading of Romans 9–11 as well, finally concluding—rightly, in this case—that Origen expected

the final redemption of all Jews (255–263). But how significant is this? As we shall shortly see, Origen anticipated the final redemption of *all* rational beings: stars, planets, demons, and even Satan himself (p. 332 above). If God saves absolutely "everyone," then, of course, he saves Jews too.

I have no general explanation for this misinterpretation of the scope of Augustine's vision of Jewish salvation. Perhaps because of all the positive things that Augustine says about Jews or about "Jews," it seems counterintuitive that he would be so hard line on this issue. But he is. It is consistent with his stance on the broader question: Most of humanity, *including most Christians,* are not among the saved, either (*Letter* 149.2,19 to Paulinus, quoted on p. 328 above). Apart from those writings of his already cited, we can look to his definitive position in *City of God,* where he repeats (quoting Paul quoting Isaiah) that in the End "only a remnant will be saved" (Rom. 11:5; *City of God* 18.46). In book twenty, he resumes discussion of the eschatological fate of the Jews. The Jews who will repent on "that day"—that is, on the apocalyptic final day—will be those "who will receive 'the spirit of grace and mercy.'" Unlike their impious parents, who gloated over Christ and who murdered him, those Jews who receive "the spirit of grace and mercy, being now members of the faith, *will not be condemned along with their impious parents*" (*City of God* 20.30). "All Israel" that is saved is a theological category indicating those Jews and those Christians who together are predestined to redemption. "All Israel" as a religious/social/ethnic category, "*the* Jews," is not saved.

18. Again, by human standards, holding people culpable for the crime of a distant ancestor would be unjust. But Augustine thinks realistically about inherited, intergenerational wrong-doing. His statement here about the Jews and the crucifixion simply parallels his more fundamental position that held all humanity to be justly and universally damned in Eden because all were "in Adam" (p. 170f above). This realism eventually sponsors his teaching, against Pelagius, on "original sin" properly so-called (see n. 20 following).

19. Origen lays out these positions in *On First Principles,* which was the first effort ever at a systematic theology—that is, at framing a system wherein different doctrinal positions were coherently coordinated. For a comparison of Paul, Origen, and Augustine on sin and the body, see P. Fredriksen and C. Shepardson, "Embodiment and Redemption"; for a comparison of the way that Origen and Augustine each understands Paul on the question of salvation, see P. Fredriksen, "The Philosopher's Paul and the Problem of Anachronism."

20. The damnation of unbaptized babies is the logical end point of Augustine's realistic interpretation of all humanity's being "in Adam": The damage caused by Adam's disobedience was inherited by all generations thereafter, rendering all humanity the *massa damnata.* His reasoning on unbaptized babies runs like this: To be saved, one must be "in Christ." To be in Christ, one must be baptized. Therefore, the unbaptized are not saved, because they are not in Christ. But such condemnation of the unbaptized would not be just if they had committed no sin; therefore, since God is just, the unbaptized must have sinned. Babies, too young to have committed a sin of their own, accordingly must have the sin of another. That sin must be the sin of Adam, because these babies were also in Adam. Church liturgy supports this view, for babies are baptized *in remissione peccatorum,* "for the remission of sins." Augustine's Pelagian opponents argued that this line of reasoning proved the opposite:

Such a god would be a caricature of justice. An overview of how Augustine thought himself into this position may be found in P. Fredriksen, "Beyond the Body/Soul Dichotomy." For Augustine's pre-Pelagian articulation of this view on unbaptized babies, see *A Literal Commentary on Genesis* 10.11,19. For his sharper statement of the same idea in the course of that later controversy, see e.g., *Christ's Grace and Original Sin* 2.40,45.

On the effects of the Origenist controversy and of its Latin avatar, the Pelagian controversy, Elizabeth Clark notes: "With the condemnation of both Origenism and Pelagianism, the last chance for a fruitful unification of Eastern and Western Christianity met with defeat. Their condemnation made effective in the West the flourishing of a Christian theology whose central concerns were human sinfulness, not human potentiality; divine determination, not human freedom and responsibility; God's mystery, not God's justice" (*The Origenist Controversy*, 250). For the ways that Jerome was involved in these arguments, see ibid., 159–193; for the way that the Pelagian controversy represents a Latin transmutation of the quarrels around Origen, see ibid., 194–244.

21. See Fredriksen, "Apocalypse and Redemption in Early Christianity," for a review of this aspect of ancient Christian political theology, with full notes.

22. There is a noticeable and important distinction between Eusebius' reuse of biblical imagery and Augustine's, visible even in the tiny sample from both men that we have here. When Eusebius conjures the rebuilt messianic Jerusalem, that "messiah" corresponds to Jerusalem's current contractor, Constantine. When Augustine applies Luke's Parable of the Great Banquet to the situation vis-à-vis the Donatists, the emperors, like the bishops, are represented by the text's "servants." See Markus, *Saeculum*, 45–52, for especially clear and concise observations.

23. Robert Markus' great classic *Saeculum* remains the premier discussion of this aspect of Augustine's mature thinking, his "secularization" of the church, 105–132; of the empire, 45–104; and of the times, 1–4. (These three themes are summarized in ibid., chap. 6.) Augustine's intellectual accomplishment in this regard sits oddly next to my generalization about happy and unhappy gods, happy and unhappy humans. If current circumstances do not in principle signal divine will, then human happiness or unhappiness becomes even more contingent. (Nothing to do either way.) And if the entire relationship with the deity is defined by the universal consequences of an ancient sin, the god's emotional vacillations are unreadable, unknowable, and moot.

24. Brown provides elegiac reflection on the associations available in Augustine's use of *peregrinatio* as definitive of current Christian experience (*Augustine of Hippo*, chap. 27, "Civitas Peregrina").

25. This interpretation vigorously dissents from the one offered by Jeremy Cohen, *Living Letters of the Law.* In his first chapter, Cohen names six elements that supposedly describe Augustine's "Doctrine of Jewish Witness": Only when five of the six are present, Cohen says, is Augustine's thought fully mature or fully realized (*Living Letters* 41). The point of his chart on p. 41 is to establish the late date of Augustine's "full doctrine" and thus to create the strongest contrast possible between his earlier writings and his later works. Two of these themes, Cohen claims, do not show up in *Against Faustus* at all, namely, (1) "Ps 59:12, 'Slay them not': Christians must let Jews live as Jews" and (2) "Jews must be refuted in proof of Christianity" even if they will not admit

defeat because they cannot understand what they read. A third theme—(3) that Jewish perseverance in their own religious customs, despite Greek and, later, Roman hegemony is praiseworthy and of testimonial value—does indeed appear in *Against Faustus*, Cohen says, but it is "less than fully explicit."

1. Cohen's misconstrual of "Cain" contributes to some of the oddities of his chart, though it does not explain all of them. As we have seen, Augustine cites Psalm 59 only quite late; but when he does, it is to *exactly* the same point that he made in evoking Genesis 4:15 earlier—namely, that Christians must not force Jews to abandon the practice of Judaism. In *Letter* 149.1,9, Augustine explains Psalm 59 by reference to Cain in Genesis 4:15, and he states there his interpretation of what both of these passages condemn: the separation of Jews from Jewish practice. So, while Psalm 59 does not appear in *Against Faustus*, the idea that "Christians must let Jews live as Jews" certainly does (*Against Faustus* 12.12–13).

2. "Refuting Jews from scripture even though they cannot understand," Cohen claims, is a theme missing from *Against Faustus*. In fact, Augustine does encourage Christians to undertake this exercise in *Against Faustus*. Christians should cite all the Old Testament prophecies to the Jews, he says there; and because the Jews know biblical literature intimately, "we can argue with them about actual events," even though Jews are divinely prevented from understanding (*Against Faustus* 12.44).

3. Cohen claims that the theme that Jewish loyalty to their Law is praiseworthy, and that this loyalty enhances their service of witness to the church, is "only implicitly present" in *Against Faustus*. But Augustine forthrightly states there that this Jewish loyalty is *revera multum mirabile*, "a miracle to be greatly in awe of" (*Against Faustus* 12:13). Exiled Israel, loyal to their Law, provides a uniquely valuable service of witness to the church (*Against Faustus* 12.23).

In sum, even by Cohen's own measure—namely, these themes that he identifies—*Against Faustus*, alone of all the texts he lists, expresses all six themes. The only item lacking is the citation to Psalm 59; but the meaning of Psalm 59 is given in Augustine's exegesis of the mark of Cain.

26. "Scripture for Augustine is as much a source of understanding as of data. Hence one striking and regular feature of his procedure is easily misconstrued: his reliance on proof-texts. Especially in works composed between his conversion [in 386] and his succession to Valerius in the see of Hippo [396], Augustine will often work out a theory or doctrine without undue reliance on any particular biblical text. Later in life, sometimes much later, he will come upon a text which seems a peculiarly appropriate support for the position already reached. When that happens, Augustine will often resort to quoting the newly discovered text mentioning neither the other texts which had previously led him to form the doctrine in question nor arguments on which the doctrine could be, and was, independently based," John Rist, *Augustine*, 20.

Rist goes on to note the career of Rom. 5:12 in Augustine's late theology (see also ibid., 124 n. 93). In the instance of Psalm 59, we luckily have the in-between stages preserved in Augustine's two sermons on that psalm and in his letter to Paulinus, wherein the interpretation of the psalm is tied to his understanding of Cain in Genesis 4.

EPILOGUE

1. Markus provides copious references to Augustine's own writings that justify anti-pagan coercion (*Saeculum*, 29–38). Another violent incident occurred nine years later at Calama, during which Christian clergy attempted to disrupt a pagan religious procession, and in turn, the pagans attacked the attackers, among whom was Possidius, Augustine's protégé and eventual biographer (*Letters* 90 and 91). Augustine insisted that the pagans be punished (ibid. 91.2). See also J. O'Donnell's remarks (*Augustine*, 185–190).

2. In Brown, *Augustine of Hippo*, chaps. 19–21 and 28 narrate the course of this controversy *in nuce;* see also Stephen Mitchell's more recent discussion in *A History of the Later Roman Empire*, chap. 8, on the post-Constantinian politics of religious identity; for the Donatists in particular, see 279–282.

3. Many of these laws hit the wealthy where it hurt most: in the pocketbook. Brown comments: "The Imperial laws fell erratically on African society. They drove a wedge between rich and poor, town and countryside. The Donatists lost their bishops and the support of the upper classes. One landowner, Celer, had had poems inscribed in his honor in the forum. Now he found out that, as a Donatist, he could not hold office, that he could not protect his property by litigation nor pass it on to his heirs by valid testament. After 405, therefore, such men found it wise to conform to the established religion," *Augustine of Hippo*, 240–241.

4. Brent Shaw, "African Christianity," provides a wonderful analysis of the council of Carthage in 411; S. Lancel, who established the critical text of the council's transcripts, describes the catholic strategy in *Saint Augustine*, 289–307. See too O'Donnell, *Augustine*, 229–245.

5. Augustine invokes God's hidden justice in this connection, too: "God, through a secret though just design [*occulta dispositione . . . sed iusta*], has predestined some people to the ultimate penalty [that is, damnation]. It is doubtless better, then, if the overwhelming majority of the Donatists were collected and reabsorbed . . . while the few perish in their own flames. Better that, truly, than that all Donatists, on account of their sacrilegious dissent, be burned in the fires of Hell" (*Letter* 204.2), said in regard to the suicidal coup de théâtre of Timgad's Donatist bishop.

6. "We have no context to explain how or why the Jews there could have had the temerity to beat an archdeacon publicly in the city's theatre," comments F. Millar about this incident from 435 C.E. ("Jews in the Greek East," 5). On the centrally located Jewish buildings (Sardis in Lydia, Aphrodisias in Caria, Apamea in Syria II, and Gerasa in Roman Arabia), see ibid., 7–14. S. Bradbury reviews the evidence on Jewish/Christian riots, and names ten cities where destruction or "hostile take-overs" of synagogues occurred or are reported as having occurred: The sites range from the edge of Persia (Callinicum) to the Italian peninsula and North Africa to Minorca (Magona; *Letter of Severus*, 53–54); see too the older itemization in J. Juster, *Les Juifs dans l'empire romain*, 1:464 n. 3. Imperial directives that reassert Jewish prerogatives appear in the *Theodosian Code* 16.8.9 (in 393 C.E.), 8.12 (in 397), 8.20 (in 412), and 8.25–27 (in 423). As Bradbury notes, "The very repetition of these laws indicates the recurrence of the problem" (*Letter of Severus* 54); but it also indicates the emperors' resolve to reduce occasions of urban vi-

olence. On Roman law and the Jews, most recently, see A. Linder, "The Legal Status of the Jews in the Roman Empire." This legislation creates its own kind of trompe-l'oeil. Gathered into grand compendia such as the *Theodosian Code* and the *Code of Justinian* in the fifth and sixth centuries, these earlier laws originated as letters and thus as discrete communications sent to particular imperial officers in one part or another of the empire; see esp. Millar, "Jews in the Greek East," 4; and Millar, *A Greek Roman Empire,* 7–13, and passim.

7. "The simple fact that the patronage network in Magona began with the head of the synagogue would have had far-reaching implications for the general prestige of the Jewish minority and their interaction with the Christian majority," S. Bradbury observes (*Letter of Severus* 43). He provides a rich and full description and analysis of Minorca's Jewish gentry in the introduction to his critical edition of Severus' letter (ibid., 25–43).

    Severus describes Theodorus' young sister-in-law, Artemisia, as a *femina nobilissima,* "a woman of the highest rank" (*Letter of Severus* 24.1). Through her, Theodorus' family was related to Litorius, a recent past governor of the Balearic Islands and currently a high military officer and count. Evidence about Litorius, intriguingly, cannot settle the question of his own religious affiliation, whether Christian, Jewish, or pagan. (Bradbury considers this last identification the least likely; ibid., 37). If Litorius, Artemisia's father, were Jewish, he provides another conspicuous example of the imperial government's not enforcing its own laws: Jews had been debarred from high military and civic offices since 408 (*Code of Theodosius* 16.8.16; the ban was repeated in 418, in 424, and again in 438). Finally, Severus speaks about another member of this family group, Innocentius, who was learned both in Jewish Law and in Latin and Greek literature (*Letter of Severus* 18.15). Pagans are curiously absent from Severus' narrative, perhaps, as Bradbury suggests (ibid., 29) because they play no role in the events of February 418.

8. See Bradbury, *Letter of Severus* 16–25, on traditions surrounding the discovery of Stephen's relics. Severus mentions that the Christians' first approach *en force* to the Jews of Magona occurred when Theodorus "by chance" was off the island. Summoned home, Theodorus "returned and frightened many people by his authority, and although he did not extinguish our ardor for the struggle, he did calm it for a little while" (*Letter of Severus* 7.1–2). Severus (or Consentius, his ghost writer) loads his description of events with the vocabulary of martial engagement: The two populations are "two armies" (6.4); their engagement is a "war" (7.3); Christian arguments are "weapons prepared in advance as the battle loomed" (8.1). Except for some stone throwing, however, actual violence seems directed to the synagogue building and not to Jews themselves (though see 13.10–12, a happy incident caused by an errant stone).

9. "Certain miraculous things," Consentius explains to Augustine, "were performed among us at the bidding of the Lord. When the blessed priest, the brother of your Paternity, Bishop Severus, along with others who had been present, recounted these things to me, he broke down my resolution [Consentius had resolved not to essay literary compositions] by the great force of his love, and he borrowed from me some words and phrases—no more than

that—so that he could write a letter that contained the narrative of these events" (*Letter* *12.13.5-6).

10. S. Bradbury discusses this collection of Stephen's miracles in his edition, *Letter of Severus*, 13-14. For Augustine's efforts against millenarian expectations, see Fredriksen, "Apocalypse and Redemption in Early Christianity"; specifically in regard to Jewish conversion, see S. Bradbury, *Letter of Severus*, 43-57.

11. See P. Fredriksen, "Secundum Carnem," for full argument and references.

━━ PRIMARY BIBLIOGRAPHY ━━

AUGUSTINE

Only those works of Augustine's that figure importantly in *Augustine and the Jews* appear here, cited according to my English title together with the standard Latin title and with a readily available English translation.

A full list of Augustine's works, together with their various editions and translations, may be found in the one-volume encyclopedia *Augustine through the Ages,* edited by Allan Fitzgerald (Grand Rapids, MI: Eerdmans 1999). Interested readers might also consult the saint's own website, maintained by James J. O'Donnell of Georgetown University: www9.georgetown.edu/faculty/jod/augustine. Collections of Latin texts and English translations are linked to that page.

About Lying (de mendacio)
    Deferrari, R. *Saint Augustine: Treatises on Various Subjects.* Fathers of the Church. Vol. 16. Washington, DC: Catholic University of America Press, 1952.
Against the Academics (contra academicos)
    O'Meara, John J. *Against the Academics.* Ancient Christian Writers 12. New York: Newman Press, 1951.
Against Faustus (contra Faustum Manichaeum)
    Stothert, R. *Reply to Faustus the Manichaean.* Nicene and Post-Nicene Fathers, 155–345. Series 1. Vol. 4. Grand Rapids, MI: Eerdmans, 1974. Originally published 1872.
Against Fortunatus (acta seu disputatio contra Fortunatum Manichaeum)
    Newman, A. H. *Acts or Disputation against Fortunatus the Manichee.* Nicene and Post-Nicene Fathers, 113–124. Series 1. Vol. 4. Grand Rapids, MI: Eerdmans, 1974. Originally published 1872.
Answer to Petilian (contra litteras Petiliani Donatistae)
    King, J. R. *Answer to the Letters of Petilian, Bishop of Cirta.* Nicene and Post-Nicene Fathers, 519–628. Series 1. Vol. 4. Grand Rapids, MI: Eerdmans, 1974. Originally published 1872.
Answers to Simplicianus (de diversis quaestionibus ad Simplicianum)
    Burleigh, J. H. S. "To Simplicianus," *Augustine: Earlier Writings,* 376–406. Philadelphia: Westminster, 1953.
Christian Teaching (de doctrina christiana)
    Green, R. P. H. *De Doctrina Christiana.* Oxford: Clarendon Press, 1995.

Christ's Grace and Original Sin (de gratia Christi et de peccato originali)
Schaff, Philip. Nicene and Post-Nicene Fathers. Series 1. Vol. 5. New York: Christian Literature Publications, 1886.

City of God (de civitate Dei)
Bettenson, Henry. *City of God.* New York: Penguin Books, 1972.

Commentary on Galatians (epistolae ad Galatas expositio)
Plumer, E. A. *Augustine's Commentary on Galatians.* Oxford: Oxford University Press, 2003.

Confessions (Confessiones)
Sheed, F. J. *The Confessions of St. Augustine.* New York: Sheed & Ward, 1943.
Wills, Garry. *Confessions.* New York: Penguin Group USA, 2006.
Chadwick, Henry. *Confessions.* New York: Oxford University Press, 1991.
O'Donnell, James J. *Augustine: Confessions.* 3 vols. Oxford: Clarendon Press, 1992.

Faith and the Creed (de fide et symbolo)
Burleigh, J. H. S. *Augustine: Earlier Writings,* 349–369. Philadelphia: Westminster, 1953.

Faith in Things Unseen (de fide rerum invisibilium)
Campbell, Michael G. *Faith in the Unseen. The Works of Saint Augustine.* I/8. Hyde Park, NY: New City Press, 2005.

Free Will (de libero arbitrio)
Burleigh, J. H. S. *Augustine: Earlier Writings,* 106–217. Philadelphia: Westminster, 1953.

Genesis, against the Manichees (de Genesi contra manichaeos)
Teske, Roland J. *Saint Augustine on Genesis.* Fathers of the Church 84. Washington, DC: Catholic University of America Press, 1991.

Letters (epistulae)
Teske, Roland J. *The Works of Saint Augustine.* II/1–4. Hyde Park, NY: New City Press, 2001–2005.

Literal Interpretation of Genesis (de Genesi ad litteram)
Taylor, J. H. *The Literal Meaning of Genesis.* Ancient Christian Writers 41–42. New York: Newman Press, 1982.

Manichaean Morals (de moribus Manichaeorum)
Stothert, R. *The Morals of the Manichees.* Nicene and Post-Nicene Fathers, 65–89. Series 1. Vol. 4. Grand Rapids, MI: Eerdmans, 1974. Originally published 1872.

Morals of the Church (de moribus ecclesiae catholicae)
Stothert, R. *The Morals of the Church.* Nicene and Post-Nicene Fathers, 37–63. Series 1. Vol. 4. Grand Rapids, MI: Eerdmans, 1974. Originally published 1872.

Notes on Romans (expositio 84 propositionum ex epistola ad Romanos)
Fredriksen, Paula. *Augustine on Romans.* Society of Biblical Literature, Text and Translation Series, 3–39. Chico, CA: Scholars Press, 1982.

On Order (de ordine)
Russell, Robert P. *Divine Providence and the Problem of Evil.* Fathers of the Church 1. Washington, DC: Catholic University Press, 1948.

On the Two Souls, against the Manichees (de duabus animabus contra manichaeos)
Teske, Roland. *The Two Souls. The Works of Saint Augustine,* 117–134. I/19. The Manichaean Debate. Hyde Park, NY: New City Press, 2006.

On Various Questions (de diversis 83 quaestionibus)
Mosher, David. *Eighty-Three Different Questions.* Fathers of the Church 70. Washington, DC: Catholic University of America Press, 1982.

Retractations (retractationes)
   Bogan, Mary I. *The Retractations.* Fathers of the Church 60. Washington, DC:
      Catholic University of America Press, 1968.
Sermon against the Jews (Tractatus adversus Iudaeos)
   Ligouri, M. *Sermon against the Jews.* Fathers of the Church 27, 387–414.
      Washington, DC: Catholic University of America Press, 1955.
Sermons (sermones)
   E. Hill, *Sermons. The Works of Saint Augustine.* III/1–11. Hyde Park, NY: New City
      Press, 1990–1997.
Sermons on the Gospel of John (Tractatus in evangelium Iohannis)
   Rettig, John W. *Tractates on the Gospel of John.* Fathers of the Church 78–79, 88, 90,
      92. Washington, DC: Catholic University of America Press, 1988–1995.
Sermons on the Psalms (enarrationes in Psalmos)
   Boulding, Maria. *Expositions of the Psalms. The Works of Saint Augustine.* III/15–17.
      Hyde Park, NY: New City Press, 2000.
Soliloquies (soliloquia)
   Burleigh, J. H. S. *Augustine: Earlier Writings,* 23–63. Philadelphia: Westminster, 1953.
True Religion (de vera religione)
   Burleigh, J. H. S. *Augustine: Earlier Writings,* 225–283. Philadelphia: Westminster,
      1953.
Unfinished Commentary on Romans (epistolae ad Romanos inchoate exposito)
   Fredriksen, Paula. *Augustine on Romans.* Society of Biblical Literature, Text and
      Translation Series, 53–89. Chico, CA: Scholars Press, 1982.
Unfinished Literal Commentary on Genesis (de Genesi ad litteram imperfectus liber)
   Teske, Roland. *Saint Augustine on Genesis.* Fathers of the Church 84. Washington,
      DC: Catholic University of America Press, 1991.
Usefulness of Belief (de utilitate credendi)
   Burleigh, J. H. S. *Augustine: Earlier Writings,* 287–323. Philadelphia: Westminster,
      1953.

JEWISH TEXTS

I usually cite biblical texts according to the Revised Standard Version, and intertestamental texts from the *Oxford Annotated Revised Standard Version with Apocrypha.* A larger collection of intertestamental Jewish writings can be found in *The Old Testament Apocrypha and Pseudepigrapha,* 2 vols., edited by J. H. Charlesworth (New York: Doubleday, 1985). For the Greek text of the Jewish scriptures, I used *The Septuagint* (Grand Rapids, MI: Zondervan Publishing House, 1970). For English translations of the great rabbinic corpora, see (1) for the Mishnah, the edition by H. Danby (London: Oxford University Press, 1950); (2) for the Jerusalem Talmud, the volumes edited under the direction of J. Neusner, *The Talmud of the Land of Israel* (Chicago: University of Chicago Press, 1982–); and (3) for the Babylonian Talmud, the volumes under the general editorship of I. Epstein (London: Soncino Press, 1978; originally published 1935–1952).

   Dead Sea Scrolls in English. Trans. Geza Vermes. 3rd ed. Harmondsworth, UK:
      Penguin, 1962.
   Josephus. *Jewish Antiquities.* Trans. H. St. J. Thackeray. Loeb Classical Library. 7
      vols. Cambridge, MA: Harvard University Press, 1930–1965.

——. *The Jewish War.* Trans. H. St. J. Thackeray. Loeb Classical Library. 2 vols. Cambridge, MA: Harvard University Press, 1927–1928.

——. *The Life* and *Against Apion.* Trans. H. St. J. Thackeray. Loeb Classical Library. Cambridge, MA: Harvard University Press, 1926.

Philo. *Works.* Loeb Classical Library. 10 vols. 2 suppl. vols. Cambridge, MA: Harvard University Press, 1929–1936.

Philo's Flaccus: The First Pogrom. Introduction, trans., and commentary P. W. van der Horst. Atlanta: Society of Biblical Literature, 2003.

Avot de-Rabbi Natan. The Fathers According to Rabbi Nathan. Transl. Judah Goldin. New Haven, CT: Yale University Press, 1955.

CHRISTIAN TEXTS

For the New Testament, I most often referred to the Revised Standard Version. For the Greek text, I used *Novum Testamentum Graece et Latine,* edited by E. Nestle et al. (Stuttgart: Deutsche Bibelgesellschaft, 1984).

Ambrose. *Political Letters and Speeches.* Trans. Carole Hill. Liverpool, UK: Liverpool University Press, 2005.

Athenagoras. *Apologia pro Christianis, Legatio, and de Resurrectione.* Ed. and trans. W. Schoedel. Oxford Early Christian Texts. Oxford: Clarendon Press, 1972.

John Chrysostom. *Discourses against Judaizing Christians.* Trans. Paul W. Harkins. Fathers of the Church 68. Washington, DC: Catholic University of America Press, 1999.

Clement of Alexandria. *The Miscellanies; or Stromata.* Ante-Nicene Fathers, 349–462. Vol. 2. Peabody, MA: Hendrickson Publishers, 1994. Originally published 1885.

Cyprian. *Three Books of Testimonies against the Jews* (*To Quirinius*). Ed. A. Roberts and J. Donaldson. Ante-Nicene Fathers, 507–557. Vol. 5. Peabody, MA: Hendrickson Publishers, 1994. Originally published 1886.

Ephrem. *St. Epfraim's Prose Refutations.* Vol. 1. Ed. C. W. Mitchell. London: Williams and Norgate, 1912.

——. *St. Epfraim's Prose Refutations.* Vol. 2. Ed. E. A. Bevan and F. C. Burkitt. London: Williams and Norgate, 1921.

Epiphanius. *The Panarion of Epiphanius of Salamis.* Trans. Frank Williams. New York and Leiden: E. J. Brill, 1987.

Eusebius. *The History of the Church.* Trans. G. A. Williamson. London and New York: Penguin Books, 1989.

——. *In Praise of Constantine.* Trans. H. A. Drake. Berkeley: University of California Press, 1976.

Irenaeus. *Against Heresies.* Trans. Dominic J. Unger, with John Dillon. Ancient Christian Writers 55. New York: Paulist Press, 1992.

Justin Martyr. *Dialogue with Trypho.* Ante-Nicene Fathers, 194–270. Vol. 1. Peabody, MA: Hendrickson Publishers, 1994. Originally published 1885.

——. *First Apology.* Ed. A. Roberts and J. Donaldson. Ante-Nicene Fathers, 163–187. Vol. 1. Peabody, MA: Hendrickson Publishers, 1994. Originally published 1885.

——. *Second Apology.* Ante-Nicene Fathers, 188–193. Vol. 1. Peabody, MA: Hendrickson Publishers, 1994. Originally published 1885.

Melito of Sardis. "A Homily on the Passover." In *The Christological Controversy*. Trans. and ed. Richard A. Norris Jr. Philadelphia: Fortress Press, 1980.

Minucius Felix. *Octavius*. Trans. Gerald H. Rendall. Loeb Classical Library, 315–437. Cambridge, MA: Harvard University Press, 1984.

Nag Hammadi Library. Ed. James M. Robinson. Rev. ed. San Francisco: Harper San Francisco, 1990.

Origen. *Contra Celsum*. Trans. Henry Chadwick. Cambridge: Cambridge University Press, 1953.

———. *On First Principles*. Trans. G. W. Butterworth. Gloucester, MA: Peter Smith, 1973.

Philostorgius. *Church History*. Trans. P. R. Amidon. Atlanta: Society of Biblical Literature, 2007.

Possidius. *The Life of Saint Augustine*. Introduction and notes M. Pellegrino. Ed. J. Rotelle. Villanova, PA: Augustinian Press, 1988.

Ptolemy. *Letter to Flora*. In *Gnosis: A Selection of Gnostic Texts*. Ed. W. Foerster, 1:154–161. 2 vols. Oxford: Oxford University Press, 1972.

Tertullian. *Adversus Marcionem*. Trans. Ernest Evans. 2 vols. Oxford: Clarendon Press, 1972.

———. *Against the Jews*. Trans. Geoffrey D. Dunn. The Early Church Fathers, 63–104. London and New York: Routledge, 2004.

———. *Apology* and *de Spectaculis*. Trans. T. R. Glover. Loeb Classical Library. Cambridge, MA: Harvard University Press, 1984.

———. *De idolatria/On Idolatry*. Ed. and trans. J. H. Waszink and J. C. M. van Winden. Leiden: E. J. Brill, 1987.

———. *Scorpiace*. Ante-Nicene Fathers, 633–648. Vol. 3. Peabody, MA: Hendrickson Publishers, 1994. Originally published 1885.

Tyconius. *The Book of Rules*. Trans. William S. Babcock. Atlanta: Scholars Press, 1989.

———. "The Book of Rules, I–III." In *Biblical Interpretation in the Early Church*. Trans. K. Froehlich, 104–132. Philadelphia: Fortress Press, 1985.

Severus of Minorca. *Letter on the Conversion of the Jews*. Ed. and trans. Scott Bradbury. Oxford: Clarendon Press, 1996.

OTHER ANCIENT TEXTS

Dio Cassius. *Roman History*. Trans. Ernest Cary. 9 vols. Loeb Classical Library. Cambridge, MA: Harvard University Press, 1970–1990.

Herodotus. *The Histories*. Trans. A. D. Godley. Loeb Classical Library. 4 vols. Cambridge, MA: Harvard University Press, 1981.

Julian. *Against the Galileans*. Ed. and trans. R. Joseph Hoffmann. Amherst, MA: Prometheus Books, 2004.

Sallustius. *Concerning the Gods and the Universe*. Ed. and trans. A. D. Nock. Hildesheim: Georg Olms, 1966.

COLLECTIONS OF ANCIENT TEXTS

Coleman-Norton, Paul R. *Roman State and Christian Church: A Collection of Legal Documents to* A.D. *535*. London: S. P. C. K., 1966.

Eidelberg, Shlomo. *The Jews and the Crusaders: The Hebrew Chronicles of the First and Second Crusades.* Madison: University of Wisconsin Press, 1977.

Gardner, Iain, and Samuel N. C. Lieu, eds. *Manichaean Texts from the Roman Empire.* New York: Cambridge University Press, 2004.

Linder, Amnon. *The Jews in the Legal Sources of the Early Middle Ages.* Detroit: Wayne State University Press, 1997.

———. *The Jews in Roman Imperial Legislation.* Detroit: Wayne State University Press, 1987.

MacMullen, Ramsey, and E. N. Lane. *Paganism and Christianity, 100–425 C.E.* Minneapolis: Fortress Press, 1992.

Mansi, J. D., ed. *Sacrorum Consiliorum Nova et Amplissima Collectio.* 31 volumes. Florence and Venice, 1759 and seq.

Musurillo, Herbert. *The Acts of the Christian Martyrs.* Oxford Early Christian Texts. Oxford: Clarendon Press, 1972.

Pharr, Clyde. *The Theodosian Code and Novels, and the Sirmondian Constitutions.* Princeton, NJ: Princeton University Press, 1952.

Stevenson, James. *A New Eusebius: Documents Illustrating the History of the Church to AD 337.* 2nd ed. W. H. C. Frend. London: S. P. C. K., 1987.

Stern, Menachem. *Greek and Latin Authors on Jews and Judaism.* 3 vols. Jerusalem: Hebrew University Press, 1974–1994.

Williams, Margaret. *Jews among Greeks and Romans: A Diasporan Sourcebook.* Baltimore: Johns Hopkins University Press, 1998.

Observations on ancient Jews and Judaism by non-Jews cited in the present work may be found in M. Stern; the various martyr stories cited in the present work may be found in H. Musurillo.

SECONDARY BIBLIOGRAPHY

Alexander, Philip S. "Jewish Elements in Gnosticism and Magic c. 70–c. 270." In *Cambridge History of Judaism*, 3:1052–1078. Cambridge: Cambridge University Press, 1999.

———. " 'Quid Athesis et Hierosolymis?' Rabbinic Midrash and Hermeneutics in the Graeco-Roman World." In *A Tribute to Geza Vermes: Essays on Jewish and Christian Literature and History*. Ed. P. R. Davies and R. T. White, 101–124. Sheffield, UK: JSOT Press, 1990.

Alfaric, Prosper. *L'évolution intellectuelle de S. Augustin.* Paris: E. Nourry, 1918.

Allgeier, Arthur. "Der Einfluss des Manichäismus auf die exegetische Fragestellung bei Augustin." In *Aurelius Augustinus: Festschrift der Görres-Gesellschaft zum 1500.* Ed. M. Grabmann and J. Mausbach, 1–13. Cologne: Bachem, 1930.

Alpert, B. S. "Un nouvel examen de la Politique anti-juive Visigothique." *Revue des études juives* 135 (1976): 3–29.

Altaner, Berthold. *Kleine patristische Schriften.* Berlin: Akademie Verlag, 1967.

Alvarez, J. "St. Augustine and Antisemitism." *Studia Patristica* 9 (1966): 340–349.

Ameling, Walter. "Die jüdischen Gemeinden im antiken Kleinasien." In *Jüdische Gemeinden und Organisationsformen von der Antike bis zur Gegenwart.* Ed. R. Jütte and A. P. Kustermann, 29–55. Vienna/Cologne: Böhlars, 1966.

Amory, P. *People and Identity in Ostrogothic Italy.* Cambridge: Cambridge University Press, 1997.

Applebaum, S. *Jews and Greeks in Ancient Cyrene.* Leiden: E. J. Brill, 1979.

———. "The Legal Status of the Jewish Communities in the Diaspora." In *The Jewish People in the First Century.* Vol. 1. Ed. S. Safrai and M. Stern, 402–463. Philadelphia: Fortress Press, 1974.

———. "The Organization of Jewish Communities in the Diaspora." In *Jewish People.* Vol. 1, 464–503.

Athanassiadi, P., and M. Frede, eds. *Pagan Monotheism in Late Antiquity.* Oxford: Clarendon Press, 1999.

Avi-Yonah, M. *The Jews of Palestine: A Political History from the Bar Kokhba War to the Arab Conquest.* Oxford: Clarendon Press, 1976.

Babcock, W. S. "Augustine and the Spirituality of Desire." *Augustinian Studies* 25 (1994): 179–199.

———. "Augustine's Interpretation of Romans (A.D. 394–396)." *Augustinian Studies* 10 (1979): 55–74.

———. "Augustine on Paul. The Case of Romans IX." *Studia Patristica* 16 (1985): 473–479.

Bachrach, B. C. "A Reassessment of Visigothic Jewish Policy, 589–711." *American Historical Review* 78 (1973): 11–34.

Bammel, C. P. "Augustine, Origen, and the Interpretation of St. Paul." *Augustinianum* 32 (1992): 341–368.

———. "Pauline Exegesis, Manichaeism and Philosophy in the Early Augustine." In *Christian Faith and Greek Philosophy in Late Antiquity.* Ed. Lionel R. Wickham and Caroline P. Bammel, 1–25. Leiden: E. J. Brill, 1993.

Barclay, J. *Jews in the Western Mediterranean Diaspora, from Alexander to Trajan [323 B.C.E. to 117 C.E.].* Berkeley: University of California Press, 1996.

Barkhuizen, J. H. "Proclus of Constantinople: A Popular Preacher in Fifth-Century Constantinople." In *Preacher and Audience: Studies in Early Christian and Byzantine Homiletics.* Ed. M. B. Cunningham and P. Allen, 179–200. Leiden: E. J. Brill, 1998.

Barnes, T. D. "Constantine and Christianity: Ancient Evidence and Modern Interpretations." *Zeitschrift für Antikes Christentum* 2 (1998): 274–94.

———. *Constantine and Eusebius.* Cambridge, MA: Harvard University Press, 1981.

———. "Legislation against the Christians." *Journal of Roman Studies* 58 (1968): 32–50.

———. " 'Monotheists All?' Review-Discussion of Edward-Goodman-Price 1999 and Athanassiadi and Frede 1999." *Phoenix* 55 (2001): 142–62.

———. *The New Empire of Diocletian and Constantine.* Cambridge, MA: Harvard University Press, 1982.

———. *Tertullian: A Historical and Literary Study.* Rev. ed. New York: Oxford University Press, 1985.

Baskin, J. R. "Rabbinic-Patristic Exegetical Contacts in Late Antiquity: A Bibliographical Reappraisal." In *Approaches to Ancient Judaism.* Ed. W. S. Green, 53–80. Atlanta: Scholars Press, 1985.

Bastiaensen, A. A. R., "Augustin commentateur de saint Paul et l'Ambrosiaster." *Sacris Erudiri* 36 (1996): 37–65.

Bauer, Walter. *Orthodoxy and Heresy in Earliest Christianity.* Mifflentown, PA: Sigler, 1971.

Beard, Mary, and John A. North, eds. *Pagan Priests: Religion and Power in the Ancient World.* Ithaca, NY: Cornell University Press, 1990.

Beard, Mary, John A. North, and S. R. F. Price. *Religions of Rome.* 2 vols. Cambridge: Cambridge University Press, 1998.

Beaucamp, J., F. Briquel-Chatonnet, and C. J. Robin. "La persécution des Chrétiens de Nagrûn et la chronologie himyarite." *Aram* 11–12 (1999–2000): 15–83.

Beaujeu, Jean. "Les apologètes et le culte du souverain." In *Le culte des souverains dans l'empire romain.* Ed. Willem den Boer, 103–136. Vandoeuvres-Genève: Olivier Reverdin, 1973.

Becker, Adam H., and Annette Yoshiko Reed, eds. *The Ways That Never Parted: Jews and Christians in Late Antiquity and the Early Middle Ages.* Tübingen: Mohr Siebeck, 2003.

BeDuhn, Jason. *The Manichaean Body in Discipline and Ritual.* Baltimore: Johns Hopkins University Press, 2000.

Berger, David. "The Attitude of St. Bernard of Clairvaux to the Jews." *Proceedings of the American Academy for Jewish Research* 40 (1972): 89–108.

——. "Mission to the Jews and Jewish-Christian Contacts in the Polemical Literature of the High Middle Ages." *American Historical Review* 91, no. 3 (1986): 576–591.

Berrouard, M.-F. *S. Augustin, Homélies sur l'évangile de saint Jean.* Bibliothèque augustinienne 73A. Brussels: Desclee, 1988.

——. "L'exégèse augustinienne de Rom. 7, 7–25 entre 396 et 418." *Rechereches augustiniennes* 16 (1981): 101–195.

Blanchetière, F. *"Aux sources de l'antijudaïsme chrétien."* *Revue d'histoire et philosophie religieuses* 53 (1973): 353–398.

Blumenkranz, B. *"Augustin et les Juifs, Augustin et le judaïsme."* *Recherches augustiniennes* 1 (1958): 225–241.

——. *Die Judenpredigt Augustin.* Paris: Études augustiniennes, 1973. Originally published 1946.

——. *"Judaeorum Convivia:* À propos du concile de Vannes (465), c. 12." In *Études d'histoire du droit canonique, dédiées à Gabriel Le Bras,* 1055–1058. Vol. II. Paris: Mouton, 1965.

——. *Juifs et Chrétiens dans le Monde Occidentale, 430–1096.* Paris: Mouton, 1960.

Bohak, G. "The Ibis and the Jewish Question. Ancient 'Anti-Semitism' in Historical Perspective." In *Jews and Gentiles in the Holy Land, in the Days of the Second Temple, the Mishnah, and the Talmud.* Ed. M. Mor, A. Oppenheimer, J. Pastor, and D. R. Schwartz, 25–43. Jerusalem: Yad Ben-Zvi Press, 2003.

Bonner, Gerald. "Les origines africaines de la doctrine augustinienne sur la chute et le péché originel." *Augustinus* XII (1967): 97–116.

——. *St. Augustine of Hippo.* Philadelphia: Westminster Press, 1963.

Bori, Pier Cesare. "The Church's Attitude Towards the Jews: An Analysis of Augustine's *Adversus Iudaeos.*" *Miscellanea Historiae Ecclesiasticae* 6 (1983): 300–311.

Bowersock, G. W. "Greek Intellectuals and the Imperial Cult in the Second Century A.D." In *Le culte des souverains dans l'empire romain.* Ed. Willem den Boer, 179–206. Vandoeuvres-Genève: Olivier Reverdin, 1973.

——. *Hellenism in Late Antiquity.* Ann Arbor: University of Michigan Press, 1990.

——. "The Imperial Cult: Perceptions and Persistence." In *Jewish and Christian Self-Definition.* Vol. 3. Ed. B. F. Meyer and E. P. Sanders, 171–182. Philadelphia: Fortress Press, 1982.

——. *Martyrdom and Rome.* New York: Cambridge University Press, 1995.

——. "Polytheism and Monotheism in Arabia and the Three Palestines." *Dumbarton Oaks Papers* 51 (1997): 1–10.

Bowersock, G. W., P. Brown, and O. Grabar, eds. *Late Antiquity: A Guide to the Postclassical World.* Cambridge, MA: Harvard University Press, 1999.

Boyarin, Daniel. *Border Lines: The Partition of Judeo-Christianity.* Philadelphia: University of Pennsylvania Press, 2004.

——. *Dying for God: Martyrdom and the Making of Christianity and Judaism.* Stanford, CA: Stanford University Press, 1999.

——. "Semantic Differences; or, 'Judaism'/'Christianity.' " *The Ways That Never Parted: Jews and Christians in Late Antiquity and the Early Middle Ages.* Ed. A. H. Becker and A. Y. Reed, 65–85. Tübingen: Mohr Siebeck, 2003.

Bradbury, S. "Constantine and the Problem of Anti-pagan Legislation in the Fourth Century." *Classical Philology* 89 (1994): 120–39.

——. "The Jews of Spain, c. 235–638." In *Cambridge History of Judaism.* Vol. 4. Ed. Steven T. Katz, 508–518. Cambridge: Cambridge University Press, 2006.

——. *Severus of Minorca. Letter on the Conversion of the Jews.* Oxford: Clarendon Press, 1996.

Brakke, D. "Athanasius." In *The Early Christian World.* Ed. Philip F. Esler, 1102–1127. New York: Routledge, 2000.

——. "Canon Formation and Social Conflict in Fourth-Century Egypt: Athanasius of Alexandria's Thirty-Ninth Festal Letter." *Harvard Theological Review* 87 (1994): 395–419.

——. "Jewish Flesh and Christian Spirit in Athanasius of Alexandria." *Journal of Early Christian Studies* 9 (2001): 453–481.

Braun, Thomas. "The Jews in the Late Roman Empire." *Scripta Classica Israelica* 17 (1998): 142–171.

Brenk, Beat. "Die Umwandlung der Synagoge von Apamea in eine Kirche." *TESSERAE: Festschrift für Josef Engemann,* 1–25. Münster: Aschendorffsche Verlagsbuchhandlung, 1994.

Brennan, B. "The Conversion of the Jews of Clermont in A.D. 576." *Journal of Theological Studies* 36 (1985): 320–337.

Brisson, Jean-Paul. *Autonomisme et christianisme dans l'Afrique romaine.* Paris: E. de Boccard, 1958.

Brown, Peter. *Augustine of Hippo: A Biography.* Berkeley and Los Angeles: University of California Press, 1967.

——. *Authority and the Sacred: Aspects of the Christianization of the Roman World.* Cambridge: Cambridge University Press, 1995.

——. *The Body and Society: Men, Women, and Sexual Renunciation in Early Christianity.* New York: Columbia University Press, 1988.

——. "Christianization and Religious Conflict." In *Cambridge Ancient History.* Vol. 13. Ed. A. Cameron and P. Garnsey, 632–664. Cambridge: Cambridge University Press, 1998.

——. *The Cult of the Saints.* Chicago: University of Chicago Press, 1981.

——. "The Diffusion of Manichaeism in the Roman Empire." In *Religion and Society in the Age of Saint Augustine,* 94–118. London: Faber & Faber, 1972.

——. "Enjoying the Saints in Late Antiquity." *Early Medieval Europe* 9 (2000): 1–24.

——. *Power and Persuasion in Late Antiquity: Towards a Christian Empire.* Madison: University of Wisconsin Press, 1992.

——. "Religious Coercion in the Later Roman Empire: The Case of North Africa." In *Religion and Society in the Age of Saint Augustine,* 301–331. London: Faber and Faber, 1972.

——. "Religious Dissent in the Later Roman Empire: The Case of North Africa." In *Religion and Society in the Age of Saint Augustine,* 237–259. London: Faber and Faber, 1972.

——. "The Rise and Function of the Holy Man in Late Antiquity." *Journal of Roman Studies* 61 (1971): 80–101.

——. "St. Augustine's Attitude toward Religious Coercion." In *Religion and Society in the Age of Saint Augustine,* 260–278. London: Faber and Faber, 1972.

Buell, D. K. "Ethnicity and Religion in Mediterranean Antiquity and Beyond." *Religious Studies Review* 26 (2000): 243–249.

——. "Race and Universalism in Early Christianity." *Journal of Early Christian Studies* 10 (2002): 429–468.

——. "Rethinking the Relevance of Race for Early Christian Self-Definition." *Harvard Theological Review* 94 (2001): 449–476.

———. *Why This New Race: Ethnic Reasoning in Early Christianity.* New York: Columbia University Press, 2005.

Buonaiuti, Ernesto. "The Genesis of St. Augustine's Idea of Original Sin." *Harvard Theological Review* 10 (1917): 159-175.

———. "Manichaeism and Augustine's Idea of the *Massa Perditionis.*" *Harvard Theological Review* 20 (1927): 117-127.

Burkett, W. *Greek Religion.* Cambridge, MA: Harvard University Press, 1985.

Burrus, Virginia. *The Making of a Heretic: Gender, Authority, and the Priscillianist Controversy.* Berkeley: University of California Press, 1995.

Cadbury, H. J. "Some Foibles in New Testament Scholarship." *Journal of Bible and Religion* 26 (1958): 213-216.

Cameron, Alan. "Gratian's Repudiation of the Pontifical Robe." *Journal of Roman Studies* 58 (1968): 96-99.

Cameron, Averil. "Byzantines and Jews: Some Recent Work on Early Byzantium." *Byzantine and Modern Greek Studies* 20 (1996): 249-274.

———. *Christianity and the Rhetoric of Empire: The Development of Christian Discourse.* Berkeley: University of California Press, 1991.

———. "Disputations, Polemical Literature and Formation of Opinion in the Early Byzantine Period." *Orientalia Lovaniensia Analecta* 42 (1991): 91-108.

———. "Jews and Heretics: A Category Error?" *The Ways That Never Parted: Jews and Christians in Late Antiquity and the Early Middle Ages.* Ed. A. H. Becker and A. Y. Reed, 345-360. Tübingen: Mohr Siebeck, 2003.

———. "The Jews in Seventh-Century Palestine." *Scripta Classica Israelica* 13 (1994): 75-93.

Cameron, Michael. "The Christological Substructure of Augustine's Figurative Exegesis." In *Augustine and the Bible.* Ed. P. Bright, 74-103. Notre Dame, IN: Notre Dame University Press, 1999.

Carleton Paget, J. "Anti-Judaism and Early Christian Identity." *Zeitschrift für Antikes Christentum* 1 (1997): 195-225.

———. "Jewish Christianity." In *Cambridge History of Judaism.* Vol. 3. Ed. W. D. Davies, J. Sturdy, and W. Horbury, 731-775. Cambridge: Cambridge University Press, 1999.

———. "Jewish Proselytism at the Time of Christian Origins: Chimera or Reality?" *Journal of the Study of the New Testament* 62 (1996): 65-103.

Carroll, James. *Constantine's Sword.* New York: Houghton Mifflin, 2001.

Castritius, H. "The Jews in North Africa at the Time of Augustine of Hippo— Their Social and Legal Position." In *Proceedings of the Ninth World Congress of Jewish Studies,* 31-37. Jerusalem: World Union of Jewish Studies, 1986.

———. " 'Seid weder den Juden noch den Heiden noch der Gemeinde Gottes ein Ärgernis' (1 Kor 10,32): Zur sozialen und rechtlichen Stellung der Juden im spätrömischen Nordafrika." In *Antisemitismus und jüdische Geschichte.* Ed. R. Erb and M. Schmidt, 47-67. Berlin: Metropol, 1987.

Chadwick, H. *Augustine.* Oxford: Oxford University Press, 1986.

———. *The Church in Ancient Society: From Galilee to Gregory the Great, Oxford History of the Christian Church.* New York: Oxford University Press, 2001.

———. *Early Christian Thought and the Classical Tradition.* Oxford: Oxford University Press, 1966.

———. "Oracles of the End in the Conflict of Paganism and Christianity in the Fourth Century." In *Mémorial André-Jean Festugière: Antiquité païenne et chrétienne.* Ed. E. Lucchesi and H. D. Saffrey, 125-129. Geneva: Patrick Cramer, 1984.

——. *Origen: Against Celsus*. Cambridge: Cambridge University Press, 1965.

——. *Priscillian of Avila: The Occult and the Charismatic in the Early Church*. Oxford: Clarendon Press, 1976.

——. "Tyconius and Augustine." In *A Conflict of Christian Hermeneutics in Roman Africa: Tyconius and Augustine*. Ed. Charles Kannengiesser, Pamela Bright, and Wilhelm H. Wuellner, 48–55. Berkeley, CA: Center for Hermeneutical Studies in Hellenistic and Modern Culture, 1989.

Clark, Elizabeth. *Ascetic Piety and Woman's Faith: Essays on Late Antique Christianity*. Lewiston, ME: Edwin Mellen Press, 1986.

——. "Augustine and the Early Christian Debate on Marriage." *Recherches augustiniennes* 21 (1986) 139–162.

——. *The Origenist Controversy. The Construction of an Early Christian Debate*. Princeton, NJ: Princeton University Press, 1992.

——. *Reading Renunciation: Asceticism and Scripture in Early Christianity*. Princeton: Princeton University Press, 1999.

Cohen, Jeremy. *Living Letters of the Law: Ideas of the Jew in Medieval Christianity*. Berkeley: University of California Press, 1999.

——. "The Mystery of Israel's Salvation: Romans 11:25–29 in Patristic and Medieval Exegesis." *Harvard Theological Review* 98 (2005): 247–281.

——. "Roman Imperial Policy toward the Jews from Constantine until the End of the Palestinian Patriarchate (ca. 429)." *Byzantine Studies* 3 (1976): 1–29.

——. " 'Slay Them Not': Augustine and the Jews in Modern Scholarship." *Medieval Encounters* 4 (1998): 78–92.

Cohen, Shaye J. D. *The Beginnings of Jewishness: Boundaries, Varieties, Uncertainties*. Berkeley: University of California Press, 1999.

——. " 'Those Who Say They Are Jews and Are Not.' " In *Diasporas in Antiquity*. Ed. S. J. D. Cohen and E. S. Frerichs, 1–45. Atlanta: Scholars Press, 1993.

——. "Was Judaism in Antiquity a Missionary Religion?" In *Jewish Assimilation, Acculturation, and Accommodation: Past Traditions, Current Issues, and Future Prospects*. Ed. M. Mor, 14–23. Lanham, MD: University Press of America, 1992.

Cole-Turner, Ronald S. "Anti-Heretical Issues and the Debate over Galatians 2:11–14 in the Letters of St. Augustine to St. Jerome." *Augustinian Studies* 11 (1980): 155–165.

Coleman, K. M. "Fatal Charades: Roman Executions Staged as Mythological Enactments." *Journal of Roman Studies* 80 (1990): 44–73.

Colorni, V. "Gli ebrei nei territori italiani a nord di Roma dal 568 agli inizi del seculo XIII." *Settimane* 26 (1980): 241–312.

Courcelle, Pierre. *Late Latin Writers and Their Greek Sources*. Cambridge, MA: Harvard University Press, 1969.

——. *Recherches sur les Confessions de saint Augustin*. Paris: E. de Boccard, 1968.

Craggo-Ruggini, L. "Intolerance: Equal and Less Equal in the Roman World." *Classical Philology* 82 (1987): 187–205.

——. "Pagani, ebrei e cristiani: Odio sociologico e odio teologico nel mondo antico." In *Gli ebrei nell'alto medioevo. XXVI Sett. di St. del Centro It. di St. sull'Alto Medioevo (30 marzo-5 apr. 1978)*, I:15–117. Spoleto: Centro Studi Alto Medioevo, 1980.

Cranz, F. E. "The Development of Augustine's Ideas on Society before the Donatist Controversy." *Harvard Theological Review* 47 (1954): 255–316.

Daniélou, J. *From Shadows to Reality: Studies in the Biblical Typology of the Fathers*. London: Burns & Oates, 1960.

———. "La typologie millénariste de le semaine dans le christianisme primitif," *Vigiliae Christianae* 2 (1948): 1–16.

De Bryn, T. S. "Constantius the *Tractator.* Author of an Anonymous Commentary on the Pauline Epistles?" *Journal of Theological Studies* 43 (1992) 38–54.

Decret, F. *L'Afrique manichéenne (IV–V siècles).* 2 vols. Paris: Études augustiniennes, 1978.

———. "Aspects de l'Église manichéenne: Remarques sur le manuscrit de Tebessa." In *Signum Pietatis: Festgabe für Cornelius Petrus Mayer OSA zum 60. Geburtstag (Cassiciacum, 40).* Ed. A. Zumkeller, 123–151. Würzburg: Augustinus-Verlag, 1989.

———. *Aspects du manichéisme dans l'Afrique romaine.* Paris: Études augustiniennes, 1970.

———. *Mani et la tradition manichéenne.* Paris: Seuil, 1974.

———. "Le manichéisme présentait-il en Afrique et à Rome des particularismes régionaux distinctifs?" *Augustinianum* 34 (1994): 5–40.

———. "L'utilisation des épîtres de Paul chez les Manichéens d'Afrique." In *Le epistole paoline nei Manichei, i Donatisti e il primo Agostino,* 29–83. Rome: Istituto Patristico Augustinianum, 1989.

De Lange, N. R. M. *Origen and the Jews.* Cambridge: Cambridge University Press, 1976.

DeRoche, V. "Polémique anti-judaïque et l'émergence de l'Islam [7e–8e Siècles]." *Revue des études byzantines* 57 (1999): 141–161.

Digeser, Elizabeth DePalma. *The Making of a Christian Empire: Lactantius and Rome.* Ithaca, NY: Cornell University Press, 2000.

Dillon, John. *The Middle Platonists: A Study of Platonism 80* B.C. *to* A.D. *200.* Ithaca, NY: Cornell University Press, 1977.

Dodds, E. R. *Pagan and Christian in an Age of Anxiety.* Cambridge: Cambridge University Press, 1965.

Dolbeau, F. *Augustin d'Hippone: Vingt-six sermons au peuple d'Afrique.* Paris: Études augustiniennes, 1996.

———. "Sermons inédits de Saint Augustin prêchés en 397." *Revue bénédictine* 101 (1991), 240–256; 102 (1992), 45–74, 267–297.

Donfried, K. P., ed. *The Romans Debate.* Minneapolis: Augsburg Press, 1977.

Drake, H. A. *Constantine and the Bishops.* Baltimore: Johns Hopkins University Press, 2000.

———. "Lambs into Lions: Explaining Early Christian Intolerance." *Past and Present* 153 (1996): 3–36.

Dreyfus, F. "La condescendance divine (*synkatabasis*) comme principe herméneutique de l'Ancien Testament dans la tradition juive et dans la tradition chrétienne." In *Congress Volume, Salamanca 1983.* Ed. J. A. Emerton, 96–107. Leiden: E. J. Brill, 1985.

Droge, Arthur J. *Homer or Moses? Early Christian Interpretations of the History of Culture.* Tübingen: J. C. B. Mohr, 1989.

Duchrow, U. *Christenheit und Weltverantwortung.* Stuttgart: Klett, 1970.

Eden, K. *Hermeneutics and the Rhetorical Tradition.* New Haven: Yale University Press, 1997.

Edwards, Douglas R. *Religion & Power: Pagans, Jews, and Christians in the Greek East.* New York: Oxford University Press, 1996.

Edwards, M. J., Martin Goodman, S. R. F. Price, and Christopher Rowland. *Apologetics in the Roman Empire: Pagans, Jews, and Christians.* Oxford: Clarendon Press, 1999.

Efroymson, D. P. "The Patristic Connection." In *Anti-Semitism and the Foundations of Christianity.* Ed. A. T. Davis, 98–117. New York: Paulist Press, 1979.

——. "Review of *Anti-Judaism and Early Christian Identity: A Critique of the Scholarly Consensus* (Miriam S. Taylor, 1994)." *The Jewish Quarterly Review* 87, no. 3–4 (1997): 380–382.

——. "Review of *Jewish Responses to Early Christians: History and Polemics, 30–150 C.E.* (Claudia Setzer, 1994)." *The Jewish Quarterly Review* 87, no. 3–4 (1997): 383–385.

——. "Whose Jews? Augustine's *Tractatus* on John." In *A Multiform Heritage.* Ed. B. G. Wright, 197–211. Atlanta: Scholars Press, 1999.

Ehrman, Bart D. *The Orthodox Corruption of Scripture.* Oxford: Oxford University Press 1993.

Eidelberg, S. *The Jews and the Crusaders: The Hebrew Chronicles of the First and Second Crusades.* Madison: University of Wisconsin Press, 1977.

Eliav, Y. Z. *God's Mountain. The Temple Mount in Time, Place and Memory.* Baltimore: Johns Hopkins University Press, 2005.

——. "Jews and Judaism, 70–429 CE." In *A Companion to the Roman Empire.* Ed. David S. Potter, 565–586. Oxford: Blackwell Publishing, 2006.

——. "The Roman Bath as a Jewish Institution: Another Look at the Encounter between Judaism and Graeco-Roman Culture." *Journal for the Study of Judaism* 31 (2000): 416–454.

Elsner, Jas. *Imperial Rome and Christian Triumph: The Art of the Roman Empire* A.D. *100–450.* Oxford History of Art. Oxford: Oxford University Press, 1998.

Étaix, Raymond. "Sermon inédit de saint Augustin sur la circoncision dans un ancien manuscript de Saragosse." *Revue des études augustiniennes* 26 (1980): 62–87.

Feldman, Louis H. *Jew and Gentile in the Ancient World: Attitudes and Interactions from Alexander to Justinian.* Princeton, N.J.: Princeton University Press, 1993.

——. "Proselytism by Jews in the Third, Fourth, and Fifth Centuries." *Journal for the Study of Judaism* 24, no. 1 (1993): 1–58.

Ferrari, Leo. "Augustine's 'Discovery' of Paul (*Confessions* 7.21, 27)." *Augustinian Studies* 22 (1991) 37–61.

——. "Paul at the Conversion of Augustine (*Confessions* VIII.12, 29–30)." *Augustinian Studies* 11 (1980): 5–20.

——. "Saint Augustine on the Road to Damascus." *Augustinian Studies* 13 (1982): 151–170.

Fine, Steven. *This Holy Place. On the Sanctity of the Synagogue during the Graeco-Roman Period.* Notre Dame, IN: University of Notre Dame Press, 1997.

Fishwick, Duncan. *The Imperial Cult in the Latin West: Studies in the Ruler Cult of the Western Provinces of the Roman Empire,* 3 vols. Leiden: E. J. Brill, 1987–2005.

Fitzgerald, Allan, ed. *Augustine through the Ages: An Encyclopedia.* Grand Rapids, MI: Wm Eerdmans, 1999.

Floëri, F. "Remarques sur la doctrine augustinienne du péché originel." *Studia Patristica* IX (1966): 416–421.

Folliet, G. "Iudaei tamquam capsarii nostri sunt. Augustin, *Ennaratio in Ps.* 40:14." *Augustinianum* 44 (2004): 443–457.

——. "La typologie du Sabbat chez S. Augustin: son interprétation millénariste entre 389 et 400." *Revue des études augustiniennes* 2 (1956): 371–390.

Fowden, G. "Bishops and Temples in the Eastern Roman Empire, A.D. 320–435." *Journal of Theological Studies* 29 (1978): 53–78.

———. *Empire to Commonwealth: Consequences of Monotheism in Late Antiquity.* Princeton, NJ: Princeton University Press, 1993.

———. "The Pagan Holy Man in Late Antiquity." *Journal of Hellenic Studies* 102 (1982): 33–59.

Frankfurter, D. "Beyond 'Jewish Christianity.' Continuing Religious Sub-Cultures of the Second and Third Centuries and Their Documents." In *The Ways That Never Parted.* Ed. A. H. Becker and A. Y. Reed, 131–143. Tübingen: J. C. B. Mohr (Paul Siebeck), 2003.

———. "Jews or Not? Reconstructing the 'Other' in Rev 2:9 and 3:9." *Harvard Theological Review* 94 (2001): 403–425.

Frede, M. "Monotheism and Pagan Philosophy in Late Antiquity." In *Pagan Monotheism in Late Antiquity.* Ed. P. Athanassiadi and M. Frede, 41–68. Oxford: Clarendon Press, 1999.

Fredriksen, Paula. "Allegory and Reading God's Book: Paul and Augustine on the Destiny of Israel." In *Interpretation and Allegory.* Ed. J. Whitman, 125–149. Leiden: Brill, 2000.

———. "Apocalypse and Redemption in Early Christianity, from John of Patmos to Augustine of Hippo." *Vigiliae Christianae* 45 (1991): 151–183.

———. "Augustine and Israel: *Interpretatio ad litteram,* Jews, and Judaism in Augustine's Theology of History." *Studia Patristica* 38 (2001): 119–135.

———. "Beyond the Body/Soul Dichotomy. Augustine on Paul against the Manichees and Pelagians." *Recherches augustiniennes* 23 (1988): 87–114.

———. "The Birth of Christianity and the Origins of Christian Anti-Judaism." In *Jesus, Judaism, and Christian Anti-Judaism: Reading the New Testament after the Holocaust.* Ed. Paula Fredriksen and Adele Reinhartz, 8–30. Louisville, KY: Westminster John Knox Press, 2002.

———. "Christians in the Roman Empire in the First Three Centuries A.D." In *Companion to the Roman Empire.* Ed. David Potter, 587–606. Oxford: Blackwell, 2006.

———. "*Excaecati Occulta Iustitia Dei:* Augustine on Jews and Judaism." *Journal of Early Christian Studies* 3 (1995): 299–324.

———. *From Jesus to Christ: The Origins of the New Testament Images of Jesus.* 2nd ed. New Haven: Yale University Press, 2000.

———. *Jesus of Nazareth, King of the Jews: A Jewish Life and the Emergence of Christianity.* New York: Knopf, 1999.

———. "Judaism, the Circumcision of Gentiles, and Apocalyptic Hope: Another Look at Galatians 1 and 2." *Journal of Theological Studies* 42 (1991): 532–564.

———. "Mandatory Retirement: Ideas in the Study of Christian Origins Whose Time Has Come to Go." *Studies in Religion/Sciences Religieuses* 35 (2006) 231–246.

———. "Paul and Augustine. Conversion Narratives, Orthodox Traditions, and the Retrospective Self." *Journal of Theological Studies* 37 (1986): 3–34.

———. "Paul, Purity, and the *Ekklêsia* of the Gentiles." In *The Beginnings of Christianity.* Ed. Jack Pastor and Menachem Mor, 205–217. Jerusalem: Yad Ben-Zvi Press, 2005.

———. "The Philosopher's Paul and the Problem of Anachronism." In *St. Paul among the Philosophers.* Ed. John D. Caputo and Linda Martin Alcoff. Bloomington: Indiana University Press, in press.

———. "*Secundum Carnem:* History and Israel in the Theology of St. Augustine." In *The Limits of Ancient Christianity.* Ed. C. Klingshirn and M. Vessey, 26–41. Ann Arbor: University of Michigan Press, 1999.

————. "What 'Parting of the Ways'? Jews, Gentiles, and the Ancient Mediterranean City." In *The Ways That Never Parted: Jews and Christians in Late Antiquity and the Early Middle Ages.* Ed. A. H. Becker and A. Y. Reed, 35–63. Tübingen: J. C. B. Mohr (Paul Siebeck), 2003.

————. "What You See Is What You Get: Context and Content in Current Research on the Historical Jesus." *Theology Today* 52 (1995): 75–97.

Fredriksen, Paula, and Oded Irshai. "Christian Anti-Judaism: Polemics and Policies, from the Second to the Seventh Century." In *Cambridge History of Judaism.* Vol. 4. Ed. Steven T. Katz, 977–1034. Cambridge: Cambridge University Press, 2006.

Fredriksen, Paula, and J. Lieu. "Rival Traditions: Christian Theology and Judaism." In *The First Christian Theologians.* Ed. G. R. Evans, 85–101. Oxford: Blackwell Publishing, 2004.

Fredriksen, Paula, and C. Shepardson. "Embodiment and Redemption. The Human Condition in Ancient Christianity." In *The Human Condition: A Volume in the Comparative Religious Ideas Project.* Ed. Robert C. Neville, 133–156. Albany: State University of New York Press, 2001.

Fredriksen, Paula, and G. G. Strousma. "The Two Souls and the Divided Will." In *Self, Soul and Body in Religious Experience.* Ed. A. Baumgarten, 198–217. Leiden: Brill, 1998.

Frend, W. H. C. *The Donatist Church.* Oxford: Clarendon Press, 1952.

————. "The Donatist Church and St. Paul." In *Le epistole paoline nei Manichei, i Donatisti e il primo Agostino,* 86–123. Rome: Istituto Patristico Augustinianum, 1989.

————. "The Gnostic-Manichaean Tradition in North Africa." *Journal of Ecclesiastical History* 4 (1953): 13–27.

————. "Jews and Christians in Third-Century Carthage." In *Paganisme, Judaïsme, Christianisme.* Ed. E. de Boccard, 185–194. Paris: P. Broche, 1978.

————. *Martyrdom and Persecution in the Early Church.* Oxford: Blackwell, 1965.

————. "A Note on Jews and Christians in Third-Century North Africa." *Journal of Theological Studies* 21 (1978): 92–96.

Friesen, Steven J. *Imperial Cults and the Apocalypse of John.* New York: Oxford University Press, 2001.

Froehlich, Karlfried. *Biblical Interpretation in the Early Church.* Sources of Early Christian Thought. Philadelphia: Fortress Press, 1984.

Gager, John G. *The Origins of Anti-Semitism: Attitudes toward Judaism in Pagan and Christian Antiquity.* New York: Oxford University Press, 1983.

————. *Reinventing Paul.* New York: Oxford University Press, 2004.

Gardner, Iain, and Samuel N. C. Lieu, eds. *Manichaean Texts from the Roman Empire.* New York: Cambridge University Press, 2004.

Garnsey, P. "Religious Toleration in Classical Antiquity." In *Persecution and Toleration.* Ed. W. J. Shiels, 1–27. Oxford: Blackwell, 1984.

Gibson, E. L. "Jewish Antagonism or Christian Polemic: The Case of the Martyrdom of Pionius." *Journal of Early Christian Studies* 9 (2001): 339–358.

Goldstein, Jonathan A. *II Maccabees: A New Translation with Introduction and Commentary.* Garden City, NY: Doubleday, 1983.

Goodenough, E. R. "The Bosporus Inscriptions to the Most High God." *Jewish Quarterly Review* 47 (1956–1957): 221–244.

Goodman, Martin. "Jewish Proselytizing in the First Century." In *The Jews among Pagans and Christians.* Ed. J. Lieu, J. North, and T. Rajak, 53–78. London: Routledge, 1992.

——. *Mission and Conversion: Proselytizing in the Religious History of the Roman Empire.* New York: Oxford University Press, 1994.

——. "Modeling the 'Parting of the Ways.' " In *The Ways That Never Parted: Jews and Christians in Late Antiquity and the Early Middle Ages.* Ed. A. H. Becker and A. Y. Reed, 119–129. Tübingen: J. C. B. Mohr (Paul Siebeck), 2003.

——. "The Persecution of Paul by Diaspora Jews." In *The Beginnings of Christianity.* Ed. J. Pastor and M. Mor, 376–387. Jerusalem: Yad Ben-Zvi Press, 2005.

——. "The Pilgrimage Economy of Jerusalem in the Second Temple Period." In *Jerusalem: Its Sanctity and Centrality to Judaism, Christianity and Islam.* Ed. L. I. Levine, 69–76. New York: Continuum, 1999.

——. "Trajan and the Origins of Roman Hostility to the Jews." *Past and Present* 182 (2004): 3–29.

Gorday, P. "Jews and Gentiles, Galatians 2:11–14, and Reading Israel in Romans: The Patristic Debate." In *Engaging Augustine on Romans.* Ed. Daniel Patte and Eugene TeSelle, 199–236. Harrisburg, PA: Trinity Press International 2002.

——. *The Principles of Patristic Exegesis. Romans 9–11 in Origen, John Chrysostom and Augustine.* New York and Toronto: Edwin Mellen Press, 1983.

Gradel, Ittai. *Emperor Worship and Roman Religion.* Oxford: Clarendon Press, 2002.

Grant, R. M. *Gods and the One God.* Philadelphia: Westminster Press, 1986.

Gruen, Erich S. *Diaspora: Jews amidst Greeks and Romans.* Cambridge, MA: Harvard University Press, 2002.

——. *Heritage and Hellenism: The Reinvention of Jewish Tradition.* Berkeley: University of California Press, 1998.

——. "Jewish Perspectives on Greek Culture and Ethnicity." In *Ancient Perceptions of Greek Ethnicity.* Ed. I. Malkin, 347–373. Cambridge, MA: Harvard University Press, 2001.

Hall, Jonathan M. *Ethnic Identity in Greek Antiquity.* Cambridge: Cambridge University Press, 1997.

Hare, Douglas R. A. *The Theme of Jewish Persecution of Christians in the Gospel According to St. Matthew.* Cambridge: Cambridge University Press, 1967.

Harkins, Franklin T. "Nuancing Augustine's Hermeneutical Jew: Allegory and Actual Jews in the Bishop's Sermons." *Journal for the Study of Judaism* 26 (2005): 41–64.

Harnack, Adolf von. *The Expansion of Christianity in the First Three Centuries.* Trans. James Moffatt. Freeport: Books for Libraries Press, 1972.

——. *History of Dogma.* 5 vols. New York: Dover Publications, 1961.

Harries, Jill. *Law and Empire in Late Antiquity.* Cambridge: Cambridge University Press, 1999.

Harrison, Carol. *Rethinking Augustine's Early Theology.* Oxford: Oxford University Press, 2006.

Hasan-Rokem, Galit. *Tales of the Neighborhood: Jewish Narrative Dialogues in Late Antiquity.* Berkeley: University of California Press, 2003.

Hayman, A. P. "Monotheism: A Misused Word in Jewish Studies?" *Journal of Jewish Studies* 42, no. 1 (1991): 1–15.

Henten, J. W. van, and Friedrich Avemarie. *Martyrdom and Noble Death: Selected Texts from Graeco-Roman, Jewish, and Christian Antiquity.* New York: Routledge, 2002.

Hill, Charles E. *Regnum Caelorum: Patterns of Future Hope in Early Christianity.* Oxford: Oxford University Press, 1992.

Hirschberg, H. Z. *History of the Jews in North Africa.* 2 vols. Leiden: E. J. Brill, 1974.

Hirschman, Marc. "Rabbinic Universalism in the Second and Third Centuries." *Harvard Theological Review* 93 (2000): 101–115.

———. *A Rivalry of Genius. Jewish and Christian Biblical Interpretation.* Albany: State University of New York Press, 1996.

Hodge, Caroline Johnson. *If Sons, Then Heirs: A Study of Kinship and Ethnicity in the Letters of Paul.* New York: Columbia University Press, 2005.

Holte, Ragnar. *Béatitude et Sagesse—saint Augustin et le problème de la fin de l'homme dans la philosophie ancienne.* Paris: Études augustiniennes, 1962.

Hombert, P.-M. *Gloria Gratiae. Se glorifier en Dieu. Principe et fin de la théologie augustinienne de la grâce.* Paris: Études augustiniennes, 1996.

———. *Nouvelles recherches de chronologie augustinienne.* Paris: Études augustiniennes, 2000.

Hopkins, K. "Christian Number and Its Implications." *Journal of Early Christian Studies* 6 (1998): 185–226.

———. "Divine Emperors, or the Symbolic Unity of the Roman Empire." In *Conquerors and Slaves*, 197–242. Cambridge: Cambridge University Press, 1978.

Horbury, W. *Jews and Christians in Contact and Controversy.* Edinburgh: T&T Clark, 1998.

———. "Jews and Christians on the Bible: Demarcation and Convergence (325–451)." *Jews and Christians in Contact and Controversy*, 200–225. Edinburgh: T&T Clark, 1998.

———. "The Purpose of Pseudo-Cyprian, *Adversus Judaeos*." In *Jews and Christians in Contact and Controversy*, 180–199. Edinburgh: T&T Clark, 1998.

———. "Tertullian on the Jews in the Light of *de Spectaculis* xxx.5-6." *Journal of Theological Studies* 23 (1972): 455–59. Reprinted in *Jews and Christians in Contact and Controversy*, 176–179. Edinburgh: T&T Clark, 1998.

Horner, Timothy J. "Overcoming History with History: Eusebius' Use of Jewish History." Paper presented at the Society of Biblical Literature. Denver, 2000.

Horst, Pieter Willem van der. " 'Thou Shalt Not Revile the Gods.' The LXX Translation of Exodus 22:28 (27), Its Background and Influence." *Studia Philonica* 5 (1993) 1–8.

Hultgren, Arland J. "Paul's Pre-Christian Persecutions of the Church: Their Purpose, Locale, and Nature." *Journal of Biblical Literature* 95 (1976): 97–111.

Hunt, E. D. "Christianizing the Roman Empire: The Evidence of the Code." In *The Theodosian Code.* Ed. J. Harris and I. Wood, 143–158. London: Duckworth, 1993.

———. "The Church as Public Institution." In *Cambridge Ancient History.* Vol. 13. Ed. A. Cameron and P. Garnsey, 238–276. Cambridge: Cambridge University Press, 1998.

———. "Constantine and Jerusalem." *Journal of Ecclesiastical History* 48 (1997): 405–424.

———. "St. Stephen in Minorca: An Episode in Jewish-Christian Relations in the Early Fifth Century A.D." *Journal of Theological Studies* 33 (1982): 106–123.

———. "The Successors of Constantine." In *Cambridge Ancient History.* Vol. 13. Ed. A. Cameron and P. Garnsey, 1–43. Cambridge: Cambridge University Press, 1998.

Hunter, David. "Resistance to the Virginal Ideal in Late Fourth-Century Rome: The Case of Jovinian." *Theological Studies* 48 (1987): 45–64.

Hurtado, Larry W. *Lord Jesus Christ: Devotion to Jesus in Earliest Christianity*. Grand Rapids, MI: W. B. Eerdmans, 2003.

Irshai, O. "Confronting a Christian Empire: Jewish Culture in the World of Byzantium." In *The Cultures of the Jews*. Ed. D. Biale, 181–221. New York: Schocken Books, 2002.

———. "Dating the Eschaton: Jewish and Christian Apocalyptic Calculations in Late Antiquity." In *Apocalyptic Time*. Ed. A. I. Baumgarten, 113–53. Leiden: Brill, 2000.

———. "From Oblivion to Fame: The History of the Palestinian Church (135–303 CE)." In *Christians and Christianity in the Holy Land: From the Origins to the Latin Kingdoms*. Ed. Ora Limor and Guy G. Stroumsa, 91–139. Turnhout: Brepols, 2006.

Isaac, Benjamin H. *The Invention of Racism in Classical Antiquity*. Princeton, NJ: Princeton University Press, 2004.

Jacobs, Andrew S. "A Jew's Jew: Paul and the Early Christian Problem of Jewish Origins." *Journal of Religion* 86 (2006): 258–286.

———. *Remains of the Jews: The Holy Land and Christian Empire in Late Antiquity*. Stanford, CA: Stanford University Press, 2004.

———. "The Lion and the Lamb: Reconsidering Jewish-Christian Relations in Antiquity." In *The Ways That Never Parted. Jews and Christians in Late Antiquity and the Early Middle Ages*. Ed. A. H. Becker and A. Y. Reed, 95–118. Tübingen: J. C. B. Mohr (Paul Siebeck), 2003.

Janowitz, Naomi. "Rethinking Jewish Identity in Late Antiquity." In *Ethnicity and Culture in Late Antiquity*. Ed. Stephen Mitchell and Geoffrey Greatex, 205–219. London: Duckworth, 2000.

Jones, A. H. M. *The Greek City from Alexander to Justinian*. 2 vols. Oxford: Clarendon Press, 1940.

———. *The Later Roman Empire, 284–602: A Social, Economic, and Administrative Survey*. 2 vols. Norman: University of Oklahoma Press, 1964.

Jones, C. P. *Kinship Diplomacy in the Ancient World*. Cambridge, MA: Harvard University Press, 1999.

Juster, Jean. *Les Juifs dans l'empire romain*. 2 vols. Paris: Geuthner, 1914.

Kamesar, Adam. "The Evaluation of the Narrative Aggada in Greek and Latin Patristic Literature." *Journal of Theological Studies* 45 (1994): 37–71.

———. *Jerome, Greek Scholarship, and the Hebrew Bible: A Study of the Quaestiones Hebraicae in Genesim*. Oxford Classical Monographs. New York: Oxford University Press, 1993.

———. "The Virgin of Isaiah 7:14: The Philological Argument from the Second to the Fifth Century." *Journal of Theological Studies* 41 (1990): 52–75.

Kaster, Robert A. *Guardians of Language: The Grammarian and Society in Late Antiquity*. Berkeley: University of California Press, 1988.

Kelly, J. N. D. *Early Christian Creeds*. 3rd ed. London: Longman, 1972.

———. *Golden Mouth: The Story of John Chrysostom—Ascetic, Preacher, Bishop*. Ithaca, NY.: Cornell University Press, 1995.

———. *Jerome: His Life, Writings, and Controversies*. New York: Harper & Row, 1975.

Kimelman, Reuven. "*Birkhat Ha-Minim* and the Lack of Evidence for an Anti-Christian Jewish Prayer in Late Antiquity." In *Jewish and Christian Self-Definition*. Vol. 2: *Aspects of Judaism in the Greco-Roman Period*. Ed. A. I.

Baumgarten, E. P. Sanders, and Alan Mendelson, 226–244. Philadelphia: Fortress Press, 1981.

———. "Identifying Jews and Christians in Roman Syria-Palestine." In *Galilee Through the Centuries: Confluence of Cultures.* Ed. Eric M. Meyers, 301–333. Winona Lake, IN: Eisenbrauns, 1999.

King, Karen L. *What Is Gnosticism?* Cambridge, MA: Harvard University Press, 2003.

King. P. D. *Law and Society in the Visigothic Kingdom.* Cambridge: Cambridge University Press, 1972.

Kinzing, Wolfram. " 'Non-Separation': Closeness and Co-operation between Jews and Christians in the Fourth Century." *Vigiliae Christianae* 45 (1991): 27–53.

———. "Philosemitismus Teil I: Zur Geschichte des Begriffs." *Zeitschrift für Kirchengeschichte* 105 (1994): 202–228.

———. "Philosemitismus Teil II: Zur Historiographischen Verwendung des Begriffs." *Zeitschrift für Kirchengeschichte* 105 (1994): 361–383.

Klingshirn, William E. *Caesarius of Arles: The Making of a Christian Community in Late Antique Gaul.* Cambridge: Cambridge University Press, 1994.

Klingshirn, W. E. and M. Vessey, eds. *The Limits of Ancient Christianity: Essays on Late Antique Thought and Culture in Honor of R. A. Markus.* Ann Arbor: University of Michigan Press, 1999.

Knust, Jennifer W. *Abandoned to Lust. Sexual Slander and Ancient Christianity.* New York: Columbia University Press, 2006.

———. "Early Christian Re-writing and the History of the *Pericope Adulterae.*" *Journal of Early Christian Studies* 14 (2006): 485–536.

Kofsky, Arieh. *Eusebius of Caesarea against Paganism.* Leiden: Brill, 2000.

———. "Mamre: A Case of Regional Cult?" In *Sharing the Sacred: Religious Contacts and Conflicts in the Holy Land.* Ed. A. Kovsky and G. G. Stroumsa, 19–30. Jerusalem: Yad Izhak Ben Zvi, 1998.

Koltun-Fromm, Naomi. "A Jewish–Christian Conversation in Fourth-Century Persian Mesopotamia." *Journal of Jewish Studies* 48 (1996): 45–63.

Konstan, David. "*To Hellenikon Ethnos:* Ethnicity and the Construction of Ancient Greek Identity." In *Ancient Perceptions of Greek Ethnicity.* Ed. Irad Malkin, 29–50. Washington, DC: Center for Hellenic Studies, 2001.

Kraabel, A. T. "The Diaspora Synagogue: Archaeological and Epigraphic Evidence since Sukenik." *Aufstieg und Niedergang der römischen Welt* 19, no. 1 (1979): 477–510.

Kraemer, R. S. "Jewish Tuna and Christian Fish: Identifying Religious Affiliation in Epigraphic Sources." *Harvard Theological Review* 84 (1991): 141–162.

———. "On the Meaning of the Term 'Jew' in Greco-Roman Inscriptions." *Harvard Theological Review* 82, no. 1 (1989): 35–53.

Krauss, Samuel, and William Horbury. *The Jewish-Christian Controversy: From the Earliest Times to 1789.* Tübingen: J. C. B. Mohr, 1995.

Külzer, A. *Disputationes Graecae contra Iudaeos: Untersuchungen zur byzantinischen anti-judischen Dialogliteratur und ihren Judenbild.* Stuttgart: B. G. Taubner, 1999.

Laato, Anni Maria. *Jews and Christians in De duobus montibus Sina et Sion.* Åbo, Finland: Åbo Akademi University Press, 1998.

Ladner, Gerhart B. *The Idea of Reform. Its Impact on Christian Thought and Action in the Age of the Fathers.* Cambridge, MA: Harvard University Press, 1959.

——. "Reflections on Medieval Anti-Judaism I: Aspects of Patristic Anti-Judaism." *Viator* 2 (1971): 355-363.

Lampe, Peter. *From Paul to Valentinus: Christians at Rome in the First Two Centuries.* Minneapolis: Fortress Press, 2003.

Lancel, Serge. *Saint Augustine.* London: SCM Press, 2002.

Landes, R. " 'Lest the Millennium Be Fulfilled': Apocalyptic Expectations and the Pattern of Western Chronography, 100-800 C.E." In *The Use and Abuse of Eschatology in the Middle Ages.* Ed. D. Verhelst, W. Verbeke, and A. Welkenhuysen, 141-211. Leuven: Leuven University Press, 1988.

Lane Fox, Robin. *Pagans and Christians.* New York: Knopf, 1987.

Lassère, J.-M. *Ubique Populus.* Paris: Centre Nationale de Recherches Scientifiques, 1977.

Le Bohec, Y. "Inscriptions juives et judaïsantes de l'Afrique romaine," *Antiquités africaines* 17 (1981): 165-207.

Leeming, Bernard. "Augustine, Ambrosiaster, and the *Massa.*" *Gregorianum XI* (1930): 58-91.

Lepelley, C. *Les cités de l'Afrique romaine au Bas-Empire.* 2 vols. Paris: Études augustiniennes, 1979, 1981.

LeRoy, Guy. "Ac 9,4b dans la prédication de saint Augustin." Memoire de licence, Institute d'études théologiques, Université de Bruxelles, 1986.

Levenson, J. *The Death and Resurrection of the Beloved Son.* New Haven: Yale University Press, 1993.

Levine, A.-J. "The Earth Moved: Jesus, Sex, and Eschatology." In *Apocalypticism, Anti-Semitism and the Historical Jesus.* Ed. John S. Kloppenborg and John W. Marshall, 83-97. London and New York: T & T Clark, International 2005.

Levine, Lee I. *The Ancient Synagogue: The First Thousand Years.* New Haven: Yale University Press, 2000.

——. "Jewish Archaeology in Late Antiquity: Art, Architecture, and Inscriptions." In *Cambridge History of Judaism.* Vol. 4. Ed. Steven T. Katz, 519-555. Cambridge: Cambridge University Press, 2006.

——. "The Status of the Patriarch in the Third and Fourth Centuries: Sources and Methodology." *Journal of Jewish Studies* 47 (1996): 1-32.

Levinskaya, I. A. *The Book of Acts in Its Diaspora Setting.* Grand Rapids, MI: W. B. Eerdmans, 1996.

Lieberman, S. "The Martyrs of Caesarea." *Annuaire de l'Institut de Philologie et d'Histoire orientales et slaves.* 7 (1938-44), 395-446.

Liebeschuetz, J. H. W. G. *Continuity and Change in Roman Religion.* New York: Oxford University Press, 1979.

——. *The Decline and Fall of the Roman City.* New York: Oxford University Press, 2001.

Lieu, Judith. "Accusations of Jewish Persecution in Early Christian Sources, with Particular Reference to Justin Martyr and the Martyrdom of Polycarp." In *Tolerance and Intolerance in Early Judaism and Christianity.* Ed. G. N. Stanton and G. G. Stroumsa, 279-295. Cambridge: Cambridge University Press, 1998.

——. *Christian Identity in the Jewish and Graeco-Roman World.* New York: Oxford University Press, 2004.

——. "History and Theology in Christian Views of Judaism." In *The Jews among Pagans and Christians in the Roman Empire.* Ed. J. Lieu, J. North, and T. Rajak, 79-96. London: Routledge, 1992.

——. *Image and Reality: The Jews in the World of the Christians in the Second Century.* Edinburgh: T&T Clark, 1996.

——. *Neither Jew nor Greek? Constructing Early Christianity, Studies of the New Testament and Its World.* New York: T&T Clark, 2002.

——. " 'The Parting of the Ways': Theological Construct or Historical Reality?" *Journal for the Study of the New Testament* 56 (1994): 101–119.

——. "The Race of the God-Fearers." *Journal of Theological Studies* 46 (1995): 483–501.

Lieu, Judith, John A. North, and Tessa Rajak, eds. *The Jews among Pagans and Christians: In the Roman Empire.* New York: Routledge, 1992.

Lieu, Samuel N. C. *Manichaeism in the Later Roman Empire and Medieval China.* Tübingen: J. C. B. Mohr, 1992.

Lim, R. "Manichaeans and Public Disputation in Late Antiquity." *Recherches augustiniennes* 26 (1992): 233–272.

——. "Unity and Diversity among Western Manichaeans." *Revue des études augustiniennes* 35 (1989): 231–250

Limor, O. "Christian Sacred Space and the Jew." In *From Witness to Witchcraft. Jews and Judaism in Medieval Christian Thought.* Ed. J. Cohen, 55–77. Wolfenbüttel: Wolfenbuttler Mittelalterichen-Studien, 1996.

Linder, Amnon. *The Jews in the Legal Sources of the Early Middle Ages.* Detroit: Wayne State University Press, 1997.

——. *The Jews in Roman Imperial Legislation.* Detroit: Wayne State University Press, 1987.

——. "The Legal Status of the Jews in the Roman Empire." In *Cambridge History of Judaism.* Vol. 4. Ed. Steven T. Katz, 128–173. Cambridge: Cambridge University Press, 2006.

Löhrer, M. *Der Glaubensbegriff des Hl. Augustinus in seinen ersten Schriften bis zu den Confessiones.* Einsiedeln: Benzinger, 1955.

Lotter, Friedrich. "Die Zwangsbekehrung der Juden von Menorca um 418 im Rahman der Entwicklung des Judenrechts der Spätantike." *Historische Zeitschrift* 242 (1986): 291–326.

——. "The Forced Conversion of the Jewish Community of Minorca in 418 C.E." In *Proceedings of the Ninth World Congress of Jewish Studies,* 23–30. Jerusalem: World Union of Jewish Studies, 1986.

Luneau, A. *L'histoire du salut chez les pères de l'Église.* Paris: Beauchesne, 1964.

Lyman, Rebecca. "Hellenism and Heresy." *Journal of Early Christian Studies* 11 (2003): 209–222.

Lyonnet, Stanislaus. "Augustin et Rm. 5,12 avant la controverse pélagienne." *Nouvelle revue théologique* 7 (1967): 842–849.

——. "Rm., V,12 chez saint Augustin." In *L'Homme devant Dieu: Mélanges offerts au P.H. de Lubac.* I. Exégèse et patristique (Coll. Théologie 56), 324–339. Paris: Auber, 1964.

MacMullen, Ramsay. *Christianity and Paganism in the Fourth to Eighth Centuries.* New Haven: Yale University Press, 1997.

——. *Christianizing the Roman Empire (A.D. 100–400).* New Haven: Yale University Press, 1984.

——. "The Preacher's Audience (A.D. 350–400)." *Journal of Theological Studies* 40 (1989): 503–511.

——. "What Difference Did Christianity Make?" *Historia* 35 (1986): 322–343.

Madec, G. *Introduction aux révisions et à la lecture des oeuvres de saint Augustin.* Paris: Études augustiniennes, 1996.

———. "Sur une nouvelle introduction à la pensée d'Augustin." *Revue des études augustiniennes* 28 (1982): 100–111.

Magness, J. "The Date of the Sardis Synagogue in Light of the Numismatic Evidence." *American Journal of Archaeology* 109 (2005): 443–475.

———. "Heaven on Earth: Helios and the Zodiac Cycle in Ancient Palestinian Synagogues." *Dumbarton Oakes Papers* 59 (2007): 1–52.

Malkin, Irad, ed. *Ancient Perceptions of Greek Ethnicity.* Cambridge, MA: Harvard University Press, 2001.

Mara, M. G. *Agostino interprete di Paolo.* Milan: Paoline, 1993.

———. "Agostino e la polemica antimanichea: il ruolo di Paolo e del suo epistolario." *Augustinianum* 32 (1992): 119–143.

———. "Commentaries on the Pauline epistles." In *Encyclopedia of the Early Church.* Ed. A. D. Bernadino, 653 to 659. New York: Oxford University Press 1992.

Marafioti, D. "Il problema dell' *'initium fidei'* in sant'Agostino fino al 397." *Augustinianum* 21 (1981): 541–565.

———. *Conversion and Disenchantment in Augustine's Spiritual Career.* Villanova, PA: Villanova University Press, 1989.

———. *The End of Ancient Christianity.* Cambridge: Cambridge University Press, 1990.

———. *From Augustine to Gregory the Great: History and Christianity in Late Antiquity.* London: Variorum Reprints, 1983.

———. *Gregory the Great and His World.* Cambridge: Cambridge University Press, 1997.

———. *Sacred and Secular: Studies on Augustine and Latin Christianity.* Aldershot: Variorum Reprints, 1994.

———. *Saeculum: History and Society in the Theology of St. Augustine.* Cambridge: Cambridge University Press, 1970.

———. "Victorinus and Augustine." In *Cambridge History of Later Greek and Early Medieval Philosophy.* Ed. A. H. Armstrong, 331–406. Cambridge: Cambridge University Press, 1970.

Markus, R. A. "Alienato." Studia Patristica IX (1966): 431–450.

Marrou, H.-I. *Augustine and His Influence through the Ages.* New York: Harper and Bros., 1957.

———. *The History of Education in Antiquity.* Trans. George Lamb. Madison: University of Wisconsin Press, 1982.

———. *Saint Augustin et la fin de la culture antique.* Paris: de Boccard, 1958.

Marshall, John. "Apocalypticism and Anti-Semitism: Inner-Group Resources and Inter-Group Conflicts." In *Apocalypticism, Anti-Semitism and the Historical Jesus.* Ed. J. S. Kloppenborg with J. Marshall, 68–82. London and New York: T&T Clark International, 2005.

Martin, T. "Modus Inveniendi Paulum." In *Engaging Augustine on Romans.* Ed. D. Patte and E. TeSelle, 63–90. Harrisburg, PA: Trinity Press International, 2002.

———. "*Vox Pauli.* Augustine and the Claims to Speak for Paul. An Exploration of Rhetoric in the Service of Exegesis." *Journal of Early Christian Studies* 8 (2000): 237–272.

McKnight, Scot. *A Light among the Gentiles: Jewish Missionary Activity in the Second Temple Period.* Minneapolis: Fortress Press, 1991.

McLynn, Neil B. *Ambrose of Milan: Church and Court in a Christian Capital.* Berkeley: University of California Press, 1994.

Meeks, Wayne A. "Breaking Away: Three New Testament Pictures of Christianity's Separation from Jewish Communities." In *"To See Ourselves as Others See Us": Christians, Jews, "Others" in Late Antiquity.* Ed. Jacob Neusner and Ernst Frerichs, 93–115. Chico, CA: Scholars Press, 1985.

Meeks, Wayne, and Robert Wilken, *Jews and Christians in Antioch in the First Four Centuries of the Common Era.* Missoula, MT: Scholars Press, 1978.

Meer, F. van der, *Augustine the Bishop.* London: Sheed & Ward, 1961.

Meier, John P. *A Marginal Jew: Rethinking the Historical Jesus.* Vol. 1 of *The Anchor Bible Reference Library.* New York: Doubleday, 1991.

Mellinkoff, Ruth. *The Mark of Cain.* Berkeley: University of California Press, 1981.

Merdinger, J. E. *Rome and the African Church in the Time of Augustine.* New Haven: Yale University Press, 1997.

Miles, Margaret. *Desire and Delight. A New Reading of Augustine's Confessions.* New York: Crossroads, 1991.

Millar, Fergus. "Christian Emperors, Christian Church and the Jews of the Diaspora in the Greek East, CE 379–450." *Journal of Jewish Studies* 55 (2004): 1–24.

———. "Empire and City, Augustus to Julian: Obligations, Excuses, and Status." *Journal of Roman Studies* 73 (1993): 76–91.

———. *A Greek Roman Empire. Power and Belief under Theodosius II (408–450).* Berkeley: University of California Press, 2007.

———. "The Imperial Cult and the Persecutions." In *Le culte des souverains dans l'empire romain.* Ed. W. Van den Boer, 147–175. Geneva: Fondations Hardt, 1973.

———. "The Jews of the Graeco-Roman Diaspora between Paganism and Christianity, A.D. 312–438." In *The Jews among Pagans and Christians in the Roman Empire.* Ed. J. North, J. Lieu, and T. Rajak, 97–123. London: Routledge, 1992.

———. "Review of *Martyrdom and Persecution in the Early Church: A Study of a Conflict from the Maccabees to Donatus* (W. H. C. Frend, 1965)." *Journal of Roman Studies* 56 (1966): 231–236.

———. *The Roman Near East, 31 BC–AD 337.* Cambridge, MA: Harvard University Press, 1993.

Mitchell, Margaret M. *The Heavenly Trumpet. John Chrysostom and the Art of Pauline Interpretation.* Louisville, KY: John Knox Press, 2001.

———. "Patristic Rhetoric on Allegory: Origen and Eustathius Put 1 Samuel 28 on Trial." *Journal of Religion* 85 (2005): 414–445.

Mitchell, Stephen. *Anatolia: Land, Men, and Gods in Asia Minor.* 2 vols. New York: Oxford University Press, 1993.

———. "The Cult of Theos Hypsistos between Pagans, Jews, and Christians." In *Pagan Monotheism.* Ed. P. Athanassiadi and M. Frede, 81–148. Oxford: Clarendon Press, 1999.

———. *A History of the Later Roman Empire, A.D. 284–641.* Oxford: Blackwell Publishing, 2007.

Momigliano, Arnaldo. *Alien Wisdom: The Limits of Hellenization.* Cambridge: Cambridge University Press, 1975.

Monceaux, Paul. "Les colonies juives dans l'Afrique romaine." *Revue des études juives* 44 (1902) 1–28.

——. *Histoire littéraire de l'Afrique chrétienne.* Vols. 1 and 5. Paris: E. Leroux, 1901–1923.

Moorehead, J. *Theodoric in Italy.* Oxford: Oxford University Press, 1992.

Newman, H. "Jerome's Judaizers." *Journal of Early Christian Studies* 9 (2001): 421–452.

Niebergall, A. *Augustins Anschauung von der Gnade.* Göttingen: Vandenhoeck & Ruprecht, 1951.

Nickelsburg, G. W. E. *Jewish Literature between the Bible and the Mishnah.* Philadelphia: Fortress Press, 1981.

Nock, A. D. *Conversion: The Old and the New in Religion from Alexander the Great to Augustine of Hippo.* Baltimore: Johns Hopkins University Press, 1998. Originally published 1933.

North, John. "The Development of Religious Pluralism." In *The Jews among Pagans and Christians in the Roman Empire.* Ed. John North, Judith Lieu, and Tessa Rajak, 174–193. New York: Routledge, 1992.

O'Connell, Robert J. *Images of Conversion in St. Augustine's Confessions.* New York: Fordham University Press, 1996.

——. " 'Involuntary Sin' in the *de libero arbitrio.*" Revue des études augustiniennes 37 (1991): 23–36.

O'Donnell, J. J. *Augustine: A New Biography.* New York: HarperCollins Publishers, 2005.

Olster, D. M. *Roman Defeat, Christian Response, and the Literary Construction of the Jew.* Philadelphia: University of Pennsylvania Press, 1994.

O'Meara, John J. *The Young Augustine: The Growth of St. Augustine's Mind up to His Conversion.* New York: Longmans, 1954.

Oort, Johannes van. "Manichaeism and Anti-Manichaeism in Augustine's *Confessions.*" In *Atti del Terzo Congresso Internationale di Studi Manicheismo e Oriente Cristiano Antico.* Ed. L. Cirillo and A. van Tongerloo, 235–247. Leuven and Naples: Brepols, 1997.

Pagels, E. H. *The Gnostic Paul: Gnostic Exegesis of the Pauline Letters.* Philadelphia: Fortress Press, 1975.

——. *The Origin of Satan.* New York: Random House, 1995.

Pakter, W. "Early Western Church Law and the Jews." In *Eusebius, Christianity, and Judaism.* Ed. H. Attridge and G. Hata, 714–735. Leiden: E. J. Brill, 1992.

Panayotov, Alexander. "The Synagogue in the Copper Market of Constantinople: A Note on the Christian Attitude toward Jews in the Fifth Century." *Orientalia christiana periodica* 68 (2002): 319–334.

Parkes, J. *The Conflict of the Church and the Synagogue. A Study in the Origins of Antisemitism.* Philadelphia: The Jewish Publication Society of America, 1961. Originally published 1934.

Pearson, Birger. "1 Thessalonians 2:13–16: A Deutero-Pauline Interpolation." *Harvard Theological Review* 64 (1971): 79–94.

Pellegrino, Michel. *Les Confessions de saint Augustin.* Paris: Études augustiniennes, 1960.

Pincherle, Alberto. "Alla ricerca di Ticonio." *Studi storico-religiosi* 2 (1978): 355–365.

——. *La formazione teologica di Sant' Agostino.* Rome: Edizioni Italiane, 1947.

——. "Sulla formazione della dottrina agostiniana della Grazia." *Rivista di storia e letteratura religiosa* 11 (1975): 1–23.

———. "Da Ticonio a Sant' Agostino." *Richerche religiose* 1 (1925): 443–466.

Platz, Philip. *Der Römerbrief in der Gnadenlehre Augustins.* Würzburg: Rita-Verlag und -Druckerei, 1938.

Pollman, Karla. "La genesi dell'ermeneutica nell'Africa del secolo IV." In *Cristianesimo e specificità regionali nel Mediterraneo latino (sec. IV–VI)*, XXII Incontro di Studiosi dell'antichità cristiana, 137–145. Studia Ephemeridis Augustinianum 46. Rome: Institutum Patristicum Augustinianum, 1994.

Potter, D. "Martyrdom and Spectacle." In *Theatre and Society in the Classical World.* Ed. R. Scodel, 53–88. Ann Arbor: University of Michigan Press, 1993.

———. "Roman Religion: Ideas and Actions." In *Life, Death, and Entertainment in the Roman Empire.* Ed. D. S. Potter and D. J. Mattingly, 113–167. Ann Arbor: University of Michigan Press, 1999.

Pradels, W., R. Brandle, M. Heimgartner. "The Sequence and Dating of the Series of John Chrysostom's Eight Discourses *Adversus Iudaeos.*" *Zeitschrift für antikes Christentum* 6 (2002): 81–116.

Price, S. R. F. *Rituals and Power: The Roman Imperial Cult in Asia Minor.* Cambridge: Cambridge University Press, 1984.

Pucci ben Zeev, Miriam. *Diaspora Judaism in Turmoil, 116/117* C.E. Leuven: Peeters, 2005.

———. *Jewish Rights in the Roman World.* Tübingen: J. C. B. Mohr (Paul Siebeck), 1998.

Puech, H. C. *Le Manichéisme: Son fondateur, sa doctrine.* Paris: Civilisations du Sud, 1949.

Rabello, A. M. "Civil Jewish Jurisdiction in the Days of the Emperor Justinian (527–565): Codex Justinianus 1.9.8." *Israel Law Review* 33 (1999): 51–66.

———. "The Legal Condition of the Jews in the Roman Empire." *Aufsteig und Neidergang des römischen Welt II* 13 (1980): 662–762.

———. "The Legal Condition of the Jews under the Visigothic Kings." *Israel Law Review* 11 (1976): 216–287, 391–414, 563–590.

———. "On the Relations between Diocletian and the Jews." *Journal of Jewish Studies* 35 (1984): 147–167.

Rajak, Tessa. "Benefactors in the Greco-Jewish Diaspora." In *Geschichte—Tradition—Reflexion.* Ed. Hermann Lichtenberger, Peter Schäfer, and Hubert Cancik, 305–319. Tübingen: J. C. B. Mohr (Paul Siebeck), 1996.

———. "The Jewish Community and Its Boundaries." In *The Jews among Pagans and Christians.* Ed. J. Lieu, J. North, and T. Rajak, 9–28. London: Routledge, 1992.

———. "Talking at Trypho: Christian Apologetic as Anti-Judaism in Justin's *Dialogue with Trypho the Jew.*" In *Apologetics in the Roman Empire: Pagans, Jews, and Christians.* Ed. Martin Goodman, Mark Edwards, and Simon Price, in association with Christopher Rowland, 59–80. New York: Oxford University Press, 1999.

Raveaux, Thomas. "*Adversus Judaeos*—Antisemitismus bei Augustinus?" *Signum Pietates. Festgabe für Cornelius Petrus Mayer OSA zum 60. Geburtstag (Cassiciacum, 40).* Ed. A. Zumkeller, 37–51. Würzburg: Augustinus-Verlag, 1989.

———. "Augustinus über den jüdischen Sabbat seiner Zeit." *Revue des études augustiniennes* 28 (1982): 213–224.

Reed, A. Y. "The Trickery of the Fallen Angels and the Demonic Mimesis of the Divine." *Journal of Early Christian Studies* 12 (2004): 141–171.

——. "What the Fallen Angels Taught: The Reception-History of the Book of the Watchers in Judaism and Christianity." Dissertation. Princeton University, 2002.

Reynolds, Joyce Marie, and Robert Tannenbaum. *Jews and God-Fearers at Aphrodisias: Greek Inscriptions with Commentary.* Cambridge: Cambridge Philological Society, 1987.

Richardson, Peter. *Herod: King of the Jews and Friend of the Romans.* Columbia: University of South Carolina Press, 1996.

Ries, J. "Saint Paul dans la formation de Mani." In *Le epistole paoline nei Manichei, i Donatisti e il primo Agostino,* 7–27. Rome: Istituto Patristico Augustinianum 1989.

Rist, John M. *Augustine: Ancient Thought Baptized.* Cambridge: Cambridge University Press, 1994.

Rives, J. B. "The Decree of Decius and the Religion of Empire." *Journal of Roman Studies* 89 (1999): 135–154.

——. *Religion and Authority in Roman Carthage from Augustus to Constantine.* New York: Oxford University Press, 1995.

——. *Religion in the Roman Empire.* Oxford: Blackwell Publishing, 2007.

Robert, L. *Le martyre de Pionios, prêtre de Smyrne.* Ed. G. Bowersock and C. P. Jones. Washington, DC: Dumbarton Oaks, 1994.

Ruether, Rosemary Radford. *Faith and Fratricide: The Theological Roots of Anti-Semitism.* New York: Seabury Press, 1974.

Rutgers, Leonard Victor. *The Hidden Heritage of Diaspora Judaism.* Leuven: Peeters, 1998.

——. *The Jews in Late Ancient Rome. Evidence of Cultural Interaction in the Roman Diaspora.* Leiden: Brill, 1995.

——. "The Jews of Italy, c. 235–638." In *Cambridge History of Judaism.* Vol. 4. Ed. Steven T. Katz, 492–508. Cambridge: Cambridge University Press, 2006.

——. "Justinian's Novella 146 between Jews and Christians." In *Jewish Culture and Society under the Christian Roman Empire.* Ed. R. Kalmin and S. Schwartz, 381–403. Leuven: Peeters, 2002.

Sage, A. "*Praeparatur voluntas a Deo.*" *Revue des études augustiniennes* 10 (1964): 1–20.

Salvensen, Alison. "A Convergence of Ways? The Judaizing of Christian Scripture by Origen and Jerome." In *The Ways That Never Parted: Jews and Christians in Late Antiquity and the Early Middle Ages.* Ed. Adam H. Becker and Annette Yoshiko Reed, 233–257. Tübingen: J. C. B. Mohr (Paul Siebeck), 2003.

Salzman, M. "The Evidence for the Conversion of the Roman Empire to Christianity in Book 16 of the Theodosian Code." *Historia* 42 (1993): 362–378.

——. *The Making of a Christian Aristocracy: Social and Religious Change in the Western Roman Empire.* Cambridge, MA: Harvard University Press, 2002.

——. *On Roman Time: The Codex-Calendar of 354 and the Rhythms of Urban Life in Late Antiquity.* Berkeley: University of California Press, 1990.

——. "Superstitio in the Codex Theodosianus and the Persecution of Pagans." *Vigiliae Christianae* 41 (1987): 172–188.

Sanders, E. P. *The Historical Figure of Jesus.* London: Penguin Press, 1993.

——. *Jesus and Judaism.* Philadelphia: Fortress Press, 1985.

——. *Jewish Law from Jesus to the Mishnah.* Philadelphia: Trinity Press International, 1990.

——. *Judaism: Practice and Belief, 63 B.C.E.–66 C.E.* Philadelphia: Trinity Press International, 1992.

——. *Paul, the Law, and the Jewish People.* Philadelphia: Trinity Press, 1983.

——. *Paul and Palestinian Judaism.* Philadelphia: Fortress Press, 1977.

Schäfer, Peter. *Jesus in the Talmud.* Princeton, NJ: Princeton University Press, 2007.

——. *Judeophobia: Attitudes toward the Jews in the Ancient World.* Cambridge, MA: Harvard University Press, 1997.

Schelkle, Karl Herman. *Paulus, Lehrer der Väters. Die altkirchliche Auslegung von Romer 1–11.* Düsseldorf: Patmos, 1956.

Schreckenberg, H. *Die christlichen adversos-judaeos Texte und ihr literarisches und historisches Umfeld (1.–11. Jh.).* Frankfurt: Peter Lang, 1982.

Schürer, Emil. *The History of the Jewish People in the Age of Jesus Christ (175 B.C.–A.D. 135).* 3 vols. Rev. ed. Ed. G. Vermes et al. Edinburgh: T & T Clark, 1973–1987.

Schwartz, Seth. *Imperialism and Jewish Society, 200 B.C.E. to 640 C.E.* Princeton, NJ: Princeton University Press, 2001.

Schwartz, Yossef. "In the Name of the One and of the Many: Augustine and the Shaping of Christian Identity." In *Religious Apologetics—Philosophical Argumentation.* Ed. Y. Schwartz and V. Krech, 49–67. Tübingen: J. C. B. Mohr (Paul Siebeck), 2004.

Scott, A. *Origen and the Life of the Stars.* Oxford: Oxford University Press, 1994.

Setzer, C. "Jews in Carthage and Western North Africa, 70–235 CE." In *Cambridge History of Judaism IV.* Ed. Steven T. Katz, 68–74. Cambridge: Cambridge University Press, 2006.

——. "Jews, Jewish Christians and Judaizers in North Africa." In *Putting Body and Soul Together. Essays in Honor of Robin Scroggs.* Ed. V. Wiles et al., 185–200. Valley Forge, PA: Trinity Press International, 1997.

Shaw, B. D. "African Christianity: Disputes, Definitions, and 'Donatists.'" *Orthodoxy and Heresy in Religious Movements: Discipline and Dissent.* Ed. Malcolm R. Greenshields and Thomas A. Robinson, 4–34. Lewiston, NY: The Edwin Mellen Press, 1992.

——. "The Family in Late Antiquity: The Experience of Augustine." *Past and Present* 115 (1987): 3–51.

Shepardson, Christine. "Paschal Politics: Deploying the Temple's Destruction against Fourth-Century Judaizers." *Vigiliae Christianae* 62 (2008): 1–28.

——. *Anti-Judaism and Christian Orthodoxy: Ephrem's Hymns in Fourth-Century Syria.* Washington, DC: Catholic University of America Press, 2008.

Shoemaker, S. J. "'Let Us Go Burn Her Body.' The Image of the Jews in Early Dormition Traditions." *Church History* 68 (1999): 775–823.

Simon, Marcel. *Verus Israel: A Study of the Relations between Christians and Jews in the Roman Empire, 135–425.* New York: Oxford University Press, 1986. Originally published as *Verus Israël. Études sur les relations entre Chrétiens et Juifs dans l'empire romain,* 1948.

Simonsohn, S. *The Apostolic See and the Jews.* Toronto: Pontifical Institute of Medieval Studies, 1991.

Simonetti, Manlio. *Biblical Interpretation in the Early Church: An Historical Introduction to Patristic Exegesis.* Edinburgh: T&T Clark, 1994.

Sivan, Hagith. "Why Not Marry a Jew? Jewish-Christian Marital Frontiers in Late Antiquity." In *Law, Society, and Authority in Late Antiquity.* Ed. R. W. Mathisen, 208–219. New York: Oxford University Press, 2001.

Skarsaune, Oskar. *The Proof from Prophecy: A Study in Justin Martyr's Proof-Text Tradition.* Leiden: E. J. Brill, 1987.

Smallwood, Mary. *The Jews under Roman Rule.* Leiden: E. J. Brill, 1976.

Smith, Jonathan Z. *Drudgery Divine: On the Comparison of Early Christianities and the Religions of Late Antiquity.* Chicago: University of Chicago Press, 1990.

Souter, Alexander. *The Earliest Latin Commentaries on the Epistles of Saint Paul.* Cambridge: Cambridge University Press, 1927.

Springer, A. J. "Augustine's Use of Scripture in His Anti-Jewish Polemic." Dissertation. Southern Methodist University, 1989.

Stanton, G. "Justin Martyr's *Dialogue with Trypho:* Group Boundaries, 'Proselytes,' and 'Godfearers'." In *Tolerance and Intolerance in Early Judaism and Christianity.* Ed. G. M. Stanton and G. G. Stroumsa, 263-278. Cambridge: Cambridge University Press, 1998.

Stemberger, Günter. "Hieronymus und die Juden seiner Zeit." In *Begegnungen zwischen Christentum and Judentum in Antike und Mittelalter. Festschrift für H. Schreckenberg.* Ed. D. A. Koch and H. Lichtenberger, 347-364. Göttingen: Vandenhoeck & Ruprecht, 1993.

———. *Jews and Christians in the Holy Land: Palestine in the Fourth Century.* Edinburgh: T&T Clark, 2000.

Stendahl, Krister. "The Apostle Paul and the Introspective Conscience of the West." *Harvard Theological Review* 56 (1963): 199-215.

———. *Final Accounts. Paul's Letter to the Romans.* Minneapolis: Fortress Press, 1995.

Stern, Karen. "Inscribing Devotion and Death in Context: Deciphering the Jewish Culture of Roman North Africa (2nd-6th Centuries C.E.)." Dissertation. Brown University, 2005.

Stern, Menahem. *Greek and Latin Authors on Jews and Judaism.* 3 vols. Jerusalem: Israel Academy of Sciences and Humanities, 1974.

Stock, Brian. *Augustine the Reader: Meditation, Self-Knowledge, and the Ethics of Interpretation.* Cambridge, MA: Harvard University Press, 1996.

Stökl, Daniel Ben Ezra. "Whose Fast Is It? The Ember Day of September and Yom Kippur." In *The Ways That Never Parted: Jews and Christians in Late Antiquity and the Early Middle Ages.* Ed. A. H. Becker and A. Y. Reed, 258-282. Tübingen: Germany: J. C. B. Mohr (Peter Siebeck), 2003.

Stowers, Stanley K. "Greeks Who Sacrifice and Those Who Do Not: Toward an Anthropology of Greek Religion." In *The Social World of the First Christians: Studies in Honor of Wayne Meeks.* Ed. Michael L. White and Larry O. Yarborough, 293-333. Minneapolis: Fortress Press, 1995.

———. *A Rereading of Romans: Justice, Jews, and Gentiles.* New Haven: Yale University Press, 1994.

Struck, P. T. *The Birth of the Symbol.* Princeton, NJ: Princeton University Press, 2004.

Stroumsa, G. G. *Savoir et Salut: Gnoses de l'antiquité tardive.* Paris: Éditions du Cerf, 1992.

Stroumsa, G. G., and Sarah Stroumsa. "Aspects of Anti-Manichaean Polemic in Late Antiquity and under Early Islam." *Harvard Theological Review* 81 (1988): 37-58.

Stuckenbruck, L. T., and W. E. S. North, eds. *Early Jewish and Christian Monotheism.* London: T & T Clark, 2004.

Tardieu, M. *Le Manichéisme.* Paris: Presses universitaires de France, 1981.

———. "Principes de l'exégèse manichéenne du Nouveau Testament." In *Les règles de l'interprétation.* Ed. M. Tardieu, 123-128. Paris: Éditions du Cerf, 1987.

Taylor, Miriam S. *Anti-Judaism and Early Christian Identity: A Critique of the Scholarly Consensus.* Leiden: E. J. Brill, 1995.

TeSelle, Eugene. *Augustine the Theologian.* London: Burns & Oates, 1970.

Thompson, E. A. *The Goths in Spain.* Oxford: Clarendon Press, 1969.

Tilley, Maureen A. *The Bible in Christian North Africa: The Donatist World.* Minneapolis: Fortress Press, 1997.

———. *Donatist Martyr Stories: The Church in Conflict in Roman North Africa.* Liverpool: Liverpool University Press, 1996.

Turcan, Robert. *The Cults of the Roman Empire.* Oxford: Blackwell, 1996.

———. *The Gods of Ancient Rome.* Edinburgh: Edinburgh University Press, 2000.

Ulrich, J. *Eusebius von Caesaria und die Juden: Studien zur Rolle der Juden in der Theologie des Eusebius.* Tübingen: De Gruyter, 1999.

Unterseher, L. A. "The Mark of Cain and the Jews: Augustine's Theology of Jews and Judaism." Dissertation. Southern Methodist University, 2000.

Vanneste, A. "S. Paul et la doctrine augustinienne du péché originel." *Studium Paulinorum Congressus* II (1961): 513–522.

Visotzki, B. L. "Prolegomenon to the Study of Jewish Christianity in the Rabbinic Literature." *Association of Jewish Studies Review* 14 (1989): 47–70.

Vogler, Chantal. "Les Juifs dans le code théodosien." In *Les Chrétiens devant le fait juif.* Ed. Jacques Le Brun, 35–74. Paris: Éditions Beauchesne, 1979.

Walbank, F. W. *The Hellenistic World.* Cambridge, MA: Harvard University Press, 1981.

Walker, P. W. L. *Holy City, Holy Places? Christian Attitudes to Jerusalem and the Holy Land in the Fourth Century.* Oxford: Oxford University Press, 1990.

Wallis, R. T. *Neoplatonism.* New York: Charles Scribner's Sons, 1972.

Walters, James. *Ethnic Issues in Paul's Letter to the Romans.* Valley Forge, PA: Trinity Press, 1993.

Wander, B. *Gottesfürchtige und Sympathisanten.* Tübingen: J. C. B. Mohr (Peter Siebeck), 1998.

Ward-Perkins, Brian. *The Fall of Rome and the End of Civilization.* Oxford: Oxford University Press, 2005.

Wetzel, J. *Augustine and the Limits of Virtue.* Cambridge: Cambridge University Press, 1992.

Whitman, Jon. "From the Textual to the Temporal: Early Christian 'Allegory' and Early Romantic 'Symbol.' " *New Literary History* 22 (1991): 161–176.

Wilken, Robert L. *The Christians as the Romans Saw Them.* 2nd ed. New Haven: Yale University Press, 2003.

———. *John Chrysostom and the Jews: Rhetoric and Reality in the Late 4th Century.* Berkeley: University of California Press, 1983.

———. *Judaism and the Early Christian Mind. A Study of Cyril of Alexandria's Exegesis and Theology.* New Haven: Yale University Press, 1971.

———. *The Land Called Holy: Palestine in Christian History and Thought.* New Haven: Yale University Press, 1992.

Wiles, Maurice. *The Divine Apostle: The Interpretation of St. Paul's Epistles in the Early Church.* Cambridge: Cambridge University Press, 1969.

Wilkenhauser, A. "Die Herkunft der Idee des tausendjährigen Reich in der Johannes-Apokalypse." *Römische Quartalschrift* 45 (1937): 1–24.

Williams, A. Lukyn. *Adversus Iudaeos.* Cambridge: Cambridge University Press, 1935.

Williams, Margaret. *The Jews among the Greeks and Romans.* Baltimore: Johns Hopkins University Press, 1998.

——. "The Jews of Early Byzantine Venusia: The Family of Faustinus I, the Father." *Journal of Jewish Studies* 50 (1999): 38–52.

Wills, Garry. *Saint Augustine.* New York: Viking Penguin, 1999.

Young F. *Biblical Exegesis and the Formation of Christian Culture.* Cambridge: Cambridge University Press, 1997.

——. "The Fourth Century Reaction against Allegory." *Studia Patristica* 30 (1997): 120–125.

——. "Greek Apologists of the Second Century." In *Apologetics in the Roman Empire: Pagans, Jews, and Christians.* Ed. Martin Goodman, Mark Edwards, and Simon Price, in association with Christopher Rowland, 81–104. New York: Oxford University Press, 1999.

——. "The Rhetorical Schools and Their Influence on Patristic Exegesis." In *The Making of Orthodoxy: Essays in Honour of Henry Chadwick.* Ed. R. Williams, 182–199. Cambridge: Cambridge University Press, 1989.

——. "Typology." In *Crossing the Boundaries: Essays in Biblical Interpretation in Honour of Michael D. Goulder.* Ed. Stanley E. Porter, Paul Joyce, and David E. Orton, 29–48. Leiden: E. J. Brill, 1994.

Yuval, Israel Jacob. "The Myth of Jewish Exile from the Land of Israel." *Common Knowledge* 12 (2006): 16–34.

——. *Two Nations in Your Womb: Perceptions of Jews and Christians in Late Antiquity and the Middle Ages.* Berkeley: University of California Press, 2006.

INDEXES

JEWISH TEXTS

BOSTON PUBLIC LIBRARY

3 9999 06200 753 7

12/08

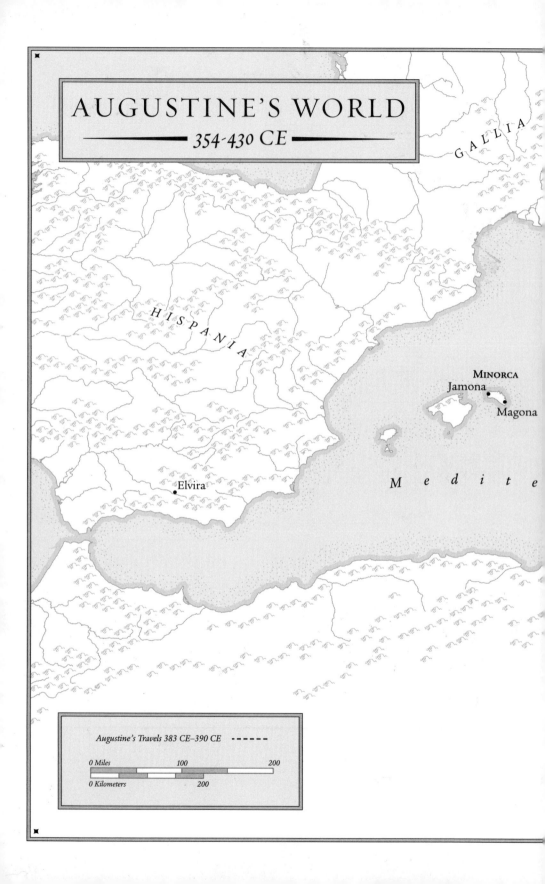

AUGUSTINE'S WORLD
354-430 CE

GALLIA

HISPANIA

MINORCA
Jamona
Magona

Elvira

M e d i t e

Augustine's Travels 383 CE–390 CE - - - - - -

0 Miles   100   200

0 Kilometers   200